Fourth Edition

Deutsch: Na klar!

An Introductory German Course

ROBERT DI DONATO
Miami University
Oxford, Ohio

MONICA D. CLYDE
St. Mary's College of California
Moraga, California

JACQUELINE VANSANT
University of Michigan, Dearborn

Contributing Writer
LIDA DAVES-SCHNEIDER

Boston   Burr Ridge, IL   Dubuque, IA   Madison, WI   New York   San Francisco   St. Louis
Bangkok   Bogotá   Caracas   Kuala Lumpur   Lisbon   London   Madrid   Mexico City
Milan   Montreal   New Delhi   Santiago   Seoul   Singapore   Sydney   Taipei   Toronto

The McGraw·Hill Companies

This is an ⊏B| book.

Deutsch: Na klar!
An Introductory German Course

Published by McGraw-Hill, an imprint of The McGraw-Hill Companies, Inc., 1221 Avenue of the Americas, New York, NY 10020. Copyright © 2004, 1999, 1995, 1991 by McGraw-Hill. All rights reserved. No part of this publication may be reproduced or distributed in any form or by any means, or stored in a database or retrieval system, without the prior written consent of The McGraw-Hill Companies, Inc., including, but not limited to, in any network or other electronic storage or transmission, or broadcast for distance learning.

This book is printed on acid-free paper.

1 2 3 4 5 6 7 8 9 0   WCK   WCK   0 9 8 7 6 5 4 2 3

ISBN 0-07-240817-0   (Student's Edition)
ISBN 0-07-249252-X   (Instructor's Edition)

Editor-in-chief: Thalia Dorwick
Publisher: William R. Glass
Sponsoring editor: Christa Harris
Director of development: Scott Tinetti
Developmental editor: Harriet C. Dishman
Executive marketing manager: Nick Agnew
Senior project manager: Christina Gimlin
Senior production supervisor: Richard DeVitto
Design manager: Violeta Diaz
Senior photo researcher: Nora Agbayani
Interior and cover designer: Andrew Ogus
Art editor: Emma Ghiselli
Editorial assistant: Jennifer Chow
Senior supplements coordinator: Louis Swaim
Cover image: © Helga Lade/Peter Arnold Inc.
Compositor: ICC
Typeface: Melior
Printer: Quebecor World Color

Because this page cannot legibly accommodate all the copyright notices, page A-89 constitutes an extension of the copyright page.

Library of Congress Cataloging-in-Publication Data

Di Donato, Robert.
    Deutsch, na klar! : an introductory German course / Robert Di Donato,
Monica D. Clyde, Jacqueline Vansant.—4th ed.
        p. cm.
    Includes index.
    ISBN 0-07-240817-0 (alk. paper)
    1. German language—Grammar.   2. German language—Textbooks for foreign
speakers—English.   I. Clyde, Monica.   II. Vansant, Jacqueline, 1954- .   III. Title.

PF3112.D48 2004
838.2′421—dc21   2002044482

http://www.mhhe.com

Contents

Einführung

Sprachtipps	Kulturtipps	Sprache im Kontext

	Wörter im Kontext	**Grammatik im Kontext**

Wörter im Kontext	Grammatik im Kontext

Sprachtipps	Kulturtipps	Sprache im Kontext

Contents **XI**

| **Wörter im Kontext** | **Grammatik im Kontext** |

Sprachtipps	Kulturtipps	Sprache im Kontext

Contents **XIII**

| Wörter im Kontext | Grammatik im Kontext |

Sprachtipps	Kulturtipps	Sprache im Kontext

Übergang: Gestern und heute

PREFACE

Welcome to the Fourth Edition of *Deutsch: Na klar!* Those of you who are familiar with this textbook know that *Deutsch: Na klar!* offers a versatile, comprehensive, and colorful program for introductory German courses. The new Fourth Edition provides an exciting, innovative package designed to suit a wide variety of approaches, methodologies, and classrooms, while still preserving many standard pedagogical features that instructors have come to trust since the publication of the first edition. Among the trusted and proven features of *Deutsch: Na klar!*, you will recognize the following:

- A rich array of authentic materials with accompanying activities and exercises
- Streamlined grammar explanations
- A commitment to the development of both receptive skills (listening and reading) and productive skills (speaking and writing)
- Abundant communicative activities, together with many interactive, as well as form-focused, activities
- The promotion of meaningful acquisition of vocabulary and structures with considerable regard to accuracy

As noted above, one of the trusted hallmarks of *Deutsch: Na klar!* is its unique approach to the use of authentic materials. Authentic materials motivate and interest students, and allow them to see the immediate application of their newly acquired skills in authentic contexts. Thus, in *Deutsch: Na klar!*, authentic materials are used to illustrate vocabulary in context, communicative functions of grammatical structures, and cultural points. Moreover, realia-based activities are extremely effective in helping students develop receptive skills.

Vocabulary and grammar are presented in a functional framework so that students begin to associate forms with functions. Vocabulary is introduced in context through the use of visuals, dialogues, short narratives, or "built-in" activities to stimulate meaningful language. **Neue Wörter**

boxes help students verify the meaning of words after they have encountered them in an initial presentation. Wherever useful, grammatical structures are contrasted with parallel structures in English. Vocabulary and grammar activities progress from controlled and form-focused to open-ended and interactive, and from receptive to productive.

A Listening Comprehension Program is tied to several activities in every chapter. Indicated in the student text with a headphone icon, some of these listening comprehension activities are designed for global comprehension, while others have been designed to give students practice in noting specific details. In a similar fashion, students learn to skim for general information and scan for specific details when reading. In both listening and reading, students are encouraged to use background knowledge and context to aid comprehension.

The Fourth Edition integrates an interview-based video **(Videoclips)** and computer-based realia into the program. Taped on location in Berlin, these interviews with native speakers of German provide authentic input directly related to the chapter theme and functions. The comprehensible yet natural speech of the interviews provides students with a window into the lives and habits of today's German citizens, thus promoting both the development of communicative skills and cultural awareness. A new Interactive Student CD-ROM expands on these interviews by giving students the opportunity to "interact" with the interviewees themselves in a simulated conversation. In addition, the Interactive Student CD-ROM offers abundant vocabulary and grammar practice, as well as additional reading, writing, and cultural activities.

The five Cs of the National Standards—Communication, Connections, Culture, Comparisons, and Communities—developed by ACTFL in collaboration with AATG, AATF, and AATSP (*Standards for Foreign Language Learning: Preparing for the 21st Century*) permeate the activities, exercises, readings, cultural and language tips, and video of *Deutsch: Na klar!* Each chapter provides opportunities for students to communicate in German in real-life situations for real purposes. Authentic materials and the new video, as well as the exercises based on them, stimulate students' thinking about their own language and culture in order to draw cross-cultural comparisons and connect their study of German language and culture with other disciplines. And finally, opportunities for students to reach out to German-speaking communities locally and globally are provided through Internet activities.

In summary, through its authentic materials, cultural features, readings, listening passages, activities, and innovative technology, *Deutsch: Na klar!* teaches skills that will help students communicate successfully in the German-speaking world.

Organization of the Text

Deutsch: Na klar! consists of a preliminary chapter **(Einführung)**, fourteen regular chapters, and a closing chapter **(Übergang).** Each of the fourteen regular chapters is developed around a major theme and has the following organization:

- Alles klar?
- Wörter im Kontext
    Themen 1, 2, 3
- Grammatik im Kontext
- Sprache im Kontext
    Videoclips
    Lesen
    Sprechen und Schreiben

Cultural collages **(Zwischenspiele),** containing visuals and activities, appear after **Kapitel 3, 6, 9, and 12,** and give students the opportunity to review, consolidate, and apply what they have learned in previous chapters to cultural topics of German-speaking countries in new contexts.

A Guided Tour through Deutsch: Na klar!

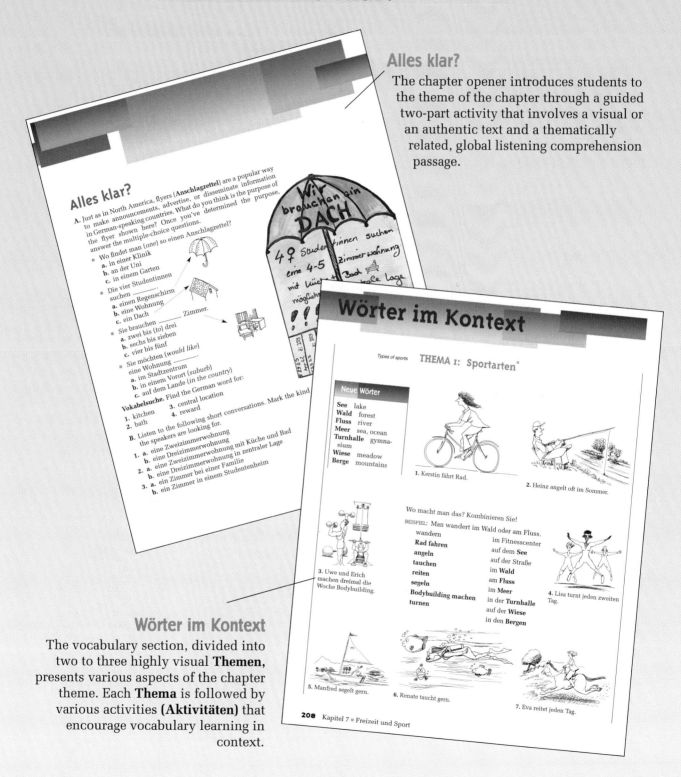

Alles klar?

The chapter opener introduces students to the theme of the chapter through a guided two-part activity that involves a visual or an authentic text and a thematically related, global listening comprehension passage.

Alles klar?

A. Just as in North America, flyers (**Anschlagzettel**) are a popular way to make announcements, advertise, or disseminate information in German-speaking countries. What do you think is the purpose of the flyer shown here? Once you've determined the purpose, answer the multiple-choice questions.

- Wo findet man (*one*) so einen Anschlagzettel?
  - a. in einer Klinik
  - b. an der Uni
  - c. in einem Garten
- Die vier Studentinnen suchen _____.
  - a. einen Regenschirm
  - b. eine Wohnung
  - c. ein Dach
- Sie brauchen _____ Zimmer.
  - a. zwei bis (*to*) drei
  - b. sechs bis sieben
  - c. vier bis fünf
- Sie möchten (*would like*) eine Wohnung _____.
  - a. im Stadtzentrum
  - b. in einem Vorort (*suburb*)
  - c. auf dem Lande (*in the country*)

Vokabelsuche. Find the German word for:
1. kitchen   3. central location
2. bath   4. reward

B. Listen to the following short conversations. Mark the kind the speakers are looking for.
1. a. eine Zweizimmerwohnung
   b. eine Dreizimmerwohnung mit Küche und Bad
2. a. eine Zweizimmerwohnung in zentraler Lage
   b. eine Dreizimmerwohnung
3. a. ein Zimmer bei einer Familie
   b. ein Zimmer in einem Studentenheim

Wörter im Kontext

Types of sports   **THEMA 1: Sportarten°**

Neue Wörter

See	lake
Wald	forest
Fluss	river
Meer	sea, ocean
Turnhalle	gymnasium
Wiese	meadow
Berge	mountains

1. Kerstin fährt Rad.

2. Heinz angelt oft im Sommer.

3. Uwe und Erich machen dreimal die Woche Bodybuilding.

Wo macht man das? Kombinieren Sie!
BEISPIEL: Man wandert im Wald oder am Fluss.

wandern   im Fitnesscenter
  Rad fahren   auf dem **See**
  angeln   auf der Straße
  tauchen   im **Wald**
  reiten   am **Fluss**
  segeln   im **Meer**
  Bodybuilding machen in der **Turnhalle**
  turnen   auf der **Wiese**
                         in den **Bergen**

4. Lisa turnt jeden zweiten Tag.

5. Manfred segelt gern.

6. Renate taucht gern.

7. Eva reitet jeden Tag.

208 Kapitel 7 ▪ Freizeit und Sport

The vocabulary section, divided into two to three highly visual **Themen**, presents various aspects of the chapter theme. Each **Thema** is followed by various activities (**Aktivitäten**) that encourage vocabulary learning in context.

Grammatik im Kontext

Grammar is presented in succinct explanations with abundant charts and examples and, whenever possible, via authentic materials. Some grammar explanations expand on points that are previewed in **Sprachtipps.**

Grammatik im Kontext

unterordnende Konjunktionen

Connecting Sentences: Subordinating Conjunctions

Subordinating conjunctions are used to connect a main clause and a dependent clause. Four frequently used subordinating conjunctions are **dass** (*that*), **ob** (*whether, if*), **weil** (*because*), and **wenn** (*whenever, if*).

Ich hoffe, **dass** du bald gesund wirst.

Weißt du, **ob** Mark krank ist?

Mark bleibt zu Hause, **weil** er eine Erkältung hat.

Ich gehe ins Fitnesscenter, **wenn** ich Zeit habe.

I hope that you'll get well soon.

Do you know whether Mark is ill?

Mark is staying at home because he has a cold.

I go to the fitness center whenever I have time.

Note:
- In dependent clauses the conjugated verb is placed at the end.
- In the case of a separable-prefix verb, the prefix is joined with the rest of the verb.
- A comma always separates the main clause from the dependent clause.

Sprache im Kontext

Videoclips

A. Watch the interviews with Sara and Ali as they talk about what they are studying, their hobbies, and how their friends would describe them. Write **S** if the phrase or word applies to **Sara** or **A** if it applies to **Ali.**

—— Medienwissenschaft   —— Schwimmen
—— Mathematik   —— spontan
—— Joggen   —— zurückhaltend (*reserved*)
—— Gitarre spielen   —— lustig
—— Zeichnen   —— fröhlich
—— Tanzen   —— sehr aktiv
—— Fahrrad fahren

B. Who does what? Watch the interviews and match each person with a profession or job.

1. —— Peter
2. —— Oliver
3. —— Alex
4. —— Jasmin
5. —— Frau Simon

a. ist Grafikdesigner
b. ist Pilot
c. ist Bankkauffrau
d. arbeitet bei KWD im Silbershop
e. ist Webdesigner

C. Watch the interviews again and jot down notes about things you have in common with the interviewees. If you have anything in common, then write a few sentences that describe the commonalities. Follow the model.

BEISPIEL: Ali studiert Mathematik. Ich studiere auch Mathematik. Saras Hobby ist Tanzen. mein Hobby ist auch Tanzen...

Sprache im Kontext

This culminating four-skills section is divided into three parts: **Videoclips,** featuring interviews with German speakers on topics presented in each chapter and reflecting the vocabulary and grammar presented. **Lesen,** an authentic reading passage with pre- and post-reading activities; and **Sprechen und Schreiben,** interactive, task-oriented activities that provide open-ended oral and written practice on the chapter theme.

The Deutsch: Na klar! vocabulary system

Vocabulary is presented by means of authentic materials, illustrations, descriptive texts, dialogues, and built-in activities. Students must first "discover" the meaning of the new vocabulary, which is highlighted in the presentation through contextual guessing. New, active vocabulary is then reflected in the **Neue Wörter** lists, which students should use to verify their contextual guessing.

BEISPIELE: Man kann auf dem Kiessee segeln.
Man kann im Jahnstadion Fußball spielen.

kegeln
Fußball spielen
tauchen, schwimmen
Tennis spielen

wandern
angeln
segeln
Schlittschuh laufen

Golf spielen
reiten
joggen

Neue Wörter

Freibad outdoor swimming pool
Hallenbad indoor swimming pool
Schwimmbad swimming pool
Sporthalle sports arena
Sportplatz athletic field
Stadion stadium
Eisstadion ice-skating rink
Tennisplatz tennis court

¹physical education

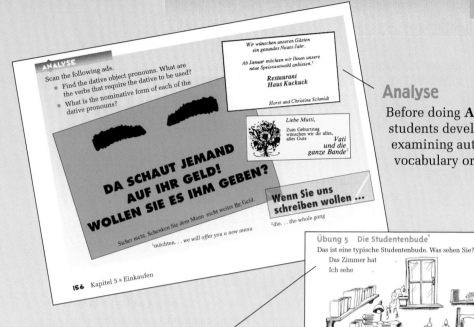

Analyse

Before doing **Aktivitäten** or **Übungen,** students develop receptive skills by examining authentic texts for specific vocabulary or grammatical structures.

Aktivitäten und Übungen

A broad range of activities and exercises allows for structured communicative practice of vocabulary and grammatical structures. Whereas some activities and exercises are tied to the audio CD and provide receptive vocabulary and grammar practice, others develop productive skills.

Icons

Icons identify pair or small-group activities, information gap, listening comprehension, as well as activities requiring an extra sheet of paper.

Hier klicken!

At relevant locations throughout the text, this new feature directs students to the **Deutsch: Na klar!** Online Learning Center (http://www.mhhe.com/dnk), which contains additional vocabulary, grammar, and cultural activities.

Sprachtipp

Expressions and "grammar for communication" are provided to assist students in carrying out a given activity. These grammar points may be elaborated on in the same or a later chapter.

Kulturtipp

Enhanced with photos or other visuals, this feature expands on the cultural information presented in the **Themen,** activities and exercises, and readings.

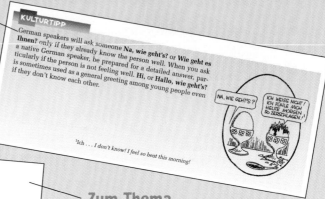

KULTURTIPP

German speakers will ask someone **Na, wie geht's?** or **Wie geht es Ihnen?** only if they already know the person well. When you ask a native German speaker, be prepared for a detailed answer, particularly if the person is not feeling well. **Hi,** or **Hallo, wie geht's?** is sometimes used as a general greeting among young people even if they don't know each other.

NA, WIE GEHT'S ?

ICH WEISS NICHT ! ICH FÜHLE MICH HEUTE MORGEN SO ZERSCHLAGEN ¹

¹Ich . . . I don't know! I feel so beat this morning!

Zum Thema

Eine Umfrage (survey). Fill out the questionnaire and compare answers in class.

A. Which holidays are important in your own family?

	WICHTIG	UNWICHTIG
1. Geburtstage	☐	☐
2. Hochzeitstage	☐	☐
3. religiöse Feiertage	☐	☐
4. nationale Feiertage	☐	☐
5. Muttertag	☐	☐
6. Vatertag	☐	☐

Sprache im Kontext **103**

Zum Thema

This section contains activities that prepare students to read the text. Students use their background knowledge or brainstorm about the topic to predict what will happen in the reading passage.

Auf den ersten Blick

In this activity, students skim the reading to get the gist or scan it for specific pieces of information in order to achieve a global understanding.

Auf den ersten Blick

A. The following text on cafés in Vienna contains many cognates and other words that look similar in English and German. Scan the text and make a list of such words.

BEISPIEL: traditionell

B. Now scan the text for compound words. Say the words aloud and try to identify their components. Can you guess their meaning from the components?

BEISPIEL: das Kaffeehaus = Kaffee + Haus = *coffeehouse, café*

Sprache im Kontext **199**

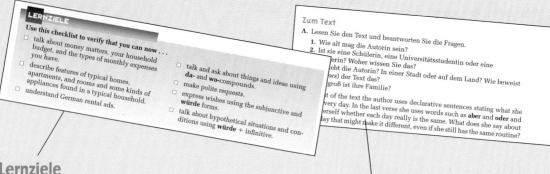

LERNZIELE

Use this checklist to verify that you can now . . .

☐ talk about money matters, your household budget, and the types of monthly expenses you have.

☐ describe features of typical homes, apartments, and rooms and some kinds of appliances found in a typical household.

☐ understand German rental ads.

☐ talk and ask about things and ideas using **da-** and **wo-**compounds.

☐ make polite requests.

☐ express wishes using the subjunctive and **würde** forms.

☐ talk about hypothetical situations and conditions using **würde** + infinitive.

Zum Text

A. Lesen Sie den Text und beantworten Sie die Fragen.

1. Wie alt mag die Autorin sein?
2. Ist sie eine Schülerin, eine Universitätsstudentin oder eine ...erin? Woher wissen Sie das?
... ebt die Autorin? In einer Stadt oder auf dem Land? Wie beweist ...ws) der Text das?
... groß ist ihre Familie?

...t of the text the author uses declarative sentences stating what she ...very day. In the last verse she uses words such as **aber** and **oder** and ...erself whether each day really is the same. What does she say about ...ay that might make it different, even if she still has the same routine?

Lernziele

Appearing at the end of every chapter, **Lernziele** function as a study aid for students to verify that they have reached the learning goals of the chapter.

Zum Text

Here students read intensively, focusing on content, vocabulary, structures, and finally, implications and interpretation.

WHAT'S NEW IN THE FOURTH EDITION?

Retaining the aspects that reviewers have praised and that have set **Deutsch: Na klar!** apart from other texts, while at the same time adding new features to keep it lively, contemporary, and up-to-date, has been our major goal during the revision process. Instructors have given us feedback on the previous edition and we have responded. We have honed the dialogues, streamlined the grammar, introduced a more systematic approach to the vocabulary, included new readings, and added a lively new video program. Major features appear in the visual *Guided Tour Through* **Deutsch: Na klar!**

The Fourth Edition has been improved in numerous ways:

- A new and exciting design that supports and enhances vocabulary presentations, grammar explanations, activities, and exercises.

- New and updated realia reflecting cultural phenomena and current vocabulary.

- **Neue Wörter** boxes, which students can use to "verify" the meaning of vocabulary they have guessed the meaning of in context.

- Streamlined grammar explanations in bulleted form that focus on key usage of particular items and transition from simple to more complex grammar use.

- Updated information on specific cultural changes, such as the focus on the euro.

- An entirely new Video Program filmed on location in Germany featuring interviews with a wide variety of native speakers reflecting the vocabulary, grammar, and cultural topics of each chapter.

- The **Übergang** chapter has been revised and updated to focus on Berlin and reflect recent developments in Germany.

- A new Online Learning Center (www.mhhe.com/dnk) provides a wide variety of activities that practice vocabulary and grammar and offer opportunities for cultural exploration. Additional features of the Online Learning Center include practice midterm and final exams, and flashcards. The **Hier klicken!** feature of the Student Edition reminds students of these activities and directs them to the Online Learning Center.

- An interactive CD-ROM provides students with additional form-focused practice. It also contains cultural and video features and a dictionary, among others.

SUPPLEMENTS

The following components of **Deutsch: Na klar!** Fourth Edition are designed to complement your instruction and to enhance your students' learning experience. Please contact your local McGraw-Hill sales representative for details concerning policies, prices, and availability of the supplementary materials, as some restrictions may apply. Available to students and instructors:

- The *Student Text* includes a grammar appendix and German-English/ English-German end vocabularies.

- The *Listening Comprehension Program* contains material tied to the listening activities in the main text. The audio CDs, provided free for in-class or at-home use, are packaged along with the student edition.

- The *Workbook,* by Jeanine Briggs, includes additional form-focused vocabulary and grammar exercises as well as abundant guided writing practice.

- The *Laboratory Manual,* by Lida Daves-Schneider and Michael Büsges, contains engaging listening comprehension activities and pronunciation practice. Available on audio CD, the *Audio Program* includes an audioscript for instructors.

- The *McGraw-Hill Electronic Language Tutor* (MHELT 2.1), available for Macintosh and IBM compatibles, contains single-response exercises from the main text.

- The dual-platform *Interactive Student CD-ROM to accompany Deutsch: Na klar!* contains additional form-focused vocabulary and grammar practice, along with other features designed to make learning German with *Deutsch: Na klar!* easier and more engaging.

- The new *Online Learning Center to accompany Deutsch: Na klar!,* located at http://www.mhhe.com/dnk, contains a variety of activities that practice vocabulary and grammar, as well as cultural activities, flashcards, and more.

Available to instructors only:

- The *Annotated Instructor's Edition* of the main text includes marginal notes, answers, and an audioscript to the in-text listening comprehension activities.

- The combined *Instructor's Manual* and *Testing Program* provides theoretical background, practical guidance, and ideas for using *Deutsch: Na klar!.* It also contains tests and exams written by Jennifer Redmann (Ripon College) and Pennylyn Dykstra-Pruim (Michigan State University).

- The *Audioscript* contains the material found on the *Audio Program.*

- The new *Video to accompany Deutsch: Na klar!* contains a wide variety of interviews with native speakers of German.

- The *McGraw-Hill Video Library of Authentic Materials: A German TV Journal* includes authentic segments from German television (ZDF) and a *User's Guide.* Topics relate directly to the main themes in the text. The *User's Guide* contains a variety of activities that can be duplicated for students.

- A *Training/Orientation Manual* by James F. Lee (Indiana University) offers practical advice for beginning language instructors and coordinators.

ACKNOWLEDGMENTS

The publisher would like to thank those instructors who participated in surveys and reviews that were indispensable in the development of *Deutsch: Na klar!* Fourth Edition. The appearance of their names does not necessarily constitute their endorsement of the text or its methodology.

Christiane Baldus, Cabrillo College
Réka Barabás, Bowling Green State University
Constance Colwell, Presbyterian College
Dayton Cook, Northern State University
James C. Danell, Jr., Martin Luther College
Lida Daves-Schneider, Riverside Community College
Nikolaus Euba, University of South Carolina
Lisa J. Graham, Washington College
John E. Harrington, North Carolina Central University
Lisabeth Hock, College of Wooster
Lynda Hoffman-Jeep, Millikin University
Mary Rita Isaacson, North Idaho College
Richard Kalfus, St. Louis Community College
Cathy Kappius, Alpena Community College
Edith H. Krause, Angelo State University
Wendell D. Kurr, Highland Community College
Victoria Moessner, University of Alaska, Fairbanks
Terry Pickett, Samford University
Hildegard Rossoll, Kent State University
Eckhard Rolz, Idaho State University
Sandra Singer, Alfred University
Donald R. Sunnen, Virginia Military Institute

John R. te Velde, Oklahoma State University
Erlis Wickersham, Rosemont College
David Witkosky, Auburn University, Montgomery
Elisabeth Wolpert, Henry Ford Community
 College

We would also like to thank the many people who worked on this book behind the scenes: Our development editor, Harriet C. Dishman, who expertly commented on all aspects of the manuscript; Stephen Newton (University of California, Berkeley) and Bettina Pohle (University of California, Berkeley), for their contributions to the **Zuschauen** section; Daniela Gibson, who, as the native reader, edited the language for authenticity; Daniela Dosch, who painstakingly compiled the German-English / English-German vocabularies; and David Sweet, who secured reprint permissions for the realia and texts. We would also like to thank Paul H. Listen for his invaluable editorial contributions.

The look of this Fourth Edition owes much to the creative talents of Andrew Ogus, who designed the interior of the book as well as the cover. We would also like to acknowledge Wolfgang Horsch for his engaging line drawings.

The authors also wish to acknowledge the editing, production, and art and design team at McGraw-Hill: Christina Gimlin, Richard DeVitto, Violeta Díaz, Nora Agbayani, and Emma Ghiselli. Thanks also to Marie Deer for her wonderful copyedit and to Stacey Sawyer for her excellent proofread, and to Nick Agnew, Rachel Amparo and the rest of the McGraw-Hill marketing and sales staff, who have so actively promoted this book over the past three editions. Finally, we would like to express our gratitude to the McGraw-Hill foreign language editorial staff: Christa Harris, our Sponsoring editor, Bill Glass, our Publisher, and Thalia Dorwick, Editor-in-chief, whose belief in the project made it a reality, and whose constant support helped bring it to completion; and, finally, Eirik Børve, whose vision made this book happen in the first place.

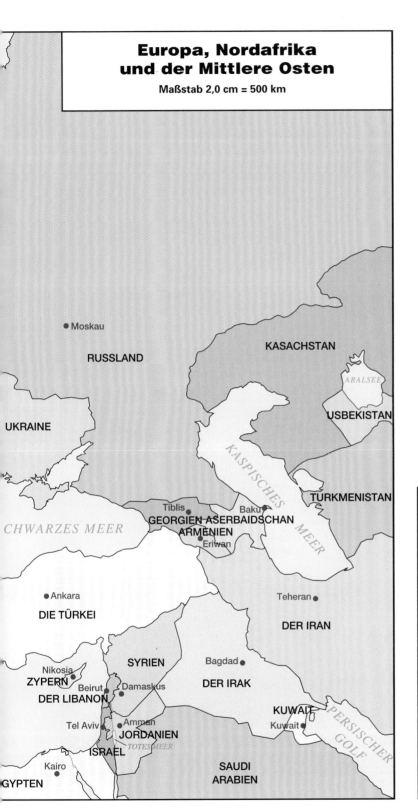

Europa, Nordafrika
und der Mittlere Osten

Maßstab 2,0 cm = 500 km

• Moskau

RUSSLAND

KASACHSTAN

ARALSEE

USBEKISTAN

UKRAINE

KASPISCHES MEER

TURKMENISTAN

Tiblis •   Baku •

GEORGIEN ASERBAIDSCHAN

ARMENIEN

• Eriwan

SCHWARZES MEER

• Ankara   Teheran •

DIE TÜRKEI

DER IRAN

SYRIEN   Bagdad •

Nikosia •

ZYPERN   Beirut •   • Damaskus   DER IRAK

DER LIBANON

KUWAIT

Tel Aviv •   • Amman   Kuwait •   *PERSISCHER*

JORDANIEN   *GOLF*

ISRAEL   *TOTESMEER*

Kairo •   SAUDI

ÄGYPTEN   ARABIEN

EU-LÄNDER (2003)	EINWOHNER (2001-2002)
	Millionen
Belgien	10,3
Dänemark	5,4
Deutschland	82,5
Finnland	5,2
Frankreich	59,3
Griechenland	10,9
Großbritannien	58,9
Irland	3,9
Italien	57,7
Luxemburg	0,4
Niederlande	16,2
Österreich	8,0
Portugal	10,1
Schweden	8,9
Spanien	40,1
GESAMT	377,7

Deutschland und Luxemburg
Einwohner
Deutschland (2002): 82,5 Mio
Luxemburg (1998): 418 000
Maßstab 2,0 cm = 100 km

Österreich

Einwohner (2001): 8 Mio
Maßstab 1,5 cm = 50 km

TSCHECHIEN

Gmünd
Horn
Krems
Donau
WIEN
Linz
Sankt Pölten
Wien
DEUTSCHLAND
OBERÖSTERREICH
Melk
Baden
Amstetten
NIEDERÖSTERREICH
Eisenstadt
Gmunden
Neusiedler See
Salzburg
Bad Ischl
Wiener Neustadt
Salzach
Liezen
Mariazell
BURGENLAND
Bodensee
Hallstatt
Salzkammergut
Bruck an der Mur
Oberwart
Bregenz
Kufstein
Sankt Johann in Tirol
Enns
VORARLBERG
Wörgl
Bischofshofen
STEIERMARK
Feldkirch
Arlberg
Kitzbühel
Zell am See
Radstadt
Sankt Georgen
Güssing
Innsbruck
Bruck
Reutte
Landeck
SALZBURG
Mauterndorf
Mur
TIROL
Osttirol
(zu Tirol)
Graz
DIE SCHWEIZ
Vintschgau
Lienz
Spittal an der Drau
Feldkirchen
Meran
Drau
KÄRNTEN
Klagenfurt
SÜDTIROL
Villach
Wörther See
UNGARN
Bozen
ITALIEN
SLOWENIEN

SCHAFFHAUSEN
Schaffhausen
DEUTSCHLAND
Kreuzlingen
BASEL
(STADT)
Rhein
THURGAU
Thur
Basel
Liestal
Frauenfeld
Bodensee
St. Gallen
St. Margrethen
FRANKREICH
Baden
Winterthur
ZÜRICH
Herisau
AUSSER-RHODEN
Delemont
BASEL
(LAND)
AARGAU
Zürich
APPENZELL
Appenzell
JURA
Aarau
Reuss
INNER-RHODEN
SOLOTHURN
Zürichsee
Solothurn
Biel
LUZERN
Zug
SANKT
Vaduz
Neuchâtel
ZUG
Einsiedeln
GALLEN
ÖSTERREICH
NEUENBURG
Luzern
SCHWYZ
Glarus
LIECHTENSTEIN
Neuenburger See
Bern
Schwyz
GLARUS
Vierwaldstätter See
Stans
Chur
Fribourg
BERNER
OBERLAND
Sarnen
NIDW.
Altdorf
Braunwald
Davos
WAADT
FREIBURG
BERN
Thun
UNTERWALDEN
OBW.
Engelberg
URI
GRAUBÜNDEN
Brienz
Brienzer See
Andermatt
Disentis
Thuner See
Interlaken
A
St. Moritz
Lausanne
Jungfrau
Grindelwald
Klosters
Montreux
Gstaad
Jungfraujoch
L
P
E
N
Genfer See
Brig
TESSIN
Genf
Sion
Rhône
Bellinzona
GENF
WALLIS
Locarno
Matterhorn
Zermatt
Lugano
NIDW = NIDWALDEN
OBW = OBWALDEN
Langensee
ITALIEN

Die Schweiz und Liechtenstein

Einwohner

Schweiz (2000): 7,2 Mio
Liechtenstein (1998): 30 000
Maßstab 2,0 cm = 50 km

Einführung

Einführung. Note: The **Einführung** aims to familiarize students with the range of activities in the book. Students will use German in simple communicative situations that focus mainly on sharing basic personal information. They will also see authentic texts throughout the book. In some cases the texts and pictures illustrate a particular point; in others they provide the reading and listening material.

Grüß dich!

In diesem Kapitel

- **Themen:** Words for greetings and farewells, getting acquainted, spelling in German, numbers, some classroom expressions
- **Kultur:** Forms of address, inquiring about someone's well-being, postal codes and country abbreviations, German-speaking countries and their neighbors

Videoclips
Wer ist wer in Berlin?

Hallo! Guten Tag! Herzlich willkommen!*

Im Tennisklub in Offenbach

TENNIS-TRAINER:	**Guten Tag! Herzlich willkommen! Mein Name ist** Pohle, Norbert Pohle. Und **wie ist Ihr Name?**
SABINE:	Sabine Zimmermann.
TRAINER:	Und Sie? **Wie heißen Sie?**
ANTONIO:	**Ich heiße** Antonio Coletti.
ARI:	Und **ich bin** Ari Pappas.

Hallo! Suggestion: Ask students if they already know any German greetings. Write them on the board.

Dialogue 1. Suggestion: Use the vocabulary in the dialogue to introduce yourself to the class and to ask students what their names are. Move from student to student, saying: *Guten Tag! Mein Name ist _____. Herzlich willkommen! Und wie ist Ihr Name?* Shake hands with students during the interaction, and point out that this is usual when greeting someone outside the classroom. Read the dialogue through, ensuring that you are clearly playing the roles of different people (i.e., draw figures on the board, use different voices, stand in different positions); have students practice dialogues in pairs.

PETER:	**Grüß dich.** Ich heiße Peter Sedlmeier.
KATARINA:	Mein Name ist Katarina Steinmetz.
PETER:	**Woher kommst du?**
KATARINA:	**Aus** Dresden. Und du?
PETER:	Aus Rosenheim.

Dialogue 2. Suggestion: Set the scene of two students meeting each other. Explain that the language is more informal. Model the dialogue and have students take roles to practice. Follow up with similar dialogues, where students introduce themselves to each other.

---

*New, active vocabulary is shown in bold print.

This is not as rude as it seems — also means "here"

pleasing

Freut mich. Don't need a!

HERR GROTE: **Frau** Kühne, **das ist Herr** Michels aus Berlin. Frau Kühne
kommt aus Potsdam.
HERR MICHELS: **Freut mich.**
FRAU KÜHNE: **Gleichfalls.**

Ein Treffen (*meeting*) in Berlin

Grüß dich! Should have an·

Kulturtipp. Note: This recurring feature introduces cultural information that relates to the topics of activities or readings in the chapter. In the early chapters they are in English to ensure that the students understand them. In later chapters they are in German.

KULTURTIPP

German speakers address one another as **Sie** or **du. Sie** (*You*) is used for strangers and acquaintances. Family members and friends address one another with **du** (*you*), as do children and, generally, students. Otherwise, only very close personal friends address one another with **du** and first names. Most adults address one another as **Herr** or **Frau** and use **Sie** although some might use first names with **Sie. Frau** is the standard title for all women, regardless of marital status.

Aktivität 1. Suggestion:
Before beginning the activity, write the necessary phrases on the board so that students can work without their books. Students should stand up and walk around the room and talk to as many different people as possible within the time limit you have set. Make sure that you monitor the students' interactions.

May I introduce?

Aktivität 2. Suggestion:
Model the interaction by introducing a couple of students to each other. To make the activity as authentic as possible, remind students to introduce people to each other who might not yet have met.

How is that spelled?

Wie schreibt man das? Point Out: While we refer to letters with an umlaut as a-, o-, or u-umlaut, these are distinct letters and sounds in German. German speakers refer to them as *ä, ö,* and *ü*. Model these sounds carefully.

An example of spelling reform changes is displayed with the word *nass*, formerly spelled *naß*.

Aktivität 1   Wie ist der Name?

Introduce yourself to several people in your class.

s1: Mein Name ist _____.
s2: Ich heiße _____.
s1: Woher kommst du?
s2: Aus _____. Und du?
s1: Aus _____.

Aktivität 2   Darf ich vorstellen?°

Introduce a classmate to another.

BEISPIEL: GINA: Paul, das ist Chris.
PAUL: Tag, Chris.
CHRIS: Hallo, Paul.

Wie schreibt man das?°

When you introduce yourself or give information about yourself, you may have to spell out words for clarification. In contrast to English, German follows fairly predictable spelling and pronunciation rules. You will gradually learn these rules throughout the course. Native speakers of German are learning new spelling rules too, since a spelling reform was instituted in 1998.

The German alphabet has the same twenty-six letters as the English alphabet, plus four other letters of its own. The four special German letters are written as follows. Note that the letter **ß** has no capital; **SS** is used instead.

Ä ä   a-Umlaut: **Bär, Käse**

Ö ö   o-Umlaut: **böse, hören**

Ü ü   u-Umlaut: **müde, Süden**

ß   sz („ess tsett"): **süß, Straße**

Hier klicken!

You'll find more about the German spelling reform in **Deutsch: Na klar!** on the World Wide Web at www.mhhe.com/dnk.

The alphabet house (**Buchstabenhaus**) on page 5 shows how German schoolchildren learn to write the letters of the alphabet. In addition to displaying individual letters, the **Buchstabenhaus** also practices such frequently used combinations as **ch, sch,** and the diphthongs.

Buchstabenhaus.
Suggestion: Have students discover which letters look different from the letter styles they learned to write in school.

Have students look at the children's handwriting in the letters to President Hoover in the **Übergang** chapter at the end of the book.

Aktivität 3. Suggestion: Have students repeat in groups of three letters. It is best to write out and point to letters on the board as they are spoken.

Follow-up: Pass out a set of cards with a letter of the alphabet on each card. Say the letters at random. As each is said, the student with the corresponding card holds it up.

Aktivität 3   Das ABC.

Repeat the letters of the German alphabet after your instructor.

Aktivität 4   B-E-R-L-I-N: So schreibt man das!°

That's how you spell it!

Listen as your instructor spells some common German words. Write the words as you hear them.

Aktivität 4. Suggestion: Say, then spell, each word. Then say the word again. You may wish to repeat the spelling. This should be a playful and low-anxiety activity. 1. *Musik* 2. *Herz* 3. *Bücher* 4. *schön* 5. *groß*

Follow-up. Keyboard: Assign each student to play a letter of the alphabet; include the umlaut letters. Then call out a familiar word in German, e.g., *Name*. Students become a living keyboard. The student who is *N* stands up, says *N*, and remains standing. Then *A*, *M*, and *E* do the same. After the word is spelled, the whole class repeats the word.

Wie schreibt man das?   **5**

Aktivität 5. Suggestion:
Demonstrate this activity by referring to the accompanying drawing first. Students turn to each other to do the activity. Have them reverse roles.

Aktivität 5 Wie bitte?°

Introduce yourself to another student and spell your name.

BEISPIEL: S1: Mein Name ist _____.
S2: Wie bitte?
S1: (*repeat your name; then spell it in German*)
S2: Ah, so!

Aktivität 6 Buchstabieren Sie!°

Aktivität 6. Suggestion:
Spot-check students' words by having several students spell the words they have written. Encourage them to come up with words other than the ones listed here.

Think of a common German word, name, product, or company name. Without saying the word, spell it in German (**auf Deutsch**) for a classmate, who writes it down and reads the word back to you.

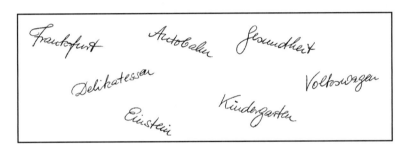

Frankfurt   Autobahn   Gesundheit

Delikatessen   Volkswagen

Einstein   Kindergarten

Hallo! Mach's gut! Point Out:
Greetings differ from region to region; e.g., Austrians who know each other will say *Servus. Hallo* and *Hi* are very popular among young people.

Suggestion: Model the greetings using various kinds of intonation and emotional states, e.g., enthusiastic and glad to see someone, sad, displeased to see someone. Have students repeat what you say and how you say it.

Hallo!—Mach's gut!°

How do people in German-speaking countries greet one another and say good-bye? Look at the following expressions and illustrations, and see whether you can guess which ones are greetings and which ones are good-byes.

German speakers use various formal and informal hellos and good-byes, depending on the situation and the person with whom they are speaking.

Saying hello:

FORMAL	CASUAL	USE
guten Morgen	Morgen	*until about 10:00 A.M.*
guten Tag	Tag	*generally between 10:00 A.M. and early evening*
guten Abend	'n Abend*	*from about 5:00 P.M. on*
grüß Gott†	grüß Gott	*southern German and Austrian for* **guten Tag**
	grüß dich	*greeting among young people*
	hallo	*any time*

Saying good-bye and good night:

FORMAL	CASUAL	USE
auf Wiedersehen	Wiederseh'n	*any time*
	mach's gut	*among young people, friends, and family*
	tschüss	*among young people, family*
gute Nacht	Nacht	*only when someone is going to bed at night*

Note: The word *tschüss*, sometimes spelled *tschüs*, is related to the French word *adieu*.

---

*The **'n** before **Abend** is short for **guten.**
†*Lit.* Greetings in the name of God.

What do you say?

Aktivität 7 Was sagt man?°

What would people say in the following circumstances?

1. ____ your German instructor entering the the classroom
2. ____ two students saying good-bye
3. ____ a person from Vienna greeting an acquaintance
4. ____ two students meeting at a café
5. ____ a mother as she turns off the lights in her child's room at night
6. ____ a student leaving a professor's office
7. ____ family members greeting one another in the morning
8. ____ a hostess and her guests saying good-bye in the evening

a. Gute Nacht!
b. Grüß dich!
c. Tschüss!
d. Mach's gut!
e. Guten Tag!
f. (Auf) Wiedersehen!
g. (Guten) Morgen!
h. Grüß Gott!
i. Hallo!
j. Guten Abend!

Aktivität 7. Suggestion: Have students look over the possible responses before answering the questions. Remind them to think about the intonation and tone of voice that they would use in each situation.

So, how's it going?

Na, wie geht's?°

German has several ways of asking *How are you?*

Wie geht es dir?
Wie geht's? } *a family member or friend*

Wie geht es Ihnen, Herr Lindemann? *an acquaintance*

You can respond in a number of different ways.

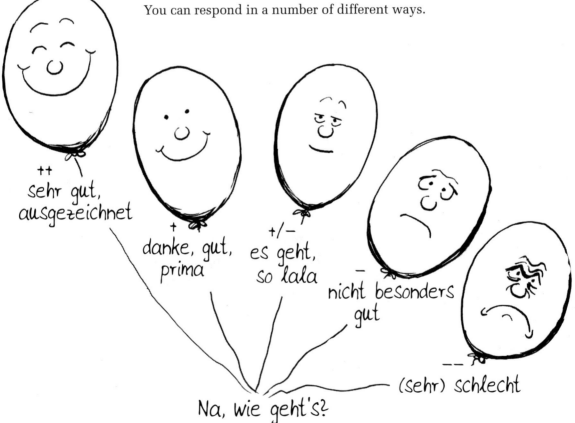

++
sehr gut, ausgezeichnet

+
danke, gut, prima

+/−
es geht, so lala

−
nicht besonders gut

−−
(sehr) schlecht

Na, wie geht's?

German speakers will ask someone **Na, wie geht's?** or **Wie geht es Ihnen?** only if they already know the person well. When you ask a native German speaker, be prepared for a detailed answer, particularly if the person is not feeling well. **Hi,** or **Hallo, wie geht's?** is sometimes used as a general greeting among young people even if they don't know each other.

Realia. Note: Reading strategies will be the focus of the **Lesen** section of **Sprache im Kontext** in each chapter. However, students should be encouraged to practice techniques such as contextual guessing when working with the realia wherever it occurs. For this reason, only a minimal amount of glossing will be provided for most of the realia.

NA, WIE GEHT'S?

ICH WEISS NICHT! ICH FÜHLE MICH HEUTE MORGEN SO ZERSCHLAGEN![1]

[1]Ich . . . *I don't know! I feel so beat this morning!*

Aktivität 8   Wie geht's?

Listen as three pairs of people greet each other and conduct brief conversations. Indicate whether the statements below match what you hear.

	JA	NEIN
Dialog 1		
a. The conversation takes place in the morning.	☐	☒
b. The greetings are informal.	☒	☐
c. The man and the woman are both doing fine.	☐	☒
Dialog 2		
a. The two speakers must be from southern Germany or Austria.	☒	☐
b. The speakers are close friends.	☐	☒
c. Both of them are doing fine.	☒	☐
Dialog 3		
a. The two speakers know each other well.	☒	☐
b. The man is feeling great.	☒	☐
c. They use a formal expression to say good-bye.	☐	☒

Aktivität 8. Note: Listening comprehension exercises will appear throughout the book. In the **Themen** section of each chapter, the focus is on new vocabulary.

Pre-listening Suggestion: Give students time to read through the information in the activity before you play the tape. Encourage them to make a habit of this, as it provides clues about what they will hear.

Post-listening Suggestion: After you have gone over the correct answers, focus on the words and expressions in each dialogue that provide the correct answers. Then play each dialogue again, so that the students can listen to them fully aware of what they are hearing.

Aktivität 9   Und wie geht es dir?

Start a conversation chain by asking one classmate how he/she is.

BEISPIEL: s1: Na, Peter, wie geht's?
　　　　　 s2: So lala. Wie geht es dir, Kathy?
　　　　　 s3: Ausgezeichnet! Und wie geht's dir,...?

Aktivität 9. Note: Make sure that questions are directed to those across the room as well as to those next to the questioner.

So zählt man auf Deutsch.°

Eins, zwei, drei...

So zählt man auf Deutsch.
Suggestion: Model the numbers from 0 to 20 and have students repeat them. Introduce new numbers two or three at a time, and begin from 1 each time to reinforce the lower numbers. Use your fingers to count from 0 to 10, but make sure you use your fingers as a German speaker would, starting with the thumb (as illustrated in the drawing). For numbers over 10 and for review, write numbers on the board or hold up flash cards as you say the numbers.

Follow-up: Pass out flash cards with numbers on them. Say numbers at random; the student with the number holds up the card.

Point Out: You might want to mention to students the two different German terms for "number." *Zahl* refers to numbers used by themselves, whereas *Nummer* refers to numbers in context. For example:*Sieben und elf sind Zahlen,* but *Heikes Nummer ist 0651-0001.*

Follow-up: Play bingo. Students draw up own cards of nine numbers between 0 and 20, or 0 and 30, and cross off numbers as you call them. The first person to cross out all numbers calls "bingo" and must then call out the crossed-out numbers so you can verify them. Have a small prize for the first three or four winners.

Point Out: In spoken German, especially on the phone, people often say *zwo* for *zwei* to avoid confusion with *drei.*

0 null	9 neun	18 achtzehn	90 neunzig
1 eins	10 zehn	19 neunzehn	100 (ein)hundert
2 zwei	11 elf	20 zwanzig	200 zweihundert
3 drei	12 zwölf	30 dreißig	300 dreihundert
4 vier	13 dreizehn	40 vierzig	1 000 (ein)tausend
5 fünf	14 vierzehn	50 fünfzig	2 000 zweitausend
6 sechs	15 fünfzehn	60 sechzig	3 000 dreitausend
7 sieben	16 sechzehn	70 siebzig	
8 acht	17 siebzehn	80 achtzig	

The numbers 21 through 99 are formed by combining the numbers 1–9 with 20–90.

21 einundzwanzig	24 vierundzwanzig	27 siebenundzwanzig
22 zweiundzwanzig	25 fünfundzwanzig	28 achtundzwanzig
23 dreiundzwanzig	26 sechsundzwanzig	29 neunundzwanzig

The numbers *one* and *seven* are written as follows:

1   7

German uses a period or a space where English uses a comma.

1.000   7 000

Zwei,
Fünf,
Neun,
Eins,
Sechs,
Eins:

Telefonische
Anzeigenannahme[1]

BERLINER MORGENPOST
Berlins größte Abonnementzeitung

In German-speaking countries, telephone numbers generally have a varying number of digits and may be spoken as follows:

24 36 71   zwei, vier – drei, sechs – sieben, eins [*or*] vierundzwanzig – sechsunddreißig – einundsiebzig

[1]Telefonische . . . *Submit your ad by phone*

Aktivität 10 Wichtige Telefonnummern°

Important phone numbers

Imagine that you are calling for information. Write the phone numbers you hear in the appropriate space.

Hier klicken!

You'll find more about telephone numbers in **Deutsch: Na klar!** on the World Wide Web at www.mhhe.com/dnk.

Aktivität 10. Suggestion: For this activity, you may wish to play the recording or simply read the script aloud. It is important to read it at normal speed. Students may ask you to repeat by saying *Wie bitte?*

Telefon-Ansagen	☎		Theater und Konzerte	1 15 17
Polizei	1 10		Feuerwehr/Rettungsleitstelle	1 12
Kinoprogramme	1 15 11		Wetter	38 53
Küchenrezepte	11 67		Zahlenlotto	11 62
Sport	11 63		Zeit	19 94

Suggestion: Remember that it takes a long time to become proficient with numbers. Students should use single digits to practice telephone numbers and postal codes. Double-digit numbers should be considered passive vocabulary and used only if necessary for house numbers. Students will have an opportunity to begin using double-digit numbers actively in **Kapitel 1.**

ANALYSE

Look over the examples of addresses (**Adressen**) from German-speaking countries. How do they differ from the way addresses are written in your country?

- Locate the name of the street (**Straße**) and the town (**Stadt**).
- Where is the house number (**Hausnummer**) placed? Where is the postal code (**Postleitzahl**) placed?
- Can you guess what the **A** before **9020 Klagenfurt** and the **CH** before **8050 Zürich-Oerlikon** represent?
- Now say each address out loud.

UNIVERSITÄT FÜR BILDUNGSWISSENSCHAFTEN KLAGENFURT

Universitätsstraße 65–67
A-9020 Klagenfurt

APOTHEKE

IN DER FRÖSCHAU

Apothekerin Helma Koch
Fröschau 38 · Tel. 0 96 61/10 22 99
92237 Sulzbach-Rosenberg

VERKEHRSMUSEUM  **DRESDEN**
Augustusstraße 1, 01067 Dresden · Tel. 0351/ 86440 · Fax 0351/8644110
http://www.verkehrsmuseum.sachsen.de
e-mail: verkehrsmuseum@verkehrsmuseum.sachsen.de

*Ferienträume ?
Wir erfüllen sie !*

TRAVELLER REISEN

*Filiale Oerlikon
CH-8050 Zürich-Oerlikon, Ohmstrasse 14*

*Telefon 01- 312 10 14
Telex 823 221
Telegramm: Travellerag Zürich*

Point Out:
CH stands for Confoederatio Helvetica (= Switzerland) and *A* for Austria.

So zählt man auf Deutsch **11**

Aktivität 11 Die Adresse und Telefonnummer, bitte!

You will hear three brief requests for addresses and telephone numbers. As you listen, mark the correct street numbers and jot down the postal codes and telephone numbers.

1. Professor Hausers Adresse ist . . .

   Gartenstraße   9   12   <u>19</u>

   <u>82067</u>   Ebenhausen/Isartal

   Die Telefonnummer ist <u>41 34 76</u>.

2. Die Adresse von Margas Fitnessstudio ist . . .

   Bautzner Straße   5   <u>15</u>   14

   <u>01093</u>   Dresden

   Die Telefonnummer ist <u>20 86 73</u>.

3. Die Adresse von Autohaus Becker ist . . .

   Landstuhler Straße   <u>54</u>   44   45

   <u>66482</u>   Zweibrücken-Ixheim

   Die Telefonnummer ist <u>1 88 42</u>.

Hier klicken!

You'll find more about the postal and country codes in **Deutsch: Na klar!** on the World Wide Web at www.mhhe.com/dnk.

KULTURTIPP

As in the United States, postal codes in Germany consist of five digits. Postal codes in Austria, Liechtenstein, and Switzerland have four digits. When mail is sent between countries in Europe, international abbreviations are used for the country names. Can you match the following country names with the correct abbreviations?

Belgien	(B)	**Rumänien**	(RO)
Dänemark	(DK)	**Russland**	(RUS)
Deutschland	(D)	**die Schweiz**	(CH)
Frankreich	(F)	**die Slowakei**	(SK)
Griechenland	(GR)	**Spanien**	(E)
Großbritannien	(GB)	**Tschechien**	(CZ)
Irland	(IRL)	**Ungarn**	(H)
Italien	(I)		
Liechtenstein	(FL)		
Luxemburg	(L)		
die Niederlande	(NL)		
Österreich	(A)		
Polen	(PL)		
Portugal	(P)		

Volkswagen –
da weiß man, was man hat.

Danke schön, Europa.

RO	DK	GR
F	CZ	A
IRL	D	PL
SK	B	GB
CH	I	L
E	NL	RUS
FL	H	P

Aktivität 12 Hin und her°: Wie ist die Postleitzahl?

Back and forth

This is the first of many activities in which you will exchange information with a partner. Here, one of you uses the chart below; the other turns to the corresponding chart in Appendix A. Take turns asking each other for the postal codes missing from your charts.

BEISPIEL: S1: Wie ist die Postleitzahl von Eisenach?
S2: D-99817. Wie ist die Postleitzahl von Bitburg?
S1: D-54634.

D-99817	Eisenach
D-54634	Bitburg
A-5020	Salzburg
CH-3800	Interlaken
D-94315	Straubing
D-06217	Merseburg
D-21614	Buxtehude
FL-9490	Vaduz

Aktivität 13 Ein Interview

A. Interview a partner using the questions provided below. Jot down the information using the grid below.

Wie heißt du?

Woher kommst du?

Wie ist deine Adresse?

Wie ist die Postleitzahl?

Wie ist deine Telefonnummer?

Name	
Wohnort	
Straße und Hausnummer	
Postleitzahl	
Telefonnummer	

B. Now tell the class about the person you interviewed.

BEISPIEL: Das ist Kerstin aus Chicago.
Die Adresse ist 678 Maple Street. Die
Postleitzahl ist 54880. Die Telefonnummer ist 555-4797.

Aktivität 12. This is the first of many information-gap activities designed to create a genuine exchange of information in a controlled context. Each student has only half the information in the chart and must ask his/her partner questions to fill in the gaps. Since this is the first information-gap activity, be sure students understand how the activity works by demonstrating the model with one student and then having the class observe two paired students performing an exchange.

Note: Point out to students that the international country abbreviations are treated as part of the postal code when mail is sent between countries.

Aktivität 13. Suggestion: Review with students the information sought.

Note: Some students may be reluctant to share personal information with their classmates. Be sure to let them know that they may make up fictional personal information about themselves.

Realia: Explain that **Quelle** is a well-known mail-order company in Germany.

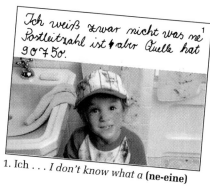

Ich weiß zwar nicht was ne¹ Postleitzahl ist, aber Quelle hat 90750.

1. Ich . . . *I don't know what a* (**ne-eine**)

Nützliche Ausdrücke im Sprachkurs°

IHR DEUTSCH**LEHRER** / IHRE DEUTSCH**LEHRERIN** SAGT:

Bitte. . .	Please . . .
Hören Sie zu.	Listen.
Schreiben Sie.	Write.
Machen Sie die Bücher auf Seite _____ auf.	Open your books to page _____.
Lesen Sie.	Read.
Machen Sie die Bücher zu.	Close your books.
Setzen Sie sich.	Be seated.
Wiederholen Sie.	Repeat.
Haben Sie Fragen?	Do you have any questions?
[Ist] Alles klar?	Is everything clear?
Noch einmal!	Once more, please; could you say that again, please?

SIE SAGEN:

Langsamer, bitte!	*Slower, please.*
Wie, bitte?	*Pardon? What did you say?*
Wie schreibt man _____?	*How do you write _____?*
Ich habe eine Frage.	*I have a question.*
Wie sagt man _____ auf Deutsch?	*How do you say _____ in German?*
Was bedeutet _____?	*What does _____ mean?*
Das weiß ich nicht.	*I don't know.*
Ich verstehe das nicht.	*I don't understand.*
Ja.	*Yes.*
Nein.	*No.*
Danke [schön].	*Thank you.*

Sie können schon etwas Deutsch!°

Even if you have never studied German before, you will soon find that you know more German than you think. For example, look at the ad on the next page taken from a German phone book's yellow pages (**gelbe Seiten**).

- What is this ad for?
- Which words are *identical* in English?
- Which words in the ad look *similar* to words you use in English?

Note: It may be necessary to "walk students through" a piece of realia to accustom them to dealing with authentic texts.

Point Out: Cognates are clues to meaning in most texts. Also encourage students to draw on their background knowledge when approaching these texts.

Words like **Motel, Hotel, Restaurant,** and **Sauna** are borrowed from other languages: **Motel** from American English, **Restaurant** and **Hotel** from French, and **Sauna** from Finnish. These words are used internationally.

Some words in the ad look similar to English words, for example **Biergarten.** You may already have seen the word **Biergarten** in English-language text. This word has been borrowed from German, along with some other German words commonly used in English, such as **Kindergarten** and **Delikatessen.** You recognize the words *beer* and *garden* in **Biergarten. Bier** and *beer,* **Garten** and *garden* have the same meaning in both languages. These words are cognates. Cognates are descended from the same word or form. Since English and German are both Germanic languages, they share many cognates. This common linguistic ancestry will help you a great deal in understanding German. Recognizing cognates is an important skill stressed throughout this textbook.

Cognates like **Bier** and **Garten** are easy to recognize. Understanding other words takes more imaginative guessing: for instance, what do you think **Hallenbad** means? Other words in the ad probably look completely unfamiliar. The word **Ruf,** for instance, is not easily guessed. The meaning can be guessed from the context, however, and you already know a synonym for this word. What is it?

Now summarize what you have found out about "Zum Dorfkrug." Add any additional information you were able to extract from the ad by guessing.

Aktivität 14   Informationen finden

An important first step in reading is identifying the type of text you have in front of you. Look for verbal as well as visual clues. Look at the texts on the next page. Write the letter of each text in front of the appropriate category in the list below (some categories will remain empty).

1. __e__ an ad for a movie
2. _____ a list of the week's bestsellers
3. __b__ a concert announcement
4. __d__ a headline
5. _____ a short news item about crime in Germany
6. __a__ an ad for a restaurant
7. __c__ a section from a TV guide

Aktivität 14. Suggestion: This activity familiarizes students with various types of texts in German. Students can work in pairs. After students complete the exercise, ask them how they were able to recognize the various categories.

CAFÉ KADENZ

Pfiffige Mischung aus Bistro, Café, Restaurant und Bar. Schlemmerfrühstück, großes Kaffeeangebot, kleine, leckere Gerichte, ausgesuchte Weine und Cocktails verlocken dazu, in einem Hauch von Wiener Caféhausatmosphäre zu genießen.

Täglich geöffnet
von 10.00 - 01.00 Uhr
Jüdenstr. 17 • 37073 Göttingen
Übrigens: Auch Sonntags geöffnet
Tel. 0551/ 4 72 08

a.

SYMPHONISCHES ORCHESTER BERLIN

Heute, 16 Uhr   PHILHARMONIE

Dirigent: **László Kovács**
Solist: **Boris Bloch**

Kodály: Tänze aus Galanta
Tschaikowsky: Konzert für Klavier und Orchester Nr. 2, G-Dur, op. 44
Rimsky-Korsakoff: „Scheherazade" Symphonische Suite aus „Tausend und eine Nacht"

b.

20.15   **KABEL 1**

FILM   **Lawrence von Arabien**

Kairo, 1916: Im Auftrag seiner Regierung vereint der britische Offizier Thomas E. Lawrence (Peter O'Toole, l.), mit Anthony Quinn) die Wüstenstämme Arabiens zu einer schlagkräftigen Armee und führt sie in den Aufstand gegen die Türken.

c.

Hunger in Afrika
Reicher Kontinent
in Not

d.

e.
Metropolis

Aktivität 15 Sie verstehen schon etwas Deutsch!°

You already understand some German!

You have learned that you can use visual and verbal cues to understand a considerable amount of written German. Now you will hear some short radio announcements and news headlines. Listen for cognates and other verbal clues as you try to understand the gist of what is being said. As you hear each item, write its number in front of the topic(s) to which it corresponds. Not all the topics below will be mentioned.

Aktivität 15. Suggestion: Play the recording twice, once for students to complete the exercise and the second time to check responses.

__1__ Automobil	_____ Musik	__3__ Sport
_____ Bank	_____ Politik	_____ Tanz
_____ Film	__4__ Restaurant	__2__ Theater
__5__ Kinder		

Aktivität 16 Freizeitspaß

Working with a partner, find out as much information as possible from the ad **Freizeitspaß.** You don't have to understand every word or sentence to get the gist.

1. What is advertised here?
2. Which words do you recognize immediately?
3. What two cognates do you see in the word **Tanzschule?**
4. In which city is the **Tanzschule** located?
5. Which words look familiar in the last sentence of the ad?
6. What could this sentence mean?

Aktivitäten 14, 15 und 16. Throughout the course, students will be confronted with texts that are above their productive ability. If students are tempted to look up words they don't recognize, encourage them to refrain. Emphasize that it is more productive to work from context and cognates as much as possible at first. When adult readers can identify the type of text they are looking at, their background knowledge of the world and the subject will help them to decipher meaning, particularly when cognates are present. The object is to expose students to authentic real texts written for German speakers rather than simplified ones devised specifically for foreign language learners. It is important that students develop productive reading strategies in German, strategies that they probably use automatically in English but that may not come naturally in dealing with a foreign language text.

KULTURTIPP

Wo spricht man Deutsch? (*Where is German spoken?*)

Naturally, German is spoken in Germany, but it is also spoken in many other countries. Which of the following countries have relatively large German-speaking populations?

☐ Argentinien
☐ Bosnien
☐ Brasilien
☐ Italien
☐ Liechtenstein
☐ Luxemburg
☐ Österreich
☐ Polen
☐ Rumänien
☐ die Schweiz
☐ Tschechien
☐ Ungarn

German is the official language of Germany (**Deutschland**), Austria (**Österreich**), and Liechtenstein. It is one of four official languages of Switzerland (**die Schweiz**) and one of three official languages of Luxembourg and Belgium. German is also spoken in regions of France, Denmark, Italy, the Czech Republic, Poland, Rumania, Bosnia and Herzegovina, Hungary, Latvia, Lithuania, Estonia, Russia, and the Ukraine. Altogether, between 120 and 140 million Europeans speak German as their first language—more than the number of people in Europe who speak English as their first language.

German is also spoken by many people as a first language in other countries such as Brazil, Argentina, Canada, and the United States (Pennsylvania Dutch). In Namibia, German is spoken by a sizable minority. It is estimated that outside Europe, an additional 20 million people speak German as their first language.

According to U.S. Department of Commerce figures, over 50 million U.S. citizens claim German descent.

At present, approximately 20 million people worldwide are learning German in formal courses. Two-thirds of these people live in eastern Europe.

Maps: For more detail on Europe and the principal German-speaking countries, refer students to the maps in the front of this book.

Note: Namibia is a former German colony.

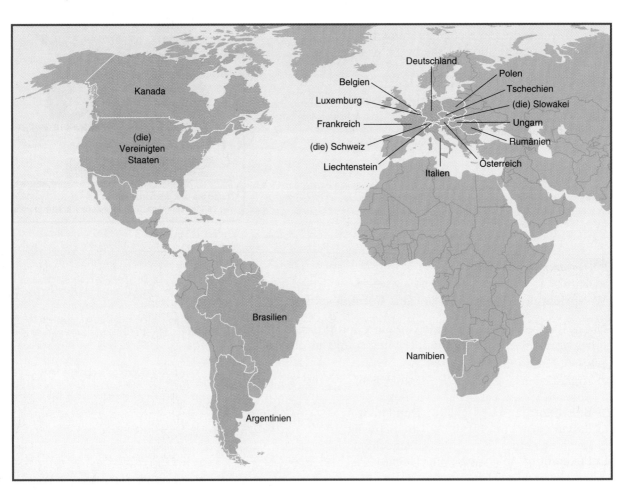

Videoclips

A. Michael, our moderator for the interviews you will see throughout **Deutsch: Na klar!,** asks people their names in two different ways. Watch the video segment and complete the following questions.

1. Using the informal form, he asks Dennis: "_____ _____ du?"
2. Using the formal form, he asks Herr Borowsky: "_____ _____ Sie?"

B. Several people respond to the above questions in one of two ways. Watch and complete the following.

1. „Hallo! _____ Name _____ Dennis".
2. „Ich _____ Beatrice. Guten Morgen!"
3. „_____ _____ ist Kurt Borowsky".

C. Now concentrate on the segments with Peter, Jasmin, and Frau Simon. Complete their profiles.

Peter	„Guten Tag! _____ _____ ist Peter Junkel". „Ich _____ _____ Berlin-Spandau". „Die _____ ist Bechsteinweg Numero (*number*) 10 in _____ Berlin". „Meine Telefonnummer ist _____ ".
Jasmin	„_____ Tag! Mein _____ ist Jasmin Walter. _____ komme _____ Berlin. _____ _____ ist die Lietzenburgerstraße Numero 20 in _____ Berlin. Meine Telefonnummer ist _____ ".
Frau Simon	„Guten Tag, _____ _____ Malle Simon und wohne in _____ auf der Schönhauser Allee". „Meine Telefonnummer ist 030/_____ ".

D. Now watch all the interviews again and listen for the following information. Select the correct response.

1. Oliver geht es...
   a. glänzend. **b.** sehr gut. **c.** so lala.
2. Jan wohnt...
   a. in Berlin. **b.** in Hamburg. **c.** in Hannover.
3. Harald kommt ursprünglich (*originally*)...
   a. aus Hannover. **b.** aus Berlin. **c.** aus Leipzig.
4. Nicolettas Adresse ist...
   a. Lietzenburgerstraße 13. **b.** Pappelallee 35. **c.** Schönhauser Allee 41.
5. Saras Postleitzahl ist...
   a. 10557 Berlin. **b.** 12203 Berlin. **c.** 10437 Berlin.
6. Herr Borowsky kommt...
   a. aus Hamburg. **b.** aus Düsseldorf. **c.** aus Berlin.
7. Michael fragt: „Wie Heißt due?" Ali sagt: ...
   a. „Mein Name ist Ali". **b.** „Ich bin der Ali". **c.** „Ich heiße Ali".

Wortschatz

Wortschatz: Vocabulary lists are organized into conceptual groups, where possible, or into grammatical categories. Students should use these lists as a study checklist.

Zur Begrüßung — Greetings

grüß dich	hello, hi (*among friends and family*)
guten Abend	good evening
(guten) Morgen	good morning
(guten) Tag	hello, good day
hallo	hello (*among friends and family*)
herzlich willkommen	welcome

Beim Abschied — Saying Good-bye

(auf) Wiedersehen	good-bye
gute Nacht	good night
Mach's gut.	Take care, so long. (*informal*)
tschüss	so long, bye (*informal*)

Bekannt werden — Getting Acquainted

Frau; die Frau	Mrs., Ms.; woman
Herr; der Herr	Mr.; gentleman
der Lehrer /die Lehrerin	teacher
Das ist . . .	This is . . .
Wie heißt du?	What's your name? (*informal*)
Wie ist dein Name?	What's your name? (*informal*)
Wie heißen Sie?	What's your name? (*formal*)
Wie ist Ihr Name?	What's your name? (*formal*)
Woher kommst du?	Where are you from? (*informal*)
Woher kommen Sie?	Where are you from? (*formal*)
Ich bin . . .	I'm . . .
Ich heiße . . .	My name is . . .
Ich komme aus . . .	I'm from . . .
Mein Name ist . . .	My name is . . .
bitte	please; you're welcome
danke	thanks
danke schön	thank you very much
Freut mich.	Pleased to meet you.

(continued)

gleichfalls	likewise
und	and

Auskunft erfragen — Asking for Information

ja	yes
nein	no
Wie bitte?	Pardon? What did you say?
Wie heißt . . .	What is the name of . . .
die Stadt?	the town; city?
die Straße?	the street?
Wie ist . . .	What is . . .
deine/Ihre Telefonnummer?	your (*informal/ formal*) telephone number?
die Adresse?	the address?
die Hausnummer?	the street address?
die Postleitzahl?	the postal code?

Nach dem Befinden fragen — Asking About Someone's Well-being

Na, wie geht's?	How are you? (*casual*)
Wie geht's?	How are you (*informal*)?
Wie geht's dir?	How are you (*informal*)?
Wie geht es Ihnen?	How are you (*formal*)?
ausgezeichnet	excellent
danke, gut	fine, thanks
nicht besonders gut	not particularly well
prima	great, super
so lala	OK, so-so
schlecht	bad(ly), poor(ly)
sehr gut	very well; fine; good

Im Deutschunterricht — In German Class

Das weiß ich nicht.	I don't know.
Ich habe eine Frage.	I have a question.
Ich verstehe das nicht.	I don't understand.

Langsamer, bitte.	Slower, please.	80 achtzig	300 dreihundert
Was bedeutet _____?	What does _____ mean?	90 neunzig	1 000 (ein)tausend
Wie bitte?	Pardon? What did you say?	100 (ein)hundert	2 000 zweitausend
Wie sagt man _____ auf Deutsch?	How do you say _____ in German?	200 zweihundert	3 000 dreitausend
Wie schreibt man _____?	How do you write _____?		

Zahlen / Numbers

Zahlen		Numbers	
0	null	13	dreizehn
1	eins	14	vierzehn
2	zwei	15	fünfzehn
3	drei	16	sechzehn
4	vier	17	siebzehn
5	fünf	18	achtzehn
6	sechs	19	neunzehn
7	sieben	20	zwanzig
8	acht	30	dreißig
9	neun	40	vierzig
10	zehn	50	fünfzig
11	elf	60	sechzig
12	zwölf	70	siebzig

Deutschsprachige Länder und ihre Nachbarn / German-speaking Countries and Their Neighbors

Deutschsprachige Länder und ihre Nachbarn	German-speaking Countries and Their Neighbors
Belgien	Belgium
Dänemark	Denmark
Deutschland	Germany
Frankreich	France
Italien	Italy
Liechtenstein	Liechtenstein
Luxemburg	Luxembourg
die Niederlande (*pl.*)	Netherlands
Österreich	Austria
Polen	Poland
die Schweiz	Switzerland
die Slowakei	Slovakia
Slowenien	Slovenia
Tschechien	Czech Republic
Ungarn	Hungary

LERNZIELE°

Learning goals

Use this checklist to verify that you can now . . .

- ☐ introduce yourself and others.
- ☐ say the alphabet and spell.
- ☐ use common greetings.
- ☐ ask about someone's well-being and respond to inquiries about your own well-being.
- ☐ read numbers and count.
- ☐ give your telephone number and address, and ask others for theirs.
- ☐ understand and use some basic classroom expressions.
- ☐ recognize cognates and use them to understand the gist of simple texts.
- ☐ name some European countries and identify the countries where German is spoken.

Lernziele: Learning goals are given at the end of every chapter. Show students how the goals relate to information and activities in the chapter. You may wish to have your students look at this list before they begin work in the chapter. Encourage them to use this checklist to monitor their progress and to assist them during review.

Über mich und andere

Was machen diese
Studenten?
a. Sie spielen Tennis.
b. Sie spielen Karten.
c. Sie sagen, „Tag, wie
   geht's?"

Kapitel 1. Suggestion: You
may preview the theme of this
chapter by describing yourself
and sharing some personal
information (where you are
from, where you live, etc.).
Some of this will be review
from the Einführung. Other
information can be introduced
using mime and pictures.

Videoclips

Beruf, Studium und
Hobbys

In diesem Kapitel

- **Themen:** Personal characteristics, hobbies and interests
- **Grammatik:** Nouns, gender, and definite articles; personal pronouns;
  infinitives and present tense; word order; asking questions; **denn**
  and **ja**
- **Kultur: Einwohnermeldeamt,** foreigners in Germany

Alles klar? Beginning with this chapter, the **Alles klar?** section introduces the major chapter topic through illustrations and other visuals that set the tone for the chapter. Students will be asked to react to them and to express their own opinions.

Alles klar?

If this activity is done in class, give students time to scan the information requested as well as the documents. Then call on individuals for responses. Or have them work in pairs, allowing three to four minutes to complete the activity. Otherwise, have students do the activity as homework.

A. One of the things you will learn to do in German is to give information about people in different contexts and situations. People give information about themselves in personal documents—documents they use in everyday life—as, for example, in personal IDs. Let's take a close look at one such ID.

Try to find the following information in the personal ID:

- What is the full name of the ID holder?
- When was he born?
- What is his nationality?
- Where does he live?
- What information is provided after the word **Größe?**
- What color are his eyes?
- What does the word **Unterschrift** refer to?

Vokabelsuche (*word search*).
Find the German word for:

1. birthdate   *Geburtstag*
2. nationality   *Staatsangehörigkeit*
3. color of eyes   *Augenfarbe*
4. height   *Größe*

B. You will now hear five speakers introduce themselves. As you listen, see whether you can hear what cities they are from.

1. Berlin   Leipzig   <u>München</u>
2. Rostock   <u>Köln</u>   Luzern
3. <u>Wien</u>   Jena   Mainz
4. Düsseldorf   Graz   <u>Leipzig</u>
5. Erfurt   <u>Zürich</u>   Frankfurt

Gegenwärtige Anschrift
Adresse:

Flensburg
Teichstraße 14

Größe:

183 cm

Augenfarbe:

braun

PERSONALAUSWEIS
Name:

Tiemann

Vorname:

Hauke

Geburtstag:

24.05.76

Staatsangehörigkeit:

Deutsch

Gültig bis:

30.08.2005

Unterschrift:

Hauke Tiemann

Alles klar! Part B.
Suggestion: You may wish to have your students look at the color maps of Germany, Austria, and Switzerland at the front of the book as they listen.

Alles klar?   **23**

Wörter im Kontext

information

THEMA 1: Persönliche Angaben°

Wer sind diese Leute? Scan the information, then create a profile of each person.

1. Mein Name ist Harald Lohmann. Ich **bin** am 23. Mai 1956 in Dessau **geboren** und **wohne** jetzt in Magdeburg. **Ich bin Hochschullehrer von Beruf.** Meine Adresse ist Bahnhofstraße 20. Ich bin 1,82 Meter groß.

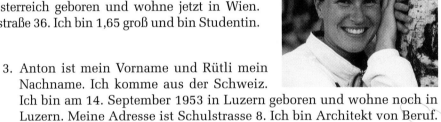

2. Mein Nachname ist Lercher und mein Vorname Daniela. Ich bin am 7. Januar 1979 in Graz in Österreich geboren und wohne jetzt in Wien. Meine Adresse ist Mozartstraße 36. Ich bin 1,65 groß und bin Studentin.

3. Anton ist mein Vorname und Rütli mein Nachname. Ich komme aus der Schweiz. Ich bin am 14. September 1953 in Luzern geboren und wohne noch in Luzern. Meine Adresse ist Schulstrasse 8. Ich bin Architekt von Beruf. Ich bin 1,79 groß.

Schreiben Sie Steckbriefe (*profiles*) von diesen Personen:

1. Vorname: Harald
   Nachname:
   Geburtstag:
   Geburtsort:
   Größe:
   Beruf:
   Wohnort:
   Straße und Hausnummer:
   Land:

2. Vorname:
   Nachname: Lercher
   Geburtstag:
   Geburtsort:
   Größe:
   Beruf:
   Wohnort:
   Straße und Hausnummer:
   Land:

Neue Wörter

bin...geboren was
  born
wohne live
ich bin...von Beruf
  my profession is . . .
Hochschullehrer
  university instructor

Wörter im Kontext. Each chapter is divided into three sections: **Wörter im Kontext, Grammatik im Kontext,** and **Sprache im Kontext.** The first section provides opportunities to acquire new vocabulary and expressions by exploring authentic materials, dialogues, and visuals. Students are asked to analyze the materials and figure out the meaning of words on their own. The activities of this section practice and recycle the vocabulary. Some grammar is previewed in short notes titled **Sprachtipp.** Activities are targeted at getting students to interact.

3. Vorname:
   Nachname: Rütli
   Geburtstag:
   Geburtsort: *Place of birth?*
   Größe:
   Beruf: *Profession?*
   Wohnort: *Living Place?*
   Straße und Hausnummer:
   Land: *Country?*

SPRACHTIPP

To ask how tall someone is, say:
Wie groß bist du? or **Wie groß sind Sie?**

   In stating their height, German speakers use the metric system. If you are 1.63 m (163 cm) tall, you can express it as follows: **Ich bin eins dreiundsechzig (groß)**. In German, it's written **1,63 m.**

1 cm (Zentimeter)	= 0.39 in. (inch)
1 in. (inch)	= **2.54 cm (Zentimeter)**

Sie ist 1,56 m groß   Er ist 1,94 m groß

Sprachtipp. This recurring feature focuses on an item of idiomatic usage of the language, or it briefly previews a grammar point that is explained in detail in the grammar section of the same or of a later chapter.

Aktivität I Interessante Personen

Listen to the following statements about the people in the profiles and say whether they are true (**das stimmt**) or false (**das stimmt nicht**).

	DAS STIMMT	DAS STIMMT NICHT
1. a.	☒	☐
b.	☐	☒
c.	☒	☐
d.	☐	☒
e.	☒	☐
f.	☒	☐
2. a.	☒	☐
b.	☐	☒
c.	☒	☐
d.	☒	☐
e.	☐	☒

Aktivität 1. Play each section of the activity separately. Once students have filled in the answers, ask them to turn to a partner to verify their answers. When going over the information in class, pay particular attention to incorrect information. For instance, *Herr Lohmann ist (nicht) Journalist. Er ist Hochschullerer.*

Jetzt = now, immediately

	DAS STIMMT	DAS STIMMT NICHT
3. a.	☒	☐
b.	☒	☐
c.	☒	☐
d.	☐	☒
e.	☐	☒

Jetzt sind Sie dran! (*Now it's your turn!*)

Mein Nachname ist _____.

Mein Vorname ist _____.

Ich komme aus _____.

Ich wohne in _____.

Meine Adresse ist _____.

Ich bin __ , ____ groß.

Hier klicken!

You'll find more about the **Einwohnermeldeamt** in **Deutsch: Na klar!** on the World Wide Web at www.mhhe.com/dnk.

KULTURTIPP

Everyone who lives in Germany must register with the **Einwohnermeldeamt** (residents' registration office) within two weeks of moving to a new community. This applies to everyone, even students living in a community only temporarily. The **Einwohnermeldeamt** must also be notified when one moves from one place to another.

Aktivität 2   Eine neue Studentin

Julie, who recently arrived in Berlin, is registering at the **Einwohnermeldeamt.** Listen to the interview between the official and Julie. What information does the official ask her for? Check **ja** if the information is asked for, **nein** if it is not.

	JA	NEIN
BEISPIEL: Vor- und Nachname	☒	☐
1. Wohnort in den USA	☒	☐
2. Beruf	☒	☐
3. Geburtsort	☐	☒
4. Geburtstag	☒	☐
5. Telefonnummer	☐	☒
6. Straße und Hausnummer	☒	☐
7. Postleitzahl	☐	☒

Aktivität 3.   Follow-up suggestion: Wrap up with a poll of who lives where and who was born where, based on the information that students have gathered.

Ask!

Suggestion.   Point out the meaning of *dein* and that the ending *-e* reflects a feminine noun.

Aktivität 3   Fragen Sie!

A. Unscramble the following to form questions for a short interview.

1. dein / wie / Name / ist /, bitte?

2. Adresse / ist / deine / wie?

3. deine / Telefonnummer / wie / ist?

4. Geburtsort / was / dein / ist?

5. groß / bist / wie / du?

Aktivität 3. Note: Some students may be reluctant to share personal information with their classmates, especially at the beginning of the semester. Be sensitive to this and let them know that they may provide made-up personal information.

B. Now use the questions to interview two people in your class.

C. Tell the class what you've found out.
- Das ist _____.
- (Tims/Elizabeths) Adresse ist _____.
- Seine/Ihre Telefonnummer ist _____.
- Er/Sie ist in _____ geboren.
- Er/Sie ist __, ____ groß.

Aktivität 4 Wie groß bist du? Wie alt bist du?

Figure out your height in meters with the help of the conversion chart. Then exchange this information with one or two people in the class.

BEISPIEL: s1: Wie groß bist du?
           s2: Ich bin 1,64 (eins vierundsechzig) groß.
           s1: Wie alt bist du?
           s2: Ich bin dreiundzwanzig.

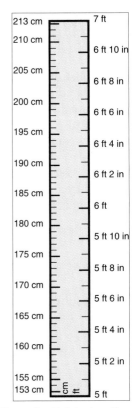

THEMA 2: „Glücksrad Fortuna"

ANSAGER: Guten Abend, meine Damen und Herren. Willkommen im Studio bei Glücksrad Fortuna. Und hier kommt Quizmaster Dieter Sielinski.

HERR SIELINSKY: Guten Abend und herzlich willkommen. Und hier ist unsere Kandidatin. Wie ist Ihr Name, bitte?

FRAU LENTZ: Lentz, Gabi Lentz.

HERR SIELINSKY: Woher kommen Sie, Frau Lentz?

FRAU LENTZ: Aus München.

HERR SIELINSKY: Na, und **wie finden Sie** Berlin denn?

FRAU LENTZ: **Ganz toll,** faszinierend. Aber München ist auch toll.

HERR SIELINSKY: So? Und was sind Sie von Beruf, Frau Lentz?

FRAU LENTZ: Ich bin Programmiererin.

HERR SIELINSKY: Und haben Sie Hobbys?

FRAU LENTZ: **Aber natürlich! Lesen, Reisen, Wandern, Kochen,** und ich mache **Kreuzworträtsel.**

HERR SIELINSKY: So, na dann **viel Glück heute Abend.**

FRAU LENTZ: **Danke sehr.**

Thema 2.   To introduce the new vocabulary, play or read the dialogues to the class. Remind students that they do not need to understand every word at first; rather they should use the context to arrive at the meaning of words they do not know. The **Analyse** that follows will also aid comprehension.

Neue Wörter

wie finden Sie...?
 how do you like. . .?
ganz toll   super
Lesen   reading
Reisen   traveling
Wandern   hiking
Kochen   cooking
Kreuzworträtsel
 crossword puzzles
viel Glück   good
 luck
heute Abend   tonight
danke sehr   thanks
 a lot

Neue Wörter

Sag mal Tell me
was machst du?
what are you doing?
jetzt now
hier here
ich lerne I'm
learning
Deutsch German
ich studiere I'm
studying; major-
ing in
Universität univer-
sity
bleibst du? are you
staying?
nächstes Jahr next
year

Ein Gespräch an der Uni

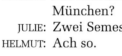

HELMUT: Grüß Gott! Helmut
Sachs.
JULIE: Guten Tag! Ich heiße
Julie Harrison.
HELMUT: Woher kommst du,
Julie?
JULIE: Ich komme aus
Cincinnati.
HELMUT: Cincinnati, wo ist
denn das?
JULIE: In den USA, im
Mittelwesten, im
Bundesstaat Ohio.
HELMUT: **Sag mal, was machst du jetzt hier?**
JULIE: Ich **lerne Deutsch** am Sprachinstitut. Und du?
HELMUT: Ich **studiere** Physik an der T.U.
JULIE: Was ist die T.U. denn?
HELMUT: Die Technische **Universität.** Und wie lange **bleibst** du hier in
München?
JULIE: Zwei Semester. **Nächstes Jahr** bin ich wieder in Ohio.
HELMUT: Ach so.

—staying

ANALYSE

Look at the dialogues again and locate the following information.

Glücksrad Fortuna

- How does the quizmaster ask his guest what her name is?
- What phrase does the quizmaster use to ask Frau Lentz where she is from?
- What does the quizmaster ask to find out Frau Lentz's profession?
- What question does he ask to find out about her hobbies?
- What question does he ask to find out if Frau Lentz likes Berlin?

Ein Gespräch an der Uni

- How do Helmut and Julie greet each other?
- How does Helmut ask Julie where she is from? How does this differ from the same question asked by the quizmaster?
- What phrase does Helmut use to ask Julie what she is doing in Munich?
- Helmut doesn't know where Cincinnati is. What does he ask Julie to get that information?

To say that you are studying at a university or to state your major, use the verb **studieren.**

Ich **studiere** Physik in München.

To say you are studying specific material, such as for a test, use **arbeiten** or **lernen.**

Ich **lerne** heute Abend für eine Chemieprüfung.
Ich **arbeite** auch für die Matheprüfung.

To say that you are learning or taking a language, use the verb **lernen.**

Ich **lerne** Deutsch.

studieren

arbeiten

lernen

Aktivität 5   Steht das im Dialog?

Mark whether the statements below are correct or incorrect, based on the information found in the dialogues in **Thema 2.**

	DAS STIMMT	DAS STIMMT NICHT
1. Der Quizmaster heißt Dieter Sielinsky.	☒	☐
2. Gabi Lentz kommt aus Augsburg.	☐	☒
3. Frau Lentz ist Professorin von Beruf.	☐	☒
4. Tanzen ist ein Hobby von Frau Lentz.	☐	☒
5. Frau Lentz findet Berlin zu groß.	☐	☒
6. Julie lernt Deutsch in München.	☒	☐
7. Helmut studiert Mathematik.	☐	☒
8. Julie bleibt zwei Jahre in München.	☐	☒

You may have already noticed that people address each other in different ways. In German, people are addressed either formally, with **Sie,** or informally, with **du.**

du (*you*): informal, one person
Sie (*you*): formal, one or more people, always capitalized

Another form, **ihr,** is used to address more than one person informally. It is the plural of **du.**

Use **du** (or **ihr** in plural) for:	Use **Sie** (in singular or plural) for:
a family member	a stranger
a close friend	an acquaintance
a fellow student	anyone you would address with a title, such as **Herr** or **Frau**
a child	
an animal	

du
Sie

ihr - plural of du

Aktivität 6. Suggestion:
Students can work in pairs.
Call on individuals to supply
responses. After the exercise
has been completed, students
can act out the dialogue.

Aktivität 6   Fragen und Antworten°

Match each question in the left-hand column with a possible answer from the right-hand column. More than one answer is possible.

1. __c d__ Wie heißen Sie?
2. __f g__ Woher kommst du?
3. __a e__ Was machen Sie hier?
4. __b__ Wo ist das?

a. Ich studiere hier.
b. Das ist im Mittelwesten.
c. Mein Name ist Meier.
d. Ich heiße Keller.
e. Ich lerne Deutsch.
f. Ich komme aus Deutschland.
g. Ich bin aus Kalifornien.

What are these people saying
to each other?

Aktivität 7. Suggestion:
Have students work in pairs,
taking turns saying a sentence
and marking an X in the
appropriate column. Check
responses to several items or
to all, keeping in mind that
some of the expressions might
fall into both categories.

Aktivität 7   Was sagen diese Leute zueinander?°

Determine whether the following phrases and questions would be used by two students addressing each other, by a professor and a student, or by both pairs of speakers.

	ZWEI STUDENTEN	PROFESSOR UND STUDENT
1. Was studierst du?	☒	☐
2. Grüß dich!	☒	☐
3. Auf Wiedersehen.	☒	☒
4. Wie heißt du?	☒	☐
5. Guten Tag!	☒	☒
6. Wie heißen Sie?	☐	☒
7. Was machst du hier?	☒	☐
8. Was studieren Sie?	☐	☒
9. Tschüss!	☒	☐
10. Mach's gut!	☒	☐

Aktivität 8   Eine Konversation

When rearranged, the following sentences form a short conversation between Herr Brinkmann and Frau Garcia, who are just getting acquainted. Number the items in order to create the conversation. Then perform it with a partner.

Aktivität 8. Suggestion:
Write this or a similar dialogue
out on a transparency and cut it
up so that each utterance is on
a separate piece. Have
students arrange the sentences
correctly, on the overhead.
These pieces can function as
cues when they act out the
dialogue.

__10__ Ich finde Hamburg interessant.
__7__ Und was machen Sie hier?
__3__ Wie bitte?
__2__ Guten Tag. Mein Name ist Brinkmann.
__6__ Ich komme aus Florida.
__4__ Brinkmann.

__1__ Guten Tag. Ich heiße Garcia.
__11__ Ach so!
__9__ Wie finden Sie Hamburg?
__8__ Ich besuche Freunde. visit
__5__ Woher kommen Sie?

Aktivität 9 Kurzdialoge°

Brief dialogues

Listen to the brief conversational exchanges and indicate in each case whether the response to the first question or statement is logical (**logisch**) or illogical (**unlogisch**).

Aktivität 9. Suggestion: Play the recording twice or say each item twice. When checking responses, replay each recorded item or read it aloud. Then ask students to give a correct response to all items marked "illogical."

	LOGISCH	UNLOGISCH
1.	☒	☐
2.	☐	☒
3.	☒	☐
4.	☒	☐
5.	☐	☒
6.	☒	☐
7.	☐	☒
8.	☒	☐
9.	☐	☒
10.	☒	☐

Aktivität 10 Was studierst du?

A. Find your major in the following list. Then, by asking questions, try to find at least one other classmate who has the same major as you.

Note: Provide students with majors not listed if the need arises. Note also the list in Appendix B.

BEISPIEL: S1: Was studierst du?
S2: Ich studiere Geschichte. Und du?
S1: Ich studiere Informatik.

History

• Vorlesungsverzeichnis •

Betriebswirtschaft°	Mathematik
Biologie	Musik
Chemie	Pädagogik
Deutsch/Germanistik	Philosophie
Englisch/Anglistik	Physik
Französisch/Romanistik	Politik
Geschichte°	Psychologie
Informatik	Public Relations
Kunst°	Soziologie
Marketing	Spanisch/Romanistik
Maschinenbau°	Volkswirtschaft°

management

history

art

engineering / economics

B. Now report back to the class. Does anyone have the same major as you?

BEISPIEL: Ich studiere Informatik. Candice und Ben studieren auch Informatik. Wir lernen Deutsch.

THEMA 3: Eigenschaften°

Hm? Wie ist er? Ist er **exzentrisch** oder **langweilig**? Und **was macht ihm Spaß**? Diskutieren?

maybe! perhaps

Vielleicht ist er **ernst** und **ruhig**? Und Hobbys? Vielleicht **Kochen und Musik hören.**

Ist sie **freundlich**? tolerant? Hat sie Freunde? Sie ist **sympathisch**. Und Hobbys? Ja **bestimmt Bücher** lesen und Filme sehen.

Sie ist **bestimmt sportlich. Was macht ihr Spaß**? Wandern?

Neue Wörter

langweilig boring
Was macht ihm / ihr Spaß? What does he/she like to do?
diskutieren to discuss, discussing
ernst serious
ruhig quiet
Kochen cooking
Musik hören listening to music
freundlich friendly
sympathisch likable
bestimmt definitely
Bücher books
sportlich athletic

that's me!

Neue Wörter

faul lazy
fleißig hardworking
lustig fun-loving
nett nice
praktisch practical
treu loyal
gehen to go
Computerspiele spielen to play computer games
essen to eat, eating
Karten spielen to play cards
tanzen to dance, dancing
Zeitung newspaper

So bin ich!° Check the characteristics that apply to you.

☐ chaotisch
☐ dynamisch
☐ ernst
☐ exzentrisch
☐ **faul**
☐ **fleißig**
☐ freundlich
☐ interessant
☐ konservativ
☐ langweilig

☐ liberal
☐ **lustig**
☐ **nett**
☐ **praktisch**
☐ **romantisch**
☐ ruhig
☐ sympathisch
☐ tolerant
☐ **treu**

Meine Eigenschaften.
Suggestion: Point out to students that the opposite meaning of some adjectives can be expressed by adding the prefix *un-* or *in-*, e.g., *unfreundlich* and *intolerant.*

Das macht mir Spaß! Check off your interests and hobbies.

☑ Bücher lesen
☑ ins Café **gehen**
☐ **Computerspiele spielen**
☐ Diskutieren
☑ **Essen**
☐ Fernsehen
☑ Fotografieren
☐ im Internet surfen
☐ **Karten spielen**

☑ Kochen
☑ Musik
☑ Deutsch lernen
☑ Reisen
☑ Sport
☑ **Tanzen**
☑ Videos machen
☑ Wandern
☑ **Zeitung** lesen

Herr Wölf ist fleißig, romantisch und nett. Bücher lesen, Zeitung lesen, reisen und tanzen machen ihm Spaß.

SPRACHTIPP

One way to say that you like (doing) something is by using the expression **Spaß machen.**

Fotografieren **macht mir Spaß.**	*I like photography.*
Was macht dir Spaß?	*What do you like (to do)?*

Aktivität 11 Ratespiel: Wie bin ich? Was macht mir Spaß?

Write down two adjectives that describe you and one of your interests. Do not write your name. Your instructor will collect and distribute everyone's list. Then each class member will read a description out loud, while the others try to guess who the writer is.

BEISPIEL: Ich bin dynamisch und exzentrisch. Im Internet surfen macht mir Spaß.

Aktivität 11. This activity allows students to link pieces of information together. It prepares them for constructing longer sentences later on.

Related Activity. Brainstorm with the class for names of famous people (*der Präsident, die Königin von England, der Bundeskanzler, die Frau des Präsidenten,* singers, actors, etc.). Which qualities do students associate with these people?

Aktivität 12 Eine Beschreibung

Turn to a partner and describe a famous person whom you admire or someone who has been important in your life. Make sure you use at least three adjectives. Also say what the person likes to do.

Aktivität 13 Wichtig° oder nicht?

1. Make a list of three characteristics and three interests that you consider important in a friend.
2. Tally the results on the board.
   Which characteristic is most important for the class?
   Which interest is most frequently mentioned?

°Important

Grammatik im Kontext

Nomen, Genus und bestimmte Artikel

Nouns, Gender, and Definite Articles°

°Nomen, Genus und bestimmte Artikel

Nouns in German can be easily recognized because they are capitalized.

German nouns are classified by grammatical gender as either masculine, feminine, or neuter. The definite articles **der, die,** and **das** (all meaning *the* in German) signal the gender of nouns.

MASCULINE: der	FEMININE: die	NEUTER: das
der Mann	die Frau	das Haus
der Beruf	die Adresse	das Buch
der Name	die Straße	das Semester

Grammatik im Kontext. This section aims to give students a concise explanation of basic grammar. Specific points brought up previously in a **Sprachtipp** are elaborated. Exercises reinforce grammar points and incorporate them into meaningful contexts that parallel the chapter themes. Listening exercises focus on grammar points as well. Whenever possible, grammar points are illustrated by authentic materials. Make sure to integrate these visuals into the discussion of a grammar point by asking students to analyze them. Grammar sections should be previewed in class and then assigned for homework.

**Der Test. Das Abo.
Die Uhr.**

Frankfurter Allgemeine

FAZette

FAZhion

FAZimile

Einmalige Sonder-Aktion

Zwanzig Jahre
F.A.Z.-Studentenabonnement frei Haus

The grammatical gender of a noun that refers to a human being generally matches biological gender; that is, most words for males are masculine, and words for females are feminine. Aside from this, though, the grammatical gender of German nouns is largely unpredictable.

Even words borrowed from other languages have a grammatical gender in German, as you can see from the following newspaper headline.

Fußball ist der Hit

Since the gender of nouns is generally unpredictable, you should make it a habit to learn the definite article with each noun.

Sometimes gender is signaled by the ending of the noun. The suffix **-in,** for instance, signals a feminine noun.

der Amerikaner, die Amerikaner**in**
der Freund, die Freund**in**
der Professor, die Professor**in**
der Student, die Student**in**

Suggestion: Point out to students other endings associated with particular genders.

Compound nouns (**Komposita**) are very common in German. They always take the gender of the final noun in the compound.

der Biergarten = das Bier + der Garten
das Telefonbuch = das Telefon + das Buch
die Telefonnummer = das Telefon + die Nummer

Übung 1. Suggestion: Play the recording for students twice: once to do the exercise and again to check responses.

Übung 1　Was hören Sie?

Circle the definite article you hear in each of the following questions and statements.

1. <u>der</u>　die　das
2. der　<u>die</u>　das
3. der　die　<u>das</u>
4. der　<u>die</u>　das

5. <u>der</u>　die　das
6. der　<u>die</u>　das
7. der　die　<u>das</u>
8. <u>der</u>　die　das

Übung 2　Hier fehlen die Artikel.

Complete each sentence with the missing article—**der, die,** or **das.**

1. _Die_ Studentin aus Cincinnati lernt Deutsch am Sprachinstitut.
2. _Der_ Student studiert Physik an der T.U.
3. _Die_ Frau aus München findet Berlin ganz toll. *- super*
4. Was ist _das_ Hobby von Frau Lentz?
5. _Die_ Adresse vom Hotel ist bestimmt im Telefonbuch.
6. Wie heißt _das_ Land südlich von Österreich?
7. Fußballtrainer? _Der_ Beruf ist interessant, aber oft stressig.
8. _Das_ Kreuzworträtsel ist sehr kompliziert.
9. _Der_ Freund von Ute studiert Informatik.

die Hausfrau   das Telefonbuch
der Biergarten   die Telefonnummer

Übung 3   Wörter bilden° *der Gartenmann*

Creating words

Create compound nouns using the words supplied.

BEISPIEL: der Garten + das Haus = das Gartenhaus

| das Bier | die Frau | das Haus | die Nummer |
| das Buch | der Garten | der Mann | das Telefon |

Übung 3. Suggestion: Add variety to the exercise by pairing students. Ask each pair to come up with as many compound words as possible.

Personal Pronouns°

Personalpronomen

A personal pronoun stands for a person or a noun.

Mein Name ist **Ebert. Ich** bin Architekt.

*My name is **Ebert. I** am an architect.*

Du bist immer so praktisch, **Gabi.**

You** are always so practical, **Gabi.

Der Wagen ist toll. Ist **er** neu?

***The car** is fabulous. Is **it** new?*

Then call on pairs to offer their compounds and help them determine which ones are actual words.

	SINGULAR	PLURAL
1st person	ich *I*	wir *we*
2nd person	du *you (informal)* Sie *you (formal)*	ihr *you (informal)* Sie *you (formal)*
3rd person	er *he; it* sie *she; it* es *it*	sie *they*

Übung 3. Variation: One student calls out a noun from the list at random, another student tries to form a compound with this word. Have students record all possibilities on the board.

Note:

- The pronoun **ich** is not capitalized unless it is the first word in a sentence.
- German has three words to express *you:* **du, ihr,** and **Sie.**

  Use **du** (or **ihr,** plural) for . . .   Use **Sie** (always capitalized) for . . .

a family member	a stranger
a close friend	an acquaintance
a fellow student	anyone you would address with
a child, an animal	a title, such as **Herr** or **Frau**

- The pronouns **er, sie** (*she*), and **es** reflect the grammatical gender of the noun or person for which they stand (the antecedent).

Ich bin rundum Spitze[1]
mit pan-ADRESS

[1]*Ich. . . I am really sharp. (I am great in every way.)*

Mark und Anja sind Studenten.	*Mark and Anja are students.*
Er kommt aus Bonn und **sie** kommt aus Wien.	*He comes from Bonn, and she comes from Vienna.*
Wie ist **der Film? —Er** ist wirklich lustig.	*How is the film? It is really funny.*
Wo ist **die Zeitung? —Sie** ist hier.	*Where is the newspaper? It is here.*
Wo ist **das Buch? —Es** ist nicht hier.	*Where is the book? It is not here.*

Übung 4   Du, ihr oder Sie?

How would you address the following people?

1. Frau Lentz aus München
2. Ute und Felix, zwei gute Freunde
3. Sebastian, ein guter Freund
4. Herr Professor Rauschenbach
5. Herr und Frau Zwiebel aus Stuttgart
6. eine Studentin in der Mensa
7. ein Tourist aus Kanada
8. ein Vampir

Übung 5   Herr und Frau Lentz

Working with a partner, take turns asking and answering questions. Use the pronoun **er** or **sie** in each answer.

BEISPIEL: s1: Wie ist Frau Lentz? (nett und freundlich)
　　　　　 s2: Sie ist nett und freundlich.

1. Wo wohnen Herr und Frau Lentz?　　Sie wohnen in München.
2. Was ist Frau Lentz von Beruf?　　Sie ist Programmiererin.
3. Was ist Herr Lentz von Beruf?　　Er ist Koch im Hofbräuhaus.
4. Wie groß ist Frau Lentz?　　Sie ist 1,63 m groß.
5. Und wie groß ist Herr Lentz?　　Er ist 1,90 m groß.

What do you think?   ## Übung 6   Was meinst du?°

Ask a partner for his/her opinion. Create questions with the words in column A, completing each blank with information of your choice. Then have your partner answer your question by choosing an appropriate adjective from column B. Follow the model.

BEISPIEL: s1: Wie ist der Film „Casablanca"?
　　　　　 s2: Er ist ausgezeichnet.

A	B
der Film _____	ausgezeichnet
das Buch _____ es ist	langweilig
das Wetter (*weather*) in _____ es ist	gut
die Studentenzeitung _____ sie ist	nicht besonders gut
das Essen im Studentenwohnheim _____ es ist	lustig
der _____ kurs* (z. B. Deutschkurs)	interessant
	schlecht
	ganz toll

---

* Refer to the list of subjects in **Aktivität 10, Was studierst du?,** earlier in this chapter.

The Verb: Infinitive and Present Tense°

In German, the basic form of the verb, the infinitive, consists of the verb stem plus the ending **-en** or, sometimes, just **-n.**

VERB STEM	ENDING	INFINITIVE
komm	**-en**	kommen
wander	**-n**	wandern

The present tense is formed by adding different endings to the verb stem. These endings vary according to the subject of the sentence.

Here are the present-tense forms of three common verbs.

	kommen	**finden**	**heißen**
ich	komm**e**	find**e**	heiß**e**
du	komm**st**	find**est**	heiß**t**
er sie es	komm**t**	find**et**	heiß**t**
wir	komm**en**	find**en**	heiß**en**
ihr	komm**t**	find**et**	heiß**t**
sie/Sie	komm**en**	find**en**	heiß**en**

Note:

- German has four different endings to form the present tense: **-e, -(e)st, -(e)t,** and **-en.** English, in contrast, has only one ending, -(*e*)s, for the third-person singular (*comes, goes*).

- Verbs with stems ending in **-d** or **-t** (**fin<u>d</u>en, arbei<u>t</u>en**) add an -e before the **-st** or **-t** ending (**du fin<u>d</u>est, er arbei<u>t</u>et**).

- Verbs with stems ending in **-ß, -s,** or **-z** (**hei<u>ß</u>en, rei<u>s</u>en, tan<u>z</u>en**) add only a **-t** in the **du** form (**du hei<u>ß</u>t, rei<u>s</u>t, tan<u>z</u>t**).

SPRACHTIPP

An infinitive can be used as a noun.

| Mein Hobby ist **Kochen.** | *My hobby is **cooking**.* |
| **Wandern** macht Spaß. | ***Hiking** is fun.* |

- Identify the different verb endings in the illustrations.
- What are the subjects in each of the sentences? Are they in the singular or in the plural?
- What is the infinitive form of the verbs?

Analyse. Note: The purpose of this type of exercise is to take a closer look at the grammatical structure or usage of a grammar point just introduced.

¹*discover*

Use of the Present Tense

The present tense in German may express either something happening at the moment or a recurring or habitual action.

Wolfgang spielt Karten.	*Wolfgang is playing cards.*
Antje arbeitet viel.	*Antje works a lot.*

It can also express a future action or occurrence, particularly with an expression of time.

Nächstes Jahr lerne ich Spanisch.	*Next year I'm going to learn Spanish.*

German has only one form of the present tense, whereas English has three different forms.

Hans **tanzt** wirklich gut.
{ *Hans **dances** really well.*
*Hans **is dancing** really well.*
*Hans **does dance** really well.*

Übung 7　Ergänzen Sie die Verben.

Supply the missing verb endings.

1. Ich heiß_____ Wolfgang Ebert.
2. Ich studier_____ Mathematik in Zürich.
3. Ich mach_____ oft Musik mit Freunden.
4. Wolfgangs Freundin heiß_____ Gisela.
5. Sie studier_____ auch Mathematik.
6. Wolfgang und Gisela find_____ Mathematik interessant.
7. Wolfgang mach_____ oft Musik mit (*with*) Freunden.
8. Gisela tanz_____ wirklich gut.
9. Gisela mach_____ nächstes Jahr ein Praktikum (*internship*).

Übung 8　Kombinieren Sie.

Combine elements from the two columns to create sentences.

BEISPIEL: Wolfgang studiert Mathematik.

1. ich	heißt Gisela
2. Wolfgang	studieren in Zürich
3. Wolfgang und Gisela	tanzt wirklich gut
4. Wolfgangs Freundin	machen oft Musik
5. mein Freund und ich	findest Mathematik sehr interessant
6. ihr	machst ein Praktikum
7. wir	studiert Mathematik
8. du	heiße Gisela

Übung 9　Kleine Szenen

Supply the missing verb endings and then role-play each scene.

Szene 1 (drei Personen)
A: Darf ich vorstellen? Herr Witschewatsch. Er komm_____ aus Rosenheim.
B: Ah, guten Tag, Herr Wischewas.
C: Nein, nein, ich heiß_____ Witschewatsch.
B: Ach so, Sie heiß_____ Wischewasch?
C: Nein, Wit-sche-wat-sch.
B: Oh, Entschuldigung (*Excuse me*), ich hör_____ nicht gut.

Szene 2 (zwei Personen)
A: Ich hör_____, Sie komm_____ aus Rosenheim?
B: Nein, nein, ich komm_____ nicht aus Rosenheim. Ich komm_____ aus Rüdesheim, Rüdesheim am Rhein.
A: Ach, meine Freundin Antje komm_____ auch aus Rüdesheim.

Szene 3 (drei Personen)
A: Wie find_____ ihr Andreas?
B: Ich find_____ Andreas echt langweilig.
C: Ich auch. Er nerv_____ mich (*He gets on my nerves.*).
A: Sabine find_____ Andreas super.
C: Na, und er find_____ Sabine total langweilig.

Szene 4 (zwei Personen)
A: Guten Morgen, meine Damen und Herren. Willkommen in Dresden. Heute besuch_____ wir das Verkehrsmuseum.
B: Das Verkehrsmuseum? Ich bleib_____ im Hotel!

VERKEHRS-
MUSEUM DRESDEN
JOHANNEUM
AM NEUMARKT
TEL. 4953002
MONTAGS GE-
SCHLOSSEN

HENNIGER

The Verb **sein**

The irregular verb **sein** is used to describe or identify someone or something.

Marion **ist** Studentin.
Sie **ist** sehr sympathisch.

sein			
ich	**bin**	wir	**sind**
du	**bist**	ihr	**seid**
er sie } es	**ist**	sie	**sind**
Sie	**sind**		

¹*eagle*

That's the way he is.

Übung 10   So ist er.°

Everyone is picking on Thomas. Complete the sentences with the appropriate form of **sein.**

1. Die Freundin von Thomas sagt: „Du _____ so konservativ, Thomas."
2. Thomas sagt: „Wie bitte? Das stimmt nicht. Ich _____ sehr liberal."
3. Der Vater von Thomas sagt: „Thomas _____ nicht sehr praktisch."
4. Die Mutter von Thomas sagt: „Wir _____ zu kritisch. Thomas _____ sehr intelligent und sensitiv."
5. Der Chef von Thomas sagt zu Thomas: „Herr Berger, Sie _____ nicht besonders fleißig."
6. Thomas denkt: „Ihr _____ alle unfair. Ich _____ ein Genie!"

Wortstellung

Word Order° in Sentences

One of the most important rules of German word order is the fixed position of the conjugated verb (the verb with the personal ending).

First Element (Subject, Adverb, etc.)	Second Element (Verb)	Other Elements
Ich	studiere	Informatik in Deutschland.
Nächstes Jahr	mache	ich ein Praktikum.
Heute	besuchen	wir das Verkehrsmuseum.

Note:

- The conjugated verb is always the second element in a sentence.
- The subject of the sentence can either precede or follow the verb.

Übung 11 Gabis Freund

Restate the information in each sentence by starting with the boldfaced word or words.

BEISPIEL: Gabis Freund heißt **Klaus.**
Klaus heißt Gabis Freund.

1. Klaus ist Musiker **von Beruf.**
2. Er wohnt **jetzt** in Berlin.
3. Er findet **Berlin** ganz fantastisch.
4. Er spielt **oft** im Jazzclub.
5. Sein Hobby ist **Motorrad fahren.**
6. Er arbeitet **nächstes Jahr** in Wien.

Übung 12 Wer macht was und wann?

Create two sentences for each group of words.

BEISPIEL: besuchen / das Museum / heute / wir →
Wir besuchen heute das Museum. [or]
Heute besuchen wir das Museum.

1. Karten / wir / spielen / heute Abend
2. bei McDonald's / Peter / arbeitet / jetzt
3. ich / sehr interessant / finde / Berlin
4. spielen / wir / morgen / Tennis mit Boris
5. das Museum / Herr Schaller / nächstes Jahr / besucht / in Dresden

Übung 13 Meine Pläne°

plans

Tell a partner two things you may do today and tomorrow (**morgen**). Tell the class about them.

BEISPIEL: Heute spiele ich Karten. Morgen spiele ich Tennis →
Heute spielt Bob Karten. Morgen spielt er Tennis.

Asking Questions°

Fragen stellen

There are two types of questions. We refer to them as *word questions* and *yes/no questions.*

Word Questions

Wann kommst du?	***When** are you coming?*
Was machst du?	***What** are you doing?*
Wer ist das?	***Who** is that?*
Wie ist Berlin?	***How** do you like Berlin?*
Wo wohnst du?	***Where** do you live?*
Woher kommen Sie?	***Where** are you from?*

[1] am. . . *on the weekend*

Note:

- Word questions begin with an interrogative pronoun. They require specific information in the answer.
- The conjugated verb is the second element in a word question.
- German uses only one verb form to formulate a question, in contrast to English.

Wo **wohnst** du? $\begin{cases} \textit{Where } \textbf{\textit{do}} \textit{ you } \textbf{\textit{live}}? \\ \textit{Where } \textbf{\textit{are}} \textit{ you } \textbf{\textit{living}}? \end{cases}$

Kommst Du?

Yes/No Questions

Kommst du bald?	*Are you coming soon?*
Studiert Gabi in Berlin?	*Is Gabi studying in Berlin?*
Heißt der Professor Kuhn?	*Is the professor's name Kuhn?*

Note:

- A yes/no question begins with the conjugated verb and can be answered with either **ja** or **nein.**
- The verb is immediately followed by the subject.

SPRACHTIPP

To convey strong curiosity or surprise, add the particle **denn** to your question.

Was machst du **denn**?   *What are you doing?* (strong curiosity)

Arbeitest du **denn** heute?   *Are you working today?* (surprise)

Ich heiße Petra, bin 28 Jahre alt, 168 cm groß und arbeite in einem Ingenieurbüro.

Jürgen ist 25 Jahre alt, 185 cm groß, blond, sportlich-schlank, gut aussehend und sympathisch.

Übung 14   Zwei Menschen

Read the two personal ads and answer the questions.

1. Wie heißt der Mann?
2. Wie heißt die Frau?
3. Wie alt ist die Frau?
4. Wie alt ist der Mann?
5. Wie groß ist der Mann?
6. Wie groß ist die Frau?
7. Wie ist Jürgen? (drei Adjektive)
8. Was macht Petra?

Übung 15   Ergänzen Sie.

Complete each question with an interrogative pronoun: **wer, was, wie, woher,** or **wo.**

1. _____ heißt du?
2. _____ kommst du denn?

3. _____ studierst du denn?
4. _____ findest du Heidelberg?
5. _____ wohnst du denn?
6. _____ studiert Mathematik in Zürich?

Übung 16   Formulieren Sie passende Fragen.

Formulate a word question for each answer.

BEISPIEL: _____? Ich komme aus Kanada.→
         Woher kommst du?

1. _____   Ich heiße Peter.
2. _____   Ich wohne in Essen.
3. _____   Ich studiere da Medizin.
4. _____   Ich komme aus Süddeutschland.
5. _____   Nächstes Jahr mache ich ein Praktikum.
6. _____   Meine Familie wohnt in Nürnberg.
7. _____   Ich finde Hamburg sehr schön.

Übung 17   Ja und nein

What questions would trigger the following answers?

BEISPIEL: _____? Ja, ich komme aus Hamburg. →
         Kommen Sie aus Hamburg?

1. _____?   Nein, ich bin nicht Frau Schlegel; ich bin
                    Frau Weber.
2. _____?   Ja, wir wohnen in Köln.
3. _____?   Ja, ich finde Köln sehr interessant.
4. _____?   Nein, ich arbeite nicht bei der Telekom.
5. _____?   Ja, Köln ist sehr groß.
6. _____?   Wir spielen oft Karten.

Übung 18   Zur Information

Take a survey. Formulate five questions. Use them to find someone who does these, or similar, things.

BEISPIEL: S1: Wer wohnt im Studentenwohnheim?
          S2: Ich wohne im Studentenwohnheim. [oder]
               Matt wohnt im Studentenwohnheim.

Wer	spielen	oft	Tennis, Fußball, Karten
	wohnen	jetzt	in der Disko
	lernen	manchmal	schwimmen
	sein	nie	faul, fleißig, langweilig
	machen	immer	im Studentenheim
			ein Praktikum

Übung 19 Wie bitte?

Übung 19. Suggestion: Have students fill in the blanks with information of their choice. Then have them do a role play, making statements and asking questions to repeat the information.

Imagine that you did not entirely catch what someone said to you. Working with a partner, take turns filling in the blanks with information of your own choice, making a statement, and asking the other person to repeat the information.

BEISPIEL: s1: Ich heiße Karl-Heinz Rüschenbaum.
s2: Wie bitte? Wie heißt du?
s1: Karl-Heinz Rüschenbaum.
s2: Ach so!
s1: Ich komme aus. . . (usw. [*and so on*])

1. Ich heiße _____.
2. Ich komme aus _____.
3. Das ist in _____.
4. Ich studiere _____.
5. _____ ist sehr interessant.
6. Nächstes Jahr studiere ich in _____.

Student life

Übung 20 Das Studentenleben°

A. You will hear some information about a German university student. Compare what you hear with the statements below. If a statement is incorrect, find the correct answer from among the choices in parentheses.

	DAS STIMMT	DAS STIMMT NICHT
1. Die Studentin heißt Claudia. (___ Katrin, _X_ Karin)	☐	☒
2. Sie kommt aus Göttingen. (_X_ Dresden, ___ Bremen)	☐	☒
3. Der Familienname ist Renner. (___ Reuter, ___ Reiser)	☒	☐
4. Sie studiert jetzt in Tübingen. (_X_ Göttingen, ___ Dresden)	☐	☒
5. Sie studiert Mathematik. (___ Jura, _X_ Informatik)	☐	☒
6. Sie wohnt bei einer Familie. (_X_ im Studentenwohnheim, ___ allein)	☐	☒
7. Sie geht oft schwimmen. (___ wandern, ___ Tennis spielen)	☒	☐
8. Sie geht oft ins Café. (___ in die Disko, ___ ins Museum)	☒	☐

B. Now formulate yes/no questions based on the statements in Part A. Ask another student in your class to verify the information.

BEISPIEL: s1: Heißt die Studentin Claudia?
s2: Nein, sie heißt Karin.

Sprache im Kontext

Videoclips

A. Watch the interviews with Sara and Ali as they talk about what they are studying, their hobbies, and how their friends would describe them. Write **S** if the phrase or word applies to **Sara** or **A** if it applies to **Ali.**

_____ Medienwissenschaft   _____ Schwimmen
_____ Mathematik   _____ spontan
_____ Joggen   _____ zurückhaltend (*reserved*)
_____ Gitarre spielen   _____ lustig
_____ Zeichnen   _____ fröhlich
_____ Tanzen   _____ sehr aktiv
_____ Fahrrad fahren

> **Sprache im Kontext.** The goal of this section is to activate the four skills through a variety of activities. The section opens with a video activity, includes a reading with accompanying exercises, and culminates in writing and speaking assignments. In the video and reading sections, students are not expected to understand everything. Particularly in the initial chapters, global comprehension is the goal.

B. Who does what? Watch the interviews and match each person with a profession or job.

1. _____ Peter   **a.** ist Grafikdesigner
2. _____ Oliver   **b.** ist Pilot
3. _____ Alex   **c.** ist Bankkauffrau
4. _____ Jasmin   **d.** arbeitet bei KWD im Silbershop
5. _____ Frau Simon   **e.** ist Webdesigner

C. Watch the interviews again and jot down notes about things you have in common with the interviewees. If you have anything in common, then write a few sentences that describe the commonalities. Follow the model.

BEISPIEL: Ali studiert Mathematik. Ich studiere auch Mathematik. Saras Hobby ist Tanzen. mein Hobby ist auch Tanzen…

> **Lesen.** These sections focus on developing effective reading strategies. Here, basic techniques such as skimming, scanning, and reading for specific information are introduced. You should stress recognizing cognates and guessing from context. Although the texts are not meant to be read aloud in class, it may be useful to deal with certain parts of the readings as a class activity, especially at the beginning of the course. Prereading activities, called **Auf den ersten Blick,** will require students to brainstorm and speculate about the text. We recommend doing **Auf den ersten Blick** in class the day before the reading is assigned. Such an approach will provide you with an opportunity to clear up any potential misunderstandings or false assumptions about the main topic of the text. In the section titled **Zum Text,** students work with the text to acquire vocabulary and gather more detailed information.

Lesen

Zum Thema°

About the topic

Where do the students in your German class come from? Were all students in the class born in the same country? What nationalities and ethnic groups are represented? How many students can speak more than one language? How many students have bilingual parents?

Auf den ersten Blick°

Auf den ersten Blick.
Students will need a lot of reassurance and encouragement to develop a positive attitude toward reading authentic material. The texts will seem daunting if approached word for word, but with proper application of the strategies suggested here, students will learn to enjoy taking risks when exploring an unknown text. The

1. Look at the title and the text itself. What type of text do you think this is? What led you to your conclusions?
2. Label the exchanges in the dialogue with *S1 (Speaker 1)* and *S2 (Speaker 2)*.
3. Now read the dialogue aloud with a partner, each taking one of the two roles.
4. Skim the text for references to geographical locations and references to a person's appearance.
5. From the context, what do you think **reden** and **aussehen (siehst. . . aus, sehe aus)** mean?

readings have been left largely unglossed so that students are compelled to guess meanings. Emphasize to students that they should avoid using the dictionary. In going over the text with them in class you may wish to point out the meaning of certain words, after students have tried to guess their meanings.

DIALOG

von Nasrin Siege

„Du redest so gut deutsch. Wo kommst du denn her?"

„Aus Hamburg."

„Wieso? Du siehst aber nicht so aus!"

„Wie sehe ich denn aus?"

5   „Na ja, so schwarzhaarig und dunkel..."

„Na und?"

„Wo bist du denn geboren?"

„In Hamburg."

„Und dein Vater?"

10   „In Hamburg."

„Deine Mutter?"

„Im Iran."

„Da haben wir's!"

„Was denn?"

15   „Dass du keine° Deutsche bist!"   *no*

„Wer sagt das?"

„Na ich!"

„Warum?"

Reading. "*Dialog*" by Nasrin Siege appeared in *Texte dagegen,* a volume of fiction against xenophobia and racism. Note the use of colloquialisms such as splitting the interrogative *woher.*

Even if students don't know the exact meaning of a word, they may be able to categorize it. This is a skill that will help them to use a dictionary judiciously. Depending on one's purpose in reading, knowing the general category of something may be sufficient for a general understanding of a text.

Zum Text°

1. What can you find out about the birthplace, place of residence, citizenship of Speaker 2? What else can you find out about him or her?

2. Consider what you've learned about different forms of "you" in German. Speculate: How old are the two speakers? How well do they know each other? Where might this dialogue take place? How do you think it started?
3. Why is the nationality of Speaker 2 an issue for Speaker 1?

Hier klicken!

You'll find information about the topic of foreigners in Germany in **Deutsch: Na klar!** on the World Wide Web at www.mhhe.com/dnk.

KULTURTIPP

More than seven million foreigners make up roughly 9% of Germany's population and contribute to the country's economic growth. Most Germans and foreigners live in peaceful coexistence; however, incidents of discrimination and even violence against foreigners have occurred, especially following the economic difficulties in the wake of the unification of Germany in 1990. The German government strives to promote tolerance toward foreigners through media campaigns, and the governments of the German states try to integrate children of foreigners into the German school system.

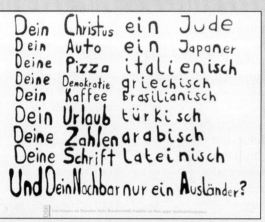

Plakat gegen Rassismus und Ausländerfeindlichkeit (antiforeigner sentiments), *gesehen in einer Hamburger U-Bahn Station*

Sprechen und Schreiben°

Speaking and writing

Aktivität 1 Ein Interview

Interview a classmate you have not already met to find out

- his/her name
- where he/she comes from
- where he/she was born
- where his/her father/mother is from
- what he/she is studying

1. As a class, formulate the questions in German for the interview, using the appropriate form of *you.*
2. Interview your partner.
3. Report your findings to the class.

Aktivität 2 Ein Bericht°

report

Using the answers to your questions in **Aktivität 1,** write a summary of your interview.

Wortschatz

Eigenschaften	Characteristics
alt	old
ernst	serious
exzentrisch	eccentric
fantastisch	fantastic
faul	lazy
fleißig	hardworking, diligent
freundlich/unfreundlich	friendly/unfriendly
groß	tall; big, large
gut	good, well
Er tanzt gut.	He dances well.
interessant	interesting
kompliziert	complicated
konservativ	conservative
langweilig	boring
lustig	cheerful; fun
nett	nice
praktisch/unpraktisch	practical/impractical
romantisch	romantic
ruhig	quiet
sportlich	athletic
stressig	stressful
sympathisch/ unsympathisch	likable/unlikable
toll! (coll.)	super!
ganz toll!	super! great!
treu	loyal

Substantive	Nouns
der Amerikaner / die Amerikanerin	American
der Beruf	profession, occupation
Was sind Sie von Beruf?	What do you do for a living?
das Buch	book
(das) Deutsch	German (language)
das Essen	food; eating
der Freund / die Freundin	friend
der Geburtstag	birthday, date of birth
der Geburtsort	birthplace
das Hobby	hobby
der Hochschullehrer / die Hochschullehrerin	university instructor
das Interesse	interest

das Jahr	year
nächstes Jahr	next year
der Journalist / die Journalistin	journalist
der Mann	man
die Mensa	student cafeteria
die Musik	music
der Name	name
der Nachname	family name, surname
der Vorname	first name, given name
das Praktikum	internship
ein Praktikum machen	to do an internship
der Professor / die Professorin	professor
das Semester	semester
der Student / die Studentin	student
die Universität	university
der Wohnort	place of residence
die Zeitung	newspaper

Verben	Verbs
arbeiten	to work
besuchen	to visit
bleiben	to stay, remain
diskutieren	to discuss
essen	to eat
fahren	to drive, ride
Motorrad fahren	to ride (drive) a motorcycle
finden	to find
Wie findest du...?	How do you like . . . ?; What do you think of . . . ?
fragen	to ask
gehen	to go
heißen	to be called, be named
hören	to listen, hear
kochen	to cook
kommen	to come

lernen	to learn, study	was	what
lesen	to read	wer	who
machen	to do; to make	wie	how
Kreuzworträtsel	to do crossword	wo	where
machen	puzzles	woher	from where
reisen	to travel		
sagen	to say, tell		
sag mal	tell me		
sein	to be	**Sonstiges**	**Other**
spielen	to play	**Aber natürlich!**	But of course!
Computerspiele	to play computer	**auch**	also
spielen	games	ich auch	me too
Karten spielen	to play cards	**bestimmt**	definitely
studieren	to study	**danke sehr**	thanks a lot
tanzen	to dance	**Das macht mir Spaß.**	That's fun.
wandern	to hike	**echt** (*coll.*)	really
wohnen	to reside, live	**echt langweilig**	really boring
		Entschuldigung.	Excuse me.
		ganz	very
Personalpronomen	**Personal Pronouns**	**heute**	today
		heute Abend	this evening
ich	I	**hier**	here
du	you (*informal sing.*)	**ich bin geboren**	I was born
er	he; it	**immer**	always
sie	she; it; they	**jetzt**	now
es	it	**nächstes Jahr**	next year
wir	we	**nicht**	not
ihr	you (*informal pl.*)	**oft**	often
Sie	you (*formal sing./pl.*)	**sehr**	very
		viel	a lot, much
Interrogativpronomen	**Interrogative Pronouns**	**Viel Glück!**	Good luck!
		Viel Spaß!	Have fun!
wann	when	**wirklich**	really

LERNZIELE

Use this checklist to verify that you can now . . .

☐ give personal information about yourself (and others) such as your name, address, telephone number, home town, height, and place of birth.

☐ mention a few subjects you are studying.

☐ describe your personal characteristics and those of others.

☐ understand and apply concepts of grammatical gender.

☐ name some of your hobbies and interests.

☐ conjugate regular verbs in the present tense.

☐ use simple declarative sentences to make statements.

☐ use the irregular verb **sein.**

☐ use formal and informal ways of addressing people.

☐ understand word order in statements and questions.

☐ ask "information" and "yes/no" questions.

☐ apply basic reading strategies in order to identify types of texts, recognize cognates, and understand the gist of some types of texts through contextual guessing.

Wie ich wohne

Kapitel 2. Suggestion:
Introduce the theme of this
chapter by focusing on the
students' concern for housing.
Is housing also a problem in
your community? State in
simple German where you live,
and briefly describe your home.
Ask students where they live.
Be tolerant if their answers are
only partially in German and
grammatically incorrect, and be
prepared to help them with their
answers.

Wo sind die Studenten?
a. An der Universität
b. Im Supermarkt

Point out: These students are
searching for housing or jobs at
das Schwarze Brett, typical of
German universities.

Videoclips

So wohnen sie.

In diesem Kapitel

- **Themen:** Types of housing, furnishings, daily activities
- **Grammatik:** Noun plurals; nominative and accusative case of nouns, articles, and interrogative pronouns; **haben**; verbs with stem-vowel changes; negation with **nicht** and **kein**; demonstrative pronouns
- **Kultur:** Living arrangements, the euro, purchasing items

Alles klar?

Alles klar? A. Suggestion:
Give students several minutes
to scan both the questions and
the flyer from a university
bulletin board, *das Schwarze
Brett,* before responding.

A. Just as in North America, flyers (**Anschlagzettel**) are a popular way to make announcements, advertise, or disseminate information in German-speaking countries. What do you think is the purpose of the flyer shown here? Once you've determined the purpose, answer the multiple-choice questions.

- Wo findet man (*one*) so einen Anschlagzettel?
  - **a.** in einer Klinik
  - **b.** an der Uni
  - **c.** in einem Garten
- Die vier Studentinnen suchen _____.
  - **a.** einen Regenschirm
  - **b.** eine Wohnung
  - **c.** ein Dach
- Sie brauchen _____ Zimmer.
  - **a.** zwei bis (*to*) drei
  - **b.** sechs bis sieben
  - **c.** vier bis fünf
- Sie möchten (*would like*) eine Wohnung _____.
  - **a.** im Stadtzentrum
  - **b.** in einem Vorort (*suburb*)
  - **c.** auf dem Lande (*in the country*)

Vokabelsuche. Find the German word for:

1. kitchen   3. central location
2. bath   4. reward

B. Listen to the following short conversations. Mark the kind of apartment the speakers are looking for.

1. **a.** eine Zweizimmerwohnung
   b. eine Dreizimmerwohnung
2. **a.** eine Zweizimmerwohnung mit Küche und Bad
   b. eine Dreizimmerwohnung in zentraler Lage
3. **a.** ein Zimmer bei einer Familie
   b. ein Zimmer in einem Studentenheim

Follow-up: You may "narrate"
the flyer to the students. Or,
with the help of the questions,
individual students can explain
sections of the flyer.

Realia.   This flyer was distributed at the university in Göttingen and demonstrates the imagination required to obtain student housing. The reward of 50 euros reflects how keen competition for housing is.

In German-speaking countries, the kitchen and bathroom are not counted as "rooms" when describing the number of rooms in an apartment. Thus, a **Zweizimmerwohnung** has one bedroom and a living room, while a **Dreizimmerwohnung** has two bedrooms and a living room. An **Appartement** is a studio, or efficiency apartment.

Apartments are expensive in German-speaking countries. Students either live in a **Studenten(wohn)heim,** a residence hall, or share living accommodations such as an apartment to cut expenses. Many students prefer living in a **Wohngemeinschaft (WG),** a co-op in which each student has a private room, while kitchen and bath facilities are shared.

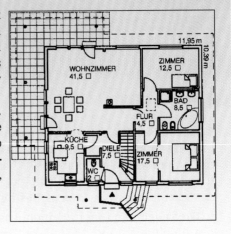

Suggestion: After students read the **Kulturtipp,** have them determine what size apartment is depicted in the floor plan.

Thema 1. Suggestion: Once students have worked with the dialogue, ask them questions such as the following: *Was sucht Ulla? Wo gibt es ein Zimmer? Wie sieht das Zimmer aus? Wie hoch ist die Miete? Wo liegt die Wohnung?*

Wörter im Kontext

Neue Wörter

Was ist denn los?
What's the matter?
ich suche: suchen to look for
dringend desperately
Wohnung apartment
Zimmer room
so teuer very expensive
nichts nothing
frei free, available
vielleicht maybe, perhaps
etwas something
da here; there
schönes beautiful
möbliertes: mobliert furnished
hoch high
Miete rent
nur only
recht quite
preiswert reasonable

THEMA 1: Auf Wohnungssuche°

In search of an apartment

*Ulla und Stefan treffen sich (meet) vor der Mensa der Uni Freiburg. Ulla hat ein großes **Problem.***

STEFAN: Tag, Ulla! Wie geht's?
ULLA: Ach, nicht besonders.
STEFAN: **Was ist denn los?**
ULLA: Ich **suche dringend** eine **Wohnung** oder ein **Zimmer.** Wohnungen sind aber alle **so teuer.**
STEFAN: Ist denn **nichts frei** im **Studentenheim?**
ULLA: Hier in Freiburg? Bestimmt nicht!
STEFAN: Hier ist die Zeitung von heute. **Vielleicht** gibt es (*there is*) doch **etwas.** Ah, hier, Wohnungsanzeigen. **Da,** schau mal: **schönes, möbliertes** Zimmer.
ULLA: Wie **hoch** ist die **Miete?**
STEFAN: **Nur** 250 Euro.
ULLA: Das ist **recht preiswert.** Wo ist das Zimmer?
STEFAN: In Zußdorf.

ULLA: In Zußdorf?! Kommt nicht in Frage! Das ist viel zu weit weg.

STEFAN: Na, **da hast du Recht.** Preiswert ist es, **aber** Zußdorf ist nicht **gerade zentral gelegen.**

Mark whether the following statements are correct (**das stimmt**) or incorrect (**das stimmt nicht**) based on the information in the dialogue.

	DAS STIMMT	DAS STIMMT NICHT
1. Stefan sucht ein Zimmer.	☐	☒
2. Im Studentenheim ist nichts frei.	☒	☐
3. Stefan findet eine Wohnungsanzeige in der Zeitung.	☒	☐
4. Das Zimmer ist nicht möbliert.	☐	☒
5. Die Miete ist nicht sehr hoch.	☐	☒
6. Zußdorf ist nicht zentral gelegen.	☒	☐

Wo wohnen Sie?
- ☐ Appartement
- ☐ Haus
- ☐ Studentenwohnheim
- ☐ **Wohngemeinschaft (WG)**
- ☐ Wohnung
- ☐ Zimmer

Wie wohnen Sie? Ich wohne...
- ☐ allein (*alone*)
- ☐ bei den Eltern (*with my parents*)
- ☐ bei einer Familie

Ich habe...
- ☐ einen **Mitbewohner** / eine **Mitbewohnerin**
- ☐ einen Hund (*dog*)
- ☐ eine Katze
- ☐ einen Goldfisch
- ☐ ein **Handy**

Beschreiben Sie Ihre Wohnung / Ihr Zimmer! / Ihr Haus!

Sie/Es hat...
- ☐ ein **Arbeitszimmer**
- ☐ eine schöne Aussicht (*view*)
- ☐ ein **Badezimmer / Bad**
- ☐ einen **Balkon**
- ☐ ein **Esszimmer**
- ☐ ein (zwei/drei) **Fenster**
- ☐ eine **Garage**
- ☐ einen **Garten**
- ☐ eine **Küche**
- ☐ ein (zwei/drei) **Schlafzimmer**
- ☐ ein **Wohnzimmer**
- ☐ **Computeranschluss**

Sie/Es ist...
- ☐ groß
- ☐ **klein**
- ☐ **dunkel**
- ☐ **hell**
- ☐ möbliert
- ☐ **unmöbliert**
- ☐ preiswert
- ☐ teuer
- ☐ zentral gelegen
- ☐ **weit von der Uni**

Die Miete ist...
- ☐ hoch
- ☐ **niedrig**

SPRACHTIPP

Das ist **ein** Balkon. Das ist **eine** Küche. Das ist **ein** Badezimmer.

When a masculine noun is used as a direct object, **ein** changes to **einen**.

Mein Haus hat **einen** Balkon, eine Küche und ein Badezimmer.

---

da hast du Recht you're right

aber but

gerade just, exactly

zentral gelegen centrally located

Wo und wie wohnen Sie? Expressions using the dative case should be treated as lexical items. Dative prepositions will be covered in **Kapitel 5,** prepositions that take either the dative or accusative in **Kapitel 6.**

Suggestion: Remind students that *sie* is used to refer to *Wohnung* and *es* to *Zimmer* or *Haus.*

Neue Wörter

Handy cell phone

Mitbewohner/ Mitbewohnerin roommate, housemate

Arbeitszimmer study

Badezimmer/Bad bathroom

Esszimmer dining room

Fenster window

Küche kitchen

Schlafzimmer bedroom

Wohnzimmer living room

Computeranschluss computer connection

groß big

klein small

dunkel dark

hell bright

unmöbliert unfurnished

weit von der Uni far from the university

niedrig low

Aktivität 1. Suggestion: Go over the ads with students before starting the listening comprehension. Focus on those details that are most pertinent to the exercise.

Kulturtipp. Suggestion: Write a few prices on the board and have students practice saying them.

Point out. Note the different sizes of the bills.

Aktivität 1　Wir brauchen eine Wohnung / ein Zimmer.

Scan the five ads from people looking for housing. Label the ads from 1 to 5 in the order in which you hear them.

> Freundl. junger 37-jähriger Eng-lischlehrer su. 1 Zi. in WG um mit euch Deutsch zu sprechen und es besser zu lernen. ☎ 570 56 39
>
> _4_

> Freundlicher Schauspieler[4] aus Hamburg sucht Zi in WG vom 1. Mai bis 1. August in München. ☎ 637 88 78, ♂ Manfred
>
> _2_

> Musiker (24) sucht Zimmer oder Raum in WG zum 1.6. oder etwas früher. ☎ 040/439 84 20 Markus (rufe zurück[1]) PS.: Zahle[2] bis 250 Euro incl.[3]
>
> _5_

> Fotodesignerin, 22, sucht preis-wertes Zimmer in junger WG, möglichst zentral zum 1.7.03. ☎ 352 78 39 abends, Nicht-raucherin.
>
> _1_

> Architekturstudentin (25) sucht zum 1. od. 15.5. ruhiges Zim. bis 200 Euro incl. in WG ☎ 857 63 90 (oder 50 72 58)
>
> _3_

[1]rufe. . . _call back_　[2]_pay_
[3]incl. = inclusive _including utilities_　[4]_actor_

KULTURTIPP

On January 1, 2002, the European Union adopted the euro (€) as its currency. The currency has seven denominations of bills and eight different coins; the bills are 5, 10, 20, 50, 100, 200, and 500 €, and the coins are 2 €, 1 €, and 50, 20, 10, 5, 2, and 1 cent. The front side of each coin is the same in all countries, but on the reverse, each nation can choose motifs particular to that country. Here are some examples of the euro in Germany.

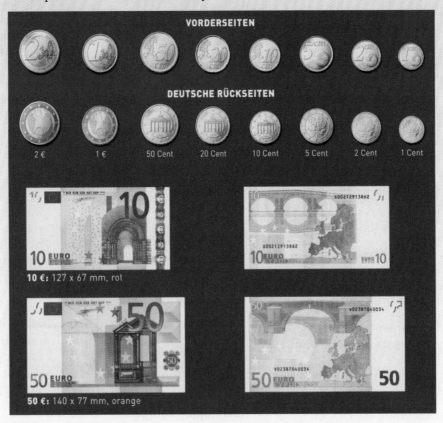

10 €: 127 x 67 mm, rot

50 €: 140 x 77 mm, orange

In German, attributive adjectives—that is, adjectives in front of nouns—take endings.

Ich suche ein möbliert**es** Zimmer.   *I'm looking for a furnished room.*

Predicate adjectives—that is, adjectives used after the verb **sein**—do not take endings.

Das Zimmer ist möbliert.   *The room is furnished.*

You will learn more about attributive adjective endings in **Kapitel 9.**

Aktivität 2   Wer braucht eine Wohnung?

Schritt 1: Look over the five ads from **Aktivität 1** and complete the following:

1. Der junge Englischlehrer sucht...
   a. eine Wohnung   b. ein Zimmer in einer WG   c. ein Appartement
2. Der Musiker braucht ein Zimmer...
   a. zum 1. Juli   b. zum 1. Juni   c. zum 1. August
3. Der Schauspieler sucht ein Zimmer...
   a. in München   b. in Hamburg   c. in Zürich
4. Die Fotodesignerin sucht...
   a. ein Zimmer   b. eine Wohnung   c. eine Nichtraucherin
5. Für das Zimmer zahlt die Architekturstudentin...
   a. bis 250 Euro   b. bis 200 Euro   c. bis 300 Euro

Schritt 2: Now look over the ads again and say as much as you can about each, giving more detailed information.

BEISPIEL: Ein Englischlehrer sucht ein Zimmer in einer WG.
           Er ist 37.
           Er ist freundlich und nett.

Aktivität 3   Eine Anzeige° schreiben

°ad

Using the newspaper ads on the previous page as models, create a simple ad in the following format. Trade ads with another person, who will read yours to the class.

$$\left\{\begin{array}{l}\text{Student}\\\text{Studentin}\\\text{??}\end{array}\right\} \text{sucht} \left\{\begin{array}{l}\text{großes}\\\text{kleines}\\\text{ruhiges}\\\text{helles}\\\text{möbliertes}\\\text{unmöbliertes}\\\text{??}\end{array}\right\} \text{Zimmer mit} \left\{\begin{array}{l}\text{Telefon}\\\text{Bad}\\\text{Küche}\\\text{Garten}\\\text{Computeranschluss}\end{array}\right\} \text{in} \left\{\begin{array}{l}\text{einer WG}\\\text{einem Haus}\\\text{zentraler Lage}\\\text{??}\end{array}\right\} \text{bis zu Euro \_\_.}$$

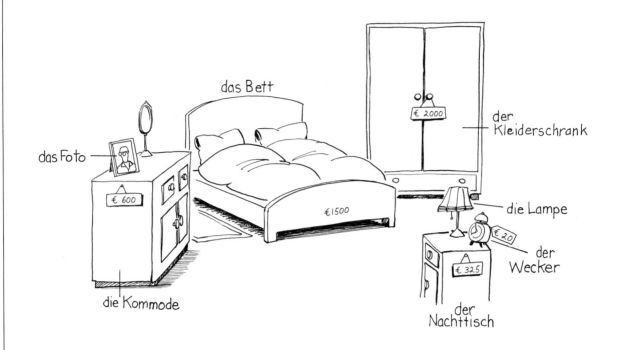

Was haben Sie **schon** in Ihrem Zimmer / in Ihrer Wohnung?

Ich habe...
- ☐ einen **Fernseher**
- ☐ eine **Lampe**
- ☐ einen **CD-Spieler**

- ☐ ein **Radio**
- ☐ einen Computer
- ☐ ??

Ich brauche noch...
- ☐ einen **DVD-Spieler**
- ☐ ein **Bücherregal**

- ☐ ein Handy
- ☐ ??

Was **kostet** das?
- ☐ der DVD-Spieler kostet 200 Euro.
- ☐ die Lampe kostet 70 Euro
- ☐ ??

Aktivität 4   Ulla hat jetzt endlich° ein Zimmer.   *finally*

Listen as Ulla tells her friend Karin about the room she has just found. As
you listen, check off the items that Ulla already has.

- ☒ ein Bett
- ☐ ein Bücherregal
- ☐ eine Lampe
- ☒ einen Schreibtisch
- ☒ einen Sessel
- ☒ einen Stuhl
- ☐ ein Telefon
- ☒ einen Tisch

Purchases

Aktivität 5 Einkäufe°

Schritt 1: Look at the department store displays at the beginning of **Thema 2** and give your opinion of the furniture and other items shown.

BEISPIEL: S1: Wie findest du   den Computer?
                         das Bett?
                         die Lampe?
        S2: Sehr schön. Und wie findest du ____?

REAKTIONEN

zu(*too*)...	teuer	praktisch
sehr...	hässlich	(un)bequem
nicht...	schön	billig
	preiswert	toll

Schritt 2: Bring in several photos of pieces of furniture you have in your room, apartment, or house, or bring in several from magazines. Show them to a partner and, using the model and the vocabulary in **Schritt 1,** ask them to react.

Neue Wörter

hässlich ugly
bequem comfortable
billig inexpensive, cheap

> **SPRACHTIPP**
>
> When a masculine noun is used as a direct object, **der** changes to **den.** The articles **das** and **die** remain unchanged.
>
>   Wie findest du **den** Computer?
>   Wie findest du **das** Bett und **die** Lampe?

Aktivität 6 Ein Gespräch im Kaufhaus

Listen as Ulla talks with a salesperson. Then answer the true/false questions and correct any false statements.

Hier klicken!

You'll find more about home furnishings in German-speaking countries in **Deutsch: Na klar!** on the World Wide Web at www.mhhe.com/dnk.

	DAS STIMMT	DAS STIMMT NICHT
1. Ulla braucht nur eine Lampe.	☐	☒
2. Ulla findet die italienische Lampe schön.	☒	☐
3. Die Lampe aus Italien ist nicht teuer.	☐	☒
4. Ulla kauft eine Lampe für 25 Euro.	☒	☐
5. Das Kaufhaus führt (*carries*) keine (*no*) Bücherregale.	☒	☐

THEMA 3: Was wir gern machen

Was machen diese Leute gern? Match each caption with
the corresponding drawing.

1. _____ Herr Wurm **liest** gern Bücher.
2. _____ Frau Schlemmer **isst** gern.
3. _____ Ernst Immermüd **schläft** gern.
4. _____ Uschi Schnell **fährt** gern **Motorrad.**
5. _____ Gerhard Glotze **sieht** gern **Videos.**
6. _____ Frau Renner **läuft** gern.

SPRACHTIPP

In some German verbs, the stem vowel
changes from **e** to **i, e** to **ie,** or **a** to **ä** in
certain verb forms. Do you recognize
the verbs in bold type? You will learn
these stem-changing verbs later in this
chapter.

a.

b.

c.

d.

e.

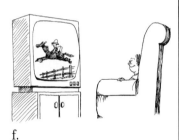

f.

Was machen Sie gern?

	JA	NEIN
Hören Sie gern Musik?	☐	☐
Tanzen Sie gern Tango?	☐	☐
Essen Sie gern Fisch?	☐	☐
Fahren Sie gern **Auto**?	☐	☐
Kochen Sie gern?	☐	☐
Schreiben Sie gern Briefe?	☐	☐
Schwimmen Sie gern?	☐	☐
Telefonieren Sie gern mit einem Handy?	☐	☐
Laufen Sie gern?	☐	☐
Lesen Sie gern Bücher?	☐	☐

Suggestion: Have students
check off two or three things
they like to do and then have
them say what they enjoy
doing.

In **Kapitel 1** you learned to express what you like to do, using the expression **Spaß machen** (*to be fun*).

Another common way to say you like to do something is to use the adverb **gern** with a conjugated verb.

Ich schwimme **gern**.	*I like to swim.*
Ich esse **gern** Fisch.	*I like to eat fish.*

If you want to say you dislike doing something, use **nicht gern.**

Ich schwimme **nicht gern**.	*I don't like to swim.*
Ich esse **nicht gern** Fisch.	*I don't like to eat fish.*

Note that **(nicht) gern** usually precedes direct objects.

Ich spiele **gern** Tennis.	*I like to play tennis.*
Frau Spitz hört **nicht gern** laute Musik.	*Ms. Spitz does not like to listen to loud music.*

- What activities are described in the ad and headline?
- Can you rephrase the following sentences using **(nicht) gern**?

  1. Wandern macht mir Spaß.
  2. Arbeiten macht mir keinen (*no*) Spaß.

Warum ich so gern in Hamburg arbeite
Von WOLFGANG JOOP, Hamburg
Ich lebe und arbeite in Hamburg.

Point out. *gerne* is a variant of *gern.*

Aktivität 7   Hin und her: Machen sie das gern?

Find out what the following people like to do or don't like to do by asking your partner.

BEISPIEL: s1: Was macht Denise gern?
s2: Sie reist gern. Was macht Thomas nicht gern?
s1: Er fährt nicht gern Auto.

	GERN	NICHT GERN
Thomas	arbeiten	Auto fahren
Denise	reisen	kochen
Niko	Eis essen	Karten spielen
Anja	laufen	Bier trinken
Sie		
Ihr Partner / Ihre Partnerin		

Aktivität 8   Zwei Leipziger°

Two people from Leipzig

Answer the questions about the Knobels, using the information below.

1. Was trinkt Frau Knobel gern? Und Herr Knobel?
2. Was essen die Knobels gern?
3. Was für (*what kind of*) Musik hören sie gern?
4. Was liest Herr Knobel gern? Und Frau Knobel?
5. Wer kocht gern?
6. Wer fährt gern einen BMW?

Aktivität 8. Suggestion:
Make up a chart like the
biographies shown. Then have
students interview one or two
other people. This can be
followed by a class discussion
of what students like.

[1] *pasta dishes*
[2] *skirts*
[3] *doing sports*
[4] *meatloaf*

Name: *Marianne Knobel*
Alter: *54*
Lieblingsgetränk: *Rotwein*
Lieblingsessen: *Nudelgerichte* [1]
Lieblingskleidung: *Jeans, Röcke* [2]
Lieblingskomponist: *Gustav Mahler*
Lieblingsauto: *Nissan Sunny*
Hobbys: *Bücher lesen, Kochen, Sport* [3]

Name: *Martin Knobel*
Alter: *58*
Lieblingsgetränk: *Bier*
Lieblingsessen: *Hackbraten* [4]
Lieblingskleidung: *Jeans, Pullover*
Lieblingskomponist: *Ludwig van Beethoven*
Lieblingsauto: *BMW M5*
Hobbys: *Zeitung lesen, ins Kino gehen*

Aktivität 9   Wer macht was gern?

Schritt 1: Find out who likes to do the following things by asking different classmates the questions on the next page. If they answer *yes*, have them sign their name in the blank to the right (or keep track by jotting down the people's names on a separate sheet).

BEISPIEL: S1: Siehst du gern Filme?
S2: Ja, ich sehe gern Filme.

1. Wanderst du gern? _____
2. Hörst du gern laute Musik? _____
3. Liest du gern Bücher? _____
4. Surfst du gern im Internet? _____
5. Isst du gern Brokkoli? _____
6. Fährst du gern Motorrad? _____

Schritt 2: Now ask three people in your class: **"Was machst du gern und was machst du nicht gern?"** Jot down their responses and report them to the class.

BEISPIEL: Jeff reist gern, aber (*but*) er tanzt nicht gern.
Sharon spielt gern Karten, aber sie kocht nicht gern.
Dave hört gern Musik, aber er arbeitet nicht gern.

Grammatik im Kontext

Substantive im Plural

The Plural of Nouns°

**The Plural of Nouns.
Suggestion:** Introduce plurals by mentioning in the plural several items that you have recently purchased. Let students hear plural nouns in a natural context. This can be accompanied by visuals, or you can write items on the board or use an overhead projector.

Point out: Noun plurals cannot be acquired overnight. At this point students need to familiarize themselves with the different possibilities of plural formation rather than to memorize long lists.

German forms the plural of nouns in several different ways. The following chart shows the most common plural patterns and the notation of those patterns in the vocabulary lists of this book.

SINGULAR	PLURAL	TYPE OF CHANGE	NOTATION
das Zimmer	die Zimmer	*no change*	-
die Mutter	die Mütter	*stem vowel is umlauted*	¨
der Tag	die Tage	*ending -e is added*	**-e**
der Stuhl	die Stühle	*ending -e is added and stem vowel is umlauted*	¨**e**
das Haus	die Häuser	*ending -er is added and stem vowel is umlauted*	¨**er**
die Lampe	die Lampen	*ending -n is added*	**-n**
die Frau	die Frauen	*ending -en is added*	**-en**
die Studentin	die Studentinnen	*ending -nen is added*	**-nen**
das Radio	die Radios	*ending -s is added*	**-s**

Note:

- The definite article (*the*) in the plural is **die** for all nouns, regardless of gender.

- Nouns ending in **-er** do not, with a few exceptions, change this ending in the plural.

SINGULAR	PLURAL
der Amerika**ner**	die Amerika**ner**
der Verkäu**fer**	die Verkäu**fer**
das Zimm**er**	die Zimm**er**
der Comput**er**	die Comput**er**

However, the stem vowel may change, as follows:

die M**u**tter	die M**ü**tter
der V**a**ter	die V**ä**ter

- Feminine nouns ending in **-in** form the plural by adding **-nen** to the singular.

SINGULAR	PLURAL
die Amerikaner**in**	die Amerikaner**innen**
die Mitbewohner**in**	die Mitbewohner**innen**

- Feminine nouns ending in **-e** form the plural by adding **-n** to the singular.

SINGULAR	PLURAL
die Küch**e**	die Küch**en**
die Miet**e**	die Miet**en**

- Nouns ending in vowels other than **-e** usually form the plural by adding **-s.**

SINGULAR	PLURAL
das Handy	die Handy**s**
das Kino	die Kino**s**
das Sofa	die Sofa**s**

SPRACHTIPP

In order to use gender-inclusive language, Germans frequently write **Student/in, Amerikaner/in,** or even, for the plural of such nouns, **StudentInnen, AmerikanerInnen.**

Übung 1   Wie viele

List items in your classroom, students in your class, and things that you and your friends have.

BEISPIEL: Das Klassenzimmer hat 27 Stühle und 25 Studenten.

Das Klassenzimmer hat...	Fenster (-)	Student (-en)	Freundin (-nen)
Ich habe...	Tür (-en)	Studentin (-nen)	Uhr (-en)
Mein Zimmer hat...	Stuhl (¨e)	Buch (¨er)	Problem (-e)
	Tisch (-e)	Freund (-e)	??

The Nominative and Accusative Cases°

In English, the subject and the direct object in a sentence are distinguished by their placement. The subject usually precedes the verb, whereas the direct object usually follows the verb.

In German, however, the subject and the object are not distinguished by their placement in the sentence. Instead, subjects and objects are indicated by grammatical cases. In this chapter you will learn about the nominative case (**der Nominativ**) for the subject of the sentence (as well as the predicate noun) and the accusative case (**der Akkusativ**) for the direct object and the object of certain prepositions.

German typically signals the case and the grammatical gender of a noun through different forms of the definite and indefinite articles that precede a noun.

Der bestimmte Artikel

The Definite Article°: Nominative and Accusative

You are already familiar with the nominative case. Those are the forms you used in **Kapitel 1.** Here are the nominative and the accusative case forms of the definite article (*the*).

NOMINATIVE	ACCUSATIVE
Der Stuhl kostet 70 Euro.	Ich kaufe **den** Stuhl.
The chair costs 70 Euro.	*I am going to buy the chair.*
Wo ist **die** Zeitung?	Ich brauche **die** Zeitung.
Where is the newspaper?	*I need the paper.*
Wie ist **das** Zimmer?	Ich miete **das** Zimmer.
How is the room?	*I am going to rent the room.*

	SINGULAR			PLURAL
	Masculine	*Feminine*	*Neuter*	*All Genders*
Nominative	der Stuhl	die Zeitung	das Zimmer	die Stühle
Accusative	**den** Stuhl	die Zeitung	das Zimmer	die Stühle

Note:

- Only the masculine definite article has a distinct accusative form: **den.**
- The plural has only one article for all three genders: **die.**

Weak Masculine Nouns°

A few common masculine nouns have a special accusative singular form. Five nouns of this type are:

NOMINATIVE	ACCUSATIVE
der **Mensch**	den Mensch**en**
der **Student**	den Student**en**
der **Herr**	den Her**rn**
der **Name**	den Name**n**
der **Kunde**	den Kunde**n**

Note:

- Weak masculine nouns, as they are called, are indicated in the vocabulary lists of this book by the notation (**-en** *masc.*) or (**-n** *masc.*).

Übung 2 Wie finden Sie das Zimmer?

What do you think of this typical **Studentenbude** (*student room*)?

BEISPIEL: Ich finde den Stuhl nicht bequem.

Ich finde...

das Zimmer	nicht	praktisch
das Bücherregal	zu	hässlich
der Stuhl	sehr	klein
die Schuhe		modern
der Sessel		schön
der Schreibtisch		bequem
der Wecker		groß

The Indefinite Article°: Nominative and Accusative

Here are the nominative and accusative forms of the indefinite article (*a/an*).

NOMINATIVE

Das ist **ein** Stuhl.
That is a chair.

Das ist **eine** Zeitung.
That is a newspaper.

Das ist **ein** Zimmer.
That is a room.

ACCUSATIVE

Ich brauche **einen** Stuhl.
I need a chair.

Wo finde ich hier **eine** Zeitung?
Where do I find a newspaper here?

Ich brauche **ein** Zimmer.
I need a room.

	SINGULAR			PLURAL
	Masculine	*Feminine*	*Neuter*	*All Genders*
Nominative	ein Stuhl	eine Zeitung	ein Zimmer	Stühle
Accusative	**einen** Stuhl	eine Zeitung	ein Zimmer	Stühle

Note:

- Only the masculine indefinite article has a distinct accusative form: **einen.**
- There is no plural indefinite article.

Was ist das?

ein Fussballspieler

Nominative and Accusative Interrogative Pronouns°

To ask about the subject of a sentence, use **wer** (*who*) or **was** (*what*). To ask about the direct object, use **wen** (*whom*) or **was** (*what*).

Wer braucht Geld?
Was ist ein Handy?

Who needs money?
What is a cell phone?

Wen besucht Frau Martin?
Was braucht der Mensch?

Whom is Mrs. Martin visiting?
What does a person need?

Übung 3   Neu in Göttingen

You will now hear a conversation between Stefan and Birgit. As you listen, check off what Stefan already has and what he still needs for his new apartment. Not all items are mentioned; leave them blank.

	DAS HAT STEFAN	DAS BRAUCHT STEFAN
1. eine Stereoanlage	☐	☐
2. eine Zimmerpflanze	☐	☐
3. eine Uhr	☐	☐
4. einen Couchtisch	☐	☐
5. einen Computer	☐	☐
6. einen Schreibtisch	☐	☒
7. ein Bücherregal	☐	☒
8. eine Kaffeemaschine	☐	☒
9. einen Schlafsack (*sleeping bag*)	☒	☐
10. ein Bett	☐	☒
11. einen Sessel	☐	☐

Übung 4   Was brauchen Sie noch?

You are shopping for several items. Referring to the items and prices under
Thema 2: Auf Möbelsuche im Kaufhaus in this chapter, create short conversational exchanges with a partner.

BEISPIEL: S1: Ich brauche eine Lampe.
           S2: Hier haben wir Lampen.
           S1: Was kostet die Lampe hier?
           S2: 130 Euro.
           S1: Das ist zu teuer. [oder:]
                Das ist preiswert.

Here are some additional noun plurals:

Betten	Sessel	Uhren
Handys	Sofas	Videorecorder
Kaffeemaschinen	Stereoanlagen	Wecker
Radios		

Übung 5   Die Studentenbude°

student room

Das ist eine typische Studentenbude. Was sehen Sie?

Das Zimmer hat _____.
Ich sehe _____.

das Papier — der Papierkorb

Übung 5. Suggestion: Have
students furnish a fantasy room
with a certain number of
objects. Each draws a picture of
the room and furnishings. Then,
in pairs, each person tries to
find out what is in the partner's
room.

Grammatik im Kontext   **67**

Übung 6. Suggestion: Give students several minutes to scan the ad in order to think of several items. Have students compare lists. One student can report what another has on his or her list. This activity also works well in pairs, with each student taking a turn asking *Was kaufst du?* If the activity is done in pairs, encourage students to comment on the items to be bought by adding such information as *Das finde ich praktisch.*

Übung 6   Was kaufen Sie?

Sie haben 900 Euro. Was kaufen Sie?

BEISPIEL: Ich kaufe den Tisch für _____ Euro und das Bett für _____ Euro.

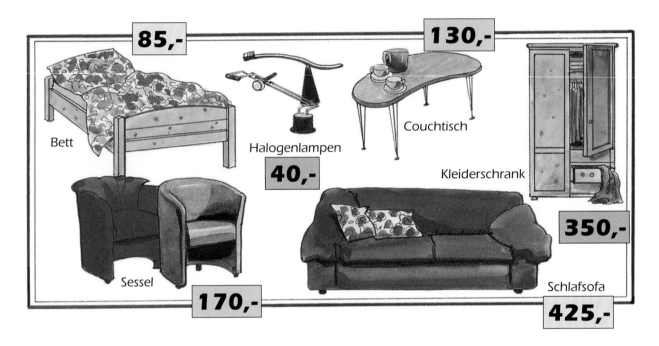

The Verb haben

The irregular verb **haben** (*to have*), like many other verbs, needs an accusative object (a direct object) to form a complete sentence.

Wir haben **eine Vorlesung** um zwei Uhr.   *We have a lecture at two o'clock.*

Anja hat **einen Schreibtisch.**   *Anja has a desk.*

haben			
ich	habe	wir	haben
du	**hast**	ihr	habt
er sie es	**hat**	sie	haben
Sie haben			

Lesen Sie den Dialog.

Ein Gespräch zwischen zwei Studenten. Es ist 12 Uhr mittags.

JÜRGEN: Grüß dich, Petra. Hast du Hunger?
PETRA: Warum fragst du?
JÜRGEN: Ich geh' jetzt essen. Ich hab' Hunger. Kommst du mit?
PETRA: Na, gut. Da kommt übrigens Hans. Der hat bestimmt auch Hunger.
HANS: Habt ihr zwei vielleicht Hunger?
PETRA: Ja, und wie! Aber ich hab' nicht viel Zeit. Um zwei haben wir nämlich eine Vorlesung.

- Which forms of the verb **haben** can you find in the dialogue?
- The **ich**-form of **haben** appears without the ending **-e**. What could be the reason for this?

Analyse. Explain to students that in casual spoken German, the *-e* of the *ich*-form is usually dropped. The full form with *-e* is standard for written and formal spoken German.

Übung 7 Hast du Hunger?

Complete the sentences with **haben** or **sein**.

Jürgen, Petra und Hans _____ [1] Studenten. Es _____ [2] gerade Mittagszeit. Jürgen _____ [3] Hunger. Er fragt Petra: „ _____ [4] du Hunger?" Hans _____ [5] Petras Freund. Hans und Petra _____ [6] um zwei eine Vorlesung. Sie _____ [7] nicht viel Zeit. Und Jürgen _____ [8] nicht viel Geld (*money*). Er fragt Hans „ _____ [9] du etwas Geld?"

Negation with **nicht** and the Negative Article **kein**°

Verneinung

In **Kapitel 1** you learned to negate a simple statement by adding the word **nicht** (*not*) before a predicate adjective.

Die Lampe ist **nicht** billig.   *The lamp is not cheap.*

You can also use **nicht** to negate an entire statement, or just an adverb.

Karin kauft die Lampe **nicht**.   *Karin is not buying the lamp.*

Ralf schreibt **nicht** besonders gut. *Ralf doesn't write particularly well.*

One other important way to express negation is by using the negative article **kein** (*no, not a, not any*), which parallels the forms of **ein**.

—Hast du **einen** Computer?   *Do you have a computer?*

—Nein, ich habe **keinen** Computer.   *No, I don't have a computer.*

—Hast du Geld?   *Do you have any money?*

—Nein, ich habe **kein** Geld.   *No, I do not have any money.*

—Ist das **eine** Zeitung?   *Is that a newspaper?*

—Das ist **keine** Zeitung!   *That isn't a newspaper!*

Salamander Schuh & Sport
Inh. E. Neuhausen

**Große Füße —
kein Problem**

ÜBERGRÖSSEN
SALAMANDER
SERVICE

**Damenschuhe bis Gr. 44
Herrenschuhe bis Gr. 49**

Altkalkarer Straße 17
Telefon 0 28 24 / 59 69

Note:

- Use **kein** to negate a noun that is preceded by an indefinite article or no article at all.

	SINGULAR					PLURAL	
	Masculine		Feminine		Neuter	All Genders	
Nominative	kein	Sessel	keine	Lampe	kein	Sofa	keine	Stühle
Accusative	keinen	Sessel	keine	Lampe	kein	Sofa	keine	Stühle

Zwei Störche und ein Frosch

[1]Die. . . That line never fails.

Übung 8 Immer diese Ausreden!°

Excuses, excuses!

Everyone has a different excuse for turning down an invitation. Listen and check off the excuse given by each person.

1. Reinhard...
   - ☐ hat keine Zeit.
   - ☐ hat keine Lust.
   - ☒ hat kein Geld.
2. Erika...
   - ☐ hat keinen Freund.
   - ☐ hat keine Zeit.
   - ☒ hat keine Lust.
3. Frau Becker...
   - ☒ trinkt keinen Kaffee.
   - ☐ hat keine Lust.
   - ☐ hat keine Zeit.
4. Jens und Ulla...
   - ☐ haben kein Examen.
   - ☒ haben keine Zeit.
   - ☐ haben keinen Hunger.
5. Peter...
   - ☒ hat keine Lust.
   - ☐ hat kein Geld.
   - ☐ hat kein Auto.

Übung 9 Ein Frühstück°

Breakfast

Was ist hier komisch (*funny*)? In Grimm's fairy tale "The Frog Prince," a prince turned into a frog is transformed back into the prince when kissed by a beautiful princess. The cartoon on the left draws on this story for its comical effect. Circle the correct option in each statement.

1. Die zwei Störche (*storks*) suchen ein/kein Frühstück.
2. Der Frosch hat ein/kein Problem.
3. Störche essen gern / nicht gern Frösche zum Frühstück.
4. Der Frosch ist ein/kein Prinz.
5. Der Frosch ist sehr / nicht sehr intelligent.
6. Die Störche essen heute ein/kein Frühstück.
7. Ich finde den Cartoon komisch / nicht komisch.

Übung 10 Wer hat das nicht?

Find out what your fellow students do not have.

BEISPIEL: s1: Wer hat kein Handy? →
          s2: Sieben Studenten haben kein Handy.

Suggestion: Have students take turns asking a question. Students raise their hand in response. Another student counts raised hands and states the answer.

Wer hat kein-...?

Computer	Motorrad
Stereoanlage	Kommode
Schreibtisch	Teppich
Lampe	Regal
Telefon	Stühle
Sessel	Wecker
Fernseher	Nachttisch
Sofa	Videorecorder
Bett	Handy
Zimmerpflanzen (*pl.*)	Poster (*pl.*)
Radio	DVD-Spieler
Auto	

Verbs with Stem-Vowel Changes

A number of common verbs have vowel changes in the present tense.

	fahren	**schlafen**	**laufen**	**essen**	**sehen**	**lesen**	**nehmen**
ich	fahre	schlafe	laufe	esse	sehe	lese	nehme
du	**fährst**	**schläfst**	**läufst**	**isst**	**siehst**	**liest**	**nimmst**
er sie es	**fährt**	**schläft**	**läuft**	**isst**	**sieht**	**liest**	**nimmt**
wir	fahren	schlafen	laufen	essen	sehen	lesen	nehmen
ihr	fahrt	schlaft	lauft	esst	seht	lest	nehmt
sie/Sie	fahren	schlafen	laufen	essen	sehen	lesen	nehmen

Note:

- The vowel changes are in the second-person singular (**du**) and the third-person singular (**er, sie, es**).
- The verb **nehmen** (*to take*) has additional consonant changes: **du** *nimmst;* **er, sie, es** *nimmt.*

Verbs with vowel changes in the present tense will be indicated in the vocabulary sections of this book as follows: **schlafen (schläft).**

Suggestion: Ask students to come up with 2 or 3 statements for each to show the couple's differences.

Übung 11   Kontraste

Mr. and Mrs. Wunderlich don't have a lot in common. Create a profile of each of them using the phrases provided.

BEISPIEL: Frau Wunderlich fährt gern Motorrad.
         Herr Wunderlich fährt gern Auto.

Herr Wunderlich	fährt gern Motorrad.
Frau Wunderlich	sieht gern Horrorfilme um Mitternacht.
	isst gern Sauerkraut.
	sieht gern „Glücksrad Fortuna" im Fernsehen.
	nimmt gern ein Glas Wein beim Essen.
	schläft beim Lesen ein (*falls asleep while reading*).
	liest jeden Tag Zeitung.
	liest jeden Tag nur das Horoskop.
	läuft jeden Tag im Park.
	isst kein Sauerkraut.
	fährt gern Auto (einen alten Volkswagen).

Übung 12   Was machen sie gern?

1. Ich _____ gern italienisch, Karin _____ gern chinesisch. (essen)
2. Klaus und Petra _____ heute im Restaurant. (essen) Petra _____ Fisch und Klaus _____ ein Wiener Schnitzel. (nehmen)
3. Hans braucht eine Lampe. Er _____ eine supermoderne Lampe im Kaufhaus. (sehen)
4. Ilse _____ gern Auto. Morgen _____ wir nach Berlin. (fahren)
5. Herr Renner _____ jeden Tag im Park. Dort _____ viele Jogger. (laufen)
6. Was _____ du gern? Ich _____ gern Zeitung. (lesen)

Übung 13   Was machen Sie gern, manchmal, nie, oft?

Tell a partner several things you do or don't like to do and how often: **gern, manchmal** (*sometimes*), **nie** (*never*), **oft.** Report to the class what you've learned.

BEISPIEL: S1: Ich esse gern, ich tanze manchmal, ich laufe nie.
         S2: John isst gern, tanzt manchmal und läuft nie.

gern	arbeiten	schwimmen
manchmal	Auto/Motorrad fahren	tanzen
nie	einen Hamburger essen	wandern
oft	Karten/Tennis/Fußball spielen	Zeitung lesen
	laufen	
	reisen	
	schlafen	

Demonstrative Pronouns°

Demonstrativpronomen

ROBERT: Hat Thomas Hunger?

KARIN: **Der** hat immer Hunger. [*Instead of*: Er hat immer Hunger.]

HERR HOLZ: Was kostet der Sessel hier?

VERKÄUFER: **Der** kostet nur 150 Euro.

FRAU HOLZ: Gut, **den** nehmen wir.

ULLA: Wie findest du die Lampe?

ROBERT: **Die** finde ich prima.

In conversational German, demonstrative pronouns, identical to the definite articles, may be used instead of personal pronouns. Since demonstratives are more emphatic than personal pronouns, they are usually placed at the beginning of a sentence.

Übung 14   Fragen und Antworten

Answer, replacing the nouns or names with demonstrative pronouns.

BEISPIEL: Was macht Frau Schlemmer schon wieder? →
Die isst schon wieder.

1. Was macht Ernst Immermüd schon wieder?

   _____ schläft schon wieder.

2. Was macht Uschi Schnell schon wieder?

   _____ fährt schon wieder Motorrad.

3. Was kostet die Zeitung?

   _____ kostet zwei Euro.

4. Was kostet der Stuhl?

   _____ kostet 35 Euro.

5. Nimmst du den Stuhl?

   Ja, _____ nehme ich.

6. Liest du das Horoskop?

   Nein, _____ lese ich nie.

Sprache im Kontext

Videoclips

A. Listen to what the following people say about where they live and complete the information.

1. Wiebke hat eine _____. Sie hat vier _____, eine _____ und ein _____. Die Wohnung hat ungefär _____ Quadratmeter. Wiebke und ihr Mann _____ gern.

2. Nicoletta wohnt in Berlin-Kreuzberg in einer _____. Es ist eine _____. Man kann eine Wohnung über die Mitwohnzentrale, über die _____, über _____ oder am Schwarzen Brett finden.

3. Claudia hat eine helle _____ im vierten Stock. Das Wohnzimmer hat eine _____, einen Schreibtisch mit einem _____, verschiedene _____, einen _____ und Regale mit CDs. Die Wohnung war nicht _____.

4. Harald _____ in Berlin-Kreuzberg in einer alten Fabrik. Die Wohnung hat eine große Küche, zwei _____ und ein _____. Harald _____ gern vegetarisch und auch Fisch.

B. Watch the interviews with Sabina and Claudia. Listen as they say what they still need for their apartments. Who needs what?

C. Now describe your house, apartment, or room.

Lesen

Wie und wo wohnen junge Leute in Deutschland? In this section you will look at texts in which young people in Germany tell how they live.

Zum Thema

Wie wohnen Sie?

A. Take a few moments to complete the questionnaire; then interview a partner to see how he/she answered the questions.

Wo wohne ich?

1. Ich wohne _____.
   a. in einem Studentenheim
   b. in einer Wohnung
   c. bei meinen Eltern
   d. in meinem eigenen (*own*) Haus
   e. privat in einem Zimmer
   f. ??

   all words that end in -ung are feminine (die).

2. Ich teile (*share*) mein Zimmer / meine Wohnung / mein Haus mit _____.
   a. einer anderen Person
   b. zwei, drei, vier,...Personen
   c. niemand anderem. Ich wohne allein.

   Most nouns ending in -e are also die.

3. Ich habe _____.
   a. eine Katze (*cat*)
   b. einen Hund (*dog*)
   c. einen Goldfisch
   d. andere Haustiere (eine Kobra, einen Hamster,...)
   e. keine Haustiere

4. Ich wohne gern/nicht gern _____.
   a. in einer Großstadt
   b. in einer Kleinstadt
   c. auf dem Land

   exceptions: der Blume der Straße

Wie wohnen Sie?
Suggestions: This may be done as a partner activity, with students jotting down the answers on a separate sheet.

Follow-up: The first four answers can be linked in a third-person report. Call on several students to do this. Record answers to the first four questions on the board to develop a class profile, e.g., *Drei Studenten wohnen bei ihren Eltern. Zwölf Studenten wohnen in einer Wohnung. Vier Studenten wohnen in einem Studentenheim.*

5. Als Student hat man hier _____ Probleme, eine Wohnung zu finden.
  a. keine
  b. manchmal
  c. große

6. Die Mieten sind hier _____.
  a. niedrig
  b. hoch

B. Report to the class what you found out about your partner.

Auf den ersten Blick

In the following passages students in Bonn, the former capital of West Germany, and Rostock, a city in northeastern Germany, tell about their living arrangements. Skim through the texts, and for each one organize the vocabulary you recognize into the following categories.

PERSON	HOUSING	OBJECTS FOUND IN ROOM
BEISPIEL: Katja	Studentenwohnheim	Betten, Schreibtisch, Esstisch, Regale...

SO WOHNE ICH

Name: *Katja Meierhans*
Wohnort: *Rostock*
Hauptfächer: *Mathematik, Chemie*

Während des Studiums wohne ich im Studenten-
5 wohnheim mit noch einer[1] Studentin auf einem Zimmer; Gemeinschaftswaschräume[2] und WCs[3] für den ganzen Flur[4] (22 Zimmer); im Raum sind Betten, Schreibtisch, Esstisch, viele Regale, viele Schränke. Ich bin zufrieden.[5] Zu Hause
10 (300 km von Rostock) wohne ich bei meinen Eltern. Wir haben mein Zimmer zusammen ausgebaut,[6] deshalb[7] ist es natürlich mehr nach meinen Wünschen. Ich fahre gern nach Hause, aber in Rostock bin ich unabhängiger.[8]

15 **Name:** *Christina Stiegen*
Wohnort: *Niederkassel (Rheidt)*
Hauptfächer: *Politologie, Italienisch*

Ich wohne in einer Wohnung etwas außerhalb von[9] Bonn. Die Wohnung hat 52m², zwei
20 Zimmer, Küche, Diele,[10] Bad. Ich teile mir[11] die Wohnung mit meinem Freund, der auch in Bonn studiert. Es handelt sich um[12] eine Dachwohnung.[13]

Name: *Jennifer Wolcott*
25 **Wohnort:** *Mönchengladbach*
Hauptfächer: *Englisch, Politische Wissenschaften*

Ich wohne in einem Zimmer (12m²) in einem Studentenwohnheim. In dem Zimmer sind ein großer Schreibtisch mit Schubladen,[14] ein
30 Bett, ein Regal, ein Kleiderschrank und ein Waschbecken[15] mit Spiegel.[16] Ich habe einen Teppich[17] hingelegt, Pflanzen auf die große Fensterbank[18] gestellt, noch ein Regal (für meine vielen Bücher und meine Stereoanlage).
35 Außerdem habe ich Bilder, Poster und Erinnerungen[19] an die weißen Wände gehängt. Ich teile Bad/Toiletten und eine große Küche mit zwanzig Studenten.

Name: *Peter Kesternich*
40 **Wohnort:** *Euskirchen*
Hauptfächer: *Englisch, Geschichte*

Ich wohne in einem Zimmer bei meinen Eltern. Ich fahre jeden Morgen mit dem Zug[20] zur Uni (ca. 50 Min.). Das ist für mich praktischer (und billiger), als in Bonn ein Zimmer zu suchen.

[1]*noch... one other* [2]*common washrooms* [3]*toilets* [4]*floor* [5]*content, satisfied* [6]*renovated* [7]*for that reason* [8]*more independent* [9]*etwas... just outside of* [10]*front hall* [11]*teile... share* [12]*Es... It is* [13]*attic apartment* [14]*drawers* [15]*sink* [16]*mirror* [17]*carpet* [18]*windowsill* [19]*mementos, souvenirs* [20]*train*

Hier klicken!

You'll find more about housing in German-speaking countries in **Deutsch: Na klar!** on the World Wide Web at www.mhhe.com/dnk.

Zum Text. The goal is not to
have students understand every
word but to read the text to
complete the task.

Zum Text

A. Read the texts more thoroughly and look at these drawings. Which description most closely matches which drawing?

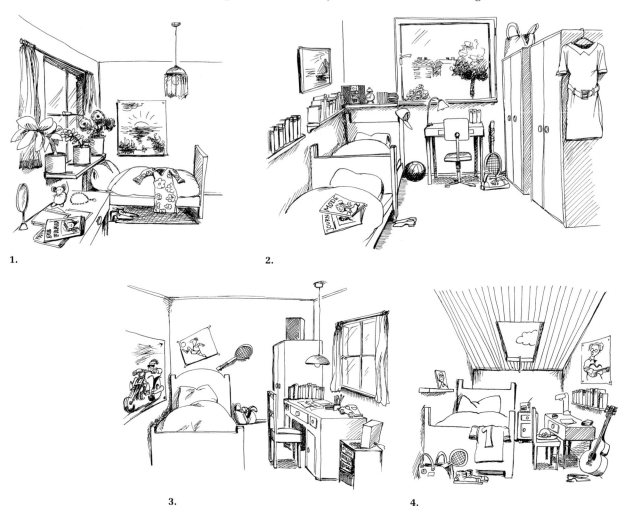

1.

2.

3.

4.

B. Look at the chart below and then scan the texts for specific information in order to complete it. If there is no information given for a particular category, leave that space blank.

NAME	WOHNORT	WIE ER/SIE WOHNT	WAS IM ZIMMER IST	WEITERE INFORMATIONEN

1. Using the information in the chart, construct sentences about the students. Have the rest of the class guess which person you are describing.
2. Using the information in the chart, describe one of the people by creating true and false statements. The rest of the class has to say whether your statements are true or false.

Sprechen und Schreiben

Aktivität 1   Mitbewohner(in) gesucht°!

°sought

Imagine that you live in an apartment with two or three other roommates and that one of the roommates has just moved out. Working with one or two other students and using the housing ads in the **Wörter im Kontext** section as a guide, create an ad about your apartment. Begin your ad as follows:

> **Mitbewohner(in) gesucht! Zimmer in**
>
> _____ **zimmerwohnung/Haus frei.**

Aktivität 2   Zusammenwohnen, aber mit wem?°

°Living together, but with whom?

A. Now pair up with someone who was not in your group in **Aktivität 1** and interview him/her to see whether you are compatible. Use the questions below as a point of departure and add your own questions to reflect your personal needs. Then switch roles. Repeat the interview with at least one other person.

S1 asks:
- how large the room is
- if the room is furnished
- how much the rent is
- if they have a telephone, garden, garage

S2 asks the other person whether he/she:
- smokes (**rauchen**)
- has a pet (**ein Haustier**)
- has a car
- uses the telephone (**telefonieren**) a lot
- often has friends over (**Besuch haben**)
- plays loud music (**laute Musik**)

B. After you've interviewed a couple of prospective roommates or house-mates, meet with your original group from **Aktivität 1**, compare notes, and then report to the class about whom you chose.

BEISPIEL: Wir vermieten das Zimmer an Jeanine. Sie ist sehr nett und sympathisch. Sie spielt keine laute Musik. . .

Aktivität 2. Suggestion: Students formulate questions as a group; the instructor or a student can put them on the board or overhead. The questions can also be assigned as homework that you can quickly check before students interview one another.

Wortschatz

Im Kaufhaus / At the Department Store

das **Bett, -en**	bed
der **CD-Spieler, -**	CD player
der **Computer, -**	computer
der **Computeranschluss, ⸚e**	computer connection
der **DVD-Spieler, -**	DVD player
der **Fernseher, -**	TV set
das **Foto, -s**	photograph
das **Handy, -s**	cell phone
der **Kleiderschrank, ⸚e**	clothes closet
die **Kommode, -n**	dresser
die **Lampe, -n**	lamp
das **Poster, -**	poster
das **Radio, -s**	radio
das **Regal, -e**	shelf
das **Bücherregal, -e**	bookcase, bookshelf
der **Sessel, -**	armchair
das **Sofa, -s**	sofa
die **Stereoanlage, -n**	stereo
der **Stuhl, ⸚e**	chair
das **Telefon, -e**	telephone
der **Teppich, -e**	rug, carpet
der **Tisch, -e**	table
der **Couchtisch, -e**	coffee table
der **Nachttisch, -e**	nightstand
der **Schreibtisch, -e**	desk
die **Uhr, -en**	clock
der **Videorecorder, -**	video recorder, VCR
der **Wecker, -**	alarm clock

Das Haus / The House

das **Bad, ⸚er**	bathroom
der **Balkon, -s**	balcony
das **Fenster, -**	window
die **Garage, -n**	garage
der **Garten, ⸚**	garden, yard
das **Haus, ⸚er**	house
die **Küche, -n**	kitchen
die **Terrasse, -n**	terrace, patio
die **Tür, -en**	door
die **Wand, ⸚e**	wall

das **Zimmer, -**	room
das **Arbeitszimmer, -**	workroom, study
das **Badezimmer, -**	bathroom
das **Esszimmer, -**	dining room
das **Schlafzimmer, -**	bedroom
das **Wohnzimmer, -**	living room

Sonstige Substantive / Other Nouns

das **Auto, -s**	car
der **Euro, -s**	euro
das **Geld** _, -er_	money
das **Kaufhaus, ⸚er**	department store
der **Kunde, -n** (-n _masc._)	(male) customer
die **Kundin, -nen**	(female) customer
der **Mensch, -en** (-en _masc._)	person, human being
die **Miete** _, – n_	rent
der **Mitbewohner, -/die Mitbewohnerin, -nen**	roommate
das **Motorrad, ⸚er**	motorcycle
das **Papier, -e**	paper
der **Papierkorb, ⸚e**	wastebasket
das **Problem, -e**	problem
das **Studenten(wohn)heim, -e**	dormitory
der **Tag, -e**	day
der **Verkäufer, -** / die **Verkäuferin, -nen**	salesperson
das **Video, -s**	video(tape)
die **Wohngemeinschaft, -en (WG)**	shared housing
die **Wohnung, -en**	apartment
die **Zeit, -en**	time
die **Zimmerpflanze, -n**	houseplant

(handwritten note: Plural?)

Verben / Verbs

brauchen	to need
haben (hat)	to have
Durst haben	to be thirsty
gern haben	to like (_a person or thing_)
Hunger haben	to be hungry

Lust haben	to feel like (*doing something*)	**hässlich**	ugly
Recht haben	to be correct	**hell**	bright(ly), light
Zeit haben	to have time	**hoch**	high(ly)
kaufen	to buy	**klein**	small
kosten	to cost	**möbliert**	furnished
laufen (läuft)	to run, jog	**unmöbliert**	unfurnished
lesen (liest)	to read	**niedrig**	low
nehmen (nimmt)	to take	**noch**	still; yet
schlafen (schläft)	to sleep	**nur**	only
schreiben	to write	**preiswert**	a bargain, inexpensive(ly)
schwimmen	to swim	**recht**	quite, rather
sehen (sieht)	to see	**recht preiswert**	quite inexpensive, reasonable
sprechen (spricht)	to speak	**schon**	already
suchen	to look for	**schön**	nice(ly), beautiful(ly)
trinken	to drink	**selten**	rare(ly)
		so	so
Adjektive und Adverbien	**Adjectives and Adverbs**	**teuer**	expensive(ly)
		viel/viele	much/many
aber	but, however	**vielleicht**	maybe, perhaps
bequem	comfortable, comfortably	**wieder**	again
billig	inexpensive(ly), cheap(ly)	**Sonstiges**	**Other**
da	there	**etwas**	something; somewhat, a little (*adverb*)
dringend	urgent(ly)	**kein**	no, none, not any
dunkel	dark	**nichts**	nothing
frei	free(ly)	**warum**	why
gerade	just, exactly	**Was ist denn los?**	What's the matter?
gern	gladly	**weit weg von...**	far away from . . .
gern + *verb*	to like to do something	**zentral gelegen**	centrally located
gross	big, large		

LERNZIELE

Use this checklist to verify that you can now . . .

☐ read and understand German housing ads.

☐ describe the way you (and others) live.

☐ talk about prices in German.

☐ describe some of the furnishings and other items you (and others) have and need.

☐ give your opinions about types of housing, furnishings, and other objects.

☐ describe some activities you (and others) like or don't like to do.

☐ form the plural of nouns you have learned in this and previous chapters.

☐ form sentences and questions using (accusative) direct objects.

☐ recognize and use special masculine nouns.

☐ use common expressions with **haben.**

☐ form negative sentences and questions using **kein** and **nicht.**

☐ recognize and use verbs with stem-vowel changes in the present tense.

☐ recognize and use demonstrative pronouns in the nominative and accusative cases.

☐ scan texts for specific information.

Familie und Freunde

Wo isst die Familie?
a. Zu Hause im Garten.
b. Im Restaurant.

Kapitel 3. Introduce the chapter theme (family, days and dates, special events) by talking about your own experiences: How large is your family? Are certain dates, months, times of the year important in your family?

Videoclips
Familien und Feste

In diesem Kapitel

- **Themen:** Family members, days of the week, months, holidays, ordinal numbers
- **Grammatik:** Possessive adjectives; accusative case; prepositions with accusative; **werden; wissen** and **kennen**
- **Kultur:** German holidays and celebrations

Alles klar?

Families are important in every culture. We define ourselves most often in terms of our family background. Even with the fast pace of modern life, family members take time to come together for important celebrations such as weddings, birthdays, and holidays.

A. Below you see a picture of Bernd Thalhofer's family with his relatives labeled. Your knowledge of cognates and contextual guessing will help you understand what these words mean. Look at the picture and identify the words for mother, father, sister, brother-in-law, and niece. Now, can you guess at what family celebration the picture was taken?

meine Schwägerin Gabriele   mein Schwiegervater Horst   meine Kusine Uta   meine Schwester Alexandra

mein Neffe Sebastian

mein Bruder Werner

meine Mutter Helene

mein Neffe Thomas   meine Nichte Nicole   meine Frau Bettina   **Das bin ich: Bernd**

B. Now listen as Bernd's sister, Alexandra, describes her family. As you listen, indicate whether the following statements are correct or incorrect.

	DAS STIMMT	DAS STIMMT NICHT
1. Das Foto zeigt Familie Thalhofer bei einer Geburtstagsfeier.	☐	☒
2. Familie Thalhofer wohnt in Leipzig.	☐	☒

3. Alexandra Thalhofer hat zwei Brüder. ☒ ☐
4. Ihr Bruder Bernd und seine Frau, Bettina, sind
   Lehrer von Beruf. ☒ ☐
5. Alexandra plant eine Reise nach Kanada. ☐ ☒
6. Alexandras Bruder Werner hat zwei Kinder. ☒ ☐
7. Alexandras Eltern sind nicht auf dem Foto. ☐ ☒

Wörter im Kontext

A family tree

THEMA 1: Ein Familienstammbaum°

Bernd Thalhofers Familie

[1]geb. = geborene   *maiden name*

Wer ist wer? How is each relative related to you?

1. der **Bruder**
2. der **Enkel**
3. die **Enkelin**
4. die **Geschwister** (*pl.*)
5. die **Großeltern** (*pl.*)
6. die **Großmutter (Oma)**
7. der **Großvater (Opa)**
8. die **Kusine**
9. der **Neffe**
10. die **Nichte**
11. der **Onkel**
12. der **Schwager**
13. die **Schwägerin**
14. die **Schwester**
15. die **Tante**
16. der **Vetter**

a. Mein ____9____: der Sohn meines (*of my*)Bruders oder meiner (*of my*) Schwester
b. Meine ____14____: die Tochter meiner Eltern
c. Meine ____10____: die Tochter meines Bruders oder meiner Schwester
d. Meine ____15____: die Schwester meines Vaters oder meiner Mutter
e. Mein ____2____: der Sohn meines Sohnes oder meiner Tochter
f. Mein ____12____: der Mann meiner Schwester
g. Meine ____4____: die Söhne und Töchter meiner Eltern
h. Meine ____6____: die Mutter meines Vaters oder meiner Mutter
i. Mein ____11____: der Bruder meines Vaters oder meiner Mutter
j. Mein ____1____: der Sohn meiner Eltern
k. Mein ____16____: der Sohn meines Onkels und meiner Tante
l. Meine ____3____: die Tochter meines Sohnes oder meiner Tochter
m. Meine ____13____: die Frau meines Bruders
n. Meine ____5____: die Eltern meiner Eltern
o. Meine ____8____: die Tochter meines Onkels und meiner Tante
p. Mein ____7____: der Vater meines Vaters oder meiner Mutter

Neue Wörter

Enkel grandson
Enkelin granddaughter
Frau wife
Geschwister (*pl.*) siblings
Oma grandma
Opa grandpa
Mann husband
Neffe nephew
Nichte niece
Schwager brother-in-law
Schwägerin sister-in-law
Sohn son
Tochter daughter

Note: You may want to mention the French-derived variants **Cousin** and **Cousine** for **Vetter** and **Kusine**.

SPRACHTIPP

As in English, to indicate that somebody is related to another person, add an **-s** to the person's name—though without an apostrophe.

Das ist Bernd **Thalhofers** Familie.
Bernds Eltern heißen Werner und Helene.

Another way to indicate relationships is with the preposition **von** (*of*).

Das ist die Familie **von** Bernd Thalhofer.
Die Eltern **von** Bernd heißen Werner und Helene.

The **von** construction is preferred if a name ends in an **-s** or **-z**.

Die Frau **von** Markus heißt Julia.
Das Haus **von** Familie Lentz ist sehr modern.

Aktivität 1 Wer ist das?

Unscramble the letters to find out which family member each item represents. The vocabulary at the top of the previous page will help you.

1. feeNf
2. eTtna
3. esKnui
4. treeVt
5. chNeti

6. klnOe
7. sewrStche
8. drerBu
9. tmßGorture
10. rVaet

Aktivität 2 Ein Interview

A. Ask a person in your class about his/her family.

1. Wie heißen deine Eltern?
2. Wie viele Geschwister hast du?
3. Wie heißen deine Geschwister?
4. Wo wohnt deine Familie?
5. Wie alt sind deine Geschwister?
6. ??

B. Report back to the class about your partner's family.

BEISPIEL: Jennys Familie wohnt in Salt Lake City. Jenny hat fünf Brüder und drei Schwestern. Ihre Brüder heißen Mark und Stephen. . .

Aktivität 2. Suggestion: Before doing this activity, brainstorm possible questions with students for number 6. Then have students work in pairs to interview each other, taking notes. Ask several students to report their findings.

SPRACHTIPP

To indicate that someone is related only through one parent, compounds can be formed using **Stief-** (*step*) and **Halb-** (*half*). The German equivalent to English *great* is the prefix **Ur-**.

Maria ist meine **Stiefschwester.**   *Maria is my stepsister.*
Mein **Halbbruder** heißt Jens.   *My half-brother is named Jens.*

Wilhelmine ist meine **Urgroßmutter.**   *Wilhelmine is my great-grandmother.*

Aktivität 3 Generationen: Wer ist wer?

Aktivität 3. Suggestion: Students can work in pairs to ask and answer the questions.

A. Look closely at the family portrait on page 85 and answer the questions.

1. Wie viele Generationen sind auf diesem Foto?
2. Wie heißen die Frauen mit Vornamen?
3. Wie heißen die zwei jüngsten (*youngest*) Frauen? Wie alt sind sie?
4. Wer ist die älteste (*oldest*) Frau? Wie alt ist sie?
5. Wer ist die Mutter von Susanne und Nicole?
6. Wer ist die Großmutter von Frauke?
7. Wer ist die Tochter von Pauline?

Landkinder: Tochter Susanne, 18; Großmutter Alma, 63; Tochter Nicole, 19; Urgroßmutter Pauline, 87; Mutter Frauke, 40

B. Suggestion: This activity is a summary of **A.** To reinforce new vocabulary, do as a whole-group activity or as homework.

Aktivität 4. Suggestion: Students should first scan the realia and the accompanying questions. Then ask them to complete the activity in pairs or threes, asking each other the questions. Afterward, elicit responses from the students as a whole group. Ask students what the family's last name is (*Volkswagen*).

Realia. This ad congratulates *Volkswagen* on the occasion of its 50th birthday.

B.   Now fill in the missing information.

1. Susanne ist Fraukes _____.
2. Pauline ist Susannes und Nicoles _____ und Fraukes _____.
3. Alma ist Paulines _____ und Susannes und Nicoles _____.
4. _____ spielt gern Fußball. Sie ist Paulines Enkelin.
5. Alma hat zwei Enkelinnen, _____ und _____. Und wer ist das in der Mitte? Sie gehört (*belongs*) auch zur Familie.

Aktivität 4   Ein merkwürdiger° Stammbaum

peculiar

A very special family is celebrating its birthday. What is the name of the family?

1. Welche Namen kennen Sie, welche Namen kennen Sie nicht?
2. Wer fehlt (*is missing*) in diesem Stammbaum? Ich sehe keine/keinen _____.
3. Wer hat keinen Namen?
4. Das Insekt hier ist ein Käfer. Wie heißt „Käfer" auf Englisch?
5. Wissen Sie, wie alt der Großvater ungefähr (*roughly*) ist?

   a. ungefähr 100 Jahre
   b. ungefähr 60–70 Jahre
   c. ungefähr 10 Jahre

6. Wie heißt die „Käfer" Familie?

DER GROSSVATER.

DIE SCHWESTER KARMANN GHIA.   DER BRUDER KÄFER.

DER ONKEL ILTIS.   DIE TANTE GOLF.   DER NEFFE PASSAT.

DER VETTER POLO.   DIE COUSINE JETTA.   DER COUSIN SANTANA.   DER ENKELIN SCIROCCO.

Wir gratulieren der ganzen Familie.

Der Kalender. Suggestion: Introduce days of the week and have students repeat them. On which days do you have German class?

Introduce months by mentioning events that occur in each month, e.g., *Das zweite Semester beginnt im Januar. Der Valentinstag ist im Februar.* Write only the name of the month on the board as you do this. Students will become accustomed to hearing *im Januar, im Juni,* etc.

Point out: All months are masculine, but the definite article is not usually used with the month.

THEMA 2: Der Kalender: Die Wochentage und die Monate

die Monate	
Januar	Juli
Februar	August
März	September
April	Oktober
Mai	November
Juni	Dezember

Oktober

Montag	Dienstag	Mittwoch	Donnerstag	Freitag	Samstag	Sonntag
4	5	6	7	1	2	3
11	12	13	14	8	9	10
18	19	20	21	15	16	17
25	26	27	28	22	23	24
				29	30	31

Aktivität 5 Welcher Tag ist das?

Newspaper ads often abbreviate the days of the week. Can you identify which days of the week these abbreviations represent?

1. Mo _____
2. Fr _____
3. Do _____
4. So _____
5. Mi _____
6. Sa _____
7. Di _____

> ### SPRACHTIPP
>
> Use the following phrases to say the day or month when something takes place.
>
> —Wann wirst du 21?
> —Ich werde **am Samstag** 21.
>
> —Wann hast du Geburtstag?
> —Ich habe **im Dezember** Geburtstag.

Aktivität 6 Wie alt bist du?

Interview several classmates to learn their ages and birthdates.

BEISPIEL: S1: Wie alt bist du?
　　　　　 S2: Ich bin 23.
　　　　　 S1: Wann wirst du 24?
　　　　　 S2: Ich werde im August 24. Und du?

Aktivität 7 Eine Einladung° zum Geburtstag

invitation

Listen and take notes as Tom and Heike talk about an upcoming birthday party. Read the questions first before listening to the conversation.

1. Wer hat Geburtstag? *Heike*
2. Wann ist der Geburtstag? *Samstag*
3. Wo ist die Party? *bei Heike zu Hause*
4. Wer kommt sonst noch (*else*)? *Gabi, Jürgen, Heikes Eltern und Geschwister*
5. Kommt die Person am Telefon, oder nicht? *Ja, er kommt.*

Aktivität 7. Suggestion: Students should scan the questions before listening to the dialogue. Play the tape once; students answer as many questions as they can, based on one listening. Play the tape a second time and have students complete any unfinished questions.

Aktivität 8 Hin und her: Verwandtschaften°

relationships

Ask a partner questions about Bernd's family. How is each person related to Bernd?

BEISPIEL: S1: Wie ist Gisela mit Bernd verwandt?
S2: Gisela ist Bernds Tante.
S1: Wie alt ist sie denn?
S2: Sie ist 53.
S1: Wann hat sie Geburtstag?
S2: Im Februar.

Additional activity: Have students create a similar chart with real family members, keeping kinship terms but changing names and ages.

PERSON	VERWANDTSCHAFT	ALTER	GEBURTSTAG
Gisela	Tante	53	Februar
Alexandra	Schwester	25	März
Werner	Schwager	36	Dezember
Andreas	Großvater	70	Juni
Sabine	Kusine	19	August

THEMA 3: Feste und Feiertage°

Geburtstagswünsche

Celebrations and holidays

Germans express birthday wishes in many ways. Here are some typical birthday wishes taken from German newspapers.

Heike
wird heute
„21"
Herzlichen Glückwunsch

Lieber Vater und Opa!
Zu Deinem 85. Geburtstag gratulieren
*Hansi –Waltraud – Angela – Torsten
Birgit – Peter – Jan und Marco*

Hallo Belinda!
Viel Glück und alles Gute
zum 18.
wünschen Mutti und Papa
und der ganze Clan.
W. W. B. U. S. U. J. D. M.
S. W. P. S. W. und Chris

**Ralf hat
Geburtstag!**
Alles Gute!

Liebe Oma *Marie Sudhoff*
zu Deinem **80. Geburtstag** wünschen Dir
Deine Kinder, Enkel und Urenkel alles
Liebe und Gute.

Neue Wörter

wird (werden)
becomes, turns
**Herzlichen
Glückwunsch (zum
Geburtstag)** Happy
birthday!
gratulieren
congratulate
Alles Gute! All the
best!
wünschen wish

ANALYSE

Answer these questions about the birthday greetings in **Thema 3.**

- Find at least two different expressions of good wishes in the ads.
- Who are the family members who are sending birthday greetings to Belinda? to Marie Sudhoff?
- Marie Sudhoff is being addressed as "**liebe Oma.**" To which family member does the term **Oma** refer? What is another word for **Oma?**
- One birthday greeting gives no name but says only "**lieber Vater und Opa.**" Is this ad directed to one or two people? What clue(s) helped you arrive at your answer? What is another word for **Opa?**

Feiertage in der Familie Thalhofer

Valentinstag ist relativ **neu** für viele Deutsche. Bernd und Alexandra **kennen** diesen Tag aus den USA. Muttertag ist für Frau Thalhofer nicht so **wichtig,** aber ihre Familie gibt ihr **oft** Blumen.

Neue Wörter

neu new
kennen know
wichtig important
Hochzeit wedding
heiratet (heiraten)
  is getting married
plant (planen) is
  planning
Familienfest family
  gathering
natürlich natural(ly)
es gibt there is
Geschenke presents
Weihnachten
  Christmas
feiert (feiern)
  celebrate
am Heiligen Abend
  on Christmas Eve
Silvester New Year's
  Eve
um Mitternacht at
  midnight

Dieses Jahr gibt es eine **Hochzeit** in Bernds Familie. Seine Kusine Sabine **heiratet** nämlich im Mai. Die

Familie **plant** ein großes **Familienfest** mit einem Abendessen in der Marxburg am Rhein. Bernds Großeltern feiern dieses Jahr ihre goldene Hochzeit.

Bernd hat im April Geburtstag. Dieses Jahr feiert er mit seiner Frau Bettina bei

Freunden in Berlin. **Natürlich** feiern sie auch bei den Eltern in Leipzig, und **es gibt** auch eine kleine **Party** und natürlich auch **Geschenke.**

Weihnachten hat eine lange **Tradition. Am Heiligen Abend** gibt es Geschenke und ein Familienessen. Auch am ersten Weihnachtstag (25. Dezember) **feiert** die Familie zusammen. Am zweiten Weihnachtstag (26. Dezember) besucht die Familie die Großeltern, Tanten und Onkel.

Silvester sind Thalhofers oft bei Freunden. **Um Mitternacht** gibt es dann oft ein kleines Feuerwerk im Garten. Manchmal bleiben sie aber auch zu Hause.

To form most ordinal numbers (*first, second, third,* and so on) in German, add the suffix **-te** or **-ste** to the cardinal number. Note that the words for *first, third, seventh,* and *eighth* are exceptions to the rule.

eins	**erste**	neun	neun**te**
zwei	zwei**te**	zehn	zehn**te**
drei	**dritte**	elf	elf**te**
vier	vier**te**	zwölf	zwölf**te**
fünf	fünf**te**	dreizehn	dreizehn**te**
sechs	sechs**te**	. . .	. . .
sieben	**sieb(en)te**	zwanzig	zwanzig**ste**
acht	**achte**		

Ordinal numbers are normally used with the definite article.

Freitag ist **der erste** Oktober.

To talk about dates for special occasions, you can say:

Wann hast du Geburtstag? —**Am 18. (achtzehnten)** September.

Weihnachten is **am 25. (fünfundzwanzigsten)** Dezember.

Note that ordinal numbers are written with a period: **der 4. Juli; am 4. Juli.**

Suggestion: Practice dates with ordinal numbers using the calendar at the beginning of Thema 2 or a current calendar: *Was ist Samstag?—Samstag ist (der zweite) Oktober. Und Sonntag?—Sonntag ist (der dritte) Oktober. Und was ist morgen? Morgen ist _____?*

Hier klicken!

You'll find more about holidays and festivals in German-speaking countries in **Deutsch: Na Klar!** on the World Wide Web at www.mhhe.com/dnk.

Legal holidays in German-speaking countries are largely religious holidays. The most important ones are Christmas (**Weihnachten**), New Year (**Neujahr**), and Easter (**Ostern**) and are celebrated for two days each. An important nonreligious holiday in Germany is the Day of German Unity (**Tag der deutschen Einheit**) on October 3.

There are a number of regional holidays as well. Mardi Gras (**Karneval** in the Rhineland and **Fasching** in southern Germany) is celebrated before Lent in early spring. People get one day off work to participate in the merriment in and out of doors. Germans in northern and eastern regions do not celebrate Mardi Gras.

Germans go all out for family celebrations such as weddings, silver and golden wedding anniversaries, and birthdays with a round number, such as 40, 50, or 60.

Karneval in Köln

Aktivität 9 Feste und Feiertage

Match up the German holidays and celebrations with their English equivalents.

1. _____ Weihnachten
2. _____ Karneval
3. _____ Geburtstag
4. _____ Ostern
5. _____ Silvester
6. _____ Hochzeit
7. _____ der Heilige Abend
8. _____ Tag der deutschen Einheit

a. Mardi Gras
b. Christmas Eve
c. Easter
d. Labor Day
e. birthday
f. wedding
g. Memorial Day
h. German Unity Day
i. Christmas
j. New Year's Eve

Aktivität 10 Geburtstagsgrüße

Choose several of the following words and phrases to create birthday greetings for someone.

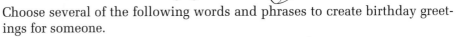

alles Gute   du wirst   ich gratuliere   liebe _____

herzlichen Glückwunsch   lieber _____   viel Glück   zum   Geburtstag

wir gratulieren   wünscht / wünschen dir

zu deinem _____ Geburtstag   _____ wird _____

Aktivität 11 Eine Einladung zu einer Party

Invite someone to a party, using the expressions provided.

BEISPIEL: S1: Ich mache am Sonntag eine Party. Kommst du?
            S2: Am Sonntag? Vielen Dank. Ich komme gern. [oder]
                Vielen Dank. Leider kann ich nicht kommen.

OTHER EXCUSES

Es tut mir Leid.

Ich bin leider nicht zu Hause.

Ich fahre nämlich nach _____.

Mein Vater / Meine Mutter usw. (and so on) hat nämlich auch Geburtstag.

Aktivität 11. Suggestion: Have students circulate and do this activity with a number of different students. Encourage them to give other reasons for not being able to go. Stress that they may either accept or decline the invitation.

Neue Wörter

Es tut mir Leid. I'm sorry.
leider unfortunately
nämlich namely, that is to say
morgen tomorrow

90 Kapitel 3 ▪ Familie und Freunde

When stating your reason for an action, use the adverb **nämlich** in the explanation.

Ich kann nicht kommen. Ich fahre **nämlich** nach Hamburg.
I cannot come. The reason is, I am going to Hamburg.

Note that there is no exact equivalent of **nämlich** in English.

Grammatik im Kontext

Possessive Adjectives°

Possessivartikel

Possessive adjectives (e.g., *my, your, his, our*) indicate ownership or belonging.

—Wie ist **Ihr** Name?   *What is your name?*
—**Mein** Name ist Schiller.   *My name is Schiller.*

Wie heißt **deine** Schwester?   *What's your sister's name?*

Each possessive adjective corresponds to a personal pronoun.

SINGULAR		PLURAL	
PERSONAL PRONOUN	**POSSESSIVE ADJECTIVE**	**PERSONAL PRONOUN**	**POSSESSIVE ADJECTIVE**
ich	**mein** *my*	wir	**unser** *our*
du	**dein** *your (informal)*	ihr	**euer** *your (informal)*
Sie	**Ihr** *your (formal)*	Sie	**Ihr** *your (formal)*
er	**sein** *his; its*		
sie	**ihr** *her; its*	sie	**ihr** *their*
es	**sein** *its*		

Possessive Adjectives.
Note: Students have already been exposed to a number of possessive adjectives in every chapter. Relate a personal anecdote containing possessive adjectives; have students clap their hands every time they hear one.

Possessives—short for possessive adjectives—take the same endings as the indefinite article **ein.** Unlike **ein,** however, they also have plural forms. They agree in gender, case, and number with the nouns they modify.

The nominative and accusative forms of **mein** and **unser** illustrate the pattern for all possessives.

	SINGULAR			PLURAL
	Masculine	*Neuter*	*Feminine*	*All Genders*
Nominative	mein Freund unser Freund	mein Buch unser Buch	mein**e** Oma unser**e** Oma	mein**e** Eltern unser**e** Eltern
Accusative	mein**en** Freund unser**en** Freund	mein Buch unser Buch	mein**e** Oma unser**e** Oma	mein**e** Eltern unser**e** Eltern

Note: Point out to students that they will frequently see **du** and **ihr** forms, as well as possessives, capitalized in letters; however, this convention has become obsolete with the new spelling reform.

Note: You may want to point out that the **e** of **unser** is also frequently dropped when an ending is added.

Note:

- The masculine singular possessive adjective is the only one for which the accusative form differs from the nominative: **Mein → meinen, unser → unseren.**
- The formal possessive adjective **Ihr** (*your*) is capitalized, just like the formal personal pronoun **Sie** (*you*).
- The possessive adjective **euer** (*your*) drops the **e** of the stem when an ending is added: **euere → eure, eueren → euren.**

Ruth Brandt,
Unsere Omi ist das Liebste, was wir haben, das wollen wir ihr heute einmal sagen:
WIR LIEBEN DICH

Deine Kinder
Deine Enkelkinder

[1]das... the dearest thing that
[2]just

An- und Verkauf von Büchern und Schallplatten

Vorsicht
Lesen gefährdet eure Dummheit!

Modernes Antiquariat
LeseZEICHEN
Hindenburgplatz 64
Tel. 43933

- Scan the Valentine's Day greetings taken from a German newspaper and identify all possessive adjectives.
- In each case, determine whether the possessives refer to a male or female individual or to several people. What is the gender of each name or noun?

Analyse. Suggestion:
Have students create their own valentine messages, using expressions found in the ads and possessive adjectives.

Herzliche Grüße zum Valentinstag

Liebe Beate,
ich liebe Dich

Dein Rainer

GF100037

**Für meine Lieben
Helmut und Sandra**
einen lieben Gruß und ein dickes Küsschen[2]
Eure Doris Ma GF100081

Hallo Maus!
Nun ist es doch schon das 4. Jahr!

In Liebe Deine Katze
GE90558

**Guten Morgen,
mein Tiger**
Die Welt[1] ist wieder schön durch Dich.
Dein Stern von Rio GD81183

Lieber Andre!
Alles Liebe zum Valentinstag.

Dein Häschen
GF100036

Liebe Christina
Zum Valentinstag herzliche Grüße und alles Liebe und Gute wünscht
Dir Dein Vater
GC114748

---

[1]*world*
[2]*ein. . . a big kiss*

Übung 1   Herzlichen Glückwunsch!

You will hear eight congratulatory messages taken from a radio program. Write down who receives the greetings (**der Empfänger**) and who sends them (**der Absender**). Include the possessive adjectives you hear, if any. Follow the example.

Ubung 1. Note: It is a common practice on local radio stations to have a program for reading congratulatory messages.

	EMPFÄNGER	ABSENDER
1.	*unsere Mutter*	*deine Kinder*
2.	unser Opa	deine Enkel
3.	Uwe	deine Freundin
4.	unser Vater	deine Söhne
5.	unsere Tochter	deine Eltern
6.	Eltern	eure Kinder
7.	meine Kinder	eure Mutter
8.	Gabi	dein Tiger

Übung 2 Suchen

Complete each sentence with the appropriate possessive adjective.

BEISPIEL: sie (Frau Müller): Wo ist *ihr* Wagen? Sie sucht *ihren* Wagen (*car*).

1. er (Herr Müller): Wo ist _____ Frau? Er sucht _____ Frau.
2. sie (Herr und Frau Müller): Wo sind _____ Kinder? Sie suchen _____ Kinder.
3. du: Wo ist _____ Schwester? Suchst du _____ Schwester?
4. ihr: Wo sind _____ Eltern? Ihr sucht _____ Eltern.
5. wir: Wo ist _____ Großvater? Wir suchen _____ Großvater.
6. ich: Wo ist _____ Handy? Ich suche _____ Handy schon den ganzen Tag.

Übung 3. Suggestion: Have students work in pairs, assigning one conversation per pair. Then have each pair act out its conversation. As students listen to the conversations being acted out, have them fill in the possessives as they hear them.

everyday life

Übung 3 Kleine Gespräche im Alltag°

Complete the minidialogues with appropriate possessive adjectives.

1. CLAUDIA: Hier ist _____ neue Telefonnummer.
   STEFAN: Gut, und _____ neue Adresse?
   CLAUDIA: _____ neue Adresse ist Rosenbachweg 2.

2. LILO: Und dies hier ist _____ Freund.
   HELGA: Wie heißt er denn?
   LILO: _____ Name ist Max.
   HELGA: Max? Na, so was! So heißt nämlich _____ Hund.

3. HERR WEIDNER: Und was sind Sie von Beruf, Frau Rudolf?
   FRAU RUDOLF: Ich bin Automechanikerin.
   HERR WEIDNER: Und was ist _____ Mann von Beruf?
   FRAU RUDOLF: _____ Mann ist Hausmann.
   HERR WEIDNER: Hausmann?

4. FRAU SANDERS: Ach, wie niedlich! Ist das _____ Tochter?
   FRAU KARSTEN: Ja, das ist _____ Tochter.
   FRAU SANDERS: Und ist das _____ Hund?
   FRAU KARSTEN: Ja, das ist _____ Hund. Das ist der Caesar.

5. INGE: Kennst du _____ Freund Klaus?
   ERNST: Ich kenne Klaus nicht, aber ich kenne _____ Schwester.
   INGE: Morgen besuchen wir _____ Eltern in Stuttgart.

6. KLAUS: Morgen fahren Inge und ich nach Stuttgart. Da wohnen _____ (*her*) Eltern.
   KURT: Wie fahrt ihr denn?
   KLAUS: Wir nehmen _____ (*my*) Wagen.
   KURT: _____ Wagen?
   KLAUS: Na, klar. Warum denn nicht?
   KURT: _____ Wagen gehört ins Museum, nicht auf die Autobahn.

7. POLIZIST: Ist das _____ Wagen?
   FRAU KUNZE: Ja, leider ist das _____ Wagen.
   POLIZIST: Hier ist Parkverbot.

Übung 4   Persönliche Angaben

A. Complete a personal profile of yourself. Add one or two items of your own choice.

_____ Name ist _____.

_____ Adresse ist _____.

_____ Telefonnummer ist _____.

_____ Familie wohnt in _____.

_____ Mutter heißt _____.

_____ Vater heißt _____.

_____ Geschwister heißen _____.

_____ Wagen/Motorrad ist ein _____.

_____ Geburtstag ist im _____. (z.B. Juli)

_____ Lieblingsessen (*favorite food*) ist _____.

_____ Lieblings_____ ist _____. (z.B. Lieblingsprofessor, Lieblingsrestaurant)

B. Exchange personal profiles with someone in your class and report about him/her to the class.

BEISPIEL: Das ist Sam Lee. Seine Telefonnummer ist 354–8762.
              Sein Lieblingsessen ist Pizza.

Personal Pronouns in the Accusative Case°

Personalpronomen im Akkusativ

You have already learned the personal pronouns for the nominative case. Here are the corresponding accusative forms.

SINGULAR		PLURAL	
NOMINATIVE	ACCUSATIVE	NOMINATIVE	ACCUSATIVE
ich	**mich** *me*	wir	**uns** *us*
du	**dich** *you (informal)*	ihr	**euch** *you (informal)*
Sie	**Sie** *you (formal)*	Sie	**Sie** *you (formal)*
er	**ihn** *him; it*		
sie	**sie** *her; it*	sie	**sie** *them*
es	**es** *it*		

Note:

- The third-person singular pronouns **ihn, sie,** and **es** must agree in gender with the noun to which they refer.
- In the accusative case, **ihn** can mean *him* or *it,* and **sie** can mean *her* or *it* depending on the gender of the noun to which they refer.

—Kennst du **meinen Freund?**   *Do you know my friend?*
—Ja, ich kenne **ihn.**   *Yes, I know him.*

—Brauchst du **deinen Wagen** heute?   *Do you need your car today?*
—Na klar brauche ich **ihn.**   *But of course I need it.*

—Hast du **meine Telefonnummer?**   *Do you have my phone number?*
—Ich glaube, ich habe **sie.**   *I think I have it.*

Personal Pronouns in the Accusative Case. Suggestion: Provide some quick drills to practice the third-person pronouns, particularly with inanimate objects. *Kennen Sie die Stadt (die Straße, den Film, das Buch)?* Have students respond only with accusative pronouns.

ANALYSE

- Identify all personal pronouns in the ads and announcements and determine whether they are in the nominative or in the accusative case.
- Provide the English meaning of each phrase.

Analyse. Suggestion: Go over the items, reading them aloud and brainstorming with the class what they refer to.

Wir sind da, wo Sie uns brauchen.

Gourmets lieben ihn.

Mein Schatz, [1]
Ich liebe Dich.
Deine Jutta

GA140650

[1]mein. . . *my dear*

Übung 5   Wer kennt wen?

Supply the missing direct-object pronouns.

1. Ich kenne _____ (du).
2. Herr Müller kennt _____ (ich).
3. Ich kenne _____ (er).
4. Frau Schmidt kennt _____ (wir).
5. Herr und Frau Schmidt kennen _____ (ihr).
6. Kennt ihr _____ (Herrn und Frau Schmidt)?

Übung 6. Suggestion: Assign individual conversations to pairs of students. Have each pair act out its conversation. Also suitable as homework.

Übung 6   Im Café Kadenz

Several students are conversing at different tables at the Café Kadenz. Complete the blanks with appropriate personal pronouns in the nominative or the accusative case.

1. A: Wie findest _____ den Professor Klinger?
   B: Also, ich finde _____ unmöglich. _____ kommt nie pünktlich. Wir warten (*wait*) und warten, dann kommt _____ endlich und hält seine Vorlesung, keine Diskussion, keine Fragen, nichts. _____ ist echt langweilig.
   A: Ich verstehe _____ nicht, Karin. Warum gehst du dann hin?
2. C: Machst du jetzt das Linguistik-Seminar?
   D: Ja, ich brauche _____ für mein Hauptfach (*major*).
3. E: Und wie findest du deine Mitbewohner im Wohnheim?
   F: Ich finde _____ ganz prima. Da sind zwei Italienerinnen aus Venedig. _____ sind wirklich nett. Ich verstehe _____ allerdings nicht immer.

96   Kapitel 3 ▪ Familie und Freunde

4. G: Im Lumière läuft der Film „Himalaya". Kennst du _____?

H: Nein, aber die Filmkritiker finden _____ ausgezeichnet.

5. I: Da kommt endlich unser Kaffee. Wie trinkst du _____?

J: Gewöhnlich trinke ich _____ schwarz.

6. K: Meine Eltern besuchen _____ nächste Woche. Das ist immer stressig.

L: Ja, ich verstehe _____ gut.

Übung 7 Wie findest du das?

With a partner, create five questions regarding student life. Then interview several people in your class.

BEISPIEL: S1: Wie findest du die Vorlesungen von Professor Ziegler?
S2: Ich finde sie ausgezeichnet. Und du?
S1: Ich finde sie zu lang.

Übung 7. Note: Have students first figure out which questions they would like to ask; allow for variations and additional items not on the list. Then have students ask each other questions while mingling. Have several students present their questions and the answers they received.

Essen in der Mensa	ausgezeichnet
Kaffee in der Mensa	faul
Leben (*life*) an der Uni	sympathisch
Uni-Zeitung	langweilig
Studenten an der Uni	schlecht
Mitbewohner im Studentenheim	gut
Professor _____	freundlich
Film _____	interessant
Freund/Freundin	arrogant
??	??

Prepositions with the Accusative Case°

Präpositionen mit dem Akkusativ

You have already seen and used a number of German prepositions.

Ich studiere Architektur **in** Berlin.
Ich brauche eine Lampe **für** meinen Schreibtisch.

The use of prepositions, in English as well as in German, is highly idiomatic. An important difference, however, is that German prepositions require certain cases; that is, some prepositions are followed by nouns or pronouns in the accusative case, others by nouns or pronouns in other cases. In this chapter, we focus on prepositions that always require the accusative case.

Wir sind für Sie da!

Der freundliche Kunden-Service

Wir tun etwas **gegen** den Hunger.	We are doing something against hunger.
Es ist **gegen** fünf Uhr.	It's around five o'clock.
Herr Krause fährt **durch** die Stadt.	Mr. Krause drives through town.
Er braucht ein Geschenk **für** seine Tochter.	He needs a gift for his daughter.
Er geht **ohne** seine Frau einkaufen.	He goes shopping without his wife.
Die Geburtstagsfeier beginnt **um** sechs.	The birthday party begins at six.
Er sucht einen Parkplatz und fährt dreimal **um** den Marktplatz (**herum**).	He looks for a parking space and drives around the marketplace three times.

Accusative Prepositions.
Note: Telling time is formally presented in **Kapitel 4.** In this chapter students will work only lexically with expressions of time such as *um 4.*

ACCUSATIVE PREPOSITIONS	
durch	through, across
für	for
gegen	against; around (*with time*)
ohne	without
um	at (*with time*)
um (... herum)	around (*a place*)

Um. . . herum. Suggestion: Practice *um. . . herum* by demonstrating it and having students say what you are doing, e.g., *Sie gehen um den Tisch herum, um den Stuhl herum.*

Note:

- When the preposition **um** is used to indicate movement around something, the word **herum** is often added to the end of the sentence.
  um die Stadt (**herum**)

- Three accusative prepositions often contract with the article **das.**

  durch das → **durchs** Zimmer

  für das → **fürs** Auto

  um das → **ums** Haus

Übung 8 Dieter braucht ein Geschenk

Choose the correct preposition.

1. Dieter braucht dringend ein Geburtstagsgeschenk _____ (um/für) seine Freundin Sonja.
2. Leider hat Sonja schon alles, aber _____ (ohne/durch) Geschenk geht es nicht.
3. Dieter gibt _____ (für/um) sieben Uhr abends eine kleine Party _____ (für/ohne) sie.
4. Sonja hat Partys gern, aber sie ist _____ (gegen/ohne) große Partys.
5. Dieter fährt also in die Stadt. Er fährt dreimal _____ (um/durch) den Marktplatz herum. Er sucht einen Parkplatz. Er findet nichts.

6. Er fährt und fährt _____ (um/durch) die Straßen.
7. Er sucht und sucht _____ (für/ohne) Erfolg (*success*). Was nun?
8. Er parkt illegal—er tut alles _____ (ohne/für) Sonja.
9. Was macht Sonja Spaß? Kochen! Also ein Kochbuch _____ (durch/für) Vegetarier. (Sonja ist nämlich Vegetarierin.)
10. Im Buchladen geht Dieter _____ (für/um) den Tisch mit (*with*) Kochbüchern herum.
11. Es gibt tausend Kochbücher _____ (für/gegen) Vegetarier. Was tun?

Übung 9　Geschenke

Bernd needs Christmas presents for his friends and relatives. Choose gifts for his friends and relatives from the drawings. Who will get what gift?

BEISPIEL: Sein Bruder hat keine Uhr. →
　　　　　Die Armbanduhr ist für seinen Bruder.

die Krawatte　　　das Buch　　　das Armband

der Fotoapparat　　das Fotoalbum　　die Armbanduhr

der Nasenring　　das Fitness-Video　　der Wanderstock

1. Sein Freund Marco ist etwas exzentrisch.
2. Seine Tante Gisela liest gern.
3. Seine Eltern reisen und fotografieren viel.
4. Sein Großvater wandert gern.
5. Sein Onkel Karl hat schon alles.
6. Seine Schwester Alexandra fährt oft nach Spanien.
7. Seine Freundin Gabi trägt gern Schmuck (*jewelry*).
8. Seine Kusine Uta ist ein Fitnessfan.

Geschenke. Suggestion: Have students do *Übung 9* as a partner activity. Exchange roles for each item. Personalize this exercise by having students say for whom they need a gift. Students respond by making suggestions: e.g., s1: *Ich brauche ein Geschenk für meine Mutter.* s2: *Ein Buch ist immer gut.*

The Irregular Verbs werden and wissen

Two common verbs that show irregularities in the present tense are **werden** (*to become*) and **wissen** (*to know*).

Heidewitzka, Herr Kapitän!
Der beste Opa der Welt wird 60!

Es gratulieren:
David
Inge
Ulf
Uwe
Sandra
Schira
Afra

Helmut
2.7. 2003

	werden	*wissen*
ich	werde	**weiß**
du	**wirst**	**weißt**
er sie es	**wird**	**weiß**
wir	werden	wissen
ihr	werdet	wisst
sie/Sie	werden	wissen

Realia. „Heidewitzka, Herr Kapitän!" is the beginning of a popular song.

Sandra, 8 Jahre: *Meine Mutter Martina, mein Bruder Kelvin, Meine Schwester Andrea, mein Vater Uli und ich beim Fahrrad fahren*

Übung 10   Kennen Sie eigentlich meine Familie?

Complete the sentences using the appropriate form of **werden**.

1. Ich _____ im September 16 Jahre alt.
2. Meine zwei Kusinen _____ am Samstag 13.
3. Mein kleiner Bruder Bernd _____ im November 11.
4. Meine kleine Schwester Sara _____ dieses Jahr 3 Jahre alt.
5. Mein Vater hat im Dezember Geburtstag. Er _____ 38 Jahre alt.
6. Mein Großvater fragt immer: „Wann _____ du fünfzehn?" Er vergisst (*forgets*), dass ich schon fünfzehn bin!

Übung 11 Eine Umfrage: Wer wird wann wie alt?

Do a class poll:

1. Wer _____ dieses Jahr _____ Jahre alt?
2. Wie viele Leute _____ dieses Jahr 19?
3. Wann _____ du 50? 100? (Ich werde in 30 Jahren 50.)
4. Wann _____ dein Freund oder deine Freundin 19, 21, 25?

Using the Verbs wissen and kennen

ZEITUNGSLESER WISSEN MEHR!

Mich kennt keiner[1]

Wer kennt Goethe?

[1]nobody

The verbs **wissen** and **kennen** both mean *to know.* **Wissen** means *to know facts,* while **kennen** means *to know or be acquainted/familiar with a person or thing.*

Ich **weiß** deine Telefonnummer nicht.	*I don't know your phone number.*
Ich **kenne** Herrn Meyer nicht persönlich, aber ich **weiß,** wer er ist.	*I don't know Mr. Meyer personally, but I know who he is.*

Note:

- **Wissen** is often used with indirect questions (Ich **weiß,** wer Goethe ist.)

Übung 12 Die neue Mitbewohnerin

Wendy, an exchange student from San Diego, is new in Göttingen and lives in a dorm. Listen to Wendy's questions and check off the appropriate negative responses.

	WEISS ICH NICHT.°	KENNE ICH NICHT.°
1.	☒	☐
2.	☐	☒
3.	☒	☐
4.	☒	☐
5.	☒	☐
6.	☒	☐
7.	☐	☒
8.	☒	☐

Don't know. (casual)

Übung 11. Suggestion: Have students ask a variation of question 1 of a number of classmates and write down their answers. (*Wie alt wirst du dieses Jahr?* Then ask the whole class the questions in the exercise. Students answer with information gathered about a classmate (e.g., *Barbara wird dieses Jahr 22; in 78 Jahren wird sie 100.*).

Wissen/Kennen. **Suggestion:** Practice *kennen* first by asking a number of simple questions that students answer simply with *nein/ja.* (*Kennen Sie . . . Professor/Film/Buch/das Spiel . . . ?*) Then practice *wissen* with simple questions (*Wie viele Studenten studieren Deutsch?*) that allow students to answer: *Das weiß ich nicht.* Finally, add the idea of an indirect question: *Wissen Sie, wo ich wohne?* Keep questions brief to avoid complications with the end position of the verb.

Johann Wolfgang von Goethe, 1749–1832

Übung 12. Suggestion: Make sure students understand the distinction between the two phrases. The ones used here represent a more casual way of speaking. Allow a first listening where everyone notes their answers; a second time around, compare answers.

Grammatik im Kontext **101**

Übung 13. Suggestion: Do the first example with the whole class to make sure students know Goethe and *Die Leiden des jungen Werther*. Then have pairs read each segment of the exercise.

Übung 13   Wissen oder kennen?

Complete the minidialogues with the correct form of **wissen** or **kennen.**

1. A: _____ du Goethe?

   B: Nein, aber ich _____, wer er ist.

   A: _____ du seinen Roman, „Die Leiden (*sufferings*) des jungen Werther"?

   B: Nein, den _____ ich nicht. Aber mein Professor _____ ihn bestimmt.

2. C: _____ du, welcher Film heute im Odeon läuft?

   D: Das _____ ich nicht. Aber Toni, der _____ das bestimmt. Der _____ alles.

3. E: Wo wohnt ihr eigentlich jetzt?

   F: In der Schillerstraße. _____ du die?

   E: Nein. Ich _____ aber, wo die Goethestraße ist.

4. G: _____ ihr schon, wo ihr nächstes Semester studiert?

   H: Nein, wir _____ nur, dass wir nicht hier bleiben.

5. I: Ich _____, wo eine Wohnung frei wird.

   J: Wo denn?

   I: In der Weenderstraße.

   J: Die _____ ich nicht. Wo ist die denn?

6. K: Ihr _____ doch den Peter?

   L: Peter Schnitzler?

   K: Nein, Peter Sudhoff.

   L: Tut mir Leid, den _____ wir nicht.

inquisitive

Übung 14   Ein neugieriger° Mensch

Find out what your partner knows by taking turns asking each other questions.

BEISPIEL: S1: Kennst du den neuen Film von Steven Spielberg?

   S2: Nein, den kenne ich nicht. Kennst du den neuen Film von Wolfgang Peterson?

   S1: Ja, den kenne ich.

Kennst du...	Weißt du...
das neue Buch von _____ ?	die Telefonnummer von _____ ?
den neuen Film von _____ ?	die Adresse von _____ ?
die Mutter / den Vater von _____ ?	den Vornamen von Herrn / Frau _____ ?
Herrn Professor _____ ?	wie alt _____ ist?
Frau Professor _____ ?	wann _____ Geburtstag hat?
die Rockgruppe _____ ?	wann das nächste Semester beginnt?
die Stadt _____ ?	

Sprache im Kontext

Videoclips

In these videoclips, the people interviewed are talking about their families and various celebrations. As you watch, listen to what they say and think how you would respond to the interviewer's questions.

A. Watch the interviews with Doris and Kurt Borowsky. Mark the following statements **richtig (R)** or **falsch (F)**.

1. Doris

_____ Doris ist verheiratet.

_____ Sie hat zwei Kinder.

_____ Die Kinder heißen Tina und Matthias.

_____ Die Familie feiert Weihnachten, Velentinstag und Ostern.

_____ Das Lieblingsfest von Doris Weihnachten.

_____ Doris hat heute Geburtstag.

2. Herr Borowski

_____ Herr Borowsky wohnt in Berlin.

_____ Er hat eine kleine Familie.

_____ Er hat drei Enkelkinder.

_____ Er hat einen Bruder und zwei Schwestern.

_____ Er ist 67 Jahre alt.

_____ Er hat am 10. Februar ist Geburtstag.

B. Now listen again to the questions asked by Michael, the interviewer. Write down four questions he asks and use them to interview two other students in the class. Then report your findings about one of the students to the class.

Lesen

Zum Thema

Eine Umfrage (*survey*). Fill out the questionnaire and compare answers in class.

A. Which holidays are important in your own family?

	WICHTIG	UNWICHTIG
1. Geburtstage	☐	☐
2. Hochzeitstage	☐	☐
3. religiöse Feiertage	☐	☐
4. nationale Feiertage	☐	☐
5. Muttertag	☐	☐
6. Vatertag	☐	☐

Zum Thema. Suggestion. Give students several minutes to complete the questionnaire. Then turn it into a listening activity, recording the number of student responses on the board; e.g., *Wie viele finden Geburtstage wichtig? Familienfest zum Muttertag? Zum Vatertag?* In this way a class profile will emerge.

B. How do you celebrate Mother's Day and Father's Day?

	ZUM MUTTERTAG		ZUM VATERTAG	
	JA	NEIN	JA	NEIN
1. Wir haben ein großes Familienfest.	☐	☐	☐	☐
2. Wir gehen ins Restaurant.	☐	☐	☐	☐
3. Ich kaufe ein Geschenk für meine Mutter / meinen Vater.	☐	☐	☐	☐
4. Ich mache an diesem Tag nichts Besonderes.	☐	☐	☐	☐
5. ??	☐	☐	☐	☐

Auf den ersten Blick

A. Skim the text to the left and guess the theme. Look at the pictures, the headings, and familiar words. These texts are probably:

1. fathers talking about the importance of Father's Day.

2. young people telling about their fathers on Father's Day.

3. young people talking about how they celebrate Father's Day.

Explain your answer.

B. Scan the text for the vocabulary that fits under the following rubrics:

☐ words related to family

☐ types of presents

Zum Text

A. Guessing from context. The verb **feiern** and the noun **Feier** are key words in this text. If you don't know what they mean, what clues can you use to help you guess?

B. Now read the statements by the three young people in order to answer the following questions. As you work through the text, note which words you have to look up, if any, to find the information.

1. Wer findet den Vatertag wichtig?

2. Wer geht aus essen?

3. Wer kauft ein Geschenk zum Vatertag?

4. Wer geht mit dem Vater ins Konzert?

5. Wer feiert Muttertag mehr als Vatertag?

Wolfgang Fellier in Innsbruck

fragt junge Leute:

Feierst du den Vatertag?

RADISLAV JOVIC, 13:
Ja, ich feiere den Vatertag schon. Ich finde, er ist genauso wichtig wie[1] der Muttertag. Ein Geschenk bekommt mein Vater auch, dafür gebe ich gerne mein Taschengeld[2] aus. Ich werde ihm ein Rasierwasser[3] oder ein Parfüm kaufen.

WERNER KLICOVA, 15:
Wir feiern heute, obwohl gar nicht Vatertag ist. Ich werde meinen Vater nämlich zu einem Konzert einladen. Eigentlich feiere ich das ganze Jahr über Vatertag, weil ich einfach super mit ihm auskomme.[4] Er hat eine ähnliche Frisur[5] wie ich und ist viel mehr ein cooler Kollege als ein autoritärer Elternteil.

TANJA PESCOSTA, 16:
Wir werden alle zusammen essen gehen, und der Vater bekommt auch ein Geschenk, aber eine Feier, so intensiv wie beim Muttertag, gibt es bei uns nicht. Das liegt wohl daran,[6] dass man die Arbeit der Mutter besser mitbekommt. Mein Vater freut sich[7] allerdings sehr über die Anerkennung am Vatertag.

[1]genauso. . . *just as important as*

[2]*pocket money*

[3]*aftershave*

[4]*get along*

[5]ähnliche. . . *similar hairstyle*

[6]Das. . . *That's probably because*

[7]freut. . . *is glad*

Zum Text. Note: It is important to do contextual guessing exercises in class. When students' guesses are off the mark, you can guide them to make better guesses by having them articulate what led them to their guess and teaching them to look for evidence to confirm their guesses. Reassure your students that we all make false assumptions about texts. The goal is to learn how to move on until they can confirm their assumptions.

C. Close reading

1. Opinions in the text are often cued by the phrase **Ich finde. . .** Locate this phrase in the text. Do you agree with the opinion expressed?

2. Reread the text and locate evidence for the following.

   ☐ Indication that Mother's Day and Father's Day have different importance.
   ☐ Speculation on reasons for the difference.
   ☐ Evidence that some of the speakers have traditional expectations of men and women.

Sprechen und Schreiben

Aktivität 1   Eine Person vorstellen

Work in small groups. Bring in a picture of your family, a family member, a friend, or a magazine picture depicting a family and describe the person or people in the picture to your group.

BEISPIEL: Das ist meine Mutter. Sie heißt Barbara. Sie ist 44 Jahre alt. Sie hat im April Geburtstag. Sie ist sehr aktiv. Sie kocht gern und läuft gern.

Aktivität 2   Ein Bericht

Write a short report about yourself and your family, or write about a friend and his/her family. Include in your report:

- wie groß die Familie ist und wo sie wohnt
- wann Sie Geburtstag haben
- was Sie und andere Familienmitglieder (*family members*) gern machen (kochen, tanzen usw.)
- Lieblings. . . (-sport, -komponist, -musiker)
- Probleme (kein Geld, zu viel Geld. . .)

Aktivität 1. Suggestion: As each student describes his or her picture, the others take notes. One student in each group should be called on to report on one of the photos described.

Aktivität 2. Suggestion: Have students form groups of five. One narrates the report he or she wrote to the group; the others take notes, and one of them reports to the whole class.

Additional activity.   Hand out Uwe Timm's poem "Erziehung" and read it aloud in the class. Have students guess what it is about. Have them guess the meaning of the word *Erziehung*.

Wortschatz

Der Stammbaum	Family Tree		
der **Bruder,** ÷	brother	die **Geschwister** (*pl.*)	siblings
die **Eltern** (*pl.*)	parents	die **Großeltern** (*pl.*)	grandparents
der **Enkel,** -	grandson	die **Großmutter,** ÷	grandmother
die **Enkelin, -nen**	granddaughter	der **Großvater,** ÷	grandfather
die **Familie, -n**	family	die **Kusine, -n**	(female) cousin
die **Frau, -en**	wife	der **Mann,** ÷er	husband
		die **Mutter,** ÷	mother

der **Neffe, -n** (**-n** *masc.*)	nephew	die **Hochzeit, -en**	wedding
die **Nichte, -n**	niece	der **Kalender, -**	calendar
die **Oma, -s**	grandma	(der) **Karneval**	Mardi Gras
der **Onkel, -**	uncle		(*Rhineland*)
der **Opa, -s**	grandpa	der **Muttertag**	Mother's Day
der **Schwager, ∺**	brother-in-law	das **Neujahr**	New Year's Day
die **Schwägerin, -nen**	sister-in-law	(das) **Ostern**	Easter
die **Schwester, -n**	sister	die **Party, -s**	party
der **Sohn, ∺e**	son	(das) **Silvester**	New Year's Eve
die **Tante, -n**	aunt	die **Tradition, -en**	tradition
die **Tochter, ∺**	daughter	der **Valentinstag**	Valentine's Day
der **Vater, ∺**	father	das **Weihnachten**	Christmas
der **Vetter, -n**	(male) cousin	der **Weihnachtsbaum, ∺e**	Christmas tree

Die Wochentage	**Days of the Week**	**Verben**	**Verbs**
der **Montag**	Monday	**feiern**	to celebrate
am **Montag**	on Monday	**geben (gibt)**	to give
der **Dienstag**	Tuesday	**gratulieren**	to congratulate
der **Mittwoch**	Wednesday	**heiraten**	to marry
der **Donnerstag**	Thursday	**kennen**	to know (*be acquainted with a person or thing*)
der **Freitag**	Friday		
der **Samstag** / der **Sonnabend**	Saturday		
		planen	to plan
der **Sonntag**	Sunday	**werden (wird)**	to become, be
		wissen (weiß)	to know (*something as a fact*)

Die Monate	**The Months**	**wünschen**	to wish
der **Januar***	January		
im **Januar**	in January	**Adjektive und Adverbien**	**Adjectives and Adverbs**
der **Februar**	February	**leider**	unfortunately
der **März**	March	**morgen**	tomorrow
der **April**	April	**nämlich**	namely, that is to say
der **Mai**	May	**natürlich**	natural(ly)
der **Juni**	June	**neu**	new
der **Juli**	July	**verwandt mit**	related to
der **August**	August	**wichtig**	important
der **September**	September		
der **Oktober**	October		
der **November**	November	**Ordinalzahlen**	**Ordinal Numbers**
der **Dezember**	December	**erste**	first
		der **erste Mai**	May first
		am **ersten Mai**	on May first
Feste und Feiertage	**Holidays**	**zweite**	second
das **Familienfest, -e**	family gathering	**dritte**	third
(der) **Fasching**	Mardi Gras (*southern Germany, Austria*)	**vierte**	fourth
		fünfte	fifth
der **Geburtstag, -e**	birthday	**sechste**	sixth
das **Geschenk, -e**	gift, present		
der **Heilige Abend**	Christmas Eve		

*****Jänner** is used in Austria.

sieb(en)te	seventh
achte	eighth
neunte	ninth
zehnte	tenth
elfte	eleventh
zwölfte	twelfth
dreizehnte	thirteenth
zwanzigste	twentieth

Possessivartikel	**Possessive Adjectives**
mein	my
dein	your (*informal sg.*)
sein	his; its
ihr	her; its; their
unser	our
euer	your (*informal pl.*)
Ihr	your (*formal*)

Akkusativ-präpositionen	**Accusative Prepositions**
durch	through
für	for
gegen	against; around (+ *time*)
ohne	without

um	at (+ *time*)
um (... herum)	around (*spatial*)

Akkusativ-pronomen	**Accusative Pronouns**
mich	me
dich	you (*informal sg.*)
ihn	him; it
sie	her; it; them
es	it
uns	us
euch	you (*informal pl.*)
Sie	you (*formal*)

Sonstiges	**Other**
Alles Gute!	All the best!
es gibt	there is, there are
Herzlichen Glückwunsch zum Geburtstag!	Happy birthday!
der Hund, -e	dog
um Mitternacht	at midnight
Wann hast du Geburtstag?	When is your birthday?
Welches Datum ist heute/morgen?	What is today's/tomorrow's date?

LERNZIELE

Use this checklist to verify that you can now . . .

- describe how you are related to other people.
- talk about your family and friends.
- name several holidays and describe some of the things people do on those holidays.
- congratulate people on special occasions.
- say the day, month, or date when an event takes place.

- describe personal ownership or a relationship using the possessive adjectives.
- refer to people and things using accusative personal pronouns.
- recognize and use accusative prepositions.
- use **werden, wissen,** and **kennen** appropriately.

Persönlichkeiten: Drei Kurzbiographien

Wolfgang Amadeus Mozart (1756–1791)

*Wolfgang Amadeus Mozart,
ca. 1783*

Geburtsort: Salzburg
Geburtsdatum:
27. Januar 1756
Sternzeichen:
Wassermann[1]
Vater: Leopold
Mutter: Maria
Anna

Geschwister: Marianne, genannt „Nannerl"
Verheiratet[2] mit: Constance geb. Weber
Kinder: Karl und Wolfgang
Wohnort: Wien
Beruf: Kapellmeister und Komponist
Hauptwerke: Opern (z.B. „Don Giovanni",
„Die Zauberflöte"); 41 Symphonien;
Kirchenmusik (z.B. „Krönungsmesse",[3]
„Requiem"); Konzerte und Kammermusik (z.B.
„Eine kleine Nachtmusik")
Hobbys: Musik, Tanzen, Geselligkeit,[4]
Reisen
Lieblingskomponist: Joseph Haydn

*Leopold Mozart und seine Kinder
Wolfgang und „Nannerl", 1763*

*Paula Modersohn-Becker: Worpsweder Land-
schaft, um 1900*

Paula Modersohn-Becker (1876–1909)

*Paula Modersohn-Becker,
Selbstbildnis*

Geburtsort: Dresden
Geburtsdatum:
8. Februar 1876
Sternzeichen:
Wassermann
Vater: Woldemar
Mutter: Mathilde
Geschwister: sechs;
vier jüngere, zwei
ältere
Verheiratet mit: Otto
Modersohn
Kinder: Mathilde

Wohnort: zuletzt in
Worpswede[5]
Beruf: Malerin
Hauptwerke: Landschaftsmalerei,[6] Porträts,
Stilleben
Hobbys: Musik, Tanzen, Kochen, Lesen,
Zeichnen
Lieblingsdichter: Rainer Maria Rilke

[1]*Aquarius* [2]*married* [3]*Coronation Mass* [4]*conviviality* [5]*Worpswede ist ein Künstlerdorf in
der Nähe von Bremen.* [6]*landscape painting*

Albert Einstein (1879–1955)

Geburtsort: Ulm
Geburtsdatum: 14. März 1879
Sternzeichen: Fisch
Vater: Hermann
Mutter: Pauline
Geschwister: Maria („Maja")
Verheiratet mit: zuerst Mileva, dann Elsa
Kinder: Hans und Eduard
Wohnort: zuletzt in Princeton, New Jersey
Beruf: Physiker (Nobelpreis, 1921)
Hauptwerk: Relativitätstheorie
Hobbys: Musik, Geige[1] spielen, Segeln[2]
Lieblingskomponist: Mozart
Lieblingsphilosoph: Immanuel Kant

[1]*violin* [2]*sailing*

(links) Albert Einstein als Kind, mit seiner Schwester Maja

Aktivität 1 Darf ich vorstellen?

Suppose you had to introduce Mozart, Einstein, or Modersohn-Becker to someone at a party. Make three statements about each that characterize who they are.

BEISPIEL: Darf ich vorstellen, das ist Herr/Frau. . .
Er/Sie ist. . .
Er/Sie schreibt/malt/wohnt in. . .

Aktivität 2 Rollenspiel

Imagine that you could interview the people you just read about. With a partner, select one of the three, then create the interview. You could begin as follows:

BEISPIEL: s1: Wo sind Sie geboren, Frau Modersohn-Becker?
s2: In Dresden.
s1: Sind Sie verheiratet?. . .

(rechts) Albert Einstein beim Segeln

Aktivität 3 Ein Steckbrief°

wanted poster

Choose a well-known historical person and gather information to write a **Steckbrief** about her or him. Present the information in class without revealing who the person is. Let the members of the class guess her or his identity.

KAPITEL 4

Mein Tag

Wo ist das?
a. Im Hotel.
b. In der Fußgängerzone
(*pedestrian mall*).

Kapitel 4. Suggestion:
Introduce this chapter by talking
about your daily routine, i.e.,
what you do at different times of
the day, when you get up, go to
bed, eat, etc. Ask students
yes/no questions about the
same topics. Incorporate
adverbs of time and modals.

Videoclips

Ein Tag im Leben von
Jan, Jasmin und Beatrice

In diesem Kapitel

- **Themen:** Times of day, telling time, entertainment
- **Grammatik:** Separable-prefix verbs, modal verbs, the imperative
- **Kultur:** German theater

Alles klar?

A. In diesem  (Brief) sehen Sie fünf (Bilder). Die Bilder stehen für fünf Wörter oder Ausdrücke. Die Ausdrücke sind in alphabetischer Ordnung.

   Fahrrad

   Haus(e)

   Herz

   Sonntag

   Tasse Kaffee

Lesen Sie den Brief nun mit den Wörtern.

Realia. Suggestion: Have students scan the note to determine (1) what kind of text it is and (2) what it might be about.

B. Sie hören jetzt eine telefonische Einladung. Hören Sie bitte zu und markieren Sie die richtige Information.

1. Die Einladung ist für _____.
   a. Sonntag
   b. Samstag
   c. Freitag
2. Erika und Thomas wollen _____.
   a. Dirk zu Kaffee und Kuchen einladen
   b. mit Dirk auf eine Party gehen
   c. mit Dirk ins Café gehen
3. Dirk soll _____ kommen.
   a. um 3 Uhr
   b. um 5 Uhr
   c. um 4 Uhr

Wörter im Kontext

THEMA 1: Die Uhrzeit

Wie spät ist es?
Wie viel Uhr ist es?

Thema 1. Point Out: Both *Wie viel Uhr ist es?* and *Wie spät ist es?* are used to ask "What time is it?" *Wie viel Uhr...* is somewhat more formal than *Wie spät...* The examples on the left are considered informal; those on the right are considered more formal.

Suggestion: Present times using an actual clock (or one made from a paper plate), moving the hands to correspond to the times in the examples. Students repeat the times. Check students' comprehension by reviewing the examples in random order, using the clock, and asking students to say what time it is.

Es ist eins. Es ist **ein Uhr.**
Es ist dreizehn Uhr.

Es ist zehn (Minuten) **nach** eins. Es ist ein Uhr zehn.
Es ist dreizehn Uhr zehn.

Es ist **Viertel nach** eins. Es ist ein Uhr fünfzehn.
Es ist dreizehn Uhr fünfzehn.

Es ist **halb** zwei. Es ist ein Uhr dreißig.
Es ist dreizehn Uhr dreißig.

Es ist zwanzig (Minuten) **vor** zwei. Es ist ein Uhr vierzig.
Es ist dreizehn Uhr vierzig.

Es ist **Viertel vor** zwei. Es ist ein Uhr fünfundvierzig.
Es ist dreizehn Uhr fünfundvierzig.

Es ist zehn (Minuten) vor zwei. Es ist ein Uhr fünfzig.
Es ist dreizehn Uhr fünfzig.

Eine **Minute** hat sechzig **Sekunden**, eine **Stunde** sechzig Minuten und ein Tag vierundzwanzig Stunden.

Aktivität I Zeitansagen°

Markieren Sie die Uhrzeiten, die Sie hören.

1. a. 7.38	**b.** 17.35	**c.** 17.30
2. a. 3.06	**b.** 2.06	**c.** 20.16
3. a. 14.00	**b.** 14.15	**c.** 14.05
4. a. 12.25	**b.** 10.24	**c.** 11.25
5. a. 19.45	**b.** 9.45	**c.** 19.40
6. a. 13.00	**b.** 3.40	**c.** 13.40
7. a. 0.15	**b.** 0.05	**c.** 0.45
8. a. 20.05	**b.** 20.50	**c.** 21.50

SPRACHTIPP

In official timetables—for instance, in radio, television, movie, and theater guides—time is expressed according to the twenty-four-hour system.

1.00–12.00 Uhr	*1:00 A.M. to 12:00 noon*
13.00–24.00 Uhr	*1:00 P.M. to 12:00 midnight*

Midnight may also be referred to as **0 (null) Uhr.**

When writing time in numbers, German speakers usually separate hours and minutes with a period, instead of a colon as in English.

Analyse. Suggestion: Have students give time in both the twelve- and twenty-four-hour systems.
Realia. This cartoon appeared in *P.M.* magazine.

ANALYSE

Sehen Sie sich die Zeichnung an und beantworten Sie die Fragen.

- Wie spät ist es in New York?
- Wie spät ist es in Tokio?
- Wie spät ist es in Bombay?
- Die vierte Uhr zeigt (*shows*) die „gute alte Zeit". Warum hat der Mann wohl (*probably*) diese Uhr gern?

  a. Er hat Kuckucksuhren gern.
  b. Heute ist alles so hektisch.
  c. Die Kuckucksuhr geht langsamer als die anderen Uhren.
  d. ??

Aktivität 2   Wie viel Uhr ist es? Wie spät ist es?

BEISPIEL: Wie viel Uhr ist es? (Wie spät ist es?) →
Es ist Viertel nach sieben.

1. 2. 3.

4. 5. 6. 7.

SPRACHTIPP

To find out at what time something takes place, ask:

Um wie viel Uhr ____ ?

To say at what time something takes place, use the following expressions:

um ein Uhr (1.00 Uhr)	**um ein Uhr dreißig (1.30 Uhr)**
um ein Uhr zehn (1.10 Uhr)	**um ein Uhr vierzig (1.40 Uhr)**
um ein Uhr fünfzehn (1.15 Uhr)	**um ein Uhr fünfundvierzig (1.45 Uhr)**

Aktivität 3   Was macht Hans-Jürgen am Wochenende?

Sehen Sie sich die Bilder an und ergänzen Sie Hans-Jürgens Pläne für das **Wochenende.**

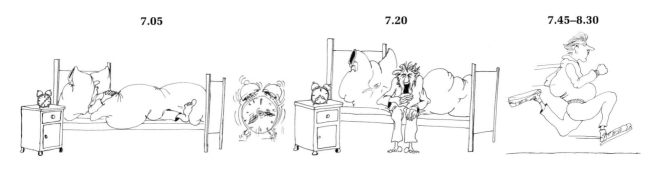

7.05   7.20   7.45–8.30

1. Um ____ schläft Hans-Jürgen noch. Dann klingelt der Wecker.
2. Um ____ **steht** er endlich **auf.**
3. Von ____ bis ____ geht er joggen.

9.30

11.20

12.15

Neue Wörter

steht. . . auf:
  aufstehen   gets up
frühstückt:
frühstücken   eats
  breakfast
ruft. . . an: anrufen
  calls up
trifft: treffen   meets

4. Um _____ **frühstückt** er und liest die Zeitung.
5. Um _____ **ruft** er einen Freund **an.**
6. Um _____ **trifft** er eine Freundin im Café.

13.40

15.00

19.15

7. Um _____ geht er einkaufen.
8. Um _____ spielt Hans-Jürgen Fußball auf dem Sportplatz.
9. Um _____ ist er mit Freunden im Kino.

Aktivität 4   Mein Zeitbudget

A.   Wie viel Zeit verbringen (*spend*) Sie **gewöhnlich** mit diesen Dingen?
Tragen Sie in die Tabelle auf Seite 116 ein, wie viel Zeit Sie **pro Woche**
mit jeder Tätigkeit verbringen. Fragen Sie dann einen Partner / eine
Partnerin:

1. Wie viel Zeit verbringst du mit _____ (Lesen, Essen, Arbeiten usw.)?
2. Wie viel Zeit hast du für dich?

Neue Wörter

Fernsehen   watching
  television
pro Woche   per week
gewöhnlich   usually

Tätigkeit	Montag bis Freitag	Wochenende	Insgesamt
Vorlesungen Labor Lesen Schreiben			
Nebenarbeit			

Essen:
   Frühstück
   Mittagessen
   Abendessen			

Einkaufen Sport Schlafen			

Zeit für mich:
   Fernsehen
   Zeitung/Bücher lesen
   Freunde besuchen
   Musik hören			

B. Berichten Sie, wie Ihr Partner / Ihre Partnerin seine/ihre Zeit verbringt.

BEISPIEL: Laura verbringt drei Stunden pro Woche mit Fernsehen.

THEMA 2: Hans-Jürgens Wochenplan

Dies ist Hans-Jürgens Wochenplan für die nächsten vier Tage.

Note: Tell students that Hans-Jürgen is a cousin of Bernd Thalhofer (Bernd was introduced in **Kapitel 3**). Hans-Jürgen studies at the FU in Berlin. You can point out where the places in the *Wochenplan* are located.

Neue Wörter

Woche week
Fitnesscenter gym
Bahnhof train station
abholen to pick up
Vortrag lecture
streichen to paint
Bibliothek library
ausruhen to rest

Wochenplan   Oktober

Zeit	Tagesplan
	15. Donnerstag
8.00	Karin im **Fitnesscenter** treffen
12.00	mit Thomas essen
14.00	Mutter am **Bahnhof abholen**
19.00	**Vortrag:** Uni
	16. Freitag
7.00	schwimmen gehen
10.00	mit Astrid zu IKEA fahren
15.00	Erika und Thomas in der Stadt treffen: Kaffee trinken
20.00	mit Astrid und Max ins Kino gehen

Zeit	Tagesplan
	17. Samstag
9.00	Küche bei Frau Stegemeier **streichen**
14.00	Kurt in der **Bibliothek** treffen
21.00	Kneipentour mit Jutta und Christina
	18. Sonntag
	AUSRUHEN!

Was möchte Hans-Jürgen machen—und wann? Sehen Sie sich Hans-Jürgens Wochenplan an und ergänzen Sie seine Pläne.

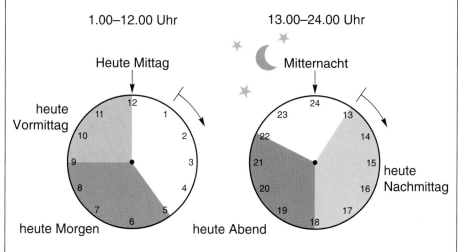

am Donnerstag, 15. Oktober

☐ **Heute Morgen** möchte Hans-Jürgen ins Fitnesscenter gehen.
☐ Heute Mittag möchte er _____.
☐ **Heute Nachmittag** möchte er _____.
☐ Heute Abend möchte er zu einem _____ gehen.

SPRACHTIPP

To say *this morning, this evening*, etc., combine **heute** with a period of the day such as **Morgen: heute Morgen** = *this morning*. Do the same for phrases combined with *tomorrow*: **morgen Nachmittag** = *tomorrow afternoon*; **heute Abend** = *this evening*.

The phrase for *tomorrow morning* is either **morgen früh** or **morgen Vormittag** (to avoid the awkward **morgen Morgen**).

The times of day can also combine with the days of the week: **Samstagabend** = *Saturday evening*. Note that these are written as one word.

am Freitag, 16. Oktober

☐ **Morgen früh** möchte Hans-Jürgen schwimmen gehen.
☐ Morgen Vormittag möchte er _____.
☐ Morgen Nachmittag möchte er _____.
☐ **Morgen Abend** möchte er _____.

am Samstag, 17. Oktober

☐ Samstagmorgen möchte Hans-Jürgen Frau Stegemeiers Küche streichen.
☐ Samstagnachmittag möchte er _____.
☐ Samstagabend möchte er _____.

Und Sie? Was möchten Sie machen—und wann?

Thema 2: Have students complete the sentences following Hans-Jürgen's *Wochenplan*.

Neue Wörter

Morgen morning; tomorrow
Mittag noon
Nachmittag afternoon
Abend evening
früh early
Vormittag morning, before noon
Nacht night

Further practice: Write the following on the board: _____ *möchte ich* _____. Have the class stand up. Each student completes the sentence using words of his or her own choice. As they complete their sentences, students sit down.

Note: Point out to students that in combination with *heute* and *morgen* (tomorrow), the words *Morgen* (morning), *Vormittag, Mittag*, and *Nachmittag* remain separate words and are capitalized, but that in combination with days of the week they form compounds.

SPRACHTIPP

When you do something on a regular basis, use the following adverbs to express the day or the time.

montags	**morgens**
dienstags	**vormittags**
mittwochs	**mittags**
donnerstags	**nachmittags**
freitags	**abends**
samstags/sonnabends	**nachts**
sonntags	

In German, general time precedes specific time.

GENERAL   SPECIFIC

Ich habe donnerstags um 13.00 Uhr Chemie.

GENERAL   SPECIFIC

Ich komme heute Abend um 7 Uhr vorbei.

Aktivität 5. Sven's schedule appears here; Frank's appears in Appendix A.

Note: This schedule is based on the schedule at the *Burgstraße Gymnasium* in Kaiserslautern. Tell students that most schools have a recess or break (*Pause*), usually in the morning. See if they can determine when the *große Pause* takes place. Both Sven and Frank have classes on Saturday morning, but only on the 2nd and 4th Saturday of the month. A growing trend in Germany is to do away with Saturday classes altogether.

Aktivität 5   Hin und her: Zwei Stundenpläne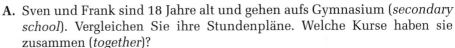

A. Sven und Frank sind 18 Jahre alt und gehen aufs Gymnasium (*secondary school*). Vergleichen Sie ihre Stundenpläne. Welche Kurse haben sie zusammen (*together*)?

BEISPIEL: S1: Welchen Kurs hat Sven dienstags um acht?
S2: Dienstags um acht hat Sven Informatik. Welchen Kurs hat Frank dienstags um acht?
S1: Dienstags um acht hat Frank Physik.

B. Sven und Frank möchten Tennis spielen. Wann ist die beste Zeit? Wann haben sie beide frei?

Zeit	Montag	Dienstag	Mittwoch	Donnerstag	Freitag	Samstag
8 - 8⁴⁵	Englisch	Informatik	Chemie	Physik	frei	Deutsch
8⁴⁵ - 9³⁰	Englisch	Informatik	Chemie	Physik	Kunst	Deutsch
9³⁵ - 10²⁰	Religion	Deutsch	Erdkunde	Deutsch	Sozialkunde	
10⁴⁰ - 11²⁵	Religion	Mathematik	Mathematik	Mathematik	Deutsch	
11³⁰ - 12¹⁵	Erdkunde	Kunst	Sozialkunde	Geschichte	Geschichte	
12¹⁵ - 13⁰⁰	Mathematik	Physik	Informatik	Englisch	Chemie	
13¹⁵ - 14⁰⁰				Sport		
14⁰⁰ - 14⁴⁵				Sport		

Svens Stundenplan

Aktivität 6 Wie sieht Ihr Stundenplan aus?°

How does your schedule look?

Schritt 1: Schreiben Sie Ihren Stundenplan. Wann sind Ihre Kurse? Wann arbeiten Sie? Dann vergleichen Sie Ihren Stundenplan mit dem von zwei anderen Studenten/Studentinnen in Ihrem Kurs.

BEISPIEL: S1: Was hast du donnerstags um 10?
          S2: Donnerstags um 10 habe ich _____. Und du?
          S1: Ich habe _____.

Aktivität 6. Point Out: Refer students to the list of academic subjects in Appendix B.

Schritt 2: Wer hat Kurse mit Ihnen zusammen? Berichten (*Report*) Sie der Klasse.

Aktivität 7 Bist du heute Abend zu Hause?

Sie wollen einen Freund / eine Freundin besuchen.

- Sagen Sie, wann Sie vorbeikommen und wie lange Sie bleiben möchten.
- Benutzen Sie Ausdrücke wie **heute Abend** und **morgen Abend.**
- Geben Sie die genaue Uhrzeit an.

Benutzen Sie folgendes Sprechschema.

Aktivität 7. Suggestion: Follow up with questions such as *Wann kommt _____ vorbei?* to elicit responses such as *_____ kommt Samstagnachmittag um vier vorbei.*

S1	S2
1. Bist du _____ zu Hause?	**2a.** Ja, ich bin zu Hause. **b.** Nein, ich bin leider nicht zu Hause.
3a. Kann ich dann _____ vorbeikommen? **b.** Schade. Wann kann ich denn mal vorbeikommen?	**4a.** Ja, gern. Ich sehe dich also _____. **b.** Kannst du _____ kommen?
5a. Schön. **b.** Ja, gern.	**6.** Wie lange kannst du denn bleiben?
7. _____ Stunde(n).	

THEMA 3: Kino, Musik und Theater

JAN: Ich **gehe** heute Abend **ins Theater.** Willst du mit?
ULLA: Nein, danke. Ich bin kein Theaterfan. Ich möchte **lieber ins Kino.**
JAN: So. Du bist ein Kinofan. Was für (*what kind of*) **Filme** siehst du denn gern?
ULLA: **Am liebsten** Horrorfilme und Psychothriller—die sind so **spannend.**

Was für Filme sehen Sie gern?

☐ Horrorfilme   ☐ **Krimis**
☐ **Komödien**   ☐ Science-fiction-Filme
☐ Psychothriller   ☐ Abenteuerfilme
☐ Liebesfilme   ☐ Wildwestfilme

lieber rather
ins Kino to the
  movies
am liebsten most;
  preferably
spannend suspense-
  ful; exciting
Komödien comedies
Krimis detective
  stories
Tragödien tragedies
Theaterstücke plays
Opern operas

Was sehen Sie gern auf der Bühne (*on stage*)?

☐ **Tragödien**
☐ Lustspiele (*comedies*)
☐ Musicals

☐ **Theaterstücke**
☐ **Opern**
☐ Tanz und **Ballett**

Was für **Musik** hören Sie gern?

☐ klassische Musik
☐ Heavy Metal
☐ Rockmusik
☐ Techno
☐ alternative Musik

☐ Jazz
☐ Soul
☐ Western-Musik
☐ Rap
☐ Electroclash

Aktivität 8   Zwei Einladungen°

invitations

Sie hören zwei Dialoge. Wer spricht? Wohin möchten die Sprecher gehen? Warum ist es nicht möglich (*possible*)? Markieren Sie die richtige Information.

DIALOG 1

1. Die Sprecher sind...
   a. ein Professor und ein
      Student.
   b. zwei Studentinnen.
   c. eine Studentin und ein
      Freund.

2. Der eine Sprecher möchte...
   a. zu Hause arbeiten.
   b. ins Kino.
   c. ins Konzert.

3. Die Sprecherin muss leider...
   a. arbeiten.
   b. in eine Vorlesung (*lecture*).
   c. einen Brief schreiben.

DIALOG 2

1. Die Sprecher sind...
   a. zwei Studenten.
   b. zwei Professoren.
   c. ein Student und eine Freundin.

2. Die eine Sprecherin möchte...
   a. ins Kino.
   b. in eine Vorlesung.
   c. Karten spielen.

3. Der andere Sprecher...
   a. hat eine Vorlesung.
   b. hat Labor.
   c. muss in die Bibliothek.

generally

Aktivität 9   Was machst du so° am Wochenende?

Interviewen Sie Studenten/Studentinnen in der Klasse und finden Sie folgende Personen. Wer „ja" antwortet, muss unterschreiben.

AM WOCHENENDE

1. _____ Wer geht tanzen, spazieren, laufen oder wandern?
2. _____ Wer steht früh auf?
3. _____ Wer steht spät auf?
4. _____ Wer räumt das Zimmer, die Wohnung, den
      Kleiderschrank auf?
5. _____ Wer geht ins Kino, ins Theater, in die Oper, ins Konzert,
      in die Disko?
6. _____ Wer lädt Freunde ein?
7. _____ Wer sieht fern?

Aktivität 10   Was hast du vor?°

What are you planning to do?

Schauen Sie sich die Programme für Kino, Theater und Musik an. Sagen Sie, wohin Sie gehen wollen.

Vorverkauf Hardenbergstr. 6, Mo.- Fr. von 8 -16.30 Uhr

15. März, 16.00 Uhr und 20.00 Uhr sowie
2. und 3. Mai, jeweils 20.00 Uhr
4. Mai, 18.00 Uhr und 15. Juni, 18.00 Uhr

ICC BERLIN

Das Musical-Ereignis!
Endlich in deutscher Sprache!

PHANTOM DER OPER

Von Arndt Gerber u. Paul Wilhelm
nach dem Roman von G. Leroux
**Internationales Musical-Ensemble
mit Ballett, Chor und Orchester**

Karten: Kasse ICC und alle Vorverkaufsstellen

Theater in Berlin

KOMÖDIE AM KU´DAMM
19.30 Uhr **TAXI, TAXI**
Turbulenter Schwank
THEATER am KU´DAMM
Zusätzlich am Wochenende
Wilhelm heeßt er
Revue-Musical

47 02 10 10

FAME

Das Musical
im
Schiller Theater
Tickets: 030 · 31 11 31 11

THEATER	Montag, 10. 3.	Dienstag, 11. 3.
Deutsche Oper Berlin 341 02 49	20.00 Kammermusik im Foyer: **Ensemble „das neue Werk" Berlin**	17.00 Foyer: **„Klein-Siegfried"**
Berliner Kammerspiele 391 55 43	**Biedermann und die Brandstifter** von Max Frisch Freitag und Sonnabend 18.00 Uhr	

19.6.
Theaterwerkstatt
Charlottenburg
Neil Simon
Brooklyn Memoiren
Cafétheater Schalotte,
1000 Berlin 10
Behaimstr. 22, 20 Uhr

S1	S2
1. Was hast du am Samstag vor?	2. Ich gehe ins Theater / in die Oper / ? Willst du mit?
3. Was gibt es denn?	4. Ein Musical / eine Oper / ? von (+ *name*).
5a. So? Wann fängt er/es/sie denn an? b. Ach, ich bleibe lieber zu Hause.	6a. ————. b. Schade.

Kulturhaus Spandau
Heute: 21.00 Uhr
Spandauer Harfenfestival
Alte Sprache & Neue Musik
Moderne chinesische
Harfenmusik
Mauerstr. 6, 333 40 21
Spandauer Altstadt

To say where you are going, use the following expressions.

Ich gehe
- ins Kino.
- ins Theater.
- ins Konzert.
- in die Oper.
- in die Disko.

Hier klicken!

Weiteres zum Thema Konzert
und Theater finden Sie bei
Deutsch: Na klar! im World-
Wide-Web unter
www.mhhe.com/dnk.

In Deutschland gibt es in den Groß- und Kleinstädten über 400 öffentliche und private Theater. Der deutsche Staat subventioniert (*subsidizes*) die meisten von ihnen. Deshalb sind die Preise für die Theaterkarten nicht zu teuer. Viele Deutsche haben ein Theaterabonnement (*subscription*). Die deutschen Theater spielen gerne klassische Stücke, die oft modernisiert oder politisiert sind. Das macht sie aktuell und interessant.

Stadttheater Göttingen

Grammatik im Kontext

Separable-Prefix Verbs°

Verben mit trennbaren Präfixen

You are already familiar with sentences like the following:

Susanne und Peter **kommen** per Fahrrad **vorbei.**

*Susanne and Peter **are coming** by on their bikes.*

Ich gehe heute tanzen. **Kommst** du **mit?**

*I am going dancing today. Will you **come along?***

German, like English, has many two-part verbs that consist of a verb and a short complement that affects the meaning of the main verb. Examples of such two-part verbs in English are *to come by, to come along, to call up, to get up.*

Wüstenrot-Rendite[1]-Programm mit 470 Euro pro anno.

Jede Million fängt klein an.[2]

Ich rufe an.... (Telefonieren ist einfach)[3]

Realia. *Jede Million fängt klein an* is a well-known ad slogan for *Wüstenrot*, a German investment house. The text of the ad (not shown here) encourages savers to begin with a small amount to start out on the road to becoming millionaires.

[1] *yield on investment*
[2] fängt... an: *begins*
[3] *simple*

Kommen. . . vorbei, fängt. . . an, rufe. . . an, and **kommst. . . mit** are examples of such two-part verbs in German. They are also called separable-prefix verbs. In the infinitive, the separable part of these verbs forms the verb's prefix. The prefixes are always stressed.

ánrufen   **án**fangen   vor**béi**kommen   **mít**kommen

In a statement or a question, the prefix is separated from the conjugated verb and placed at the end of the sentence.

—**Kommst** du heute Abend **vorbei?**

Are you coming by tonight?

—Ja, aber ich **rufe** vorher **an.**

Yes, but I'll call first.

Here are examples of some commonly used separable-prefix verbs.

VERB	BEISPIEL
abholen (holt...ab) to pick up	Ich **hole** dich um 6 Uhr **ab.**
anfangen (fängt...an) to begin	Wann **fängt** die Vorlesung **an**?
anrufen (ruft...an) to call up	Ich **rufe** dich morgen **an.**
aufhören (hört...auf) to end, quit	Der Regen **hört** nicht **auf.**
aufräumen (räumt...auf) to straighten up	Er **räumt** sein Zimmer **auf.**
aufstehen (steht...auf) to get up	Er **steht** um 9 Uhr **auf.**
aufwachen (wacht...auf) to wake up	Wann **wachst** du gewöhnlich **auf**?
einkaufen (kauft...ein) to shop	Herr Lerche **kauft** immer morgens **ein.**
einladen (lädt...ein) to invite	Ich **lade** dich zum Essen **ein.**
einschlafen (schläft...ein) to fall asleep	Ich **schlafe** gewöhnlich nicht vor Mitternacht **ein.**
mitkommen (kommt...mit) to come along	**Kommst** du **mit**?
mitnehmen (nimmt...mit) to take along	**Nimmst** du einen Regenschirm **mit**?
vorbeikommen (kommt... vorbei) to come by	Wir **kommen** Sonntag **vorbei.**
vorhaben (hat...vor) to plan to do	Was **hast** du heute **vor**?
zurückkommen (kommt... zurück) to come back	Wann **kommst** du **zurück**?

So geben Sie Ihre Anzeige¹ auf:²

01 30/81 80 10

07 11/1 82-13 49
Faxaufträge am Anzeigenschluß nur bis 16 Uhr!

★34200#

Coupon ausfüllen, und einsenden

¹ad
²geben... auf *place*

Separable-prefix verbs are listed in the vocabulary of this book as follows:

  auf•hören   ein•schlafen (schläft ein)   vor•haben (hat vor)

Note:

■ A separable-prefix verb shows all the same stem-vowel changes or other irregularities in the present tense as the base verb.

  Hans **schläft** immer lange.   Er **schläft** gewöhnlich erst um 23 Uhr **ein.**

  Er **nimmt** den Schirm.   Er **nimmt** den Schirm **mit.**

Die Satzklammer

The Sentence Bracket°

Separable-prefix verbs show a sentence structure that is characteristic for German: The conjugated verb and its complement form a bracket around the core of the sentence. The conjugated verb is the second element of the sentence, and the separable prefix is the last element.

```
                    ┌──────── SATZKLAMMER ────────┐
Ich      rufe      dich heute Abend      an.
Wann     kommst    du heute              vorbei?
Peter    geht      leider nicht          mit.
```

Another example of the sentence bracket (**Satzklammer**) can be seen in sentences with compound verbs such as **einkaufen gehen** (*to go shopping*), **tanzen gehen** (*to go dancing*), and **spazieren gehen** (*to go for a walk*).

```
                    ┌──────── SATZKLAMMER ────────┐
Ich                gehe     morgens                   einkaufen.
Klaus und Erika    gehen    Sonntag mit Freunden      tanzen.
Daniel             geht     mit dem Hund              spazieren.
```

In the sentences above, the verb **gehen** and the infinitives **einkaufen, tanzen,** and **spazieren** form a bracket around the sentence core. You will encounter the concept of the sentence bracket in many other contexts involving verbs.

Übung 1   Daniels Tagesablauf

Daniel ist Künstler (*artist*), aber die Kunst (*art*) allein bringt nicht genug Geld ein. Sie hören jetzt eine Beschreibung von Daniels Tagesablauf. Kreuzen Sie alle passenden Antworten an.

1. Wann wacht Daniel gewöhnlich auf?
   a. <u>sehr früh</u>
   b. sehr spät
   c. um 5 Uhr
2. Wohnt Daniel allein oder mit jemandem zusammen?
   a. allein
   b. <u>mit seinem Bruder</u>
   c. mit seiner Freundin
3. Was tut Daniel für die Familie Schröder?
   a. <u>Er geht einkaufen.</u>
   b. <u>Er geht mit dem Hund spazieren.</u>
   c. <u>Er macht Reparaturen.</u>
4. Wann fängt Daniels Arbeit im Hotel an?
   a. um 6 Uhr
   b. <u>um 7 Uhr</u>
   c. um 5 Uhr
5. Wann kommt Daniel nach Hause zurück?
   a. um 12 Uhr nachts
   b. um 6 Uhr abends
   c. <u>so gegen 3 Uhr nachmittags</u>
6. Was macht Daniel dann zuerst?
   a. <u>Er geht schlafen.</u>
   b. Er geht einkaufen.
   c. Er räumt das Zimmer auf.
7. Wann fängt Daniels Leben für die Kunst an?
   a. <u>spät nachmittags</u>
   b. am Wochenende
   c. so gegen Mitternacht
8. Wie verbringt Daniel manchmal seinen Abend?
   a. Er sieht fern.
   b. <u>Er lädt Freunde ein.</u>
   c. <u>Er ruft Freunde an.</u>
9. Wann schläft Daniel gewöhnlich ein?
   a. um 12 Uhr nachts
   b. <u>nicht vor 1 Uhr nachts</u>
   c. so gegen halb eins

Übung 1. Suggestion: Have students scan the questions and possible answers before listening to the passage for the first time. Allow students time to answer the questions. Let students listen a second time in order to complete the exercise before going over the answers together.

Grammatik im Kontext   **125**

Übung 2. Suggestion: Do as a whole-class activity. Allow students to add as much detail as possible.

Additional Activity: Copy the audio script and white-out the prefixes of all separable-prefix verbs appearing in the text. Make copies for the entire class. This can also be done as additional homework or to reinforce new vocabulary and practice narrating a series of events.

Übung 3. Suggestion: Have students work alone to fill in the prefixes. Then have them work in pairs to rearrange the sentences and practice "making a date" in German.

Übung 2 Was Daniel macht

Erzählen Sie jetzt mit Hilfe der Fragen und Antworten in Übung 1, was Daniel jeden Tag macht.

BEISPIEL: Daniel wacht gewöhnlich sehr früh auf.

Übung 3 Eine Verabredung°

Die folgenden Sätze stellen eine Konversation zwischen Hans und Petra dar. Ergänzen Sie zuerst die Verben mit den fehlenden (*missing*) Präfixen. Arrangieren Sie dann die Sätze als Dialog, und üben Sie den Dialog mit einem Partner / einer Partnerin.

_____ Um acht. Ich komme um halb acht _____ und hole dich _____.

_____ Ja, ich gehe ins Kino. Im Olympia läuft ein neuer Film mit Keanu Reeves. Kommst du _____?

_____ Schön. Hinterher lade ich dich zu einem Bier _____.

_____ Gerne. Wann fängt der Film denn _____?

__1__ Hast du für heute Abend schon etwas _____?

A date

Übung 4. Suggestion: Have students work in pairs, taking turns reading a statement and then commenting. Have them jot down their partner's answers. A few students will be asked to report back to the class what their partner does.

Übung 4 Was ich so mache

Was machen Sie **immer, manchmal, selten, nie, oft, gewöhnlich?** Vergleichen Sie sich (*compare yourself*) mit den Personen in den folgenden Sätzen.

BEISPIEL: Hans schläft gewöhnlich in der Vorlesung ein. →
         Ich schlafe nie in der Vorlesung ein.

1. Daniel steht gewöhnlich sehr früh auf.
2. Er geht nie am Wochenende einkaufen.
3. Lilo geht oft mit ihrem Hund spazieren.
4. Hans räumt selten sein Zimmer auf.
5. Lilo schläft gewöhnlich beim Fernsehen ein.
6. Daniel lädt manchmal abends Freunde ein.
7. Daniel schläft selten vor 1 Uhr nachts ein.
8. Lilo ruft ihre Eltern oft an.
9. Daniel geht selten mit Freunden aus.

Übung 5. Suggestion: Have students scan the verbs and phrases to be used in their responses before starting the interviews.

Übung 5 Wie sieht dein Tag aus?

A. Arbeiten Sie zu zweit und stellen Sie einander folgende Fragen. Schreiben Sie die Antworten auf. Formulieren Sie Ihre Antworten mit Hilfe der Verben auf Seite 127.

■ Was machst du jeden Tag?

■ Was machst du oft?

■ Was machst du manchmal?

■ Was machst du nie?

vor sechs Uhr aufstehen

einkaufen ... gehen

beim Fernsehen einschlafen

Zimmer aufräumen

nach Mitternacht einschlafen

jemand *(someone)* anrufen

mit Freunden ausgehen

BEISPIEL: Ich stehe oft vor sechs Uhr auf. Ich schlafe nie beim Fernsehen ein.

B. Geben Sie jetzt einen kurzen Bericht von etwa vier Sätzen.

BEISPIEL: Keith steht nie vor sechs Uhr auf. Er räumt auch nie sein Zimmer auf. Er geht manchmal einkaufen. Jeden Tag geht er mit Freunden aus.

Modal Auxiliary Verbs°

Modalverben

Modal auxiliary verbs (for example, *must, can, may*) express an attitude toward an action.

Morgen **möchten** wir Tennis **spielen.**	*Tomorrow we **would like to play** tennis.*
Am Wochenende **wollen** wir Freunde **besuchen.**	*On the weekend we **want to visit** friends.*
Ich **kann** morgen **vorbeikommen.**	*I **can come by** tomorrow.*

The examples show:

- The modal auxiliary verb is in the second position in a statement.
- Its complement—the verb that expresses the action—is in the infinitive form and stands at the end of the sentence.

Note:

- In German, sentences with modal auxiliaries and a dependent infinitive demonstrate the pattern of the sentence bracket (**Satzklammer**).
- The modal is in second position in a statement, and the infinitive is at the end of the statement.

<table>
<tr><td></td><td colspan="3" align="center">── SATZKLAMMER ──</td></tr>
<tr><td>Morgen</td><td>**möchten**</td><td>wir Tennis</td><td>**spielen.**</td></tr>
<tr><td>Peter</td><td>**muss**</td><td>morgen leider</td><td>**arbeiten.**</td></tr>
<tr><td>Ich</td><td>**kann**</td><td>dich heute</td><td>**besuchen.**</td></tr>
<tr><td>Heute Abend</td><td>**wollen**</td><td>wir ins Kino</td><td>**gehen.**</td></tr>
</table>

Grammatik im Kontext **127**

¹novels

German has the following modal verbs.

dürfen	to be allowed to, may	**Dürfen** wir hier rauchen? *May we smoke here?*
könn	to be able to, can	Ich **kann** dich gut verstehen. *I can understand you well.*
mögen	to like, care for	**Mögen** Sie Bücher? *Do you like books?*
müssen	to have to, must	Er **muss** heute arbeiten. *He has to work today.*
sollen	to be supposed to, shall	Wann **sollen** wir vorbeikommen? *When are we supposed to come by?*
wollen	to want to, plan to do	**Willst** du mitgehen? *Do you want to go along?*

Note: Point out to students the older spelling *muß, mußt, müßt* in the ad.

The Present Tense of Modals

Modals are irregular verbs. With the exception of **sollen,** they have stem-vowel changes in the singular. Note also that the first- and third-person singular forms are identical and have no personal ending.

	dürfen	können	mögen	müssen	sollen	wollen
ich	**darf**	**kann**	**mag**	**muss**	**soll**	**will**
du	darfst	kannst	magst	musst	sollst	willst
er sie es	**darf**	**kann**	**mag**	**muss**	**soll**	**will**
wir	dürfen	können	mögen	müssen	sollen	wollen
ihr	dürft	könnt	mögt	müsst	sollt	wollt
sie	dürfen	können	mögen	müssen	sollen	wollen
Sie	dürfen	können	mögen	müssen	sollen	wollen

Realia. It is relatively rare nowadays to be asked to show one's ticket on a bus, streetcar, or subway. A *Kontrolleur* may come around asking all passengers to prove they have paid their fare by showing their tickets.

„Darf ich einmal Ihren Fahrschein sehen!"

Möchte (*would like to*), one of the most common modal verbs, is the subjunctive of **mögen**. Note that the first- and third-person singular forms are identical.

Wir **möchten** morgen Tennis **spielen**.　　*We would like to play tennis tomorrow.*

möchte			
ich	**möchte**	wir	möchten
du	möchtest	ihr	möchtet
er sie es	**möchte**	sie	möchten
Sie möchten			

Note:

- The modal **mögen** is generally used without a dependent infinitive.

    Er **mag** seine Arbeit im Hotel.　　*He likes his work in the hotel.*

- The infinitive may be omitted in a sentence when its meaning is understood.

    Ich **muss** jetzt in die Vorlesung (**gehen**).　　*I have to go to the lecture now.*

    Ich **möchte** jetzt nach Hause (**gehen**).　　*I would like to go home now.*

    Er **will** das nicht (**machen**).　　*He doesn't want to do that.*

ANALYSE

Scan the headlines and visuals.

- Identify all modal auxiliary verbs in the headlines and visual. Give the English equivalents of the sentences.
- What verbs express the action in those sentences?
- Mark the two parts of each sentence bracket.

Analyse. Suggestion: Include realia illustrating modals from the previous page. Encourage students to guess the meaning whenever possible.

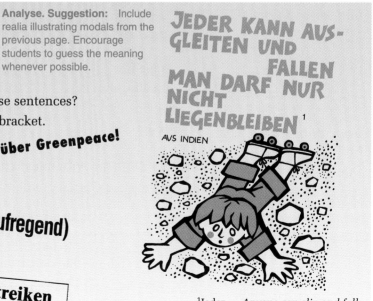

JEDER KANN AUSGLEITEN UND MAN DARF NUR NICHT FALLEN LIEGENBLEIBEN[1]

AUS INDIEN

Ich möchte mehr Informationen über Greenpeace!

So schön (spannend, aufregend) kann Fernsehen sein

Die Studenten wollen streiken

[1]Jeder. . . *Anyone can slip and fall; the trick is not to stay down.*

Übung 6   Was kann man da machen?

BEISPIEL: in der Bibliothek →

    s1: Was kann man in der Bibliothek machen?
    s2: Da kann man Bücher lesen!

1. im Restaurant   **a.** Filme sehen
2. im Kino   **b.** einkaufen
3. im Internet Café   **c.** tanzen
4. in der Disko   **d.** Kaffee trinken
5. im Kaufhaus   **e.** Bücher lesen
6. im Park   **f.** essen
7. in der Bibliothek   **g.** spazieren gehen
     h. am Computer arbeiten
     i. Zeitung lesen

SPRACHTIPP

The indefinite pronoun **man** (*one, people, you, they*) is used to talk about a general activity.

  Man darf hier nicht parken.

  You (One) may not park here. (Parking is not allowed here.)

Man is used with the third-person singular verb form.

Übung 7. Suggestion:
Personalize this exercise by asking students to state what is allowed where they live: *Darf man hier (auf dem Unigelände) rauchen? Darf man hier parken?*

rather

Übung 8. Suggestion: Model the example with a student to convey the meaning of *lieber.* Point out that *lieber* is the comparative form of *gern.* Do the exercise as a whole-class activity and have the student who has just answered initiate the next set of questions.

Übung 7   Was darf man hier machen oder nicht machen?

BEISPIEL: Man darf hier nicht parken.

 1.
 2.
 3.

 4.
 5.
 6.

campen   spielen
schnell fahren   rauchen (*smoke*)
schwimmen   von 8 bis 14 Uhr parken
parken

Übung 8   Was möchtest du lieber° machen?

Fragen Sie einen Partner / eine Partnerin, was er/sie lieber machen möchte.

BEISPIEL: lange schlafen oder Tennis spielen? →

    s1: Was möchtest du lieber machen: lange schlafen oder Tennis spielen?
    s2: Ich möchte lieber Tennis spielen.

1. Zeitung lesen oder im Internet surfen?
2. fernsehen oder einkaufen gehen?

3. ins Café oder ins Kino gehen?
4. deine Familie anrufen oder eine E-Mail schreiben?
5. ein Picknick machen oder spazieren gehen?
6. eine Party zu Hause machen oder ausgehen?
7. zu Hause bleiben oder Freunde besuchen?

Übung 9   Im Deutschen Haus

Chris und Jeff wohnen im Deutschen Haus an einer amerikanischen Universität. Sie sollen so oft wie möglich deutsch miteinander sprechen. Hören Sie zu, und kreuzen Sie die richtige Information an.

Übung 9. Point Out: Is there a German house on your campus? If so, provide students with some information about it.

	DAS STIMMT	DAS STIMMT NICHT
1. Chris muss für einen Test arbeiten.	☒	☐
2. Chris stört (*disturbs*) seinen Mitbewohner Jeff.	☒	☐
3. Jeff wird jetzt auch müde (*tired*).	☒	☐
4. Chris kann nur laut (*out loud*) lernen.	☒	☐
5. Chris geht in die Bibliothek.	☐	☒

Übung 10   Was sind die Tatsachen°?

facts

Was wissen Sie über die beiden Bewohner des Deutschen Hauses? Bilden Sie Sätze.

Chris	soll	ins Badezimmer gehen
Jeff	muss	deutsche Grammatik lernen
	kann	ein A bekommen
	will	nur laut Deutsch lernen
	möchte	Jeff nicht stören
		auch arbeiten
		jetzt auch schlafen
		nicht arbeiten
		lesen

Übung 11   Pläne für eine Party

Brigitte, Lisa und Anja haben endlich ein Dach (*roof*) über dem Kopf: eine Wohnung auf einem alten Bauernhof (*farm*). Jetzt planen sie eine Party. Setzen Sie passende Modalverben in die Lücken ein.

BRIGITTE: Also wen _____[1] (*want to*) wir denn einladen?

LISA: Die Frage ist: Wie viele Leute _____[2] (*can*) wir denn einladen? Wir haben ja nicht so viel Platz.

ANJA: Im Wohnzimmer _____[3] (*can*) bestimmt zwanzig Leute sitzen.

LISA: Und tanzen _____[4] (*can*) wir im Garten.

ANJA: Und wer _____[5] (*is supposed to*) für so viele Leute kochen?

LISA: Ich _____[6] (*want*) lieber nur ein paar Leute einladen.

ANJA: Wir sagen, jeder _____[7] (*is supposed to*) etwas zum Essen mitbringen.

BRIGITTE: Ich _____[8] (*would like to*) Kartoffelsalat mit Würstchen machen.

LISA: Gute Idee. Das ist einfach, und das _____[9] (*like*) alle.

ANJA: Tut mir leid, aber ich _____[10] (*like*) Kartoffelsalat nicht.

BRIGITTE: Ich _____[11] (*can*) auch was Italienisches machen, Pizza oder Lasagne.

LISA: Wir _____[12] (*may*) aber nicht nur Bier servieren, wir _____[13] (*have to*) auch Mineralwasser oder Cola servieren, für die Autofahrer.

Übung 12 Ein Picknick im Grünen

Einige Mitbewohner im internationalen Studentenwohnheim planen ein Picknick. Wer bringt was mit?

BEISPIEL: Andreas will ein Frisbee mitbringen. Er soll auch Mineralwasser besorgen.

Jürgen aus München	wollen	Brot und Käse (*cheese*)	kaufen
Stephanie aus den USA	müssen	Mineralwasser	mitbringen
die Zwillinge aus Italien: Paola und Maria	möchte	Bier	machen
Nagako aus Tokio	sollen	eine Decke (*blanket*) zum Sitzen	
Michel aus Frankreich		ein Radio	
ich		ein Frisbee	
		eine Pizza	
		Kartoffelsalat	
		eine Kamera	

Übung 13 Kommst du mit?

Übung 13. Suggestion: This activity is best done with students circulating in class. Assign several students to act as observers who jot down the different excuses they hear and report them to the class afterward.

Arbeiten Sie mit einem Partner / einer Partnerin zusammen. Laden Sie ihn/sie ein, etwas mit Ihnen zu unternehmen (*do*). Er/Sie soll die Einladung ablehnen (*decline*) und einen Grund (*reason*) dafür angeben.

BEISPIEL: s1: Ich will heute Tennis spielen. Möchtest du mitkommen?
s1: Nein, leider kann ich nicht. Ich muss nämlich arbeiten.

s1	s2
heute Abend ins Rockkonzert gehen	arbeiten
in die Disko gehen	meine Eltern besuchen
nach (+ *place*) fahren	zu Hause bleiben (Mein Wagen ist kaputt.)
ins Grüne fahren	mein Zimmer aufräumen
Tennis spielen	Deutsch lernen
Mini-Golf spielen	??
zu einer Party gehen	
??	

The Imperative°

The imperative is the verb form used to make requests and recommendations and to give instructions, advice, or commands. You are already familiar with imperative forms used in common classroom requests.

Wiederholen Sie bitte.	*Repeat, please.*
Hören Sie zu!	*Listen!*
Sagen Sie das auf Deutsch.	*Say that in German.*

These are examples of formal imperatives, used for anyone you would address as **Sie.** There are two additional imperative forms, used for informally addressing one or several people whom you would address individually as **du.** Imperatives in written German often end in an exclamation point, especially to emphasize a request or a command.

The Imperative. Suggestion: Introduce imperatives through Total Physical Response (TPR) techniques. Have students carry out several typical classroom actions: *Stehen Sie auf! Machen Sie die Tür auf! Gehen Sie an die Tafel! Öffnen Sie Ihr Buch!*

OVERVIEW OF IMPERATIVE FORMS

Infinitive	Formal	Informal Singular	Informal Plural
kommen	**Kommen Sie** bald.	**Komm** bald.	**Kommt** bald.
fahren	**Fahren Sie** langsam!	**Fahr** langsam!	**Fahrt** langsam!
anrufen	**Rufen Sie** mich **an.**	**Ruf** mich **an.**	**Ruft** mich **an.**
sprechen	**Sprechen Sie** langsam!	**Sprich** langsam!	**Sprecht** langsam!
arbeiten	**Arbeiten Sie** jetzt!	**Arbeite** jetzt!	**Arbeitet** jetzt!
sein	**Seien Sie** freundlich.	**Sei** freundlich.	**Seid** freundlich.

Formal Imperative

The formal imperative is formed by inverting the subject **(Sie)** and the verb in the present tense.

Note:

- The formal imperative has the same word order as a yes/no question; only punctuation or intonation identifies it as an imperative.

- The imperative of the verb **sein** is irregular.

  Seien Sie bitte freundlich!   *Please be friendly.*

Particles and **bitte** with the Imperative

Requests or commands are often softened by adding the word **bitte** and particles such as **doch** and **mal. Bitte** can stand at the beginning, in the middle, or at the end of the sentence. The particles **doch** and **mal** follow the imperative form. They have no English equivalent.

Bitte nehmen Sie Platz

Hören Sie **bitte** zu!	*Please listen.*
Bitte nehmen Sie Platz.	*Please have a seat.*
Kommen Sie **doch** heute vorbei.	*Why don't you come by today?*
Rufen Sie mich **mal** an.	*Give me a call (some time).* (*Why don't you give me a call some time?*)

office hour

Übung 14. Note: The listening text focuses on distinguishing a yes/no question (rising intonation) from a formal request (falling intonation).

Suggestion: Once students have completed the listening part and marked their answers, go over each sentence once more and illustrate the differences in intonation. Have students repeat questions and then turn them into requests by changing their intonation and vice versa. In the case of questions, have students provide possible answers as well.

Übung 14 In der Sprechstunde°

Mary Lerner geht zum Professor in die Sprechstunde. Kreuzen Sie an, ob es um eine Frage oder eine Aufforderung (*command*) geht.

	FRAGE	AUFFORDERUNG		FRAGE	AUFFORDERUNG
1.	☐	☒	**8.**	☒	☐
2.	☐	☒	**9.**	☐	☒
3.	☐	☒	**10.**	☒	☐
4.	☒	☐	**11.**	☒	☐
5.	☐	☒	**12.**	☐	☒
6.	☒	☐	**13.**	☒	☐
7.	☐	☒	**14.**	☐	☒

Informal Imperative

The singular informal imperative is used for anyone you address with **du.** It is formed for most verbs simply by dropping the **-st** ending from the present tense **du-** form of the verb.

kommen: du **kommst**	→	**Komm!**
anrufen: du **rufst an**	→	**Ruf an!**
arbeiten: du **arbeitest**	→	**Arbeite!**
sprechen: du **sprichst**	→	**Sprich!**
nehmen: du **nimmst**	→	**Nimm!**
But: **sein: du bist**	→	**Sei!**

Verbs that show a vowel change from **a** to **ä** (or **au** to **äu**) in the present tense have no umlaut in the imperative.

du fährst → **Fahr!**

du läufst → **Lauf!**

Schreib mal wieder.

Deutsche Post AG

Flieg mit mir
Die Welt zu Ihren Füßen

Eine abgehobene Geschenkidee

[1]Flieg...*Fly with me*

Mach Dir ein paar schöne Stunden... geh ins **Kino**

The plural informal imperative is used to request something from several persons whom you individually address with **du.**

Kommt doch mal zu uns.	*Why don't you come see us. (lit., Come to us.)*
Fahrt jetzt nach Hause.	*Drive home now.*
Gebt mir bitte etwas zu essen.	*Please give me something to eat.*
Seid doch ruhig!	*Be quiet!*

This imperative form is identical to the **ihr**-form of the present tense, but without the pronoun **ihr.**

Übung 15   Macht das, bitte!

Ergänzen Sie die Tabelle.

GENIESS[1] DIE KLEINE PAUSE.
SAG JA ZU YES.

Leicht wie Biscuit.
Locker wie frische Torte.

[1]enjoy

FORMAL	INFORMAL SING.	INFORMAL PL.
1. Kommen Sie, bitte!	Komm, bitte!	_____, bitte!
2. _____ leise, bitte!	Sprich leise, bitte!	_____ leise, bitte!
3. Laden Sie uns bitte ein.	_____ uns bitte _____.	_____ uns bitte ____.
4. _____ doch ruhig!	Sei doch ruhig!	_____ doch ruhig!
5. Fahren Sie langsam!	_____ langsam!	Fahrt langsam!
6. Rufen Sie mich mal an.	_____ mich mal _____.	Ruft mich mal an.
7. _____ das Buch mit.	_____ das Buch mit.	Nehmt das Buch mit.
8. Machen Sie schnell!	Mach schnell!	_____ schnell!
9. Hören Sie doch auf!	_____ doch ____!	_____ doch ____!

Übung 16   Wir duzen einander unter Studenten.°

*We students say **du** to each other.*

Stellen Sie sich vor, Sie sind neu im Studentenwohnheim und reden alle Ihre Mitbewohner zuerst mit **Sie** an. Jetzt müssen Sie **du** lernen, denn alle Studenten duzen einander. Setzen Sie die Imperativsätze in die **du**-Form.

BEISPIEL: Bitte, kommen Sie herein. → Bitte, komm herein.

1. Bitte, sprechen Sie etwas langsamer.
2. Laden Sie mich bitte auch zur Party ein.
3. Arbeiten Sie nicht so viel.
4. Fahren Sie doch am Wochenende mit mir nach Heidelberg.
5. Bleiben Sie doch noch ein bisschen.
6. Besuchen Sie mich mal.
7. Rufen Sie mich morgen um 10 Uhr an.
8. Gehen Sie doch mit ins Kino.
9. Kommen Sie doch morgen vorbei.
10. Nehmen Sie die Zeitung mit.
11. Sehen Sie mal, hier ist ein Foto von meiner Familie.

Übung 16. Suggestion: This exercise lends itself to variations; do a quick oral drill of reversing the exercise by providing a *du*-imperative and asking students to express it in a formal imperative.

Übung 17   Pläne unter Freunden

Sie möchten Ihren Freunden sagen, was sie alles tun sollen. Machen Sie aus den Fragen Imperativsätze. Benutzen Sie dabei auch **doch, mal** oder **bitte.**

BEISPIEL: Kommt ihr heute Abend vorbei? →
          Kommt bitte heute Abend vorbei!

1. Ladet ihr mich ein?
2. Ruft ihr mich morgen an?
3. Holt ihr mich ab?
4. Sprecht ihr immer deutsch?
5. Hört ihr zu?
6. Geht ihr mit?
7. Kommt ihr morgen vorbei?

Übung 17. Suggestion: Stress the distinction in the intonation of a question and a request when doing this exercise.

Übung 18. Point Out: The phrase *Sei so gut/nett und. . .* and its variations are used in polite conversation in connection with a request. Have students add the appropriate forms of *Sei / Seid / Seien Sie so gut/nett* to *Ruf mich morgen an! Komm morgen vorbei! Öffnen Sie bitte das Fenster! Geht jetzt! Mach die Tür zu!*

Übung 18   Situationen im Alltag

Ergänzen Sie die passende Form des Imperativs von **sein.**

1. Ich muss Sie warnen: Autofahren in Deutschland ist ein Abenteuer. _____ bitte vorsichtig!
2. Sie gehen mit zwei Freunden ins Konzert. Diese Freunde sind nie pünktlich und das irritiert Sie. Sie sagen zu ihnen: „_____ aber bitte pünktlich!"
3. Ihr Mitbewohner / Ihre Mitbewohnerin im Studentenwohnheim ist sehr unordentlich. Sie erwarten Ihre Eltern zu Besuch und bitten ihn/sie: „_____ so nett und räum deine Sachen auf!"
4. Drei Mitbewohner im Studentenwohnheim spielen um drei Uhr morgens immer noch laute Musik. Sie klopfen irritiert gegen die Wand und rufen: „Zum Donnerwetter, _____ endlich ruhig!"
5. Frau Kümmel zu Frau Honig: „_____ bitte so nett und kommen Sie morgen vorbei!"

Sprache im Kontext

Videoclips

A. Wie sind die Tagesroutinen von Jan und Beatrice? Was machen sie morgens und abends? Schauen Sie sich die Interviews mit Jan und Beatrice an und ergänzen Sie die Tabelle.

	JAN	BEATRICE
MORGENS	*7 Uhr — aufstehen*	
ABENDS		
		0–1 Uhr — ins Bett gehen

B. Schauen Sie sich das Interview mit Jasmin an und ergänzen Sie die Informationen.

1. Jasmin _____ um 8 Uhr.
2. Um ____ oder ____ Uhr kommt sie von der Arbeit nach Hause.
3. Sie geht ungefähr um 22 Uhr ins _____.
4. Am Wochenende ____ sie lange, macht Sport oder geht _____.
5. Sie geht gern ____ ____.

C. Und Sie? Machen Sie eine Tabelle für Ihre eigene (*own*) Tagesroutine. Erzählen Sie dann einem Partner/einer Partnerin, wie Ihr typischer Tag aussieht.

Lesen

The reading here describes daily routines and everyday pleasures.

Zum Thema

Immer das Gleiche (*the same thing*)?

A. Ergänzen Sie die Tabelle. Wie sieht Ihr Alltag aus? Und Ihr Geburtstag?

MEIN ALLTAG		MEIN GEBURTSTAG	
Uhrzeit	*Aktivität*	*Uhrzeit*	*Aktivität*
	aufstehen		
	ins Bett gehen		

B. Machen Sie etwas Besonderes (*something special*) an Ihrem Geburtstag, oder ist er wie jeder andere Tag? Berichten Sie mit Hilfe der Tabelle.

BEISPIEL: Gewöhnlich stehe ich um 7 Uhr auf. Aber an meinem Geburtstag schlafe ich lange.

Auf den ersten Blick

Überfliegen Sie (*skim*) den Text auf der nächsten Seite, „Immer das gleiche." Suchen Sie Wörter, die in die folgenden Kategorien passen: **Schule, zu Hause** und **unterwegs** (*on the road*).

BEISPIEL: SCHULE: lernen...
          ZU HAUSE: kleine Geschwister...
          UNTERWEGS: viele Menschen...

von Christine Wuttke

Jeden Tag das gleiche.
Ich geh' in die Schule,
lern was—oder auch nicht.
Sehe immer die vielen Menschen,
5 die unterwegs sind,
entweder mit der Straßenbahn[1]
oder zu Fuß
oder auch mit dem Auto.
Und ich fahr lächelnd[2] an den
10 Autoschlangen[3] vorbei.
Auch wenn[4] man als Radfahrer
Mühe[5] hat, vorwärtszukommen,
ist man doch oft schneller.
In der Schule sind es dann überall
15 dieselben Erzählungen[6] der Lehrer:
Ihr lernt für euch, nicht für mich.
Und was sonst noch so typisch ist.
In den Arbeiten frage ich mich,
was das Klima[7] ist, was der Transformator ist,
20 oder was ist der Satz aus der Wassermusik.
Und ich kann mal wieder nur abgucken.[8]
Endlich wieder zu Hause,
haben die kleineren Geschwister sogar
mal das Fernsehen abgestellt[9] und spielen
25 im Kinderzimmer.
Dann geh' ich zum Klavierunterricht,[10]
zu Freunden oder in die Stadt,
und zähle die Werbeplakate[11]
an den Schaufenstern.
30 Abends im Bett denke ich dann,
wie „friedlich"[12] der Tag doch wieder war.
Immer das gleiche.

Oder ist es nicht jeden Tag was Besonderes,[13]
was man erlebt[14]?
35 Aber doch das gleiche?
Sehe ich nicht jeden Tag andere Leute
auf den Straßen?
Reden die Lehrer nicht doch immer
was anderes?
40 Schreiben sie nicht jedesmal andere Arbeiten,
in denen[15] man auch mal was weiß?
Aber es ist jeden Tag das gleiche.

*Immer das Gleiche (the same): Straßenverkehr in der
Großstadt, München*

Reading. Note: You may want to point out to students that
the spelling reform rules require capitalization of *Gleiche*,
used this way, whereas it is not capitalized in the poem.

Point out: The word *Arbeiten* (line 18) refers to an in-class
test (also called *Klassenarbeit*).

Point out: *Wassermusik* (line 20) refers to Händel's
famous instrumental music suite *Water Music*.

[1]*street car* [2]*smiling* [3]*rows of cars* [4]*Auch... Even if*
[5]*difficulty* [6]*stories* [7]*climate* [8]*to copy from someone/
cheat* [9]*haben... abgestellt turned off* [10]*piano lesson*
[11]*advertising posters* [12]*peaceful* [13]*was... something
special* [14]*experiences* [15]*which*

As you read a text, you may be tempted to look up most of the words you do not know. Before reaching for the dictionary, however, try to guess the meaning of words from the context. If you find you really must use a dictionary, consider the following:

- Many compound words are not listed in dictionaries. To discover their meaning, look up the components and determine the meaning of the compound from the definitions of its components.

- Some forms found in texts differ from those listed in dictionaries. For example, nouns and pronouns are listed in the nominative singular; verbs are listed under their infinitive forms.

- Some words have multiple meanings. Choose the correct meaning of the word based on its use in the text.

For practice in using a dictionary, do the following exercise:

- Can you figure out what **Autoschlange** means by looking up its components?
- Under which entry would you find **jeden?** And what about the phrase **ich fahr... vorbei?**
- How many different meanings can you find for the word **Satz?** Which of those meanings most closely fits the context of the word as it is used in the poem **Immer das gleiche**?
- Cross-check your definition by looking up the assumed English equivalent in the English-German section of your dictionary.
- Underline all words in the text that you do not understand. Choose five and look them up. In what form do they appear in the dictionary? How many meanings are given? Which meaning best fits the context?

Zum Text

A. Lesen Sie den Text und beantworten Sie die Fragen.

1. Wie alt mag die Autorin sein?
2. Ist sie eine Schülerin, eine Universitätsstudentin oder eine Lehrerin? Woher wissen Sie das?
3. Wo lebt die Autorin? In einer Stadt oder auf dem Land? Wie beweist (*shows*) der Text das?
4. Wie groß ist ihre Familie?

B. In most of the text the author uses declarative sentences stating what she does every day. In the last verse she uses words such as **aber** and **oder** and asks herself whether each day really is the same. What does she say about each day that might make it different, even if she still has the same routine?

Sprechen und Schreiben

Aktivität 1   Nicht immer das Gleiche!

A. Imagine that you find yourself transported to a desert island. Make two lists. The first should outline your usual routine. The second will include those things that you can or can't do, you want or don't want to do, or you need or don't need to do, now that you are on the island.

B. Compare your list with those of your classmates. Working in small groups, prepare a letter that you might put in a bottle telling of your life on the island.

Using a dictionary.
Suggestion: Assign students the task of finding the titles, call numbers, and locations of the German-English dictionaries in your library.

Aktivität 1. Suggestion: Write on the board the two categories *Zu Hause* and *Auf der Insel*. Have students brainstorm possible activities for each category.

Additional Activity. Have students write a composition about their daily routine.

poem **Aktivität 2   Ein Gedicht°**

Schreiben Sie ein Gedicht mit dem Titel „Immer das Gleiche". Tauschen Sie (*trade*) Ihr Gedicht mit dem von einem Partner / einer Partnerin aus. Lesen Sie das Gedicht vor.

Wortschatz

Tageszeiten	Times of Day
der **Morgen**	morning
der **Vormittag**	morning, before noon
der **Mittag**	noon
der **Nachmittag**	afternoon
der **Abend**	evening
die **Nacht**	night
heute Morgen	this morning
heute Nachmittag	this afternoon
morgen früh	tomorrow morning
morgen Abend	tomorrow evening
morgens	in the morning, mornings
vormittags	before noon
mittags	at noon
nachmittags	in the afternoon, afternoons
abends	in the evening, evenings
nachts	at night, nights
montags	Mondays, on Monday(s)
dienstags	Tuesdays, on Tuesday(s)
mittwochs	Wednesdays, on Wednesday(s)
donnerstags	Thursdays, on Thursday(s)
freitags	Fridays, on Friday(s)
samstags; sonnabends	Saturdays, on Saturday(s)
sonntags	Sundays, on Sunday(s)

Unterhaltung	Entertainment
das **Ballett, -e**	ballet
die **Disko, -s**	disco
in die Disko gehen	to go to a disco
das **Fernsehen**	watching television
der **Film, -e**	film

das **Kino, -s**	cinema, (movie) theater
ins Kino gehen	to go to the movies
die **Komödie, -n**	comedy
das **Konzert, -e**	concert
ins Konzert gehen	to go to a concert
der **Krimi, -s**	crime, detective, mystery film or book
die **Musik**	music
die **Oper, -n**	opera
in die Oper gehen	to go to the opera
das **Theater, -**	(stage) theater
ins Theater gehen	to go to the theater
das **Theaterstück, -e**	play (stage) drama
die **Tragödie, -n**	tragedy

Verben mit trennbaren Präfixen	Verbs with Separable Prefixes
ab•holen	to pick up (*from a place*)
an•fangen (fängt an)	to begin
an•rufen	to call up
auf•hören (mit)	to stop (*doing something*)
auf•räumen	to clean up, straighten up
auf•stehen	to get up; to stand up
auf•wachen	to wake up
aus•gehen	to go out
aus•ruhen	to rest
ein•kaufen (gehen)	to (go) shop(ping)
ein•laden (lädt ein)	to invite
ein•schlafen (schläft ein)	to fall asleep
fern•sehen (sieht fern)	to watch television
mit•kommen	to come along

mit•nehmen (nimmt mit)	to take along
vorbei•kommen	to come by
vor•haben (hat vor)	to plan (*to do*)
zurück•kommen	to return, come back

Modalverben / Modal Verbs

dürfen (darf)	to be permitted to; may
können (kann)	to be able to; can
mögen (mag)	to care for; to like
möchte	would like to
müssen (muss)	to have to; must
sollen	to be supposed to; ought, should
wollen (will)	to want to; to plan to

Uhrzeiten / Time

die Minute, -n	minute
die Sekunde, -n	second
die Stunde, -n	hour
Um wie viel Uhr?	At what time?
Wie spät ist es? / Wie viel Uhr ist es?	What time is it?
Es ist eins. / Es ist ein Uhr.	It's one o'clock.
halb: halb zwei	half: half past one, one-thirty
nach: fünf nach zwei	after: five after two
um: um zwei	at: at two
Viertel: Es ist Viertel nach/vor zwei.	quarter: It's a quarter after/to two.
vor: fünf vor zwei	to, of: five to/of two

Sonstiges / Other

frühstücken	to eat breakfast
spazieren gehen	to go for a walk
Ich gehe spazieren.	I'm going for a walk.
streichen	to paint (a wall or house)
treffen	to meet
der Bahnhof, ⸚e	train station
die Bibliothek, -en	library
das Fitnesscenter, -	gym
die Tasse, -n	cup
eine Tasse Kaffee	a cup of coffee
der Vortrag, ⸚e	lecture
die Woche, -n	week
pro Woche	per week
das Wochenende, -n	weekend
am liebsten: möchte am liebsten	would like to (do) most
doch	(*intensifying particle used with imperatives*)
früh	early
gemütlich	cozy, cozily
gewöhnlich	usual(ly)
lieber: möchte lieber	would rather
mal	(*softening particle used with imperatives*)
man	one, people, you, they
Hier darf man nicht parken.	You may not park here.
spannend	suspenseful, exciting
spät	late

LERNZIELE

Use this checklist to verify that you can now . . .

- ☐ tell the time.
- ☐ state at what time something takes place.
- ☐ describe your daily routine.
- ☐ talk about the kinds of entertainment you like.
- ☐ invite someone to an event or to go out with you.
- ☐ use verbs with separable prefixes in the present tense.
- ☐ use the modal verbs in the present tense.
- ☐ make general statements using **man.**
- ☐ make requests and recommendations, give instructions, advice, or commands using imperative forms.

Einkaufen

Was machen diese Leute?
a. Sie kaufen auf dem Markt ein.
b. Sie gehen ins Kino.

Kapitel 5. Suggestion: Approach the material in this chapter by talking about things you need and where you would buy them. Talk about what you are wearing and where you buy your clothes. Recycle vocabulary from previous chapters, e.g., **Kapitel 2,** in which shopping was first introduced. You could also talk about what you eat for certain meals and review time by mentioning when you eat. Be sure to involve students by asking questions.

Videoclips
Einkaufen: was und wo?

In diesem Kapitel

- **Themen:** Types of foods, names of stores and shops, clothes, colors
- **Grammatik:** Dative case; **wo, wohin,** and **woher; der-**words
- **Kultur:** European clothing sizes, shopping, prices, weights and measures

Alles klar?

A. Hertie ist eine Kaufhauskette (*department store chain*) in Deutschland. Was kann man alles bei Hertie kaufen? Wo findet man es?

BEISPIELE: Man kann da Computer kaufen. Computer findet man im vierten Stock.

Man kann da Bücher kaufen. Bücher findet man im Erdgeschoss.

	JA	NEIN	IN WELCHEM STOCK?
Autos	☐	☒	____
Haustiere	☐	☒	____
Lebensmittel	☒	☐	U
Pullover	☒	☐	1, 2
Schreibwaren	☒	☐	E
Schuhe	☒	☐	2
Sofas	☐	☒	____
Sportartikel	☒	☐	2
Telefonapparate	☒	☐	4
Teppiche	☒	☐	3

4 — HERTIE · Die 4. Dimension moderner Technik
- Computer/HIFI/TV/Video/CD-Center
- Foto – Optik/Filme/Fotoannahme
- Elektro Groß- und Kleingeräte
- Beleuchtung/Lampen
- Telefon-Shop/Braun-Shop

Kundendienst/Bankschalter/Kartenvorverkauf

3
Bettwaren/Bettwäsche/Frottierwaren
Gardinen/Dekostoffe/Tischwäsche
Teppiche/Orientteppiche/Bodenbeläge
Geschenkartikel/Seidenblumen
Glas/Porzellan
Haushaltswaren/Heimwerker/Autozubehör
Handarbeiten/Stoffe

2 — HERTIE TREND
Jeans-Wear
Mode-Boutiquen
Cafe „Trend"
Kinderkonfektion/Baby-Wäsche
Schuhe/Sport/Fahrräder/Camping
Friseursalon

1
Damenkonfektion/Damenhüte
Damenwäsche/Miederwaren/Bademoden
Lederbekleidung/Pelze/Trachten
Herrenkonfektion/Herrenartikel/Wäsche
Herren-Strickwaren   HERTIE-Reisebüro

E[1]
Lederwaren/Reisegepäck
Lotto/Toto/Tabak – Zeitschriften
Modewaren/Schirme/Handschuhe
Parfümerie/Kosmetik/Drogerie/Parfümerie „ORLY"
Schreibwaren/Bücher
Strümpfe/Strumpfboutique „Hot-Socks"
Uhren/Schmuck

U[2] SCHLEMMER LAND **HERTIE** Lebensmittel
GUT IST UNS NICHT GUT GENUG

Realia. Suggestion: Give students several minutes to skim the information in class, or else assign the text for homework. Have students formulate statements similar to the ones in the examples. Be sure to personalize the material by asking students what they need or would like to buy at *Hertie*. Explain that *Hertie* is a typical large department store. Ask students what differences they notice in the goods and services offered at a department store like *Hertie* and those with which they are familiar. (For example, most department stores like *Hertie* do not sell furniture, but they do include a supermarket.)

[1]E = Erdgeschoss (*ground floor*)
[2]U = Untergeschoss (*basement*)

B. Sie hören nun vier Ansagen (*announcements*) im Kaufhaus. Markieren Sie, was die Sprecher beschreiben.

1. Kosmetik <u>Kameras</u> Fahrräder
2. Schmuck Betten <u>Schuhe</u>
3. Bücher <u>Kaffeemaschinen</u> Lederjacken
4. Jeans Lampen <u>Videorecorder</u>

Wörter im Kontext

THEMA 1: Kleidungsstücke

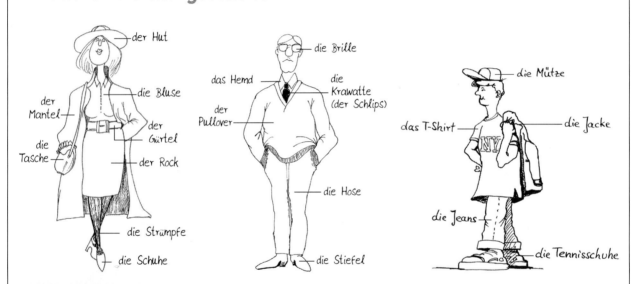

Neue Wörter

Anzug suit
Badeanzug (women's) bathing suit
Hausschuhe slippers
Kleid dress
Sakko sport coat
Schal scarf
Socken socks

Was haben Sie alles zu Hause in Ihrem Kleiderschrank (*closet*)? Kreuzen Sie an.

☐ einen **Anzug**
☐ einen **Badeanzug**
☐ **Hausschuhe**
☐ einen Jeansrock
☐ ein **Kleid**
☐ einen Parka
☐ einen **Rucksack**

☐ ein **Sakko**
☐ einen **Schal**
☐ eine Skihose
☐ **Socken**
☐ ein **Sporthemd**
☐ einen Wintermantel

Das Koffer-Memo zeigt eine Liste von Kleidungsstücken für den Urlaub.

- Welche Kleidungsstücke sind für den Winter? Welche sind für den Sommer?
- Welche Sachen auf dieser Liste tragen Sie besonders gern?
- Suchen Sie aus der Liste vier zusammengesetzte Wörter (*compounds*).

Bilden Sie nun Ihre eigenen Wörter.

Analyse. Point Out: *Trainings- und Jogginganzüge = Trainingsanzüge und Jogginganzüge.* The hyphen after *Trainings-* stands for the word shared with the following compound (*Anzüge*).

BEISPIEL: Bade- + Hose = Badehose

Bade-
Cord-
Baumwoll-
Trainings-   +
Leder-
Regen-

Anzug
Mantel
Hose
Hemd
Jacke
Schuhe

Aktivität 1   Eine Reise nach Südspanien

Sie hören ein Gespräch zwischen Bettina und Markus. Sie planen für die Semesterferien eine Reise an die Küste von Südspanien mit einer Gruppe von Freunden. Was nimmt man da mit? Sind die Aussagen richtig oder falsch?

	RICHTIG	FALSCH
1. Bettina und Markus nehmen einen Koffer und einen Rucksack mit.	☐	☒
2. Markus nimmt Shorts, ein paar T-Shirts und Jeans mit.	☐	☒
3. Bettina braucht unbedingt einen neuen Badeanzug.	☒	☐
4. Markus empfiehlt ihr, sie soll einen Bikini in Spanien kaufen.	☐	☒
5. Markus hat einen besonderen Gürtel für sein Geld.	☒	☐
6. Bettina steckt ihr Geld in die Schuhe.	☒	☐

Aktivität 2   Was tragen Sie gewöhnlich?

Sagen Sie, was Sie in den folgenden Situationen tragen.

BEISPIEL: Ich trage gewöhnlich Jeans und ein T-Shirt zur Uni. Zur Arbeit trage ich ein Sporthemd, eine Hose und ein Sakko.

zur Arbeit
zur Uni
im Winter
im Urlaub auf Hawaii
zu einem Rockkonzert
zu Hause
auf einer Fete
zu einer Hochzeit
??

einen Anzug
einen Badeanzug
ein Kleid
ein Abendkleid
einen Wintermantel
Jeans
ein T-Shirt
ein Sporthemd
eine Hose
ein Sakko
??

Koffer-Memo[1]

Für den Urlaub—
was nimmt man mit?

☐ T-Shirts	**€5,-**
☐ Shorts	**€6,-**
☐ Cordhosen	**€10,-**
☐ Regenmantel	**€9,-**
☐ Sandalen	**€8,-**
☐ Badeanzug	**€7,-**
☐ Badehose	**€6,-**
☐ Blusen	**€8,-**
☐ Röcke	**€9,-**
☐ Kleider	**€12,-**
☐ Hemden	**€7,-**
☐ Sweatshirts	**€8,-**
☐ Baumwollhosen	**€9,-**
☐ Trainings- und Jogginganzüge	**€16,-**
☐ Sportschuhe	**€7,-**
☐ Unterwäsche	**€3,-**
☐ Jacke	**€15,-**
☐ Handschuhe	**€11,-**
☐ Stiefel	**€23,-**
☐ Pullover	**€9,-**
☐ Mütze	**€5,-**

[1]*suitcase*

Aktivität 2. Suggestion: Discuss what students are wearing in class that day.

The impersonal expression **es gibt** means *there is* or *there are.* It can also be used to say where you can get something. The object of **es gibt** is always in the accusative case.

Es gibt in dieser Stadt einen Markt.	*There is a market in this town. (It exists.)*
Wo gibt es schicke Blusen?	*Where can you get stylish blouses?*

Use the preposition **bei** and the name of the place to say where you can get something.

Blusen gibt es **bei** Gisie.	*You can get blouses at Gisie's (shop).*

Schicke Blusen
Wo?
bei
Gisie
Papendiek 29

Aktivität 3. Note: *clothing*
Bekleidung is a collective noun. It is not generally found in the plural or with the indefinite article. To indicate one or more particular items of clothing, German uses the term *Kleidungsstück.*

Aktivität 3   Ich brauche neue Bekleidung.°

Was brauchen Sie, und wo gibt es das? Was kostet das?

BEISPIEL: s1: Ich brauche dringend einen Anzug. Wo gibt es hier Anzüge?
s2: Anzüge gibt es bei Strauss.
s1: Weißt du, wie viel ein Anzug da kostet?
s2: Es gibt Anzüge für 48 Euro.

Pullover (Pulli)
Stiefel
Jacke
Hose
Bluse
Sakko
Rock
Anzug
??

STRAUSS FÜR MÄNNER
Ausstatter-Anzüge, Sakkos, Hosen und Hemden sind jetzt enorm reduziert.

HERREN-ANZÜGE 3-teilig mit Weste.
Schurwolle 198.- 48.-

HERREN-ANZÜGE sportliche Modelle in normalen, schlanken und Spezial-Größen 119.- 98.- 48.-

HERREN-SAKKOS von elegant bis sportlich.
Viele Modelle 78.- 58.- 28.-

SPORTSWEAR-JACKEN 80.- 65.- 38.-

FLANELL-STRETCHHOSEN
Schurwolle 48.- 38.- 18.-

MARKEN-HEMDEN 38.- 28.- 18.-

FLANELL-HEMDEN 20.- 12.-

HERREN-STRICKPULLOVER
mit Cashmere 32.- 28.- 22.-

und auf alle Artikel dieser Anzeige erhalten Sie zusätzlich
20% Rabatt

HERREN-LEDERSCHUHE
klassisch 68.- 38.-

Bonn In der Sürst 1 · Bad Godesberg Koblenzer Straße 63

Strauss 1902
your private innovation
www.strauss1902.de

SONDERANGEBOTE
IN DER
HERRENABTEILUNG!!

ab €48,-

Modellbeispiel
Stiefel reduziert
ab €49,-

Moon Boots und gefütterte Gummistiefel ab €20,-

Schuhkauf =
ohne Parkprobleme

Otten & Leenders
Ihr Schuhzentrum
in Kleve
Mittelweg 48

Aktivität 4   Koffer packen!°

Let's pack our bags!

Spielen Sie in Gruppen von vier bis fünf Personen. So spielt man es:

BEISPIEL: s1: Ich packe fünf Bikinis in meinen Koffer.
s2: Ich packe fünf Bikinis und Sportschuhe in meinen Koffer.
s3: Ich packe fünf Bikinis, Sportschuhe und Ledersandalen in meinen Koffer.

Wer etwas vergisst (*forgets*) oder falsch sagt, scheidet aus (*drops out*).

THEMA 2: Beim Einkaufen im Kaufhaus

Bernd Thalhofer geht einkaufen, denn er braucht ein paar neue Hemden.

VERKÄUFER: Bitte schön. Kann ich Ihnen **helfen?**

BERND: Ich brauche ein paar neue **Sporthemden.**

VERKÄUFER: Welche **Größe** brauchen Sie?

BERND: Größe 42.

VERKÄUFER: Und welche **Farbe?**

BERND: Grün oder blau.

VERKÄUFER: **Wie gefällt Ihnen dieses gestreifte** Hemd in Marineblau? Sehr dezent (*tasteful*) und **modisch.**

BERND: Ich finde, **die Farbe steht mir** nicht. Haben Sie das in Hellblau?

VERKÄUFER: Ja, hier ist ein Hemd in Hellblau.

BERND: Ist das aus Baumwolle oder Synthetik?

VERKÄUFER: Das ist 100 Prozent Baumwolle. Möchten Sie es **anprobieren?**

BERND: Nein, das ist nicht **nötig.** Größe 42 **passt** mir bestimmt. Wie viel kostet dieses Hemd?

Point Out: After the preposition *in,* colors are capitalized, e.g., *ein Hemd in Hellblau.*

VERKÄUFER: 40 Euro.

BERND: Gut. Ich nehme drei Hemden.

VERKÄUFER: **Alle** in Hellblau?

BERND: Nein, geben Sie mir bitte zwei in Blau und ein Hemd in Weiß.

VERKÄUFER: **Das macht zusammen** 120 Euro. Bitte **zahlen** Sie vorne an der **Kasse!**

BERND: Danke schön.

VERKÄUFER: Bitte sehr.

Beim Einkaufen im Kaufhaus. **Suggestion:** Begin by looking at the picture. What is happening? Where can you buy a shirt? Introduce new words using pictures, mime, and classroom situations. After students have heard the dialogue and then read it, assign pairs to role-play it.

Neue Wörter

helfen (helfen) help
Größe size
Farbe color
Wie gefällt Ihnen...? How do you like...?
dieses this
modisch fashionable
Die Farbe steht mir. The color looks good on me.
anprobieren (anprobieren) try on
nötig necessary
passt (passen) fits
das macht zusammen all together
zahlen (zahlen) pay
Kasse cashier, check-out

kariert

gestreift

weiß
rot
orange
gelb
grün
blau
lila
beige
braun
grau
schwarz

Aktivität 5   Im Kaufhaus

Ergänzen Sie die fehlenden Informationen aus dem Dialog im Thema 2.

1. Der Kunde braucht _____.
2. Der Verkäufer möchte _____ und _____ wissen.
3. Der Kunde braucht _____ 42.
4. Größe 42 _____ ihm.
5. Das Hemd in Marineblau _____ ihm nicht.
6. Das Hemd ist aus _____.
7. Der Kunde _____ 120 Euro für drei Hemden.

KULTURTIPP

European sizes vary greatly from American sizes.

Für Damen: Kleider, Mäntel, Jacken, Blusen

in USA	6	8	10	12	14	16
in Deutschland	34	36	38	40	42	44

Für Herren: Mäntel, Anzüge, Sakkos

in USA	36	38	40	42	44
in Deutschland	46	48	50	52	54

Herrenhemden

in USA	14	14½	15	15½	16	16½
in Deutschland	36	37	38	39	40	42

Schuhgrößen für Damen

in USA	5½	6½	7½	8½	9½	10½	11½	12½
in Deutschland	36	37	38/39	39/40	41	42	43/44	44/45

Schuhgrößen für Herren

in USA	6½	7½	8½	9½	10½	11½	12½	13½
in Deutschland	39/40	41	42	43/44	44/45	46	47	48/49

Kleine Preise auch für große Größen! Tolle Angebote,[1] wie z.B. sportliche Pullover in modischen Dessins

ab **€50,-**

[1]Tolle... *great deals*

In many stores you will also find the sizes S, M, L, and XL (small, medium, large, and extra-large) for clothing. In addition, shoes are sometimes labeled with American sizes.

Kulturtipp. Suggestion: Have students figure out their German clothing and shoe sizes. Use the information in a brief listening activity by asking questions such as *Wer hat Schuhgröße 42?* or *Wer hat Kleidergröße 36?* Students raise their hands to respond when an item applies to them.

Aktivität 6. Suggestion: Play each dialogue once so students get the gist of it. Then play each one a second time while students complete the chart. Check students' responses by calling on individuals to report.

Aktivität 6:   Gespräche im Geschäft

Was brauchen die Leute? In welcher Größe und in welcher Farbe? Ergänzen Sie die Tabelle.

	WAS?	IN WELCHER GRÖSSE?	IN WELCHER FARBE?
Dialog 1	Schuhe	44	Schwarz
Dialog 2	Hose	38	Blauweiß
Dialog 3	Bluse	38	Rot
Dialog 4	Wintermantel	44	Dunkelblau

SPRACHTIPP

To talk about how clothing fits, how it looks, and whether you like it, you can use the following expressions.

Gefällt Ihnen dieses Hemd?	*Do you like this shirt?*
Ja, es **gefällt mir.**	*Yes, I like it.*
Größe 42 **passt ihr** bestimmt.	*Size 42 will fit her for sure.*
Das Hemd **steht dir** gut.	*The shirt looks good on you.*

Aktivität 7 Wer trägt was?

Finden Sie folgende Personen und bilden Sie Fragen. Wer **ja** sagt muss rechts unterschreiben (*sign*).

BEISPIEL: Wer trägt gern rot?
Frage: Trägst du gern rot?

FRAGE UNTERSCHRIFT

1. Wessen (*Whose*) Lieblingsfarbe ist lila? _____

2. Wem steht Blau sehr gut? _____

3. Wem steht Grün nicht gut? _____

4. Wer trägt gern bunte (*colorful*) Sachen? _____

5. Wer trägt gern gestreifte oder karierte Sachen? _____

6. Wer trägt Größe 39 in Hemden oder Größe 10 in Blusen? _____

7. Wer braucht die Schuhgröße 42? _____

Aktivität 8 Wer trägt was?

Beschreiben Sie, was und welche Farben jemand in Ihrem Deutschkurs trägt. Sagen Sie den Namen der Person nicht. Die anderen im Kurs müssen erraten (*guess*), wer das ist.

BEISPIEL: Diese Person trägt eine Bluse. Die Bluse ist rotweiß gestreift. Sie trägt auch Jeans; die sind natürlich blau. Und ihre Schuhe sind, hm, lila. Wer ist das? —Das ist Winona.

Aktivität 9 Ein Gespräch

Schritt 1: Benutzen Sie die Wörter und Ausdrücke im Kasten und schreiben Sie ein Gespräch zwischen einem Verkäufer / einer Verkäuferin und einem Kunden / einer Kundin.

Aktivität 8. Suggestion: The day before you plan on doing this activity, tell students to come to class the next day wearing something unusual.

Hier klicken!

Weiteres zum Thema Einkaufen finden Sie bei **Deutsch: Na klar!** im World-Wide-Web unter www.mhhe.com/dnk.

Farbe
Ich möchte gern _____.
kosten
Größe
mir zu groß
_____ Euro
passt mir (nicht)
preiswert
Wie gefällt Ihnen _____?
Bitte sehr.
mir zu klein
mir zu teuer
anprobieren
Ich brauche _____.
steht mir (nicht)
Das macht zusammen _____.
Ich nehme _____.
Danke schön.

Schritt 2: Spielen Sie jetzt das Gespräch mit einem Partner / einer Partnerin.

SPRACHTIPP

The dative case is used with adjectives, sometimes in conjunction with the adverb **zu** (*too*).

300 Euro für dieses Kleid? Das ist **mir zu teuer.**

300 euros for this dress? That's too expensive (for me).

THEMA 3: Lebensmittel

Jeden Tag bis 20 Uhr! Samstag immer bis 16 Uhr!

Südafrikanische Trauben blau Handelskl. I, kg

MultiKNÜLLER €2,50

TopCi Apfelsaft klar oder naturtrüb 100 % Fruchtgehalt, ohne Zuckerzusatz, Liter-Flasche

MultiKNÜLLER €1,00 ohne Pfand
€1,50 incl.0,30 DM Pfand

Zyprische Frühkartoffeln Speise- und Salatware Handelsklasse I, 1,5-kg-Netz

MultiKNÜLLER €1,75

In Selbstbedienung: Frische Truthahn-Oberkeulen kg

MultiKNÜLLER €3,50

„Herta" Schinken-aufschnitt in den Sorten: Hawaii- oder Country-Schinken, 100 g

MultiKNÜLLER €1,50

Bauer Frucht-joghurt 3,5 % Fett, versch. Sorten, 250-g-Becher

MultiKNÜLLER €-,35

Dr. Oetker „Vitalis Müsli" verschiedene Sorten, 750-g-Packung

MultiKNÜLLER €2,75

Zarter Gulasch Rind und Schwein gemischt, kg

MultiKNÜLLER €4,99

Deutsche Hähnchen bratfertig, gefroren, Handelskl. A, 950-g-Stück

Multi MINI DAUER-TIEF-PREIS €1,49

Holländischer Westberg Schnittkäse 45 % Fett i. Tr., milder, leicht nußartiger Geschmack, 100 g am Stück

MultiKNÜLLER €-,50

Lebensmittel. Suggestion: Use pictures to help introduce the vocabulary, or lead students through the ad, and have them guess the meaning of the new vocabulary.

Suggestion: Tell your students the current exchange rate. Are the prices higher or lower than they expect?

A. In welche Kategorie gehört das? Ordnen Sie die Wörter einer passenden Kategorie auf der nächsten Seite zu.

Äpfel	**Brötchen**	**Karotten**
Apfelsaft	**Butter**	Kartoffeln
Apfelstrudel	**Cola**	**Käse**
Aufschnitt	**Eier**	**Kekse**
Bananen	**Eis**	Knäckebrot
Bier	**Erdbeeren**	Kräutertee
Blumenkohl	**Gurken**	**Kuchen**
Brokkoli	**Hähnchen**	**Make-up**
Brot	**Joghurt**	**Milch**

Mineralwasser	Schinken	Truthahn
Müsli	Schnitzel	Vollkornbrot
Pfeffer	Schweinefleisch	Wasser
Rasiercreme	Shampoo	Weintrauben
Rindfleisch	Steak	Wurst
Rohmilch	Tee	Zahnpasta
Saft	Toilettenpapier	Zucker
Salz	Tomaten	

Thema 3. Suggestion: Interview different students. Ask them
- what kinds of fruits and vegetables they like to eat.
- what kinds of meat products they like to eat (or whether they are vegetarians).
- what kinds of beverages they usually buy.

BACKWAREN: Brot, . . . Apfelstrudel, Brötchen, Kekse, Knäckebrot, Kuchen

OBST UND GEMÜSE: Kartoffeln, . . . Äpfel, Bananen, Blumenkohl, Brokkoli, Erdbeeren, Gurken, Karotten, Tomaten, Weintrauben

BIOKOST (*organic foods*): Vollkornbrot, . . . Kräutertee, Müsli, Rohmilch

FLEISCHWAREN: Steak, . . . Aufschnitt, Hähnchen, Rindfleisch, Schinken, Schnitzel, Truthahn, Wurst

GETRÄNKE: Cola, . . . Apfelsaft, Bier, Mineralwasser, Saft, Tee, Wasser

ANDERE LEBENSMITTEL: Pfeffer, . . . Butter, Eier, Eis, Joghurt, Käse, Milch, Salz, Tee, Zucker

TOILETTENARTIKEL: Shampoo, . . . Make-up, Rasiercreme, Toilettenpapier, Zahnpasta

B. Mini-Umfrage: Was essen Sie gewöhnlich zum **Frühstück**? Zum **Mittagessen**? Zum **Abendessen**?

Note: Point out the differences between traditional American meals and traditional German meals.

KULTURTIPP

Viele Deutsche kaufen heute in großen, modernen **Supermärkten** ein. Es gibt aber immer noch viele Spezialgeschäfte, besonders in kleinen Städten, wie die **Metzgerei**, die **Bäckerei**, die **Konditorei**, den **Getränkeladen** und den **Obst- und Gemüsestand** auf dem Markt. **Medikamente** auf Rezept kann man in Deutschland nicht in einer **Drogerie** kaufen, sondern nur in einer **Apotheke**. Im **Bioladen** gibt es Produkte, die nicht mit chemischen Mitteln behandelt (*treated*) sind.

Neue Wörter

Obst fruit
Gemüse vegetables
Fleisch meat
Getränke beverages

Äpfel apples
Aufschnitt cold cuts
Blumenkohl cauliflower
Brot bread
Brötchen roll
Eier eggs
Eis ice cream; ice
Erdbeeren strawberries
Gurken cucumbers
Hähnchen chicken
Kartoffeln potatoes
Käse cheese
Kekse cookies
Kuchen cake
Rasiercreme shaving cream
Rindfleisch beef
Saft juice
Schinken ham
Schnitzel cutlet
Schweinefleisch pork
Truthahn turkey
Wasser water
Weintrauben grapes
Wurst sausage
Zahnpasta toothpaste
Zucker sugar

frisch fresh
gefroren frozen
zart tender

Metzgerei butcher shop
Konditorei pastry shop
Laden store
Drogerie toiletries and sundries store
Apotheke pharmacy
Bioladen natural foods store

Sprachtipp. Point Out: The American pound is 454 grams, whereas the metric pound is 500 grams. One liter is slightly more than a quart. One U.S. gallon = 3.78 liters. Normally prices are written with a comma separating *Euro* and *Cents*.

Suggestion: Practice the metric system and reading prices by asking students how much the items in the ads in *Thema 3* cost in various quantities.

SPRACHTIPP

The metric system is used in German-speaking countries. The following abbreviations for weights and measures are commonly used:

1 kg = 1 Kilogramm = 1000 Gramm = 2 Pfund

500 g = 500 Gramm = 1 Pfund

1000 ml = 1000 Milliliter

0,75 l = 0,75 Liter

1 l = 1 Liter

Other abbreviations used are:

Kl. I = Klasse I (*top quality*)

Stck. = Stück (*piece*)

Aktivität 10. Suggestion: Make sure students understand how to work with the chart: Place check marks under correct store and write in what the item is and its price. Play each dialogue once. Then let students listen a second time, pausing after each dialogue to let them write down the information.

Aktivität 10 Wo? Was? Wie viel?

Sie hören drei Dialoge: in einer Bäckerei, auf dem Markt und in einer Metzgerei. Kreuzen Sie das richtige Geschäft an. Ergänzen Sie die Tabelle.

	MARKT	BÄCKEREI	METZGEREI	WAS?	PREIS?
Dialog 1			X	Würstchen Aufschnitt	€8,50
Dialog 2		X		Brötchen Schwarzbrot	€3,20
Dialog 3	X			Erdbeeren Tomaten	€4,20

SPRACHTIPP

The following words will help you organize your writing and help you put statements in order of occurrence.

zuerst first

deshalb therefore

dann then

zuletzt finally

Using these connectors will enable you to narrate effectively in German. Remember that if you begin your sentence with one of these connectors, your verb will immediately follow it.

Aktivität 11　Einkaufstag für Jutta

Jutta muss einkaufen. Sie gibt nämlich eine Party. Schreiben Sie einen Text zu jedem Bild. Benutzen Sie Elemente aus beiden Spalten (*columns*) unten.

　　So beginnt die Geschichte:

　　Jutta gibt am Wochenende eine Party. Deshalb geht sie heute
　　　einkaufen...

Dort kauft sie...	Obst und Gemüse—alles ganz frisch.
Zuletzt geht sie...	Brot, Brötchen und Käsekuchen.
Zuerst geht sie...	und geht nach Hause.
Da gibt es...	zur Bäckerei.
Dann geht sie...	zum Lebensmittelgeschäft.
Jutta braucht auch...	zur Metzgerei.
Deshalb geht sie auch...	Würstchen zum Grillen.
Jetzt hat sie alles...	Kaffee, Zucker, Milch und Käse.
In der Bäckerei kauft sie...	zum Markt.
Am Obst- und Gemüsestand	Blumenkohl und Kartoffeln.
kauft sie...	Äpfel, Bananen und
	Weintrauben—alles ganz frisch.

Aktivität 11. Suggestion: Have students work in pairs. They should first scan the pictures to see where Jutta is going. Review the meaning of vocabulary: *zuerst, zuletzt, deshalb, jetzt*. Students match up sentence halves and then match sentences and pictures. Call on pairs to supply a description for each picture, thereby creating a *Bildgeschichte*.

Follow-up: Have students supply a description for each picture without referring to a written text.

Aktivität 12. Suggestion: Have students work in pairs. They should first scan the ads and then preview vocabulary with the whole group. Set a time limit of about five minutes to draw up the lists. Spot-check several pairs by asking *Was kaufen Sie mit Ihren 10 Euro?*

Aktivität 12   Preiswert einkaufen!

Stellen Sie sich vor, Sie haben nur 10 Euro für Essen und Trinken übrig und müssen damit ein ganzes Wochenende auskommen. Wählen Sie Waren aus den Anzeigen (*ads*) aus. Vergleichen Sie (*compare*) Ihre Listen im Plenum.

BEISPIEL: Wir kaufen ein Bauernbrot für €–,90;
200 g Kalbsleberwurst für €–, 65;
1 Kilo Tomaten für €1,95 und eine
Schwarzwälder Kirschtorte für €4,95.

[1]*farmer's bread*   [2]*pumpernickel*   [3]*whole food three-grain*   [4]*Schwarzwälder. . . Black Forest cherry torte*

Aktivität 13. Note: This interactive activity allows for personal choices. Review the vocabulary first, then have students do the activity in pairs. Call on several pairs to role-play a dialogue for the whole class, using the outline on the next page.

Aktivität 13   Ein Menü für eine Party

A. Sie planen mit einem Freund / einer Freundin ein Menü für eine Party am Wochenende. Was wollen Sie servieren? Hier sind einige Vorschläge (*suggestions*). Wählen Sie Dinge aus jeder Gruppe aus.

zum Essen: Würstchen, Steaks, Hamburger, Kartoffelsalat, Kartoffelchips, Pommes frites, Salat, Gemüse, ??

zum Nachtisch: Eis, Pudding, frische Erdbeeren, Käsekuchen, ??

zum Trinken: Mineralwasser (Sprudel), Bier, Wein, Limonade, ??

S1	S2
1. Wollen wir _____ grillen?	**2a.** Gut. Machen wir _____ mit _____ und _____. **b.** Nein, ich möchte lieber _____ mit _____ und _____.
3a. Und zum Nachtisch? **b.** Na gut, und _____?	**4.** _____.Was sollen wir dazu trinken?
5. _____.	**6a.** Na, gut. **b.** Also, _____ schmeckt doch nicht dazu. Ich schlage vor (*suggest*), wir trinken _____.

B. Tragen Sie Ihre Partypläne im Plenum vor.

Grammatik im Kontext

The Dative Case°

Der Dativ

As you have learned, the nominative case is the case of the subject; the accusative case is used for direct objects and with a number of prepositions. These cases are signalled by special endings of articles and possessive adjectives, as well as by different forms for personal pronouns.

NOMINATIVE		ACCUSATIVE
Subject		*Direct Object*
Wer	braucht	einen Mantel?
Uwe	braucht	einen Mantel.

NOMINATIVE		ACCUSATIVE
Subject		*Prepositional Object*
Der Mantel	ist	für Uwe.

The dative case, like the accusative, serves several distinct functions; it is used primarily:

- for indirect objects (indicating the person to/for whom something is done)
- with certain verbs
- with specific prepositions

As with the other cases, special forms of pronouns and endings for articles and possessive adjectives signal the dative case. The dative object answers the question **wem?** (*whom?, to/for whom?*).

Wem zeigt der Verkäufer drei Ringe?	**To whom** is the salesman showing three rings?
Er zeigt sie **Herrn Ebert.**	He's showing them to **Mr. Ebert.**
Wem kauft Herr Ebert einen Ring?	**For whom** is Mr. Ebert buying a ring?
Er kauft ihn **seiner Frau.**	He's buying it for **his wife.**

Analyse. Suggestion: Review accusative case endings and personal pronouns before approaching dative objects through the **Analyse.** Do this as a whole group.

Personal Pronouns in the Dative

The following chart shows the personal pronouns in the dative case.

NOMINATIVE	DATIVE		NOMINATIVE	DATIVE	
ich	**mir**	*to/for me*	wir	**uns**	*to/for us*
du	**dir**	*to/for you (informal)*	ihr	**euch**	*to/for you (informal)*
Sie	**Ihnen**	*to/for you (formal)*	Sie	**Ihnen**	*to/for you (formal)*
er	**ihm**	*to/for him; to/for it*			
sie	**ihr**	*to/for her; to/for it*	sie	**ihnen**	*to/for them*
es	**ihm**	*to/for it*			

ANALYSE

Scan the following ads.

- Find the dative object pronouns. What are the verbs that require the dative to be used?
- What is the nominative form of each of the dative pronouns?

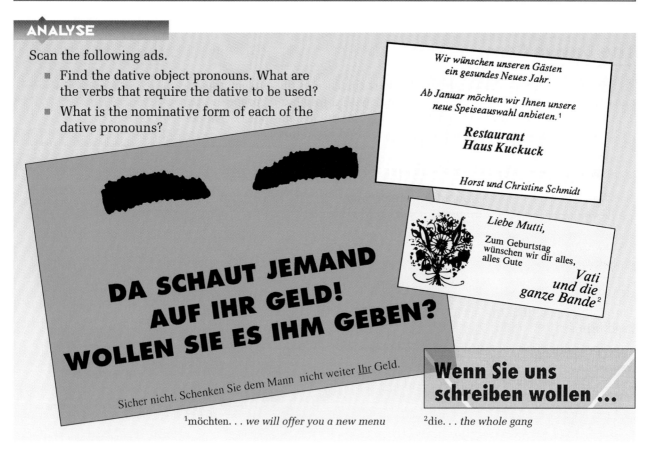

Wir wünschen unseren Gästen
ein gesundes Neues Jahr.

Ab Januar möchten wir Ihnen unsere
neue Speiseauswahl anbieten.[1]

**Restaurant
Haus Kuckuck**

Horst und Christine Schmidt

Liebe Mutti,
Zum Geburtstag
wünschen wir dir alles,
alles Gute
*Vati
und die
ganze Bande*[2]

DA SCHAUT JEMAND
AUF IHR GELD!
WOLLEN SIE ES IHM GEBEN?

Sicher nicht. Schenken Sie dem Mann nicht weiter <u>Ihr</u> Geld.

**Wenn Sie uns
schreiben wollen ...**

[1]möchten. . . *we will offer you a new menu*   [2]die. . . *the whole gang*

Übung I Hallo, wie geht's?

Ergänzen Sie die fehlenden Personalpronomen im Dativ.

mir	ihm	uns	ihnen
dir	ihr	euch	Ihnen

1. A: Hallo, Brigitte, wie geht es _____?
   B: Danke, es geht _____ gut.
   A: Und wie geht's deinem Freund?
   B: Ach, es geht _____ nicht besonders gut. Er ist sauer. Sein neues Auto ist schon kaputt.
   A: Das tut _____ aber Leid.

2. C: Hallo, Petra und Christoph. Na, wie geht es _____ denn?
   D: Danke, es geht _____ gut.
   C: Und was machen die Kinder?
   D: Ach, es geht _____ immer viel zu gut.

3. E: Guten Tag, Herr Professor Distelmeier.
   F: Guten Tag, Herr Liederlich. Wie geht es _____?
   E: Es geht _____ schlecht. Meine Tante Adelgunde hat einen Nervenzusammenbruch, auf Tahiti.
   F: Das tut _____ Leid. Was kann ich für Ihre Tante machen?
   E: Nichts. Aber ich muss _____ helfen. Ich muss sofort nach Tahiti. Übrigens, ... meine Semesterarbeit ist nicht fertig. Kann ich sie einen Monat später einhändigen (*turn in*)? Sie wissen, meine Tante...
   F: Ihre Tante ist _____ EGAL! Ich gebe _____ zwei extra Tage für die Semesterarbeit. Auf Wiedersehen!

Articles and Possessive Adjectives in the Dative

The following chart shows the dative endings for articles and possessive adjectives. Note that the masculine and neuter endings are identical.

MASCULINE	NEUTER	FEMININE	PLURAL
dem (k)ein**em** } Mann mein**em** **dem** Kunden	dem (k)ein**em** } Kind mein**em**	der (k)ein**er** } Frau mein**er**	den } Männern keinen } Frauen mein**en** } Kindern **den** Kunden

Geben Sie Ihrem Haar einen modischen Kick...

Note:

- Nouns in the dative singular do not normally take an ending, except for the special masculine nouns that take an **-n** or **-en** in the accusative as well (Kapitel 2).

Nominative	Accusative	Dative
der Kunde	den Kunde**n**	dem Kunde**n**
der Student	den Student**en**	dem Student**en**

- In the dative plural, all nouns add **-n** to the plural ending, unless the plural already ends in **-n,** except for a few nouns whose plural ends in **-s.**

	Plural	Dative Plural
	die Männer	den Männer**n**
	die Frauen	den Frauen
but:	die Autos	den Autos
	die Handys	den Handys

The Dative Case for Indirect Objects

As in English, many German verbs take both a direct object and an indirect object. The direct object, in the accusative, will usually be a thing; the indirect object, in the dative, will normally be a person.

		DATIVE indirect object	ACCUSATIVE direct object
Michael	schenkt	**seiner Freundin**	einen Ring.
Der Verkäufer	zeigt	**ihm**	drei Ringe.
Der Kunde	gibt	**dem Verkäufer**	seine Scheckkarte.

Following are examples of verbs that take two objects in German:

empfehlen (empfiehlt)	to recommend
geben (gibt)	to give
glauben	to believe
kaufen	to buy
leihen	to lend, borrow
sagen	to tell, say
schenken	to give as a gift
schicken	to send
schreiben	to write
wünschen	to wish
zeigen	to show

Note: German does not distinguish between "lend" and "borrow." Both English verbs are rendered into German by *leihen.* Thus, *Ich leihe dir Geld.* I'll lend you some money. *Ich leihe mir Geld.* I'm borrowing some money (for myself).

Position of Dative and Accusative Objects

Ich gebe **meinem Bruder ein Handy** zum Geburtstag.

I'm giving my brother a cell phone for his birthday.

Ich gebe **es meinem Bruder.**

I'm giving it (the cell phone) to my brother.

Wann gibst du **es ihm?**

When are you giving it to him?

Note:

- The dative object precedes the accusative object when the accusative object is a noun.
- The dative object follows the accusative object when the direct object (accusative) is a pronoun.

Übung 2   Situationen im Alltag

Sie hören fünf Dialoge. Kreuzen Sie für jeden Dialog den Satz an, der zu dem Thema passt.

1. Hans braucht unbedingt etwas Geld.
   - ☒ Sein Freund kann ihm nichts leihen.
   - ☐ Sein Freund gibt ihm einen Scheck.
2. Zwei Studentinnen brauchen Hilfe.
   - ☐ Ein Freund gibt ihnen etwas Geld.
   - ☒ Ein Herr zeigt ihnen den Weg zum Café.
3. Helmut hat Geburtstag.
   - ☒ Marianne schreibt ihm eine Karte.
   - ☐ Marianne schenkt ihm eine CD.
4. Eine Studentin erzählt einem Studenten über ihren Tagesablauf.
   - ☒ Sie empfiehlt ihm Yoga.
   - ☐ Sie hat keine Zeit für Yoga.
5. Achim sagt, er lebt nur von Brot und Wasser.
   - ☐ Er hat kein Geld.
   - ☒ Man kann ihm nicht alles glauben, was er sagt.

Übung 2. Suggestion: Have students listen to each mini-dialogue in succession. Expand the questions about each situation. Incorporate the dative verbs in as many questions as possible. Ask students to summarize each dialogue orally.

Wer, wen, or wem?

Here is a summary of the interrogative pronouns that ask about a person in the nominative, accusative, and dative cases.

Wer hat morgen Geburtstag?

Who has a birthday tomorrow?

Wen lädst du ein?

Whom are you inviting?

Wem schenkst du den Kalender?

To whom are you giving the calendar?

Wem leihst du nie Geld?

(To) whom do you never lend any money?

NOMINATIVE	ACCUSATIVE	DATIVE
wer (*who*)	**wen** (*whom*)	**wem** (*to/for whom*)

Übung 3   Wer, wen oder wem?

Formulate questions that would be answered by the underlined word or words in each statement.

BEISPIEL: Ulrike schenkt <u>ihrem Bruder</u> eine Jacke zum Geburtstag.
Wem schenkt Ulrike eine Jacke zum Geburtstag?

1. <u>Heike</u> schenkt ihrem Bruder einen Wecker zum Geburtstag.
2. Markus lädt <u>seine Schwester</u> nicht zum Geburtstag ein! (Nicht sehr nett!)
3. Antje leiht <u>ihrer Freundin</u> 100 Euro für die Party am Wochenende.
4. Ich rufe <u>meine Eltern</u> immer am Wochenende an.
5. Der Professor zeigt <u>den Studenten</u> eine Landkarte von Deutschland.
6. Der Verkäufer empfiehlt <u>der Kundin</u> einen preiswerten Computer.
7. <u>Die Kundin</u> muss an der Kasse zahlen.

Übung 4   So ein Stress!

Horst hat eine große Familie und viele Freunde. Wem schenkt Horst was?

BEISPIEL: Sein Onkel hört gern klassische Musik.
a. Er schenkt seinem Onkel ein Musikvideo.
b. Er schenkt ihm ein Musikvideo.

1. Seine Oma fährt allein nach Hawaii.
2. Sein Bruder ist sportlich sehr aktiv. Sein Wagen ist kaputt. Er hat kein Geld.
3. Sein Vetter Klaus findet Fische interessant.
4. Seine Schwester Heike telefoniert pausenlos.
5. Seine Freundin Ute will nach Südspanien reisen.
6. Seine Tante Adelgunde liebt exzentrische Mode.
7. Sein Vater hat schon alles.
8. Seine Mutter trinkt morgens, mittags und abends Kaffee.
9. Seine Eltern planen eine Reise nach Spanien.

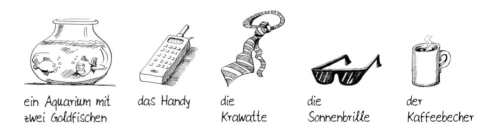

ein Aquarium mit zwei Goldfischen   das Handy   die Krawatte   die Sonnenbrille   der Kaffeebecher

der Reiseführer   die Inline-Skates   der Rucksack   der Hut

Verbs with a Dative Object Only

A number of common German verbs always take an object in the dative case. Note that these dative objects usually refer to people.

danken	Ich **danke** dir für die Karte.	*I thank you for the card.*
gefallen	Wie **gefällt** Ihnen dieses Hemd?	*How do you like this shirt?**
gehören	Der Mercedes **gehört** meinem Bruder.	*The Mercedes belongs to my brother.*
helfen	Der Verkäufer **hilft** dem Kunden.	*The salesperson is helping the customer.*
passen	Größe 48 **passt** mir bestimmt.	*Size 48 will surely fit me.*
stehen	Das Kleid **steht** dir gut.	*The dress looks good on you.*

A number of frequently used idiomatic expressions also require dative objects.

Wie geht es **dir?**	*How are you?*
Das tut **mir** Leid.	*I'm sorry.*
Das ist **mir** egal.	*I don't care.*

Verbs that take only a dative object are indicated in the vocabulary lists of this book as follows: (+ *dat.*)

Übung 5   Ein schwieriger° Kunde

difficult

Ergänzen Sie den Dialog mit passenden Verben und Pronomen im Dativ. Suchen Sie passende Verben aus der folgenden Liste:

danken, empfehlen, gefallen (gefällt), helfen, Leid tun, passen, stehen, (zu) teuer sein, zeigen.

Übung 5. Suggestion: Review the meanings of the verbs first. Then let students work in pairs to complete the dialogue. Have several pairs role-play the completed dialogue for the class.

VERKÄUFER: Kann ich _____^{1} _____^{2}? (*help you*)

KUNDE: Ja. Ich brauche ein Geschenk für meine Freundin. Können Sie _____^{3} vielleicht etwas _____^{4}? (*recommend to me*)

VERKÄUFER: Eine Bluse vielleicht?

KUNDE: _____^{5} Sie _____^{6} bitte eine Bluse in Größe 50. (*Show me*)

VERKÄUFER: Größe 50? Ist das nicht zu groß?

KUNDE: Ich glaube, Größe 50 _____^{7} _____^{8} bestimmt. (*fits her*)

VERKÄUFER: Hier habe ich eine elegante Seidenbluse. In Schwarz.

KUNDE: Nein, Schwarz _____^{9} _____^{10} nicht. (*look good on her*)

VERKÄUFER: Wie _____^{11} _____^{12} diese Bluse in Lila? (*do you like*)

KUNDE: Schrecklich. Diese Farbe _____^{13} _____^{14} überhaupt nicht. (*I like*)

VERKÄUFER: Hier habe ich ein Modell aus Paris für 825 Euro. Ich garantiere, diese Bluse _____^{15} _____^{16} bestimmt. (*she will like*)

KUNDE: Sie machen wohl Spaß. Das ist _____^{17} _____.^{18} (*too expensive for me*)

Lit.: How does this shirt please you?

VERKÄUFER: Kann ich _____¹⁹ etwas anderes _____²⁰? (*show you*)

KUNDE: Können Sie _____²¹ vielleicht ein T-Shirt _____²²? (*show me*)

VERKÄUFER: Ja, natürlich. Hier habe ich ein ganz...

KUNDE: Oh, je. Es ist schon halb sechs. Es tut _____²³ _____.²⁴ (*I'm sorry.*) Ich muss sofort gehen. Ich _____²⁵ _____²⁶ für Ihre Hilfe. (*thank you*) Auf Wiedersehen.

Übung 6. Follow-up: Expand this activity by bringing a number of clothing items that students describe and express their opinion about.

honest

Übung 6   Sei ehrlich°!

Wem gehört das? Wie gefällt Ihnen das? Führen Sie ein Gespräch mit einem Partner / einer Partnerin.

BEISPIEL: s1: Wem gehört der große Hut?
s2: Der gehört meiner Schwester Jutta.
s1: Der Hut gefällt mir. Er steht ihr gut!

Wem gehört/gehören... ?

... gefällt/gefallen...   die karierte Hose

... steht... gut / überhaupt nicht   der große Hut

... passt... gut/nicht   die langen Stiefel

... zu groß / zu eng / zu kurz   das komische Hemd

Michael (mein Freund)   Jutta (meine Schwester)   Mark (mein Vater)   Sabine (meine Kollegin)

Prepositions with the Dative Case

Prepositions that require the dative case of nouns and pronouns include:

aus	from, out of	Richard kommt gerade **aus** dem Haus.
		Alexandra kommt **aus** Jena.
	(made) of	Das Hemd ist **aus** Baumwolle.
bei	near	Die Bäckerei ist **beim** Marktplatz.
	at (the place of)	Schicke Blusen gibt es **bei** Gisie.
	for, at (a company)	Manfred arbeitet **bei** VW.
	with	Sybille wohnt **bei** ihrer Großmutter.
mit	with	Herr Schweiger geht **mit** seiner Frau einkaufen.
		Katja wohnt **mit** ihrer Freundin Beate zusammen.
	by (means of)	Wir fahren **mit** dem Bus.

Täglich frische Brötchen aus der
Bäckerei Johann Baers
Reichswalde · Dorfanger 15
Telefon 02821/49916

nach	to	Der Bus fährt **nach** Frankfurt. Ich fahre jetzt **nach** Hause.
	after	**Nach** dem Essen gehen wir einkaufen.
seit	since	**Seit** gestern haben wir schönes Wetter.
	for (time)	**Seit** einem Monat kauft sie nur noch Bio-Brot.
von	from	Das Brot ist frisch **vom** Bäcker. Frank kommt gerade **vom** Markt.
	by (origin)	Dieses Buch ist **von** Peter Handke.
zu	to	Wir gehen heute **zum** Supermarkt. Dirk muss schon um fünf Uhr **zur** Arbeit.
	at	Er ist jetzt wieder **zu** Hause.
	for	**Zum** Frühstück gibt es Müsli.

Note:

- **Nach Hause** and **zu Hause** are set expressions. **Nach Hause** is used to say that someone is *going* home, while **zu Hause** means someone is *at* home.

- The following contractions are common:

bei dem → **beim**	Jürgen kauft sein Brot nur **beim** Bäcker.
von dem → **vom**	Er kommt gerade **vom** Markt.
zu dem → **zum**	Er muss jetzt noch **zum** Bäcker.
zu der → **zur**	Dann geht er **zur** Bank.

Übung 7   Ein typischer Tag

Sie hören eine Beschreibung von Maxis Tagesablauf. Was stimmt?
Was stimmt nicht? Geben Sie die richtige Information an.

	DAS STIMMT	DAS STIMMT NICHT
1. Maxi wohnt seit einem Monat in Göttingen.	☒	☐
2. Maxi wohnt allein in einer Wohnung.	☐	☒
3. Sie kann zu Fuß zur Universität gehen.	☒	☐
4. Maxi kommt gerade aus der Bibliothek.	☐	☒
5. Dann geht sie in die Mensa.	☐	☒
6. Maxi und Inge gehen zum Supermarkt.	☒	☐
7. Beim Bäcker kaufen sie ein Brot.	☐	☒
8. Maxi muss noch zur Bank.	☒	☐

[1]Vom. . . From grain to bread

Übung 8   Auskunft° geben

Ergänzen Sie die fehlenden Präpositionen.

1. Sag mal, wo gibt es hier denn schicke Blusen?—_____ Gisie.
2. Die Bluse steht dir gut. Ist sie _____ Baumwolle (*cotton*) oder Synthetik?
3. Ist diese Bluse neu? —Ja, sie ist ein Geschenk _____ meiner Mutter.
4. Das Brot schmeckt ausgezeichnet. Woher hast du es?—Es ist _____ der Bäckerei.
5. Gehst du zu Fuß zum Supermarkt? —Nein, ich fahre _____ dem Wagen.
6. Bitte, komm nach dem Einkaufen sofort _____ Hause.
7. Ich plane schon _____ drei Monaten eine Grillparty.
8. Wollen wir die Party _____ dir oder _____ mir _____ Hause machen?

Übung 9   Michaels Tag

Setzen Sie die fehlenden Präpositionen, Artikel und Endungen ein.

1. Michael wohnt _____ sein_____ Bruder zusammen in einer alten Villa in Berlin.
2. Er geht schon _____ 6 Uhr _____ _____ Haus.
3. Er fährt _____ sein_____ Moped _____ Arbeit.
4. Er arbeitet _____ Hotel Zentral.
5. Er arbeitet da schon _____ ein_____ Jahr. Die Arbeit gefällt ihm sehr.
6. Er arbeitet _____ Leute_____ _____ vielen Länder_____ zusammen, z. B. _____ Jugoslawien, Spanien, Afghanistan und Amerika.
7. Abends _____ d_____ Arbeit trifft er oft ein paar Freunde.
8. Dann geht er _____ sein_____ Freunde_____ in eine Kneipe.
9. Michael kocht gern. _____ Frühstück gibt es oft so etwas wie Rührei _____ Zwiebeln und Zucchini.
10. Das ist ein Rezept _____ Mexiko.
11. Er hat das Rezept _____ sein_____ Freundin Marlene.

Übung 10   Seit wann ist das so?

Arbeiten Sie mit einem Partner / einer Partnerin zusammen. Stellen Sie Fragen.

BEISPIEL: s1: Seit wann wohnst du hier?
           s2: Seit drei Semestern.

1. Deutsch lernen
2. Auto fahren können
3. den Professor / die Professorin kennen
4. hier wohnen
5. an dieser Uni studieren
6. ??

Point out: *Seit wann* is used with the present tense in German, but when it means *for how long*, it is used with the past progressive tense in English: *(for) how long have you been studying German?*

Interrogative Pronouns° wo, wohin, and woher

The interrogative pronouns **wo** and **wohin** both mean *where.* **Wo** is used to ask where someone or something is located, **wohin** to ask about the direction in which someone or something is moving. **Woher** is used to ask where someone or something comes from.

Wo bist du denn jetzt?	Zu Hause.
Wo wohnst du?	In Berlin.
Wo kauft Maxi ihr Brot?	Beim Bäcker.
Wohin gehst du? (**Wo** gehst du **hin**?)	Zur Bibliothek.
Wohin fährst du? (**Wo** fährst du **hin**?)	Nach Deutschland.
Woher kommen die Orangen? (**Wo** kommen die Orangen **her**?)	Aus Spanien.
Woher hast du die gute Wurst? (**Wo** hast du die gute Wurst **her**?)	Vom Metzger.

Note that the words **wohin** and **woher** are frequently split (**wo... hin, wo... her**), especially in conversation.

Übung 11   Wo, wohin, woher?

Bilden Sie die Fragen zu den Antworten.

BEISPIEL: Ich muss heute noch <u>zur Bank</u>. →
            Wohin musst du heute noch? [*oder*]
            Wo musst du heute noch hin?

1. Brötchen gibt es <u>beim Bäcker</u>.
2. Mark muss heute noch <u>zur Metzgerei</u>.
3. Sein Freund kommt gerade <u>vom Bioladen</u>.
4. Die Studentinnen trinken einen Kaffee <u>im Café Kadenz</u>.
5. Wir gehen später <u>zum Supermarkt</u>.
6. Antje ist heute <u>zu Hause</u>.
7. Die Leute kommen gerade <u>aus dem Kino</u>.
8. Sie gehen jetzt alle <u>nach Hause</u>.

The der-Words dieser, jeder, and welcher

The demonstrative adjectives **dieser** (*this*) and **jeder** (*every*) and the interrogative adjective **welcher** (*which*) have the same endings as the definite article. Like the definite article, they signal the gender, case, and number of the noun that follows them. For this reason they are frequently called **der**-words.

Dieser Mantel passt mir gut.	*This coat fits me well.*
Ich kann nicht **jede** Farbe tragen.	*I cannot wear every color.*
Welches Hemd möchten Sie?	*Which shirt would you like?*
Diese Schuhe sind unbequem.	*These shoes are uncomfortable.*

The plural of **jeder** is **alle**.

Jeder Student trägt Jeans.	*Every student wears jeans.*
Alle Studenten tragen Jeans.	*All students wear jeans.*

All **der**-words follow this pattern of endings:

	MASCULINE	NEUTER	FEMININE	PLURAL
Nominative	dies**er**	dies**es**	dies**e**	dies**e**
Accusative	dies**en**	dies**es**	dies**e**	dies**e**
Dative	dies**em**	dies**em**	dies**er**	dies**en**

Übung 12   Mini-Dialoge im Geschäft

Setzen Sie die passende Form von **dieser, jeder/alle** oder **welcher** ein.

1. A: Was kostet _____ Anzug?
   B: Wir haben _____ Woche ein Sonderangebot. _____ Anzug im Laden kostet nur 275 Euro.
2. C: Wie finden Sie _____ Mantel?
   D: _____ Mantel meinen Sie?
3. E: Wie viel kostet _____ Hemd?
   F: _____ Hemden kosten 65 Euro.
4. G: Was kosten _____ Stiefel hier?
   H: _____ Stiefel meinen Sie?
5. I: Sind _____ Blusen aus Baumwolle?
   J: Ja, _____ Blusen in unserem Laden sind aus Baumwolle.
6. K: Haben Sie _____ Rock in meiner Größe?
   L: _____ Größe brauchen Sie denn?
7. M: Passt die Bluse zu _____ Rock?
   N: _____ Bluse meinen Sie?

Sprache im Kontext

Videoclips

A. Schauen Sie sich das Interview mit Sara an. Lesen Sie die Fragen und streichen (*cross out*) Sie die Antwort durch, die nicht stimmt.

BEISPIEL: Was trägt Sara jetzt? [Jacke, ~~Hut~~, Bluse]

1. Welche Blusengröße hat Sara? [38, 83]
2. Welche Schuhgröße hat sie? [51, 41]
3. Was nimmt Sara mit in Urlaub? [Jeans, Bikini, kurze Hosen]
4. Was trägt sie zu Hause? [Pyjama, Shorts, Kleider]

5. Sara kauft Lebensmittel. Was für Gemüse kauft sie? [Gurke, Karotten, grüne Bohnen]
6. Was für Obst kauft sie? [Äpfel, Erdbeeren, Orangen]
7. Sara muss auch Kosmetik kaufen. Was muss sie kaufen? [Zahnpasta, Shampoo, Toilettenpapier]

B. Schauen Sie sich das Interview mit Harald an und beantworten Sie die Fragen.

1. Was für eine Hemdengröße hat Harald?
2. Was für eine Schuhgröße hat er?
3. Was trägt er im Sommerurlaub?
4. Was trägt er zur Arbeit?
5. Was für Lebensmittel kauft er?

C. Schauen Sie sich das Interview mit Jasmin an. Was für Getränke kauft sie?

D. Jasmin nennt auch ein Rezept für Auberginen. Wie bereitet (*prepare*) sie sie vor?

Lesen

Zum Thema

A. Wo kaufen Sie ein? Kreuzen Sie an, wo Sie oft, manchmal oder nie einkaufen.

	OFT	MANCHMAL	NIE
auf dem Flohmarkt	☐	☐	☐
auf dem Markt	☐	☐	☐
im Supermarkt	☐	☐	☐
in der Drogerie	☐	☐	☐
in der Apotheke	☐	☐	☐
in einer Boutique	☐	☐	☐
in einem Einkaufszentrum	☐	☐	☐
aus einem Versandkatalog	☐	☐	☐
im Internet	☐	☐	☐

B. Schauen Sie sich die Liste in A an. Sagen Sie, was man dort kaufen kann.

C. Interviewen Sie jemanden im Kurs. Machen Sie eine Umfrage!

1. Kaufst du gern ein?
2. Wie oft gehst du einkaufen? (jeden Tag, einmal/zweimal/dreimal in der Woche, ?)
3. Wo kaufst du am liebsten ein?
4. Hast du jemals etwas im Internet gekauft? Was? Warum (nicht)?

Auf den ersten Blick

Lesen Sie den Titel und überfliegen (*scan*) Sie die ersten paar Zeilen des Textes.

1. Was für ein Text ist dies?
   a. ein Artikel aus einer Zeitung
   b. ein Dialog
   c. eine Werbung für einen Hutladen
2. Suchen Sie im Text zusammengesetzte Wörter mit **Hut** oder **Hüte**. Versuchen Sie zu erraten (*guess*), was diese Wörter bedeuten, z. B. **Filzhüte** = Filz + Hüte; **Filz** = *felt;* **Hüte** = *Plural von* **Hut**.

Auf den ersten Blick. Have students work with the cognates. Point out how new German expressions are coined using English words even when English already has a different expression for a given concept; for example, *Shopping City* (German) instead of *shopping mall* (English).

3. Überfliegen Sie die ersten vier Zeilen. Was ist Ihre Meinung zu den Aussagen a–c, unten? Wo sehen Sie einen Beweis (*evidence*) für Ihre Meinung?

 a. Die Verkäuferin und der Kunde führen ein ganz normales Gespräch in einem Hutladen.

 b. Die Verkäuferin stellt ganz normale Fragen.

 c. Der Kunde ist schwierig.

IM HUTLADEN

von Karl Valentin

VERKÄUFERIN:	Guten Tag. Sie wünschen?
KARL VALENTIN:	Einen Hut.
VERKÄUFERIN:	Was soll das für ein Hut sein?
K. V.:	Einer zum Aufsetzen.[1]

5   VERKÄUFERIN: Ja, anziehen können Sie niemals einen Hut, den muß man immer aufsetzen.

        K. V.: Nein, immer nicht—in der Kirche[2] zum Beispiel kann ich den Hut nicht aufsetzen.

  VERKÄUFERIN: In der Kirche nicht—aber Sie gehen doch nicht
10   immer in die Kirche.

        K. V.: Nein, nur da und hie.

  VERKÄUFERIN: Sie meinen nur hie und da[3]!

        K. V.: Ja, ich will einen Hut zum Auf- und Absetzen[4].

  VERKÄUFERIN: Jeden Hut können Sie auf- und absetzen! Wollen Sie
15   einen weichen[5] oder einen steifen[6] Hut?

        K. V.: Nein—einen grauen.

  VERKÄUFERIN: Ich meine, was für eine Fasson[7]?

        K. V.: Eine farblose[8] Fasson.

  VERKÄUFERIN: Sie meinen, eine schicke Fasson—wir haben allerlei
20   schicke Fassonen in allen Farben.

        K. V.: In allen Farben?—Dann hellgelb!

  VERKÄUFERIN: Aber hellgelbe Hüte gibt es nur im Karneval[9]—einen hellgelben Herrenhut können Sie doch nicht tragen.

        K. V.: Ich will ihn ja nicht tragen, sondern aufsetzen.

25   VERKÄUFERIN: Mit einem hellgelben Hut werden Sie ja ausgelacht.[10]

        K. V.: Aber Strohhüte[11] sind doch hellgelb.

  VERKÄUFERIN: Ach, Sie wollen einen Strohhut?

        K. V.: Nein, ein Strohhut ist mir zu feuergefährlich[12]!

  VERKÄUFERIN: Asbesthüte[13] gibt es leider noch nicht! —Schöne
30   weiche Filzhüte hätten wir.

---

[1]zum... *for putting on*   [2]*church*   [3]hie... = hier und da *now and then*
[4]*to take off (a hat)*   [5]*soft*   [6]*firm, stiff*   [7]*shape*   [8]*colorless*   [9]*Mardi Gras*
[10]*ridiculed*   [11]*straw hats*   [12]*flammable, a fire hazard*   [13]*asbestos hats*

K. V.: Die weichen Filzhüte haben den Nachteil,[14] daß man sie nicht hört, wenn sie einem vom Kopf auf den Boden fallen.[15]

35 VERKÄUFERIN: Na, dann müssen Sie sich eben einen Stahlhelm[16] kaufen, den hört man fallen.

K. V.: Als Zivilist darf ich keinen Stahlhelm tragen.

VERKÄUFERIN: Nun müssen Sie sich aber bald entschließen,[17] was Sie für einen Hut wollen.

K. V.: Einen neuen Hut!

40 VERKÄUFERIN: Ja, wir haben nur neue.

K. V.: Ich will ja einen neuen.

VERKÄUFERIN: Ja, aber was für einen?

K. V.: Einen Herrenhut!

VERKÄUFERIN: Damenhüte führen wir nicht!

45 K. V.: Ich will auch keinen Damenhut!

VERKÄUFERIN: Sie sind sehr schwer zu bedienen,[18] ich zeige Ihnen einmal mehrere Hüte!

K. V.: Was heißt mehrere, ich will doch nur einen. Ich habe ja auch nur einen Kopf.[19]

. . .

---

[14]*disadvantage*   [15]*auf... fall to the ground*   [16]*steel helmet*   [17]*sich... to decide*
[18]*schwer... difficult to serve*   [19]*head*

Note: This reading is an excerpt; the rest of the text ends in yet more frustration and absurdities, with, finally, no sale.

Zum Text

Lesen Sie den Dialog mit verteilten Rollen im Kurs vor.

1. Was will der Kunde eigentlich? Wo sagt er genau, was er will?
2. Finden Sie Beispiele im Text, wo und wie der Kunde die Verkäuferin irritiert. Wie reagiert die Verkäuferin?
3. Humor in einer fremden Sprache ist oft schwer zu verstehen. Karl Valentin war ein beliebter Humorist. Finden Sie diesen Dialog komisch oder humorvoll? Wenn ja, was macht ihn komisch?
4. Sie lesen hier nur einen Auszug aus dem Dialog. Glauben Sie, dass der Kunde schließlich einen Hut kauft? Was würden Sie als Verkäufer/ Verkäuferin mit diesem Kunden machen?

Hier klicken!

Weiteres zum Thema Internet-Shopping finden Sie bei **Deutsch: Na klar!** im World-Wide-Web unter www.mhhe.com/dnk.

Sprechen und Schreiben

Aktivität I   Meinungsforschung°

Opinion poll

Stellen Sie sich vor, Sie arbeiten bei einem Institut für Meinungsforschung. Das Institut möchte wissen, wofür Studenten und Studentinnen ihr Geld ausgeben. Interviewen Sie drei Studenten und Studentinnen, die nicht in Ihrem Deutschkurs sind. Notieren Sie dabei Namen, Alter und Hauptfach (*major*).

A. Stellen Sie folgende Fragen:

- Wofür geben Sie das meiste Geld aus?

  ☐ Miete   ☐ Studiengebühren (*tuition*)
  ☐ Auto   ☐ Essen
  ☐ Kleidung   ☐ etwas anderes
  ☐ Unterhaltung

- Gehen Sie gern einkaufen?

- Was kaufen Sie, und wie oft kaufen Sie es?

  WAS SIE KAUFEN   WIE OFT SIE ES KAUFEN

  ☐ Bücher   einmal   ⎫   ⎧ in der Woche
  ☐ Kleidung   zweimal   ⎬   ⎨ im Monat
  ☐ CDs   dreimal   ⎭   ⎩ im Jahr
  ☐ Lebensmittel   jeden Tag
  ☐ ein Auto   alle fünf Jahre
  ☐ Kaffee/Bier

B. Wofür geben Studenten und Studentinnen ihr Geld aus? Was haben Sie herausgefunden? Bilden Sie kleine Gruppen, und tauschen (*exchange*) Sie die Informationen aus, die Sie gesammelt haben (*have gathered*). Geben Sie nachher im Plenum einen Bericht ab.

advertisement   **Aktivität 2   Web-Werbung**°

Arbeiten Sie in Gruppen zu dritt. Sie arbeiten für eine Werbeagentur. Sie müssen für eine Firma eine Werbung für das Web entwerfen (*design*). Wählen Sie ein Produkt aus, und zeichnen (*draw*) Sie die Werbung. Wie sieht die Werbung aus? Wie viel Text wollen Sie haben?

Wortschatz

Lebensmittel	Groceries, Food
Obstsorten	**Types of Fruit**
der **Apfel**, ∵	apple
die **Banane**, -n	banana
die **Erdbeere**, -n	strawberry
das **Obst**	fruit
die **Weintraube**, -n	grape
Gemüsesorten	**Types of Vegetables**
der **Blumenkohl**	cauliflower
der **Brokkoli**	broccoli
das **Gemüse**	vegetables

die **Gurke**, -n	cucumber
die **Karotte**, -n	carrot
die **Kartoffel**, -n	potato
die **Tomate**, -n	tomato
Backwaren	**Baked Goods**
das **Brot**, -e	(loaf of) bread
das **Brötchen**, -	roll
der **Keks**, -e	cookie
der **Kuchen**, -	cake
Fleischwaren	**Meats**
der **Aufschnitt**	cold cuts

das **Fleisch**	meat	die **Metzgerei, -en**	butcher shop
das **Rindfleisch**	beef	der **Obst- und**	fruit and vegetable
das **Schweinefleisch**	pork	**Gemüsestand, ⸚e**	stand
das **Hähnchen**	chicken	der **Supermarkt, ⸚e**	supermarket
der **Schinken, -**	ham		
das **Schnitzel, -**	cutlet		
das **Steak, -s**	steak		
der **Truthahn, ⸚e**	turkey		**Articles of**
die **Wurst, ⸚e**	sausage	**Kleidungsstücke**	**Clothing**
Getränke	**Beverages**	der **Anzug, ⸚e**	suit
das **Bier, -e**	beer	der **Badeanzug, ⸚e**	bathing suit
die **Cola, -s**	cola	die **Bluse, -n**	blouse
das **Getränk, -e**	drink	der **Gürtel, -**	belt
der **Saft, ⸚e**	juice	das **Hemd, -en**	shirt
der **Apfelsaft, ⸚e**	apple juice	das **Sporthemd, -en**	casual shirt
der **Tee**	tea	die **Hose, -n**	pants, trousers
das **Wasser**	water	der **Hut, ⸚e**	hat
das **Mineralwasser**	mineral water	die **Jacke, -n**	jacket
Milchprodukte	**Dairy Products**	die **Jeans**	jeans
die **Butter**	butter	das **Kleid, -er**	dress
das **Ei, -er**	egg	die **Krawatte, -n**	necktie
das **Eis**	ice cream; ice	der **Mantel, ⸚**	coat
der **Joghurt**	yogurt	die **Mütze, -n**	cap
der **Käse**	cheese	der **Pullover, -**	pullover sweater
die **Milch**	milk	der **Rock, ⸚e**	skirt
Sonstige Lebensmittel	**Other Foods**	das **Sakko, -s**	sport coat
das **Müsli, -**	granola; cereal	der **Schal, -s**	scarf
der **Pfeffer**	pepper	der **Schlips, -e**	necktie
das **Salz**	salt	der **Schuh, -e**	shoe
der **Zucker**	sugar	der **Hausschuh, -e**	slipper
		der **Tennisschuh, -e**	tennis shoe
		die **Socke, -n**	sock
Toilettenartikel	**Toiletries**	der **Stiefel, -**	boot
das **Make-up**	make-up	der **Strumpf, ⸚e**	stocking; sock
die **Rasiercreme, -s**	shaving cream	das **T-Shirt, -s**	T-shirt
das **Shampoo, -s**	shampoo		
das **Toilettenpapier**	toilet paper		
die **Zahnpasta**	toothpaste	**Sonstige**	
		Substantive	**Other Nouns**
Geschäfte	**Stores, Shops**	das **Abendessen**	evening meal
die **Apotheke, -n**	pharmacy	die **Brille, -n**	(pair of) eyeglasses
die **Bäckerei, -en**	bakery	die **Farbe, -n**	color
die **Drogerie, -n**	toiletries and sundries store	das **Frühstück**	breakfast
		die **Größe, -n**	size
die **Konditorei, -en**	pastry shop	die **Kasse, -n**	cash register; check-out, cashier
der **Laden, ⸚**	store		
der **Bioladen, ⸚**	natural foods store	der **Koffer, -**	suitcase
der **Getränkeladen, ⸚**	beverage store	das **Medikament, -e**	medicine
der **Markt, ⸚e**	(open-air) market, marketplace	das **Mittagessen**	midday meal; lunch
		der **Rucksack, ⸚e**	backpack
		die **Tasche, -n**	handbag, purse

Farben

Farben	Colors
beige	beige
blau	blue
braun	brown
gelb	yellow
grau	gray
grün	green
lila	purple
orange	orange
rot	red
schwarz	black
weiß	white

Verben

Verben	Verbs
an•probieren	to try on
danken (+ *dat.*)	to thank
empfehlen (empfiehlt)	to recommend
gefallen (gefällt) (+ *dat.*)	to be pleasing
Wie gefällt Ihnen...?	How do you like . . . ?
gehören (+ *dat.*)	to belong to (*a person*)
glauben	to believe
helfen (hilft) (+ *dat.*)	to help
leihen	to lend; borrow
passen (+ *dat.*)	to fit
schenken	to give (*as a gift*)
schicken	to send
schmecken (+ *dat.*)	to taste (good)
stehen (+ *dat.*)	to look good (*on a person*)
Die Farbe steht mir.	The color looks good on me.
tragen (trägt)	to wear; carry
zahlen	to pay
zeigen	to show

Sonstige Adjektive und Adverbien / Other Adjectives and Adverbs

Sonstige Adjektive und Adverbien	Other Adjectives and Adverbs
frisch	fresh(ly)
gefroren	frozen
gestreift	striped
kariert	plaid
modisch	fashionable, fashionably
nötig	necessary
zart	tender

der-Wörter / der-Words

der-Wörter	der-Words
alle	all; every
dieser	this
jeder	each, every
welcher	which

Dativpronomen / Dative Pronouns

Dativpronomen	Dative Pronouns
mir	(to/for) me
dir	(to/for) you (*informal sg.*)
ihm	(to/for) him/it
ihr	(to/for) her/it
uns	(to/for) us
euch	(to/for) you (*informal pl.*)
ihnen	(to/for) them
Ihnen	(to/for) you (*formal*)

Dativpräpositionen / Dative Prepositions

Dativpräpositionen	Dative Prepositions
aus	from; out of, (made) of
bei	at; near; with
mit	with; by means of
nach	after; to
seit	since; for (+ *time*)
von	of; from; by
zu	to; at; for

Sonstiges / Other

Sonstiges	Other
das macht zusammen	all together, that comes to
egal: Das ist mir egal.	I don't care.
nach Hause	(to) home
wem?	(to/for) whom?
wohin?	(to) where?
zu Hause	at home

Use this checklist to verify that you can now . . .

- ☐ name articles of clothing.
- ☐ name where you can buy articles of clothing.
- ☐ name colors and patterns.
- ☐ identify your clothing sizes using the German sizing system.
- ☐ offer opinions about clothing using verbs like **gefallen, passen,** and **stehen.**
- ☐ identify some basic foods and the shops where you would purchase them in Germany.

- ☐ express weights and measures using the metric system.
- ☐ understand German prices.
- ☐ use **der-**words.
- ☐ understand the dative case and its use with verbs and prepositions.
- ☐ identify direct and indirect objects.
- ☐ differentiate between **wo** and **wohin.**

Wir gehen aus

Was serviert der Kellner?
a. Wurst und Pommes frites.
b. Schweinebraten.

Kapitel 6. Suggestion:
Describe a recent visit to a restaurant. Discuss with the class which kinds of restaurants are in town, and which ones they like.

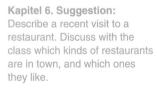

Videoclips
Bedienung, bitte

In diesem Kapitel

- **Themen:** Places to eat and drink, ordering in a restaurant
- **Grammatik:** Two-way prepositions; describing location (**hängen, liegen, sitzen, stecken, stehen**); describing placement (**hängen, legen, setzen, stecken, stellen**); expressing time with prepositions; simple past tense of **sein, haben,** and modal verbs
- **Kultur:** Regional food specialties, menus, sharing tables in restaurants, paying the bill, the importance of coffeehouses

Alles klar?

Offenbach-Stuben

Berlin Prenzlauer Berg
Stubbenkammerstraße 8

Seit 1970 gibt es die Offenbach-Stuben im Herzen des Alten Berlins. Die fünf Räume bieten für ca. 100 Personen Platz und sind bestens geeignet für kleine und größere Betriebs- oder Familienfeste. Speisekarte und Innendekoration erinnern an die Komische Oper. Wir bieten unseren Gästen neben Spezialitäten der deutschen und internationalen Küche auch Berliner Regionalgerichte. Berühmte Gäste aus Kultur und Politik speisten schon hier, wie Leonard Bernstein, François Mitterrand und Richard von Weizsäcker. Nach einem anregenden Theaterabend, oder wann immer Sie zu später Stunde Gastfreundschaft suchen: Offenbach-Stuben erwarten Sie täglich ab 18.00 Uhr.

Tischbestellung erbeten unter Telefon (030) 445 85 02.
Kreditkarten: VISA, EUROCARD, AMEX, DINERS

Note: *FU* stands for *Freie Universität.* In general, *Asta* stands for *Allgemeiner Studierender Ausschuss.* The FU in Berlin uses the designation *Allgemeiner StudentInnen Ausschuss.* This organization helps students with academic problems, financial aid (BAföG), and housing. In Berlin, Asta holds itself responsible for raising the political awareness of students and cultivating relationships among international students.

A. Die Offenbach-Stuben ist ein Restaurant in Berlin.

- Was kann man in den Offenbach-Stuben essen?
- Wie viele Plätze gibt es im Restaurant?
- Wie kann man dort zahlen?
- Wann kann man dort essen?

- Wer hat schon einmal dort gegessen?
- In welcher Straße befindet sich das Restaurant?
- Wie alt ist das Restaurant?

B. Doris hat die Uni gewechselt und studiert jetzt in Berlin. Sie ist beim Info-Büro des Astas an der FU. Hören Sie jetzt ihr Gespräch mit der Asta-Referentin (*adviser*) und ordnen Sie die Charakterisierungen dem richtigen Restaurant zu.

RESTAURANT	CHARAKTERISIERUNG
1. _____ Brazil	**a.** gemütlich **e.** österreichische Küche
2. _____ Kartoffelkeller	**b.** in der Oranienburger Straße **f.** rappelvoll (*coll. crowded*)
3. _____ Kellerrestaurant	**c.** macht viel Spaß **g.** Rezepte von Helene Weigel
4. _____ Ristorante Italiano	**d.** nicht so teuer **h.** vegetarisch

Wörter im Kontext

THEMA 1: Lokale

Realia. These restaurant and café ads represent the cities of Berlin, Bonn, Regensburg, Vienna and the villages of Born and Oberstdorf.

Neue Wörter

tägl. = täglich daily
geöffnet open
Küche cuisine;
  kitchen
geschlossen closed
zum Mitnehmen
  food to go, take-out
Ruhetag day that a
  business is closed

18 Biere vom Fass
Gastlichkeit auf
Wirtshaus
zum
Nußbaum
Alt-Berliner Art

Mühlenstube
Gastlichkeit & Atmosphäre

Speisegaststätte & Café
auch geeignet für
Reisegruppen,
Vereins- und Familienfeiern

Nordstraße 27   18375 Born/Darß

Pizzeria Ristorante
Da Bizi
WARME KÜCHE VON 11—23 UHR
(Sonntag geschlossen)
1030 WIEN, FASANG. 7   **78 91 37**
(PIZZA auch zum Mitnehmen)

ALTSTADTSTÜBERL
Griechisches
Restaurant

Tändlergasse 4

Tägl. geöffnet von 11.30 – bis 14.30 u. 17.00 – 24.00 Uhr
Dienstag von 17.00 – 24.00 Uhr

SURYA
INDISCHES RESTAURANT

Genießen Sie in indischer
Atmosphäre unsere Spezialitäten,
Huhn, Lamm, vegetarische
Speisen zu kleinen Preisen.

Grolmanstraße 22 · 10623 Berlin-Charlbg.
(am Savignyplatz)
☎ 312 91 23 · täglich 12.00 - 1.00 Uhr

Berghaus
Schönblick
Tel. 08322/4030

Ihr Treffpunkt   **TERRASSE**
unsere

bei Steaks und   **BERGGRILL**
Forellen vom

und auch sonst . . .
**Für Ihr leibliches Wohl geben
wir uns die größte Mühe!**

Zimmer für kleine oder große
Gruppen (von 1 - 90 Pers.)
Kein Ruhetag

Restaurant Ads.
Suggestion: Focus
students' attention on one
piece of realia at a time,
asking questions such as
*Was für Gerichte bietet das
Restaurant an? Was kann
man dort trinken? Möchten
Sie dort essen?*

Kaiser von China
China Restaurant

● In der Kaiserpassage 18 / Eingang Wesselstraße.
  53113 Bonn · Telefon (02 28) 65 88 30
● **Restaurant Hong Kong**
  Brassertufer 1 · 53111 Bonn · Tel. (02 28) 65 17 06
● **Restaurant Hongdi / Siegburg**
  mit schönem Biergarten am Mühlenbach · Auf der Kälke 1-3,
  beim Kreishaus · 53721 Siegburg · Tel. (0 22 41) 5 69 94

HONGDI

Wo gibt es das?

Schauen Sie sich die Anzeigen im **Thema 1** an. In welches Lokal können Leute gehen, die

- gern griechisch essen?
- gern im Biergarten sitzen?
- gern Bier vom Fass trinken?
- etwas zum Mitnehmen möchten?
- Vegetarier sind?
- ein großes Familienfest feiern möchten?
- gern auf der Terrasse sitzen?

Und Sie? In welches Lokal möchten Sie gehen? Warum?

German has many different words for places where one can eat or drink something.

das **Café**	café serving mainly desserts—**Kaffee und Kuchen**—but also offering a limited menu
der **Gasthof** / das **Gasthaus**	small inn with pub or restaurant
die **Gaststätte**	full-service restaurant
der **Imbiss**	fast-food stand; snack counter
die **Kneipe**	small, simple pub or bar; typical place where students gather (**Studentenkneipe**)
das **Lokal**	general word for an establishment that serves food and drinks
das **Restaurant**	generic word for *restaurant*
das **Wirtshaus**	pub serving mainly alcoholic beverages and some food

Often the word **Stube** or **Stüberl** will appear as a part of the name, as in **Altstadtstüberl** or **Mühlenstube. Stube** is an older word for *room* and suggests a cozy atmosphere.

Eine Wirtshaustür in München

Sprachtipp. Point Out: Lass
is the informal imperative form
of lassen.

SPRACHTIPP

To suggest to a friend that you do something together, you can
use the expression **Lass uns (doch)... :**

Lass uns doch ins Restaurant gehen!   *Let's go to a restaurant!*
Lass uns türkisch essen!   *Let's eat Turkish food!*

Aktivität 1   Lass uns essen!

Sie haben Hunger. Der Magen knurrt schon. In kleinen Gruppen, besprechen
Sie, wie Sie essen möchten. Wozu entscheiden Sie sich?

s1: Lass uns essen. Sag mir, wie?
s2: Lass uns vegetarisch essen.
s3: Nein, lass uns... essen.

Realia.   *Der Magen knurrt mir*
translates "*My stomach is
growling.*" Use the "*Knurr!
Knuurr!*" realia, a faxable
invitation and response form, to
practice *Lass uns...* in
preparation for **Aktivität 1.**
One student proposes, "Lass
uns essen. Sag mir, wie."
Another student responds,
"Lass uns vegetarisch essen."
Several expressions (*Ohne
misch = ohne mich; Wenisch =
wenig; Gar nisch = gar nicht*);
are deliberately misspelled in
order to rhyme with words like
Griechisch, Hektisch, and *Fisch.*
After students have made their
statements, ask: *Was isst man,
wenn man italienisch,
amerikanisch usw. isst?*

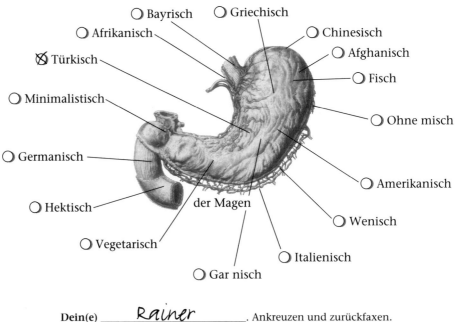

Knurr! Knuurr!

Lass uns essen. Sag mir, wie:

○ Bayrisch   ○ Griechisch
○ Afrikanisch   ○ Chinesisch
⊗ Türkisch   ○ Afghanisch
                              ○ Fisch
○ Minimalistisch
                              ○ Ohne misch
○ Germanisch
                              ○ Amerikanisch
○ Hektisch   der Magen
                              ○ Wenisch
○ Vegetarisch
            ○ Gar nisch   ○ Italienisch

Dein(e) _____*Rainer*_____ . Ankreuzen und zurückfaxen.

Aktivität 2. Suggestion:
1. Have students answer the
questions at home. 2. Have
students work in small groups
to answer these questions.
Ensure that they change the
questions from the Sie-form to
the du-form. In each case,
follow up with a class
discussion of students'
preferences.

Aktivität 2   Umfrage

Beantworten Sie die Fragen.

1. Gehen Sie oft aus essen? Wie oft? Einmal die Woche, einmal im Monat?
2. Essen Sie gern griechisch, chinesisch, italienisch... ?
3. Wie heißt Ihr Lieblingsrestaurant? Welche Spezialitäten gibt es dort?

4. Wann hat Ihr Lieblingsrestaurant Ruhetag? Ist es an allen Tagen der Woche geöffnet?
5. Was trinken Sie normalerweise, wenn Sie ausgehen?
6. Gibt es Cafés in Ihrer Stadt? Was kann man dort essen und trinken?

Aktivität 3 Ich habe Hunger. Ich habe Durst.

Wo gibt es was zu essen und zu trinken in Ihrer Stadt?

Vorschläge (*Recommendations*) für Essen und Trinken:

Pizza, Bier (vom Fass), griechische Küche, indische Spezialitäten (z.B. Lamm), internationale Küche (z.B. chinesische oder italienische Spezialitäten), ein Eis, eine Tasse Kaffee.

Aktivität 3. Suggestion: You could use ads from restaurants from a different city. These need not necessarily be from Europe. If you have a German-language paper in your area, use that.

S1	S2
1. Ich habe Hunger. Ich habe Durst.	**2.** Magst du _____? Isst du gern _____? Möchtest du _____?
3. Ja. Wo kann man das bekommen?	**4.** Im _____.
5. Wann ist es geöffnet? Ist es heute geöffnet?	**6a.** Ich weiß es nicht genau. **b.** Täglich von _____ bis _____.

Geselligkeit in einer Kneipe

THEMA 2: Die Speisekarte, bitte!

JOH.MATZ BRAUHAUS

Im Hause gebraute Biere nach dem Deutschen Reinheitsgebot von 1516.

Frisch vom Grill und aus der Pfanne

1. **Schweinshaxen** (1000 g)
   mit Sauerkraut und Kartoffelpüree .... € 9,00
2. **Spanferkel auf Biersauce**
   mit Bratkartoffeln und Krautsalat .... € 9,50
3. **Bayrischer Leberkäs'**
   mit Spiegelei und Bratkartoffeln .... € 6,50
4. **Nürnberger Rostbratwürst'l**
   mit Sauerkraut und Kartoffelpüree .... € 7,00
5. Argentinisches **Rumpsteak** (200 g)
   mit Zwiebeln, Champignons und Bratkartoffeln .... € 14,00
6. **Rumpsteak** nach Art des Hauses (200 g, scharf)
   mit Zwiebeln, Paprika, Pepperoni,
   Knoblauchbutter und Pommes frites .... € 14,00
7. **Roastbeef** (kalt)
   auf Salatkranz mit Remouladensauce
   und Bratkartoffeln .... € 10,00
8. Geschnetzeltes «**Züricher Art**»
   mit Reis oder Butterspätzle .... € 11,50
9. **Matjes** nach «**Hausfrauenart**»
   mit Apfelsahne, Zwiebelringe und Bratkartoffeln .... € 6,50
10. Bayrischer **Käseteller**
    mit Brot und Butter .... € 7,00
11. **Vegetarischer Teller**
    Gemüserosti auf Käsesauce .... € 6,00

Alle Gerichte wahlweise auch mit Pommes frites.

Unsere Salatbar

12. Salat «**Niçoise**» mit Gurken, Tomaten,
    grünem Salat, Paprika, Ei, Thunfisch und Oliven .... € 6,50
13. Kleiner **Salat** mit Gurken, Tomaten,
    grünem Salat und Paprika .... € 3,00
14. **Bauernsalat** mit Schafskäse, Tomaten,
    grünem Salat, Zwiebeln, Oliven, Kräutervinaigrette .... € 6,50
15. «**Joh. Matz**» mit frischen, knackigen Blattsalaten
    der Saison, Streifen vom Schweizer Käse, gekochtem
    Schinken, Tomaten, Gurken, Ei u. Island-Dressing .... € 6,50

Biere

Matz Pilsener naturtrüb	0,2 l	€	1,20
Matz Pilsener naturtrüb	0,4 l	€	2,40
Matz Pilsener naturtrüb **herb**	0,2 l	€	1,20
Matz Pilsener naturtrüb **herb**	0,4 l	€	2,40

Für den kleinen Hunger

16. **2 Münchener Weißwürste**
    mit süßem Senf und Brot .... € 4,00
17. **Sauerfleisch** mit Salatbeilage u. Bratkartoffeln .... € 5,50
18. Hausgebeizter **Graved Lachs**
    auf Kartoffelpuffer mit einer Senf-Dill-Honigsauce .... € 6,50
19. **Ofenkartoffel** mit Sour-Creme .... € 2,00
20. **Gulaschsuppe** .... € 3,00
21. **Chili «Con Carne»** dazu Baguette .... € 4,50

Dessert

22. **Rote Grütze** mit Vanillesauce .... € 3,50
23. **Kaiserschmarren** mit Kompott .... € 4,00
24. Kleiner «**Eiweißschock**»
    Magerquark mit frischen Früchten,
    Nüssen und Honig .... € 3,50
25. **Vanilleeis**
    mit heißen Himbeeren und Sahnehaube .... € 4,00
26. **Eisbecher «Matz Brauhaus»**
    Sahneeis mit Früchten .... € 3,50

Alkoholfreies

Coca Cola, Fanta, Sprite	0,2 l	€	1,50
Sprudel	0,25 l	€	1,50
Apfelsaft	0,2 l	€	2,00
Orangensaft	0,2 l	€	2,00
Schweppes **Soda**	0,2 l	€	2,00
Schweppes **Bitter Lemon**	0,2 l	€	2,00
Schweppes **Tonic Water**	0,2 l	€	2,00
Spezi	0,4 l	€	3,00

JOH. MATZ · Gasthaus-Brauerei
Eppendorf
Robert-Koch-Straße 36 / Ecke Kümmellstraße
(gleich hinter C&A) · 20249 Hamburg
Tel. (040) 46 50 33 · Fax (040) 46 50 34
Geöffnet ab 17.00 Uhr
Warme Speisen 17.00–24.00 Uhr

Suchen Sie die Wörter unten auf der Speisekarte im Thema 2. Können Sie vom Kontext erraten (*guess*), wie die Wörter auf Englisch heißen?

Suggestion: Have students prepare this for homework. Discuss in class.

1. __h__ die **Bratkartoffeln**
2. __l__ der **Champignon**
3. __e__ der **Eisbecher**
4. __d__ das **Gericht**
5. __i__ der **Grill**
6. __j__ der **Leberkäs**
7. __n__ die **Olive**
8. __b__ die **Paprika**
9. __p__ die **Pfanne**
10. __f__ die **Pommes frites**
11. __r__ der **Reis**
12. __c__ die **Sahne**
13. __s__ der **Salat**
14. __t__ das **Sauerkraut**
15. __m__ der **Senf**
16. __g__ das **Spiegelei**
17. __k__ der **Sprudel**
18. __q__ der **Teller**
19. __u__ die **Tomate**
20. __a__ die **Weißwurst**
21. __o__ die **Zwiebel**

a. Bavarian white sausage
b. bell pepper
c. cream; whipped cream
d. dish (*a prepared item of food*)
e. dish of ice cream
f. french fries
g. fried egg
h. fried potatoes
i. grill; barbecue
j. meat loaf, Bavarian style
k. mineral water
l. mushroom
m. mustard
n. olive
o. onion
p. pan, skillet
q. plate
r. rice
s. salad; lettuce
t. sauerkraut
u. tomato

Eine Mahlzeit (*meal*) besteht oft aus mehreren Gängen (*courses*): **Vorspeise, Hauptgericht, Beilage** und **Nachspeise (Nachtisch).** Ordnen Sie die Speisen in die richtige Kategorie ein.

alkoholfreies Bier
Apfelstrudel
Eis
gemischter Salat
Hühnerbrust
Kartoffelpüree

Käsekuchen
Krabbencocktail
Lachs
Pommes frites
Reis
Sauerkraut

Schweinebraten
Sprudel
Suppe
Wein
Wiener Schnitzel

Neue Wörter

Vorspeise appetizer
Hauptgericht main dish
Beilage side dish
Nachspeise dessert
Nachtisch dessert
Schweinebraten pork roast
Hühnerbrust chicken breast

VORISPEISEN
Suppe
Krabbencocktail
gemischter Salat

HAUPTGERICHTE
Hühnerbrust
Lachs
Schweinebraten
Wiener Schnitzel

BEILAGEN
Kartoffelpüree
Reis
Pommes frites
Sauerkraut

NACHSPEISEN
Apfelstrudel
Käsekuchen
Eis

GETRÄNKE
Sprudel
alkoholfreies Bier
Wein

Every area of Germany has its own regional specialties. The menu shown in **Thema 2** features some typical Bavarian dishes. Favorites are **Schweinshaxen** (*pig's feet*), **Spanferkel** (*suckling pig*), **Leberkäs** (*a type of liver paté*), and **Weißwurst** (*a type of veal sausage*). Meat is frequently pork (**Schweine-fleisch**). Beef (**Rindfleisch**) is also found on menus but is much more expensive. Germans are diet-conscious; therefore, many restaurants have introduced lighter fare such as chicken breast (**Hühnerbrust**) and turkey (**Truthahn** or **Pute**). Favorite dessert items include **Rote Grütze,** a compote made from crushed strawberries, currants, and cherries, and—in Bavaria—**Kaiserschmarren,** a sweet crepelike omelet.

Ein stolzer (proud) *Wirt mit köstlichen* (delicious) *Gerichten aus seinem Restaurant*

Be prepared to get a bottle of **Sprudel** (*mineral water*) if you request water in a restaurant, and don't expect to get a lot of ice with it. It is not customary to serve a guest tap water, whether in a restaurant or a private home.

Aktivität 4   So viele Speisen!

Aktivität 4. Suggestion: Have students work in pairs, taking turns saying the items in each line aloud and deciding on the correct answer. When the activity is completed, check it by calling on individuals for responses.

Welche Speisen gehören nicht in die Kategorie? Streichen Sie aus, was nicht dazu gehört.

BEISPIEL: Rumpsteak, Münchner Weißwürste, ~~Vegetarischer Teller~~

1. Kleiner Salat, Käsekuchen, Bauernsalat
2. Weißwürste, Schweinshaxen, Pommes frites
3. Rote Grütze, Rumpsteak, Vanilleeis
4. Kartoffelpüree, Gulaschsuppe, Sauerkraut
5. Bier, Apfelsaft, Spiegelei

Aktivität 5   Was bestellen° Norbert und Dagmar?

are ordering

Hören Sie zu und ergänzen Sie die Tabelle.

Hier klicken!

Weiteres zum Thema Restaurant und Gerichte finden Sie bei **Deutsch: Na klar!** im World-Wide-Web unter www.mhhe.com/dnk.

	NORBERT	**DAGMAR**
Vorspeise	Gulaschsuppe	Gulaschsuppe
Hauptgericht	Spanferkel mit Bratkartoffeln	Nürnberger Rostbratwürst'l mit Kraut und Kartoffelpüree
Getränk	Bier	alkoholfreies Bier

Aktivität 6 Was sollen wir bestellen?

Schauen Sie sich die Speisekarte auf Seite 180 an und besprechen Sie zu zweit oder zu dritt, was Sie bestellen möchten. Pro Person können Sie nur 20 Euro ausgeben.

BEISPIEL: Ich nehme (Nummer 20) Gulaschsuppe als Vorspeise. Als Hauptgericht nehme ich (Nummer 16) Münchener Weißwürste mit Senf und Brot. Und als Nachspeise nehme ich (Nummer 23) Kaiserschmarren.

		Notieren Sie Ihre Bestellung:
Vorspeise:	€ 3,00	Vorspeise: _____
Hauptgericht:	€ 4,00	Hauptgericht: _____
Nachspeise:	€ 4,00	Nachspeise: _____
Summe:	€ 11,00	Summe: _____

Aktivität 6. Suggestion: First have students scan the menu given earlier, or one that you have brought in. Have them jot down what they would order without spending more than 20 Euro. Then ask them to tell each other what they would like and how much it would cost. Have students report back to the class on what others have ordered. Challenge them to come up with the most interesting meal for the least amount of money.

Aktivität 7 Im Restaurant

Bilden Sie kleine Gruppen. Eine Person spielt den Ober oder die Kellnerin und nimmt die Bestellungen der Gäste an.

S1	**S2**
OBER/KELLNERIN	GAST
1. Bitte schön. Was darf's sein?	**2.** Ich möchte gern _____.
3. Und zu trinken?	**4.** Bringen Sie mir bitte _____.
5. Sonst noch was? (*Anything else?*)	**6a.** Ja, _____. **b.** Nein, das ist alles.

Aktivität 7. Suggestion: Group students in fours. Have them choose one to be the server. They could use their food selections from the previous activity, so that they concentrate on their language rather than choosing the food. Discuss the **Sprachtipp** earlier in the chapter about addressing the server in a restaurant.

Im Restaurant. Suggestion: You may need to point out certain clues to the students. For example, in A the woman is handing the waiter some money. The man in B has nothing but flowers on the table. The man standing in F is pointing to the chair in front of him. Have students act out the mini-dialogues after they have matched them with the pictures.

KULTURTIPP

When you are in a restaurant and want to get the server's attention, it is polite to say **bitte schön.** Young people often call out **hallo,** but this is very informal. In more formal restaurants, you may hear people call **Herr Ober** if the server is male. Use the generic term **Bedienung (bitte)** to call for a server.

In all but the most exclusive restaurants in German-speaking countries, it is acceptable for people to ask to share a table if it is very crowded. Simply ask: **Ist hier noch frei?** The answer might be: **Ja, hier ist noch frei.** Or: **Nein, hier ist besetzt.**

THEMA 3:   Im Restaurant

Welches Bild passt zu welchem Mini-Dialog?

a.

b.

c.

d.

e.

f.

1. __b__ — Herr **Ober,** die **Speisekarte,** bitte!

2. __d__ — Wir möchten **bestellen.**
— Ja, bitte, was **bekommen** Sie?
— Ich nehme die gegrillte Hühnerbrust.

3. __a__ — Zahlen bitte!
— Das macht zusammen 28,40 Euro.
— 30,– Euro.
— **Vielen Dank.**

4. __f__ — **Entschuldigen Sie,** bitte! **Ist hier noch frei?**
— Nein, **hier ist besetzt,** aber **da drüben** ist **Platz.**

5. __c__ — Herr Ober, ich habe **Messer, Löffel** und **Serviette,** aber keine **Gabel.**
— Und ich habe keine Serviette.

6. __e__ — Hier ist es aber **ziemlich voll. Hoffentlich** müssen wir nicht lange auf einen Platz **warten.**

> Ist hier noch frei?

Aktivität 8   Im Brauhaus Matz

Zwei Freunde, Jens und Stefanie, sind im Brauhaus Matz. Hören Sie zu, und ergänzen Sie den Text mit Informationen aus dem Dialog.

Stefanie und Jens suchen ____einen Platz____[1] in einem

Restaurant. Es ist ziemlich ____voll____.[2] Jens sieht

zwei ____Leute____ an einem ____Tisch____.[3] Da ist noch

____Platz____[4] für zwei Leute. Er geht an den Tisch und

fragt: „Ist ____hier noch frei____?"[5] Die Antwort am ersten Tisch

ist: „____Nein____."[6] Die Antwort am zweiten Tisch

ist: „____Ja____."[7]

Aktivität 9 Ist hier noch frei?

Bilden Sie mehrere Gruppen. Einige Personen suchen Platz.

S1	S2
1. Entschuldigen Sie. Ist hier noch frei?	**2a.** Ja, hier ist noch ____. **b.** Nein, hier ist leider ____. Aber da drüben ist noch ____.
3a. Danke schön. **b.** (*geht zu einem anderen Tisch*)	

Aktivität 9. Suggestion: Set up the classroom so that half the class is sitting in groups of two or three. The other half plays lone restaurant patrons, individually approaching a group and initiating a conversation.

KULTURTIPP

When adding up your restaurant bill (**Rechnung**), your server will often ask whether you want to pay separately (**getrennt**) or together (**zusammen**). When paying, you do not have to add a tip, as it is always included in your bill. The menu sometimes indicates this by stating:

Bedienungsgeld und
Mehrwertsteuer
enthalten.

*Tip (service fee) and
value-added tax
(federal sales tax)
included.*

It is customary to round up the figures on your bill to the next euro, but this practice is entirely up to the individual.

Kuffler

Spatenhaus
an der Oper

**** SPATENHAUS MÜNCHEN ***
61 BARUTCU

TI: 950/1   RG# 2934   **Rechnung** G.: 1
26AUG'02 16:55

3 @ 3.50
WEIZENBIER 0.5   10.50
1 PFIFFERL KLEIN   14.60
1 SCHWEINEBRATEN   12.70
BARZAHLUNG   37.80

5.21 MWST16% INCL.   37.80
61 RG GEBUCHT   17:45

VIELEN DANK FÜR IHREN BESUCH

FIRMA
NAME
ADRESSE
FÜR DIE RICHTIGKEIT

Aktivität 10. Follow-up: Put the activity and the dialogues in context by telling students about paying the bill in a German restaurant.

Aktivität 10 Wir möchten zahlen, bitte.

Was haben diese Leute bestellt? Wie viel kostet es? Kreuzen Sie an, was Sie hören.

		GETRÄNKE		ESSEN		BETRAG
Dialog 1		2 Bier	X	Knackwürste*		€10,00
		3 Cola		Weißwürste		€15,00
	✗	3 Bier		Bockwürste†	X	€18,50
			X	Sauerkraut		
				Brot		

---

*a type of German frankfurter
†a type of German sausage similar to a hot dog in flavor and consistency

		GETRÄNKE		ESSEN		BETRAG
Dialog 2		2 Tassen Tee		2 Stück Käsekuchen		€6,25
	X	2 Tassen Kaffee	X	1 Stück Käsekuchen		€4,25
		1 Tasse Kaffee	X	1 Stück Obsttorte	X	€9,55
Dialog 3		2 Bier	X	Leberknödelsuppe*		€35,40
	X	5 Bier	X	Schweinskotelett	X	€39,40
		3 Bier	X	Brezeln		€43,40
			X	Weißwürste		
				Sauerkraut		

Two-Way Prepositions. Suggestion: First review prepositions that take accusative only and dative only. Note: The two-way prepositions refer primarily to location. Model the difference between using the dative or accusative and utilizing typical classroom situations, e.g., stand next to a table and say *Ich stehe am Tisch.* Move to the door. . . *Ich gehe an die Tür.*

Grammatik im Kontext

Wechselpräpositionen

Auf dem Bauernhof kann man gut frisches Obst und Gemüse kaufen.

Two-Way Prepositions°

So far you have learned two kinds of prepositions: prepositions that are always used with the accusative case and others that are always used with the dative case.

In addition, a number of prepositions take either the dative or the accusative, depending on whether they describe a location or a direction. The most common two-way prepositions are these:

an	at, near, on
auf	on, on top of, at
hinter	behind, in back of
in	in
neben	next to
über	above, over
unter	under, beneath, below; among
vor	in front of; before
zwischen	between

*liver dumpling soup

Note:

- When answering the question **wo,** these prepositions take the dative case.

WO?	STATIONARY LOCATION (DATIVE)
Wo kauft man Brot?	In **der** Bäckerei.
Wo zahlt der Kunde?	An **der** Kasse.
Wo kauft man frisches Gemüse?	Auf **dem** Bauernhof.
Wo soll ich warten?	Vor **dem** Geschäft.

- When answering the question **wohin,** they take the accusative case.

WOHIN?	DIRECTION (ACCUSATIVE)
Wohin geht Frau Glättli?	In **die** Bäckerei.
Wohin geht der Kunde?	An **die** Kasse.
Wo gehst du hin?	Auf **den** Markt.
Wo geht Herr Sauer hin?	In **das** Geschäft.

- The following contractions are common:

an dem → **am**	Das Kaufhaus steht **am** Markt.
an das → **ans**	Geh doch **ans** Fenster!
in dem → **im**	Frau Kraus isst **im** Restaurant.
in das → **ins**	Nikola geht gleich **ins** Geschäft.

CAFE DERKS
BÄCKEREI KONDITOREI

Ihr Fachgeschäft[1]
für Brot
und feinste
Backwaren

**Derks, am Markt
Derks, am Rathaus**

[1]*specialty store*

ANALYSE

Suchen Sie in den folgenden Anzeigen Präpositionen mit Dativ- oder Akkusativobjekten. Ordnen Sie sie ein.

WO? (DATIV)	WOHIN? (AKKUSATIV)
BEISPIEL: im alten Forsthaus	_____

Analyse. Suggestion: Let students skim the ads first. The exercise can be done as homework or as class activity. Once all prepositional phrases have been identified, ask students to form simple content questions that would be answered by a prepositional phrase, such as *Was kann man im alten Forsthaus machen?*

Restaurant
Schubert-Stüberln

Küchenchef
Franz Zimmer

hinter dem Burgtheater, vis-à-vis der Universität,
beim Dreimäderlhaus

Schreyvogelgasse 4, 1010 Wien
Telefon für Tischreservierung 63 71 87

Mach Dir ein paar schöne Stunden... geh ins Kino

Parken! Problemlos!

3.000 kostenlose Parkplätze direkt vor der Tür.

Fahren Sie in unser großes Parkhaus an der Pelkovenstraße.

PP

Kulinarische Notizen

Ein Brevier für Genießer.

Biergartenromantik im alten Forsthaus

OLYMPIA
Einkaufszentrum

Hanauer Straße · Telefon 1 41 60 02

Übung 1.
Suggestion: Have students working in pairs ask each other questions and note their partner's answers. Have several students report back about what their partners like or do not like to do.

Übung 1   Am Feierabend°

After work

Was machst du gern/oft/manchmal/nie am Feierabend?

BEISPIEL: s1: Gehst du gern ins Café?
s2: Ja, ich gehe gern ins Café. [*oder*] Nein, ich gehe nicht gern ins Café.

der Biergarten	die Kneipe	der Supermarkt
das Café	das Restaurant	das Theater
das Fitnesszentrum	der Sportclub	??
das Kino	die Stadt	

Einkaufszettel
250 g Aufschnitt
Käsekuchen
150 g Emmentaler Käse
6 Brötchen
12 Würstchen zum Grillen
1 Pfund Kaffee
Schwarzbrot
2 Flaschen Sprudel
4 Tomaten
<u>nicht vergessen:</u>
Wörterbuch
Tennisschuhe

Übung 2   Wo kauft Mark ein?

Mark muss heute einkaufen. Hier ist sein Einkaufszettel. Wo gibt es das?

BEISPIEL: Käsekuchen →
Käsekuchen gibt es in der Konditorei.

die Bäckerei	die Metzgerei
die Buchhandlung	das Schuhgeschäft
die Konditorei	der Supermarkt
der Markt	

Übung 3   Ein Einkaufszentrum

Wie kommt man dahin und was kann man dort machen? Schauen Sie sich die Werbung (unten) an und beantworten Sie die Fragen.

BEISPIEL: Wie kommt man zum Einkaufszentrum Spahn? →
Man kommt mit dem Bus dahin.

NÜTZLICHE WÖRTER
die Boutique
der Bus
die Buslinie
die Cafeteria
der Parkplatz
die Spielecke
das Studio

Preiswert und sympathisch

Mit dem Bus zu Spahn
Linie 1 Linie 19
Linie 5 Linie 20

Service zuhause

Großraum-Parkplatz

Rund um's Bett

Geschenk-Boutique

Caféteria

Gardinen-Komplett-Service

Kinder-Spielecke

Lampen-Studio

1. Mit welcher Buslinie kann man dahin fahren?
2. Wo gibt es etwas zu essen?
3. Wo kann man Lampen kaufen?
4. Wo kann man parken?
5. Wo gibt es Geschenke zu kaufen?
6. Wohin kann man seine Kinder bringen?

Suggestion: Have students work in pairs, taking turns asking and answering the questions.

Übung 4   Wo sollen wir nur parken?

Sie und ein Freund / eine Freundin haben heute Nachmittag viel vor. Sie wollen mit dem Wagen in die Stadt. Wo können Sie parken?

BEISPIEL: Sie wollen ins Kino. →
  Lass uns hinter dem Kino parken.

1. Sie wollen ins Kino.
2. Sie müssen zum Bahnhof.
3. Sie gehen ins Theater.
4. Sie wollen im Kaufhaus und auf dem Markt einkaufen.
5. Sie wollen im Stadtpark spazieren gehen.
6. Sie wollen ins Museum.
7. Sie wollen in den Bierkeller im Rathaus (*town hall*).

Übung 4. Suggestion: The exercise will elicit a variety of answers. Encourage students to make counterproposals: *Lass uns hinter dem Kino parken. Nein, lass uns vor dem Kino parken.* The drawing also lends itself to describing where something is located: *Wo liegt der Bahnhof?*

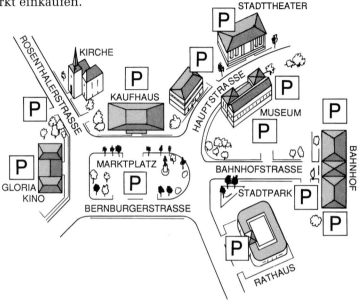

Describing Location

The verbs **hängen, liegen, sitzen, stecken,** and **stehen** indicate where someone or something is located.

hängen	to be (hanging)
liegen	to be (lying)
sitzen	to be (sitting)
stecken	to be (placed)
stehen	to be (standing)

When a two-way preposition is used with one of these verbs indicating location, the object of the preposition is in the dative case. Remember, the interrogative pronoun **wo** asks where someone or something is located.

Describing Location. Suggestion: These verbs can be practiced first by using simple classroom situations: *Wo liegt Jeffs Buch? (unter dem Tisch); Wo steht der Stuhl? (neben der Tur).*

Wo hängt das Bild?	*Where is the picture hanging?*
Es hängt **im** Museum.	*It's hanging in the museum.*
Wo liegt die Rechnung?	*Where is the bill?*
Sie liegt **neben der** Serviette.	*It's next to the napkin.*
Wo sitzen die Studenten?	*Where are the students sitting?*
Sie sitzen **auf einer** Bank **im** Park.	*They're sitting on a bench in the park.*
Wo steckt der Schlüssel?	*Where is the key?*
Er steckt **im** Wagen.	*It's in the car.*
Wo steht der Wagen?	*Where is the car?*
Er steht **auf dem** Parkplatz **beim** Markt.	*It's in the parking lot by the market.*

Übung 5. Follow-up: Have students write a paragraph describing the *Idylle im Grünen*.

Additional activity: Bring in pictures from your picture file and have students describe where things are located.

Übung 5   Idylle im Grünen

Claudia und Jürgen verbringen (*are spending*) einen Samstagnachmittag im Grünen. Beantworten Sie die Fragen zum Bild.

1. Wo liegt Jürgen?
2. Wo sitzt Claudia?
3. Wo hängt eine Spinne?
4. Wo sitzt der Hund?
5. Wo sitzt der Vogel?
6. Wo steht der Picknickkorb?
7. Wo steckt die Weinflasche?
8. Wo liegt das Buch?

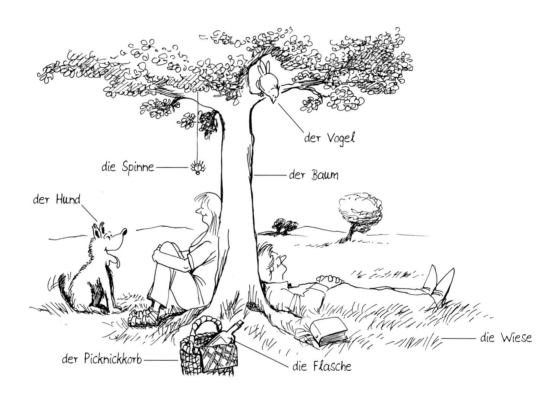

pub with a beer garden

Übung 6   In einem Gartenlokal°

Ergänzen Sie das passende Verb: **hängen, liegen, sitzen, stecken** oder **stehen.**

Andreas und Thomas ____¹ in einem Gartenlokal. Das Lokal heißt „Im Forsthaus". Es ____² sehr schön im Grünen nicht weit von Bonn. Vor dem Lokal ____³ viele Autos. Im Biergarten ____⁴ Papierlaternen. Auf dem Tisch vor Andreas und Thomas ____⁵ zwei Gläser Bier. Unter dem Tisch direkt neben ihnen ____⁶ ein Dackel (*dachshund*). Er gehört zu den Gästen am Nebentisch. Um den Tisch ____⁷ vier Leute. Der Ober ____⁸ jetzt neben Andreas. Ein Bleistift (*pencil*) ____⁹ in seiner Tasche. Die Rechnung ____¹⁰ schon auf dem Tisch.

Describing Placement

The verbs **legen, setzen,** and **stellen,** as well as **hängen** and **stecken,** can indicate where someone or something is being put or placed.

hängen	to hang, to put/place
legen	to lay, to put/place
setzen	to set, to put/place
stecken	to put/place
stellen	to stand, to put/place

When a two-way preposition is used with one of these verbs indicating placement, the object of the preposition is in the accusative case. Remember, the interrogative pronoun **wohin** asks where someone or something is being put or placed.

Wohin hängt der Mann den Mantel?	*Where is the man hanging the coat?*
Er hängt ihn **an den** Haken.	*He's hanging it on the hook.*
Wo legt der Kellner die Rechnung **hin?**	*Where is the waiter putting the bill?*
Er legt sie **auf den** Tisch.	*He's laying it on the table.*
Wohin setzt die Frau das Kind?	*Where is the woman putting the child?*
Sie setzt es **auf den** Stuhl.	*She's putting him/her on the chair.*
Wo steckt die Kellnerin das Geld **hin?**	*Where is the waitress putting the money?*
Sie steckt es **in die** Tasche.	*She's putting it in the purse.*
Wohin stellt der Kellner den Stuhl?	*Where is the waiter putting the chair?*
Er stellt ihn **an den** Tisch.	*He's placing it at the table.*

SPRACHTIPP

The verb **setzen** is frequently used with a personal pronoun that reflects the subject of the sentence. Used in this reflexive way, the verb means *to sit down.*

Ich setze **mich** an den Tisch.	*I sit down at the table.*
Wir setzen **uns.**	*We sit down.*

In the third-person singular and plural this reflexive pronoun is always **sich.**

Die Studenten setzen **sich** auf die Bank.	*The students sit down on the bench.*

Übung 7　Im Lokal

Andreas trifft ein paar Freunde im „Kartoffelkeller". Ergänzen Sie die Sätze mit **hängen, legen, setzen, stecken** oder **stellen.**

1. Andreas und drei Studienfreunde _____ sich an einen Tisch beim Fenster.
2. Andreas _____ seinen Rucksack unter den Stuhl.
3. Michael _____ seinen Rucksack an seinen Stuhl.
4. Endlich kommt der Kellner und _____ die Speisekarte auf den Tisch.
5. Die vier bestellen zuerst etwas zu trinken. Der Kellner _____ vier Colas auf den Tisch.
6. Da kommt noch ein Freund, Phillipp, an den Tisch zu ihnen. Andreas _____ noch einen Stuhl an den Tisch.
7. Phillipp _____ sich neben Andreas.
8. Er _____ seine Bücher auf den Tisch.
9. Sein Handy _____ er in seinen Rucksack.

Additional Activity. Have students work in pairs with one student doing what the other student tells him/her to do. Put the following example on the board: *Leg das Buch bitte unter den Tisch!*

SPRACHTIPP

The verb **stehen** is used idiomatically to say that something has been stated (in print).

—Hier gibt es auch vegetarische Kost.　　*They have vegetarian food here.*
—Wo **steht** das?　　*Where does it say that?*

Übung 8　Ein Abend im Kartoffelkeller!

Ergänzen Sie die Sätze mit einem passenden Verb: **liegen, sitzen, stehen, legen, setzen** oder **stellen.**

1. Im Zentrum von Berlin _____ das Restaurant „Kartoffelkeller".
2. Im Restaurant ist es heute sehr voll. An allen Tischen _____ schon Leute und einige suchen noch Platz.
3. Ein paar Leute _____ draußen vor dem Lokal und warten, dass jemand geht.
4. Man _____ hier auch sehr gemütlich. Und die Preise sind nicht so hoch. Deshalb ist es unter Studenten populär.
5. Endlich kommt eine Kellnerin und _____ die Speisekarte auf den Tisch.
6. Auf der Speisekarte _____: „Spezialität unseres Hauses ist Kartoffelsuppe mit Brot."
7. Die Kellnerin _____ neben dem Tisch und wartet auf die Bestellung.
8. Am Nebentisch _____ einige Studenten und diskutieren laut.
9. Ein Student _____ sich an die Theke (*counter*) und bestellt ein Bier.
10. Der Kellner _____ das Bier vor ihn auf die Theke.

Übung 9　Die verlorene Theaterkarte

Michael kann seine Theaterkarte nicht finden. Wo steckt sie wohl? Eine Person denkt sich aus, wo die Karte ist. Die anderen müssen raten (*guess*), wo die Karte ist.

BEISPIEL: S1: Steckt die Theaterkarte in seiner Hosentasche?
　　　　　S2: Nein.
　　　　　S1: Liegt die Theaterkarte auf dem Schreibtisch?
　　　　　S2: Nein. (usw.)

Übung 9. Suggestion: Have students say how Michael should clean up his room by saying where he should put things.

Expressing Time with Prepositions

The following two-way prepositions always take the dative case when expressing time:

vor drei Tagen	*three days ago*
vor dem Theater	*before the play*
in einer Stunde	*in one hour*
zwischen 5 und 7 Uhr	*between 5 and 7 o'clock*

Vor und nach dem Theater an die schönste Bar in der Stadt

Paletti

direkt im **Stadtkino**

You have learned several other prepositions expressing time—not two-way prepositions—that also take the dative case.

nach dem Theater	*after the play*
seit einem Jahr	*for a year*
von 5 bis 7 Uhr	*from 5 to 7 o'clock*

The prepositions **um** and **gegen** always take the accusative case.

bis (um) 5 Uhr	*until 5 o'clock*
(so) gegen 7 Uhr	*around 7 o'clock*

Note: In German, expressions of time always precede expressions of place.

	TIME	PLACE
Wir kommen	**so gegen zehn Uhr**	nach Hause.
Ich gehe	**heute**	ins Kino.

Übung 10   Was machst du gewöhnlich um diese Zeit?

Arbeiten Sie mit einem Partner / einer Partnerin zusammen.

BEISPIEL: S1: Was machst du nach dem Deutschkurs?
  S2: Da gehe ich in die Bibliothek.

von ____ bis ____	arbeiten
zwischen ____ und ____	schlafen
so gegen ____	essen
um ____	ausgehen
vor ____	einkaufen gehen
nach ____	fernsehen
??	??

Expressing Events in the Past

Like English, German has several tenses to express events in the past. The most common are the simple past tense (**das Imperfekt**) and the present perfect tense (**das Perfekt**).

- The present perfect tense (introduced in **Kapitel 7**) is preferred in conversation.
- The simple past tense is used primarily in writing. However, in the case of **haben, sein,** and the modals, the simple past is more common in conversation. In this chapter you will learn the simple past tense of these verbs; the simple past tense of all other verbs will be introduced in **Kapitel 10.**

The Simple Past Tense of sein and haben

	sein	haben
ich	war	hatte
du	warst	hattest
er, sie, es	war	hatte
wir	waren	hatten
ihr	wart	hattet
sie	waren	hatten
Sie	waren	hatten

ANALYSE

Read the cartoon.

- What forms of the verbs **haben** and **sein** are used?
- The answer to the friend's question contains no verb or object because they are understood. What would the complete sentence be?
- How would the friend pose her questions if the speakers were adults addressing each other formally?

Du warst in Paris? Hattest du denn keine Schwierigkeiten[1] mit deinem Französisch?

Ich nicht, aber die Franzosen!

[1]*difficulties*

Übung 11   Ausreden und Erklärungen°

Ergänzen Sie **haben** oder **sein** im Imperfekt.

1. A: Warum ____ Sie gestern und vorgestern nicht im Deutschkurs, Herr Miller?
   B: Es tut mir Leid, Herr Professor, aber meine Großmutter ____ krank (*sick*).

Excuses and explanations

Übung 11. Suggestion: Have students work in pairs.

2. C: Rolf, ____ du gestern Abend noch in der Bibliothek?

D: Nein, die ____ geschlossen. Außerdem ____ ich keine Lust zum Arbeiten. Ich ____ aber im Kino!

3. E: Warum ____ Michael und Peter nicht auf der Party bei Ulla?

F: Sie ____ keine Zeit.

4. G: Ihr ____ doch gestern im Café Käuzchen, nicht?

H: Nein, wir ____ im Café Kadenz. Im Käuzchen ____ es zu voll.

G: Wie ____ es denn?

H: Die Musik ____ gut, aber der Kaffee ____ schlecht.

5. I: Frau Steinmetz, warum ____ Sie gestern nicht in der Vorlesung?

J: Ich ____ beim Zahnarzt (*dentist*). Ich ____ Zahnschmerzen (*toothache*).

Übung 12 Wo warst du denn?

Übung 12. Suggestion: You may wish to reuse this activity after introducing the simple past tense of modals. Have students expand on their answers:
s1: *Wo warst du denn heute Nachmittag?* s2: *Ich war im Kino.* s1: *Wie war's denn?*
s2: *Nicht besonders gut. Ich konnte den Film nicht verstehen.*

Fragen Sie Ihren Partner / Ihre Partnerin!

BEISPIEL: s1: Wo warst du denn Freitagabend?

s2: Da war ich im Theater.

s1: Wie war's denn?

s2: Sehr langweilig.

WO	WIE
auf dem Sportplatz	interessant
auf einer Party	langweilig
bei Freunden	nicht besonders gut
im Kino	schön
im Restaurant	??
im Theater	
zu Hause	
??	

The Simple Past Tense of Modals

	dürfen	**können**	**mögen**	**müssen**	**sollen**	**wollen**
ich	durfte	konnte	mochte	musste	sollte	wollte
du	durftest	konntest	mochtest	musstest	solltest	wolltest
er, sie, es	durfte	konnte	mochte	musste	sollte	wollte
wir	durften	konnten	mochten	mussten	sollten	wollten
ihr	durftet	konntet	mochtet	musstet	solltet	wolltet
sie	durften	konnten	mochten	mussten	sollten	wollten
Sie	durften	konnten	mochten	mussten	sollten	wollten

Note:

■ As with **haben** and **sein,** the first- and third-person singular forms and first- and third-person plural forms of the simple past tense of modals are identical.

■ Modals have no umlaut in the simple past tense.

Peter **wollte** gestern in die Disko. Ich **musste** aber zu Hause bleiben.	*Peter wanted to go to the disco yesterday. But he had to stay home.*
Wir **konnten** keinen Parkplatz finden.	*We couldn't find a parking space.*

Suggestion: You may want to point out to students the alternate spelling of the preterite of *müssen* with *ß* instead of *ss*.

¹*In case*

Übung 13   Kleine Probleme

Ergänzen Sie die fehlenden Modalverben im Imperfekt.

Gestern Abend waren wir im Theater. Wir ____¹ (wollen) in der Nähe vom Theater parken. Da ____² (dürfen) man aber nicht parken. Wir ____³ (können) keinen Parkplatz auf der Straße finden. Deshalb ____⁴ (müssen) wir ins Parkhaus fahren. Katrin ____⁵ (sollen) vor dem Theater auf uns warten. Sie ____⁶ (müssen) lange warten. Nach dem Theater ____⁷ (wollen) wir noch ins Café Kadenz. Da ____⁸ (können) wir keinen Platz bekommen. Wir ____⁹ (müssen) also nach Hause fahren.

Übung 14   Bei mir zu Hause

Wie war das bei Ihnen zu Hause?

BEISPIEL: Als (*As a*) Kind mochte ich keinen Fisch essen.
　　　　Mein Vater wollte abends in Ruhe die Zeitung lesen.

ich	dürfen	Fisch/Brokkoli/Salat essen
wir Kinder	können	Gemüse essen
mein Vater	mögen	am Wochenende das Auto waschen
??	müssen	jeden Tag Hausaufgaben machen
	sollen	abends in Ruhe die Zeitung lesen
	wollen	abends nicht fernsehen
		nur am Wochenende ins Kino gehen
		um zehn im Bett sein
		??

Übung 15 Hin und her: Warum nicht?

Fragen Sie Ihren Partner / Ihre Partnerin, warum die folgenden Leute nicht erschienen sind (*didn't show up*).

BEISPIEL: s1: Warum war Andreas gestern Vormittag nicht in der Vorlesung?
s2: Er hatte keine Lust.

PERSON	WANN	WO	WARUM
Andreas	gestern Vormittag	in der Vorlesung	keine Lust haben
Anke	Montag	zu Hause	arbeiten müssen
Frank	gestern Abend	auf der Party	keine Zeit
Yeliz	heute Morgen	in der Vorlesung	schlafen wollen
Mario	Samstag	im Café	kein Geld haben
Ihr Partner / Ihre Partnerin			

Sprache im Kontext

Videoclips

A. Schauen Sie sich das Interview mit dem Besitzer des Restaurants an und ergänzen Sie die Sätze.

1. Das Restaurant heißt ___.

   a. Geigenhafen
   b. Gugelhof
   c. Gartenlaube

2. Es gibt Spezialitäten vom ___, von Baden und von der Schweiz.

   a. Elsass
   b. Rheinland
   c. Bayern

3. Eine Spezialität des Restaurants ist ___.

   a. Lamm provenzal
   b. Tarte flambée
   c. Steak tartare

B. Schauen Sie sich die Szene im Restaurant an, wo die Gäste Essen bestellen. Wer bestellt was?

1. ___ Michael   3. ___ Ali   a. Putenspieß   c. Schweineschnitzel
2. ___ Claudia   4. ___ Sara   b. Kartoffelauflauf   d. Tomatensuppe

C. Die Gäste sprechen über ihre Essgewohnheiten. Hören Sie zu und beantworten Sie folgende Fragen.

1. Wo isst Ali gern?   4. Wer isst gern Falafel?
2. Was isst Claudia gern?   5. Was für Fastfood isst Claudia gern?
3. Was ist Saras Lieblingsessen?

D. Und Sie? Was essen und trinken Sie gern, wenn Sie ins Restaurant gehen?

Lesen

Zum Thema

In meiner Freizeit. Arbeiten Sie in Gruppen und beantworten Sie die folgenden Fragen. Vergleichen Sie dann Ihre Antworten im Plenum (*with the whole group*). Gibt es Gemeinsames (*commonalities*)? Was für ein Bild ergibt sich über die Freizeit?

1. Wohin gehen Studenten und Studentinnen, wenn sie etwas Freizeit haben? am Abend? am Wochenende?
2. Wohin gehen Sie, wenn Sie in der Freizeit etwas trinken möchten?
3. Lesen Sie Zeitungen oder Zeitschriften (*magazines*) in Ihrer Freizeit? Wenn ja, welche? Wo lesen Sie sie?
4. Gibt es ein populäres Lokal in Ihrer Nähe, wo man einen guten Kaffee oder Tee trinken kann?
5. Wo gehen Sie hin, wenn Sie Ruhe haben möchten?
6. Was kann man alles in einem Café machen?

KULTURTIPP

The First Coffeehouse
Legend has it that when the Turkish army fled Vienna in 1683, they left behind sacks of coffee beans. Though no one knows for sure who got the coffee, Georg Franz Kolschitzky is said to have been awarded 500 sacks for his service during the siege of Vienna; the story goes that he opened the first coffeehouse. The earliest official records, however, show that Johannes Diodato was awarded a license to sell coffee on January 17, 1685.

Auf den ersten Blick

A. The following text on cafés in Vienna contains many cognates and other words that look similar in English and German. Scan the text and make a list of such words.

BEISPIEL: traditionell

B. Now scan the text for compound words. Say the words aloud and try to identify their components. Can you guess their meaning from the components?

BEISPIEL: das Kaffeehaus = Kaffee + Haus = c*offeehouse, café*

Hier klicken!

Weiteres zum Thema Kaffee-häuser und Cafés finden Sie bei **Deutsch: Na klar!** im World-Wide-Web unter www.mhhe.com/dnk.

Auf den ersten Blick.
Suggestion: Have students do this for homework in preparation for discussion of the text. Students compare their lists of cognates and compound words in class with a partner. Alternately, have students complete **Auf den ersten Blick** in class and do the **Zum Text** section as homework.

Das Kaffeehaus ist für den Wiener der traditionelle Treffpunkt untertags. Hier kannst du stundenlang in Ruhe bei einem Kaffee sitzen, Zeitung lesen (in fast allen 5 „Alt-Wiener-Kaffeehäusern" liegen internationale Zeitungen aus), mit jemandem plaudern,[1] Schach[2] oder—in manchen Kaffeehäusern—auch Billard spielen. Man trinkt natürlich Kaffee. Den großen oder den 10 kleinen Braunen oder Schwarzen oder die Melange (ein Milchkaffee). Kleine Imbisse sind zu haben, aber auch die Kaffeehausküche sollte man nicht unterschätzen. Allerdings sind die Preise wegen[3] der 15 kalkulierten langen Aufenthaltszeit[4] des Gastes höher als[5] im Beisl.[6]

(Aus *live Wien für junge Leute,* Vienna Tourist Board)

[1]*chat or gossip*
[2]*chess*
[3]*because of*
[4]*stay*
[5]*höher... als higher than*
[6]*restaurant (Austrian), similar
to a* Kneipe

In einem Wiener Kaffeehaus

Zum Text

Zum Text A. Suggestion:
Various students should
formulate the questions for the
rest of the class, e.g., *Kann
man im Kaffeehaus Briefe
schreiben?*

A. Was kann man in einem Kaffeehaus machen? Steht das im Text oder nicht?

	STEHT IM TEXT	STEHT NICHT IM TEXT
1. Briefe schreiben	☐	☒
2. Kaffee trinken	☒	☐
3. Musik spielen	☐	☒
4. Zeitung lesen	☒	☐
5. etwas essen	☒	☐
6. Schach oder Billard spielen	☒	☐
7. Klavier (*piano*) spielen	☐	☒
8. stundenlang plaudern	☒	☐

B. Nennen Sie drei Kaffeegetränke.

C. Vokabelübung

1. Bilden Sie Komposita. Wählen Sie Wortteile aus jeder Spalte.

   BEISPIEL: Kaffee + -häuser = Kaffeehäuser

A		B
Kaffee		-punkt
Treff		-lang
Milch	+	-häuser
unter		-kaffee
stunden		-schätzen

2. Ergänzen Sie den Text mit den Komposita.

   Lotte und ich treffen uns jeden Dienstag in der Stadt. Unser normaler
   ____¹ ist ein Kaffeehaus im ersten Bezirk.* Es gibt sehr viele ____² in
   Wien. Dort kann man ____³ sitzen. Ich trinke immer einen ____.⁴ Die
   Wiener sagen „Melange" dazu. Manchmal esse ich auch dort. Es ist
   nicht schlecht. Man soll das Essen in den Kaffeehäusern nicht ____.⁵
   Es kostet allerdings mehr als in einem Restaurant oder Beisl, weil die
   Aufenthaltszeit normalerweise länger ist.

Sprechen und Schreiben

Aktivität 1   Ein Literatenkaffeehaus in Wien

Es kommen viele berühmte (*famous*) Leute ins Literatenkaffeehaus. Spielen
Sie eine Szene in kleinen Gruppen. S1 spielt den Kellner / die Kellnerin. S2,
S3 und S4 sind berühmte Personen. Können die anderen erraten (*guess*), wer
Sie sind? Sagen Sie den Namen nicht, aber benehmen (*act*) Sie sich wie diese
Person.

Aktivität 2   Ihr Lieblingslokal

Schreiben Sie einen Absatz (*paragraph*) über Ihr Lieblingslokal. Wo liegt es?
Was machen Sie dort? Was mögen Sie? Warum? Wie oft gehen Sie dorthin?
Wie ist die Atmosphäre?

Zum Text C. Suggestion:
Have students work in pairs to
complete this exercise. Check
responses quickly and have
students use the compound
nouns in the *Lückentext* that
follows.

Aktivität 1. Suggestion:
Have students focus on
famous people from the
German-speaking world.
Brainstorm and come up
with a list of people and their
characteristics: who they
are, what they do, what they
like and dislike. Assign students
the task of finding information
about one of the people,
reporting briefly during the
next class.

*The First District in Vienna is in the center of the city.

Wortschatz

Lokale / Eating and Drinking Establishments

das **Café, -s**	café
die **Gaststätte, -n**	full-service restaurant
der **Imbiss, -e**	fast-food stand
die **Kneipe, -n**	pub, bar
das **Lokal, -e**	restaurant, pub, bar
das **Restaurant, -s**	restaurant
das **Wirtshaus, ̈er**	pub

Im Restaurant / In the Restaurant

Gänge / Courses

die **Vorspeise, -n**	appetizer
das **Hauptgericht, -e**	main dish
die **Beilage, -n**	side dish
die **Nachspeise, -n**	dessert
der **Nachtisch, -e**	dessert

Getränke / Beverages

Bier vom Fass	draft beer
das **Pilsener, -**	Pilsner beer
der **Sprudel**	mineral water
der **Wein, -e**	wine

Speisen / Foods

die **Bratkartoffeln** (*pl.*)	fried potatoes
die **Brezel, -n**	pretzel
der **Eisbecher, -**	dish of ice cream
die **Hühnerbrust**	chicken breast
der **Käsekuchen**	cheese cake
der **Leberkäs**	*liver paté* (*Bavarian style dish made of liver*)
die **Olive, -n**	olive
die **Paprika**	bell pepper
die **Pommes frites** (*pl.*)	french fries
der **Reis**	rice
die **Sahne**	cream; whipped cream
der **Salat, -e**	salad; lettuce
das **Sauerkraut**	sauerkraut
der **Schweinebraten, -**	pork roast
der **Senf**	mustard
das **Spiegelei, -er**	fried egg (*sunny-side up*)
die **Suppe, -n**	soup
die **Weißwurst, ̈e**	white sausage
das **Wiener Schnitzel, -**	Wiener schnitzel, breaded veal cutlet
die **Zwiebel, -n**	onion

Sonstige Substantive / Other Nouns

die **Bedienung**	service
der **Biergarten, ̈**	beer garden (restaurant)
die **Gabel, -n**	fork
das **Gericht, -e**	dish (*of prepared food*)
der **Grill**	grill, barbeque
der **Kellner, -** / die **Kellnerin, -nen**	waiter / waitress, server
die **Küche**	food, cuisine; kitchen
der **Löffel, -**	spoon
das **Messer, -**	knife
der **Ober, -**	waiter
die **Pfanne, -n**	pan
der **Platz, ̈e**	place, seat
die **Rechnung, -en**	bill
der **Ruhetag, -e**	*day that a business is closed*
die **Serviette, -n**	napkin
die **Speisekarte, -n**	menu
der **Teller, -**	plate

Verben / Verbs

bekommen	to get
Was bekommen Sie?	What will you have?
bestellen	to order
entschuldigen	to excuse
Entschuldigen Sie!	Excuse me!
hängen	to hang; to be hanging
lassen	to let
Lass uns (doch)...	Let's . . .
legen	to lay, put (*in a lying position*)
liegen	to lie; to be located
setzen	to set; to put (*in a sitting position*)
sitzen	to sit

stecken	to place, put (*inside*); to be (*inside*)
stehen	to stand; to be located
stellen	to stand up; place, put (*in a standing position*)
warten	to wait

Adjektive und Adverbien / Adjectives and Adverbs

alkoholfrei	nonalcoholic
besetzt	occupied, taken
Hier ist besetzt.	This place is taken.
da drüben	over there
geöffnet	open
geschlossen	closed
getrennt	separate(ly)
hoffentlich	I hope
täglich	daily
vegetarisch	vegetarian
voll	full; crowded
ziemlich	somewhat, rather

Wechsel-präpositionen / Dative/Accusative Prepositions

an	at, on, to, near
auf	on, on top of, at
hinter	behind, in back of
in	in; to (*a place*)

neben	next to, beside
über	over, above
unter	under, below, beneath; among
vor	before, in front of
zwischen	between

Präpositionen (Temporal) / Prepositions (Temporal)

bis (um): bis (um) fünf Uhr	until: until five o'clock
(so) gegen: (so) gegen fünf Uhr	around/about: around five o'clock
in (+ *dat.*): in zwei Tagen	in: in two days
nach: nach Dienstag	after: after Tuesday
seit: seit zwei Jahren	since, for: for two years
von: von zwei bis drei Uhr	from: from two to three o'clock
vor (+ *dat.*): vor zwei Tagen	ago: two days ago
zwischen: zwischen zwei und drei Uhr	between: between two and three o'clock

Sonstiges / Other

Ist hier noch frei?	Is this place taken?
Vielen Dank!	Many thanks!
zum Mitnehmen	(food) to go; take-out

LERNZIELE

Use this checklist to verify that you can now . . .

☐ identify various types of eating and drinking establishments found in German-speaking countries.

☐ say what foods you like or dislike.

☐ order food and drink from a menu in a German restaurant.

☐ identify various German foods.

☐ describe location or direction using two-way prepositions.

☐ ask about location or direction using **wo** and **wohin.**

☐ make suggestions, using **lass uns doch.**

☐ express time using accusative, dative, and two-way prepositions.

☐ express events in the past, using the simple past tense of **haben, sein,** and the modal verbs.

Zweites Zwischenspiel

Die deutsche Regionalküche

Das Essen ist in jeder Kultur wichtig.[1] Mehrere Faktoren (z.B. Geschmack,[2] Klima und geographische Lage) bestimmen die Speisen, die man in einer bestimmten Region isst.

Aktivität 1   Die deutsche Küche[3]

Kennen Sie typische Gerichte aus deutschsprachigen Ländern? Stellen Sie mit einem Partner / einer Partnerin eine Liste zusammen.

Aktivität 2   Kulinarische Geographie

Können Sie die Gegenden oder Orte auf der Landkarte auf S. xxv–xxviii finden, die mit den folgenden Speisen verbunden sind?

Berliner Pfannkuchen[4]
Dresdner Stollen[5]
Emmentaler Käse
Frankfurter Würstchen
Leipziger Allerlei[6]

Limburger Käse
Linzer Torte[7]
Nürnberger Lebkuchen[8]
Salzburger Nockerln[9]
Westfälischer Schinken[10]
Wiener Schnitzel
Wiener Würstchen

Wiener oder Frankfurter?

Manche Speisen haben verschiedene Namen, je nachdem, wo man sie isst.

Weil's Wurst ist

von Gerhard C. Krischker

in wien
heißen die wiener
frankfurter
dafür heißen
in frankfurt die frankfurter
wiener

[1]important [2]taste [3]cuisine [4]jelly-filled donut [5]fruit cake [6]mixed vegetables [7]jam-filled tart [8]gingerbread [9]soufflé made of baked egg whites and sugar [10]cured raw ham

Ein Käsesortiment

Wurstsorten

Aktivität 3 Ein einheimisches[1] Gericht

Gibt es Speisen oder Gerichte, die für Ihre Gegend typisch sind? Schreiben Sie ein Gedicht darüber oder über Ihre Lieblingsspeise!

So isst man...

Manche Speisen kann man nicht so leicht essen. Lesen Sie die folgenden Hinweise aus dem Buch *Wenn Sie mich so fragen.*

FRAGE: Wie isst man Spargel[2]* richtig?

ANTWORT: Sie können ihn heutzutage[3] ohne weiteres[4] mit dem Messer schneiden und mit der Gabel essen. Denn die modernen Messer oxydieren nicht, und deshalb kann der Spargel nicht mehr „nach Messer" schmecken. Wenn ich allerdings[5] zu einem richtigen Spargelessen eingeladen werde, esse ich ihn auch heute noch zünftig nach alter Art, also mit den Fingern.

FRAGE: Zur Hochzeit haben wir Kuchengabeln geschenkt bekommen. Deckt[6] man sie eigentlich zu jedem Kuchen[7]?

ANTWORT: Nein, nur wenn man Torte, Obst oder einen anderen feuchten[8] Kuchen anbietet. Trockenen Kuchen oder Gebäck kann man mit der Hand nehmen und ohne Gabel essen. Größere Kuchenstücke essen sich leichter von Hand gebrochen.

Aktivität 5. Note: Guide students in formulating their expressions following patterns in the example, in particular the use of the perfect tense.

[1]*local* [2]*asparagus* [3]*nowadays* [4]*ohne... without concern* [5]*however* [6]*set* [7]*zu... whenever cake is served* [8]*moist* [9]*customs*

Aktivität 4 So esse ich das

Zeigen Sie, wie man die folgenden Speisen isst.

Pommes frites	Kartoffelpüree
Schweinebraten	Grüner Salat
Suppe	Bockwurst
Tomaten	Käsekuchen
Eis	

Kuchen und Gebäck

Aktivität 5 Andere Länder, andere Sitten[9]

Suchen Sie sich eine Stadt in einem deutschsprachigen Land aus und suchen Sie im Internet, ob Sie etwas über regionale Küche oder Restaurants in dieser Stadt herausfinden können. Berichten Sie im Plenum, was Sie herausgefunden haben.

BEISPIEL: Ich habe in Bern, in der Schweiz, das Restaurant „Bürgerhaus" gefunden. Es liegt in der Nähe der Neuen Gasse 20, im Herzen der Stadt und nur zwei Minuten vom Bahnhof. Es gibt da traditionelle Küche und türkische Spezialitäten.

*Die „Spargelzeit" fängt traditionell in der Mitte des Sommers an. Man isst frischen, weißen Spargel mit Kartoffeln und Kochschinken.

Freizeit und Sport

Diese Leute…
a. angeln
b. machen Windsurfing

Kapitel 7. Suggestion: To introduce the material of this chapter, talk about leisure-time activities that you and other people enjoy. Bring in pictures and discuss them with your class.

Videoclips
Pläne für die Freizeit

In diesem Kapitel

- **Themen:** Sports and leisure pastimes, locations, seasons, weather expressions
- **Grammatik:** Coordinating conjunctions, present perfect tense
- **Kultur:** Sports, hobbies, and clubs

Alles klar?

A. Schauen Sie sich das Freizeit-Budget der Deutschen an.

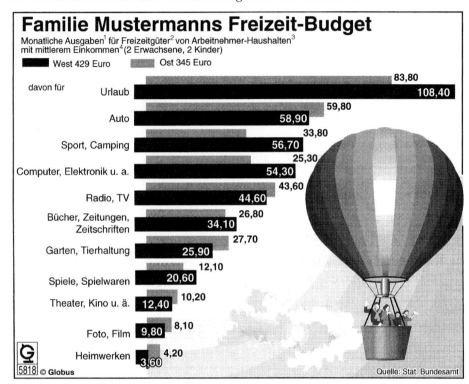

Familie Mustermanns Freizeit-Budget

Monatliche Ausgaben[1] für Freizeitgüter[2] von Arbeitnehmer-Haushalten[3] mit mittlerem Einkommen[4] (2 Erwachsene, 2 Kinder)

West 429 Euro | Ost 345 Euro

davon für	Ost	West
Urlaub	83,80	108,40
Auto	59,80	58,90
Sport, Camping	33,80	56,70
Computer, Elektronik u. a.	25,30	54,30
Radio, TV	43,60	44,60
Bücher, Zeitungen, Zeitschriften	26,80	34,10
Garten, Tierhaltung	27,70	25,90
Spiele, Spielwaren	12,10	20,60
Theater, Kino u. ä.	10,20	12,40
Foto, Film	8,10	9,80
Heimwerken	4,20	3,60

G 5818 © Globus

Quelle: Stat. Bundesamt

[1]*expenditures*
[2]*leisure goods*
[3]*households of working people*
[4]mit... *with median incomes*

Realia. Suggestions: 1. Have students scan the graphic and guess the meaning of words they do not know. 2. Ask students to comment on differences between German and American expenditures on leisure activities.

- Wie viel geben die Deutschen für ____ aus?
  a. Auto   **c.** Computer, Elektronik
  b. Radio, Fernsehen   **d.** ??

- Wie viel Geld geben Sie im Monat ungefähr für die Freizeit aus?

- Wofür (*For what*) geben Sie Geld aus? Wie viel?

BEISPIEL: Ich gebe ungefähr 20 Dollar im Monat fürs Kino aus. Ich gebe nichts für Garten und Haustiere (*pets*) aus.

B. Sie hören nun drei kurze Dialoge. Wie verbringen Ulrike, Wolfgang und Antje ihre Freizeit?

1. Ulrike
   a. Tanzen   **b.** Schwimmen   **c.** Kochen   **d.** Lesen
2. Wolfgang
   a. Fußball   **b.** Fernsehen   **c.** Lesen   **d.** Rad fahren
3. Antje
   a. ins Kino gehen   **b.** Kochen   **c.** Musik spielen   **d.** im Internet surfen

Wörter im Kontext

Types of sports

THEMA 1: Sportarten°

Sportarten. Suggestion:
Have students work in pairs.

Neue Wörter

See lake
Wald forest
Fluss river
Meer sea, ocean
Turnhalle gymna-
  sium
Wiese meadow
Berge mountains

1. Kerstin fährt Rad.

2. Heinz angelt oft im Sommer.

3. Uwe und Erich
machen dreimal die
Woche Bodybuilding.

Wo macht man das? Kombinieren Sie!

BEISPIEL: Man wandert im Wald oder am Fluss.

wandern	im Fitnesscenter
Rad fahren	auf dem **See**
angeln	auf der Straße
tauchen	im **Wald**
reiten	am **Fluss**
segeln	im **Meer**
Bodybuilding machen	in der **Turnhalle**
turnen	auf der **Wiese**
	in den **Bergen**

4. Lisa turnt jeden zweiten
Tag.

5. Manfred segelt gern.

6. Renate taucht gern.

7. Eva reitet jeden Tag.

Die Karte „Naherholung" zeigt, welche Sportmöglichkeiten es in und um Göttingen gibt. Schauen Sie sich die Bildsymbole auf der Karte an. Welche Sportarten kann man hier treiben? Wo kann man das machen?

BEISPIELE: Man kann auf dem Kiessee segeln.
Man kann im Jahnstadion Fußball spielen.

kegeln

Fußball spielen

tauchen, schwimmen

Tennis spielen

wandern

angeln

segeln

Schlittschuh laufen

Golf spielen

reiten

joggen

NAHERHOLUNG

Freibad Nikolausberg
Bowling-Center
Freibad Weende Sportanlage
Sportplatz Maschpark Squash- und Tennis-Center
Institut für Leibesübungen[1]
Trimm-Pfad
Sporthalle am MPG
Freibad Grone
Hallenbad
Schillerwiese Wörthhalle
Keglerheim
Freibad Göttingen
Bismarckturm
Tennisanlage
Kehr
Jahnstadion
Kiessee
Sporthalle Geismar
Freibad Rosdorf
Diemardener Warte
Wendebach-Stausee

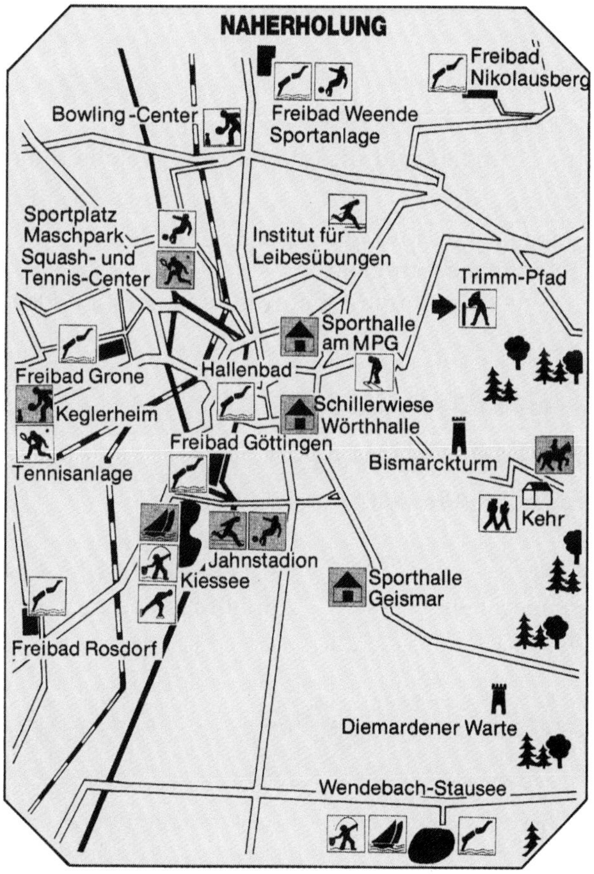

[1]*physical education*

Neue Wörter

Freibad outdoor swimming pool
Hallenbad indoor swimming pool
Schwimmbad swimming pool
Sporthalle sports arena
Sportplatz athletic field
Stadion stadium
Eisstadion ice-skating rink
Tennisplatz tennis court

Note: Point out that the various sports facilities are often combined with place names, for example, *Freibad Nikolausberg, Sporthalle Geismar,* and *Freibad Rosdorf.* Bowling has almost completely replaced the traditional game of ninepins, *Kegeln.*

SPRACHTIPP

To say how often you do something, use the following expressions:

jeden Tag	every day
einmal die Woche	once a week
zweimal die Woche	twice a week
dreimal im Monat	three times a month
einmal im Jahr	once a year

Aktivität 1   Was braucht man für diese Sportarten?

Bilden Sie Sätze mit Elementen aus beiden Spalten (*columns*).

BEISPIEL: Zum Wandern braucht man Wanderschuhe.

zum Angeln	ein Fahrrad (*bicycle*)
zum Reiten	ein Segelboot
zum Wandern	einen Ball
zum Tauchen	eine Angelrute (*fishing pole*)
zum Fußball spielen	ein Pferd (*horse*)
zum Rad fahren	Wanderschuhe
zum Segeln	Schwimmflossen (*fins*)

Aktivität 2   Ein Gespräch über Sport

Bilden Sie kleine Gruppen und diskutieren Sie. Welche Sportarten treiben Sie gern? Wie oft?

BEISPIEL: s1: Ich jogge gern, und ich wandere auch gern.
s2: Wie oft machst du das?
s1: Ich gehe einmal im Monat wandern, aber ich jogge jeden Tag.

Hier klicken!

Weiteres zum Thema Freizeit und Sport finden Sie bei **Deutsch: Na klar!** im World-Wide-Web unter www.mhhe.com/dnk.

THEMA 2: Hobbys und andere Vergnügungen°

pleasures

Wie **verbringen** Sie Ihre **Freizeit?** Kreuzen Sie an!

☐ **Sport treiben**
☐ Musik hören
☐ mit Freunden ausgehen
☐ Motorrad fahren

☐ spazieren gehen
☐ Briefmarken (*stamps*) **sammeln**
☐ **Spielkarten** sammeln

Neue Wörter

Freizeit verbringen to spend free time
Sport treiben to play sports
sammeln to collect
Spielkarten playing cards
zeichnen to draw
malen to paint (pictures)
Schach spielen to play chess
faulenzen to do nothing, be lazy

Sie gehen oft ins Museum.

Sie fotografiert.

Sie malt.

☐ ins Museum gehen
☐ **Karten** spielen
☐ Ski fahren
☐ Computerspiele spielen

☐ **zeichnen**
☐ fotografieren
☐ Klavier spielen
☐ **malen**

Er arbeitet am Wagen.

Sie spielen Schach.

Er faulenzt.

☐ **Schach spielen**   ☐ Camping gehen
☐ fernsehen   ☐ am Wagen arbeiten
☐ **faulenzen**   ☐ im Garten arbeiten
☐ Windsurfing gehen   ☐ ??
☐ lesen

Vergleichen Sie Ihre Liste mit der Liste von zwei Personen im Kurs. Können Sie drei gemeinsame Dinge finden?

Aktivität 3   In der Freizeit

Sie hören drei junge Leute über ihre Freizeit sprechen. Kreuzen Sie an, was sie machen.

1. Nina...
   a. __X__ hört Musik.
   b. __X__ geht mit Freunden aus.
   c. _____ spielt Computerspiele.
   d. __X__ fotografiert.
   e. _____ zeichnet.
   f. __X__ malt.

2. Thomas...
   a. __X__ hat keine Freizeit.
   b. __X__ träumt (*dreams*) vom
           Motorrad fahren.
   c. __X__ fährt Ski im Traum.
   d. _____ arbeitet am Wagen.
   e. _____ geht Camping.
   f. _____ spielt Fußball.

3. Annette...
   a. _____ geht Windsurfen.
   b. __X__ geht zum Flohmarkt.
   c. __X__ spielt Karten.
   d. __X__ sammelt Spielkarten.
   e. _____ sammelt Briefmarken.
   f. __X__ surft im Internet.

Aktivität 4 Wie hast du deine Freizeit verbracht?°

Aktivität 4. Suggestion: First have students scan the range of possibilities. This activity can be done with the whole group. Encourage students to link several pieces of information. Brainstorm other activities with the group, providing new vocabulary as needed.

Fragen Sie einen Partner / eine Partnerin: Wie hast du in den letzten acht Tagen deine Freizeit verbracht?

BEISPIEL: Ich habe Musik gehört. Ich bin mit Freunden ausgegangen.
Ich habe jeden Tag ferngesehen.

mit Freunden	bin … ausgegangen
mit einem Freund	bin … in die Disko / ins Kino gegangen
mit einer Freundin	habe … Musik gehört/gespielt
allein	habe … ferngesehen
	habe … im Garten gearbeitet

KULTURTIPP

In ihrer Freizeit treiben viele Deutsche gern Sport; besonders beliebt sind Fußball, Rad fahren, Schwimmen und Tennis. Andere bleiben lieber zu Hause und machen Gartenarbeit, pflegen (*take care of*) ihren Wagen, spielen mit ihren Haustieren, sammeln Briefmarken, lesen oder sehen fern. Viele Deutsche haben ein Hobby, das sie in einem Verein (*club*) ausüben. In vielen Städten gibt es Gesangs- und Heimatvereine sowie (*as well as*) Vereine für Schützen (*archery*), Amateurfunker (*ham radio operators*) und Kegler.

Sport ist eine beliebte Freizeitaktivität.

Aktivität 5 Möchtest du mitkommen?

Machen Sie eine Verabredung (*date*).

S1	S2
1. Ich gehe heute Bowling. Möchtest du mitkommen? ins Kino. ins Theater. in ein Rockkonzert. ins Stadtbad.	**2a.** Ja, gern, um wie viel Uhr denn? **b.** Ich kann nicht.
3a. Um _____ Uhr. Nach dem Abendessen um _____. Nach der Vorlesung (*lecture*) um _____. **b.** Warum denn nicht?	**4a.** Wo wollen wir uns treffen (*meet*)? **b.** Ich muss arbeiten. Ich habe kein Geld. keine Zeit. keine Lust.
5a. Vor dem Kino. Vor der Bibliothek. Im Studentenheim. Bei mir zu Hause. **b.** Schade.	**6.** Gut. Ich treffe dich dann um _____.

Aktivität 6 Pläne für einen Ausflug°

excursion

Verena und Antje machen Pläne fürs Wochenende. Sie wohnen beide in Düsseldorf. Hören Sie sich den Dialog an, und markieren Sie dann die richtigen Antworten.

	DAS STIMMT	DAS STIMMT NICHT	KEINE INFORMATION
1. Verena und Antje planen einen Ausflug.	☒	☐	☐
2. Sie wollen im Neandertal wandern.	☐	☒	☐
3. Es dauert nur eine Stunde bis zum Neandertal.	☐	☒	☐
4. Der Weg führt durch den Wald.	☒	☐	☐
5. Auf dem Wege dahin wollen sie ein Picknick machen.	☐	☐	☒
6. Antje will ihren Freund Stefan einladen.	☒	☐	☐

Jahreszeiten und Wetter.
Suggestions: 1. Bring in pictures showing different kinds of weather conditions. 2. Talk about the local weather during the different seasons. 3. Talk about the weather in German-speaking countries.

THEMA 3: Jahreszeiten und Wetter

Die **Jahreszeiten:** der **Frühling**, der **Sommer**, der **Herbst**, der **Winter**. Welches Bild passt zu welcher Jahreszeit?

Der Berliner Wannsee im <u>Sommer</u>.

Am Kornmarkt in Heidelberg im <u>Winter</u>.

Der Grundlsee in Österreich im <u>Herbst</u>.

Das Städtchen Creuzburg im <u>Frühling</u>.

Das Wetter

DIE SONNE	DIE WOLKEN	DER REGEN	DAS GEWITTER	DER SCHNEE
Die Sonne scheint.	**Es ist bewölkt.**	**Es regnet.**	**Es gibt ein Gewitter.**	**Es gibt Schnee.**
Es ist sonnig.	**Es ist kühl.**	**Es ist regnerisch.**	**Es blitzt und donnert.**	**Es schneit.**
Es ist angenehm/ heiter/warm/heiß.		**Es gibt einen Schauer.**	**Es ist schwül.**	**Es ist kalt.**

Was assoziieren Sie mit Winter, Sommer, Frühling und Herbst?

BEISPIEL: Die Blätter fallen von den Bäumen. →
Das ist Herbst.

1. Die Blätter (*leaves*) **fallen** von den Bäumen. Es kann auch regnerisch werden.
2. Leute schwimmen im Freibad. An manchen Tagen ist der **Himmel wolkenlos.**
3. Es regnet viel und die Blumen blühen. Man braucht oft einen **Regenschirm.**
4. Die Tage sind kurz. Für viele Menschen **dauert** diese Jahreszeit zu lang.
5. Es wird **kühler** und die Tage werden kürzer.
6. Es ist sehr heiß und manchmal sogar schwül.
7. **Drinnen** ist es schön warm, **draußen** aber wirklich **kalt. Die Sonne scheint** selten. Ein starker **Wind** bläst und der Himmel ist oft **bewölkt.**

Neue Wörter

angenehm pleasant
heiter bright
schwül humid
Himmel sky
wolkenlos cloudless
Regenschirm umbrella
dauert lasts
kühler cooler
heiß hot
drinnen inside
draußen outside
Wetterbericht weather report
Hagel hail

Aktivität 7   Der Wetterbericht

Welcher **Wetterbericht** passt zu welchem Bild?
1. _____ Im Norden beginnt es zu regnen, und morgen regnet es den ganzen Tag. Am Abend: **Regen,** eventuell auch **Hagel.**

a.

b.

c.   d.   e.

f.

2. ____ Im Moment ist es **bewölkt.** Die **Temperatur** heute Nachmittag ist nur 7 **Grad,** aber heute Abend wird es **kalt** und **windig.**

3. ____ In der Karibik ist es sonnig, heiter und warm. Wir haben den ganzen Tag **angenehme** Temperaturen. Morgen wird es wieder heiß.

4. ____ Im Süden gibt es Gewitter. **Es blitzt und donnert.**

5. ____ **In den Bergen** schneit es im Moment. Die Skifahrer sind begeistert über den Schnee.

6. ____ Im Rheinland gibt es heute Morgen **Nebel,** nachher einzelne **Wolken.** Auch morgen neblig und kühl.

Aktivität 8   Das Wetter in Europa

A. Lesen Sie den Text zum Wetterbericht und beantworten Sie die folgenden Fragen.

Neue Wörter

Grad   degrees
windig   windy
Gewitter   thunder-storms
es blitzt   there's lightning
es donnert   it's thundering
in den Bergen   in the mountains
es schneit   it's snowing
Nebel   fog

Das Hochdruckgebiet über Polen bestimmt weiterhin das Wetter in Deutschland. Nachts bleibt es noch empfindlich kalt.

In Berlin und Brandenburg überwiegend sonnig und niederschlagsfrei. Höchste Temperaturen am Tage zwischen 13 und 17 Grad, in Berlin um 16 Grad. Schwacher Wind aus Südwest. Nachts meist gering bewölkt und trocken, Temperaturrückgang auf 3 bis -1 Grad, in Berlin auf 2 Grad.

Übriges Deutschland: Im Norden in den Frühstunden vereinzelt noch Nebelfelder, sonst den ganzen Tag über sonniges Wetter. Höchste Temperaturen zwischen 10 Grad an der Küste und bis 20 Grad am Oberrhein. Meist schwacher Wind aus südöstlicher Richtung. Nachts im Norden zeitweise wolkig, aber überwiegend trocken. Sonst gering bewölkt oder aufklarend.

Aktivität 8. Suggestion: Begin by having students glance over the map, noting the temperatures in various cities. If they are accustomed to Fahrenheit readings, make comparisons with Celsius so that they get a sense of the season. Have them read the short text and work in pairs or groups to answer the four questions under the weather map. Note the significance of the second sentence, *Nachts bleibt es noch empfindlich kalt,* in determining that the month is more likely March than October. Go over the answers as a class. For part B, a quick geography review may be in order. Assign each pair or group a certain city, region, or country. They then describe the weather in that locale using the example as a model. Remind students to use the text for Akt. A and the map for Akt. B.

1. Dieser Wetterbericht ist wahrscheinlich für einen Tag im __d__.
   a. Juli
   b. Oktober
   c. Januar
   d. März

2. Nachts soll es __b__.
   a. warm werden
   b. kalt bleiben
   c. Nebel geben
   d. regnen

3. Im Norden soll es tagsüber __c__.
   a. windig sein
   b. bewölkt sein
   c. sonnig sein
   d. kalt werden

4. An der Küste ist die Höchsttemperatur etwa (*about*) __d__.
   a. 20° C
   b. −1° C
   c. zwischen 13° und 17° C
   d. 10° C

B. Schauen Sie sich jetzt die Wetterkarte auf Seite 215 an, und sagen Sie, wie das Wetter in den verschiedenen Gebieten ist.

BEISPIEL: In Skandinavien ist es ziemlich kalt aber heiter. Die Höchsttemperatur ist 7 Grad.

Skandinavien

Berlin

Spanien

Griechenland

Russland

??

Aktivität 9. Suggestion: First have students scan the possibilities. Then let them hear the weather reports and fill in the information. Check students' responses by asking *Wie ist das Wetter in ____?* Students use the information on their chart in their responses.

Aktivität 9 Wetterberichte im Radio

Sie hören fünf kurze Wetterberichte für fünf Städte in Europa. Kreuzen Sie die richtigen Informationen an und notieren Sie die Temperaturen in Grad Celsius.

Hier klicken!

Weiteres zum Thema Wetter finden Sie bei **Deutsch: Na klar!** im World-Wide-Web unter www.mhhe.com/dnk.

	ZÜRICH	WIEN	BERLIN	PARIS	LONDON
sonnig	☒	☐	☐	☐	☐
warm	☒	☐	☐	☒	☐
bewölkt bis heiter	☐	☐	☒	☐	☐
(stark) bewölkt	☐	☒	☐	☐	☒
Nebel	☐	☐	☐	☐	☒
Schauer	☐	☐	☒	☐	☐
Regen	☐	☐	☐	☐	☒
Wind	☐	☐	☐	☒	☐
Gewitter	☐	☒	☐	☐	☐
Grad Celsius	20–25	18	20	29	10

Aktivität 10. Suggestion: The activity can be done in pairs, with students jotting down what their partner says so they can report back to the whole group afterward.

Aktivität 10 So ist das Wetter in...

Woher kommen Sie? Wie ist das Wetter dort?

BEISPIEL: Ich komme aus San Franzisko. Dort ist das Wetter im Sommer oft kühl und neblig. Im Frühling ist es meistens sonnig. Und im Winter regnet es.

Aktivität 11 Ihr Wetterbericht

Schreiben Sie einen Wetterbericht für Ihr Gebiet (*area*).

BEISPIEL: Das Wetter für Donnerstag: schwül und heiß. Temperaturen: 30–35 Grad Celsius. Das Wetter für morgen: morgens Nebel, dann sonnig, um 30 Grad.

Grammatik im Kontext

Connecting Ideas: Coordinating Conjunctions°

koordinierende Konjunktionen

Coordinating conjunctions connect words, phrases, or sentences. You already know **und** and **oder.**

> Herr **und** Frau Baumann sitzen vor dem Fernseher.
> War der Film langweilig **oder** amüsant?

Other coordinating conjunctions are the following:

aber but, however   **sondern** but, rather   **denn** because, for

Erst muss ich heute arbeiten,	**und**	dann gehe ich Tennis spielen.
Ich spiele gern Tennis,	**aber**	mein Freund spielt lieber Karten.
Willst du mit zum Sportplatz,	**oder**	willst du zu Hause bleiben?
Ich möchte zum Sportplatz,	**denn**	da gibt es ein Fußballspiel.
Ich bleibe nicht zu Hause,	**sondern**	ich gehe zum Sportplatz.

Note:

- When used to connect sentences, coordinating conjunctions do not affect word order. Each sentence can be stated independently of the other.

Expressing a Contrast: **aber** vs. **sondern**

Das Spiel war kurz, **aber** spannend.	*The game was short but exciting.*
Der Film hat **zwar** nicht lang gedauert, **aber** er war sehr interessant.	*(Admittedly) the movie didn't last long, but it was very interesting.*
Es ist **nicht** warm, **sondern** kalt draußen.	*It isn't warm but rather cold outside.*
Das ist **kein** Regen, **sondern** Hagel!	*That's not rain but hail!*

The conjunction **aber** is normally used to juxtapose ideas. The adverb **zwar** may be used with **aber** to accentuate the juxtaposition. If, however, a negative (**nicht** or **kein**) is part of the first contrasted element *and* two mutually exclusive ideas are juxtaposed, **sondern** must be used.

mutually exclusive: nicht warm, **sondern** kalt (warm/kalt)
                          kein Regen, **sondern** Hagel (Regen/Hagel)

not mutually exclusive: kurz, **aber** spannend (kurz, spannend)
                              nicht lang, **aber** interessant (nicht lang, interessant)

Note: Point out that the combination of *zwar... aber* is very common. The contrast becomes clear when expressed as: on the one hand, on the other hand. The position of *zwar* parallels *nicht*:
   Es ist draußen zwar kalt, aber sonnig. Es ist draußen nicht kalt, sondern warm.

Übung 1 Wie ist das Wetter?

Gebraucht man hier **aber** oder **sondern?** Ergänzen Sie die Sätze.

1. Gestern war es zwar kalt, ____ sonnig.
2. Bei uns gibt es im Winter keinen Schnee, ____ nur viel Regen.
3. Im Frühling wird es hier nie heiß, ____ im Sommer wird es manchmal sehr heiß.
4. Die Sonne scheint zwar, ____ ich glaube, es gibt heute ein Gewitter.
5. Es gibt heute keinen Regen, ____ Schnee.
6. Heute ist das Wetter angenehm, ____ morgen wird es heiß.
7. Es regnet zwar nicht, ____ ich nehme doch lieber einen Regenschirm mit.
8. Bei dem Regen gehe ich nicht spazieren, ____ bleibe lieber zu Hause.

Übung 2 Freizeitpläne

Ergänzen Sie: **und, aber, oder, denn, sondern.**

Jörg ____[1] seine Freundin Karin planen einen Ausflug ____[2] ein Picknick. Die Frage ist: wohin ____[3] wann? Heute geht es leider nicht, ____[4] es regnet, ____[5] morgen haben beide keine Zeit. Also müssen sie bis zum Wochenende warten. Sie wollen diesmal nicht mit dem Auto ins Grüne fahren, ____[6] mit ihren Fahrrädern. Das dauert zwar länger (*longer*), ____[7] es macht bestimmt mehr Spaß. Sie wollen an einen See, ____[8] da können sie schwimmen gehen. Danach wollen sie ein Picknick im Wald ____[9] am See machen. Karin ist nicht für die öffentlichen (*public*) Picknickplätze, ____[10] da sind meistens zu viele Leute, Kinder ____[11] Hunde, Onkel ____[12] Tanten. Jörg lädt seinen Freund Andreas ein, ____[13] der kann leider nicht mit. Es tut ihm Leid, ____[14] er muss arbeiten.

Expressing Events in the Past: The Present Perfect Tense°

das Perfekt

In German, the present perfect tense is used conversationally to talk about past events, although a number of common verbs (**sein, haben,** and the modals) generally use the simple past tense in conversation. There is essentially no difference in meaning between the two tenses.

UWE: Gestern **habe** ich Fußball **gespielt.**	*I played soccer yesterday.*
KLAUS: Wer **hat** denn **gewonnen?**	*Who won?*
UWE: Wir **haben** fünf zu null **verloren.** Dann **sind** wir in die Kneipe **gegangen.**	*We lost five to zero. Then we went to the pub.*

Note:

- The present perfect tense in German consists of two parts: the present tense of the auxiliary verb **haben** or **sein** and a past participle.
- The auxiliary verb (**haben** or **sein**) and the past participle form a sentence bracket (**Satzklammer**).

	SATZKLAMMER		
Unsere Mannschaft	**hat**	5 zu 0	**verloren.**
Dann	**sind**	wir in die Kneipe	**gegangen.**

ANALYSE

Uwe und Klaus reden über ihr Lieblingsthema: Fußballvereine (*soccer teams*).

UWE: Hast du schon gehört? Bayern München hat gestern gegen Dynamo Dresden verloren. Null zu zwei!

KLAUS: Unglaublich! Hast du das in der Zeitung gelesen?

UWE: Ich habe es im Fernsehen gesehen.

KLAUS: Wie lange hat das Spiel gedauert?

UWE: Etwas über zwei Stunden. Dynamo Dresden hat sehr gut gespielt. Letzte Woche haben sie auch gegen Bremen gewonnen; eins zu null.

KLAUS: Ja, aber gegen den FC [Fußballclub] Nürnberg haben sie drei zu null verloren.

- Identify the past participles in the dialogue.
- What endings do these participles have?
- With what syllable do nearly all of the participles begin?
- What are the infinitives of these verbs?

Formation of the Past Participle°

das Partizip Perfekt

German, like English, distinguishes between two types of verbs: weak verbs (**schwache Verben**) and strong verbs (**starke Verben**). They form their past participles differently.

Weak Verbs

Ich habe **gehört,** Dynamo Dresden hat sehr gut **gespielt.**

I heard that Dynamo Dresden played very well.

Wir haben lange **gewartet.**

We waited for a long time.

Note:

- Weak verbs form the past participle by combining the verb stem with the prefix **ge-** and the ending **-(e)t.**
- The ending **-et** is used when the verb stem ends in **-t, -d,** or a consonant cluster.

INFINITIVE	PREFIX	STEM	ENDING	PAST PARTICIPLE
hören	ge-	hör	-t	gehört
wandern	ge-	wander	-t	gewandert
warten	ge-	wart	-et	gewartet
öffnen	ge-	öffn	-et	geöffnet

Point out. This is a program cover of the popular *Karl-May-Spiele* performed each year in Bad Segeberg, Schleswig-Holstein.

Übung 3   In meiner Kindheit

Drei Leute erzählen über ihre Hobbys als Kinder. Was hat ihnen Spaß gemacht? Was stimmt, und was wissen wir nicht?

	DAS STIMMT	KEINE INFORMATION
1. Herr Harter hat...		
Trompete gespielt	☒	☐
Insekten gesammelt	☒	☐
viel Fernsehen geschaut	☐	☒
2. Frau Beitz hat...		
mit ihrer Katze gespielt	☐	☒
die Tiere (*animals*) im Zoo gefüttert (*fed*)	☒	☐
Comic-Hefte gesammelt	☐	☒
3. Herr Huppert hat...		
Bücher von Karl May gelesen	☒	☐
gern Cowboy gespielt	☒	☐
im Schulorchester gespielt	☐	☒
Fußball gespielt	☒	☐

Übung 4   Haben Sie das als Kind gemacht?

Übung 4. Suggestion: For variation, have students say what they liked particularly well: *Briefmarken sammeln hat mir Spaß gemacht (Ich habe gern Briefmarken gesammelt)*, etc.

Point Out: the expression *Spaß gemacht* requires changing the infinitives to gerunds, which are capitalized.

Kreuzen Sie an, was Sie als Kind gern, manchmal oder nie gemacht haben. Bilden Sie dann Sätze nach dem Muster.

BEISPIEL: Als Kind habe ich gern gemalt, aber ich habe nie mit Puppen gespielt.

	GERN	MANCHMAL	NIE
Briefmarken sammeln	☐	☐	☐
Insekten sammeln	☐	☐	☐
Comic-Hefte sammeln	☐	☐	☐
__??__ sammeln	☐	☐	☐
mit Puppen (*dolls*) spielen	☐	☐	☐
Klavier oder Gitarre spielen	☐	☐	☐
Fußball oder Baseball spielen	☐	☐	☐
die Tiere im Zoo füttern	☐	☐	☐
Cowboy und Indianer spielen	☐	☐	☐
Fernsehen schauen	☐	☐	☐
Kaugummi (*gum*) oder Süßigkeiten (*sweets*) kaufen	☐	☐	☐
malen	☐	☐	☐
Pop Musik hören	☐	☐	☐
Hausarbeiten machen	☐	☐	☐
angeln	☐	☐	☐
Computerspiele spielen	☐	☐	☐

Übung 5 Im Nudelhaus

Wie haben Inge und Claudia den Abend verbracht? Setzen Sie das Partizip Perfekt ein.

Realia. This bill is from a restaurant called *Nudelhaus* in Göttingen.

Inge und Claudia haben ein gemütliches Restaurant in der Stadt ____¹ (suchen). Im Nudelhaus war es sehr voll. Der Kellner hat sie ____² (fragen): Wollen Sie warten? Sie haben ziemlich lange auf einen Platz ____³ (warten). Der Kellner hat die Speisekarte auf den Tisch ____⁴ (legen). Am Nebentisch haben einige Leute Karten ____⁵ (spielen). Sie haben laut ____⁶ (lachen [*to laugh*]). Das Essen hat sehr gut ____⁷ (schmecken). Es hat nur 15,00 Euros ____.⁸ (kosten) Auf dem Weg nach Hause hat Claudia am Kiosk eine Zeitung ____⁹ (kaufen). Dann hat sie noch etwas an ihrer Seminararbeit ____¹⁰ (arbeiten).

```
        NUDELHAUS
       ROTE STR. 13
      37073 GöTTINGEN
      TEL: 0551/42263

    #0001        06-01-02

    RECHNUNG-#       35

    GAST/TISCH#     3

  2 HEFEWEIZEN       €4,00
  1 GRUENE SCHINKEN €5,50
  1 VOLLKORNNUDELN  €5,25

  BAR-TL      €14,75

   ES BEDIENTE SIE
           KELLNER 1
```

Strong Verbs

Heute morgen **habe** ich Zeitung **gelesen.**

This morning I read the newspaper.

Dann **habe** ich einen Kaffee **getrunken.**

Then I drank a cup of coffee.

Danach **bin** ich zum Fitness center **gegangen.**

After that I went to the gym.

Note:

- Strong verbs form the past participle by placing the prefix **ge-** before the stem of the verb and adding the ending **-en.**
- Many strong verbs show vowel and consonant changes in the past participle.

INFINITIVE	PREFIX	STEM	ENDING	PAST PARTICIPLE
lesen	**ge-**	les	**-en**	gelesen
gehen	**ge-**	gang	**-en**	gegangen
sitzen	**ge-**	sess	**-en**	gesessen
trinken	**ge-**	trunk	**-en**	getrunken

Following are other familiar strong verbs and their past participles. A complete list of strong and irregular verbs is in Appendix C.

INFINITIVE	PAST PARTICIPLE	INFINITIVE	PAST PARTICIPLE
bleiben	(ist)* geblieben	schlafen	geschlafen
essen	gegessen	schreiben	geschrieben
fahren	(ist) gefahren	sehen	gesehen
finden	gefunden	sein	(ist) gewesen
geben	gegeben	stehen	gestanden
helfen	geholfen	werden	(ist) geworden
kommen	(ist) gekommen		
laufen	(ist) gelaufen		
nehmen	genommen		

Übung 6   Fragen und Antworten

Folgen Sie dem Beispiel.

BEISPIEL: Wohin seid ihr gestern Abend gegangen? (ins „Nudelhaus")
→ Wir sind ins „Nudelhaus" gegangen.

1. Wo seid ihr gestern Abend gewesen? (im „Nudelhaus")
2. Was hast du da gegessen? (grüne Schinkennudeln)
3. Und was hast du dazu getrunken? (ein Hefeweizen = *wheatbeer*)
4. Hat es dort auch Unterhaltung gegeben? (Musik)
5. Habt ihr noch andere Freunde da gesehen? (niemand)
6. Wie lange seid ihr im „Nudelhaus" geblieben? (etwa eine Stunde lang)
7. Bist du dann sofort nach Hause gegangen? (noch zur Bibliothek)

Mixed Verbs

A few verbs include features of both weak and strong verbs in the past participle. Like weak verbs, the participles of mixed verbs end in **-(e)t**; like most strong verbs, the verb stem undergoes a change.

INFINITIVE	PAST PARTICIPLE
bringen	gebracht
kennen	gekannt
wissen	gewusst

---

*Indicates a verb that uses **sein** as its auxiliary. See The Use of **haben** or **sein** in the Present Perfect Tense, on page 224 of this chapter.

Verbs with Inseparable Prefixes°

Verben mit untrennbaren Präfixen

Inseparable prefixes are syllables like **be-, er-, ge-,** and **ver-** . A verb with such a prefix forms the past participle without an additional **ge-** prefix. Verbs with inseparable prefixes may be weak or strong.

INFINITIVE	PAST PARTICIPLE
bestellen	bestellt
erzählen	erzählt
gefallen	gefallen
gewinnen	gewonnen
verlieren	verloren

Verbs Ending in -ieren

Verbs ending in **-ieren** also form the past participle without adding a prefix. These verbs are all weak.

INFINITIVE	PAST PARTICIPLE
diskutieren	diskutiert
fotografieren	fotografiert

[1]*starting at*

Verbs with Separable Prefixes°

Verben mit trennbaren Präfixen

Separable-prefix verbs form the past participle by inserting the **ge-** prefix between the separable prefix and the verb stem. These verbs may be weak or strong.

INFINITIVE	PAST PARTICIPLE
anrufen	angerufen
aufstehen	(ist) aufgestanden
ausgehen	(ist) ausgegangen
einladen	eingeladen
einschlafen	(ist) eingeschlafen
mitnehmen	mitgenommen
zurückkommen	(ist) zurückgekommen

Übung 7   Kleine Situationen

Ergänzen Sie das Partizip Perfekt.

1. Gestern hat in der Zeitung ____ (stehen): Großer, graugetigerter Kater, rotes Halsband mit Glöckchen ____ (verlieren). Wer hat ihn ____ oder ____ (sehen, finden)? Er hört auf den Namen Charly.
2. In den letzten Tagen ist es recht kalt ____ (werden).
3. Wir haben gestern Abend noch lange über die Probleme mit dem Studium ____ (diskutieren). Ich bin erst um drei Uhr nachts ____ (einschlafen). Und dann bin ich um sechs Uhr ____ (aufstehen). Kein Wunder, dass ich heute kaputt bin.
4. Wir haben für acht Uhr einen Tisch im Nudelhaus ____ (reservieren). Wir haben alle eine Pizza ____ (bestellen).

Verloren/Gefunden

Großer, graugetigerter Kater, rotes Halsband mit Glöckchen. Wer hat ihn gesehen oder gefunden? Hört auf den Namen Charly. Finderlohn.

5. A: Wo hast du deinen Freund kennen _____ (lernen)?

   B: Jemand hat ihn zu einer Party _____ (einladen).

6. C: Wie hat es euch im Nudelhaus _____ (gefallen)?

   D: Sehr gut. Warum bist du nicht _____ (mitkommen)?

   C: Ich habe nicht _____ (wissen), wo ihr wart.

The Use of **haben** or **sein** in the Present Perfect Tense

Auxiliary **haben**

Suggestion: Practice a number of the verbs by asking personalized questions such as *Wie alt sind Sie? Wann sind Sie (21) geworden? Wann sind Sie gestern Abend schlafen gegangen? Sind Sie sofort eingeschlafen? Wann sind Sie aufgewacht? Sind Sie sofort aufgestanden?* (A variation of this will be practiced later in **Übung 12.**)

Point out: **Tanzen** expresses movement, but not from one place to another; therefore its present perfect tense is formed with **haben**.

Most verbs use **haben** as the auxiliary verb in the present perfect tense.

Unsere Mannschaft **hat** das Fußballspiel **gewonnen.**	*Our team won the soccer game.*
Die Fans **haben** auf den Straßen **getanzt.**	*The fans danced in the streets.*

Auxiliary **sein**

Sein is used with verbs that indicate movement from one place to another (e.g., **gehen** and **fahren**).

Rudi **ist** zum Fußballplatz **gegangen.**	*Rudi went to the soccer field.*
Nach dem Spiel **ist** er nach Hause **gefahren.**	*After the game he went home.*

Other verbs that show motion from one place to another are **kommen (ist gekommen), laufen (ist gelaufen),** and **fliegen (ist geflogen).**

Sein is also used with verbs that indicate a change of condition (e.g., **werden** and **aufwachen**).

Gestern **ist** Peter 21 **geworden.**	*Yesterday Peter turned 21.*
Ich **bin** heute spät **aufgewacht.**	*I woke up late today.*

The verbs **werden** and **aufwachen** in the examples above express a change of condition, such as a change in age **(ist 21 geworden)** or a transition from sleeping to being awake **(ist aufgewacht).** Other verbs that show a change of condition are **aufstehen (ist aufgestanden)** and **einschlafen (ist eingeschlafen).**

Several other important verbs using **sein** in the present perfect tense are **sein, bleiben,** and **passieren.**

Wo **ist** Rudi gestern **gewesen?**	*Where was Rudi yesterday?*
Wir **sind** zu Hause **geblieben.**	*We stayed home.*
Unsere Mannschaft hat verloren? Wie **ist** das **passiert?**	*Our team lost? How did that happen?*

Note:

- Verbs conjugated with **sein** in the present perfect tense will be listed in the vocabulary sections as follows: **einschlafen (schläft ein), ist eingeschlafen.**

Übung 8 Kleine Gespräche im Alltag

Ergänzen Sie **sein** oder **haben.**

1. LINDA: Tag, Hans! _____ ihr gestern Abend noch ins Kino gegangen?
    HANS: Ja, wir _____ einen alten Film mit Charlie Chaplin im Rialto gesehen. Und du, was _____ du gestern Abend gemacht?
    LINDA: Ich _____ zu Hause geblieben und _____ gearbeitet.
    HANS: Wir _____ dann hinterher noch ein Bier getrunken. Ich _____ erst nach eins ins Bett gekommen.

2. KARL: Mein neuer Wagen ist schon kaputt.
    UTE: Wie _____ denn das passiert?
    KARL: Ich _____ gegen einen Baum gefahren.

3. SABINE: Ich _____ gestern mit Gabi telefoniert. Sie _____ gerade aus Hamburg zurückgekommen.
    NINA: Wie _____ es ihr denn dort gefallen?
    SABINE: Gut. Aber es _____ jeden Tag geregnet.

4. MARTIN: Gestern _____ Stefan dreißig geworden.
    GABI: Mein Gott, so alt? Das _____ ich gar nicht gewusst.

Übung 9 Hin und her: Wochenende und Freizeit

Warum haben Sie das gemacht? Stellen Sie Ihrem Partner / Ihrer Partnerin Fragen, um die Gründe (*reasons*) zu erfahren.

BEISPIEL: S1: Warum ist Dagmar ins Alte Land gefahren?
S2: Sie wollte auf einem Bauernhof Obst kaufen.

**Fremdenverkehrsverein[1]
Altes Land e. V.[2]**

[1]*Tourism Office*
[2](= eingetragener Verein) *registered association*

WER	WAS	WARUM
Dagmar	ins Alte Land fahren	auf einem Bauernhof Obst kaufen wollen
Thomas	in den Sportclub gehen	Bodybuilding machen wollen
Jürgen	zu Hause bleiben	seine Lieblingssendung im Fernsehen sehen wollen
Stefanie	Hans anrufen	auf die Party nicht kommen sollen
Susanne	sehr lange schlafen	die ganze Woche schwer arbeiten müssen

Übung 10 Brigitte und Rainer: Ein modernes und fast unglaubliches Märchen

Ergänzen Sie die Verben im Perfekt.

Brigitte _____ Rainer bei einem Musikfest kennen _____ (lernen).[1]

Brigitte _____ mit einer Jugendgruppe Trompete _____ (spielen).[2]

Rainer _____ unter den Zuhörern _____ (sitzen).[3] Später _____ alle _____ (tanzen).[4] Rainer _____ _____ (aufstehen) und an Brigittes Tisch _____ (kommen).[5] Er _____ mit ihr _____ (tanzen).[6] Leider _____ er ihr beim Tanzen mehrmals auf die Füße _____ (treten)![7] Brigitte _____ ihm aber

trotzdem ihre Telefonnummer ____ (geben).[8] Gleich am nächsten
Tag ____ Rainer Brigitte ____ (anrufen).[9] Am Wochenende ____ er sie
zu Hause ____ (besuchen).[10] Er ____ ihr Blumen ____ (mitbringen).[11]
Letzte Woche ____ die beiden ____ (heiraten).[12]

Übung 11   Früher und heute

Achim hat seinen Lebensstil geändert (*changed*). Bilden Sie Sätze nach dem
Beispiel.

BEISPIEL: Früher hat er viel gearbeitet, aber jetzt faulenzt er nur.

FRÜHER		JETZT
1. im Studentenheim wohnen	→	in einer WG mit sechs Leuten leben
2. Geschichte studieren	→	den ganzen Tag Gedichte schreiben
3. immer Bier trinken	→	nur noch Mineralwasser trinken
4. alles essen	→	Vegetarier sein
5. jeden Tag in die Kneipe gehen	→	selten in die Kneipe gehen
6. klassische Musik hören	→	nur laute Rockmusik spielen
7. viel Sport treiben	→	nur vor dem Fernseher sitzen
8. seine Mutter immer zum Geburtstag anrufen	→	das immer vergessen (*to forget*)

Übung 12   Mein Wochenende

A. Sprechen Sie mit jemand über Ihr Wochenende. Folgen Sie dem Beispiel.

BEISPIEL: S1: Was hast du letztes Wochenende gemacht?
            S2: Zuerst habe ich meine Freundin angerufen.
            S1: Und dann?
            S2: Dann bin ich ins Fitnesscenter gegangen.
            S1: Und danach?
            S2: Danach habe ich gearbeitet.

Hier sind einige mögliche Aktivitäten:

> sehr lange schlafen
>
> um ... Uhr aufstehen
>
> die Zeitung lesen
>
> frühstücken
>
> jemand (*someone*)
>   anrufen
>
> Karten/Fußball/Tennis mit
>   jemand spielen
>
> jemand besuchen
>
> ins Fitnesscenter / zu einer Party / ins
>   Kino gehen
>
> arbeiten

B. Berichten Sie dann im Plenum.

Übung 11. Suggestion:
As a first step, have students do
sentences in the left-hand
column first, without
combining them with the right-
hand column. Have them
determine first whether a
verb is strong or weak and
what auxiliary verb it requires.

Follow-up: Ask students to
come up with statements that
express what they used to do
and what they do now.

Übung 12. Suggestion: Have
students scan the list of
expressions first and check
those that apply to them. Ask
them to add activities that are
not listed and pertain to what
they did, e.g., *arbeiten*. Then
have student pairs create the
dialogue. Ask several pairs to
report to the class about their
partner's weekend.

Sprache im Kontext

Videoclips

A. Jan, Dennis und Beatrice sprechen über ihre Freizeit. Was machen sie nicht in der Freizeit? Streichen Sie die Aktivitäten durch, die sie *nicht* machen.

1. Jan...
   verbringt seine Freizeit
      im Freien
   geht ins Kino
   trifft Freunde
   sieht fern
   macht Sport

2. Dennis...
   geht ins Kino
   geht ins Museum
   treibt Sport
   trifft Freunde

3. Beatrice...
   geht ins Kino
   trifft gern Freunde
   macht Sport
   hört Musik

B. Herr Borowsky verbringt seine Freizeit ein bisschen anders. Wie verbringt er seine Freizeit?

C. Welche Sportarten treiben Jan und Dennis?

D. Wo haben diese Leute den Urlaub verbracht? Kombinieren Sie.

1. _____ Jan
2. _____ Beatrice
3. _____ Herr Borowsky
4. _____ Dennis

   a. in Ägypten
   b. in Wien
   c. in Guatemala
   d. auf den Kanarischen Inseln und in Bayern

E. Und Sie? Was machen Sie in der Freizeit? Wo haben Sie letztes Jahr Ihren Urlaub verbracht?

Lesen

Zum Thema

A. Wie viel Freizeit hat man in verschiedenen Ländern? Schauen Sie sich die Tabelle „Ferien im Vergleich" an. Beantworten Sie die folgenden Fragen mit Hilfe der Tabelle auf der nächsten Seite.

1. Wie viele Urlaubstage haben die Finnen? Wie viele bezahlte Feiertage?
2. Welche Länder haben mehr bezahlte Feiertage als (*than*) Deutschland?
3. Welche Länder haben weniger (*fewer*) Urlaubstage als Deutschland?
4. Wie viele bezahlte Feiertage haben die US-Amerikaner?
5. Welche Länder in dieser Tabelle haben weniger Urlaubstage als die USA? Überrascht Sie das?

FERIEN IM VERGLEICH

	Urlaubstage	bezahlte Feiertage	
Finnland	38	9	47 *gesamt*
Italien	35	8	43
Deutschland	30	11	41
Spanien	25	14	39
Niederlande	31	7	38
Frankreich	25	10	35
Großbrit.	25	8	33
Japan	18	13	31
USA	12	11	23

Quelle: Institut der deutschen Wirtschaft

Finnen haben mehr als doppelt so viele Urlaubs- und Feiertage wie US-Bürger

FOCUS-Magazin

B. Was machen die Deutschen in ihrer Freizeit? Schauen Sie sich die Entspannungshitliste an. Vergleichen Sie Ihre Freizeitbeschäftigungen mit denen der Deutschen.

■ Was machen Sie gern in Ihrer Freizeit?

■ Stehen Ihre Freizeitaktivitäten auf der Liste?

C. Machen Sie eine Liste der sechs beliebtesten Freizeitaktivitäten in Ihrer Klasse. Vergleichen Sie Ihre Klasse mit den Deutschen.

1. Was ist die beliebteste Freizeitbeschäftigung in Ihrer Klasse?
2. Was steht an zweiter Stelle (*place*) für die Klasse?
3. Steht diese Aktivität auf der Liste der Deutschen?
4. Welche Unterschiede (*differences*) und Ähnlichkeiten (*similarities*) gibt es?

ENTSPANNUNGSHITLISTE

Die beliebtesten Freizeitbeschäftigungen der Deutschen

Musik hören	41
fernsehen	35
Zeitung lesen	35
gut Essen gehen	29
feiern, Freunde treffen	24
Auto fahren	21

Quelle: Verbraucheranalyse '96

Medien beherrschen den größten Teil der Freizeit am Feierabend und am Wochenende

FOCUS-Magazin

Note: These two tables lend themselves well to discussion of cultural contrasts.

Auf den ersten Blick

A. Schauen Sie sich den Text „Vergnügungen" auf der nächsten Seite an. Um was für einen Text handelt es sich? Woher wissen Sie das?

Assoziationen. Suggestion: Do these associations with the whole group. Write the associations on the board as students give them.

B. Assoziationen: Woran denken Sie?

BEISPIEL: Schnee → Winter, Spaß, Schneemann, kalt, weiß

1. Reisen
2. Schwimmen
3. freundlich sein
4. bequeme Schuhe
5. Hund
6. Schokolade
7. gute Musik
8. Kinder

von Bertolt Brecht

Der erste Blick[1] aus dem Fenster am Morgen
Das wiedergefundene alte Buch
Begeisterte Gesichter[2]
Schnee, der Wechsel der Jahreszeiten
5 Die Zeitung
Der Hund
Die Dialektik
Duschen, Schwimmen
Alte Musik
10 Bequeme Schuhe
Begreifen[3]
Neue Musik
Schreiben, Pflanzen
Reisen
15 Singen
Freundlich sein.

Bertolt Brecht 1898–1956

[1]*glance* [2]Begeisterte... *enthusiastic faces*
[3]*understanding*

Vergnügungen. Suggestion:
Bring in additional information
about Bertolt Brecht.

Zum Text

A. Die Wörter **Duschen, Pflanzen, Reisen** können die Pluralformen sein von: **Dusche** (*shower*), **Pflanze** (*plant*), **Reise** (*trip*); oder sie können auch Verbalformen sein: **Duschen** = *taking a shower;* **Pflanzen** = *planting;* **Reisen** = *traveling.* Wie versteht Brecht diese Wörter wahrscheinlich? Als Dinge (Objekte) oder als Aktivitäten? Warum ist das wichtig?

B. Sind Brechts Vergnügungen ungewöhnliche oder ganz normale Vergnügungen? Welche finden Sie ungewöhnlich? Warum?

Hier klicken!

Weiteres über Bertolt Brecht finden Sie bei **Deutsch: Na klar!** im World-Wide-Web unter
www.mhhe.com/dnk.

Sprechen und Schreiben

Aktivität 1   Ihr Gedicht

Schreiben Sie ein Gedicht mit dem Titel „Vergnügungen". Tauschen Sie Ihr Gedicht mit dem von einem Partner / einer Partnerin aus. Lesen Sie das Gedicht Ihres Partners / Ihrer Partnerin vor.

Aktivität 2   Eine Ferienreise

Viele Leute reisen gern in ihrer Freizeit. Schreiben Sie einen Absatz über eine Reise, die Sie einmal gemacht haben. Was haben Sie alles getan und gesehen? Wo und was haben Sie gegessen? Wie lange waren Sie unterwegs? Wie war das Wetter?

Wortschatz

Sport und Vergnügen	**Sports and Leisure**
angeln	to fish
Bodybuilding machen	to do body-building, weight training
faulenzen	to be lazy, lie around
der **Fußball, ¨e**	soccer; soccer ball
Fußball spielen	to play soccer
joggen	to jog
die **Karte, -n**	card
malen	to paint
Rad fahren (fährt Rad), ist Rad gefahren	to bicycle, ride a bike
reiten, ist geritten	to ride (horseback)
sammeln	to collect
Schach spielen	to play chess
Schlittschuh laufen (läuft), ist gelaufen	to ice skate
segeln	to sail
die **Spielkarte, -n**	playing card
der **Sport,** *pl.* **Sportarten**	sports, sport
Sport treiben, getrieben	to play sports
tauchen	to dive
Tennis spielen	to play tennis
turnen	to do gymnastics
zeichnen	to draw

Orte	**Locations**
der **Berg, -e**	mountain
das **Eisstadion,** *pl.* **Eisstadien**	ice-skating rink
der **Fluss, ¨e**	river
das **Freibad, ¨er**	outdoor swimming pool
das **Hallenbad, ¨er**	indoor swimming pool
das **Meer, -e**	sea, ocean
das **Schwimmbad, ¨er**	swimming pool
der **See, -n**	lake
die **Sporthalle, -n**	sports arena
der **Sportplatz, ¨e**	athletic field
das **Stadion,** *pl.* **Stadien**	stadium
der **Tennisplatz, ¨e**	tennis court

die **Turnhalle, -n**	gymnasium
der **Wald, ¨er**	forest
die **Wiese, -n**	meadow

Die Jahreszeiten	**Seasons**
das **Frühjahr**	spring
der **Frühling**	spring
der **Herbst**	autumn, fall
der **Sommer**	summer
der **Winter**	winter

Das Wetter	**Weather**
das **Gewitter, -**	thunderstorm
der **Grad**	degree(s)
35 Grad	35 degrees
der **Hagel**	hail
der **Himmel**	sky
der **Nebel**	fog
der **Regen**	rain
der **Regenschauer, -**	rain shower
der **Regenschirm, -e**	umbrella
der **Schnee**	snow
die **Sonne**	sun
Die Sonne scheint.	The sun is shining.
der **Sonnenschein**	sunshine
die **Temperatur, -en**	temperature
der **Wetterbericht, -e**	weather report
der **Wind, -e**	wind
die **Wolke, -n**	cloud
blitzen	to flash
Es blitzt.	There's lightning.
donnern	to thunder
Es donnert.	It's thundering.
regnen	to rain
Es regnet.	It's raining.
schneien	to snow
Es schneit.	It's snowing.
angenehm	pleasant
bewölkt	overcast, cloudy
heiß	hot
heiter	fair, bright
kalt	cold
kühl	cool

neblig	foggy	**Sonstiges**	**Other**
regnerisch	rainy	die **Freizeit**	freetime
schwül	muggy, humid		
sonnig	sunny	**denn**	because, for
warm	warm	**draußen**	outside
windig	windy	**drinnen**	inside
wolkenlos	cloudless	**einmal**	once

Verben   **Verbs**

Sonstiges   **Other**

die **Freizeit** — freetime

denn — because, for
draußen — outside
drinnen — inside
einmal — once
   einmal die Woche — once a week
   einmal im Monat — once a month
   einmal im Jahr — once a year
zweimal — twice
dreimal — three times
früher — earlier, once, used to (*do, be, etc.*)

gestern — yesterday
jeden Tag — every day
oder — or
sondern — but, rather

Verben   **Verbs**

bringen, gebracht — to bring
dauern — to last; to take
fallen (fällt), ist gefallen — to fall
fliegen, ist geflogen — to fly
passieren, ist passiert — to happen
reservieren — to reserve
verlieren, verloren — to lose
(Zeit) verbringen, verbracht — to spend (time)

LERNZIELE

Use this checklist to verify that you can now . . .

☐ discuss typical leisure-time activities in German-speaking countries.

☐ talk about different types of sports and leisure-time activities you engage in.

☐ talk about the weather in various seasons and places.

☐ form compound sentences using the coordinating conjunctions.

☐ distinguish between **aber** and **sondern** and use them appropriately.

☐ talk about events in the past, using the present perfect tense.

Wie man fit und gesund bleibt

Was kann man hier machen?
a. Stress reduzieren.
b. Einkaufen gehen.

Kapitel 8. Introduce the chapter by talking about the things people do to stay fit and healthy. Recycle vocabulary on sport and food during this introduction. Personalize the discussion to include what students in the class do.

Videoclips
Gesund leben

In diesem Kapitel

- **Themen:** Health and fitness, the human body, common illnesses and complaints, morning activities
- **Grammatik:** Subordinating conjunctions, reflexive pronouns and verbs
- **Kultur:** Health spas in Germany, **Apotheken** and **Drogerien**

Alles klar?

A. Schauen Sie sich die Anzeige für Baden-Baden an, einen Kurort (*spa*) in Deutschland. Was kann man in Baden-Baden unternehmen (*do*)? Machen Sie eine Liste.

BEISPIEL: SPORT UNTERHALTUNG GESUNDHEIT

schwimmen ins Theater gehen in die Sauna gehen

B. Was machen diese Leute in Baden-Baden? Kreuzen Sie an.

	HERR/FRAU LOHMANN	HERR KRANZLER	FRAU DIETMOLD
Golf	☐	☒	☐
Karten spielen	☒	☐	☐
Massage	☒	☐	☒
Mini-Golf	☐	☐	☒
Sauna	☐	☒	☐
Schwimmen	☐	☒	☐
Spazierengehen	☒	☐	☐
Tanzen	☐	☐	☒
Theater	☐	☐	☒
Thermalbad	☒	☒	☒
Tischtennis	☐	☐	☒
Trinkkur	☐	☒	☒
Wandern	☐	☒	☐

Realia. Suggestion: Take a few minutes to introduce the idea of the *Kurort*. Have students look at a map to see if they can find towns with the word *Bad* in the name. *Baden-Baden:* This is a segment of an ad by the *Bäder-und Kurverwaltung* of the city of Baden-Baden, which is world famous for its spas and gambling casinos. Note the word *Casino* in one of the ad's activities squares.

Hier klicken!

Weiteres zum Thema
Kurorte finden Sie bei
Deutsch: Na klar! im World-
Wide-Web unter
www.mhhe.com/dnk.

KULTURTIPP

There are many health spas (**Heilbäder und Kurorte**) throughout Germany, and Germans often spend several weeks at a spa after an illness or when they feel stressed from work. If rest and recuperation (**Kur und Erholung**) are recommended by a physician, the national health care system (**Krankenkasse**) will subsidize such a stay, although this type of benefit is becoming less common. Due to increasing health care costs, as well as fewer demands for **Kur und Erholung** at health spas, these resorts are having to reinvent themselves. Many still advertise the traditional **Kur** but offer additional activities such as exercise programs, family excursions, and at some, even gambling. At some health spas people go on a **Trinkkur:** at prescribed intervals they drink a glass of the healthful mineral waters for which some spas are famous.

Wörter im Kontext

Neue Wörter

TINA
Gesundheit health
tue (tun) do
versuche (versuchen) try
Arbeit work
meistens mostly
zu Fuß on foot
Kräutertee herb tea
ab und zu now and then

WALTER
deshalb for that reason
rauche (rauchen) smoke
nie never
d.h. = das heißt that is
wenig little, few
regelmäßig regularly
besonders especially
Luft air
mich fit halten to stay fit

THEMA 1: Fit und gesund

Was machen diese Leute, um **fit** zu bleiben?

TINA: Für meine **Gesundheit tue** ich viel. Ich esse vegetarisch, **versuche** so gut es geht, den **Stress** in meinem Leben zu reduzieren. Zur **Arbeit** gehe ich **meistens zu Fuß**. Ich trinke viel **Kräutertee** und nur selten Alkohol, und **ab und zu** ein Glas Wein zum Essen.

WALTER: **Fitness** ist mir sehr wichtig. **Deshalb rauche** ich **nie** und esse gesund, **d.h. (das heißt)** wenig Fleisch und viel Gemüse. Ich treibe **regelmäßig** Sport, **besonders** an der frischen **Luft**. Ich möchte **mich fit halten**.

ANITA: **Mindestens** zweimal im Jahr **mache** ich **Urlaub**, denn meine Arbeit ist sehr **anstrengend**. Ich bin nämlich **Krankenschwester**. Ich **achte auf** meine Gesundheit und esse nur **Ökolebensmittel, entweder** direkt vom Bauernhof **oder** vom **Naturkostladen**. Ich mache jede Woche Yoga. Da kann ich **mich** richtig **entspannen**.

Neue Wörter

ANITA
mindestens   at least
Urlaub machen   to go on vacation
anstrengend strenuous
Krankenschwester nurse
achte auf (achten auf) pay attention to
Ökolebensmittel organic foods
entweder... oder either . . . or
Naturkostladen health food store
mich entspannen relax

Aktivität 1   Meine Fitnessroutine

A. Was machen Sie, um fit und gesund zu bleiben? Kreuzen Sie an!

1. ☐ joggen
2. ☐ ins Fitnesscenter gehen
3. ☐ vegetarisch essen
4. ☐ meditieren
5. ☐ Urlaub machen
6. ☐ wenig Alkohol trinken
7. ☐ Stress reduzieren
8. ☐ nicht rauchen
9. ☐ viel Gemüse/Obst essen
10. ☐ viel an die frische Luft gehen
11. ☐ viel zu Fuß gehen
12. ☐ Yoga machen
13. ☐ viel Wasser trinken
14. ☐ ??

B. Sagen Sie nun (*now*), wie oft Sie das tun.

BEISPIEL: Ich trinke jeden Tag viel Wasser.

nie	jeden Tag
selten	mindestens/meistens einmal/zweimal die Woche
ab und zu	einmal/zweimal/dreimal im Jahr
manchmal	??
regelmäßig	

C. Sagen Sie nun, warum Sie das tun oder nicht tun.

BEISPIELE: Ich jogge nicht. Das ist mir zu langweilig.
Ich esse vegetarisch. Das ist gut für die Gesundheit.

macht mir (keinen) Spaß	ist zu anstrengend
ist gut/schlecht für die Gesundheit	ist (un)gesund
macht krank	reduziert Stress
kostet zu viel Geld	ist mir zu langweilig
habe keine Zeit/Lust dazu (*for that*)	??

Aktivität 2 Beim Fitnessberater°

Spielen Sie ein Gespräch zwischen einem Fitnessberater und einer Klientin. Was darf man tun? Was soll man nicht tun?

BEISPIEL: S1: Darf ich Wein trinken?
S2: Ja, aber nicht zu viel. Trinken Sie lieber viel Wasser.
S1: Und wie viele Stunden sollte ich pro Nacht schlafen?
S2: Mindestens sieben Stunden.

Fleisch essen	Kräutertee trinken
Vitamintabletten einnehmen	Kaffee trinken
Urlaub machen	??
Sport treiben	

Aktivität 2. Suggestion: Encourage students to be as creative as possible. Follow up by selecting one or two pairs to perform their conversation in front of the class.

Der menschliche Körper. Suggestion: Introduce body parts using TPR and follow with a game of *Simon says*.

Dialogue. Suggestion: Introduce the new words before students listen to the dialogue. Then ask them to describe briefly what is wrong with Christoph and how long he has been sick. Utilize the drawing to describe Christoph's illness. Have students role-play the dialogue.

THEMA 2: Der menschliche Körper°

body

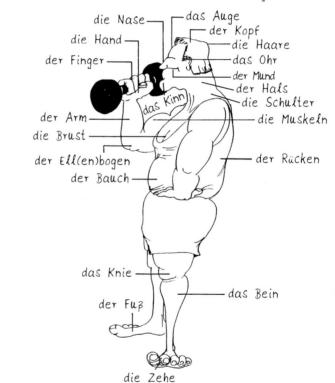

die Nase, das Auge, der Kopf, die Hand, die Haare, der Finger, das Ohr, der Mund, der Hals, das Kinn, die Schulter, der Arm, die Muskeln, die Brust, der Ell(en)bogen, der Rücken, der Bauch, das Knie, das Bein, der Fuß, die Zehe

Neue Wörter

klingst (klingen) sound
deprimiert depressed
ich fühle mich (sich fühlen) I feel
hundsmiserabel really lousy
Was fehlt dir? What's wrong with you?
Erkältung cold
sogar even
Grippe flu
tut mir weh (weh tun) hurts
kaum scarcely
schlucken swallow
mir ist schlecht I feel bad, I feel sick to my stomach
Fieber fever
Halsschmerzen sore throat
Husten cough
Schnupfen runny nose, sniffles

Ein Telefongespräch

CHRISTOPH: Schmidt.
UTA: Hallo, Christoph? Hier ist Uta.
CHRISTOPH: Ja, grüß dich, Uta.
UTA: Nanu! Was ist denn los? Du **klingst** ja so **deprimiert**.
CHRISTOPH: Ich liege im Bett. **Ich fühle mich hundsmiserabel.**
UTA: **Was fehlt dir** denn?
CHRISTOPH: Ich habe eine **Erkältung**, vielleicht **sogar** die **Grippe**. Der Hals **tut mir weh**, ich kann **kaum schlucken, mir ist schlecht**. Ich habe **Fieber, Halsschmerzen, Husten** und **Schnupfen**. Ich

habe auch **Kopfschmerzen** und bin
so **müde** und **schlapp**. Und morgen
muss ich eine Arbeit bei Professor
Höhn **abgeben**.

> Ich fühle mich hundsmiserabel.

UTA: **So ein Pech.** Warst du schon
beim **Arzt**?

CHRISTOPH: Nein.

UTA: Wie lange bist du denn
schon **krank**?

CHRISTOPH: Seit **fast** zwei Wochen
schon.

UTA: Du bist **verrückt**! Geh
doch **gleich** zum Arzt.
Er kann dir sicher was*
verschreiben.

CHRISTOPH: Aber ich kriege (*get*) bestimmt keinen **Termin**.

UTA: **Das macht nichts.** Geh einfach in die **Sprechstunde**.

CHRISTOPH: Na gut. Ich danke dir für den **Rat**.

UTA: **Nichts zu danken**... Ich wünsche dir **gute Besserung**!

Neue Wörter

Kopfschmerzen
 headache
müde tired
schlapp worn-out
abgeben drop off,
 give to
so ein Pech what bad
 luck!
Arzt doctor
fast almost
verrückt crazy
gleich right away
verschreiben
 prescribe
Termin appointment
Das macht nichts.
 That doesn't matter.
Sprechstunde office
 hours
Rat advice
nichts zu danken
 don't mention it
gute Besserung get
 well soon

Aktivität 3   Im Aerobic-Kurs

Sie hören eine Aerobic-Lehrerin beim Training im Aerobic-Kurs. Nummerieren Sie alle Körperteile in der Reihenfolge von 1–10, so wie Sie sie hören. Einige Wörter auf der Liste kommen nicht im Hörtext vor.

_1_ Arme	_5_ Füße	_3_ Knie	_10_ Muskeln
___ Bauch	_7_ Hals	_6_ Kopf	_2_ Rücken
___ Beine	___ Hände	_9_ Ohren	_8_ Schultern
_4_ Finger			

Aktivität 4   Das Telefongespräch

Ergänzen Sie den Lückentext. Die Information finden Sie in dem Telefonespräch im **Thema 2**.

Christoph klingt sehr ____[1] am Telefon, denn er fühlt sich ____.[2] Der ____[3] tut ihm weh und er kann kaum ____.[4] Er hat auch ____.[5] Seit zwei Wochen ist er ____.[6] Er war noch nicht beim ____.[7] Uta empfiehlt (*recommends*) ihm, in die ____[8] zu gehen. Uta wünscht ihm ____[9] ____.[10]

Aktivität 5   Beschwerden°

Complaints

Was fehlt diesen Leuten? Was sollten sie dagegen tun? Markieren Sie Ihre Antworten. Aktivität 5. Suggestion: Students should look over all possibilities before listening to each dialogue. After each dialogue is played, pause to let students respond.

DIALOG 1

Leni hat:	Rückenschmerzen.	eine Erkältung	Kopfschmerzen
Doris empfiehlt:	Geh zum Arzt.	Leg dich ins Bett.	Nimm Aspirin.

***Was,** as used here, is a shortened form of the pronoun **etwas**. It occurs often in colloquial German.

DIALOG 2

Doris hat:	Kopfschmerzen	Bauchschmerzen	Fieber
Leni empfiehlt:	<u>Geh zum Arzt.</u>	<u>Trink Kamillentee.</u>	Leg dich ins Bett.

DIALOG 3

Patient hat:	<u>keine Energie</u>	Halsschmerzen	<u>kann nicht schlafen</u>
Arzt empfiehlt:	<u>mehr Schlaf</u>	<u>Kur im Schwarzwald</u>	Tabletten gegen Stress

SPRACHTIPP

Use the following phrase to talk about how you feel:

   Ich **fühle mich** nicht wohl.   *I don't feel well.*

The person with the symptoms refers to himself or herself with a pronoun in the dative case.

   Mir ist schlecht.   *I feel sick to my stomach.*
   Mir ist warm/kalt.   *I feel warm/cold.*

The verb **fehlen** with the dative case is frequently used to ask "What is the matter?"

   Was fehlt dir denn?   *What's the matter with you?*
   Was fehlt ihm denn?   *What's the matter with him?*

Use the verb **wehtun** with the dative case to say that something hurts.

Die Füße **tun** { mir / ihm / ihr } **weh.**   *My / His / Her feet hurt.*

Für den Hals – jederfalls: EMSER PASTILLEN

EMS

EMSER PASTILLEN[1]
Naturkraft gegen Erkältung

Aktivität 6 Was fehlt dir denn?

Fragen Sie Ihren Partner / Ihre Partnerin: „Was fehlt dir denn?"
Antworten Sie auf seine/ihre Beschwerden mit einem guten Rat.

BEISPIEL: s1: Ich fühle mich so schlapp.
           s2: Geh nach Hause und leg dich ins Bett.

Aktivität 6. Follow-up:
Each student writes a complaint on a slip of paper (no names). Slips are collected and redistributed. As slips are read by individuals, other students give advice.

[1]*lozenges*

BESCHWERDEN	RATSCHLÄGE
Ich fühle mich so schlapp.	Nimm ein paar Aspirin.
Der Hals tut mir weh.	Geh...
Ich kann kaum schlucken.	in die Sauna.
Ich habe...	nach Hause.
Kopfschmerzen.	zum Arzt.
Rückenschmerzen.	Leg dich ins Bett.
Halsschmerzen.	Nimm mal Vitamin C.
Husten.	Trink heißen Tee mit Rum.
Schnupfen.	??
eine Erkältung.	
Fieber.	
Ich kann nicht schlafen.	
Mir ist schlecht.	
Ich habe zu viel gegessen.	

[2]*natural remedy*
[3]*valerian (medicinal plant) content*

Eine „gute Nacht"

Das Naturheilmittel[2] **mit besonders hohem Baldrian-Gehalt**[3]

Zirkulin Baldrian

Zirkulin rote baldrian-dragées

extra stark 45

238   Kapitel 8 ■ Wie man fit und gesund bleibt

THEMA 3: Morgenroutine

Morgenroutine. **Suggestion:** Introduce vocabulary using TPR.

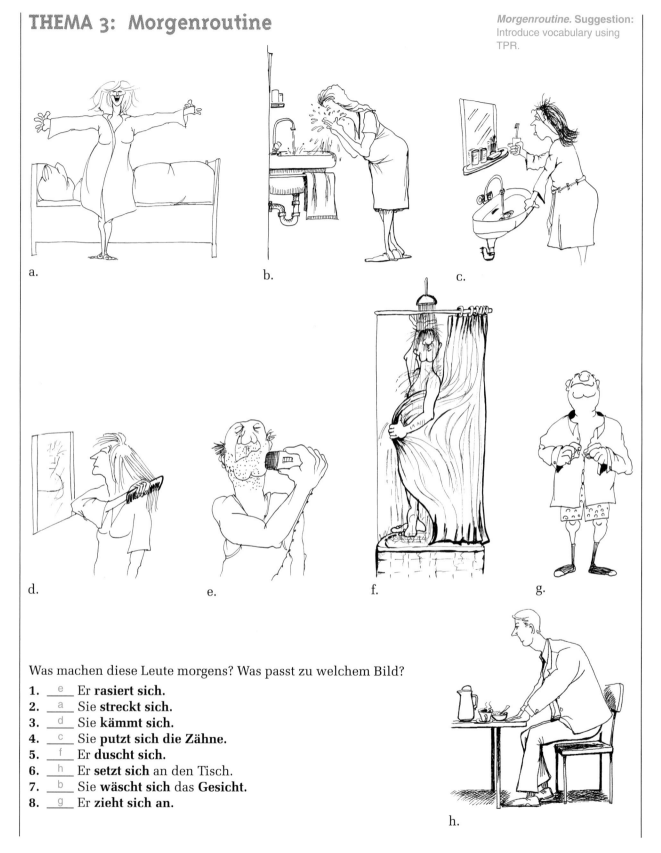

a.

b.

c.

d.

e.

f.

g.

Was machen diese Leute morgens? Was passt zu welchem Bild?

1. __e__ Er **rasiert sich.**
2. __a__ Sie **streckt sich.**
3. __d__ Sie **kämmt sich.**
4. __c__ Sie **putzt sich die Zähne.**
5. __f__ Er **duscht sich.**
6. __h__ Er **setzt sich** an den Tisch.
7. __b__ Sie **wäscht sich** das **Gesicht.**
8. __g__ Er **zieht sich an.**

h.

Aktivität 7   Meine Routine am Morgen

Was machen Sie jeden Morgen? Hier sind einige Dinge, die man morgens oft macht. In welcher Reihenfolge machen Sie alles jeden Morgen? Nummerieren Sie die Aktivitäten unten von 1 bis 8.

_____ Ich ziehe mich an.

_____ Ich dusche mich.

_____ Ich wasche mir das Gesicht.

_____ Ich kämme mich.

_____ Ich strecke mich.

_____ Ich rasiere mich.

_____ Ich setze mich an den Frühstückstisch.

_____ Ich putze mir die Zähne.

Aktivität 8   Hin und her: Meine Routine—deine Routine

Jeder hat eine andere Routine. Was machen diese Leute und in welcher Reihenfolge? Machen Sie es auch so?

BEISPIEL: S1: Was macht Alexander morgens?

S2: Zuerst rasiert er sich und putzt sich die Zähne. Dann kämmt er sich. Danach setzt er sich an den Tisch und frühstückt.

WER	WAS ER/SIE MORGENS MACHT
Alexander	zuerst / sich rasieren / sich die Zähne putzen dann / sich kämmen danach / sich an den Tisch setzen / frühstücken
Elke	zuerst / sich anziehen dann / sich die Zähne putzen danach / sich kämmen
Tilo	zuerst / sich duschen / sich rasieren dann / sich an den Tisch setzen / frühstücken danach / sich die Zähne putzen
Kamal	zuerst / sich das Gesicht waschen dann / frühstücken danach / sich rasieren / sich anziehen
Sie	zuerst / ?? dann / ?? danach / ??
Ihr Partner / Ihre Partnerin	zuerst / ?? dann / ?? danach / ??

Grammatik im Kontext

Connecting Sentences: Subordinating Conjunctions°

unterordnende Konjunktionen

Subordinating conjunctions are used to connect a main clause and a dependent clause. Four frequently used subordinating conjunctions are **dass** (*that*), **ob** (*whether, if*), **weil** (*because*), and **wenn** (*whenever, if*).

Ich hoffe, **dass** du bald gesund wirst.	*I hope that you'll get well soon.*
Weißt du, **ob** Mark krank ist?	*Do you know whether Mark is ill?*
Mark bleibt zu Hause, **weil** er eine Erkältung hat.	*Mark is staying at home because he has a cold.*
Ich gehe ins Fitnesscenter, **wenn** ich Zeit habe.	*I go to the fitness center whenever I have time.*

Note:

- In dependent clauses the conjugated verb is placed at the end.
- In the case of a separable-prefix verb, the prefix is joined with the rest of the verb.
- A comma always separates the main clause from the dependent clause.

MAIN CLAUSE	DEPENDENT CLAUSE
Er bleibt zu Hause,	weil er eine Erkältung **hat.**
Ich weiß nicht,	ob er schon beim Arzt gewesen **ist.**
Ich bin sicher,	dass er **mitkommt.**

If the dependent clause precedes the main clause, the main clause begins with the conjugated verb, followed by the subject.

DEPENDENT CLAUSE	MAIN CLAUSE
Weil Mark krank ist,	**bleibt** er zu Hause.
Wenn wir Zeit haben,	**gehen** wir am Wochenende ins Fitnesscenter.
Ob Hans Zeit hat,	**weiß** ich nicht.

Indirect Questions

An indirect question begins with an introductory clause followed by a question. Interrogative pronouns function like subordinating conjunctions in indirect questions. The conjugated verb is placed at the end.

DIRECT QUESTION	INDIRECT QUESTION
Warum kauft Herr Stierli so viel Vitamin B?	Ich weiß nicht, **warum** Herr Stierli so viel Vitamin B **kauft.**
Was hat er vor?	Ich möchte wissen, **was** er **vorhat.**

A yes/no question is introduced by the conjunction **ob** in the indirect question.

Geht er zu einer Party?	Ich möchte wissen, **ob** er zu einer Party **geht.**

success

Übung 1   Ein großer Erfolg°

Schauen Sie sich den Cartoon „Herr Stierli" an. Beantworten Sie die Fragen, indem Sie die Konjunktion **weil** benutzen (*use*).

Realia. The cartoon *Herr Stierli* makes fun of society at an international party. Herr Stierli is greeted in English, German, and French (*Comment allez-vous?* = "How are you?"). The German phrase *Ich habe die Ehre* ("I am honored") is a formal way of acknowledging someone socially, especially in southern Germany and Austria.

Übung 1. Note: Explain that the expression "Vitamin B" is sometimes used figuratively as it is here: "B" stands for *Beziehungen* = connections. Thus a dose of vitamin B means you need connections. Herr Stierli, by ingesting large amounts of vitamin B, is able to make lots of connections at the party and is the most popular guest.

von René Fehr

1. Warum ist Herr Stierli zur Apotheke gegangen? (Er wollte Vitamin B kaufen.)
2. Warum hat er fünf Packungen Vitamin B gekauft? (Er brauchte mehr Energie.)
3. Warum war Herr Stierli sehr stolz (*proud*)? (Er war sehr beliebt bei den Gästen.)
4. Warum hatte er so großen Erfolg? (Er hatte vor der Party viel Vitamin B eingenommen.)

What's your opinion?

Übung 2   Was meinen Sie?°

BEISPIEL: s1: Obst ist die beste Nahrung (*food*).
　　　　　　s2: Ich bezweifle, dass Obst die beste Nahrung ist.

Essen macht Spaß

Jeder Deutsche trinkt im Leben 3060 Liter Bier

REDEMITTEL

Ich bezweifle, dass...

Ich glaube auch, dass...

Ich bin sicher, dass...

1. Vitamin C ist gut gegen Erkältungen.
2. Klassische Musik ist gut gegen Stress.
3. Rauchen gefährdet (*endangers*) die Gesundheit.
4. Yoga reduziert Stress.
5. Gesund ist, was gut schmeckt.
6. Hühnersuppe ist gut gegen Erkältungen.
7. Bier macht dick.
8. Vegetarisches Essen ist ideal.
9. Zu viel Zucker macht aggressiv.
10. Knoblauch (*garlic*) hilft gegen Vampire!

MOZART GEGEN STRESS

Übung 2. This exercise can be done in pairs, students taking turns expressing their opinions about the statements. Follow up with a survey in class: *Wer glaubt, dass (Bier dick macht)? Wer bezweifelt, dass; Wer behauptet dass,... ?*

Übung 3 Wie gesundheitsbewusst° sind Sie?

health-conscious

Fragen Sie einen Partner / eine Partnerin, was er/sie für Fitness und die Gesundheit tut, und warum.

Übung 3. Note: Ensure that students use the *weil* construction. Review use of *denn* and *nämlich* to express reasons.

BEISPIEL: S1: Gehst du regelmäßig ins Fitnesscenter?
　　　　　 S2: Nein.
　　　　　 S1: Warum nicht?
　　　　　 S2: Weil ich das langweilig finde.

S1: FRAGEN	S2: ANTWORTEN
vegetarisch essen	finde das langweilig
Vitamintabletten einnehmen	kostet zu viel
zu Fuß zur Arbeit / zur Uni gehen	mag ich (nicht)
Kräutertee/Kaffee trinken	reduziert den Stress
rauchen	macht mir (viel/keinen) Spaß
Yoga machen	habe keine Zeit dazu
regelmäßig ins Fitnesscenter gehen	ist sehr gesund/ungesund
Biolebensmittel kaufen	

KULTURTIPP

To purchase prescription drugs in Germany, you have to go to an **Apotheke.** Nonprescription drugs must also be purchased at an **Apotheke.** Nonprescription drugs are not as common in Germany as in the United States or Canada. Toiletries, vitamins, and personal care items are carried by **Drogerien.**

Medikamente gibt es in der Apotheke.

Grammatik im Kontext　**243**

Übung 4 Das mache ich, wenn...

Sagen Sie, wann Sie das machen.

BEISPIEL: Ich gehe zum Arzt, wenn ich krank bin.

Ich gehe zum Arzt,...	Ich brauche Zahnpasta.
zum Zahnarzt,...	Ich habe zu viel gegessen.
in die Sauna,...	Ich brauche Aspirin.
in die Drogerie,...	Ich fühle mich hundsmiserabel.
in die Apotheke,...	Ich habe die Grippe.
Ich bleibe im Bett,...	Ich fühle mich schlapp.
Ich nehme viel Vitamin C ein,...	Ich habe eine Erkältung.
Ich esse Hühnersuppe,...	Ich bin krank.
Ich trinke Kräutertee,...	Ich habe Zahnschmerzen.
	??

Übung 5. Suggestion: Have students scan the possibilities before making four statements about themselves. Then have students work in pairs, taking turns asking questions and responding. Have them begin each question by asking, for example, *Was tust du, wenn du eine Erkältung hast?* etc.
Follow-up: Ask the class questions like *Wer isst Hühnersuppe, wenn er/sie eine Erkältung hat?* You may want to point out that chicken soup for a cold is not a widely-known folk remedy in Germany.

Übung 5 Was tun Sie gewöhnlich?

Sagen Sie, was Sie in diesen Situationen machen.

BEISPIEL: Wenn ich eine Erkältung habe, trinke ich viel Kräutertee.

Wenn ich eine Erkältung habe,	im Bett bleiben
Wenn ich nicht einschlafen kann,	Kräutertee trinken
Wenn ich gestresst bin,	heiße Milch mit Honig (*honey*) trinken
Wenn ich mich schlapp fühle,	Rotwein mit Rum trinken
Wenn ich schlecht gelaunt bin (*am in a bad mood*),	in die Sauna gehen
	viel Vitamin C einnehmen
	Hühnersuppe essen
	ein Buch lesen
	meditieren
	??

think it over

Übung 6 Ich muss es mir überlegen.°

Stefans Freunde wollen Bungee-jumping gehen, und er soll mitmachen. Stefan ist aber sehr skeptisch. Was will er genau wissen?

BEISPIEL: Wo kann man das lernen? →
      Er will wissen, wo man das lernen kann.

Er will wissen,...

1. Wo kann man das tun?
2. Wie gefährlich (*dangerous*) ist das eigentlich?
3. Warum muss es ausgerechnet Bungee-jumping sein?
4. Was für Kleidung muss man dabei tragen?
5. Muss man nicht zuerst ein Training machen?
6. Wer macht sonst noch mit?
7. Wer hat diese verrückte Idee gehabt?

Reflexive Pronouns and Verbs°

When the subject and pronoun object of a sentence refer to the same person, the object is called a reflexive pronoun.

Wir informieren **uns** über Fitnesscenter.

We're informing ourselves about fitness centers.

Die Studenten informieren **sich** über die Kosten.

The students inform themselves about the costs.

Informieren **Sie sich** bitte zuerst über die Kosten.

Please inform yourself first about the costs.

Note:

- Reflexive pronouns are identical to personal pronouns except for the third-person singular and plural forms and the formal **Sie**-form, all of which are **sich.**

- The reflexive pronoun comes after the conjugated verb. However, it follows pronoun subjects in questions and the formal imperative.

> Christoph fühlt **sich** nicht wohl.
> Fühlst du **dich** nicht wohl?
> Informieren Sie **sich** zuerst!

Wander-Vögel

informieren sich
jeden Samstag im
REISE-JOURNAL
der Rheinischen Post

Reflexive Pronouns. Suggestion: Introduce reflexive pronouns and verbs by recycling some of the verbs used in the **WiK:** *Ich halte mich mit Tennis fit. Wie halten Sie sich fit?* **Point out:** The reflexive pronoun is not always expressed in English: "Mr. Stierli keeps fit" (*Herr Stierli hält sich fit*).

Reflexive Pronouns

ACCUSATIVE	DATIVE		ACCUSATIVE	DATIVE	
mich	mir	*myself*	uns	uns	*ourselves*
dich	dir	*yourself*	euch	euch	*yourselves*
sich	sich	*yourself (formal)*	sich	sich	*yourselves (formal)*
sich	sich	*himself/herself*	sich	sich	*themselves*

Verbs with Accusative Reflexive Pronouns

German uses reflexive pronouns much more extensively than English. Some verbs are always used with a reflexive pronoun.

Infinitive: **sich setzen** (*to sit down*)	
ich setze **mich**	wir setzen **uns**
du setzt **dich**	ihr setzt **euch**
er sie es } setzt **sich**	sie setzen **sich**
Sie setzen **sich**	

Verbs that are always used with a reflexive pronoun in the accusative include the following:

sich ausruhen	to rest
sich beeilen	to hurry
sich entspannen	to relax
sich erholen	to recuperate
sich erkälten	to catch cold
sich (hin)legen	to lie down
sich (hin)setzen	to sit down
sich (wohl) fühlen	to feel (well)

„Bitte entspannen Sie sich!"

Verbs with Reflexive Pronouns in the Accusative or Dative

Common verbs with a reflexive pronoun in either the accusative or dative include the following:

sich anziehen	to get dressed
sich kämmen	to comb one's hair
sich verletzen	to injure oneself
sich waschen	to wash oneself

The expression **sich die Zähne putzen** (*to brush one's teeth*) is commonly used only with a dative reflexive pronoun.

ACCUSATIVE	DATIVE
Ich wasche **mich**.	Ich wasche **mir** das Gesicht.
Ich kämme **mich**.	Ich kämme **mir** die Haare.
Ich ziehe **mich** an.	Ich ziehe **mir** die Jacke an.
Ich habe **mich** verletzt.	Ich habe **mir** den Fuß verletzt.
—	Ich putze **mir** die Zähne.

Note:

- The reflexive pronoun is in the dative case (indirect object) whenever the sentence also has a direct object in the accusative case (**das Gesicht, die Haare, die Jacke,** etc.).

Schauen Sie sich den Cartoon an.

- Lesen Sie, was Wurzel denkt, und identifizieren Sie die Sätze mit reflexiven Verben.
- Wie fühlt sich Wurzel heute?
- Fühlt er sich gewöhnlich so gut? Wie oft hat er sich schon so gefühlt?
- Warum fühlt er sich am Ende ganz deprimiert?

Analyse. Suggestion: Use the cartoon as a point of departure to ask students: *Wie fühlen Sie sich heute?*

Realia. *Wurzel* is the German name for the cartoon dog Fred Basset.

¹unusual
²sign

Übung 7   Beim Arzt

Sie hören eine Besprechung zwischen Herrn Schneider und seinem Arzt. Markieren Sie die richtigen Antworten auf die Fragen.

1. Warum hat Herr Schneider einen Termin beim Arzt?
   a. Er hat einen chronischen Schluckauf (*hiccups*).
   b. Er hat sich beim Fitnesstraining verletzt.
   c. Er fühlt sich so schlapp.

2. Was ist die Ursache (*cause*) seines Problems?
   a. Seine Arbeit bringt viel Stress mit sich.
   b. Er sitzt den ganzen Tag am Schreibtisch.
   c. Seine Arbeit ist so langweilig.

3. Was empfiehlt ihm der Arzt?
   a. Er soll sich eine andere Arbeit suchen.
   b. Er soll sich im Schwarzwald vom Stress erholen.
   c. Er soll Sport treiben.

4. Wie reagiert Herr Schneider auf diese Vorschläge?
    a. Er ist sehr enthusiastisch.
    b. Er hat keine Zeit für eine Kur im Schwarzwald.
    c. Er interessiert sich nicht für Sport.

5. Was verschreibt ihm der Arzt?
    a. Einen täglichen Spaziergang.
    b. Regelmäßig meditieren.
    c. Vitamintabletten.

6. Warum meint der Arzt, dass Herr Schneider mit seinen Nerven am Ende ist?
    a. Er hat einen Schluckauf.
    b. Er hat einen nervösen Tick und weiß es nicht.
    c. Er redet zu viel und zu schnell.

[1]each time

Übung 8   Morgenroutine

Morgens geht es bei der Familie Kunze immer recht hektisch zu. Ergänzen Sie die fehlenden Reflexivpronomen.

Zuerst duscht _____[1] Herr Kunze. Dann rasiert er _____.[2] Seine Frau ruft: „Bitte, beeil _____,[3] ich muss _____[4] auch noch duschen."

Cornelia, die siebzehnjährige Tochter, erklärt: „Ich glaube, ich habe _____[5] erkältet. Ich fühle _____[6] so schlapp. Ich lege _____[7] wieder hin." Frau Kunze zu Cornelia: „Zieh _____[8] bitte sofort an! Du fühlst _____[9] so schlapp, weil du so spät ins Bett gegangen bist." Cornelia: „Ich ziehe _____[10] ja schon an."

Frau Kunze zu Thomas, dem siebenjährigen Sohn: „Es ist schon halb acht, und du musst _____[11] noch kämmen. Hast du _____[12] überhaupt schon gewaschen?"

Sabine, die zwölfjährige Tochter, duscht _____¹³ schon seit fünfzehn Minuten.

Herr und Frau Kunze setzen _____¹⁴ endlich an den Frühstückstisch. Herr Kunze zu seiner Frau: „Wir müssen _____¹⁵ beeilen. Wo sind die Kinder?" Er ruft ungeduldig: „Könnt ihr _____¹⁶ nicht ein bisschen beeilen? Es ist schon acht Uhr."

So ist es jeden Morgen: Alle müssen _____¹⁷ beeilen.

Übung 9 Ratschläge°

Advice

Was kann man Ihnen in diesen Situationen raten?

BEISPIEL: S1: Ich habe die Grippe.
  S2: Leg dich ins Bett. [oder]
    Du musst dich ins Bett legen.

1. Sie haben die Grippe.
2. Sie haben sich erkältet.
3. Sie fühlen sich hundsmiserabel.
4. Sie haben den ganzen Tag in der Bibliothek verbracht.
5. Sie müssen in einer Minute an der Bushaltestelle sein.
6. Sie haben sich die große Zehe verletzt.

sich beeilen
sich gut erholen
sich ins Bett legen
sich entspannen
sich (ins Café) setzen
sich warm anziehen
??

Trimm Dich am Feierabend

Übung 10 Wie oft machen Sie das?

Fragen Sie jemand, wie oft er/sie die folgenden Dinge macht.

BEISPIEL: sich die Zähne putzen →
  S1: Putzt du dir jeden Tag die Zähne?
  S2: Natürlich putze ich mir jeden Tag die Zähne.

sich die Zähne putzen   nie
sich die Haare kämmen   ab und zu
sich rasieren   oft
sich die Haare waschen   jeden Tag/Morgen/Abend
sich duschen

Übung 10. Suggestion: Point out that some of the pronouns will be dative, others accusative. Go over the verbs first to determine this. Then have students work in pairs.

Expressing Reciprocity

A reflexive pronoun is used to express reciprocity.

Martina und Jörg **lieben sich.**	*Martina and Jörg love each other.*
Sie **treffen sich** im Park.	*They meet (each other) in the park.*
Sie **kennen sich** seit zwei Wochen.	*They have known each other for two weeks.*
Sie **rufen sich** oft an.	*They call each other frequently.*

Übung 11 Der neue Freund

Martina erzählt ihrer Freundin Katrin über ihren neuen Freund Jörg. Benutzen Sie die Verben unten in einem kleinen Bericht.

Hier ist der Anfang:
Wir haben uns vor zwei Wochen kennen gelernt.

1. sich kennen lernen (wo und wann)
2. sich anrufen (wie oft)
3. sich treffen (wo, wie oft)
4. sich sehr gut verstehen
5. sich lieben

Sprache im Kontext

Videoclips

A. Im Interview erklären diese Leute, warum sie ihre Lebensmittel im Bioladen kaufen. Verbinden (*Connect*) Sie die Person mit dem Grund (*reason*).

1. Frau Simon
2. Maria
3. Peter

Der Biokäse schmeckt besser als in einem normalen Supermarkt.

Bauern gebrauchen keine Chemikalien für die Bioprodukte.

Biosäfte sind gesünder als die herkömmlichen Säfte.

B. Und Sie? Kaufen Sie auch im Bioladen ein? Warum? (Warum nicht?)

C. Welche Symptome haben diese Leute, wenn sie krank sind? Markieren Sie Oliver und/oder Maria.

OLIVER	MARIA	
☐	☐	hat oft eine Erkältung
☐	☐	hat Halsschmerzen
☐	☐	hat Fieber und Husten
☐	☐	hat Schnupfen
☐	☐	hat manchmal die Grippe

D. Welche Symptome haben Sie, wenn Sie krank sind?

E. Und was machen diese Leute, wenn sie krank sind?
1. Oliver badet heiß, schwitzt (*sweats*), _____ sich ins Bett, _____ viel und trinkt _____.
2. Maria legt sich auf die _____, trinkt Tee mit Honig und versucht, abzuschalten (*switch off*).

F. Was machen Sie, wenn Sie krank sind?

Lesen

Auf den ersten Blick

A. Wie gesund essen Sie? Der Text, „Ernährungsaktion für Studenten", auf der nächsten Seite ist ein Fragebogen aus einer deutschen Studenten-Zeitschrift zum Thema „richtiges Essen", das heißt, gesund essen. Schauen Sie sich die Fragen links neben dem Bild an. Wie wichtig ist Ihnen...

	IST MIR SEHR WICHTIG	IST MIR EGAL
Zeit zum Essen?	☐	☐
richtiges Essen?	☐	☐
Ihr Gewicht (*weight*)?	☐	☐

B. Kreuzen Sie an, was stimmt. Ein großes Problem ist für mich:

1. Ich habe keine Zeit zum Essen. ☐
2. Ich muss unbedingt abnehmen. ☐
3. Das Essen in der Mensa ☐
4. Ich esse gern—und oft—Pommes (mit Mayonnaise?), Hamburger, Schokoriegel (*chocolate bar*). ☐

C. Ich habe eigentlich...

1. keine Probleme mit Essen. ☐
2. kein Problem mit meinem Gewicht. ☐

Formulieren Sie mit Hilfe der Aussagen in A, B und C etwas über sich.

BEISPIEL: Richtiges Essen ist mir wichtig. Ich habe kein Problem mit Essen und Gewicht. Pommes esse ich gern, aber nicht mit Mayonnaise.

Zum Text

Füllen Sie nun den Fragebogen auf Seite 252 aus. Vergleichen Sie Ihre Antworten in kleinen Gruppen. Was haben Sie erfahren? Berichten Sie im Plenum darüber.

Machen Sie eine Umfrage in der Klasse.

1. Was sind Stressfaktoren in Ihrem Leben?
   - ☐ Arbeit
   - ☐ Studium
   - ☐ Familie
   - ☐ Geld
   - ☐ Leben in der Stadt
   - ☐ Fahren auf der Autobahn
   - ☐ Mein Leben ist stressfrei
   - ☐ ??

2. Wie erholen Sie sich vom Stress?
   - ☐ ein Buch lesen
   - ☐ faulenzen
   - ☐ mit Freunden plaudern
   - ☐ Sport treiben
   - ☐ fernsehen
   - ☐ Musik hören oder spielen
   - ☐ meditieren
   - ☐ ??

ERNÄHRUNGSAKTION FÜR STUDENTEN

Keine Zeit zum Essen
oder keine Kohle?[1]
Essen Nebensache?
Zwischendurch mal Pommes
mit Mayo, Hamburger
oder ein Schokoriegel?[2]
Oder ernährungbewusst
nach Vollwertart?[3]
Reicht die Mensa?
So ganz egal ist das alles nicht.
Aber: gelten die alten
Vorstellungen[4] über
richtiges Essen und
richtiges Gewicht[5]
tatsächlich noch?
Oder ist das alles ein alter Hut?

Sind Sie mit Ihrem Gewicht zufrieden?[6]

☐ nein, ich möchte _____ kg abnehmen

☐ nein, ich möchte _____ kg zunehmen

☐ ja, ich bin zufrieden

Haben Sie schon einmal versucht, Gewicht abzunehmen?

☐ ja, 1 bis 3 mal
☐ ja, 3 bis 10 mal
☐ ja, öfter als 10 mal
☐ nein, noch nie

Wie oft essen Sie in der Mensa?

☐ täglich
☐ mehrmals die Woche
☐ mehrmals im Monat
☐ selten/nie

Leben Sie allein oder mit anderen zusammen?

☐ allein
☐ mit Partner
☐ mit Eltern
☐ in einer Wohngemeinschaft

Wie viele Hauptmahlzeiten am Tag bereiten Sie selbst für sich zu?

☐ eine
☐ zwei
☐ drei

Wie viel Geld haben Sie im Monat für Essen und Trinken zur Verfügung?[7]

☐ bis €100,–
☐ €100,–bis €200,–
☐ mehr als €200,–

Wie oft essen, bzw. trinken Sie folgende Lebensmittel? (bitte ankreuzen)
(1) täglich, (2) mehrmals pro Woche, (3) mehrmals pro Monat, (4) selten/nie

1	2	3	4	
☐	☐	☐	☐	Vollkornbrot
☐	☐	☐	☐	Milch/Quark/Joghurt
☐	☐	☐	☐	Käse
☐	☐	☐	☐	Wurst/Schinken
☐	☐	☐	☐	Fleisch
☐	☐	☐	☐	Gemüse
☐	☐	☐	☐	Salate
☐	☐	☐	☐	Obst
☐	☐	☐	☐	Süßigkeiten
☐	☐	☐	☐	Fruchtsaft ohne Zucker
☐	☐	☐	☐	Cola/Limonade
☐	☐	☐	☐	Mineralwasser

Vorname: _____
Name: _____
Straße, Nr.: _____
PLZ[8] (neu) _____
Wohnort: _____

Geschlecht:
☐ weiblich   ☐ männlich

Alter: _____ Jahre

Bisherige Studiendauer:
_____ Semester

Fachrichtung:
☐ Naturwissenshaften/Medizin
☐ Rechts-/Wirtschafts-/Sozialwissenschaften
☐ andere Geisteswissenschaften
☐ andere Fachrichtungen:

Ihr Körpergewicht: _____ km

Ihre Körpergröße: _____ cm

---

[1]money (*slang*) [2]*chocolate bar* [3]ernährungsbewusst... *nutrition-conscious using natural foods*
[4]gelten... *do the old notions apply* [5]*weight* [6]*satisfied* [7]zur... *at your disposal* [8]*Postleitzahl*

Auf den ersten Blick

A. Der Text „Erholungstypologie" zeigt vier verschiedene Typen von Menschen. Schauen Sie sich die Bilder an.

Wie lebt...

1. der Jahresurlauber?
2. der Erholungsverweigerer?
3. der tägliche Genießer?
4. der aktive Besessene?

a. Er arbeitet Tag und Nacht.
b. Er muss immer sportlich aktiv sein.
c. Nur einmal im Jahr fährt er in Urlaub.
d. Jeden Tag erholt er sich.

B. Mit welchem „Typ" können Sie sich identifizieren?

Erholungstypologie

1 DER JAHRESURLAUBER

Schuftet elf Monate durch und will im Jahresurlaub sein Erholungsdefizit aufholen. Wird häufig wegen des abrupten Wechsels zwischen Hektik und Ruhe in den Ferien krank, weil er zu **schnell „umschaltet"** und seinen Körper dadurch belastet. Ist zudem in Gefahr, Herz, Kreislauf und Immunsystem durch Erholungsmangel **auf Dauer zu schädigen**

2 DER ERHOLUNGSVERWEIGERER

Fühlt sich unersetzlich. Befürchtet immer, im Beruf etwas zu verpassen und hat verlernt, sich mit sich selbst zu beschäftigen. Kann Urlaub nicht aushalten, weil er **Nichtstun als Belastung** empfindet. Läßt bei sich selbst und bei anderen kein Durchhängen zu. Ignoriert Warnsignale seines Körpers und ist in Gefahr, **chronisch krank** zu werden

Note: If students don't notice it on their own, point out that only men are portrayed in this text. Let them talk about whether they think the four types would be portrayed differently if they were women.

Reading: This text is unglossed so that students can work on contextual guessing and learn to judge which words are essential for general understanding. Because of this, it is very important to do **Auf den ersten Blick** as a classroom activity.

Additional group activity: Have students list the words they don't know. See how many they can guess from context and which words can be considered unimportant for a general understanding of the text. Coach them on their guesses and act as a dictionary for any essential words that they don't know.

Additional activities: The text has many examples of words from the same word family, e.g., *wechseln, Wechsel, Abwechslung; belasten, Belastung; Betätigung, Tätigkeit.* Have students find the words in the text. Then, rather than having them look up each word in a dictionary, ask them to figure out the meanings of related words after looking up just one word in the family. Encourage them to use what they know about suffixes, prefixes, and capitalization in German to help determine whether the word is a noun, verb, or adjective/adverb. Remind them to draw from the context in which these words appear to help come up with a possible meaning.

③ DER TÄGLICHE GENIESSER

Gönnt sich Abwechslung vom All-tag. Macht kleine Pausen. Erholt sich vom täglichen Stress durch Entspannung (gutes Essen, Musikhören, Fernsehen, Sport). *Bleibt gesund,* weil er immer wieder zwischen Tätigkeit und Muße so-wie zwischen Aktion und Ruhe wechselt und damit für die Belastungen von Kör-per und Psyche *Ausgleich schafft*

④ DER AKTIVE BESESSENE

Ist süchtig nach Aktivität. Will im-mer besser sein als andere und setzt sich auch in der Freizeit unentwegt *selbst unter Druck.* Kehrt damit die erholsame Wirkung von sportlichen Be-tätigungen ins Gegenteil. Quält seinen Körper, statt ihm die notwendige Ruhe zu verschaffen und wird dadurch immer *weniger leistungsfähig*

Zum Text

A. Der Text „Erholungstypologie" beschreibt vier Typen (Typ 1, 2, 3 und 4) und gibt für jeden Typus eine Beschreibung des Verhaltens (*behavior*) und dessen Auswirking (*effect*) auf die Gesundheit. Dazu gibt der Text auch den Grund (*reason*) dafür an. Lesen Sie den Text durch, und suchen Sie die notwendigen Informationen, um folgende Tabelle auszufüllen.

	VERHALTEN	AUSWIRKUNG AUF DIE GESUNDHEIT	GRUND
Typ 1:	*schuftet elf Monate durch*	*ist in Gefahr, Herz zu schädigen*	*weil er zu schnell umschaltet*
Typ 2:	_____	_____	_____
Typ 3:	_____	_____	_____
Typ 4:	_____	_____	_____

B. Intensiver lesen. Find in the text all the examples of the structure **zwischen _____ und _____.** Note the words that appear in these construc-tions. What is the relationship between the two nouns in each instance?

Sprechen und Schreiben

Aktivität 1 Ihre Erholungstypologie

Welche Erholungstypologie trifft auf Sie zu? Beschreiben Sie sich. Die Klasse soll dann versuchen, Ihre Typologie aufzustellen (*to establish*). Die Klasse soll Ihnen Vorschläge geben, wenn Ihre Erholungstypologie ungesund ist.

Aktivität 2 Was haben Sie letzte Woche für Ihre Gesundheit getan?

Führen Sie eine Woche lang Tagebuch (*diary*) über Ihre Aktivitäten. Haben Sie Sport getrieben? Haben Sie zu viel gearbeitet? Haben Sie gesund gegessen? Machen Sie eine Liste mit positiven und negativen Dingen.

BEISPIEL:	DATUM	POSITIV	NEGATIV
	am 12.11.	Ich habe Tennis gespielt.	Ich habe nicht lange genug geschlafen.

Hier klicken!

Weiteres zum Thema Gesundheit finden Sie bei **Deutsch: Na klar!** im World-Wide-Web unter www.mhhe.com/dnk.

Wortschatz

Körperteile	**Parts of the Body**
der **Arm**, -e	arm
das **Auge**, -n	eye
der **Bauch**, ⸚e	stomach, belly
das **Bein**, -e	leg
die **Brust**, ⸚e	chest; breast
der **Ell(en)bogen**, -	elbow
der **Finger**, -	finger
der **Fuß**, ⸚e	foot
das **Gesicht**, -er	face
das **Haar**, -e	hair
der **Hals**, ⸚e	throat, neck
die **Hand**, ⸚e	hand
das **Kinn**, -e	chin
das **Knie**, -	knee
der **Kopf**, ⸚e	head
der **Mund**, ⸚er	mouth
der **Muskel**, -n	muscle
die **Nase**, -n	nose
das **Ohr**, -en	ear
der **Rücken**, -	back

die **Schulter**, -n	shoulder
die **Zehe**, -n	toe

Gesundheit und Fitness	**Health and Fitness**
die **Arbeit**, -en	work; assignment; paper
der **Arzt**, ⸚e / die **Ärztin**, -nen	physician, doctor
die **Erkältung**, -en	cold
das **Fieber**	fever
die **Fitness**	fitness
die **Gesundheit**	health
die **Grippe**	flu
der **Husten**	coughing, cough
der **Krankenpfleger**, / die **Kranken-schwester**, -n	nurse
der **Kräutertee**	herbal tea
die **Luft**, ⸚e	air
der **Naturkostladen**, ⸚	health food store
die **Ökolebensmittel** (*pl.*)	organic foods

der **Rat**	advice		

der **Rat** — advice
die **Schmerzen** (*pl.*) — pains
  die **Halsschmerzen** — sore throat
  die **Kopfschmerzen** — headache
der **Schnupfen** — nasal congestion; head cold

die **Sprechstunde, -n** — office hours
der **Stress** — stress
der **Termin, -e** — appointment

Reflexive Verben — **Reflexive Verbs**

sich **an•ziehen, angezogen** — to get dressed
sich **aus•ziehen, ausgezogen** — to get undressed
sich **beeilen** — to hurry up
sich **duschen** — to shower
sich **entspannen** — to relax
sich **erholen** — to get well, recover
sich **erkälten** — to catch a cold
sich **fit halten (hält), gehalten** — to keep fit, in shape
sich **fühlen** — to feel
sich **(hin•)legen** — to lie down
sich **(hin•)setzen** — to sit down
sich **informieren (über)** — to inform oneself (about)
sich **kämmen** — to comb (one's hair)
sich **rasieren** — to shave
sich **strecken** — to stretch
sich **treffen (mit)** — to meet (with)
sich **verletzen** — to injure oneself
sich **waschen (wäscht), gewaschen** — to wash oneself
sich **(die Zähne) putzen** — to clean, brush (one's teeth)

Sonstige Verben — **Other Verbs**

abgeben (gibt ab), abgegeben — to drop off, give to
achten auf — to pay attention to
rauchen — to smoke
schlucken — to swallow
tun, getan — to do
verschreiben, verschrieben — to prescribe
versuchen — to try, attempt
weh•tun, weh getan (+ *dat.*) — to hurt
  Das tut mir weh. — That hurts.
zu Fuß gehen — to go on foot, to walk

Adjektive und Adverbien — **Adjectives and Adverbs**

ab und zu — now and then, occasionally
anstrengend — tiring, strenuous
besonders — especially
deprimiert — depressed
deshalb — for that reason
d.h. (= das heißt) — that is, i.e.
entweder... oder — either . . . or
fast — almost
fit — fit, in shape
gesund — healthy, healthful, well
gleich — immediately
hundsmiserabel (*coll.*) — sick as a dog
kaum — scarcely
krank — sick, ill
manchmal — sometimes
meistens — mostly
mindestens — at least
müde — tired
nie — never
regelmäßig — regular(ly)
schlapp — weak, worn out
sogar — even
verrückt — crazy
wenig — little, few

Unterordnende Konjunktionen — **Subordinating Conjunctions**

dass — that
ob — whether
weil — because
wenn — if, when

Sonstiges — **Other**

Das macht nichts. — That doesn't matter.
klingen — to sound
  Du klingst so deprimiert. — You sound so depressed.
Gute Besserung! — Get well soon!
Mir ist schlecht. — I'm sick to my stomach.
Nichts zu danken. — No thanks necessary; Don't mention it.
So ein Pech! — What a shame! (What bad luck!)
Urlaub machen — to go on vacation
Was fehlt Ihnen/dir? — What's the matter?

Use this checklist to verify that you can now . . .

- ☐ talk about fitness and describe the things you do to stay healthy and fit.
- ☐ name the parts of the human body.
- ☐ name some common illnesses and describe how you feel when you are sick.
- ☐ describe common grooming habits.

- ☐ form compound sentences using subordinating conjunctions.
- ☐ use accusative and dative reflexive pronouns and verbs in the present tense and in the present perfect tense.
- ☐ use reflexive verbs to express reciprocity.

KAPITEL 9

In der Stadt

Ein Blick auf die Stadt
Leipzig. Leipzig ist nicht
weit von...
a. Berlin
b. München
c. Hamburg

Kapitel 9. Suggestion:
Introduce the chapter by telling
students where you spent your
last vacation or where you are
planning to go on your next
one. Ask students *Wo waren
Sie letztes Jahr in den Ferien?
Wo verbringen Sie Ihre Ferien
am liebsten? In den Bergen?
Am Meer? Zu Hause? Wohin
würden Sie gern reisen?*

Videoclips
Hier gefällt es mir!

In diesem Kapitel

- **Themen:** Places in the city, hotel and lodging expressions, ask for and give directions
- **Grammatik:** Genitive case, attributive adjectives
- **Kultur:** Services of tourist information offices

Alles klar?

A. Die alte Residenzstadt Dresden liegt im Bundesland Sachsen südlich von Berlin an der Elbe. Es gibt viele Sehenswürdigkeiten (*tourist attractions*) in und um die Stadt. Man kann z.B. den Zoologischen Garten besuchen oder zum Schloss (*castle*) Weesenstein fahren.

Realia. Point out old spelling **Schloß**.

Tiergartenstraße 1
01219 Dresden

Tel. (0351) 471 54 45
Fax (0351) 471 86 25

2200 Tiere in 400 Arten[1] erwarten Ihren Besuch. Interessante Tierbeobachtungen[2] zu jeder Jahreszeit, ein Streichelzoo[3] und gepflegte Gastronomie machen uns besonders attraktiv für Familien. Sie erreichen den Zoo Dresden mit Bus oder Straßenbahn. Ein Parkplatz befindet sich am Haupteingang. Öffnungszeiten: Winter 8.30-16.30 Uhr Sommer 8.30-18.30 Uhr

ZOO DRESDEN

SCHLOSS WEESENSTEIN
– ein königliches Schloß –

Mittelalterliche Burg,[4] barocker Park, Schloß als Wohnsitz sächsischer Könige[5] im 19. Jahrhundert

Museum • Konzerte • Erlebnisgastronomie • Vermietung von Sälen[6]
Sommer: 9-18 Uhr · Winter: 9-17 Uhr

20 km von der Dresdner Residenz entfernt[7]
B 172 bis Heidenau/Abzweig Altenberg

Schloß Weesenstein • Am Schloßberg 1, Weesenstein
01809 Müglitztal • Tel./Fax: 035027-5426

[1]*species*   [2]*animal watching*   [3]*petting zoo*   [4]*fortress*   [5]*sächsischer... of Saxon kings*   [6]*halls, large rooms*   [7]*von... away from the Dresden residence*

Suchen Sie in den Werbungen (*advertisements*) die fehlenden Informationen.

1. Schloss Weesenstein hat einen barocken __Park__.
2. Das Schloss ist __20 km__ von der Dresdner Residenz entfernt.
3. Wer gern Musik hört, kann dort __Konzerte__ besuchen.
4. Wer Kunst (*art*) gern hat, kann ins __Museum__ gehen.
5. Im 19. Jahrhundert lebten sächsische __Könige__ im Schloss.
6. Der Zoo Dresden ist attraktiv für __Familien__.
7. Man erreicht den Zoo mit __Bus__ und __Straßenbahn__.
8. Für Autos gibt es einen Parkplatz am __Haupteingang__.

Was würden Sie lieber besuchen, den Zoo oder das Schloss? Warum?

B. Sie machen eine Stadtführung (*guided tour*) durch Dresden. Der Fremdenführer (*tour guide*) erzählt einige Tatsachen über die Stadt. Hören Sie zu und kreuzen Sie an, was stimmt und was nicht stimmt.

Hier klicken!

Weiteres zum Thema Dresden finden Sie bei **Deutsch: Na klar!** im World-Wide-Web unter www.mhhe.com/dnk.

Auf der Suche nach Unterkunft. Suggestion: Have students work in groups. Each group chooses a type of lodging and then decides what factors are most important.

	DAS STIMMT	DAS STIMMT NICHT
1. Heute leben etwa 470 000 Einwohner in Dresden.	☒	☐
2. Die erste deutsche Lokomotive kommt aus Dresden.	☒	☐
3. Bierdeckel, Kaffeefilter und Shampoo hat man in Dresden entwickelt.	☐	☒
4. In Dresden hat Richard Wagner die erste deutsche Oper geschrieben.	☐	☒
5. Die Stadt hat viel Kultur anzubieten: Musik, Museen und Theater.	☒	☐
6. Dresden gilt als die europäische Hauptstadt des Films.	☐	☒

Wörter im Kontext

THEMA 1: Auf der Suche nach Unterkunft°

accommodations

Tel.: 0351 459 01 69

Fax: 0351 459 50 36

florentina & st.caspar

HOTELSCHIFFE

STRESS ÜBER BORD

- 140 Kabinen mit Dusche/WC, Radio, Satelliten-TV, Selbstwahltelefon[1]
-2 Restaurants, Wintergarten, Terrassencafé, Biergarten

An den idyllischen Elbwiesen, inmitten[2] der historischen Altstadt freuen wir uns auf Ihren Besuch.[3]

Terrassenufer, Pf 120186 • 01003 Dresden

HOTEL VISA

CHIPPENDALE'S GASTRONOMIE SERVICE GmbH

Breitscheidstraße 47 01462 Cossebaude/Dresden Telefon: (0351) 439 61 61 Telefax: (0351) 439 91 39

- ca. 3 Min. von der Autobahn DD-Altstadt unmittelbar an der Stadtgrenze[4] Dresdens gelegen
- zentrale Lage für viele Ausflugsziele[5]
- 25 modern eingerichtete Zimmer mit DU, WC, SAT-TV, Radiowecker
- EZ € 60 / DZ € 70
- reichhaltiges Frühstücksbuffet (inkl.)
- Gruppenpreise auf Anfrage
- Pensionsverpflegung[6] für Reisegruppen

HOTEL & RESTAURANT

An der Rennbahn

An der Rennbahn
★★★

Mit freundlicher Empfehlung FAMILIE BOLZ

- zwischen Großen Garten und Rennbahn[7] gelegen
- 10 Autominuten bis zum Zentrum der Stadt
- 22 komfortabel eingerichtete Zimmer mit DU, WC, Fön, Farb-TV, Telefon und Minibar
- EZ € 65,– bis 70,–
- DZ € 90,– bis 110,–
- inkl. reichhaltiges Frühstück
- Gruppenpreise € 50,– pro Person und Nacht
- Küche mit sächsischen und internationalen Spezialitäten
- Gartenrestaurant

Winterbergstraße 96 • 01237 Dresden - Reick Telefon (0351) 2 54 00 30 • Telefax (0351) 2 52 27 85

[1]*direct-dial telephone* [2]*in the center* [3]*freuen... we look forward to* [4]*city limit* [5]*excursion destinations* [6]*full room and board provisions* [7]*racetrack*

SPRACHTIPP

Die folgenden Abkürzungen sind typisch:

EZ = das Einzelzimmer *single room*

DZ = das Doppelzimmer *double room*

DU = die Dusche *shower*

WC = die Toilette (Engl. *water closet*) *toilet*

inkl. = inklusive *included, including*

Was ist Ihnen wichtig, wenn Sie in einem **Hotel,** einer **Pension** oder einer **Jugendherberge übernachten** wollen? Die **Unterkunft** sollte...

- ☐ **in der Nähe** des Bahnhofs liegen.
- ☐ in der **Innenstadt** (im Zentrum) liegen.
- ☐ ein Restaurant im Haus haben.
- ☐ Kabelfernsehen oder Radio haben.
- ☐ in ruhiger **Lage** sein.
- ☐ Sauna im Haus haben.
- ☐ Bad/**Dusche/WC** im Zimmer haben.

- ☐ Frühstück **im Preis enthalten.**
- ☐ einen **Parkplatz** in der Nähe haben.
- ☐ Hunde **erlauben.**
- ☐ Telefon im Zimmer haben.
- ☐ im Bad einen **Fön** haben.
- ☐ preiswert sein.
- ☐ **günstig liegen** (z.B. im Zentrum).

Neue Wörter

Pension bed and breakfast
Jugendherberge youth hostel
übernachten to stay overnight
Unterkunft lodging
in der Nähe near
Lage location
im Preis enthalten included in the price
erlauben allow
Fön hair dryer
günstig liegen be conveniently located

Aktivität 1 Zwei telefonische Zimmerbestellungen

Was stimmt? Markieren Sie die richtigen Antworten.

ERSTES TELEFONGESPRÄCH

1. Der Gast braucht ein...
   a. Einzelzimmer.
   b. <u>Doppelzimmer.</u>
2. Er braucht das Zimmer für...
   a. eine Nacht.
   b. <u>mehrere (*several*) Nächte.</u>
3. Das Hotel hat ein Zimmer frei...
   a. mit Bad.
   b. <u>ohne Bad.</u>
4. Frühstück ist im Preis...
   a. nicht enthalten.
   b. <u>enthalten.</u>
5. Der Gast...
   a. nimmt das Zimmer.
   b. <u>muss ein anderes Hotel finden.</u>

ZWEITES TELEFONGESPRÄCH

1. Das Jugendgästehaus hat...
   a. nur Doppelzimmer.
   b. <u>nur Mehrbettzimmer.</u>
2. Das Haus ist...
   a. ganz neu.
   b. <u>sehr alt.</u>
3. Die Übernachtung kostet...
   a. mehr als 20 Euro.
   b. <u>weniger als 20 Euro.</u>
4. Jedes Zimmer hat...
   a. <u>WC and Dusche.</u>
   b. fünf Betten.
5. Das Gästehaus liegt...
   a. auf dem Lande.
   b. <u>in der Nähe der Innenstadt.</u>

Aktivität 1. Suggestion: Have students first scan the information requested in the first telephone conversation. Then let them listen to it on the tape. Students can work in pairs, taking turns responding to each item. Repeat this procedure with the second conversation. **Follow-up:** Exploit both conversations further through questions eliciting more detail, e.g., *Warum muss der Gast im ersten Gespräch ein anderes Hotel suchen? Wie alt ist das Jugendgästehaus genau?* **Point Out:** *Auf Wiederhören*—the final words of the first telephone conversation—is used only to end a telephone conversation.

KULTURTIPP

Tourist I (*for information*) ist für viele Besucher in deutschen Städten der erste Stopp. Meist liegt er am Hauptbahnhof oder an einem anderen zentralen Ort. Hier können Touristen viel Wissenswertes über die neue Stadt erfahren. Sie können zum Beispiel Empfehlungen für Restaurants bekommen, eine Stadtrundfahrt buchen und Prospekte (*brochures*) von der Stadt erhalten. Hier gibt es auch eine Zimmervermittlung. Da kann der Besucher ein Zimmer in einem Hotel oder einer Pension finden.

Dialogue. Note: This dialogue presents a typical situation that a visitor might encounter at a hotel. New vocabulary and expressions can be guessed from the context. **Suggestion:** Play the dialogue once, for students to get the gist. Ask a few basic questions: *Wer sind die Sprecher? Wie heißt der Gast? Wie lange möchte er bleiben?* Then ask students to scan the text once. Help them figure out the meaning of *Würden Sie bitte das Anmeldeformular ausfüllen?* by asking *Was muss ein Gast im Hotel machen, bevor er sein Zimmer bekommt?* To figure out the meaning of *im ersten Stock* and *Erdgeschoss,* refer to the realia. *Erster Stock* corresponds to second floor; *zweiter Stock* is the third floor; *Erdgeschoss* is either the ground floor or the first floor.

Point out: *Würden Sie... ausfüllen* corresponds to the English "Would you fill out . . . ," used for polite requests.

Neue Wörter

Teil A

kommt... an (ankommen) arrives

zuerst first

sich anmelden register, check in

würden Sie...
  ausfüllen would you please fill out . . .

Anmeldeformular registration form

Reisepass passport

Schlüssel key

Aufzug elevator

rechts to the right

Gepäck luggage

Koffer suitcase

übrigens by the way

links to the left

angenehmen Aufenthalt pleasant stay

Aktivität 2 Wo wollen wir übernachten?

Sie reisen mit Freunden und suchen eine Unterkunft in Dresden. Schauen Sie sich die drei Anzeigen im **Thema 1** genau an und überlegen Sie sich, in welchem Hotel Sie übernachten wollen. Gebrauchen Sie die folgenden Ausdrücke, um eine Unterkunft vorzuschlagen (*to suggest*) und geben Sie den Grund (*reason*) dafür an.

BEISPIEL: Ich schlage vor, wir übernachten im Hotelschiff „Florentina".
    Es liegt zentral und hat ein Terrassencafé.

  Ich schlage vor,...

  Mir gefällt das Hotel... besser.

  Ich brauche... im Zimmer / im Hotel.

  Das Hotel liegt...

  Das Hotel... ist mir zu teuer.

THEMA 2: Im Hotel

  *Teil A: Herr Thompson **kommt** im Hotel „Mecklenheide" **an. Zuerst muss er sich anmelden.***

REZEPTION: Guten Abend.

GAST: Guten Abend. Ich habe ein Zimmer für zwei Nächte bestellt.

REZEPTION: **Auf welchen Namen,** bitte?

GAST: Thompson.

REZEPTION: Ah, ja. Herr Thompson. Ein **Einzelzimmer** mit Bad. **Würden Sie bitte** das **Anmeldeformular ausfüllen**?

GAST: Möchten Sie auch meinen **Reisepass** sehen?

REZEPTION: Nein, das ist nicht nötig. Ihr Zimmer liegt im ersten **Stock,** Zimmer 21. Hier ist **der Schlüssel.** Der **Aufzug** ist hier **rechts.**

GAST: Danke.

REZEPTION: Wir bringen Ihr **Gepäck** aufs Zimmer. Haben Sie nur den einen **Koffer**?

GAST: Ja... **Übrigens,** wann gibt es morgens Frühstück?

REZEPTION: Zwischen 7 und 10 Uhr im **Frühstücksraum** hier gleich **links** im **Erdgeschoss.**

GAST: Danke sehr.

REZEPTION: Bitte sehr. Ich wünsche Ihnen einen **angenehmen Aufenthalt.**

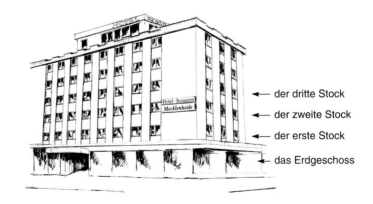

der dritte Stock

der zweite Stock

der erste Stock

das Erdgeschoss

*Teil B: Herr Thompson ruft die **Rezeption** an und **beschwert sich**, weil der Fernseher nicht **funktioniert**.*

REZEPTION: Rezeption.

THOMPSON: Guten Abend. Der Fernseher in meinem Zimmer ist **kaputt**. Es gibt kein Bild, keinen Ton, nichts.

REZEPTION: **Das tut mir Leid**, Herr Thompson. Ich schicke **sofort** jemand auf Ihr Zimmer. Wenn er den **Apparat** nicht gleich **reparieren** kann, bringen wir Ihnen einen anderen.

THOMPSON: Vielen Dank. **Auf Wiederhören.**

REZEPTION: Auf Wiederhören.

Neue Wörter

Teil B

Rezeption reception desk
beschwert sich (sich beschweren) complains
kaputt broken
Das tut mir Leid. I'm sorry.
sofort immediately
Apparat TV set
reparieren repair
auf Wiederhören good-bye (on the phone)

Aktivität 3 Im Hotel

Bilden Sie Sätze!

1. __c__ Ich habe ein Einzelzimmer
2. __e__ Würden Sie bitte das Anmeldeformular
3. __g__ Ihr Zimmer liegt
4. __f__ Wir bringen Ihr Gepäck
5. __d__ Ich wünsche Ihnen
6. __a__ Der Fernseher in meinem Zimmer

a. ist kaputt.
b. bezahlen?
c. bestellt.
d. einen angenehmen Aufenthalt.
e. ausfüllen?
f. aufs Zimmer.
g. im ersten Stock.

Hier klicken!

Weiteres zum Thema Hotel und Unterkunft finden Sie bei **Deutsch: Na klar!** im World-Wide-Web unter www.mhhe.com/dnk.

Aktivität 4 Ein Aufenthalt im Hotel Mecklenheide

Sehen Sie sich die Bilder von Herrn Thompson im Hotel an. Schreiben Sie für jedes Bild einen Satz und erzählen Sie die Geschichte von Herrn Thompson.

1.

2.

3.

4.

5.

6.

THEMA 3: Ringsum° die Stadt

All around

A. Schauen Sie auf den Stadtplan von Warnemünde, und finden Sie die Orte (*places*) rechts auf der Liste.

B. Suchen Sie die deutschen Wörter in der Liste rechts.

1. __1__ lighthouse
2. __9__ post office
3. __17__ gas station
4. __7__ light rail line
5. __4__ swimming facility
6. __29__ (ferry) harbor, dock
7. __10__ bank
8. __14__ movie house/theater
9. __5__ church
10. __8__ cemetery
11. __6__ museum
12. __24__ police (station)
13. __25__ beach

1 Leuchtturm	...
2 Kurhaus	17 **Tankstelle**
3 Hotel Neptun	18 Toiletten
4 Schwimmhalle	19 Taxi
5 **Kirche**	20 Gäste Service
6 **Museum**	
7 Bahnhof/S-Bahn	22 Sportplatz
8 Alter Friedhof	24 **Polizei**
9 **Post**	25 **Strand**
10 **Bank**	26 Surfen
...	27 Passagierkai
12 Apotheke	...
13 Telefon	29 Fähr-**Hafen**
14 Kino	30 Yacht-Hafen
15 Theater	31 Promenade

Realia. Point out: Warnemünde is located on the Baltic Sea, just north of the port of Rostock. Have students locate it on the map in the front of the book.

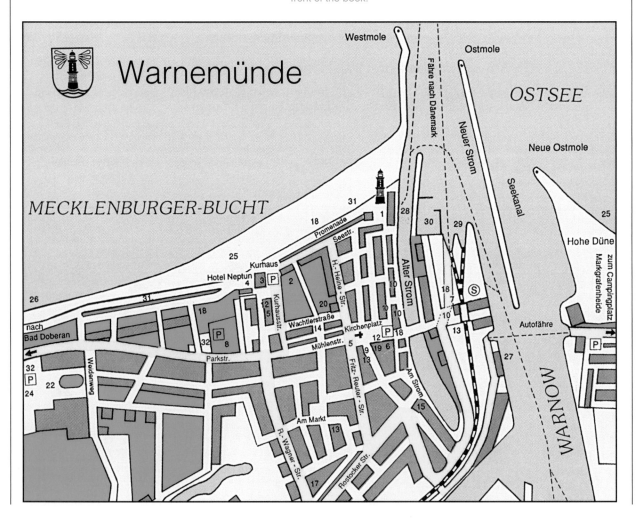

Nach dem Weg fragen

Ein Tourist steht in Warnemünde vor der Kirche und fragt nach dem Weg.

TOURIST: **Entschuldigung**, wie komme ich am besten zum Hotel Neptun?

PASSANT: **Gehen Sie** hier die Mühlenstraße **entlang**, dann **biegen** Sie rechts in die Richard-Wagnerstraße **ein.** Gehen Sie **immer geradeaus.** Das Hotel Neptun liegt **gegenüber von** der Schwimmhalle.

TOURIST: Ist es **weit** von hier?

PASSANT: Nein. **Ungefähr** 5 bis 7 Minuten zu Fuß.

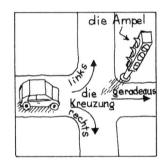

Neue Wörter

nach dem Weg fragen to ask for directions

Entschuldigung excuse me

gehen Sie... entlang (entlanggehen) go along

biegen Sie... ein (einbiegen) turn

immer geradeaus straight ahead

gegenüber von across from

weit far

ungefähr about, approximately

Aktivität 5 Drei Touristen

Drei Leute fragen nach dem Weg. Wohin wollen sie? Wie kommen sie dahin?

	DIALOG 1	DIALOG 2	DIALOG 3
Wohin man gehen will	Markt	Hotel	Post
Wie man dahin kommt	geradeaus, dann links	2 Straßen geradeaus, dann rechts	keine Auskunft

unfamiliar **Aktivität 6   Hin und her: In einer fremden° Stadt**

Sie sind in einer fremden Stadt. Fragen Sie nach dem Weg. Benutzen Sie die Tabelle.

BEISPIEL: s1: Ist das Landesmuseum weit von hier?
            s2: Es ist sechs Kilometer von hier, bei der Universität.
            s1: Wie komme ich am besten dahin?
            s2: Nehmen Sie die Buslinie 7, am Rathaus.

WOHIN?	WIE WEIT?	WO?	WIE?
Landesmuseum	6 km	bei der Universität	Buslinie 7, am Rathaus
Bahnhof	15 Minuten	im Zentrum	mit dem Taxi
Post	nicht weit	in der Nähe vom Bahnhof	zu Fuß
Schloss	15 km	außerhalb der Stadt	mit dem Auto
Opernhaus	ganz in der Nähe	rechts um die Ecke	zu Fuß, die Poststraße entlang

Aktivität 7   In Warnemünde

Schauen Sie sich den Stadtplan von Warnemünde im **Thema 3** an und fragen Sie jemand im Kurs, wie Sie am besten an einen bestimmten Ort kommen. Sie stehen vor der Kirche (Nummer 5 im Stadtplan).

BEISPIEL: s1: Entschuldigung, wie komme ich am besten zum Museum?
            s2: Gehen Sie hier geradeaus bis zum Parkplatz. Das Museum ist dann gleich an der Ecke (*corner*).

REDEMITTEL

Entschuldigung, wie komme ich am besten zum/zur ＿＿＿＿?

Wie weit ist es bis zum/zur ＿＿＿＿?

Wie komme ich zum/zur ＿＿＿＿?

Immer geradeaus.

Bis zur Kreuzung.

Gehen Sie die ＿＿＿＿ Straße entlang.

Biegen Sie links/rechts in die ＿＿＿＿ Straße ein.

Gleich an der Ecke / um die Ecke.

Es ist zehn Minuten zu Fuß.

Hier klicken!

Weiteres zum Thema Wegbeschreibung finden Sie bei **Deutsch: Na klar!** im World-Wide-Web unter www.mhhe.com/dnk.

Aktivität 8   Wie kommt man dahin?

Fragen Sie nach dem Weg in Ihrer Stadt oder auf Ihrem Campus. Wählen Sie passende Fragen und Antworten aus jeder Spalte (*column*).

BEISPIEL: s1: Entschuldigung, wo ist hier die Post?
            s2: Da nehmen Sie am besten den Bus.
            s1: Wo ist die Haltestelle (*bus stop*)?
            s2: Gleich da drüben an der Kreuzung.

FRAGEN	ANTWORTEN
Wie kommt man am besten zum Supermarkt / zur Bibliothek / zur Sporthalle?	Immer geradeaus.
	Nächste Kreuzung rechts/links.
Wie weit ist es bis ins Zentrum?	Da nehmen Sie am besten _____ (den Bus, z.B. Linie 8)
Entschuldigung, wo ist hier die Post (Bank, Mensa)?	Gleich da drüben / Gleich an der Ecke.
Wo ist die Haltestelle?	Fünf Minuten zu Fuß.
??	??

Grammatik im Kontext

The Genitive Case°

Der Genitiv

The genitive case typically indicates ownership, a relationship, or the characteristics of another noun.

Der Wagen **meines Vaters** ist in der Reparatur.	*My father's car is at the repair shop.*
Der Freund **meiner Schwester** heißt Stefan.	*The name of my sister's boyfriend is Stefan.*
Das Hotel liegt im Zentrum **der Stadt.**	*The hotel is located in the center of town.*

SINGULAR			PLURAL
Masculine	*Neuter*	*Feminine*	*All Genders*
des ⎫ Vater**s** / Gast**es** eine**s** ⎬ *but:* unser**es** ⎭ Student**en**	des ⎫ eine**s** ⎬ Hotel**s** unser**es** ⎭	der ⎫ ein**er** ⎬ Stadt unser**er** ⎭	der ⎫ ⎬ Gäste unser**er** ⎭

Note:

■ Most masculine and neuter nouns in the singular add **-s** in the genitive case. Masculine and neuter nouns of one syllable often add **-es.**

die Lage dieses Hotel**s**	*the location of this hotel*
die Unterschrift des Gast**es**	*the guest's signature*

■ Masculine nouns that add **-n** or **-en** in the dative and the accusative also add **-n** or **-en** in the genitive case.

das Gepäck des Student**en**	*the student's luggage*

■ A noun in the genitive always follows the noun it modifies.

The Genitive Case. Suggestion: Remind students that they have used the genitive case with proper names since **Kapitel 3,** e.g., *Das ist Franks Schwester. Das ist Familie Schneiders Haus.*

Nouns in the Genitive Case. Suggestion: For quick practice of genitive forms, do a substitution exercise. *Wo liegt deine Wohnung? In der Nähe... (Universität, Bahnhof, Park, Theater, Post, Einkaufszentrum, Innenstadt). Wie ist die Telefonnummer... (Freund, Freundin, Eltern, Familie, Polizei, Auskunft, Hotel, Reisebüro, Fremdenverkehrsverein)?*

Masculine Nouns Ending in -n or -en. Suggestion: Review other nouns that fall into this category: *der Kunde, der Tourist, der Mensch.* For instance, *die Unterschrift des Kunden, des Touristen.*

- In spoken German, the genitive case is often replaced by the preposition **von** and the dative case.

> in der Nähe **vom Bahnhof**   *in the vicinity of the railroad station*

To ask for the owner of something, use the interrogative pronoun **wessen** (*whose*).

> **Wessen** Koffer ist das?   *Whose suitcase is that?*
>
> **Wessen** Unterschrift ist das?   *Whose signature is that?*

Proper Names in the Genitive

> **Martinas** Koffer   *Martina's suitcase*
>
> **Herrn Kramers** Reisepass   *Mr. Kramer's passport*
>
> Hessen: das Herz **Deutschlands**   *Hesse: the heart of Germany*

Note:

- A proper name normally precedes the noun it modifies.
- Proper names in the genitive add **-s** without an apostrophe, in contrast to English.
- The name of a country or a region in the genitive case may precede or follow the noun it modifies.

Proper Names in the Genitive: Point Out: A genitive *-s* is added to names regardless of the gender of the person. If a name already ends in *-s*, you will see an apostrophe following the final *-s* to indicate that a genitive *-s* is implied. In modern German this is sometimes avoided by using the preposition **von** with names ending in *-z* or *-ss* (*das Haus von Familie Schmitz, der Wagen von Hans*). Genitive endings are also added to both parts of a masculine proper name: *Herrn Kramers Koffer,* but *Frau Kramers Tasche.*

Realia. *Kaufhaus des Westens* is the largest department store on the European continent, located in Berlin.

ANALYSE

- Identify the genitive expressions in the illustrations.
- What nouns are modified by the genitive attributes?
- Give appropriate English translations of these phrases.

Wappen der Stadt Köln

Übung 1   Was für eine Stadt ist Wien°?

Vienna

Beschreiben Sie Wien. Folgen Sie dem Beispiel.

BEISPIEL: Wien ist eine Stadt der Tradition.

Wien ist eine Stadt...   die Schlösser

die Kaffeehäuser   die Architektur

das Theater   die Kirchen

die Musik   ??

die Museen

Übung 2   Wo war Ihr Hotel?

Sie waren gerade in Wien. Beschreiben Sie die Lage des Hotels.

BEISPIEL: Unser Hotel lag in der Nähe eines Cafés.

Unser Hotel lag in der Nähe...

ein Park   die Ringstraße

ein Schloss   die Post

eine Bank   der Dom (*cathedral*)

die Donau (*Danube*)   das Rathaus

die Universität   die U-Bahn

der Bahnhof   das Stadtzentrum

Übung 3   Wem gehört das?

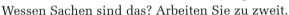

Wessen Sachen sind das? Arbeiten Sie zu zweit.

BEISPIEL: S1: Wessen Gepäck ist das?
S2: Das ist das Gepäck des Gastes.

1. der Wagen → meine Schwester
2. der Rucksack → der Student
3. der Reisepass → der Herr auf Zimmer 33
4. die Unterschrift (*signature*) → der Gast
5. die Koffer → die Touristen

Note: Übung 3 also lends itself to a review of the dative with *gehören:*
— *Wessen Wagen ist das?*
— *Der gehört meinem Bruder.*
  Or to practice the more colloquial version:
— *Das ist der Wagen von meinem Bruder.*

Übung 4   Das will sie wissen!

Frau Schimmelpfennig will alles genau wissen, bevor sie ein Zimmer reserviert. Arbeiten Sie zu zweit. Folgen Sie dem Beispiel.

BEISPIEL: Wie ist die Hotellage? → (sehr ruhig)
S1: Wie ist die Hotellage?
S2: Die Lage des Hotels ist sehr ruhig.

1. Wo ist der Hoteleingang? → (gleich um die Ecke)
2. Wer ist der Hotelbesitzer? → (ein Herr Schlüter aus Hannover)
3. Wo ist der Hotelparkplatz? → (in der Tiefgarage unter dem Hotel)
4. Wie ist die Hoteladresse? → (Weimarerstraße 137)
5. Wie weit weg ist das Stadtzentrum? → (etwa fünf Minuten mit dem Wagen)
6. Wie hoch ist der Zimmerpreis? → (90 Euro pro Person)

Suggestion: Have students convert all compound nouns into genitive constructions before beginning the exercise.

Prepositions with the Genitive. Suggestion: Practice the preposition *wegen* individually, contrasting it with *weil;* students tend to mix up these words. Do a quick substitution exercise: *Warum studieren Sie hier? Wegen...* (*die Lage, das Wetter, der Ruf der Uni / des Colleges, der Preis, die Studenten, meine Freundin, meine Eltern, mein Vater*, etc.) Now ask students to rephrase their sentences using *weil*. Repeat the question *Warum studieren Sie hier?* Provide cues using the substitution nouns: *Der Ruf der Universität (das Wetter, die Lage, etc.) ist sehr gut.* Or: *Meine Freundin studiert hier; meine Eltern haben die Universität empfohlen.* Students say. . . *weil der Ruf der Universität (das Wetter, die Lage, etc.) gut ist,* or *weil meine Freundin hier studiert,* etc.

Note: The prepositions listed here are high-frequency words. You may want to add *(an)statt* (*instead*). Note that *innerhalb* is generally used with time: *innerhalb eines Tages* (*within a day*). *Außerhalb* is always used with location.

Prepositions with the Genitive

A number of prepositions are used with the genitive case. Several common ones are:

außerhalb	*outside of*	außerhalb der Stadt
innerhalb	*inside of, within*	innerhalb einer Stunde
trotz	*in spite of*	trotz des Regens
während	*during*	während des Sommers
wegen	*because of*	wegen der hohen Kosten

In colloquial German, **trotz, während,** and **wegen** may also be used with the dative case.

Übung 5   Notizen von einer Reise nach Wien

Setzen Sie passende Präpositionen mit dem Genitiv ein.

1. _____ unserer Reise nach Wien haben wir viel gesehen.
2. _____ der hohen Hotelpreise haben wir in einer kleinen Pension übernachtet.
3. Die Pension hat _____ der Stadt gelegen.
4. _____ der vielen Touristen war es in Wien schön.
5. _____ der vielen Besucher konnten wir keine Karten für die Spanische Reitschule bekommen.

Übung 6   Erkundigungen°

Sie stehen in der Mitte des Marktplatzes und fragen nach dem Weg. Arbeiten Sie zu zweit.

inquiries

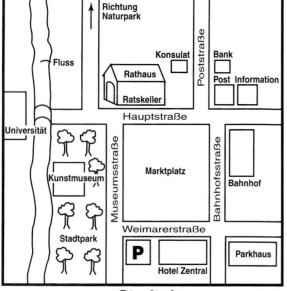

Stadtplan

FÜR DIE FRAGEN

Bitte schön, wo ist...

Entschuldigung, wie komme ich zum/zur...

Bitte, können Sie mir sagen,...

FÜR DIE ANTWORTEN

in der Nähe

in der Mitte

auf der anderen Seite

innerhalb/außerhalb

gegenüber (von)

neben

BEISPIEL: S1: Bitte schön, wo liegt das Konsulat?
S2: Es liegt in der Nähe des Rathauses auf der Poststraße.

1. das Informationszentrum
2. das Hotel Zentral
3. der Parkplatz des Hotels
4. der Naturpark (innerhalb oder außerhalb)
5. das Kunstmuseum
6. die Post
7. die Universität
8. der Ratskeller

Note: While you want to encourage students to use genitive expressions, a variety of answers is possible, including prepositional phrases in the dative or accusative.

Attributive Adjectives°

Attributive Adjektive

Predicate adjectives—adjectives used after the verbs **sein** and **werden**—take no endings. Attributive adjectives—adjectives preceding nouns—always take endings.

Attributive Adjectives. Point out: Students have seen adjectives with endings in the many texts throughout this book. Adjective endings do not interfere with understanding a text, yet they are difficult to master. However, in scanning almost any German text, students will quickly discover that only two adjective endings are used with great frequency: -e and -en.

PREDICATE ADJECTIVE	ATTRIBUTIVE ADJECTIVE
Der Bahnhof ist **alt.**	Der **alte** Bahnhof ist in der Nähe vom Hotel.
Das Hotel ist **preiswert.**	Das **preiswerte** Hotel liegt außerhalb der Stadt.
Die Bedienung ist **freundlich.**	Die **freundliche** Bedienung hat mir gefallen.

Adjectives after a Definite Article or Other **der**-Word

The two most common adjective endings are **-e** and **-en**. They are used whenever an adjective follows a definite article or other **der**-word, such as **dieser** or **jeder.***

	SINGULAR			PLURAL
	Masculine	*Neuter*	*Feminine*	*All Genders*
Nom.	der groß**e** Park	das schön**e** Wetter	die lang**e** Straße	die alt**en** Häuser
Acc.	den groß**en** Park	das schön**e** Wetter	die lang**e** Straße	die alt**en** Häuser
Dat.	dem groß**en** Park	dem schön**en** Wetter	der lang**en** Straße	den alt**en** Häusern
Gen.	des groß**en** Parks	des schön**en** Wetters	der lang**en** Straße	der alt**en** Häuser

---

*This type of adjective ending is traditionally referred to as a *weak* adjective ending.

Obst aus dem Alten Land

| | SINGULAR | | | PLURAL |
	Masculine	Neuter	Feminine	All Genders
Nom.	-e	-e	-e	-en
Acc.	-en	-e	-e	-en
Dat.	-en	-en	-en	-en
Gen.	-en	-en	-en	-en

Übung 7 Was hat Ihnen in der Stadt gefallen oder nicht gefallen?

Bilden Sie Sätze mit Adjektiven. Folgen Sie dem Beispiel.

BEISPIEL: Die Menschen waren alle sehr freundlich. →
Die freundlichen Menschen haben mir gefallen.

1. Die Häuser waren sehr alt.
2. Das Hotel war klein und gemütlich.
3. Das Frühstück im Hotel war ausgezeichnet.
4. Die Straßen waren sauber.
5. Das Bier war ausgezeichnet.
6. Der Marktplatz war klein.
7. Die Bedienung im Ratskeller war leider unfreundlich.

SPRACHTIPP

When two or more attributive adjectives modify a noun, they have the same ending.

Das **kleine historische** Hotel liegt in der Altstadt.

Die **vielen alten** Häuser haben mir gefallen.

Bei einem Volkfest in Straubing: Die vielen netten Leute haben mir gefallen.

Übung 8   Was hast du mir mitgebracht?

Sie sind von einer Reise nach Deutschland zurückgekommen. Was haben Sie allen mitgebracht? Führen Sie kurze Gespräche mit Hilfe der Zeichnungen. Wählen Sie Adjektive aus der Liste.

BEISPIEL: S1: Was hast du mir mitgebracht?
S2: Ich habe dir einen Kalender mitgebracht.
S1: Oh! Vielen Dank für den schönen Kalender.

originell	schick	toll
schön	bunt	??

Übung 9   In der Stadt

Setzen Sie passende Adjektive aus der Liste in die Lücken.

klein	alt	modern
groß	neu	(un)bequem

1. Das Rathaus liegt neben der _____ Post.
2. Neben dem _____ Rathaus ist ein Park.
3. In dem _____ Park gibt es viele Bänke zum Sitzen.
4. Auf den _____ Bänken im Park sitzen viele Leute.
5. Vor der _____ Kirche stehen viele Touristen.
6. Auf dem _____ Marktplatz kann man täglich Obst und Gemüse kaufen.
7. In dieser _____ Stadt kann man gut leben.

Übung 10 Notizen von einem Besuch

Ergänzen Sie die Endungen.

1. Das alt_____ Rathaus liegt direkt am Marktplatz.
2. Neben dem alt_____ Rathaus steht das neu_____ Opernhaus.
3. In der Nähe des alt_____ Rathauses liegt auch der Marktplatz.
4. Morgen besuchen wir das alt_____ Rathaus.
5. Die erst_____ deutsch_____ Lokomotive kommt aus Dresden.
6. Trotz des kalt_____ Wetters haben wir einen Spaziergang gemacht.
7. Der Groß_____ Garten ist der Name eines Parks in Dresden.
8. Heute besuchen wir den Groß_____ Garten.
9. Unser Hotel liegt am Groß_____ Garten.
10. Die viel_____ Touristen in Dresden kommen aus der ganz_____ Welt.

Adjectives after an Indefinite Article or Other **ein**-Word

Adjectives preceded by indefinite articles or other **ein**-words follow the same pattern as adjectives preceded by **der**-words, except in the masculine nominative and in the neuter nominative and accusative.

Heute war **ein** schön**er** Tag.	*Today was a nice day.*
Das ist **unser** neu**es** Haus.	*This is our new house.*
Ich suche **ein** preiswert**es** Hotel.	*I am looking for a reasonably priced hotel.*
Wo ist **Ihr** neu**er** Wagen?	*Where is your new car?*

	SINGULAR			PLURAL
	Masculine	*Neuter*	*Feminine*	*All Genders*
Nom.	ein groß**er** Park	ein schön**es** Haus	eine lang**e** Straße	keine neu**en** Geschäfte
Acc.	einen groß**en** Park	ein schön**es** Haus	eine lang**e** Straße	keine neu**en** Geschäfte
Dat.	einem groß**en** Park	einem schön**en** Haus	einer lang**en** Straße	keinen neu**en** Geschäften
Gen.	eines groß**en** Parks	eines schön**en** Hauses	einer lang**en** Straße	keiner neu**en** Geschäfte

SUMMARY OF ENDINGS

	SINGULAR			PLURAL
	Masculine	*Neuter*	*Feminine*	*All Genders*
Nom.	-er	-es	-e	-en
Acc.	-en	-es	-e	-en
Dat.	-en	-en	-en	-en
Gen.	-en	-en	-en	-en

Übung II Gibt es das in Ihrem Heimatort?

Stellen Sie einem Partner / einer Partnerin Fragen.

BEISPIEL: ein deutsch_____ Restaurant →
>   s1: Gibt es in deinem Heimatort ein deutsches Restaurant?
>   s2: Ja, es gibt ein deutsches Restaurant da. [oder]
>   Nein, das gibt es nicht.

1. ein französisch_____ Restaurant
2. eine bekannt_____ Universität
3. ein alt_____ Rathaus
4. eine modern_____ Fußgängerzone
5. eine historisch_____ Sehenswürdigkeit
6. einen groß_____ Flughafen
7. ein berühmt_____ Kunstmuseum
8. einen gemütlich_____ Biergarten
9. ein historisch_____ Hotel

Adjectives without a Preceding Article

An attributive adjective that is not preceded by a **der-** or an **ein-**word must take an ending that signals the case, gender, and number of the noun that follows. With the exception of the genitive singular masculine and neuter, these endings are identical to those of the **der-**words.

Wo bekommt man hier frisch**es** Obst?	*Where can you get fresh fruit?*
Hier gibt es jeden Tag frisch**e** Brötchen?	*You can get fresh rolls here every day.*
Bei schlecht**em** Wetter bleibe ich zu Hause.	*In bad weather I stay home.*

	SINGULAR			PLURAL
	Masculine	*Neuter*	*Feminine*	*All Genders*
Nom.	schön**er** Park	gut**es** Wetter	zentral**e** Lage	alt**e** Häuser
Acc.	schön**en** Park	gut**es** Wetter	zentral**e** Lage	alt**e** Häuser
Dat.	schön**em** Park	gut**em** Wetter	zentral**er** Lage	alt**en** Häusern
Gen.	schön**en** Parks	gut**en** Wetters	zentral**er** Lage	alt**er** Häuser

SUMMARY OF ENDINGS

	SINGULAR			PLURAL
	Masculine	*Neuter*	*Feminine*	*All Genders*
Nom.	-er	-es	-e	-e
Acc.	-en	-es	-e	-e
Dat.	-em	-em	-er	-en
Gen.	-en	-en	-er	-er

Note:

■ An adjective in the genitive singular masculine and neuter always takes the **-en** ending.

Circle all attributive adjectives in the illustrations. Then determine:

- the gender, case, and number of the noun.
- why a particular adjective ending is used.

ARCADE

member of

PULLMAN INTERNATIONAL HOTELS

Das **A** und **O** für Bonn!

ARCADE   OPTIMAL

Sie suchen:

- das Hotel im Herzen der Stadt
- maximalen Komfort, moderne Einrichtung[3]
- die gehobene[4] Mittelklasse
- ein Tagungshotel[6]

Wir bieten:[1]

- **zentrale Lage,** unmittelbar[2] in der Nähe der Fußgängerzone
- 147 **gastfreundliche Zimmer** mit Dusche, WC, Telefon, Kabel-TV u. Radio
- **preiswerte Übernachtung** mit reichhaltigem[5] Frühstücksbuffet, **Restaurant** mit internationaler Küche
- 3 Konferenzräume für 10—150 Personen
- eigene **Tiefgarage**

gastfreundlich   **preiswert**   **zentral**

Ältestes renommiertestes Eiscafé in KL

Eiscafé Dolomiten

Bei uns beginnt die Eiszeit - jetzt!!

★ Heiß- und Kaltspezialitäten
★ Eiskreationen mit frischen Früchten
★ Selbstgebackener Kuchen
★ Italienisches Frühstück

An Wochentagen ab 8.30 Uhr geöffnet
Kaiserslautern · Schillerstr. 2 · Tel. 06 31 / 6 31 05

[1] *offer*
[2] *directly*
[3] *furnishings*
[4] *upper*
[5] *lavish*
[6] *conference hotel*

Griechische Aprikosen
Klasse 1, 1kg
real,- spezial **€ 1,⁹⁸**

Spanische Honigmelonen
Stück
real,- spezial **€ 0,⁹⁸**

Deutscher Eissalat
Klasse 1, Stück
real,- spezial **€ 0,⁵⁰**

Deutsche Möhren
Klasse 1, 1kg
real,- spezial **€ 0,⁸⁰**

Übung 12 Kurze Gespräche

Sie hören zwei kurze Gespräche. Ergänzen Sie die Adjektivendungen, so wie
Sie sie hören.

DIALOG 1

GERD: Sag mal, seit wann hast du denn
blau__e__¹ Haare?

GABI: Seit letzt__er__² Woche. Gefallen sie dir?

GERD: Na ja, ich war an deine braun__en__³
Haare gewöhnt.

GABI: Ich habe ja auch blau__e__⁴ Augen. Die
blau__en__⁵ Haare passen gut zu meinen
blau__en__⁶ Augen.

GERD: Ein merkwürdig__er__⁷ Grund (*masc.*).
Na ja, meine Oma hat lila Haare.

DIALOG 2

PASSANT: Entschuldigung, wo ist das Rathaus?

PASSANTIN: Meinen Sie das alt__e__⁸ oder das
neu__e__⁹?

PASSANT: Oh, es gibt zwei? Ein alt__es__¹⁰ und ein
neu__es__¹¹? Ich suche das Rathaus mit
dem berühmt__en__¹² Glockenspiel.

PASSANTIN: Also, das ist das alt__e__¹³ Rathaus.
Gehen Sie geradeaus, dann die
zweit__e__¹⁴ Straße links. Das Rathaus
liegt auf der recht__en__¹⁵ Seite.

Das Rathaus in München am Marienplatz

Übung 12. Have students
complete the missing endings
before listening, then use the
listening phase to check their
work.

SPRACHTIPP

Adjectives that end in the vowel **-a** (**lila, rosa**) do not add adjective
endings. They remain unchanged.

Meine Oma hat **lila** Haare.   *My grandma has purple hair.*

Übung 13 Kleinanzeigen°: Gesucht/Gefunden

Classified ads

Ergänzen Sie die Lücken mit den passenden Adjektivendungen.

1. Studentin sucht schön ____ Zimmer in nett ____ Wohngemeinschaft.

2. Freundlich ____ Englischlehrer sucht klein ____ Wohnung in zentral ____ Lage.

3. Italienisch ____ Studentin sucht nett ____ Zimmer im Norden der Stadt.

4. **Gesucht.** Klein ____, schwarz ____ Pudel entlaufen, Nähe Stadtpark. Hört auf den Namen Papageno. Belohnung.

5. **Gefunden.** Groß____, graugetigert ____ Kater, Nähe Rosenbachstraße und Meisenweg.

6. **Gefunden.** Freundlich ____, klein ____ Katze, schwarz mit weiß ____ Nase, Landeshauptstraße, Ecke Stadtpark.

Übung 14   Hin und her: Was gibt es hier?

Fragen Sie einen Partner / eine Partnerin nach der fehlenden Information.

BEISPIEL: S1: Was gibt es beim Gasthof zum Bären?
S2: Warme Küche.
S1: Was gibt es sonst noch?
S2: Bayerische Spezialitäten.

WO?	WAS?	WAS SONST NOCH?
Gasthof zum Bären	Küche / warm	Spezialitäten / bayerisch
Gasthof Adlersberg	Biergarten / gemütlich	liegt in Lage / idyllisch
Gasthaus Schneiderwirt	Hausmusik / originell	Gästezimmer / rustikal
Hotel Luitpold	in Lage / idyllisch	Zimmer / rustikal

Adjectives Referring to Cities and Regions

Haben Sie schon einmal im Hotel **Baseler** Hof übernachtet?

Das Hotel liegt in der **Frankfurter** Innenstadt.

Wo trägt man **Tiroler** Hüte?

A city or regional name can be used attributively by adding **-er** to the name of the city or region. This is one of the rare instances where an adjective is capitalized in German. No further changes are made. One country name can also be used in this way: **die Schweiz.**

Essen Sie gern **Schweizer** Käse?

Übung 15 Berichte

Sie sind gerade von einer Reise nach Hause gekommen. Nun müssen Sie berichten.

Was hast du da gesehen oder gemacht?

BEISPIEL: S1: Was hast du in Köln gemacht?
S2: Da habe ich den Kölner Dom besichtigt.

1. in Hamburg / den Hafen besichtigt
2. in Bremen / die Stadtmusikanten gesehen
3. in Düsseldorf / die berühmte Altstadt besucht
4. in Dortmund / Bier getrunken
5. in Berlin / eine Weiße mit Schuss getrunken
   [ein Spezialgetränk aus Bier und Saft]
6. in München / Weißwurst gegessen
7. in der Schweiz / Käse gekauft
8. in Wien / Walzer getanzt

Die Bremer Stadtmusikanten

Point out: In Grimm's tale, *Die Bremer Stadtmusikanten,* four animals—a donkey, dog, cat, and rooster—end up in Bremen after many adventures. Note that *Bremer* (from *Bremen*) does not follow the rule on p. 278.

Sprache im Kontext

Videoclips

A. Hotel Jurine: Interview mit Nadine Schulz. Nadine Schulz arbeitet im Hotel. Sie gibt viele Informationen über das Hotel. Was sagt sie?

1. Der Name des Hotels ist _____ _____ des Inhabers.
2. Das Hotel hat 53 _____.
3. Ein Einzelzimmer kostet zwischen _____ und _____ Euro.
4. Ein _____ kostet zwischen 80 und 140 Euro.
5. Die Zimmer haben _____, WC, _____, Telefon, ISDN-Anschluss und Modem für Computer.

B. Wie gefällt Doris und Beatrice das Hotel? Was sagen sie?

   Das Hotel ist...

C. Michael fragt Dennis nach dem Weg zum Alexanderplatz. Was sagt Dennis? Nummerieren Sie die Sätze in der richtigen Reihenfolge.
   _____ und dann kannst du es nicht verfehlen
   _____ du gehst am besten immer geradeaus
   _____ und dann gehst du immer geradeaus circa fünf Minuten
   _____ vorne an der Ampel gehst du nach links
   _____ nächste gleich wieder rechts

Lesen

Zum Thema

A. Vorteile (*Advantages*) **und Nachteile** (*disadvantages*) **des Stadtlebens.** Arbeiten Sie zu zweit. Machen Sie eine Liste von den Vorteilen und Nachteilen des Stadtlebens.

B. Zusammenwohnen. Interviewen Sie zwei Leute im Deutschkurs und berichten Sie danach im Plenum.

   1. Was ärgert dich (*annoys you*), wenn du zu Hause bist?

   2. Was machst du, wenn deine Nachbarn/Nachbarinnen zu laut sind?

   3. Was ist wichtig für ein friedliches (*peaceful*) Zusammenleben in einer Stadt?

C. Was würden Sie machen?

   1. Sie müssen für eine Prüfung lernen, und Ihr Mitbewohner / Ihre Mitbewohnerin spielt sehr laute Musik.

   2. Sie studieren Musik und müssen jeden Tag üben. Ihre Nachbarn im Haus beschweren sich (*complain*) immer, wenn Sie spielen.

Zum Thema. C. Suggestion: Have students role-play the various situations.

Auf den ersten Blick

Auf den ersten Blick. Suggestion. A. Read the first two paragraphs of the text aloud, acting out the story, before having students answer these questions.
B. Work on contextual guessing with the students in the first two paragraphs. For example, point out that *Mietshaus* is related to *mieten* and *Haus* and see if they can infer the meaning.

A. In dem folgenden Text stehen die Verben im Imperfekt (*simple past*). Suchen Sie den Infinitiv in der zweiten Spalte.

   1. __j__ spielte   **a.** schlagen (*to hit*)

   2. __m__ gab   **b.** sprechen

   3. __i__ stieß   **c.** grüßen

   4. __f__ losging   **d.** ausziehen (*to move out*)

   5. __k__ blies   **e.** einziehen (*to move in*)

   6. __a__ schlug   **f.** losgehen (*to start, begin*)

   7. __l__ traf   **g.** anfangen

   8. __c__ grüßte   **h.** stören (*to disturb*)

   9. __e__ einzog   **i.** stoßen (*to pound*)

   10. __d__ auszog   **j.** spielen

   11. __a__ sprach   **k.** blasen (*to blow*)

   12. __g__ anfing   **l.** treffen

   13. __h__ störte   **m.** geben

B. Lesen Sie die ersten zwei Absätze (*paragraphs*). Wo findet die Geschichte statt (*takes place*)? Wie könnte die Geschichte weitergehen?

von Heinrich Hannover

Frau Amanda Klimpermunter spielte oft und gern Klavier. Aber sie wohnte in einem großen Mietshaus. Und da gab es manchmal Ärger° mit den Mietern der Nachbarwohnungen. Denn die Wände und Decken des Hauses waren dünn.° — *trouble* / *thin*

5 In der Wohnung unter Frau Klimpermunter wohnte Herr Maibaum. Wenn oben Klavier gespielt wurde, fühlte sich Herr Maibaum in seiner Ruhe gestört° und schimpfte.° Dann stieß er ein paarmal mit einem Besenstiel an die Decke. Aber Frau Klimpermunter spielte weiter. Und so schaffte sich Herr Maibaum eines Tages eine Trompete an. Und immer, wenn Frau Klimpermunters 10 Klaviermusik losging, trompetete er kräftig° dagegen. — *disturbed* / *yelled, swore* / *powerfully, vigorously*

Das störte nun den Nachbarn des Herrn Maibaum, der sich schon über das Klavier genug geärgert hatte. Und jetzt auch noch die Trompete, das war zuviel. Ein paarmal klopfte° er mit einem Holzpantoffel gegen die Wand. Aber Herr Maibaum trompetete weiter. Und so schaffte sich der Nachbar, er hieß 15 Fromme-Weise, eine Posaune an. Und immer, wenn das Klavier und die Trompete im Haus ertönten, blies er laut wie ein Elefant auf der Posaune. — *knocked*

Aber das störte nun Frau Morgenschön, die Wand an Wand mit Herrn Fromme-Weise wohnte. Ein paarmal schlug sie mit dem Kochlöffel gegen die Wand, aber das kümmerte ihren Nachbarn nicht. Und so kaufte sie sich eine 20 Flöte und düdelte° dazwischen, wenn die anderen Musikanten im Haus loslegten. — *noodled*

Das störte Herrn Bollermann, der unter Frau Morgenschön wohnte. Er kaufte sich ein Schlagzeug und haute, wenn die anderen herumtönten, kräftig auf die Pauke. Das gab nun alle Tage einen Höllenlärm im Haus, ein fürchter-25 liches Durcheinander—tüdelüdelüt-bumsbums-trärä-trara-bumspeng... Wenn man sich auf der Treppe traf, grüßte keiner den anderen, man knallte° mit den Türen, es gab immer Krach° im Haus, auch wenn keiner Musik machte. — *slammed* / *noise*

Aber dann zog Herr Hatunoglu ins Haus ein, ein Ausländer, wie man schon am Namen merkt. Er brachte eine Gitarre mit und freute sich, daß im Haus 30 musiziert wurde. „Da kann ich ja auch ein bißchen Gitarre spielen", sagte er. Aber obwohl man die Gitarre bei dem Lärm, den die anderen Hausbewohner mit ihren Instrumenten machten, gar nicht hören konnte, waren sich plötzlich alle einig: „Die Gitarre ist zu laut." Plötzlich sprachen sie wieder miteinander.

„Finden Sie nicht auch, daß der Herr Hatunoglu mit seiner Gitarre einen 35 unerträglichen Lärm macht?"

„Ja, Sie haben recht, der Mann muß raus."

Sie grüßten sich wieder auf der Treppe und hörten auf, sich gegenseitig zu nerven. Dem Herrn Hatunoglu aber machten sie das Leben schwer.° Wenn er anfing, auf der Gitarre zu spielen, klopften sie von oben und von unten und 40 von allen Seiten mit Besenstielen, Kochlöffeln und Holzpantoffeln an Wände und Decken und riefen: „Aufhören! Ruhe im Haus!" — *difficult*

„Was haben die Leute bloß gegen meine Gitarre?" fragte Herr Hatunoglu. Und eines Tages zog er aus.

Kaum war Herr Hatunoglu ausgezogen, ging der Krach im Haus wieder 45 los. Sobald Frau Klimpermunter den ersten Ton auf dem Klavier gespielt hat, packen die anderen Hausbewohner ihre Instrumente aus und legen los: Tüdelüdelüt-bumsbums-trärä-trara-bumspeng... Sie sprechen auch nicht

mehr miteinander und grüßen sich nicht mehr auf der Treppe. Und sie
knallen wieder mit den Türen. Aber abends, wenn sie völlig entnervt ins Bett
50 gehen, flüstern sie vor sich hin: „Was war das doch für eine schöne, ruhige
Zeit, als noch der Herr Hatunoglu mit seiner Gitarre im Haus wohnte."

Zum Text. A: Reproduce
the house on the board or on
a transparency. Have one
student go to the board or the
overhead projector. The rest of
the class tells her or him who
lives where, which instrument
goes where, and who is using
what to bang on the wall.

Zum Text

A. Wer wohnt wo? Setzen Sie die Namen der Bewohner in das Bild ein.
Welches Instrument gehört zu welcher Person? Welches „Schlagzeug"
gehört zu welcher Person?

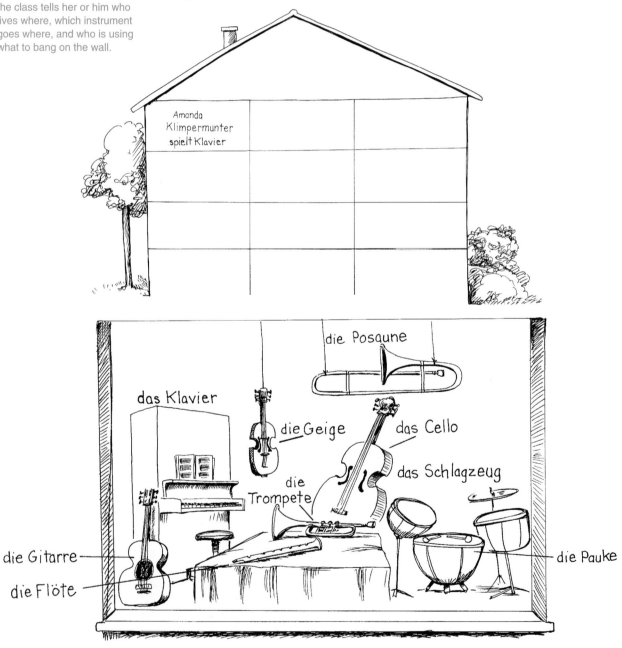

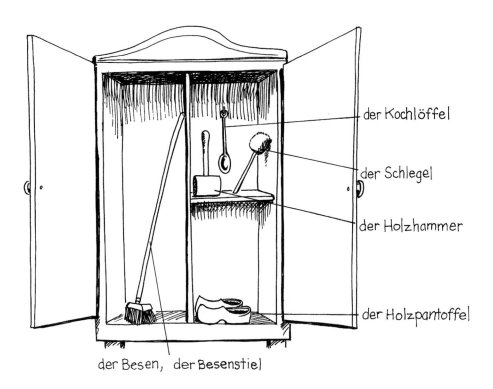

der Kochlöffel

der Schlegel

der Holzhammer

der Holzpantoffel

der Besen, der Besenstiel

B. Stimmt das? Stimmt das nicht? Oder steht das nicht im Text?

	DAS STIMMT	DAS STIMMT NICHT	DAS STEHT NICHT IM TEXT
1. Herr Hatunoglu ist unfreundlich.	☐	☒	☐
2. Nachdem Herr Hatunoglu einzieht, sprechen die Nachbarn wieder miteinander.	☒	☐	☐
3. Herr Hatunoglu spielt Gitarre und ist sehr froh, dass die anderen Bewohner so viel Musik machen.	☒	☐	☐
4. Die anderen Bewohner mögen Herrn Hatunoglu nicht, weil er so laut ist.	☒	☐	☐
5. Herr Hatunoglu lädt oft Freunde ein, und sie sind sehr laut.	☐	☐	☒
6. Sobald Herr Hatunoglu auszieht, werden die anderen Bewohner miteinander viel freundlicher.	☐	☒	☐

C. Die folgenden Wörter stehen im Text. Welches Wort gehört nicht in die Gruppe?

BEISPIEL: Holzpantoffel   Klavier   Besen →
Klavier gehört nicht dazu. Frau Klimpermunter spielt
Klavier. Die Nachbarn schlagen mit dem Holzpantoffel und
Besen gegen die Wand, wenn sie Musik hören.

1. sich etwas anschaffen   düdeln   trompeten
2. schimpfen   die Tür knallen   Krach machen
3. klopfen   schlagen   flüstern
4. anschaffen   aufhören   kaufen

Sprechen und Schreiben

Aktivität 1   Wer bin ich?

Aktivität 1. Suggestion: Collect the complaints and read some aloud or have a student read them. Have students guess which character in the story is complaining.

Wählen Sie eine Person aus der Geschichte „Die Gitarre des Herrn Hatunoglu". Beschweren Sie sich (*complain*) über die Situation im Haus aus der Perspektive dieser Person. Schreiben Sie Ihre Beschwerde (*complaint*) auf, und lesen Sie sie der Klasse vor. Die anderen müssen raten, wer Sie sind.

Aktivität 2   Ein Interview über den Krach im Haus

Interviewen Sie Herrn Hatunoglu und eine weitere Person im Haus. Schreiben Sie mindestens drei Fragen für jede Person auf. Arbeiten Sie in Gruppen zu viert. Zwei Studenten / Studentinnen übernehmen die Rollen. Die anderen interviewen die beiden.

Wortschatz

In der Stadt	In the City
die **Ampel, -n**	traffic light
die **Bank, -en**	bank
der **Hafen, :**	harbor, port
das **Hotel, -s**	hotel
die **Innenstadt, :e**	downtown
die **Jugendherberge, -n**	youth hostel
die **Kirche, -n**	church
die **Kreuzung, -en**	intersection
die **Lage, -n**	location
das **Museum,** *pl.* **Museen**	museum
der **Passant, -en (-en** *masc.*)/die **Passantin, -nen**	passer-by
die **Pension, -en**	bed and breakfast, small family-run hotel
die **Polizei**	police, police station
die **Post,** *pl.* **Postämter**	post office
der **Strand, :e**	beach
die **Tankstelle, -n**	gas station
der **Weg, -e**	way, path; road

Im Hotel	At the Hotel
das **Anmelde- formular, -e**	registration form

der **Apparat, -e**	set, appliance (*such as TV, telephone, camera*)
der **Aufenthalt, -e**	stay; layover
der **Aufzug, :e**	elevator
das **Doppelzimmer, -**	room with two beds, double room
die **Dusche, -n**	shower
das **Einzelzimmer, -**	room with one bed, single room
das **Erdgeschoss, -e**	ground floor
der **Fön, -e**	hair dryer
der **Frühstücksraum, :e**	breakfast room
das **Gepäck**	luggage
der **Koffer, -**	suitcase
die **Kreditkarte, -n**	credit card
der **Parkplatz, :e**	parking space; parking lot
der **Preis, -e**	price; cost
im Preis enthalten	included in the price
der **Reisepass, :e**	passport
die **Rezeption**	reception desk
der **Schlüssel, -**	key
der **Stock,** *pl.* **Stockwerke**	floor, story
die **Übernachtung, -en**	overnight stay

| die **Unterkunft**, ⸚e | accommodation |
| das **WC**, -s | bathroom, toilet |

LERNZIELE

Use this checklist to verify that you can now . . .

☐ describe types of lodging and amenities.

☐ register at a hotel.

☐ describe cities and various public places found there.

☐ ask for / give directions.

☐ use the genitive case to describe relationships, ownership, properties, and characteristics.

☐ use attributive adjectives to describe things.

Drittes Zwischenspiel

Die Entwicklung der Stadt

Im Laufe der Zeit hat sich das Bild der Stadt sehr verändert.[1] Viele Städte in Deutschland, wie auch anderswo in Europa, haben aber zum Teil ihren ursprünglichen[2] Charakter aus der mittelalterlichen Zeit erhalten.[3] Sie sind stolz auf ihre Vergangenheit, die oft bis ins Mittelalter und manchmal bis in die Römerzeit zurückreicht. Köln wurde zum Beispiel im Jahre 50 gegründet, Erfurt im 9. Jahrhundert. Die Geschichte Goslars reicht in das 10. Jahrhundert zurück. Gelegentlich sind sogar noch Überreste alter Bauten und Denkmäler[4] aus frühen Zeiten zu sehen.

Aktivität 1   Mittelalterliche Städte

Wie sahen Städte im Mittelalter aus? Was gehörte zum typischen Stadtbild? Kreuzen Sie an.

- ☐ Restaurants
- ☐ Gefängnis[5]
- ☐ Burg/Schloss
- ☐ Universität
- ☐ Kirche/Dom
- ☐ Bürgerhäuser[6]
- ☐ Wachttürme[7]
- ☐ Krankenhaus
- ☐ Markt
- ☐ Geschäfte
- ☐ Parks
- ☐ Bibliothek
- ☐ Schule
- ☐ Fabrik
- ☐ Stadtmauer[8]
- ☐ Rathaus[9]
- ☐ Museum
- ☐ Stadttor[10]

Aktivität 2   Nürnberg damals

Schauen Sie sich jetzt die Stadtansicht von Nürnberg aus dem Jahr 1533 an (Seite 287). Identifizieren Sie die Hauptmerkmale der Stadt.

1. _____ Burg
2. _____ Kirche
3. _____ Brücke
4. _____ Bürgerhäuser
5. _____ Stadtmauer
6. _____ Wachtturm

- ■ Welche(s) Gebäude[11] bildete(n) den Kern[12] einer mittelalterlichen Stadt? Warum?
- ■ Wer wohnte in der Stadt? Wer wohnte außerhalb der Stadt?

[1]changed [2]original [3]preserved [4]Bauten... buildings and monuments [5]prison [6]patrician houses [7]watch towers [8]city wall [9]town hall [10]city gate [11]building(s) [12]center

Erfurt

Köln

Nürnberg heute

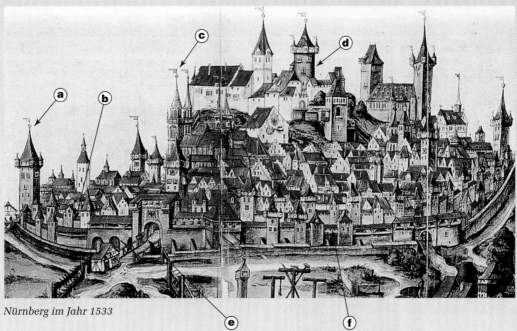

Nürnberg im Jahr 1533

Aktivität 3 Nürnberg heute

Vergleichen Sie die zwei Ansichten von Nürnberg. Obwohl Nürnberg während des Zweiten Weltkriegs fast völlig zerstört[1] wurde, sind noch einige Bauten und Denkmäler aus dem Mittelalter und der Renaissance erhalten. Wie viele der folgenden Bauten und Denkmäler können Sie auf dem Stadtplan finden?

1. St. Sebaldus Kirche (14. Jahrhundert)
2. St. Lorenz Kirche (13.–14. Jahrhundert)
3. das Rathaus (14. Jahrhundert)
4. die Stadtmauer (14.–15. Jahrhundert)
5. der Schöne Brunnen (1389–1396)
6. die Burg (11.–12. Jahrhundert)

Aktivität 4 Auf den Spuren[2] der Stadtentwicklung

Wählen Sie eine Stadt in Ihrem Land aus. Es kann auch Ihre Heimatstadt sein. Beschreiben Sie folgendes:

- Wie sah die Stadt vor 100 Jahren aus?
- Was gehörte damals zum Stadtbild?

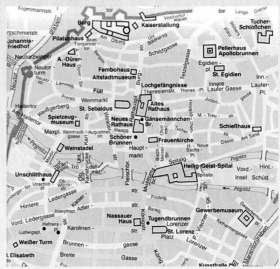

Stadtplan von Nürnberg

- Gab es einen Mittelpunkt der Stadt? Wenn ja, was gehörte dazu? Ein Markt, eine Kirche oder ein anderes Gebäude?
- Welche alten Bauten und Denkmäler sind noch in dieser Stadt erhalten? Welche sind verschwunden[3]? Warum?

[1]destroyed   [2]Auf... On the trail   [3]disappeared

Drittes Zwischenspiel   **287**

Auf Reisen

Das beliebteste Reiseziel
der Deutschen ist...
a. das Ausland, z.B.
Spanien
b. das Inland, z.B.
Süddeutschland

Kapitel 10. Suggestion: Talk
about a trip you took, focusing
on your travel preparations,
e.g., planning the trip, going to
the travel agency. Encourage
students to talk about trips they
took.

Videoclips
Wohin im Urlaub?

In diesem Kapitel

- **Themen:** Travel, vacations, means of transportation, items to take on vacation
- **Grammatik:** Comparative and superlative, adjectival nouns, simple past tense, conjunction **als,** past perfect tense
- **Kultur:** German vacations, dealing with a travel agency, buying a train ticket

Alles klar?

A. Was planen Sie für Ihren nächsten Urlaub? Was interessiert Sie? Lesen Sie die folgenden Anzeigen.

- Auf welcher Reise kann man eine Fremdsprache lernen?
- Welche Reise ist für sportliche Leute am geeignetsten (*most suited*)? Welche Sportarten kann man auf dieser Reise machen?
- Welche Reise verbindet (*connects*) Sport und Kultur?
- Was macht eine Wanderreise attraktiv?
- Was macht Ihnen persönlich in den Ferien Spaß: eine Fremdsprache lernen? Tennisspielen lernen? eine Wanderreise machen? Mountainbiking?

Diesmal Aktiv-Urlaub

BAUMELER Wanderreisen: mehr sehen, mehr erleben.[1] Auf eigenen Füßen unterwegs[2] sein, dort wo wandern sich lohnt.[3] Kleine Gruppen. Kompetente Reiseleitung. Ausgewählte[4] Hotels. Linienflug oder Busreise.

YOUNG TRAVEL Sport-Scheck Jugendreisen

Sun & Fun • Sport & Spiel • mit Board, Bike, Racket, Badehose und Bikini!

Clubdorf Tortorella • Süditalien • ab 16 Jahre

Beachlife • American Sports • Tennis • Highlife
Termine '03: 5.-19.7./19.7.-2.8./26.7.-8.9./9.8. - 23.8./23.8.-30.8.
1 Woche inkl. Halbpension,[7] Reiseleitung, Aktivprogramm
und Bus ab München pro Person **€400,–**
2 Wochen pro Person €725,–

Multi-Sportcamp • Österreich • 14 - 20 Jahre

Snowboard • Tennis • Mountainbike • Fitness
Piesendorf am Kitzsteinhorn • Termine '03: 31.5.-6.6./25.7.-14.8.
6 Tage inkl. Vollpension,[8] Multisport, Skipaß, Leihmaterial
und Betreuung pro Person **€450–**

Den Gesamt-Reisekatalog erhaltet Ihr kostenlos!
Tel.: 089/21 66-243 • Fax: 089/26 04-443

Sport-Scheck REISEN

TENNIS & KULTUR IN PRAG
€ 200,–
1 Wo inkl.: 5x2(4) Std. Tennistraining + HP + Kulturprogramm · Info + Buchung:
Tel. (089) 53 94 34 od. 53 64 35 · Fax 532 84 70
Tamar-Reisen·Häberlstraße 13·München 80337

SPANISCH in LATEINAMERIKA
z.B. Bolivien
2 Wo Einzelunterricht[5] 25 Std/Wo
Wochenend-Tourenprogramm
Unterkunft m. VP bei Gastfamilie
Kleinkinderbetreuung[6]
schon ab € 700,–
ALR Wolfgang Retz Postfach 390 153/D
Conrädstr. 16/4, Berlin 13509
Tel: (030) 805 49 30 Fax: (030) 805 15 52

[1]*to experience*
[2]*on the road*
[3]*sich... is worth (it)*
[4]*select*

[5]*one-on-one instruction*
[6]*childcare*
[7]*breakfast plus one meal*
[8]*three meals*

B. Sie hören drei Gespräche über den Urlaub. Wo haben die Urlauber ihre Ferien verbracht? Was haben sie unternommen?

WO	WAS
1. a. an der Nordsee	**a.** segeln
b. an der Ostsee	**b.** Camping
2. a. Mexiko	**a.** Spanisch lernen
b. Bolivien	**b.** tauchen
3. a. in den Dolomiten	**a.** Bergsteigen
b. im Schwarzwald	**b.** wandern

Wörter im Kontext

THEMA 1: Ich möchte verreisen

Wie fahren Sie am liebsten?

☐ mit dem **Wagen**   ☐ mit dem **Flugzeug**   ☐ mit dem **Fahrrad**

☐ mit dem **Zug** / mit der **Bahn**　　☐ mit dem **Taxi**　　☐ mit dem Motorrad
☐ mit dem **Bus**

☐ mit dem **Schiff**　　☐ **per Autostop**

Neue Wörter

sicher　safe
gefährlich　dangerous
schnell　fast
langsam　slow
verreisen　go on a
　trip

Und warum das? Was finden Sie...

am interessantesten?　　　　am langweiligsten?
am **sicher**sten?　　　　　　am **gefährlich**sten?
am **schnell**sten?　　　　　am **langsam**sten?
am praktischsten?　　　　　am unpraktischsten?

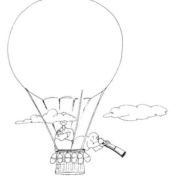

Mit dem Heißluftballon sieht man am meisten.

Zu Fuß ist es am interessantesten.

Fragen Sie jemand, wie er oder sie verreisen möchte.

BEISPIEL:　s1: Also Sven, du möchtest verreisen. Aber wie?
　　　　　s2: Mit einem Heißluftballon.
　　　　　s1: Und warum das denn?
　　　　　s2: Das ist am interessantesten.

Exercises. Suggestion: Have
students answer the questions after
you have introduced the vocabulary
using pictures. Follow up with a
class poll to find out the favorite
means of transportation and which
mode of transport students associate
with which adjective.

Wörter im Kontext　**291**

Ihre persönliche Checkliste vor der Reise – haben Sie nichts vergessen?

Bekleidung
- ☐ Unterwäsche
- ☐ Regenmantel
- ☐ **Handschuhe**
- ☐ Badehose/ Badeanzug
- ☐ Jogginganzug
- ☐ Schlafanzug
- ☐ Schal
- ☐ Sportbekleidung

Schuhwerk
- ☐ Wanderschuhe
- ☐ Hausschuhe
- ☐ Turnschuhe

Toilettensachen
- ☐ Hautcreme
- ☐ **Sonnenschutzmittel**
- ☐ Erfrischungstücher[1]
- ☐ Haarshampoo

Für Ihre Aktivitäten im Urlaub
- ☐ Kamera
- ☐ Filme
- ☐ **Reiseführer**
- ☐ Fernglas[2]
- ☐ Stadtpläne

Das sollte im Handgepäck nicht fehlen...
- ☐ Reiseapotheke
- ☐ Reiselektüre

Auch das muss mit - aber nicht im Koffer!
- ☐ **Bargeld**
- ☐ **Reiseschecks,** Euroschecks
  Achtung! Scheckkarte!
- ☐ Reisepass, **Personalausweis**
- ☐ **Fahrkarten**
- ☐ **Platzkarten**
- ☐ **Fahrplan**
- ☐ Kofferschlüssel
- ☐ Wohnungsschlüssel

[1]*towelettes* [2]*binoculars*

Neue Wörter

Reise trip
vergessen (vergessen) forgotten
Handschuhe gloves
Sonnenschutzmittel suntan lotion, sunscreen
Reiseführer travel guide
Handgepäck carry-on luggage
Bargeld cash
Reiseschecks travelers' checks
Personalausweis ID card
Fahrkarten tickets
Platzkarten seat-reservation cards
Fahrplan schedule

Aktivität 1   Alles für die Reise

Diese Wörter haben alle mit Reisen zu tun. Welches Wort in jeder Gruppe passt nicht?

1. Kamera, Film, Reiseführer, Hausschuhe
2. Badeanzug, Sportbekleidung, Stadtplan, Regenmantel
3. Bargeld, Turnschuhe, Reiseschecks, Reisepass
4. Wanderschuhe, Turnschuhe, Kofferschlüssel, Hausschuhe

Aktivität 2   Haben Sie etwas vergessen?

Schauen Sie sich die Reise-Checkliste aus **Thema 1** an und nennen Sie zwei Dinge aus der Liste, die Sie unbedingt (*absolutely*) mitnehmen würden.

BEISPIEL: Ich möchte eine Mountainbike-Tour machen. Ich nehme Sonnenschutzmittel und eine Kamera mit.

eine Wanderreise durch Europa

eine Reise nach Hawaii

eine Safari nach Afrika

eine Reise nach ____

Aktivität 2. Alternative: Have students name from the *Reise-Checkliste* three things they could manage without.

KULTURTIPP

Deutsche Arbeitnehmer bekommen im Jahr durchschnittlich (*on average*) sechs Wochen bezahlten Urlaub. Das erklärt, warum der Urlaub ein so wichtiges Thema ist. Wie kann man sechs Wochen freie Zeit sinnvoll planen? Die meisten, vor allem Familien, nehmen den größten Teil des Urlaubs im Sommer, wenn die Kinder Ferien (*school holidays*) haben. Viele Deutsche machen auch im Winter Urlaub: Sie fahren in den Bergen Ski oder suchen ein wärmeres Klima im Süden.

Strandurlaub auf der Nordseeinsel Sylt

Aktivität 3   Hin und her: Was nehmen sie mit?

Wohin fahren diese Leute im Urlaub? Was nehmen sie mit? Und warum? Ergänzen Sie die Informationen.

BEISPIEL: s1: Wohin fährt Angelika Meier in Urlaub?
        s2: Sie fährt in die Türkei.
        s1: Warum fährt sie in die Türkei?
        s2: Weil...
        s1: Was nimmt sie mit?
        s2: Sie nimmt...

Aktivität 3. Make sure students ask questions on all three categories.

PERSONEN	WOHIN?	WARUM?	WAS NIMMT ER/SIE MIT?
Angelika Meier	in die Türkei	sich am Strand erholen	Buch Sonnenbrille Badesachen
Peter Bayer	auf die Insel Rügen	Windsurfen gehen	Sonnenschutzmittel Badehose
Roland Metz	nach Thüringen	wandern Weimar besichtigen	Stadtpläne Reiseführer Wanderschuhe
Sabine Graf	nach Griechenland	eine Studienreise machen	Reiseführer Wörterbuch Kamera

SPRACHTIPP

Eine Wandertour von vier Tagen ist eine **viertägige** Wandertour. Eine Fahrt von einer Woche ist eine **einwöchige** Fahrt. Ein Aufenthalt von fünf Monaten ist ein **fünfmonatiger** Aufenthalt. So macht man es:

    ein-   -stündig

    zwei-   -tägig

    drei-   +   -wöchig } + Adjektivendung

    ...   -monatig

Aktivität 4   Vorteile und Nachteile°

Alles hat seine Vorteile und Nachteile. Was meinen Sie?

BEISPIELE: Mit dem Fahrrad sieht man viel, aber es ist anstrengend.

   Mit dem Auto geht es schneller, aber es ist ____.

mit dem/der ____	geht es	nicht	bequem / anstrengend
Bahn (Zug)	ist es	sehr	billig / teuer
Bus	kostet es	zu	praktisch / unpraktisch
Fahrrad	sieht man		romantisch / langweilig
Flugzeug			schnell / langsam
Heißluftballon			sicher / gefährlich
Wagen (Auto)			viel / wenig

per Autostop
zu Fuß (Wandern)
??

Aktivität 4. Suggestion: Point out the **Sprachtipp** about the comparative form. Then have students scan the possibilities in the sentence builder before they complete the activity, working in pairs. Spot-check the answers by asking several students to state the advantages and disadvantages of various ways of traveling.

SPRACHTIPP

To form the comparative of an adjective or adverb, add **-er** to the basic form.

schnell → schnell**er**
(*faster*)

romantisch →
romantisch**er**
(*more romantic*)

Hier klicken!

Weiteres zum Thema Reisebüro finden Sie bei **Deutsch: Na klar!** im World-Wide-Web unter www.mhhe.com/dnk.

Neue Wörter

Reisebüro travel agency
erleben experience
vorschlagen suggest
Möglichkeiten possibilities
sonst noch anything else
unternehmen undertake, do
Angebot offer
Reiseprospekt travel brochure
buchen book
Zelt tent
damit einverstanden ist (sein) agrees with that
Fahrt trip

THEMA 2: Im Reisebüro

*Ein Gespräch im Reisebüro zwischen Frau Siemens und Herrn Bittner, einem Angestellten im **Reisebüro**.*

FRAU SIEMENS: Mein Freund und ich möchten dieses Jahr mal einen Aktivurlaub machen. Wir wollen mal was anderes **erleben**. Können Sie etwas **vorschlagen**?

HERR BITTNER: Ja, gern. Wofür interessieren Sie sich denn? Es gibt so viele **Möglichkeiten**. Sind Sie **sportlich aktiv**?

FRAU SIEMENS: Nicht besonders. Manchmal spielen wir Tennis und fahren auch schon mal Rad.

HERR BITTNER: Wie wäre es mit einer Radreise durchs Elsass—oder mit einem Segelkurs an der Ostsee?

FRAU SIEMENS: Ach, ein Segelkurs ist mir zu anstrengend. Ich kann auch nicht gut schwimmen. Und eine Radreise... ich weiß nicht. Was können wir **sonst noch unternehmen**?

HERR BITTNER: Wir haben hier ein **Angebot** für eine viertägige Wandertour im Naturpark Solling-Vogler in der Nähe von Göttingen. Hier ist ein **Reiseprospekt**. Das kann ich sofort für Sie **buchen**.

FRAU SIEMENS: Hm, klingt gut. Ich sehe hier, die Gruppen sind relativ klein, höchstens zwölf Personen und ein Reiseleiter. Wo übernachtet man denn?

HERR BITTNER: Im **Zelt** natürlich!

FRAU SIEMENS: Ach, ich weiß nicht, ob mein Freund **damit einverstanden ist**. Er liebt die **Natur** zwar, aber in der Natur übernachten? Das ist etwas anderes. Wo **beginnt** die Wandertour?

HERR BITTNER: In Holzminden. Da treffen sich die Teilnehmer mit dem Reiseleiter. Von da aus fährt die Gruppe mit dem Bus zum Park. Die **Fahrt** dauert nicht lange, und unterwegs sieht man viel Grünes.

FRAU SIEMENS: Was kostet die Reise **insgesamt**?
HERR BITTNER: **Pro Person** €300.
FRAU SIEMENS: Das ist **günstig**. Wir werden es uns überlegen. Ich **sage** Ihnen in zwei Tagen **Bescheid**. Den Koffer packe ich noch nicht. Ich **hoffe**, mein Freund ist damit einverstanden.
HERR BITTNER: Ich hoffe es auch. Bis dann. Auf Wiedersehen.
FRAU SIEMENS: Auf Wiedersehen.

Neue Wörter

insgesamt altogether
günstig good (advantageous)
sage... Bescheid (Bescheid sagen) to tell definitely; to notify
hoffe (hoffen) hope

Aktivität 5 Claudia Siemens berichtet

Claudia Siemens berichtet ihrem Freund über ihren Besuch im Reisebüro. Ergänzen Sie die Sätze durch Informationen aus dem Gespräch im **Thema 2**.

CLAUDIA: Ich war heute im Reisebüro. Ich schlage vor, wir machen _____.[1]
MANFRED: Wie lange dauert denn so eine Tour?
CLAUDIA: _____.[2]
MANFRED: Und wo übernachtet man?
CLAUDIA: _____.[3]
MANFRED: Wie viele Leute nehmen (*participate*) an so einer Tour teil?
CLAUDIA: _____.[4]
MANFRED: Was soll das denn kosten?
CLAUDIA: _____.[5]
MANFRED: Ist das nicht ein bisschen teuer?
CLAUDIA: _____.[6]
MANFRED: Was meinst *du*? Sollen wir das machen?
CLAUDIA: Also, ich finde, das ist mal was anderes.
MANFRED: Gut, dann bin ich damit _____.[7]

Aktivität 6 Pläne für einen interessanten Urlaub

Sie hören vier Gespräche im Reisebüro. Wie, wohin und warum wollen die Leute in Urlaub fahren? Wie lange wollen sie dort bleiben?

Hier klicken!

Weiteres zum Thema Reisen finden Sie bei **Deutsch: Na klar!** im World-Wide-Web unter www.mhhe.com/dnk.

Im Reisebüro. Follow-up: Have students work in pairs and come up with variations on the dialogue. The customer might have different requirements for a vacation, the travel agent different suggestions. You might want to brainstorm various possibilities before the students begin.

Aktivität 6. Follow-up: Have students tell the class *wohin*, *wie*, *warum*, and *wie lange* for their own vacation dreams.

PERSONEN	WIE?	WOHIN?	WARUM?	WIE LANGE?
1. *Nicola Dinsing*	mit dem Flugzeug	nach Sizilien	für einen Sprachkurs	vier Wochen
2. *Marianne Koch und Astrid Preuß*	keine Information	nach Korfu	zur Meditation	eine Woche
3. *Herbert und Sabine Lucht*	mit dem Flugzeug, Bus und Schiff	nach Alaska	keine Information	zwei bis drei Wochen
4. *Sebastian Thiel*	keine Information	nach Israel	für eine Studienreise	drei Wochen

Art of persuasion
Aktivität 7. Suggestion: Cue students in different pairs to react in different ways, e.g., to be cooperative, to be skeptical, to be uncooperative. Have various pairs role-play their conversations for the class.

Aktivität 7 Überredungskünste°

Versuchen Sie, einen Partner / eine Partnerin zu einem Plan für einen gemeinsamen Urlaub zu überreden (*persuade*). Die Anzeigen (*ads*) in **Alles klar?** bieten mögliche Reisen.

s1	s2
1. Ich möchte dieses Jahr nach/in ＿＿. Willst du mit?	2. Was kann man denn da unternehmen?
3. Man kann da zum Beispiel ＿＿.	4. Ist das alles? Was sonst noch?
5. Nein, man kann auch ＿＿.	6. Wo übernachtet man denn?
7. ＿＿.	8. Wie viel soll das kosten?
9. ＿＿.	10. Wie kommt man dahin?
11. ＿＿.	12a. Ich will es mir überlegen. b. Ich weiß nicht, das ist mir zu ＿＿ (teuer, langweilig usw.). c. Klingt gut. Ich komme mit.

THEMA 3:   Eine Fahrkarte, bitte!

Am Fahrkartenschalter im Bahnhof

Eine Fahrkarte, bitte! Note: Tell students about the types of trains in Germany. The fastest are the high-speed ICE (*Inter-City Express*) trains, which are equivalent to the *TGV* in France. The IC (*Inter-City*) trains travel quickly and stop only in larger cities. The D-Zug (*Durchgangszug*) travels moderately fast but makes more frequent stops, whereas the *Eilzug* is not really very fast at all and makes frequent stops in small towns.

Wo kann man was machen? Wo passiert was?

1. Am _____ kauft man Fahrkarten für den Zug.
2. Der Zug fährt von _____ 2 ab.
3. Man bekommt Informationen über Züge bei der _____.
4. Auf dem _____ kann man lesen, wann ein Zug ankommt oder abfährt.
5. Die Leute stehen auf dem _____ und warten auf den Zug.

Reiseverbindungen   Deutsche Bahn DB

VON	Bad Harzburg			Gültig[1] am Montag, dem 09.08.
NACH	Hamburg Hbf			
ÜBER				

BAHNHOF		UHR	ZUG	BEMERKUNGEN[2]
Bad Harzburg	ab	10:46	E 3622	
Hannover Hbf	an	12:25		
	ab	12:43	ICE 794	Zugrestaurant
Hamburg Hbf	an	13:56		

[1]valid [2]notes

MICHAEL: Eine Fahrkarte nach Hamburg, bitte.
BEAMTER: **Hin und zurück?**
MICHAEL: Nein, **einfach, zweiter Klasse**, bitte.
BEAMTER: Das macht €42. Das ist übrigens der Sparpreis für Jugendliche. Haben Sie Ihren Ausweis dabei?
MICHAEL: Ja, natürlich. Wann fährt denn der nächste Zug?
BEAMTER: In dreißig Minuten. In Hannover müssen Sie dann **umsteigen.**
MICHAEL: Habe ich da gleich **Anschluss?**
BEAMTER: Sie haben achtzehn Minuten Aufenthalt. Dann können Sie mit dem ICE weiter nach Hamburg fahren. Für den ICE müssen Sie allerdings noch einen Platz reservieren. Möchten Sie im Großraumwagen sitzen, oder lieber in einem Abteil?
MICHAEL: Lieber in einem Abteil. **Nichtraucher,** bitte. Wann komme ich in Hamburg an?
BEAMTER: Um 13.56 Uhr.
MICHAEL: Danke schön.
BEAMTER: Bitte sehr.

Neue Wörter

hin und zurück round-trip
einfach one-way
zweiter Klasse second class
umsteigen change trains
Anschluss connection
Nichtraucher no-smoking car

Aktivität 8   Michaels Pläne

Ergänzen Sie den Text mit Informationen aus dem Dialog oben.

Michael fährt mit dem _____[1] nach Hamburg. Er kauft seine Fahrkarte am Schalter im _____.[2] Er fährt zweiter _____.[3] Der nächste Zug nach Hannover fährt in _____[4] ab. Michael muss in Hannover _____.[5] Dort hat er gleich _____[6] an den ICE nach Hamburg. Für den ICE muss er einen _____[7] reservieren.

Aktivität 9　Am Fahrkartenschalter

Sie hören drei kurze Dialoge am Fahrkartenschalter. Setzen Sie die richtigen Informationen in die Tabelle ein.

Hier klicken!

Weiteres zum Thema Bahnfahren finden Sie bei **Deutsch: Na klar!** im World-Wide-Web unter www.mhhe.com/dnk.

INFORMATION	DIALOG 1	DIALOG 2	DIALOG 3
Fahrkarte nach	Hamburg	Salzburg	Bonn
1. oder　2. Klasse	1.	keine Information	keine Information
einfach oder hin und zurück	hin und zurück	hin und zurück	einfach
für wie viele Personen	zwei	fünf	eine
Platzkarten (ja/nein)	ja	nein	nein

Grammatik im Kontext

Comparing Things and People

Adjectives and adverbs have three forms.

basic form	Der Fahrpreis ist **günstig.** *The fare is good (in price).*
comparative	Der Sparpreis ist **günstiger.** *The discount fare is better.*
superlative	Der Super-Sparpreis ist **am günstigsten.** *The super-saver fare is the best of all.*

Comparing Two Items

The basic form of an adjective or adverb is used with the expression **so... wie** to express that two items are equal, or **nicht so... wie** if they are not equal.

Der Bus fährt **so schnell wie** der Zug. — *The bus goes as fast as the train.*

Mit einem Eurail-Pass kann man **so weit** fahren, **wie** man will. — *With a Eurail Pass you can travel as far as you want.*

Der Sparpreis ist **nicht so günstig wie** der Super-Sparpreis. — *The discount fare is not as good as the super-saver fare.*

Fahr & Spar. Die neuen Preise der neuen Bahn.

G nstig fahren Sie zum Fahrpreis. Er betr gt[1] 10 Cent pro Kilometer. **€−,10**

€90,− G nstiger fahren Sie zum Sparpreis von 90 Euro.

Am g nstigsten fahren Sie zum **€60,−** Super-Sparpreis von 60 Euro.

[1]*comes to*

Übung 1 Vergleiche

Was meinen Sie?

BEISPIEL: Segeln / Bungee-jumping →
Ich finde Segeln nicht so gefährlich wie Bungee-jumping.

anstrengend	günstig	praktisch	sicher
bequem	interessant	schön	teuer
gefährlich	langweilig		

1. eine Wanderreise / eine Busreise
2. eine Zugreise / eine Flugreise
3. eine Fahrt nach Disneyland / eine Reise nach Tahiti
4. eine Fahrt im Heißluftballon / eine Fahrradtour
5. mit der Familie reisen / mit Freunden reisen
6. im eigenen (*one's own*) Land reisen / im Ausland reisen
7. mit dem Motorrad fahren / mit dem Wagen fahren
8. im Zelt schlafen / in der Jugendherberge übernachten
9. mit Bargeld bezahlen / mit einer Kreditkarte bezahlen

Übung 1. Suggestion: Have students work in pairs. This exercise can also be used later for actual comparisons. Ask students to expand the list by making suggestions of their own using phrases such as: *ich meine, ich finde, meiner Meinung nach,...*

Comparison. Suggestion: Point out the similarities between English and German when analyzing comparisons, focusing on the *-er/-est* endings and the fact that German usually expresses the comparative and superlative forms by endings rather than by forms equivalent to "more" and "most" in English.

The Comparative° of Adjectives and Adverbs

Der Komparativ

The comparative form of an adjective or adverb is used to describe things or persons that are dissimilar in quality or quantity.

Die Schaffnerin war **freundlicher als** die Bedienung im Speisewagen.	*The conductor was friendlier than the server in the dining car.*
Mit der Bahn reist man **bequemer als** mit dem Wagen.	*One travels more comfortably by train than by car.*

Note:

- In German, the comparative is formed by adding **-er** to the basic form of the adjective or adverb.
- The conjunction **als** (*than*) links the two parts of the comparison.
- Unlike English, with its two comparative forms (*-er* and *more*), German has only one form.

freundlich	freundlich**er**	*friendlier*
bequem	bequem**er**	*more comfortable*
günstig	günstig**er**	*more advantageous*
teuer	teu**er***	*more expensive*

- Most adjectives of one syllable with the vowels **a**, **o**, and **u** in their stems have an umlaut in the comparative.

alt	**ält**er	*older*
groß	**größ**er	*bigger/taller*
kurz	**kürz**er	*smaller/shorter*

- A number of adjectives and adverbs have irregular forms in the comparative. Here are some common ones:

gern **lieber** gut **besser** hoch **höher** viel **mehr**

Dümmer als die Polizei erlaubt

---

*Note that **teuer** drops the **-e-** before the **-r** in the stem when the comparative ending is added.

Die neue Bahn

Intercity fahren wird immer schöner.

- The adverb **immer** used with a comparative form expresses that someone or something is "more and more" so.

Mit der Bahn reisen wird **immer bequemer.**	*Traveling by train is getting **more and more** convenient.*
Die Züge fahren **immer schneller.**	*Trains are going **faster and faster.***

- When used attributively, adjectives in the comparative take adjective endings.

Martina braucht einen größer**en** Koffer.	*Martina needs a bigger suitcase.*
Herr Waldmann braucht ein größer**es** Zelt.	*Mr. Waldmann needs a bigger tent.*

Realia. The larger German towns, particularly university towns, have a *Mitfahrzentrale* that brings together drivers and passengers to share the cost of car travel.

SPRACHTIPP

When used attributively, the singular adjectives **viel/mehr** and **wenig/weniger** do not take adjective endings.

Ich brauche **mehr** Geld für die Reise.	*I need more money for the trip.*
Ich habe jetzt **weniger** Zeit für Reisen.	*Now I have less time for traveling.*

Analyse. Suggestion: Assign this for homework that will be the basis of the next class discussion.

ANALYSE

- Identify all adjectives and adverbs in the two ads. Which adjectives or adverbs are in the comparative?
- One comparative form is irregular; however, you can recognize it because it is a cognate. What is this form?
- For whom is the **B & S-Karte** favorably priced? What are the conditions that make commuting cheaper for these people?
- The adjective **sicher** is used in its basic form. What would be the comparative of **sicher**?
- The **Mitfahrzentrale** is a national ride-sharing agency. The ad implies a comparison. How would you complete the comparison? **Mitfahren ist günstiger als... und macht mehr Spaß als...**

mitfahr zentrale

Mitfahren... [1]

...ist günstiger

...ist sicher

...schont die Umwelt [2]

...macht mehr Spaß

Billiger zur Arbeit. Billiger zur Schule

B & S-Karten: die Fahrkarten für Berufstätige[3] und Schüler

Ist Ihr Weg zwischen Wohnort und Arbeits- oder Schulort weiter als 50 km? Dann fahren Sie mit der B & S-Karte auf dieser Strecke[4] etwa 15% billiger Bahn.

[1]*ride-sharing* [2]*schont... protects the environment* [3]*working people* [4]*route*

Übung 2 Alles ändert sich° *is changing*

Wählen Sie ein passendes Adjektiv aus der Liste.

anstrengend   praktisch

bequem   schlecht

günstig   schnell

hoch   sicher

kurz   teuer

lang

BEISPIEL: Das Wetter wird immer _____. →
           Das Wetter wird immer schlechter.

1. Fliegen wird immer _____.
2. Mit dem Zug fahren wird immer _____.
3. Die Busse werden immer _____.
4. Schiffsreisen werden immer _____.
5. Das Leben in den Städten wird immer _____.
6. Die Autos fahren immer _____.
7. Reisen wird immer _____.
8. Die Preise gehen immer _____.
9. Die Tage werden immer _____.
10. Die Nächte werden immer _____.

Übung 3 Erzähl mal!

Ein Bekannter / Eine Bekannte von Ihnen ist gerade aus Europa zurück-gekommen. Sie wollen wissen, wie es war.

BEISPIEL: schön: Österreich oder die Schweiz →

    s1: Was ist schöner? Österreich oder die Schweiz?
    s2: Österreich ist so schön wie die Schweiz. [oder]
        Die Schweiz ist schöner als Österreich. [oder]
        Ich weiß nicht, was schöner ist.

1. interessant: Berlin oder Wien
2. groß: Wien oder Salzburg
3. romantisch: der Rhein oder die Donau
4. alt: Köln oder Leipzig
5. gemütlich: die Cafés in Wien oder die Kneipen in Berlin
6. günstig: im Hotel oder in einer Jugendherberge übernachten
7. lang: der Rhein oder die Mosel
8. schön: Norddeutschland oder Süddeutschland
9. praktisch: mit dem Zug oder mit dem Auto fahren
10. teuer: die Hotels in Deutschland oder in Österreich

Übung 3. Suggestion: Have students work in groups of three to express their opinions. Each group takes turns asking a question, while the other two groups express their opinion. Encourage students to use conversational strategies to express agreement (*Das finde ich auch*) or disagreement (*Im Gegenteil, ich finde... schöner*, etc.). **Follow-up:** Have students come up with their own comparisons regarding features of their own lives.

Übung 4   Werners Reisevorbereitungen

Werner erzählt von seinen Reisevorbereitungen. Hören Sie zu und markieren Sie die beste Ergänzung zu jedem Satz.

1. Werner braucht...
   a. mehr Geld.   **b.** <u>mehr Zeit</u>   **c.** mehr Geduld (*patience*).
2. Er braucht auch...
   a. einen kleineren Koffer.   **b.** <u>einen größeren Koffer</u>.
   c. zwei kleinere Koffer.
3. Er nimmt _____ mit.
   a. <u>die kleinere Kamera</u>   **b.** die neuere Kamera
   c. die größere Kamera
4. Dies ist Werners...
   a. <u>längster Urlaub</u>.   **b.** teuerster Urlaub.   **c.** kürzester Urlaub.

Übung 5. Follow-up: Ask students about vacation problems they have had.

Übung 5   Probleme im Urlaub

Herr Ignaz Huber aus München fährt in Urlaub. Aber überall gibt es Probleme.

BEISPIEL: Sein Mietwagen ist zu klein. →
            Er wünscht sich einen größeren Wagen.

1. Das Hotel ist zu teuer.
2. Das Hotelzimmer ist ungemütlich.
3. Das Bett ist zu kurz.
4. Das Bad ist zu klein.
5. Das Hotelpersonal ist unhöflich.
6. Das Essen ist schlecht.
7. Seine Wanderschuhe sind unbequem.
8. Das Wetter ist zu heiß.
9. Der Urlaub ist zu kurz.

Übung 6. Suggestion: Brainstorm with your students about other differences among the regions of Germany.

Übung 6   Lokalpatriotismus

Leute aus verschiedenen Gegenden sagen ihre Meinung. Ergänzen Sie die Sätze mit der Komparativform des Adjektivs oder Adverbs in Klammern.

1. Bei euch in Hamburg regnet es _____ als bei uns in Bayern. (viel)
2. Bei uns in Dresden schmeckt das Bier _____ als bei euch in München. (gut)
3. Bei uns in Bayern sind die Bierkrüge _____ als bei euch in Berlin. (groß)
4. Bei uns in Thüringen schmeckt die Wurst _____ als bei euch in Westfalen. (gut)
5. Bei uns in der Schweiz sind die Berge _____ als die bei euch im Harz. (hoch)

Der Superlativ

The Superlative° of Adjectives and Adverbs

The superlative indicates the highest degree of a quality or quantity.

Adverbs and Predicate Adjectives in the Superlative

Mit dem Zug fährt man **am bequemsten.**

Traveling by train is the most comfortable.

Ein Mietwagen ist **am praktischsten.**

A rented car is the most practical (way of traveling).

Berlin ist **am interessantesten.**

Berlin is the most interesting (of all cities).

Note:

- The superlative form of adverbs and predicate adjectives is **am _____(e)sten.**

- German has only one form of the superlative, in contrast to English (*most* and *-(e)st*).

bequem	**am bequemsten**	*the most comfortable*
freundlich	**am freundlichsten**	*the most friendly*
schnell	**am schnellsten**	*the fastest*

- Adjectives of one syllable with the vowel **a, o,** or **u** in the stem add an umlaut in the superlative.

groß	**am größten**	*biggest, largest*
hoch	**am höchsten**	*highest*
kurz	**am kürzesten**	*shortest*
lang	**am längsten**	*longest*

- Some common irregular forms are these:

gern	**am liebsten**	*most preferred*
gut	**am besten**	*best*
viel	**am meisten**	*most*

Point Out: The superlative of *oft* (*öftest-*) is rarely used; instead, *häufigst-* (*most frequently*) is used.

Was machen Berliner am liebsten?

Urlaub.

Beratung[1] und Buchung bei uns im TUI Reisebüro.

Sie haben es sich verdient.[2] *Urlaub mit der TUI.*

TUI

[1]*advice* [2]*sich... earned*

Die schönsten Rathäuser in Thüringen

Hessen-Thüringen

ADAC Freizeitservice

Übung 7 Wo mag das sein?

Ergänzen Sie die Fragen mit der Superlativform des Adjektivs oder Adverbs in Klammern.

1. Wo regnet es _____? (viel)
2. Wo sind die Berge _____? (hoch)
3. Wo schmeckt das Bier _____? (gut)
4. Wo sind die Bierkrüge _____? (groß)
5. Wo verbringt man einen Sommerabend _____ in einem Biergarten? (gern)
6. Wo singen die Gäste _____? (laut)
7. Wo fahren die Autos _____? (schnell)
8. Wo feiert man _____? (viel)
9. Wo sind die Burgen _____? (alt)
10. Wo schmeckt das Essen _____? (gut)

Attributive Adjectives in the Superlative

Die Zugspitze ist der **höchste** Berg Deutschlands.	*The Zugspitze is the highest mountain in Germany.*
Arnstadt ist die **älteste** Stadt Thüringens.	*Arnstadt is the oldest city in Thuringia.*
In Thüringen gibt es die **schönsten** Rathäuser.	*The most beautiful city halls are in Thuringia.*
Das **beste** Bier gibt es in München.	*You'll find the best beer in Munich.*

Note:

- Attributive adjectives in the superlative add **-(e)st** plus an appropriate adjective ending to the adjective.
- A definite article usually precedes the adjective in the superlative.

Die Plakette für die besten Straßen der Schweiz

Übung 8 Was machst du lieber? Was machst du am liebsten?

A. Was machst du lieber im Urlaub?

BEISPIEL: s1: Sharon, was machst du lieber im Urlaub, wandern oder am Strand liegen?
s2: Ich liege lieber am Strand. Und du, Paul?

1. selber fotografieren oder Ansichtskarten kaufen?
2. allein oder mit Freunden reisen?
3. einen Aktivurlaub machen oder faul am Strand liegen?
4. im Zelt schlafen oder in einer Jugendherberge übernachten?
5. Museen besuchen oder schwimmen gehen?
6. eine Stadt besichtigen oder einen Nationalpark besuchen?
7. ??

B. Was machst du am liebsten im Urlaub?

BEISPIEL: s1: Was machst du am liebsten im Urlaub, Nicky?
s2: Am liebsten mache ich eine Radtour. Und du, Ben?
s1: Am liebsten bleibe ich zu Hause.

mit Freunden eine Reise machen	den ganzen Tag lesen
eine Radtour machen	zu Hause bleiben
eine Wandertour machen	nette Leute kennen lernen
einen Aktivurlaub machen	Museen besuchen
interessante Orte besuchen	in teuren Hotels wohnen
Freunde besuchen	??
faulenzen	

Übung 9 Eine Reise nach Österreich

Sie planen eine Reise nach Österreich und brauchen Information. Was möchten Sie wissen?

1. Wie heißt die ____ (schön) Stadt Österreichs?
2. Wie heißt das ____ (preiswert) Hotel in Wien?
3. Wo liegen die ____ (interessant) Sehenswürdigkeiten?
4. Welches ist das ____ (alt) Schloss?
5. In welchem Café gibt es den ____ (gut) Kaffee?
6. Wo gibt es die ____ (freundlich) Leute?
7. Wie heißt der ____ (groß) Vergnügungspark in Wien?

Übung 9. Suggestion: See if your students can answer any of the questions in the exercise. If not, which Austrian towns do they know? Do they know any tourist attractions there?

Übung 10 Hin und her: Wie war der Urlaub?

Herr Ignaz Huber aus München war drei Wochen im Urlaub in Norddeutschland. Er war zwei Tage in Hamburg, eine Woche in Cuxhaven und nicht ganz zwei Wochen auf der Insel Sylt. Stellen Sie einem Partner / einer Partnerin Fragen über seinen Urlaub. Benutzen Sie den Superlativ.

BEISPIEL: s1: Wo war es am wärmsten?
s2: Am wärmsten war es in Cuxhaven.

	IN HAMBURG	IN CUXHAVEN	AUF DER INSEL SYLT
Wo war es (kalt/warm)?	20°C	25°C	15°C
Wo hat es (viel) geregnet?	zwei Tage	einen Tag	fünf Tage
Wo waren die Hotels (günstig/teuer)?	150 Euro	60 Euro mit Vollpension	200 Euro
Wo war das Hotelpersonal (freundlich)?	freundlich	sehr freundlich	unfreundlich
Wo war der Strand (schön)?	kein Strand	sehr sauber, angenehm	zu windig

KULTURTIPP

Wissenswertes über Deutschland

- Zwei Drittel allen Weins kommt aus Rheinland-Pfalz.
- Mecklenburg-Vorpommern hat 600 Seen.
- Nordrhein-Westfalen hat mehr Industrie als die anderen Bundesländer.
- Die meisten Touristen und Besucher landen auf dem Frankfurter Flughafen.
- Berlin hat über drei Millionen Einwohner.
- Meißen produziert das berühmteste Porzellan.
- Die größte Insel ist Rügen (926 km^2).
- Der längste Fluss ist der Rhein (865 km), der zweitlängste ist die Elbe (700 km).
- Der höchste Berg ist die Zugspitze (2962 m), der zweithöchste ist der Watzmann (2713 m).

Burg Katz am Rhein

Facts

Übung 11   Tatsachen° über Deutschland

Die meisten Antworten finden Sie im Kulturtipp.

BEISPIEL: Berlin ist die größte Stadt Deutschlands.

Suggestion: The preceding **Kulturtipp** contains most of the information needed for **Übung 11.** Have students locate the places indicated in the **Übung** on a map.

Bayern	ist	das nördlichste Bundesland
Bremen	hat	die meiste Industrie
Berlin	produziert	die höchsten Berge
Frankfurt		das berühmteste Porzellan
Nordrhein-Westfalen		das kleinste Bundesland
Meißen		den größten Flughafen
Mecklenburg-Vorpommern		die größte Stadt Deutschlands
Schleswig-Holstein		
Rheinland-Pfalz		den meisten Wein
??		die meisten Seen
		??

Substantivierte Adjektive

Adjectival Nouns°

Adjectives can be used as nouns. As nouns, they are capitalized.

Deutsche und Amerikaner bezahlen Rechnungen oft mit Plastik.

Germans and Americans frequently pay their bills with credit cards.

Die meisten **Deutschen** zahlen mit Scheckkarte oder in bar.

Most Germans pay with a debit card or cash.

Auch die Kreditkarte ist **nichts Ungewöhnliches.**

Even the credit card is nothing unusual.

ADJECTIVE	ADJECTIVAL NOUN
deutsch	1. der/die Deutsche (*the German man/woman*) 2. Deutsche/die Deutschen (*[the]Germans*)
bekannt	3. ein Bekannter (*a male acquaintance*) 4. eine Bekannte (*a female acquaintance*)
ungewöhnlich	5. nichts Ungewöhnliches (*nothing unusual*) 6. etwas (was) Ungewöhnliches (*something unusual*)
neu	7. etwas Neues (*something [that is] new*) 8. nichts Neues (*nothing [that is] new*) 9. das Neue (*the new [thing]*)

Note:

- Adjectival nouns follow the rules that apply to attributive adjectives.
- The gender of adjectival nouns is determined by what they designate: people are masculine or feminine (see examples 1 through 4 above).
- Abstract concepts are neuter (see examples 5 through 9 above). After **etwas, nichts, viel,** and **wenig** the adjectival noun is always neuter (see examples 5 through 8).

Übung 12   Wer sind diese Leute?

Ergänzen Sie die Sätze mit einem substantivierten Adjektiv, das mit dem **fettgedruckten** Wort verwandt ist.

BEISPIEL: —Sind Sie aus **Deutschland,** Frau Huber?
         —Ja, ich bin Deutsche.

1. Erich ist mir seit Jahren **bekannt.** Er ist ein guter ____ von mir.
2. Seine Mutter ist mir auch **bekannt.** Sie ist auch eine ____ von mir.
3. **Reich** und **arm**: Kennen Sie den Spruch: „Die ____ werden reicher, und die ____ werden ärmer"?
4. Wo ist Dieter **angestellt**? Er ist ____ bei der Post.
5. Seine Schwester ist bei der Bank **angestellt.** Sie ist Bank____.
6. Herr Lindemann ist aus **Deutschland.** Er ist ____.
7. Frau Lindemann ist auch aus **Deutschland.** Sie ist ____.
8. Viele Touristen sind aus **Deutschland.** Die ____ reisen gern.

Übung 13   So etwas!

Reagieren Sie auf die Aussagen.

BEISPIEL: s1: Die Preise werden immer höher.
         s2: Das ist nichts Neues!

ärgerlich (*annoying*)	unglaublich
neu	verrückt
ungewöhnlich	??

1. A: In Kalifornien gibt es oft Erdbeben.
   B: Das ist wirklich nichts _____.
2. C: Gestern hat man mir den Wagen gestohlen.
   D: So etwas _____!
3. E: Zum ersten April bietet das Reisebüro Fröhlich eine Reise zum Mars zum Sparpreis von 2500 Euro hin und zurück.
   F: Das ist wirklich etwas _____.
4. G: Ich besitze zwanzig Kreditkarten.
   H: Das ist doch nichts _____.

Narrating Events in the Past: The Simple Past Tense°

das Imperfekt

Simple Past Tense.
Suggestion: Review the past tense of *sein, haben,* and modals first, then do **Übung 14,** which is a pure review exercise.

You recall that in conversation about events in the past, the present perfect tense is preferred, with the exception of **haben, sein,** and modal verbs. These verbs are commonly used in the simple past tense in conversation as well as in written or formal language.

The simple past tense is generally used in German to narrate past events in writing or in formal speech. By choosing this tense, the narrator or writer generally establishes a distance from the events.

Schwache Verben

Weak Verbs°

Weak verbs form the simple past tense by adding the marker **-(e)te** to the stem.

Wir **packten** unsere Sachen in einen Rucksack.	*We packed our things in a backpack.*
Wir **warteten** auf den Bus.	*We waited for the bus.*
Die Fahrt **dauerte** drei Stunden.	*The trip took three hours.*
Wir **übernachteten** in einer Jugendherberge.	*We stayed at a youth hostel.*

reisen			
ich	reis**te**	wir	reis**ten**
du	reis**test**	ihr	reis**tet**
er sie es	reis**te**	sie	reis**ten**
Sie reis**ten**			

warten			
ich	wart**ete**	wir	wart**eten**
du	wart**etest**	ihr	wart**etet**
er sie es	wart**ete**	sie	wart**eten**
Sie wart**eten**			

Note:

- The first- and third-person singular are identical, as are the first- and third-person plural.

- Verbs with stems ending in **-t** or **-d,** as well as verbs with a consonant + **-n** in the stem (e.g., **regnen, öffnen**), add **-ete** to the stem.
- Weak verbs with separable and inseparable prefixes have the same past tense stem as the base verb.

    Ute **packte** einen Badeanzug **ein.**   *Ute packed a swimsuit.*

Übung 14   Kleine Erlebnisse° im Urlaub   *experiences*

Ergänzen Sie die Sätze mit passenden Modalverben im Imperfekt: **dürfen, können, müssen, wollen.**

1. Wir _____ per Autostop nach Spanien fahren.
2. Niemand _____ uns mitnehmen.
3. Wir _____ zwei Stunden an der Autobahn warten.
4. Ein Fahrer _____ uns bis nach Freiburg mitnehmen.
5. Wir _____ in der Jugendherberge übernachten, aber dort war kein Platz mehr.
6. Deshalb _____ wir im Park übernachten.
7. Im Park _____ man aber nicht übernachten. Es war verboten.
8. Wir _____ aber noch eine Übernachtung auf einem Bauernhof bekommen.

Eine kleine Pause
auf Reisen

Übung 15   Eine Reise nach Österreich

Rainer hat in der Schule über seine Sommerferien geschrieben. Schreiben Sie die Sätze neu im Imperfekt.

BEISPIEL: Wir haben eine Reise nach Österreich gemacht. →
         Wir machten eine Reise nach Österreich.

1. Mein Vater hat einen Wohnwagen gemietet.
2. Die ganze Familie hat in dem Wohnwagen gewohnt.
3. Auf der Autobahn sind die Autos an uns vorbei gerast.
4. Wir haben lange an der Grenze im Stau (*traffic jam*) gewartet.
5. Wir haben auf einem Campingplatz übernachtet.
6. Unser Hund hat die ganze Nacht gebellt (*barked*).
7. Es hat fast jeden Tag geregnet.
8. Wir haben alle Museen in der Stadt besucht.
9. Die Reise hat nicht viel Spaß gemacht.

Im Stau auf der Autobahn

Starke Verben # Strong Verbs°

Strong verbs change their stem vowel in the simple past tense. Many verbs that are strong in English are also strong in German. You will find a comprehensive list of strong verbs in Appendix D.

Familie Stieber **fuhr** im Urlaub nach Österreich.	*The Stieber family drove to Austria on their vacation.*
Sie **standen** lange im Stau auf der Autobahn.	*They were in a traffic jam on the Autobahn for a long time.*
Der Urlaub **fing** nicht gut **an.**	*The vacation did not start out well.*

	fahren	**stehen**	**anfangen**	**verlieren**
ich	fuhr	stand	fing an	verlor
du	fuhr**st**	stand**est**	fing**st** an	verlo**rst**
er sie es	fuhr	stand	fing an	verlor
wir	fuhr**en**	stand**en**	fing**en** an	verlor**en**
ihr	fuhr**t**	stand**et**	fing**t** an	verlor**t**
sie/Sie	fuhr**en**	stand**en**	fing**en** an	verlor**en**

Note:
- The first- and third-person singular are identical; they have no personal endings.
- A past tense stem ending in a **-d, -t,** -or **-s** adds **-est** to the **du**-form and **-et** to the **ihr**-form.
- Like weak verbs, strong verbs with separable and inseparable prefixes have the same past tense stem as the base verb.

Irregular Weak Verbs°

Unregelmäßige schwache Verben

Several verbs change their stem vowel *and* add **-te** to the changed stem in the simple past, combining aspects of both strong and weak verbs. These verbs include:

bringen → brachte	kennen → kannte
denken → dachte	wissen → wusste

The simple past tense of **werden** (*to become*) is **wurde.**

The Conjunction als

The word **als** has several important functions in German. You have learned to use it in the comparison of adjectives.

> Mit dem Zug fährt man bequemer **als** mit dem Bus.

Additionally, **als** can be used as a subordinating conjunction meaning *when*, referring to a one-time event in the past. Sentences with the conjunction **als** are often in the simple past tense, even in conversation.

Als meine Reise nach Russland begann, war es schon Winter.	*When my trip to Russia began, it was already winter.*
Als ich am Morgen aufwachte, fand ich mich mitten im Dorf.	*When I woke up in the morning, I found myself in the middle of the village.*

ANALYSE

Sonderbares° Erlebnis einer Reise

Bizarre

Der Baron von Münchhausen lebte im 18. Jahrhundert und hatte einige merkwürdige Abenteuer. Man nannte ihn auch den „Lügenbaron" (*"lying baron"*), weil man ihm seine Geschichten nicht glaubte. Lesen Sie die folgende Geschichte und identifizieren Sie alle Verben im Imperfekt. Machen Sie eine Liste von den Verben und geben Sie den Infinitiv an. Welche Verben sind stark? Welche sind schwach?

Münchhausens Reise nach Russland

Meine Reise nach Russland begann im Winter. Ich reiste zu Pferde,° weil das am bequemsten war. Leider trug ich nur leichte Kleidung, und ich fror° sehr. Da sah ich einen alten Mann im Schnee. Ich gab ihm meinen Reisemantel und ritt weiter. Ich konnte leider kein Dorf° finden. Ich war müde und stieg vom Pferd ab.° Dann band° ich das Pferd an einen Baumast° im Schnee und legte mich hin. Ich schlief tief und lange. Als ich am anderen Morgen aufwachte, fand ich mich mitten in einem Dorf° auf dem Kirchhof.° Mein Pferd war nicht da, aber ich konnte es über mir hören. Ich schaute in die Höhe° und sah mein Pferd am Wetterhahn des Kirchturms° hängen. Ich verstand sofort, was

Note: You may want to briefly review the meaning and usage of **wann** (*when* as interrogative pronoun) and **wenn** (*if, whenever*) to reinforce the use of **als** (*when*) to refer to a one-time event in the past.

Analyse. Suggestion: Introduce this exercise by telling about the Baron von Münchhausen. In a modern film version of his adventures, Münchhausen rides on a cannonball into the enemy camp and back to his own camp without harm. In another adventure, Münchhausen and his horse are about to drown in a river when he pulls himself and his horse up and out of the water by his own long ponytail. **Suggestion:** Preview unknown strong verbs first. Then assign the exercise for homework.

horse

froze
village
stieg... *got off the horse / tied*
branch of a tree

village / churchyard (cemetery)
in... *up*
am... *on the weather-vane on top of the churchtower*

snowed under
melted
gebunden... had tied
shot / halter
damage

passiert war. Das Dorf war in der Nacht zugeschneit° gewesen. In der Sonne war der Schnee geschmolzen.° Der Baumast, an den ich mein Pferd gebunden hatte,° war in Wirklichkeit die Spitze des Kirchturms gewesen. Nun nahm ich meine Pistole und schoss° nach dem Halfter.° Mein Pferd landete ohne Schaden° neben mir. Dann reiste ich weiter.

diary

Übung 16   Aus Münchhausens Tagebuch°

Ergänzen Sie die Verben im Imperfekt.

Ich _____¹ (beginnen) meine Reise nach Russland im Winter. Ich _____² (reisen) zu Pferde, weil das am bequemsten _____.³ (sein) Leider _____⁴ (frieren) ich sehr, weil ich nur leichte Kleidung _____.⁵ (tragen) Plötzlich _____⁶ (sehen) ich einen alten Mann im Schnee. Ich _____⁷ (geben) ihm meinen Mantel und _____⁸ (reiten) weiter. Bald war ich müde und _____⁹ vom Pferd _____.¹⁰ (absteigen) Ich _____¹¹ (binden) das Pferd an einen Baumast im Schnee. Dann _____¹² ich mich _____¹³ (hinlegen) und _____.¹⁴ (einschlafen) Als ich am anderen Morgen _____¹⁵ (aufwachen), _____¹⁶ (finden) ich mich mitten in einem Dorf. Ich _____¹⁷ (wissen) zuerst nicht, wo mein Pferd war. Ich _____¹⁸ (kennen) keinen Menschen in diesem Dorf.

Übung 17.   The six changes are 1. Er reiste mit Pferd und Wagen. Richtig: Er reiste zu Pferde. 2. Er sah eine alte Frau im Schnee. Richtig: Er sah einen alten Mann. 3. Er gab der Frau etwas zu essen. Richtig: Er gab dem Mann seinen Reisemantel. 4. Er konnte kein Gasthaus finden. Richtig: Er konnte kein Dorf finden. 5. Er wachte mitten auf dem Marktplatz eines Dorfes auf. Richtig: Er wachte auf dem Kirchhof in einem Dorf auf. 6. Er sah sein Pferd von der Spitze des Rathauses hängen. Richtig: Er sah sein Pferd am Wetterhahn des Kirchturms hängen.

Übung 17   Münchhausens Reise

Sie hören die Geschichte von Münchhausens Reise nach Russland mit sechs Veränderungen (changes). Können Sie sie identifizieren?

Übung 18   Wann war das?

Sagen Sie, wie alt Sie damals waren.

BEISPIEL: den Führerschein machen →
        Ich war 17 Jahre alt, als ich den Führerschein machte.

1. in den Kindergarten kommen
2. das erste Geld verdienen (*to earn*)
3. sich zum ersten Mal verlieben (*to fall in love*)
4. den Führerschein machen
5. meine Familie nach ___ umziehen (*to move*)
6. ___ (besten Freund oder beste Freundin) kennen lernen
7. meine erste Reise ins Ausland machen
8. zum ersten Mal tanzen gehen

Übung 18. Suggestion: Start this exercise by reviewing *wann*-questions. Model one question based on the suggestions for this exercise and then ask students to formulate additional questions. E.g., to *Wann hast du den*

The Past Perfect Tense°

The past perfect tense describes an event that precedes another event in the past.

Bevor wir in Urlaub fuhren, **hatten** wir alle Rechnungen **bezahlt.**	*Before we went on vacation we **had paid** all the bills.*
Nachdem wir auf Mallorca **angekommen waren,** gingen wir sofort an den Strand.	*After we **had arrived** in Mallorca, we immediately went to the beach.*

The conjunctions **bevor** and **nachdem** are commonly used to connect sentences with the simple past and past perfect tenses.

To form the past perfect, combine the simple past of **haben** (*hatte*) or **sein** (*war*) and the past participle of the main verb. Verbs using **sein** in the present perfect tense also use **sein** in the past perfect.

PRESENT PERFECT	PAST PERFECT
Ich **bin** gegangen.	Ich **war** gegangen. (*I had gone.*)
Wir **haben** bezahlt.	Wir **hatten** bezahlt. (*We had paid.*)

Führerschein gemacht?, the answer could be *Mit 16 Jahren* or simply the year, e.g., *1986*. In a second phase, introduce the conjunction *als*, asking for answers in the form shown in the **Beispiel.** Have students add one item when something special happened in their lives, e.g., *Ich war acht Jahre alt, als ich meinen Hund zum Geburtstag bekam.*

Übung 19   Die Fahrt hatte kaum begonnen

Ergänzen Sie die Sätze durch Verben im Plusquamperfekt.

1. Ich ____ schon früh aus dem Haus ____ (gehen), denn mein Flugzeug nach Frankfurt flog um 8 Uhr ab.
2. Ich ____ am Tag zuvor ein Taxi ____ (bestellen).
3. Am Flughafen fiel mir ein (*I remembered*), dass ich die Schlüssel in der Haustür ____ ____ (vergessen).
4. Kein Wunder, denn letzte Nacht ____ ich kaum ____ (schlafen).
5. Sobald ich am Flughafen ____ ____ (ankommen), rief ich eine Nachbarin (*neighbor*) an.
6. Der Flug nach Frankfurt war verspätet (*late*). Nachdem wir drei Stunden ____ ____ (warten), konnten wir endlich abfliegen.

Sprache im Kontext

Videoclips

A. Thomas Möllmann arbeitet im Reisebüro. Schauen Sie sich das Interview mit ihm an und ergänzen Sie die folgenden Informationen.

1. Ein Reiseziel, das im Moment „in" ist, ist _____.
2. Andere beliebte Reiseziele der Kunden sind _____ und die_____ _____.
3. Wie kommen die Kunden an den Urlaubsort? Die meisten Kunden _____.

    4. Herr Möllmann hat dieses Jahr eine _____ an die _____ gemacht. Er ist mit der _____ gefahren.

    5. Herr Möllmann hat vor, in ungefähr sechs Wochen nach _____ zu reisen.

    6. Herr Möllmann arbeitet seit ungefähr _____ Jahren im Reisebüro.

B. Was sind beliebte Reiseziele in Ihrem Land?

C. Alex spricht über seine Urlaubspläne und über seinen Urlaub letztes Jahr. Schauen Sie sich das Interview an und machen Sie sich Notizen in der Tabelle. Benutzen Sie dann Ihre Notizen, um wenigstens 3–4 Sätze über den Urlaub von Alex zu schreiben.

Urlaub dieses Jahr:	
Wohin? Wie lange?	
Wie kommt er dahin?	
Wo hat er gebucht?	
Urlaub letztes Jahr:	
Wo? Wie lange? Mit wem?	
Was hat er mitgenommen?	
Was hat er erlebt?	

D. Fragen Sie drei Personen in der Klasse wohin sie dieses Jahr in Urlaub fahren und wo sie letztes Jahr waren. Berichten Sie der Klasse darüber.

Lesen

Zum Thema

A. Ihr letzter Urlaub. Beantworten Sie die folgenden Fragen und vergleichen Sie Ihre Antworten untereinander.

    1. Wann haben Sie zum letzten Mal Urlaub gemacht?

    2. Wohin sind Sie gefahren? Sind Sie allein oder mit Freunden gefahren?

    3. Was haben Sie dort gemacht?

    4. Wie war das Wetter dort?

    5. Wie lange waren Sie dort?

    6. Was hat Ihnen dort (nicht) gefallen?

B. Ein Aktivurlaub. Die Werbung „Sportreisen" auf der nächsten Seite zeigt viele Möglichkeiten für einen Aktivurlaub. Schauen Sie sich die Tabelle mit einem Partner / einer Partnerin an.

    ■ Welche Sportarten gibt es?

    ■ Wo finden diese Aktivitäten statt *(take place)*?

    ■ Was macht man alles da?

    ■ Für welche Sportart muss man am fittesten sein?

    ■ Welche Reise möchten Sie machen? Warum?

SPORTREISEN ...

Sportart	Ort	Leistungen	Reisetermin	Preis	Grad*
Rafting	Colorado/ USA	zwei Übernachtungen im Hotel, Transfer, Raftingtour, Bootsführer, alle Mahlzeiten während der Tour, Camping-ausrüstung, Anreise in Eigenregie[1]	1., 8., 15. und 22.9.	ab 800 € für 7 Tage	●●
Katamaran-segeln	Levkada/ Griechenland	Flug, Übernachtungen im Appartement, kostenlose Benutzung der Katamarane und Segelflotte,[2] Teilnahme am Unterricht[3]	1., 8., 15., 22. und 29.9.	ab 715 € pro Woche	●●●
Tauchen	Villi Varu/ Malediven	Flug ab Düsseldorf, sechs Übernachtungen mit Vollpension, Sechs-Tage-Tauchpaket à 1 Tauchgang[4] täglich und 2 Haus-riff-Tauchgänge (inkl. Boot, Flasche, Blei und Bleigurt)[5]	3., 10., 17. und 24.9.	115 € pro Woche	●
Aktiv-Camp	Berchtes-gaden/ Deutschland	Schnupperkurs[6] im Klettergarten,[7] River-Rafting auf der Saalach, Mountainbike-Tour, Bergwanderung, Paragliding-Schnupper-kurs, sechs Übernachtungen mit Frühstück, Ausrüstung,[8] Führung[9]	6.–12.9.	300 €	●
Surfen	Bonaire/ Karibik	Flug ab Amsterdam, Übernachtung im Appartement mit Selbstversorgung[10] oder im Hotel mit Frühstück, Surfboard-Miete 115 Euro pro Woche	6., 13., 20. und 27.9.	ab 1100 € pro Woche	●●
Reiten	Costa Blanca/ Spanien	Flug, acht Tage mit sieben Übernachtungen im Appartement mit Selbstversorgung, Reitprogramm, Reitführung, Unterlagen, Qualifikation: sicher in den Grundgangarten,[11] gute Kondition	9.–16.9.	ab 1050 €	●●

* Zeigt den Grad der körperlichen[12] Fitneß, die der Teilnehmer[13] mitbringen muß: ●●● = sehr gut trainiert, ●● = körperlich fit, ● = auch für Anfänger[14]

[1]Anreise... *passage excluded* [2]*sailing fleet* [3]Teilnahme... *participation in instruction* [4]*dive*
[5]Blei... *weight and weight belt* [6]*sampler class* [7]*climbing garden* [8]*equipment* [9]*guide* [10]*no meals provided* [11]sicher... *secure in all the basic paces* [12]*physical* [13]*participant* [14]*beginners*

Auf den ersten Blick

A. Schauen Sie sich den Text auf Seite 316 an. Was für ein Text ist das?

1. ein Interview
2. ein Artikel
3. ein Tagebuch (*diary*)

B. Überfliegen Sie (*skim*) den Text. Wie heißt das Thema dieses Textes?

1. Julias Reise nach Deutschland
2. Tourismus in China
3. Julias Reise nach China

C. Suchen Sie die Information im ersten Abschnitt.

1. Name und Alter der „Globetrotterin des Jahres 1996"
2. Mit wem sie reiste
3. Was ihr wichtig war

Auf den ersten Blick. Note: If you do this in class, students can do the **Zum Text** as homework.

■ Julia Berg, 21, wurde im März von Deutschlands größtem Outdoor-Händler, Globetrotter Ausrüstungen in Hamburg, zur „Globetrotterin des Jahres 1996" gekürt. Zusammen mit ihrem Freund Dov Meguideche reiste sie 1995 auf dem Landweg nach China und wieder zurück nach Deutschland. Nicht die touristischen Höhepunkte, sondern die Auseinandersetzung[1] mit den Menschen bestimmten[2] ihre Reiseroute: Julia lebte in einer mongolischen Familie, beschäftigte sich[3] in China mit Tuschmalerei[4] und lernte in Thailand sowohl das Lederhandwerk als auch die Silberschmiedekunst.[5] ■

★ *Wie ist die Idee zu dieser Reise entstanden?*

1992 war ich mit einem Schüleraustausch[6] in China und zwei Jahre später habe ich an der Uni in Beijing einen Sprachkurs belegt. Damals entstand[7] der Wunsch, auf dem Landweg nach China zu reisen. Beim zweiten Aufenthalt[8] habe ich meinen australischen Freund Dov kennengelernt und wir beschlossen,[9] nach meinem Abitur gemeinsam auf Tour zu gehen.

★ *Was fasziniert Dich so an diesem Land?*

Mit 16 war ich das erste Mal in China. Der Besuch in einem nicht-westlichen Land mit seiner fremden Kultur hat mich sehr beeindruckt.[10] Ich wollte noch mehr darüber erfahren[11] und die Kultur verstehen lernen. Deshalb habe ich mich auch mit Tuschmalerei und der chinesischen Philosophie beschäftigt. Ich habe die Erfahrung gemacht,[12] dass man gerade über die Kunst viele Menschen kennenlernt und einen Einblick[13] in deren Leben erhält.

★ *Waren Deine Erlebnisse in China durchweg[14] positiv?*

Nein, es ist schwierig dort zu reisen. Vor allem die Beamten sind oft sehr unfreundlich. Aber man trifft natürlich auch viele gastfreundliche Menschen und diese Erfahrungen sind es, die mich immer wieder anziehen.

★ *Hat Dich diese Reise verändert?[15]*

Ja. Durch Situationen, in denen ich an einem Tiefpunkt[16] war und sich dann doch alles zum Guten gewendet hat,[17] habe ich mehr Zuversicht[18] bekommen. Wo ich mir früher Sorgen gemacht habe,[19] denke ich jetzt: Das wird schon irgendwie. Ich glaube aber, dass man sich hier engagieren muss. Reiseerfahrungen sollten nicht einfach „weggepackt" werden, wenn man wieder zu Hause ist.

★ *Würdest Du so eine Reise auch alleine machen?*

Es gab viele Momente, in denen ich nicht hätte[20] alleine sein wollen. Zum Beispiel wenn wir völlig verlassen „in the middle of nowhere" festsaßen.[21] Auf der anderen Seite bekommt man alleine mehr Kontakte und ist anderen Menschen gegenüber offener.

★ *Welchen Tipp möchtest Du anderen Globetrottern mit auf den Weg geben?*

Auf jeden Fall sollte man ein bisschen von der Sprache des jeweiligen Landes lernen. Das freut die Leute unheimlich[22] und sie merken, dass man Kontakt sucht. Selbst wenn man zu keiner tiefergehenden Unterhaltung fähig ist,[23] es ist eine Geste.

★ *Welche Pläne hast Du für die Zukunft?[24]*

Ich habe mit einem Ethnologiestudium begonnen und möchte am liebsten Korrespondentin im Ausland oder Reiseautorin werden. Außerdem zeichne ich momentan an meinem Kinderbuch über einen kleinen mongolischen Jungen, in dessen Familie wir eine Zeitlang gelebt haben.

Julia, vielen Dank für das Interview.

---

[1]*contact* [2]*determined* [3]*beschäftigte... occupied herself* [4]*watercolor painting* [5]*silversmithing* [6]*student exchange* [7]*arose* [8]*zweiten... second trip* [9]*decided* [10]*impressed* [11]*learn* [12]*Ich... it's been my experience* [13]*insight* [14]*always* [15]*changed* [16]*low point* [17]*turned* [18]*confidence* [19]*Sorgen... worried* [20]*would have* [21]*were stuck* [22]*tremendously* [23]*zu... is not capable of deep discussions* [24]*future*

Zum Text

A. Die folgenden Aussagen *(statements)* werden im Interview mit Julia *implizit* ausgedrückt. Finden Sie die entsprechende Information dazu *(corresponding)* im Text.

   1. Die letzte Reise nach China war Julias dritte Reise nach China.
   2. Julia ist diesmal weder *(neither)* mit dem Schiff noch *(nor)* mit dem Flugzeug nach China gereist.
   3. Julia kann wenigstens ein bisschen Chinesisch sprechen.
   4. Julia glaubt, dass man ein Land besser verstehen kann, wenn man etwas über die Kunst des Landes weiß.
   5. Vieles an der chinesischen Kultur interessiert Julia.
   6. Julia sieht Reisen als Transformation und nicht als Urlaub vom Alltag *(everyday life)*.

B. Intensiveres Lesen. Kleine Wörter und Phrasen sind oft wichtige rhetorische Signale, die die Zusammenhänge *(relationships)* zwischen Ideen und Elementen klar machen.

   - **Nicht... sondern** *(not . . . but)* zeigt einen Gegensatz *(contrast)* auf.
   - **Sowohl... als auch...** *(. . . as well as . . .)* deutet auf Inklusivität.
   - **Auf der anderen Seite** *(on the other hand)* findet man da, wo Alternativen berücksichtigt *(considered)* werden.
   - **Außerdem** *(besides, moreover)* deutet auf zusätzliche *(added)* Informationen.

   Finden Sie diese Wörter im Text. Welche Zusammenhänge zeigen diese Wörter im Interview, das Sie gelesen haben?

C. Arbeit mit dem Wörterbuch. Suchen Sie die folgenden Wörter im Text. Schlagen Sie diese in einem Wörterbuch nach. Wie viele Bedeutungen finden Sie für jedes Wort? Welche passt am besten?

küren	engagieren
anziehen	verlassen

Sprechen und Schreiben

Aktivität 1   Ein besonderes Interview

Stellen Sie sich vor, Sie arbeiten als Journalist/Journalistin und haben die Gelegenheit *(opportunity)*, Julia zu interviewen. Was möchten Sie gern fragen? Notieren Sie drei mögliche Fragen. Jemand spielt die Rolle der Julia. Die anderen interviewen sie.

Aktivität 2   Eine Werbung°

Stellen Sie sich vor, Sie arbeiten bei einer Werbeagentur und haben die Aufgabe, einen Prospekt über Ihre Heimatstadt oder eine andere Gegend *(area)* zusammenzustellen. Arbeiten Sie zuerst in Gruppen, um Ideen zu sammeln. Was finden Sie interessant an Ihrer Stadt/Gegend? Was kann man dort unternehmen? Schreiben Sie dann einen Werbetext für Ihre Stadt/Gegend.

Sprechen und Schreiben. Additional Activity: Have students bring in a photograph of a trip they took. Divide students into small groups and have them briefly tell about their trip. They can also play Baron von Münchhausen, bringing in any picture and telling a tall tale of a trip they took.

advertisement

Wortschatz

Beginning with this chapter, the vocabulary section at the end of each chapter will list strong or irregular verbs with their principal parts as follows: **bringen, brachte, gebracht** or **fahren (fährt), fuhr, ist gefahren.**

Verkehrsmittel / Means of Transportation

die **Bahn, -en**	railway; train
der **Bus,** *pl.* **Busse**	bus
das **Fahrrad, ̈er**	bicycle
das **Flugzeug, -e**	airplane
das **Schiff, -e**	ship
das **Taxi, -s**	taxicab
der **Wagen, -**	car
der **Zug, ̈e**	train

Im Reisebüro / At the Travel Agency

das **Angebot, -e**	(special) offer; selection
die **Fahrkarte, -n**	ticket
die **Reise, -n**	trip
das **Reisebüro, -s**	travel agency
der **Reiseprospekt, -e**	travel brochure

Unterwegs / En Route

die **Abfahrt, -en**	departure
die **Ankunft, ̈e**	arrival
der **Anschluss, ̈e**	connection
die **Auskunft, ̈e**	information
der **Bahnhof, ̈e**	train station
der **Bahnsteig, -e**	(train) platform
der **Fahrkarten-schalter, -**	ticket window
der **Fahrplan, ̈e**	schedule
die **Fahrt, -en**	trip; ride
die **Gepäckaufbe-wahrung**	baggage check
das **Gleis, -e**	track
die **Möglichkeit, -en**	possibility, opportunity
die **Natur**	nature
der **Nichtraucher, -**	no-smoking car
die **Platzkarte, -n**	seat reservation card
der **Reiseführer, -**	travel guide (book)

Zum Mitnehmen auf Reisen / Things to Take Along on a Trip

das **Bargeld**	cash
das **Handgepäck**	carry-on luggage
der **Handschuh, -e**	glove
die **Kamera, -s**	camera
der **Personalausweis, -e**	ID card
der **Reisescheck, -s**	traveler's check
das **Sonnenschutzmittel**	suntan lotion, sunscreen
das **Zelt, -e**	tent

Verben / Verbs

ab•fahren (fährt ab), fuhr ab, ist abgefahren	to depart, leave
beginnen, begann, begonnen	to begin, start
Bescheid sagen	to notify; to say definitely
buchen	to book (a trip)
ein•steigen, stieg ein, ist eingestiegen	to board, get into (*a vehicle*)
erleben	to experience
hoffen (auf)	to hope (for)
um•steigen, stieg um, ist umgestiegen	to transfer, change (trains)
unternehmen (unter-nimmt), unternahm, unternommen	to undertake
vergessen (vergisst), vergaß, vergessen	to forget
verreisen, ist verreist	to go on a trip
vor•schlagen (schlägt vor), schlug vor, vorgeschlagen	to suggest, propose

Adjektive und Adverbien	**Adjectives and Adverbs**	**einfach**	one-way (ticket); simple
aktiv	active(ly)	**einverstanden sein (mit)**	to agree (with), be in agreement (with)
gefährlich	dangerous(ly)		
günstig (gut)	advantageous (ly); good; favorable, favorably	**erster/zweiter Klasse fahren**	to travel first/second class
		hin und zurück	round-trip
insgesamt	altogether, total	**nachdem** (*subord. conj.*)	after
jung	young	**per Autostop reisen**	to hitchhike
kurz	short	**pro Person**	per person
lang	long	**so... wie**	as . . . as
langsam	slow(ly)	**Sonst noch etwas?**	Anything else?
schnell	quick(ly), fast	**sportlich aktiv**	active in sports
sicher	safe(ly)		
Sonstiges	**Other**		
alles	everything		
als (*subord. conj.*)	when		
bevor (*subord. conj.*)	before		

LERNZIELE

Use this checklist to verify that you can now . . .

☐ talk about travel plans to express your preferences.

☐ book a vacation through a travel agency.

☐ buy a ticket at a German railway station.

☐ ask for information regarding public transportation.

☐ talk about the kinds of things one needs when traveling.

☐ use the comparative and superlative forms of adjectives and adverbs when comparing ideas, things, and people.

☐ narrate events using the simple past tense and the past perfect tense.

☐ express a more complex series of events by using the conjunctions **als, bevor,** and **nachdem.**

Der Start in die Zukunft

Warum geht man zum Arbeitsamt?
a. Man sucht eine neue Stelle.
b. Dort kann mann sich über Reisen informieren.

Kapitel 11. Suggestion: Introduce the chapter by asking students questions about their career plans, e.g., *Was möchten Sie werden? Warum haben Sie diesen Beruf gewählt? Welche Ausbildung braucht man für diesen Beruf? Was möchten Sie auf keinen Fall werden? Was für Stellen haben Sie schon gehabt?* Write new words for professions and occupations on the board.

Videoclips
Mein Beruf—mein Leben

In diesem Kapitel

- **Themen:** World of work, professions
- **Grammatik:** Future tense, relative clauses, **was für (ein),** negating sentences with **nicht** and **kein**
- **Kultur:** Help-wanted ads, applying for a job, the German school system

Alles klar?

A. Was wollen junge Deutsche vom Beruf? Die Informationen finden Sie im Schaubild.

Realia. You may wish to point out the older spelling *daß* for *dass.*

Das wollen junge Leute vom Beruf
Von je 100 Jugendlichen sagten über ihre Berufswahl:[1]
Das wichtigste bei meinem künftigen Beruf ist...

35 ...daß ich aufsteigen[2] kann
32 ...daß ich Menschen helfen kann
46 ...Sicherheit des Arbeitsplatzes
26 ...mit interessanten Menschen zu tun haben
57 ...daß ich einen Ausbildungsplatz[3] bekomme
25 ...keine Schmutzarbeit[4]
75 ...Eignung[5]
17 Hobbys verwirklichen
16 ...guter Verdienst
90 ...Spaß am Beruf
14 ...Ansehen[6]

© Globus 5660

[1]*choice of occupation*
[2]*advance*
[3]*training position*
[4]*dirty work*
[5]*qualification*
[6]*prestige*

- Das Wichtigste an einem künftigen Beruf ist ____.
- ____ finden junge Deutsche nicht so wichtig.
- Ungefähr ein Drittel der jungen Leute will ____.
- Ein Viertel der Jugendlichen will keine ____ machen.
- Ein sicherer Arbeitsplatz ist wichtig für ____ der Jugendlichen.

B. Sie hören Gabriele Sommer über ihre Berufspläne sprechen.

- Wie ist sie auf ihre Berufswahl gekommen?
- Wo studiert sie?
- Was studiert sie?
- Was hat sie in ihrem späteren Berufsleben vor?

Wörter im Kontext

wishes

expectations

Ich möchte gern. Follow-up: Which seem to be the most frequently named expectations in the class?

Neue Wörter

stellen sich vor (sich vorstellen) imagine
Berufsleben professional life
selbständig independent(ly)
Arbeitsplatz position, workplace
mich... beschäftigen (sich beschäftigen) to occupy oneself
im Freien outdoors
Gelegenheit opportunity
im Ausland abroad
verdienen to earn
abwechslungsreich varied
Tätigkeit position; activity
Firma firm, company
Chef/Chefin manager, boss
Mitarbeiter/ Mitarbeiterin co-worker, colleague
Technik technology
Ansehen prestige
Büro office
verantwortliche responsible
herausfordern to challenge

THEMA 1: Meine Interessen, Wünsche° und Erwartungen°

Wie **stellen** Sie **sich** Ihr **Berufsleben vor?** Was erwarten Sie vom Beruf? Kreuzen Sie an.

Ich möchte gern:	WICHTIG	UNWICHTIG
▪ **selbständig** arbeiten	☐	☐
▪ einen sicheren **Arbeitsplatz** haben	☐	☐
▪ **mich im Freien beschäftigen**	☐	☐
▪ **Gelegenheit** zum Reisen haben	☐	☐
▪ **im Ausland** arbeiten	☐	☐
▪ gut **verdienen**	☐	☐
▪ eine **abwechslungsreiche Tätigkeit** haben	☐	☐
▪ bei einer großen **Firma** arbeiten	☐	☐
▪ einen **Chef** / eine **Chefin** haben, der/die meine Arbeit anerkennt (*appreciates*)	☐	☐
▪ sympathische **Mitarbeiter/Mitarbeiterinnen** haben	☐	☐
▪ Menschen helfen	☐	☐
▪ mit Computern/neuer **Technik** arbeiten	☐	☐
▪ mit Tieren zu tun haben	☐	☐
▪ Prestige/**Ansehen** haben	☐	☐
▪ im **Büro** arbeiten	☐	☐
▪ eine **verantwortliche** Position haben	☐	☐
▪ einen Beruf haben, der mich **herausfordert**	☐	☐
▪ keine Schmutzarbeit machen	☐	☐

Vergleichen Sie Ihre Antworten untereinander. Suchen Sie jemand im Kurs, mit dem Sie mehr als fünf Antworten gemeinsam haben.

Note: Mention to students that seeing a chimney sweep is considered to bring good luck!

Ein Schornsteinfeger arbeitet meistens im Freien.

Aktivität 1 Drei junge Leute

Sie hören drei junge Leute über ihre Interessen, Wünsche und Erwartungen sprechen. Was tun sie gern oder nicht gern? Was ist ihnen wichtig oder nicht wichtig?

PERSON	WAS ER/SIE (NICHT) GERN TUT	WAS IHM/IHR (NICHT) WICHTIG IST
Tina	arbeitet gern im Freien, möchte nicht gern im Büro arbeiten	nicht wichtig: großes Ansehen und viel Geld
Markus	reist gern und möchte im Ausland arbeiten	wichtig: mit Menschen zu tun haben
Andrea	arbeitet gern mit ihren Händen; interessiert sich für Maschinen, Computer	keine Information

Erste Adresse für Ihren Karrierestart

Kreativ? Flexibel? Verantwortlich?

Wir fordern Sie heraus! ✔WestLB

Aktivität 2 Hin und her: Wer macht was, und warum?

Ergänzen Sie die Informationen.

BEISPIEL: s1: Was macht Corinna Eichhorn?
s2: Sie ist Sozialarbeiterin.
s1: Warum macht sie das?
s2: Weil...

NAME	BERUF	WARUM?
Corinna Eichhorn	Sozialarbeiterin	Menschen helfen
Karsten Becker	Bibliothekar	sich für Bücher interessieren
Erika Lentz	Filmschauspielerin	mit Menschen zu tun haben
Alex Böhmer	Informatiker	mit Computern arbeiten

Aktivität 3 Berufswünsche

Fragen Sie einen Partner / eine Partnerin: „Was erwartest du von deinem Beruf? Was ist dir nicht so wichtig?" Verwenden Sie einige der folgenden Redemittel.

BEISPIEL: s1: Mir ist ein sicherer Arbeitsplatz wichtig.
s2: Ein sicherer Arbeitsplatz ist mir nicht so wichtig, aber ich erwarte, dass ich Gelegenheit zum Reisen habe.

REDEMITTEL	ERWARTUNGEN
Mir ist _____ (nicht) wichtig.	möglichst viel Geld (verdienen)
Ich erwarte, dass _____.	viel Kontakt mit Menschen (haben)
Ich möchte gern _____.	Menschen helfen
An erster Stelle kommt _____.	Spaß an der Arbeit (haben)
_____ interessiert mich (nicht).	nette Mitarbeiter/Mitarbeiterinnen (haben)
	Gelegenheit zum Reisen (haben)
	selbständig arbeiten
	im Freien arbeiten
	im Ausland arbeiten
	Ansehen (haben)
	einen sicheren Arbeitsplatz (haben)
	kreativ arbeiten
	flexible Arbeitszeit (haben)

THEMA 2: Berufe

BERUFE

Gesundheitswesen
Arzt/Ärztin
Krankenpfleger/Krankenschwester
Psychologe/Psychologin
Sozialarbeiter/Sozialarbeiterin
Tierarzt/Tierärztin
Zahnarzt/Zahnärztin

Verwaltung
Rechtsanwalt/Rechtsanwältin
Diplomat/Diplomatin
Finanzbeamter/Finanzbeamtin
Personalchef/Personalchefin

Technischer Bereich
Elektroinstallateur/Elektroinstallateurin
Ingenieur/Ingenieurin
Mechaniker/Mechanikerin
Radio- oder Fernsehtechniker/
  Radio- oder Fernsehtechnikerin

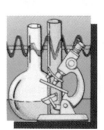

Naturwissenschaften
Biotechnologe/Biotechnologin
Chemiker/Chemikerin
Laborant/Laborantin
Meteorologe/Meteorologin
Physiker/Physikerin

Wirtschaft und Handel
Geschäftsmann/Geschäftsfrau
Informatiker/Informatikerin
Kaufmann/Kauffrau
Sekretär/Sekretärin

Verkehrswesen
Flugbegleiter/Flugbegleiterin
Flugingenieur/Flugingenieurin
Pilot/Pilotin
Reisebüroleiter/Reisebüroleiterin

Kommunikationswesen
Bibliothekar/Bibliothekarin
Dolmetscher/Dolmetscherin
Journalist/Journalistin
Nachrichtensprecher/Nachrichtensprecherin

Kreativer Bereich
Architekt/Architektin
Designer/Designerin
Fotograf/Fotografin
Künstler/Künstlerin
Musiker/Musikerin
Schauspieler/Schauspielerin
Zeichner/Zeichnerin

Aktivität 4. Suggestion: Have students work as quickly as possible in pairs or threes. Give a prize to the first group that finishes with the correct answers.

Aktivität 4   Wer macht was?

Welcher Beruf passt zu welcher Beschreibung?

BEISPIEL: Eine Architektin entwirft Häuser.

Wer...

1. __c__ spielt im Film oder auf der Bühne (*stage*)?
2. __f__ spielt in einem Orchester?
3. __a__ untersucht Patienten?
4. __g__ entwirft (*designs*) Gebäude, Häuser und Wohnungen?
5. __h__ verkauft Produkte einer Firma?
6. __b__ hat mit Computern zu tun?
7. __j__ malt Bilder?
8. __d__ arbeitet in einer Bibliothek?
9. __i__ macht Übersetzungen (*translations*)?
10. __e__ repariert Autos?

a. Arzt/Ärztin
b. Informatiker/Informatikerin
c. Schauspieler/Schauspielerin
d. Bibliothekar/Bibliothekarin
e. Automechaniker/Automechanikerin
f. Musiker/Musikerin
g. Architekt/Architektin
h. Kaufmann/Kauffrau
i. Dolmetscher/Dolmetscherin
j. Künstler/Künstlerin

Neue Wörter

Zahnarzt/Zahnärztin dentist
Rechtsanwalt/Rechtsanwältin lawyer, attorney
Geschäftsmann/Geschäftsfrau businessman/businesswoman
Informatiker/Informatikerin computer scientist
Kaufmann/Kauffrau salesman/saleswoman
Bibliothekar/Bibliothekarin librarian
Dolmetscher/Dolmetscherin interpreter
Künstler/Künstlerin artist
Schauspieler/Schauspielerin actor
Zeichner/Zeichnerin graphic artist

Aktivität 5 Was meinen Sie?

Suchen Sie Ihre Antworten auf die folgenden Fragen in der Liste von Berufen im **Thema 2.**

1. Wer hat die gefährlichste Arbeit?
2. Welcher Beruf hat das meiste Prestige?
3. Wer hat mit Tieren zu tun?
4. Wer arbeitet meistens in einem Büro?
5. Wer verdient das meiste Geld?
6. Für welche Berufe muss man studieren?
7. Welche Arbeit bringt den meisten Stress mit sich?
8. Wer hat die längsten Arbeitsstunden?
9. Wer hat die langweiligste Arbeit?

Aktivität 6 Hin und her: Berühmte° Personen

°famous

Aktivität 6. Bertha von Suttner schrieb *Die Waffen nieder.* 1891 gründete sie die Österreichische Gesellschaft der Friedensfreunde und war Vizepräsidentin des Internationalen Friedenbüreaus in Berlin. Sie hat Alfred Nobel die Idee für einen Friedens-nobelpreis vorgeschlagen. Daraufhin schuf er den Friedensnobelpreis. 1905 erhielt von Suttner selbst den Friedensnobelpreis.

Diese berühmten Menschen, die alle einen Beruf ausübten, hatten auch andere Interessen. Ergänzen Sie die Informationen.

BEISPIEL: S1: Was war Martin Luther von Beruf?
S2: Er war Priester.
S1: Was für andere Interessen hatte er?
S2: Er interessierte sich für Literatur, Musik und die deutsche Sprache.

NAME	BERUF	INTERESSEN
Martin Luther	Priester	Literatur, Musik, die deutsche Sprache
Bertha von Suttner	Schriftstellerin	die europäische Friedensbewegung
Marlene Dietrich	Schauspielerin	Ski fahren
Käthe Kollwitz	Künstlerin	Politik
Rainer Werner Fassbinder	Filmregisseur	Literatur, Theater
Willi Brandt	Politiker	Ski fahren, Lesen

Aktivität 7 Welcher Beruf ist der richtige?

Aktivität 7. Suggestion: Follow up with a class discussion to see if everyone agrees with the advice that was given. If not, what would others advise?

Machen Sie eine Liste von den Kriterien, die Ihnen im Beruf wichtig sind. Benutzen Sie die Vokabeln im **Thema 1.** Fragen Sie dann jemanden im Kurs, was für einen Beruf er/sie Ihnen empfehlen würde.

BEISPIEL: S1: Ich möchte eine abwechslungsreiche Tätigkeit haben, vielleicht im Büro arbeiten und viel Kontakt mit Menschen haben. Was empfiehlst du mir?
S2: Ich empfehle dir, Kaufmann/Kauffrau zu werden.

Thema 3: Stellenangebote und Bewerbungen

Ein Stellenangebot

Plus

Sie kennen uns als Lebensmittel-Discounter mit den kleinen Preisen. Mit über 2.700 Filialen und mehr als 24.000 Mitarbeitern sind wir auf Expansionskurs.

Wir sind Ihr Karriereplus!
Für unseren Managementnachwuchs[1] suchen wir engagierte

FACH-/HOCHSCHUL-ABSOLVENTEN/INNEN

Nach einer 6-monatigen intensiven Ausbildung übernehmen Sie einen Bezirk von 8 - 10 Filialen.

Ihr Plus:
- Sie haben Ihr Studium nach kurzer Zeit erfolgreich abgeschlossen
- Sie wollen nun auch in der Praxis möglichst schnell Verantwortung übernehmen
- Sie halten Kundenorientierung für ebenso wichtig wie wir
- Sie haben idealerweise bereits erste Erfahrungen im Handel gesammelt
- Sie bringen analytisches Denken und Entscheidungsfähigkeit[2] mit
- Sie sind mobil, flexibel und belastbar

Unser Plus:
- Zukunftssicherer Arbeitsplatz in einem erfolgreichen Großunternehmen
- Motiviertes junges Team
- Gute Karrierechancen für überdurchschnittlich engagierte Mitarbeiter
- Leistungsgerechtes[3] Gehalt und neutraler Firmenwagen

Wir freuen uns auf Ihre Bewerbung.
Bitte senden Sie Ihre aussagekräftigen[4] Unterlagen an:

Plus Warenhandelsgesellschaft mbH
Personalmanagement Dienstleistungszentrale
Herrn Günter Lippert
Wissollstr. 5-43
45478 Mülheim an der Ruhr
e-mail: glippert@plus.de

forum absolventen kongress
Köln, 12./13.06.2002
Besuchen Sie uns!
www.absolventenkongress.de

[1]*management trainees* [2]*ability to make decisions* [3]*performance-based*
[4]*pertinent*

- Was verkauft die Firma Plus?
- Was für Angestellte sucht die Firma? Nennen Sie einige Qualifikationen, die der Firma wichtig sind.
- Was bietet (*offers*) die Firma ihrem neuen Managementnachwuchs?

Stellenangebote help-wanted ads
Absolventen/innen graduates (higher education)
Ausbildung training
übernehmen take over
Bezirk area, district
Filialen branches (of a business)
erfolgreich successfully
Erfahrungen experiences
Handel trade, sales
Gehalt salary
Bewerbung application
Unterlagen documentation, papers

Neue Wörter

bewirbt sich (sich bewerben um) applies for
Stelle position, job
Lebenslauf résumé
Bewerbungsformular application form
Abitur exam at the end of Gymnasium
Abiturzeugnis report card
Abschluss completion, degree
Zeugnisse report cards, recommendations
Arbeitgeber employer
sich vorbereiten auf prepare for
Vorstellungsgespräch job interview
Arbeitsamt employment office
Berufsberater employment counselor

Hier klicken!

Weiteres zum Thema Stellenanzeigen finden Sie bei **Deutsch: Na klar!** im World-Wide-Web unter www.mhhe.com/dnk.

■ Was würde Sie bei dieser Firma interessieren?

> intensive Ausbildung
>
> sicherer Arbeitsplatz
>
> motiviertes junges Team
>
> gute Karrierechancen
>
> gutes Gehalt
>
> Firmenwagen

Wie **bewirbt** man **sich um** eine **Stelle**? Bringen Sie folgende Schritte in eine logische Reihenfolge.

_____ einen tabellarischen **Lebenslauf** schreiben

_____ ein **Bewerbungsformular** ausfüllen

__1__ Interessen, Wünsche und Erwartungen mit Familie und Freunden besprechen

_____ Unterlagen (**Abiturzeugnis** oder anderen **Abschluss** und **Zeugnisse** von früheren **Arbeitgebern**) sammeln

_____ **sich auf** das **Vorstellungsgespräch vorbereiten**

_____ die Stellenangebote in der Zeitung durchlesen

_____ Informationen über verschiedene Karrieren und Berufe sammeln

_____ zum **Arbeitsamt** an der Uni gehen und mit **Berufsberatern** sprechen

Suggestion: Introduce a fictional character and describe the steps he/she went through to apply for a job.

Aktivität 8   Ein Stellenangebot

Lesen Sie das Stellenangebot von der Firma Plus auf Seite 327 und wählen Sie passende Wörter aus der Liste, um die Sätze zu ergänzen.

> analytisches Denken
>
> Ausbildung
>
> Bewerbung
>
> Erfahrungen im Handel
>
> Fach-/Hochschulabsolventen/innen
>
> Gehalt
>
> Unterlagen
>
> verantwortlich

1. Die Firma Plus sucht _____ für ihren Managementnachwuchs.
2. Eine wichtige Qualifikation ist _____.
3. Bewerber sollten schon einige _____ gesammelt haben.
4. Die Firma bietet eine sechsmonatige _____ zum Manager.
5. Wer sich für die Firma interessiert, sollte seine _____ mit aussagekräftigen _____ an das Personalmanagement der Firma senden.

Aktivität 9   Ein Gespräch unter Freunden

Was stimmt? Was stimmt nicht? Korrigieren Sie die falschen Aussagen.

	DAS STIMMT	DAS STIMMT NICHT
1. Petra sucht einen Ausbildungsplatz.	☒	☐
2. Petra ist noch nicht zum Arbeitsamt gegangen.	☐	☒
3. Petra hat ein interessantes Stellen- angebot in der Zeitung gefunden.	☒	☐
4. Petra hat sich um eine Ausbildungs- stelle beworben.	☒	☐
5. Petra hat die Firma sofort angerufen.	☐	☒
6. Petra ist sehr enthusiastisch, weil sie die Firma gut kennt.	☐	☒
7. Die Firma verlangt, dass Bewerber Biologie studiert haben.	☐	☒

Aktivität 10   Ein Gespräch über eine Stellensuche

Führen Sie mit einem Partner / einer Partnerin ein Gespräch über eine Stel- lensuche. Sie können die Anzeigen in diesem Kapitel oder Anzeigen aus einer Zeitung zur Information benutzen.

S1	S2

1. Was wirst du ＿＿ machen?
  ■ nach dem Studium
  ■ in den Semesterferien
  ■ ??
	2. Ich werde eine Stelle ＿＿ suchen.
	  ■ in einem Büro
	  ■ bei einer Firma
	  ■ in einer Fabrik
	  ■ ??

3. Wie findet man ＿＿?	**4.** Man muss mindestens ＿＿ (2/3/4/5/?) Dinge machen: ＿＿.
	  ■ Informationen über verschiedene Berufe sammeln
	  ■ Stellenangebote in der Zeitung / im Internet durcharbeiten
	  ■ zur Arbeitsvermittlung an der Uni gehen
	  ■ Freunde/Familie/Bekannte fragen
	  ■ zum Arbeitsamt / zur Berufsberatung gehen
	  ■ ??

5. Was braucht man für eine Bewerbung?	**6.** Man muss gewöhnlich ＿＿.

7. Wie lange dauert es, bis ＿＿?	**8.** ■ ＿＿ geht schnell.
	  ■ Manchmal dauert es ＿＿.
	  ■ Meistens dauert es ＿＿ Monate.

9. Na, dann viel Glück!	**10.** Vielen Dank!

Aktivität 11 Ein Lebenslauf

Hier sehen Sie einen typischen tabellarischen Lebenslauf.

Lebenslauf

Name	Birgit Hermsen
Geburtsdatum	22. Dezember 1969
Geburtsort	Bonn
Eltern	Friedrich Hermsen Elsbeth Hermsen, geb. Marx
Ausbildungsgang	
1975-1979	Grundschule: Elisabethschule, Bonn
1979-1986	Realschule, Bonn
1984-1985	Austauschschülerin in USA (Experiment in International Living) Redwood City, Kalifornien
1986	Realschulabschluss: Mittlere Reife
1986-1988	Ausbildung als Bürokauffrau, Bonn Reisebüro Wilmers
Seit 1988	Reisebürokauffrau, Bonn Reisebüro am Markt
Familienstand	ledig
Interessen	Reisen (USA, Nepal, Australien und Neuseeland) Sport (Tennis, Reiten) Lesen und Musik

Schritt 1: Beantworten Sie die Fragen:

- Welche Schulen hat Birgit in Bonn besucht?
- Welche Ausbildung hat sie gemacht?
- Was ist ihr jetziger Beruf?
- Welche anderen Interessen hat Birgit?

Schritt 2: Nun erzählen Sie Birgits Lebenslauf in vollständigen Sätzen. Benutzen Sie folgendes Format.

BEISPIEL: Birgit ist am 22. Dezember 1969 in Bonn geboren.
   Von _____ bis _____...
   Seit...
   Danach...

Grundschule besucht

Realschule besucht

Ausbildung als Bürokauffrau gemacht

als Reisebürokauffrau in Bonn gearbeitet

Hier klicken!

Weiteres zum Thema Schule und Bildung finden Sie bei **Deutsch: Na klar!** im World-Wide-Web unter www.mhhe.com/dnk.

Mit sechs Jahren beginnt für Kinder in Deutschland die Schule. Alle Kinder gehen zuerst vier bis sechs Jahre lang gemeinsam auf **die Grundschule.** Danach trennen sich die Wege.

Ein Teil der Schüler und Schülerinnen geht dann auf **die Hauptschule,** die nach dem neunten oder zehnten Schuljahr mit dem Hauptschulabschluss endet. Danach suchen sich die meisten Schulabgänger eine Ausbildungsstelle für einen praktischen Beruf. Zweimal die Woche müssen die „Azubis" (<u>Au</u>szu<u>bi</u>ldenden oder Lehrlinge) auf **die Berufsschule** gehen. Dort lernen sie vor allem praktische Fächer, die für den künftigen Beruf wichtig sind.

Ein anderer Teil der Schüler und Schülerinnen geht von der Grundschule auf **die Realschule.** Sie endet nach dem zehnten Schuljahr mit dem **Abschluss** der **mittleren Reife.** Danach geht man auf eine **Fachschule** oder auch auf eine **Berufsschule.**

Als dritte Möglichkeit gibt es **das Gymnasium.** Das Gymnasium umfasst neun Klassen, vom fünften bis zum dreizehnten Schuljahr. Am Ende von neun Jahren machen Schüler **das Abitur.** Ohne Abitur kann man nicht studieren.

Als Alternative für die drei verschiedenen Schultypen gibt es in Deutschland heutzutage **die Gesamtschule.** Ähnlich wie in amerikanischen Schulen gehen alle Schüler zur selben Schule bis zum Abschluss; daher der Name Gesamtschule.

Der erste Schultag: der Ernst des Lebens beginnt.

Vom Kindergarten zur Universität

				Berufsqualifizierender Studienabschluß	
	Berufsqualifizierender Abschluß	Allgemeine Hochschulreife		**Universität/Technische Universität, Pädagogische Hochschule, Fachhochschule, Verwaltungsfachhochschule, Kunsthochschule, Gesamthochschule**	
	Fachschule	**Abendgymnasium/ Kolleg**			

		Berufsbildender Abschluß			Allgemeine Hochschulreife	
13		Mittlerer Bildungsabschluß		Fachhochschulreife	**Gymnasiale Oberstufe**	13
12		Berufsausbildung in Betrieb u.	Berufs- aufbau- Schule	Berufs- fach- Schule	Fach- ober- Schule	(Gymnasium, Berufliches Gymnasium, Fachgymnasium, Gesamtschule)	12
11		Berufsschule (Duales System)					11
10		Berufsgrundbildungsjahr				10

Abschlüsse an Hauptschulen nach 9 oder 10 Jahren / Realschulabschluß

10		10. Schuljahr			10
9					9
8	Sonder- schule	**Hauptschule**	**Realschule**	**Gymnasium**	**Gesamt- schule**	8
7					7
6		*Orientierungs-Stufe*			6
5		(schulformabhängig oder schulformunabhängig)			5
4					4
3	Sonder- schule	**Grundschule**			3
2					2
1					1
Sonder- kinder- garten		**Kindergarten**			

Schuljahr

Kulturtipp. Note: An excellent illustration of the information in the **Kulturtipp** is in *Transparente Landeskunde,* available from Inter Nationes, 53175 Bonn, Kennedyallee 91–103. **Suggestion:** Ask students to create a chart illustrating the American school system and describe it to a partner playing the role of a German visitor seeking information about American schools.

Grammatik im Kontext

Das Futur ## Future Tense°

You recall that in German the present tense can also refer to future action, particularly when an adverb of time is present.

Nächstes Jahr macht Sabine ein Praktikum in den USA.
Next year Sabine is going to do an internship in the USA.

Morgen schickt sie mehrere Bewerbungen ab.
Tomorrow she will send off several applications.

In German, the future tense is used most frequently to express future time when the context provides no other explicit reference to the future.

Eines Tages **werde** ich Erfolg **haben.**
Someday I will be successful.

Millionen **werden** meine Bücher **kaufen.**
Millions will buy my books.

Wir **werden** mal **sehen.**
We shall see (if that's the case).

kaufen			
ich	werde kaufen	wir	werden kaufen
du	wirst kaufen	ihr	werdet kaufen
er sie es	wird kaufen	sie	werden kaufen
Sie werden kaufen			

Note:

- The future tense is formed with the auxiliary verb **werden** and the infinitive of the main verb. The infinitive is placed at the end of the sentence.

Lesen Sie den Cartoon „Poesie" (*Poetry*).

Poesie von Erich Rauschenbach

- Identify the verbs in each sentence. Which verbs clearly refer to the present?
- How does the poet express his wishful thinking?
- For each sentence expressing the poet's hopes for the future, state the unspoken reality of his present life.

  BEISPIEL: Er hat keinen Erfolg mit seinen Gedichten.

[1] *poems*
[2] Erfolg... *be successful*
[3] in den... *praise me to the skies*
[4] *famous*
[5] mache... *continue*
[6] wie... *as before*
[7] ausgewählte... *select readership*

Expressing Probability

The future tense is also used in German to express probability, often with the adverbs **wohl** and **wahrscheinlich** (*probably*).

Consider the following hypothetical scenario concerning the unsuccessful poet of the cartoon "*Poesie.*"

Zehn Jahre später: Der Dichter, Anselmus Himmelblau fährt jetzt einen tollen BMW mit Autotelefon und Navigationssystem und wohnt in einer Villa in Spanien. Auf seiner Luxusjacht in Monte Carlo trifft sich die Prominenz der ganzen Welt...

What is probably true about Anselmus?

Er **wird wohl** endlich Erfolg haben.	*He is probably finally successful.*
Millionen **werden** jetzt **wahrscheinlich** seine Bücher **kaufen**.	*Millions are probably buying his books now.*
Er **wird wohl** sehr reich **sein**.	*He is probably very rich.*

Übung 1 Wunschträume

Was ist Ihr Wunschtraum? Was werden Sie eines Tages sein? Wo werden Sie wohnen?

BEISPIEL: Ich werde Millionär sein.
Ich werde in einem Schloss wohnen.

WAS?	WO?
Akrobat/Akrobatin beim Zirkus	auf dem Mars
Präsident/Präsidentin von…	in einem Schloss
Astronaut/Astronautin	in einer Grashütte auf Tahiti
Fußballspieler/Fußballspielerin	in einer netten kleinen Villa
Milliardär/Milliardärin	in einem Wohnwagen
berühmter Musiker / berühmte Musikerin	im Weißen Haus
berühmter Schauspieler / berühmte Schauspielerin	in einer Kommune
??	??

Übung 2 Wahrscheinlich

Führen Sie ein Gespräch. Reden Sie mit mindestens zwei Leuten.
Jemand hat gerade eine Million Dollar in der Lotterie gewonnen. Was wird er/sie wahrscheinlich mit dem Geld machen?

BEISPIEL: s1: Meine Mutter hat eine Million Dollar gewonnen.
s2: Was wird sie mit dem Geld machen?
s1: Sie wird sich wahrscheinlich einen tollen Ferrari kaufen.

WER?	WAS?
Mutter	das Geld auf die Bank bringen
Vater	einen tollen Ferrari kaufen
Eltern	nach Florida ziehen
Freundin	ein Schloss in Frankreich kaufen
Freund	vielen Leuten helfen
ich	ein tolles Motorrad kaufen
??	auf eine Insel in der Karibik ziehen
	eine Weltreise machen
	??

Describing People or Things: Relative Clauses°

Relativsätze

A relative clause provides additional information about a person or an object.

> XYZ Company is looking for bright and energetic trainees *who* are interested in a career in communications technology.

> XYZ Company is looking for trainees *whose* background includes a degree in computer science.

> XYZ Company is looking for trainees for *whom* the sky is the limit.

The Relative Pronoun°

Das Relativpronomen

In German, a relative clause is always introduced by a relative pronoun. The forms of the relative pronoun are identical to those of the definite article, except in the genitive singular and the genitive and dative plural.

	SINGULAR			PLURAL
	Masculine	*Neuter*	*Feminine*	*All Genders*
Nominative	der	das	die	die
Accusative	den	das	die	die
Dative	dem	dem	der	**denen**
Genitive	**dessen**	**dessen**	**deren**	**deren**

NOMINATIVE SUBJECT

Wir suchen Damen und Herren, **die** Ehrgeiz besitzen.

*We are looking for women and men **who** have ambition.*

ACCUSATIVE OBJECT

Wie heißt der junge Mann, **den** du gestern kennen gelernt hast?

*What is the name of the young man (**whom**) you met yesterday?*

DATIVE OBJECT

Gehören Sie zu den Menschen, **denen** ein sicherer Arbeitsplatz wichtig ist?

*Are you one of those people **to whom** a secure position is important?*

GENITIVE OBJECT

Wir sind eine Firma, **deren** Produkte weltbekannt sind.

*We are a company **whose** products are known worldwide.*

PREPOSITIONAL OBJECT

Informatikerin ist ein Beruf, **für den** ich mich interessiere.

*Being a computer scientist is an occupation **in which** I am interested.*

KONSTRUKTEURE,
denen Ihr Radius zu eng ist...

Malte Fischer
Beratung   Schlehenweg 2
und Management   D-5063 Overath
für Unternehmen   Tel. 02206/2231

Note:

- Relative pronouns correspond in gender and number to their antecedent—that is, to the noun to which they refer.

- The case of the relative pronoun is determined by its function within the relative clause. It can be the subject, an object, or a prepositional object.

- The conjugated verb is placed at the end of the relative clause.

- A relative clause in German is always set off from the rest of the sentence by a comma.

- The relative pronoun must always be expressed in German; it cannot be omitted as in English.

Der Personalchef, **den** ich kürzlich kennenlernte,...	*The personnel director I met recently . . . (The personnel director whom I met recently . . .)*
Die Berufsberaterin, **mit der** ich sprach,...	*The career adviser I spoke with . . . (The career adviser with whom I spoke . . .)*

ANALYSE

Wir suchen eine modisch interessierte, gepflegte junge Dame, die nach einem Praktikum in unserem Hause eine Lehre als

Einzelhandels- kauffrau

absolvieren[1] möchte.

Kurfürstendamm 213
10719 Berlin
Telefon 8 81 40 55

[1]eine Lehre als... absolvieren *to serve an apprenticeship as . . .*

Wir suchen noch Hausfrauen, Rentner, Studenten oder Berufstätige, die es frühmorgens in ihren Betten nicht mehr aushalten.

Wir suchen einen qualifizierten

Mitarbeiter

der mindestens ein Jahr Erfahrung mit Airlines vorweisen kann.

Lesen Sie,
was Leute lesen,
die Karriere
machen wollen.

- Identify the main clause and the relative clause(s) in each of the four ads.

- About whom or what do the relative clauses provide information?

- Where is the conjugated verb placed in each relative clause?

Übung 3　Attribute

Ergänzen Sie die Relativpronomen. Wie sagt man die Sätze auf Englisch?

A.

1. Gabriele ist eine Frau, _____ selbständig arbeiten möchte.
2. Nicholas ist ein Mann, _____ selbständig arbeiten möchte.
3. Das sind junge Leute, _____ selbständig arbeiten möchten.
4. Dies ist eine Firma, _____ junge Leute mit Verkaufstalent sucht.
5. ABC ist ein Unternehmen, _____ Azubis sucht.

B.

1. Wie heißt der Arzt, _____ du gestern kennen gelernt hast?
2. Wie heißt die Ärztin, _____ du gestern kennen gelernt hast?
3. Wie heißt der Filmschauspieler, _____ du gern kennen lernen möchstest?
4. Wie heißen die Musiker, _____ du gern hören möchtest?
5. Wie heißt das Buch, _____ du zum Geburtstag bekommen hast?

C.

1. Wir suchen eine Studentin, _____ Reisen Spaß macht.
2. Wir suchen einen Studenten, _____ Auto fahren Spaß macht.
3. Wir suchen Leute, _____ Technik Spaß macht.
4. Er ist ein Mensch, _____ Prestige sehr wichtig ist.
5. Plus ist eine Firma, _____ motivierte Manager wichtig sind.

D.

1. Dies ist eine Firma, _____ Produkte überall bekannt sind.
2. Dies ist ein Unternehmen, _____ Produkte überall bekannt sind.
3. Das sind Schulen, _____ Schüler eine gute Ausbildung bekommen.

Übung 4　Was für Leute suchen sie?

Beschreiben Sie, wer die Firmen sind und wen sie suchen.

BEISPIEL: Wir sind ein erfolgreiches Unternehmen, *das* weltbekannt ist.

1. Wir sind eine erfolgreiche Firma, (der, die, das) Ihnen gute Karrierechancen bietet.
2. Wir sind eine Firma, (dessen, deren) Produkte weltbekannt sind.
3. Unsere Firma sucht junge Leute, (der, die) Verkaufstalent besitzen.
4. Wir suchen einen Auszubildenden, (der, dem, denen) Technik Spaß macht.
5. Sind Sie eine Frau, (der, dem, denen) eine gute Ausbildung wichtig ist?
6. Unsere Firma sucht Damen und Herren, (der, die) nicht nur Geld verdienen wollen.
7. Sind Sie ein junger Mann, (die, der) eine solide Ausbildung zum Bürokaufmann möchte?

Übung 5   Qualifikationen

Die folgenden Sätze sind aus Stellenangeboten in deutschen Zeitungen. Setzen Sie die passenden Relativpronomen ein.

1. Unsere Firma sucht Abiturienten, _____ Kreativität und Flexibilität besitzen.
2. Wenn Sie eine junge Dame sind, _____ sich für technische Berufe interessiert, schicken Sie uns Ihre Bewerbung.
3. Wir suchen einen Auszubildenden (Azubi), _____ das Bäckerhandwerk lernen möchte.
4. Elektroniker ist ein Beruf, für _____ sich viele junge Leute interessieren.
5. Wir sind eine Firma, mit _____ Sie über Ihre Zukunft reden sollten.
6. Ist Ihnen die Umwelt, in _____ Sie leben, wichtig? Dann werden Sie doch Umwelt-Techniker, ein Beruf für engagierte Menschen, _____ unsere Umwelt wichtig ist.
7. Wir suchen junge Leute, _____ ein gesundes Selbstbewusstsein (*self-confidence*) haben.
8. Wir suchen junge Leute, _____ einen sicheren Arbeitsplatz suchen und _____ bei der Post Karriere machen wollen.

Übung 6   Ein gefährlicher Beruf

Herr Grimmig, Briefträger von Beruf, hat—wie Sie sehen—mal wieder einen schlechten Tag. Schauen Sie sich zuerst die zwei Bilder an.

A. Hier sind einige Tatsachen (*facts*).

- Fritz, der Hund, hasst (*hates*) Briefträger. Er hat den Briefträger, Herrn Grimmig, ins Bein gebissen.
- Der Hund gehört dem Jungen, Niko.
- Herr Sauer ist Nikos Vater. Er ist sehr böse (*angry*) über den Fall (*matter*).
- Frau Kluge, die Nachbarin, hat alles genau gesehen.
- Herr Grimmig, der Briefträger, hat die Polizei geholt.
- Der Polizist, Herr Gründlich, schreibt alles genau auf.

Übung 6. Suggestion: Focus students' attention on the first drawing. Then, working in small groups, students scan the **Tatsachen** and the second drawing. Each student in a group states a fact about one of the characters portrayed. One person in each group summarizes the facts for the whole class.

B. Sagen Sie nun mit Hilfe der Tatsachen etwas über die Situation.

BEISPIEL: Fritz ist der Hund. Tatsache: Fritz hasst Briefträger. →
         Fritz ist der Hund, der Briefträger hasst.

1. Fritz ist der Hund,...
2. Niko ist...,
3. Herr Grimmig ist...,
4. Frau Kluge ist...,
5. Herr Sauer ist...,
6. Herr Gründlich ist...,

The Interrogative Pronoun° was für (ein)

Das Interrogativpronomen

NOMINATIVE

    Was für ein Beruf ist das?   *What kind of a profession is that?*

    Was für eine Firma ist das?   *What kind of a firm is that?*

ACCUSATIVE

    Was für einen Chef hast du?   *What kind of a boss do you have?*

    Was für eine Chefin hast du?   *What kind of a boss do you have?*

DATIVE

    In **was für einer** Firma   *What kind of a firm do you work for?*
    arbeitest du?

    Mit **was für einem** Kollegen   *What kind of a colleague do you work*
    arbeitest du?   *with?*

    Mit **was für** Kollegen   *What kind of colleagues do you work*
    arbeitest du?   *with?*

Note:

- The interrogative pronoun **was für (ein)** is always followed by a noun.
- The case of the noun that follows **was für (ein)** depends on its function in the sentence. **Für** does not function as a preposition and, therefore, does not determine the case of the noun.
- With plurals, **ein** is not used; the expression shortens to **was für.**

Übung 7   Ein unkonventioneller Klub

Markieren Sie die richtige(n) Antwort(en).

1. Der eine Sprecher...
   a. liest ein Buch.   **b.** sieht fern.   **c.** schreibt ein Buch.
2. *Das literarische Oktett* ist...
   a. ein Gedicht.   **b.** der Titel eines Buches.   **c.** der Titel einer Erzählung.   **d.** der Name eines Klubs.
3. Die Autoren sind...
   a. fünf Studentinnen.   **b.** acht Studenten.   **c.** acht Hausfrauen.

4. Im Buch stehen...
   a. nur Geschichten.   **b.** nur Gedichte.
   c. hauptsächlich (*mainly*) Geschichten und ein paar Gedichte.
5. Die Themen, über die die Autoren schreiben, beziehen sich auf...
   a. Politik.   **b.** Sex.   **c.** Liebe.   **d.** Deutschland.
6. Der Leser des Buches findet das Buch...
   a. merkwürdig.   **b.** originell.   **c.** dumm.   **d.** provozierend.

Übung 8   Ein Interview

Fragen Sie mindestens drei Leute in der Klasse.

BEISPIEL: S1: Was für Filme siehst du am liebsten?
            S2: Am liebsten sehe ich Dokumentarfilme.

1. Was für Filme siehst du am liebsten? (z.B. Abenteuerfilme, Dokumentarfilme, Liebesfilme, Horrorfilme)
2. Was für einen Wagen fährst du?
3. Was für Musik interessiert dich?
4. Was für Kleidung trägst du am liebsten?
5. Was für Getränke trinkst du am liebsten?
6. Was für einen Beruf möchtest du haben?
7. In was für einer Stadt möchtest du gern leben? (z.B. Kleinstadt, Großstadt, in überhaupt keiner stadt)

Negating Sentences

Summary: The Position of **nicht**

You recall that **nicht** is used in negation when the negative article **kein** cannot be used. The position of **nicht** varies according to the structure of the sentence.

When **nicht** negates a specific sentence element, it precedes this sentence element.

Ich komme **nicht heute,** sondern morgen.

Wir haben **nicht viel Geld.**

When **nicht** negates an entire statement, it generally stands at the end of the sentence.

Petra kommt morgen leider **nicht.**

Sie gibt mir das Buch **nicht.**

However, **nicht** precedes:

- *predicate adjectives*   Petras Bewerbungsbrief ist **nicht lang.**
- *predicate nouns*   Das ist **nicht Petras Brief.**
- *verbal complements at the end of the sentence*
    a. *separable prefixes*   Sie schickt den Brief **nicht ab.**
    b. *past participles*   Sie hat sich **nicht beworben.**
    c. *infinitives*   Sie will sich **nicht bewerben.**
- *prepositional phrases*   Sie hat sich **nicht um die Stelle** beworben.

Übung 9 Das stimmt nicht!

Sagen Sie das Gegenteil (*opposite*).

1. Hans hat die Prüfung bestanden (*passed*).
2. Er kennt den Personalchef der Firma Wüstenrot.
3. Er hat seine Bewerbung zur Post gebracht.
4. Er hat den Personalchef gestern angerufen.
5. Der Personalchef hat ihn zu einem Gespräch eingeladen.
6. Der Personalchef war sehr beeindruckt von (*impressed by*) Hans.
7. Hans hat die Stelle bekommen.
8. Hans war traurig.

Negation: noch nicht / noch kein(e); nicht mehr / kein(e)... mehr

Geht Ute **schon** zur Schule?	Nein, sie geht **noch nicht** zur Schule.
Hat Dieter **schon** eine Stelle?	Nein, er hat **noch keine** Stelle.

To respond negatively to a question that includes the adverb **schon** (*already, yet*), use either **noch nicht** (*not yet*) or **noch kein** (*no . . . yet*) in your answer.

Ist Sabine **immer noch** arbeitslos?	Nein, sie ist **nicht mehr** arbeitslos.
Hat Dieter **noch** Arbeit?	Nein, er hat **keine** Arbeit **mehr.**

To respond negatively to a question that includes the adverb **noch** or **immer noch** (*still*), use either **nicht mehr** (*no longer*) or **kein... mehr** (*no . . . any longer*) in your answer.

Übung 10 Leider, noch nicht

Stellen Sie einem Partner / einer Partnerin Fragen.

1. Weißt du schon, was du mal werden willst?
2. Ist dein Bruder / deine Schwester schon mit der Ausbildung fertig?
3. Hast du schon eine Stelle für den Sommer?
4. Hast du schon die Stellenangebote in der Zeitung gelesen?
5. Hast du dich schon um eine Stelle beworben?
6. Hast du den Personalchef der Firma schon angerufen?
7. Hast du schon ein Angebot von der Firma bekommen?

Übung 11 Nein, nicht mehr

Beantworten Sie die Fragen zuerst mit **ja** und dann mit **nein**.

BEISPIEL: Studiert Barbara noch Jura? →
　　　　　 Ja, sie studiert immer noch Jura.
　　　　　 Nein, sie studiert nicht mehr Jura.

1. Wohnt Barbara noch in Heidelberg?
2. Arbeitet Andreas immer noch als Reiseführer?
3. Hat Astrid noch Arbeit?
4. Hat Klaus noch ein Motorrad?
5. Macht Astrid die Arbeit bei dem Verlag (*publishing house*) noch Spaß?

Sprache im Kontext

Videoclips

A. Schauen Sie sich die Interviews mit Oliver, Jasmin und Alex an. Wie sind sie zu ihrem Beruf gekommen? Ergänzen Sie die Sätze.

   1. Oliver ist selbständig, er ist _____. Er hat eine _____ in neuen Medien wie Fernsehen und Computeranimation gemacht. An seinem Beruf gefällt ihm die _____. Sein Beruf ist aber sehr _____.

   2. Jasmin ist _____ bei der Deutschen Bank. Wie hat sie ihre Stelle bekommen? Sie hat die_____ in der Zeitung gelesen und hat sich _____. Sie hat ihren _____ mit Passfoto an die Bank geschickt und hat ein_____ erhalten.

   3. Alex ist _____ von Beruf. Wie hat er seine Stelle bekommen? Von einer Freundin hat er erfahren, dass eine _____ frei war. Er hat sich _____. Er arbeitet seit _____ Jahren in diesem Beruf.

B. Was für Schulen haben Peter und Jasmin besucht? Kreuzen Sie an.

	PETER	JASMIN
Grundschule	☐	☐
Gesamtschule	☐	☐
Gymnasium	☐	☐
Realoberschule	☐	☐
Universität	☐	☐

C. Was wollten Oliver, Jasmin und Alex als Kinder werden? Und Sie? Was wollten Sie als Kind werden?

D. Was werden Peter, Jasmin und Alex in zwanzig Jahren tun?

E. Und Sie? Was werden Sie in zwanzig Jahren tun?

Lesen

Zum Thema

Was sind die beliebtesten Berufe?

1. Zu dritt, listen Sie drei beliebte Berufe. Nennen Sie für jeden Beruf einen Grund (*reason*), warum viele Leute sich dafür interessieren. Machen Sie dann eine Umfrage (*survey*) in der Klasse. Welche Berufe wurden am häufigsten (*most often*) genannt? Warum?

2. Die folgenden Kategorien kommen im Artikel „So kriegen Sie den Job" (Seite 346) vor. Was sollte man bedenken, wenn man zu einem Vorstellungsgespräch eingeladen ist?

   BEISPIEL: Kleidung →
   Für ein Gespräch bei einer Bank kleidet man sich am besten konservativ.

   - Kleidung
   - Haltung (*demeanor*)
   - Gestik (*gestures*)
   - Mimik (Gesichtsausdrücke)
   - Sprache
   - Make-up

Auf den ersten Blick

1. Schauen Sie sich den Titel und alle Untertitel des Textes auf der nächsten Seite an. Stellen Sie dabei das Thema des Artikels fest.

2. Welche Informationen erwarten Sie (*do you expect*) im Text? Lesen Sie den Text und versuchen Sie dabei, diese Informationen zu finden.

3. Für wen ist der Text geschrieben? Überfliegen Sie (*skim*) kurz den Text und finden Sie mindestens drei Belege (*clues*).

   BEISPIEL: Im Text steht: „Jetzt müssen Sie nur noch überzeugen, dass Sie genau <u>die Richtige</u> sind."

4. Überfliegen Sie den Text noch einmal und suchen Sie Wörter, die zu den folgenden Kategorien passen.
   a. Kleidung
   b. Haltung
   c. Gestik
   d. Mimik
   e. Sprache
   f. Make-up

Zum Thema. Suggestion: Have students report as a group, while one student records the answers on the board.

Auf den ersten Blick. Before students read the text, ask them what an article addressed specifically to women who are going for a job interview might talk about.

Bewerbungs-Gespräch

So kriegen Sie
den Job

*Oft entscheiden 15 Minuten
Vorstellungsgespräch in einer Firma
über Ihr weiteres Leben. Wir
sagen Ihnen, wie Sie sich am besten
darauf vorbereiten*

ILLUSTRATION: NILS FLIEGNER

[1]convince
[2]Wie... *How to succeed*
[3]reveal
[4]abhängig... *depends on*
[5]Essential
[6]dressed up, in costume
[7]submission
[8]avoid
[9]common
[10]finger-snapping
[11]wringing
[12]sich... verhaspeln *get muddled*
[13]exaggerate
[14]appropriately
[15]gathered
[16]company
[17]damit... *count on*
[18]sich... *are getting engaged*
[19]pregnant
[20]Stress
[21]lassen Sie sich... aus *express*
[22]to perfect
[23]demonstrate
[24]take to heart

Sie haben sich um eine neue Stelle beworben – und halten nun die Einladung zu einem persönlichen Gespräch in Händen. Jetzt müssen Sie „nur" noch überzeugen,[1] daß Sie genau die Richtige sind. Wie Ihnen das gelingt,[2] verraten[3] Ihnen hier gleich zwei Experten: Thomas Briol von der „Baumann Unternehmensberatung", einem der größten Unternehmen dieser Art in Deutschland, und Karriereberaterin Dr. Dagmar Brodersen aus Darmstadt.

Das müssen Sie beachten

Kleidung: Die Kleiderfrage ist abhängig davon,[4] in welcher Branche Sie sich vorstellen. Während Sie in einer Bank oder in einem konventionellen Unternehmen busineßlike in einem Kostüm auftreten sollten, können Sie sich in einer Werbeagentur ruhig flotter und farbiger präsentieren. Wesentlich[5] aber ist, daß Sie sich in Ihrer Kleidung wohl fühlen. Ihr Gegenüber merkt es mit absoluter Sicherheit, wenn Sie sich nur für den Termin „verkleidet"[6] haben.
Haltung: Betreten Sie den Raum, in dem das Vorstellungsgespräch stattfindet, freundlich lächelnd. Kommen Sie nicht mit heruntergezogenen Schultern und vorgebeugt herein, das signalisiert Angst oder Unterwürfigkeit.[7] Wenn Sie Ihren Gesprächspartner begrüßen, dann tun Sie dies mit einem kurzen, kräftigen Händedruck. Seien Sie ungezwungen und natürlich, und blicken Sie

Ihrem Gegenüber ruhig und offen ins Gesicht – das gibt Pluspunkte.
Gestik: Auch hier gilt, wie schon beim Betreten des Gesprächsraums, daß Sie Zeichen von Nervosität vermeiden.[8] Besonders häufig[9] ist das verräterische Fingerknipsen[10] oder das Verknoten[11] der Hände.
Mimik: Ihr Gegenüber freut sich, wenn Sie auch in dieser ernsten Gesprächssituation mal lächeln oder lachen. Ein starres Pokerface wirkt ziemlich unsympathisch.
Sprache: Sprechen Sie deutlich, verständlich und langsam. Dadurch verhindern Sie auch, daß Sie sich in der Aufregung verhaspeln.[12] Bleiben Sie trotzdem natürlich, und übertreiben[13] Sie die Selbstdarstellung nicht.
Make-up: Auch hier gilt, daß Sie sich Ihrem Stil entsprechend[14] schminken, jedoch mit Farbe eher zurückhaltend sein sollten.

Fragen, auf die Sie gefaßt sein müssen

Sicherlich werden Sie zu Ihrem Lebensweg gefragt werden. Antworten Sie nicht nur mit den Fakten, die sowieso schon Ihrem Lebenslauf zu entnehmen[15] sind, sondern geben Sie Hintergrundinformation, z.B. warum Sie gerade Ihre Ausbildung, Ihren Beruf gewählt haben. Vorbereitet müssen Sie auch auf die Frage sein, warum Sie sich gerade bei diesem Unternehmen[16] beworben haben. Und gerade als Frau müssen Sie damit rechnen,[17] nach Ihrem Privatleben ge-

fragt zu werden. Wichtig zu wissen: Auf Fragen, ob Sie sich verloben[18] oder heiraten wollen, ob Sie schwanger[19] sind oder einer Partei oder Gewerkschaft angehören, müssen Sie gar nicht bzw. dürfen Sie falsch antworten.
Wenn Sie nach Ihren persönlichen Zielen gefragt werden: Betonen[20] Sie nicht so sehr Ihre privaten Wünsche und Vorstellungen, sondern lassen Sie sich vor allem über Ihre beruflichen Interessen aus.[21]
Gefragt wird gerne auch nach den persönlichen Stärken und Schwächen. Da können Sie durchaus Schwächen zugeben, beispielsweise, daß Sie sich in einer Fremdsprache noch vervollkommnen[22] wollen. Abschließend wird man oft gefragt, ob man Nebeninteressen hat und in sportlichen, karitativen oder kirchlichen Organisationen tätig ist. Können Sie hier mit „Ja" antworten, haben Sie einen dicken Pluspunkt, weil dies als Zeichen für außergewöhnliches Engagement gewertet wird.

Fragen, die Sie unbedingt stellen sollten

Genauso wichtig wie Ihre Antworten sind aber auch Ihre Fragen: Bleiben Sie nicht stumm, sondern beteiligen Sie sich aktiv am Gespräch: Fragen Sie nach den Zielen des Unternehmens und danach, was gerade Sie dazu beitragen können. Sicherlich interessiert Sie auch alles, was mit Ihrem (künftigen) Tätigkeitsbereich zusammenhängt. Fragen Sie ruhig genau nach. Damit bezeugen[23] Sie Interesse – und machen garantiert einen guten Eindruck.
Wenn Sie das alles beherzigen,[24] könnten Sie Ihren Konkurrenten/innen um eine Nasenlänge voraus sein.

Die beliebtesten Frauen-Berufe

Künstlerin
Heil- und Pflegeberufe
Lehrerin und Dozentin
Ingenieurin und Architektin
Ärztin
Sozialberufe
Kauffrau
Psychologin
Tourismusberufe
Journalistin

(nach einer Erhebung der Bundesanstalt für Arbeit)

Zum Text

1. Die Autoren benutzen (sehr oft) den Imperativ, um den Leserinnen zu sagen, was sie während eines Vorstellungsgesprächs machen sollten oder nicht machen sollten. Suchen Sie Beispiele im Text und ordnen Sie diese in die passende Rubrik ein. Unterstreichen Sie die Tipps, die auch auf Männer zutreffen.

   WAS SIE MACHEN SOLLTEN   WAS SIE NICHT MACHEN SOLLTEN

2. Sind die folgenden Fragen im Vorstellungsgespräch zulässig (*allowed*) oder unzulässig? Ordnen Sie anhand des Textes die Fragen in die passende Rubrik. Wo steht das im Text?

   ZULÄSSIGE FRAGEN   UNZULÄSSIGE FRAGEN

   „Haben Sie vor, Kinder zu bekommen?"

   „Was haben Sie bei der Firma X gemacht?"

   „Warum haben Sie gerade diese Ausbildung gemacht?"

   „Sind Sie verheiratet?"

   „Sind Sie politisch aktiv?"

   „Gehören Sie einer Kirche an?"

   „Was sind Ihre beruflichen Ziele (*goals*)?"

   „Sind Sie schwanger?"

   „Was sind Ihre Schwächen (*weaknesses*)?"

   „Warum wollen Sie gerade bei uns arbeiten?"

3. Lesen Sie den Teil „Fragen, die Sie unbedingt stellen sollten" noch einmal. Bilden Sie dann passende Fragen für eine Person, die sich um eine Stelle bewirbt.

   BEISPIEL: Was sind die Ziele dieser Firma?

Sprechen und Schreiben

Aktivität 1   Ein Blick in die Zukunft

Arbeiten Sie zu zweit. Stellen Sie sich vor, Sie sind Hellseherin (*clairvoyant*). Jemand kommt zu Ihnen und möchte gern wissen, was die Zukunft für ihn/sie bereithält (*holds in store*). Werfen Sie einen Blick in die Zukunft.

BEISPIEL: Sie werden eines Tages eine berühmte Dichterin sein. Sie werden jedes Jahr zehn neue Gedichte schreiben...

Aktivität 2   ... gesucht!

Schreiben Sie eine Stellenanzeige (z.B. Clown gesucht). Welche Qualifikationen muss der Bewerber / die Bewerberin haben (z.B. Sinn für Humor; High-School-Abschluss)? Wie bewirbt man sich um die Stelle (z.B. Senden Sie Ihre Unterlagen an...)? Benutzen Sie die Anzeigen in diesem Kapitel als Beispiele.

Zum Text. This text uses several useful expressions with a verb + preposition. As a vocabulary-building exercise, have students identify the expressions and their meaning. Then have them use the expressions in a sentence.

Aktivität 2. Follow-up:
1. Pick the most interesting want ads produced by the students for this follow-up activity and make two copies of each ad. Divide the class into small groups, and, within each group, designate some students as interviewers and some as candidates. Give each small group two copies of one ad (one for the interviewers to share, one for the candidates to share). The interviewers in each group will brainstorm questions to ask the candidates while the candidates brainstorm questions to ask the interviewers and prepare answers for possible questions from the interviewers. 2. Have the interviewers for each group interview the corresponding candidates. Each interviewer should ask at least one question of each candidate. Each candidate should answer and ask the interviewers at least one question. 3. The interviewers in each group should convene for a couple of minutes and select one candidate for the job. Then they should announce their selection to the class and explain why that person was selected.

Wortschatz

Arbeitswelt
World of Work

der **Arbeitgeber, -** / die
  Arbeitgeberin, -nen — employer

das **Arbeitsamt, ∺er** — employment office

der **Arbeitsplatz, ∺e** — workplace; position

die **Ausbildung** — training

der **Berufsberater, -** / die
  Berufsberaterin, -nen — employment counselor

die **Bewerbung, -en** — application

das **Bewerbungs-
  formular, -e** — application form

das **Büro, -s** — office

der **Chef, -s** / die **Chefin,
  -nen** — manager, boss, head

das **Einkommen** — income

die **Erfahrung, -en** — experience

die **Filiale, -n** — branch office

die **Firma**, *pl.* **Firmen** — firm, company

das **Gehalt, ∺er** — salary

der **Handel** — trade, sales

der **Lebenslauf** — résumé

der **Mitarbeiter, -** / die
  Mitarbeiterin, -nen — co-worker, colleague

die **Stelle, -n** — position, job

das **Stellenangebot, -e** — job offer; help-wanted ad

die **Tätigkeit, -en** — position; activity

die **Unterlagen** (*pl.*) — documentation, papers

das **Vorstellungs-
  gespräch, -e** — job interview

Berufe
Professions

der **Bibliothekar, -e** / die
  Bibliothekarin, -nen — librarian

der **Dolmetscher, -** / die
  Dolmetscherin, -nen — interpreter

der **Geschäftsmann**, *pl.*
  Geschäftsleute / die
  Geschäftsfrau, -en — businessman/businesswoman

der **Informatiker, -** / die
  Informatikerin, -nen — computer scientist

der **Kaufmann**, *pl.*
  Kaufleute / die
  Kauffrau, -en — salesman/saleswoman

der **Künstler, -** / die
  Künstlerin, -nen — artist

der **Mechaniker, -** / die
  Mechanikerin, -nen — mechanic

der **Psychologe** (**-n** *masc.*),
  -n / die **Psychologin,
  -nen** — psychologist

der **Rechtsanwalt, ∺e** /
  die **Rechtsanwältin,
  -nen** — lawyer, attorney

der **Schauspieler, -** / die
  Schauspielerin, -nen — actor

der **Zahnarzt, ∺e** / die
  Zahnärztin, -nen — dentist

der **Zeichner, -** /
  die **Zeichnerin,
  -nen** — graphic artist

Sonstige Substantive
Other Nouns

der **Absolvent, -en**
  die **Absolventin,
  -nen** — graduate (*higher education*)

das **Abitur, -e** — *examination at the end of Gymnasium*

der **Abschluss, ∺e** — completion; degree

das **Ansehen** — prestige

das **Ausland** (*no pl.*) — foreign countries
  im Ausland — abroad

der **Bezirk, -e** — district, area

die **Entwicklung, -en** — development

der **Erfolg, -e** — success
  Erfolg haben — to be successful

die **Gelegenheit, -en** — opportunity

die **Grundschule, -n** — primary school

das **Gymnasium,
  Gymnasien** (*pl.*) — secondary school

der **Kontakt, -e** — contact

das **Leben** (*no pl.*) — life
  das **Berufsleben** — professional life

die **Technik, -en**	technique; technology
das **Zeugnis, -se**	report card; transcript; recommendation (from a former employer)

Verben	**Verbs**
sich beschäftigen (mit)	to occupy oneself (with)
besitzen, besaß, besessen	to own, possess
sich bewerben (um)(bewirbt), bewarb, beworben	to apply (for)
sich freuen (auf + *acc.*)	to look forward to
heraus•fordern	to challenge
her•stellen	to produce, manufacture
sich interessieren für (+ *acc.*)	to be interested in
nach•denken (über + *acc.*), dachte nach, nachgedacht	to think (about)

übernehmen (übernimmt), übernahm, übernommen	to take over
verdienen	to earn; to deserve
sich vor•bereiten (auf +*acc.*)	to prepare (for)
sich (*dat.*) vor•stellen	to imagine
sich (*acc.*) vor•stellen	to introduce

Adjektive und Adverbien	**Adjectives and Adverbs**
abwechslungsreich	varied, diverse
erfolgreich	successful(ly)
selbständig	independent(ly)
verantwortlich	responsible

Sonstiges	**Other**
im Freien	outdoors
wahrscheinlich	probably
was für (ein)	what kind of (a)
wohl	probably

LERNZIELE

Use this checklist to verify that you can now . . .

☐ describe your interests, desires, and expectations with regard to a future occupation.

☐ say what you like or dislike about work.

☐ identify some common occupations and describe the tasks involved in those occupations.

☐ are familiar with German job ads and résumés.

☐ ask and answer questions about a potential job.

☐ explain the steps involved in applying for a job.

☐ describe the main facets of the German school system.

☐ use the future tense to talk about future actions or probability.

☐ use relative clauses to describe people or things.

☐ pose questions about people or things using the expression **was für (ein).**

☐ negate sentences properly, using **nicht, kein(e), noch nicht / kein(e),** and **nicht / kein(e) mehr.**

KAPITEL 12

Haus, Haushalt und Finanzen

Warum ist der Richtkranz
(*wreath*) auf dem Dach des
neuen Hauses?
a. Man feiert, weil das
Haus fast fertig ist.
b. Man will das Haus
verkaufen.

Kapitel 12. Suggestion:
Brainstorm with students (in
German) about the different
ways they spend their money.
Have them talk about what they
do to earn money, how much
they need, and what their major
expenses are. Describe your
own housing situation. Have
students describe where they
live, where their families live,
and how and where they would
eventually like to live. Will they
prefer renting or buying a
house? Ask about the
availability of affordable
housing, a perennial problem
in Germany.

Videoclips

Beatrice, Dennis und
Jan sprechen über ihre
Finanzen

In diesem Kapitel

- **Themen:** Money matters, the house, household appliances
- **Grammatik:** Verbs with fixed prepositions, **da-** and **wo-**compounds,
  subjunctive II
- **Kultur:** The euro, BAföG

Alles klar?

A. Was würden die Personen 1 bis 9 machen, wenn sie viel Geld gewinnen würden? Lesen Sie die Aussagen unter den Bildern. Schreiben Sie dann die passende Nummer der Person neben die Frage.

Was machen Sie, wenn Sie 10 MILLIONEN Euro gewinnen?

oder 8 Millionen € oder 6 Millionen € oder 1 Million € oder...

1.

Mit dem Geld helfe ich armen[1] Menschen.

2.

Ich kaufe mir eine Eigentumswohnung.[2]

3.

Ich mache mich gleich[3] selbständig.

4.

Ich weiß noch nicht, was ich mache.

5.

Ich fahre in das Land meiner Träume.[4]

6.

Mein Traum ist ein Bauernhof mit Tieren.

7.

Wir unterstützen[5] unsere Eltern und Geschwister.

8.

Ich beantrage[6] sofort meine Rente.[7]

9.

Ich lade alle meine Freunde ein.

[1]poor
[2]condominium
[3]immediately
[4]dreams
[5]support
[6]apply for
[7]retirement

Haben Sie schon einmal überlegt, was SIE tun würden, wenn Sie plötzlich so viel Geld gewinnen?

-   __4__ Wer ist sich noch nicht sicher?
-   ____ Wer will eine Wohnung kaufen?
-   ____ Wer möchte den Armen helfen?
-   ____ Wer will etwas für seine Freunde tun?
-   ____ Wer hat Tiere gern?
-   ____ Wer interessiert sich für Reisen?
-   ____ Wer will der Familie helfen?
-   ____ Wer macht sich selbständig?
-   ____ Wer möchte sich pensionieren lassen?

Hier klicken!

Weiteres zum Thema Geld und Währung finden Sie bei **Deutsch: Na klar!** im World-Wide-Web unter www.mhhe.com/dnk.

B. „Was bedeutet euch Geld?" Diese Frage haben wir Jens, Lucia und Elke gestellt. Hören Sie ihre Antworten. Schreiben Sie J (Jens), L (Lucia) oder E (Elke) neben die zutreffenden Aussagen.

1. __E__ lange Urlaub machen und dann wieder arbeiten
2. __L__ Armen helfen
3. __J__ Geld für medizinische Forschung spenden (*donate*)
4. __L__ ein eigenes Geschäft aufmachen
5. __J__ ein neues Auto oder eine neue Wohnung kaufen
6. __E__ investieren
7. __L__ weiter studieren—vielleicht im Ausland
8. __E__ Geld für Welthungerorganisationen spenden

KULTURTIPP

Seit dem ersten Januar 2002 gibt es den Euro. Außer Deutschland haben elf europäische Länder jetzt diese einheitliche Währung. Welche Länder sind das? Belgien, Finnland, Frankreich, Griechenland, Holland, Irland, Italien, Luxemburg, Österreich, Portugal und Spanien. Für alle diese Länder war das eine große Umstellung, auch für Deutschland, wo der Euro nach 53 Jahren die D-Mark abgelöst hat.

Wie Sie in Kapitel 2 gelesen haben, es gibt 7 Euro-Scheine (*bills*) und 8 Münzen (*coins*). Die Bilder auf den Scheinen symbolisieren die Architektur Europas durch die Jahrhunderte. Die Münzen aller Länder haben eine gemeinsame Seite mit der Landkarte Europas, aber auf der Rückseite hat jedes Land eigene Motive.

Wörter im Kontext

Finanzen der Studenten. Suggestion: How do people in your country spend their money? Brainstorm with the students and compare this information with that in the graphics. To convert DM to euros, tell students to divide by 2.

THEMA 1: Finanzen der Studenten

Wie leben deutsche Studenten im Westen und im Osten? Antworten Sie mit Informationen aus dem Schaubild.

- Wie viel Geld brauchen deutsche Studenten **durchschnittlich** pro Monat?
- Wie finanzieren Studenten im Westen und Osten ihr Studium?
- Wofür **geben** deutsche Studenten im Westen/Osten das meiste Geld **aus**?
- Wofür geben sie das wenigste Geld aus?
- Was gehört alles in die Rubrik Sonstiges?

Ihr monatliches Budget:

- ■ Wofür geben Sie monatlich Geld aus und durchschnittlich ungefähr wie viel?
- ■ Wofür geben Sie das meiste Geld aus? das wenigste?
- ■ Wofür geben Sie nur ab und zu oder gar kein Geld aus?

Prozent Ihrer monatlichen **Ausgaben:**

_____ Miete

_____ **Nebenkosten (Strom, Heizung,** eigenes Telefon, Handy, Wasser)

_____ Auto (**Benzin, Reparaturen**)

_____ Fahrtkosten (öffentliche Verkehrsmittel, z.B. Bus, Flugzeug, Fahrten nach Hause)

_____ **Ernährung** (Essen und Trinken, auch Mensa, Restaurants)

_____ **Studiengebühren** (pro Semester, pro Quartal)

_____ Lernmittel (Bücher, **Hefte, Bleistifte, Kugelschreiber, Papier, Computerdisketten,** Sonstiges)

_____ Freizeit (Kino, Theater, Partys, Hobbys)

_____ **Sparen (Sparkonto,** Sparschwein)

_____ **Versicherungen**

_____ INSGESAMT (*total*)

- ■ Haben Sie genügende (*enough*) **Einnahmen**? Haben Sie am Ende des Monats etwas Geld **übrig,** oder sind Sie **pleite**? Müssen Sie sich manchmal Geld von Freunden oder Ihrer Familie leihen? Sind Sie **sparsam**?
- ■ Schauen Sie sich das Schaubild oben noch einmal an. **Vergleichen** Sie Ihre monatlichen Ausgaben mit denen eines Mitstudenten / einer Mitstudentin. Wer hat höhere monatliche Ausgaben?

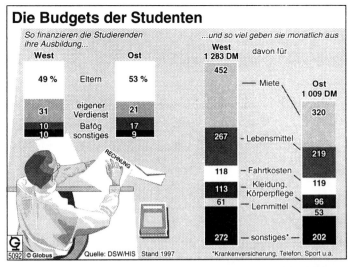

Die Budgets der Studenten

So finanzieren die Studierenden ihre Ausbildung...

...und so viel geben sie monatlich aus

	West	Ost
Eltern	49 %	53 %
eigener Verdienst	31	21
Bafög	10	17
sonstiges	10	9

West 1 283 DM / davon für — Ost 1 009 DM

davon für	West	Ost
Miete	452	320
Lebensmittel	267	219
Fahrtkosten	118	119
Kleidung, Körperpflege	113	96
Lernmittel	61	53
sonstiges*	272	202

5092 © Globus   Quelle: DSW/HIS   Stand 1997   *Krankenversicherung, Telefon, Sport u.a.

Neue Wörter

Haushalt household
durchschnittlich on average
geben... aus (ausgeben) spend
Ausgaben expenses
Nebenkosten utilities
Strom electricity
Heizung heat
Benzin gasoline
Reparaturen repairs
Ernährung food
Studiengebühren tuition
Hefte notebooks
Bleistifte pencils
Kugelschreiber ball-point pens
sparen to save
Sparkonto savings account
Versicherungen insurance
Einnahmen income
übrig left over
pleite broke
sparsam thrifty
vergleichen compare

KULTURTIPP

BAföG steht für **Bundesausbildungsförderungsgesetz.** Dieses Gesetz (*law*) regelt in Deutschland die staatliche Unterstützung von Schülern und Studenten, die ohne diese Hilfe keine Ausbildung oder Studium finanzieren könnten. BAföG besteht aus Darlehen (*loans*) und Zuschüssen (*stipends*).

Ihr monatliches Budget. Suggestion: To make this activity interactive, have students work in pairs, asking each other how much they spend on the items listed: *Wie viel gibst du für _____ aus?* Students may break down the categories in order to be more precise; e.g., *Lernmittel: Wie viel gibst du für Bücher aus? Hefte?*

Aktivität 1 Pleite oder nicht?

Schauen Sie sich Ihr monatliches Budget im **Thema 1** an. Vergleichen Sie jetzt Ihre Ausgaben mit den Ausgaben eines Partners / einer Partnerin und berichten Sie darüber. Gebrauchen Sie folgende Redemittel.

Ich gebe das meiste Geld für _____ aus.

Das wenigste Geld gebe ich für _____ aus.

Ich gebe nur ab und zu oder gar kein Geld für _____ aus.

Für _____ und _____ gebe ich mehr/weniger Geld aus als mein
   Partner / meine Partnerin.

Aktivität 2 Andreas Dilemma

Lesen Sie oder hören Sie sich den Dialog an, und ergänzen Sie die Sätze unten.

ANDREA: Sag mal, könntest du mir einen Gefallen tun?
STEFAN: Was denn?
ANDREA: Würdest du mir bis Ende der Woche 50 Euro leihen? Ich bin total pleite.
STEFAN: Fünfzig Euro? Das ist viel Geld.
ANDREA: Ich musste 100 Euro für Bücher ausgeben. Und jetzt habe ich keinen Cent mehr übrig. Ich warte auf Geld von meinen Eltern.
STEFAN: Hm, ich würde es dir gern leihen. Aber 50 Euro habe ich selber nicht mehr. Ich kann dir höchstens 20 Euro leihen.
ANDREA: Ich zahle es dir bis Ende des Monats bestimmt zurück.
STEFAN: Eben hast du gesagt, bis Ende der Woche.
ANDREA: Ja, ja. Das Geld von meinen Eltern kann jeden Tag kommen.
STEFAN: Na gut. Hier ist ein Zwanziger.
ANDREA: Vielen Dank.

Andrea hat kein _____[1] mehr; sie ist total _____.[2] Sie möchte sich von Stefan _____.[3] Sie hat nämlich ihr ganzes Geld für _____[4] ausgegeben. Deshalb hat sie jetzt nichts mehr für Essen und Trinken _____.[5] Stefan kann ihr aber _____[6] leihen. Andrea hofft, dass sie Stefan das Geld bis _____[7] zurückzahlen kann. Sie wartet auf _____.[8]

Aktivität 3 Drei Studentenbudgets

Vergleichen Sie die Ausgaben der drei Studenten auf der nächsten Seite und beantworten Sie die Fragen.

1. Wie viel Geld geben Marion, Wolfgang und Claudia insgesamt monatlich aus?
2. Wofür geben sie das meiste Geld aus?
3. Wer bezahlt die höchste Miete? Wo ist die Miete billiger?
4. Warum bezahlt Marion weniger als die zwei anderen fürs Telefon?
5. Wer hat die höchsten Kosten für Bücher und Arbeitsmittel?
6. Was ist—außer (*besides*) Miete—günstig, wenn man im Studentenwohnheim wohnt?
7. Wer unterstützt (*supports*) die drei Studenten finanziell?
8. Warum hat Marion keine Ausgaben für Verkehrsmittel?
9. Wer lebt am sparsamsten (*most thriftily*)?

Dialogue. Suggestion: With their books closed, have students listen to the dialogue once. Ask individuals to supply one fact from the dialogue. Encourage students to summarize as much as they can; then have them complete the following activity in pairs. Students read the statements aloud to one another and supply the missing information.

Hier klicken!

Weiteres zum Thema Studium und Finanzen finden Sie bei **Deutsch: Na klar!** im World-Wide-Web unter www.mhhe.com/dnk.

	MARION	WOLFGANG	CLAUDIA
Studienfach	Übersetzer (*translator*)/ Dolmetscher	Medizin	Romanistik/Politik
Studiengebühren	keine	keine	keine
Unterhalt (support)	Eltern	BAföG	Eltern
Miete	200 Euro (1 Zi, Studenten- wohnheim)	300 Euro (1 Zi, Küche, Bad außerhalb)	400 Euro (1 Zi, Küche, Bad)
Verkehrsmittel	keine (alles mit dem Fahrrad erreichbar)	40 Euro	30 Euro
Lebensmittel und Mensa	200 Euro	250 Euro	200 Euro
Bücher/Arbeitsmittel	30 Euro	70 Euro	40 Euro
Telefon	20 Euro	50 Euro (eigenes Telefon)	60 Euro (eigenes Telefon)
Freizeit	70 Euro	80 Euro	100 Euro
Fahrt nach Hause	20 Euro (Mitfahrgelegenheit) 40 Euro (mit der Bahn)	—	20 Euro
sonstiges	30 Euro	25 Euro	30 Euro

Aktivität 4 Einnahmen und Ausgaben

Vier Studenten sprechen über ihre monatlichen Einnahmen und
Ausgaben. Kreuzen Sie das Zutreffende (*the items that apply*) an.
Notieren Sie unter „Ausgaben", wie viel die Studenten für ihre
Miete ausgeben.

1. Einnahmen von:

	STEFANIE	GERT	SUSANNE	MARTIN
a. Job während des Semesters	☐	☐	☒	☒
b. Job während der Semesterferien	☒	☒	☐	☒
c. Eltern	☒	☐	☒	☒
d. Stipendium/BAföG	☐	☒	☐	☐

2. Ausgaben für:

	STEFANIE	GERT	SUSANNE	MARTIN
a. Zimmer (privat)	_____	€150	_____	_____
b. Studentenwohnheim	€100	_____	_____	_____
c. eigene Wohnung	_____	_____	_____	€200
d. Wohngemeinschaft	_____	_____	€150	_____

THEMA 2: Unsere eigenen vier Wände°

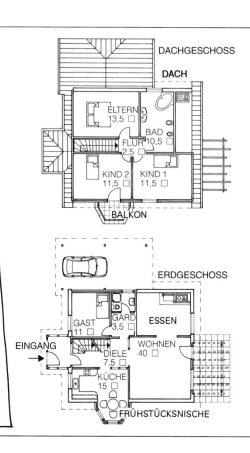

Unsere... *our own home*

Unsere eigenen vier Wände (idiomatic for "our own home"). Note: Students must refer to the floor plan to fill in the information.

Liebe Martina, lieber Jürgen!

Wir wohnen jetzt endlich in unseren eigenen vier Wänden. Vor einem Monat sind wir in unser neues Haus eingezogen. Wir schicken Euch ein Bild und eine Zeichnung des Grundrisses.[1] Wir sind sehr glücklich. Kommt uns bald mal besuchen.

Viele Grüße
Gitti und Christoph

[1] *of the floorplan*

Follow-up: Lückendiktat. Ask students to draw two rectangles on a piece of paper to represent the outlines of a floor plan. Have students draw and write the names of the floors and rooms in the blank floor plans as they are described and dictated; they can check the accuracy of their floor plan by comparing it with the one here.

Neue Wörter

eigen own
eingezogen (einziehen) moved in
Zeichnung drawing
bald soon
Dachgeschoss attic, top floor
Eingang entrance
Garderobe closet
Diele entry, foyer
Treppe staircase
nach oben upstairs

Schauen Sie sich die Zeichnung von Gittis und Christophs neuem Haus an. Ergänzen Sie dann die folgenden Sätze durch ein passendes Wort aus der Liste:

Bad	Esszimmer	Schlafzimmer
Dachgeschoss	Frühstücksnische	Terrasse
Diele	Gäste	Treppe
Erdgeschoss	Küche	Wohnzimmer

1. Das Haus hat zwei Stockwerke: ein _____ und ein _____.
2. Vom Eingang kommt man zuerst in die _____.
3. Links neben der Diele ist eine Garderobe und ein Zimmer für _____.
4. Von der Diele geht man rechts in die _____ und eine kleine _____.
5. Unten liegen noch zwei Zimmer: ein _____ und ein _____.
6. Das Wohnzimmer führt auf die _____ und in den Garten.
7. In der Diele führt eine _____ nach oben ins Dachgeschoss.
8. Im Dachgeschoss sind drei _____ und ein _____.

Aktivität 5   Die ideale Wohnung

Drei Leute (Frau Heine, Herr Zumwald und Thomas) berichten, was für eine Wohnung sie suchen, und was ihnen in der Wohnung wichtig oder unwichtig ist. Stellen Sie zuerst fest, wer welchen Wohnungstyp sucht. Dann notieren Sie in der Tabelle, was jedem wichtig (w) oder unwichtig (u) ist.

Wer sucht:

ein Zimmer in einer Wohngemeinschaft?   _____

eine Neubauwohnung in der Innenstadt?   Frau Heine

ein älteres Haus außerhalb der Stadt?   Herr Zumwald

eine gemütliche Altbauwohnung in der Stadt?   Thomas

WICHTIG/UNWICHTIG	FRAU HEINE	HERR ZUMWALD	THOMAS
Lage	w	w	w
Zentralheizung	w	w	w
Balkon	w		
Garage	u		u
Garten		w	
Teppichboden (carpeting)		u	u
Waschmaschine			w

Aktivität 6   Hin und her: Meine Wohnung—deine Wohnung

Diese Leute haben entweder eine neue Wohnung oder ein neues Haus gekauft. Wer hat was gekauft? Wie viele Stockwerke gibt es? Wie groß ist das Wohnzimmer? Wie viele WCs oder Badezimmer gibt es?

BEISPIEL: s1: Was für eine Wohnung hat Bettina Neuendorf gekauft?
s2: Eine Eigentumswohnung.
s1: Wie viele Stockwerke hat die Wohnung?
s2: Eins.
s1: Und wie viele Schlafzimmer? ...

Aktivität 6. Suggestion: Make sure students go beyond the model in asking questions: *Wie groß ist das Wohnzimmer? Hat die Wohnung ein Bad oder mehr als ein Bad?*

Note: For the personalization phase, students should imagine that they have just bought their dream home.

PERSON	TYP	STOCKWERKE	SCHLAFZIMMER	WOHNZIMMER	WC/BAD
Bettina Neuendorf	Eigentums-wohnung	eins	eins, aber auch ein kleines Gästezimmer	mit Esszimmer kombiniert 30 Quadratmeter	eins
Uwe und Marion Baumgärtner	Haus	zwei	drei: Elternschlaf-zimmer, Kinder-schlafzimmer, Gästezimmer	sehr groß mit Balkon 37 Quadratmeter	zwei Badezimmer: eins im Dach-geschoss und eins im Erdgeschoss
Sven Kersten	Eigentums-wohnung	zwei	zwei, eins als Gästezimmer benutzt	mit Esszimmer zusammen 35 Quadratmeter, Balkon vom Wohnzimmer	zwei, ein WC und ein Bad
Carola Schubärth	Haus	eins	zwei: ein Schlaf-zimmer ist Arbeitszimmer	klein 25 Quadratmeter	ein Bad
ich					
mein Partner / meine Partnerin					

Aktivität 7   Der Grundriss

A. Sie sehen hier unten einen Grundriss. Identifizieren Sie, wo das Wohn-zimmer, das Esszimmer, die Küche, das Schlafzimmer und andere Räume sind. Beschreiben Sie dann, wo die Zimmer liegen. Diese Wohnung liegt im dritten Stock eines großen Wohnhauses. Man kann die Treppe hinaufgehen oder mit dem Aufzug fahren.

Zuerst kommt man in _____.

Rechts von _____ ist _____.

Von der _____ führt eine Tür ins _____.

Neben der _____ ist ein _____ und daneben ein _____.

Vom Wohnzimmer geht man auf _____.

Unsere Eigentumswohnungen: **Ideal– für das Leben zu zweit.**

B. Zeichnen Sie nun den Grundriss Ihrer Wohnung / Ihres Hauses. (Wenn Sie in einem Studentenheim wohnen, zeichnen Sie eine Phantasiewohnung.) Geben Sie jemand die Zeichnung und beschreiben Sie ihm/ihr, wo die Zimmer liegen. Ihr Partner / Ihre Partnerin setzt die Zimmernamen in den Grundriss. Schauen Sie sich dann die Zeichnung an, um zu sehen, ob alles richtig identifiziert ist.

Beginnen Sie so: Zuerst kommt man in _____.

THEMA 3: Mieten und Vermieten

Ein Mietgesuch

Realia. This student flyer seeks a housing opportunity in Göttingen. It was found on the university's characteristic bulletin board, the so-called *Schwarzes Brett*.

Wir
(Brigitte Heyden, Mathias Elsner u. Hündin „Sarah") **suchen** günstige Wohnung, kleines Haus oder Zimmer in netter WG auf dem Lande[1] (bis ~ 12 km von Gö.[2])

Am liebsten Gemeinde[3] Obichen oder Groß Schneen u. nähere Umgebung!

Wer etwas für uns hat oder weiß, rufe bitte mögl. bald an, da[4] wir bis spätestens Ende April etwas gefunden haben müssen. Wir freuen uns über jeden Hinweis.[5]

05592/607 /395501
05592/607 /395501
05592/607 /395501
05592/607 /395501
05592/607 /395501
05592/607 /395501
05592/607 /395501
05592/607 /395501
05592/607+ /395501

[1]auf... *in the country* [2]Gö = Göttingen *university town in north central Germany* [3]*community* [4]*since* [5]*lead*

Mietangebote

1.

Land-WG sucht Mitbewohner(in)!

Wir, Bruno (26) und Britta (21), Hund und Katze, vermieten eine ganze obere Etage in einem älteren Bauernhaus 1 1/2 Zimmer, ca 38 qm.[1] Benutzbar[2] sind Küche, Bad, großer Garten. Die Miete beträgt monatlich €300,- plus €30,- Nebenkosten. 20 km von Göttingen. Ab 1. Juni.

2.

Mieter gesucht für große, helle 3 Zimmer in Neubau, ab 1. August, ca. 70 qm. Balkon, eingerichtete Küche (Spülmaschine, Kühlschrank), Waschraum mit Maschine, Zentralheizung, Teppichboden, Bad und WC, Garage. Zu Fuß ca. 15 Minuten von der Universität, 5 vom Bahnhof, 10 Minuten vom Zentrum. Tiere nicht erwünscht. Miete €400,- Nebenkosten €60,-.

[1]qm = Quadratmeter *square meters* [2]*available for use*

Neue Wörter

mieten to rent (from someone)
vermieten to rent out (to someone)
Umgebung vicinity
Katze cat
Etage floor
Bauernhaus farm house
monatlich monthly
ab 1. Juni = ab erstem Juni as of June 1st
Neubau modern building
Spülmaschine dishwasher
Kühlschrank refrigerator
Teppichboden wall-to-wall carpeting
Tiere animals

A. Lesen Sie zuerst das Mietgesuch auf der vorigen Seite. Wer sucht was und wo?

B. Lesen Sie dann die zwei Mietangebote. Welches Angebot würden Sie Brigitte und Matthias empfehlen?

    1. Ich finde Angebot Nummer _____ ideal für Brigitte und Matthias, denn es gibt dort _____.

    2. Ich würde Brigitte und Matthias Angebot Nummer _____ empfehlen, denn _____. Es gibt jedoch ein Problem: _____

Aktivität 8   Drinnen und draußen

Was passt zusammen?

1. _____ Man stellt sie im Winter an.
2. _____ Die gehören zu den Nebenkosten.
3. _____ Man stellt den Wagen dort hinein.
4. _____ Hier kocht man.
5. _____ Dort wäscht man sich.
6. _____ Der liegt auf dem Boden.
7. _____ Damit wäscht man.
8. _____ So etwas findet man meist auf dem Land.
9. _____ Der hält z.B. Milch, Käse, Fleisch und Gemüse frisch.

  a. der Teppich
  b. die Waschmaschine
  c. Strom, Heizung, Telefon
  d. die Zentralheizung
  e. der Kühlschrank
  f. die Garage
  g. das Bauernhaus
  h. die Küche
  i. das Bad

Aktivität 9   Ist die Wohnung noch frei?

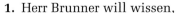

Frau Krenz hat eine große, helle Dreizimmerwohnung zu vermieten. Die Anzeige stand in der Zeitung. Herr Brunner hat auf die Anzeige hin angerufen. Er weiß, wie groß die Wohnung ist und wie hoch die Miete ist. Was will er noch von der Vermieterin wissen? Kreuzen Sie alles Zutreffende an.

Hier klicken!

Weiteres zum Thema Wohnungsangebote finden Sie bei **Deutsch: Na klar!** im World-Wide-Web unter www.mhhe.com/dnk.

1. Herr Brunner will wissen,
    ☒ ob die Heizung in den Nebenkosten einbegriffen ist.
    ☐ ob die Küche einen Mikrowellenherd hat.
    ☐ wie er vom Haus in die Innenstadt kommt.
    ☒ wo die Wohnung liegt.
    ☒ ob es einen Aufzug gibt.
    ☐ wo man parken kann.
    ☐ ob Hund und Katze willkommen sind.

2. Frau Krenz will von Herrn Brunner wissen,
    ☐ wie viele Kinder er hat.
    ☒ ob er verheiratet ist.
    ☐ ob er Arbeit hat.
    ☒ wann er vorbeikommen kann.
    ☐ wann er einziehen möchte.

Aktivität 10　Ein interessantes Angebot

Sie interessieren sich für ein Mietangebot, das Sie in der Zeitung gesehen haben und rufen deshalb den Vermieter / die Vermieterin an. Benutzen Sie die Konversationstipps.

S1 VERMIETER/VERMIETERIN	S2 ANRUFER/ANRUFERIN
1. State your last name.	2. Greet the person, state your last name, and ask whether the apartment is still available.
3. Say it is still available.	4. Ask how much the rent is.
5. State a price.	6. Ask whether this price includes all household bills.
7. State that everything is included (**inklusive**) except the heat.	8. Tell the landlord/landlady that you have a cat or dog.
9. Say that it's all right.	10. Find out where the apartment is located.
11. Give the address and location. Suggest to the caller a time when he/she can come to see it.	12. Say that the time is suitable.
13. Say good-bye.	14. Say good-bye.

Grammatik im Kontext

Verbs with Fixed Prepositions

Many German verbs require the use of fixed prepositions; these verb-preposition combinations are usually different from their English equivalents.

Ich **interessiere mich für** schnelle Autos.

I'm interested in fast cars.

Wir **warten auf** den Bus.

We are waiting for the bus.

Die Studenten **ärgern sich über** die hohen Studienkosten.

The students are annoyed about the high cost of tuition.

Verbs with Fixed Prepositions. Suggestion: Ask students for any other verbs with special prepositions that they might remember. Stress the importance of the correct use of prepositions in idiomatic speech.

The following verbs take fixed prepositions:

Angst haben vor (+ *dat.*)	*to be afraid of*
sich ärgern über (+ *acc.*)	*to be annoyed about*
bitten um	*to ask for; to request*
denken an (+ *acc.*)	*to think of*
sich freuen auf (+ *acc.*)	*to look forward to*
sich freuen über (+ *acc.*)	*to be happy about*
sich interessieren für	*to be interested in*
warten auf (+ *acc.*)	*to wait for*

Übung 1   So ist das Studentenleben

Was passt zusammen?

1. Die Studenten warten...
2. Sie haben Angst...
3. Der Professor ärgert sich...
4. Die Studenten freuen sich...
5. Der Professor denkt nur...
6. Die Studenten bitten...
7. Sie interessieren sich...

a. an seine Forschung (*research*) im Labor.
b. auf das Ende des Semesters.
c. für die Arbeit im Labor.
d. auf den Professor.
e. um mehr Zeit für die Semesterarbeit.
f. über die Studenten.
g. vor der Prüfung (*exam*).

Pronominaladverbien

Da- and wo-compounds°

Prepositional Objects: **da**-Compounds

In German, a personal pronoun following a preposition generally refers to a person or another living being.

Der Student wartet auf **die Professorin.**	*The student is waiting for the professor.*
Er wartet schon lange **auf sie.**	*He has been waiting for her for a long time.*

When the object of a preposition refers to a thing or an idea, this is represented by a **da**-compound consisting of the adverb **da** and a preposition.

Ich bin für eine Geschwindigkeitsbegrenzung auf der Autobahn.	*I am for a speed limit on the freeway.*
Viele Leute sind **dafür.**	*Many people are for it.*
Aber Markus ist **dagegen.**	*But Markus is against it.*

Note:

- **Da-** becomes **dar-** when the preposition begins with a vowel.

Marion wartet auf einen Brief von ihrem Freund.	*Marion is waiting for a letter from her boyfriend.*
Sie wartet schon lange **darauf.**	*She has been waiting for it for a long time.*

- **Da-/Dar-** can combine with most accusative and dative prepositions.
- The preposition **ohne** does not form a **da**-compound; it is always used with an accusative pronoun.

$$\begin{array}{lcl}
\text{Ich brauche Erfolg.} & \rightarrow & \\
\text{Geld.} & \rightarrow & \text{Ohne} \left\{\begin{array}{l} \text{ihn} \\ \text{es} \\ \text{sie} \end{array}\right\} \text{kann ich nicht leben.} \\
\text{Liebe.} & \rightarrow &
\end{array}$$

The Adverbs **dahin** and **daher**

The adverbs **dahin** (*there*) and **daher** (*from there*) are commonly used with verbs of motion.

Review: Go over **wo... hin** in conjunction with **da... hin** to emphasize the customary splitting of these pronouns in conversational German.

Wann fliegt Martina **nach Spanien**? —Sie fliegt morgen **dahin.**

Ich gehe heute **zur Bank.** —Ich komme gerade **daher.**

In spoken German, **dahin** is often abbreviated to **hin.**

Hans muss noch zur Bank. Er geht später **hin.**

Also in spoken German, **da** may be placed at the beginning of a sentence for emphasis, while **hin** is placed at the end of the sentence.

Gehst du oft ins Museum? **Da** gehe ich nur selten **hin.**

ANALYSE

- Identify all **da**-compounds in the following text.
- What nouns do these **da**-compounds refer to?
- Restate all **da**-compounds as prepositional objects using the nouns to which they refer.

BEISPIEL: dafür → Sabines Zimmer → für Sabines Zimmer

Sabines Zimmer im Studentenwohnheim

Sie zahlt nur 150 Euro im Monat dafür. Links an der Wand ist ein Waschbecken. Darüber hängt ein Spiegel. Daneben hängt ein Haken mit einem Handtuch. Rechts an der Wand steht ein Schreibtisch. Darauf liegen viele Bücher und Papiere. Hinten an der Wand steht ein Bett. Darunter liegen Sabines Schuhe und rechts daneben steht ein kleines Bücherregal. Dahinter ist ein Fenster. Davor steht ein Vogelkäfig. Sabines Kanarienvogel, Caruso, wohnt darin und singt pausenlos.

Übung 2   Gemeinsames und Kontraste

Sabine und ihr Freund Jürgen haben einiges, aber nicht alles gemein (*in common*).

BEISPIEL: Sie interessiert sich für klassische Musik. →
Er interessiert sich nicht *dafür.*

1. Jürgen gibt viel Geld für Unterhaltung (*entertainment*) aus.
   Sabine gibt noch mehr _____ aus.
2. Er interessiert sich überhaupt nicht für Fußball.
   Sie interessiert sich leidenschaftlich (*passionately*) _____.
3. Er hat Angst vor dem Staatsexamen.
   Sie hat auch Angst _____.
4. Sie freut sich immer über kleine Geschenke.
   Er freut sich auch _____.
5. Sie denkt immer an alle Geburtstage.
   Er denkt nie _____.
6. Er kommt immer pünktlich zur Vorlesung.
   Sie kommt nie pünktlich _____.
7. Er ärgert sich über die laute Musik im Wohnheim.
   Sie ärgert sich überhaupt nicht _____.
8. Sie freut sich auf das Ende des Studiums. Er freut sich auch _____.

No. 6. Note: Remind students that location takes a special *da-*compound.

Übung 3   Beschreibungen und Situationen

Setzen Sie passende Pronominaladverbien in die Lücken ein.

1. In meinem Zimmer steht ein Sofa. *Daneben* steht eine Stehlampe. _____
   steht ein kleiner Tisch. _____ liegen tausend Dinge.
2. —Wir wollen heute ins Kino.
   —Wann geht ihr _____?
3. Im Sommer fahre ich nach Rom. Ich freue mich schon _____.
4. Letztes Jahr hat Robert in Göttingen studiert und viel Spaß gehabt.
   Er denkt noch oft _____.
5. Gestern kam endlich ein Brief von Jürgen. Melanie hat sich sehr _____
   gefreut. Sie hat lange _____ gewartet.
6. Morgen hat Thomas eine große Prüfung (*test*). Er hat keine Angst _____.
   Aber Er muss schon um acht Uhr da sein. Er ärgert sich _____, weil er
   nämlich so früh noch nicht denken kann.

Übung 4   Eine Umfrage im Deutschkurs

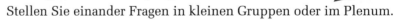

Stellen Sie einander Fragen in kleinen Gruppen oder im Plenum.

BEISPIEL: Wie viele Leute haben Angst vor Prüfungen? →
Sechs Leute haben Angst davor.

1. Wie viele Leute interessieren sich für Politik? für Sport? für Yoga?
2. Wer hat Angst vor Prüfungen?
3. Wer denkt (oft, nie, manchmal) an das Leben nach dem Studium?
4. Wie viele Leute sind für oder gegen eine nationale Krankenversicherung?
   Wer soll dafür zahlen: Arbeitgeber? Arbeitnehmer? der Staat?
5. Wer freut sich auf das Ende des Studiums? auf eine Reise im Sommer?
6. Wer ärgert sich über die hohen Preise für Bücher?

Asking Questions: **wo**-Compounds

There are two ways to formulate questions with prepositions when asking about things or ideas. One way is to use a preposition with the interrogative pronoun **was.**

Für was interessiert er sich?	*What is he interested in?*
An was denkst du?	*What are you thinking of?*
Auf was warten Sie?	*What are you waiting for?*

Another way is to combine **wo-** with a preposition to form a **wo**-compound. **Wo-** becomes **wor-** when the preposition begins with a vowel.

Wofür interessiert er sich?	*What is he interested in?*
Woran denkst du?	*What are you thinking of?*
Worauf warten Sie?	*What are you waiting for?*

Übung 5 Das möchte ich wissen!

Formulieren Sie zuerst Fragen. Arbeiten Sie dann zu zweit und beantworten Sie die Fragen abwechselnd (*taking turns*).

Wofür...	freust du dich?
Woran...	denkst du oft?
Worauf...	gibst du viel Geld aus?
Worüber...	interessierst du dich?
Wovor...	wartest du?
	hast du Angst?
	ärgerst du dich?

The Subjunctive°

Der Konjunktiv

The most important function of the subjunctive mood is to express polite requests and convey wishful thinking, conjectures, and conditions that are contrary to fact.

Expressing Requests Politely

Ich **möchte** gern bezahlen.	*I would like to pay.*
Ich **hätte** gern eine Tasse Kaffee.	*I would like a cup of coffee.*
Könntest du mir einen Gefallen tun?	*Could you do me a favor?*
Würdest du mir 50 Euro leihen?	*Would you lend me 50 Euro?*
Dürfte ich mal Ihren Pass sehen?	*May I see your passport?*

The forms **möchte, hätte, könntest, würdest,** and **dürfte** are subjunctive forms of the verbs **mögen, haben, können, werden,** and **dürfen.** They are frequently used in polite requests.

Forms of the Present Subjunctive (II)*

Present Subjunctive of Weak Verbs. Point Out: In English, "would" plus an infinitive is most often used to express nonreality, whereas German has a choice between two forms: 1. the subjunctive based on the simple past tense form, or 2. **würde** plus an infinitive. There is no difference in meaning between the two forms. More and more, the **würde** plus infinitive construction is replacing the subjunctive based on the simple past tense.

	haben	sein	können	mögen	werden	wissen
ich	hätte	wäre	könnte	möchte	würde	wüsste
du	hättest	wär(e)st	könntest	möchtest	würdest	wüsstest
er sie es	hätte	wäre	könnte	möchte	würde	wüsste
wir	hätten	wären	könnten	möchten	würden	wüssten
ihr	hättet	wär(e)t	könntet	möchtet	würdet	wüsstet
sie	hätten	wären	könnten	möchten	würden	wüssten
Sie	hätten	wären	könnten	möchten	würden	wüssten

The Present Subjunctive (II) is based on the simple past forms. Some verbs with an **-a-, -o-,** or **-u-** in the simple past form require an umlaut to be added to the vowel.

Note:

- Modals with an umlaut in the infinitive retain this umlaut in the subjunctive.

  können → konnte → könnte   *but:* sollen → sollte → sollte

  mögen → mochte → möchte

- Strong and irregular weak verbs with an **-a-, -o-,** or **-u-** in the simple past form add an umlaut to the vowel.

  sein → war → wäre   werden → wurde → würde

  haben → hatte → hätte   wissen → wusste → wüsste

- Weak verbs remain unchanged.

  kaufen → kaufte → kaufte

  wünschen → wünschte → wünschte

Übung 6   Wünsche im Restaurant

Formulieren Sie die Wünsche und Fragen sehr höflich.

BEISPIEL: Ich will ein Bier. →
Ich hätte gern ein Bier. [*oder*]
Ich möchte gern ein Bier.

1. Wir wollen die Speisekarte.
2. Ich will eine Tasse Kaffee.

---

*The forms of the subjunctive described here are also known as Subjunctive II, because they are derived from the simple past tense, the second principal part of the verb.

3. Mein Freund will ein Bier.

4. Und was wollen Sie?

5. Willst du ein Stück Kuchen?

6. Wollen Sie sonst noch etwas?

7. Wir wollen die Rechnung.

Übung 7   Im Café: Was hätten Sie gern?

BEISPIEL: ich: ein Stück Käsekuchen →
           Ich hätte gern ein Stück Käsekuchen.

1. wir: einen Platz am Fenster

2. ich: einen Espresso

3. Kerstin: einen Eiskaffee

4. Herr und Frau Haese: einen Platz in der Nichtraucherecke (*non-smoking section*)

5. wir: zwei Eisbecher mit Vanilleeis und Sahne

The Use of **würde** with an Infinitive

In spoken German, the most commonly used form of the subjunctive is **würde** plus infinitive. Like English *would,* the **würde** form can be used with almost any infinitive to express polite requests or wishes, or to give advice.

Würdest du mir **helfen**?	*Would you help me?*
Ich **würde** gerne **mitfahren**.	*I would like to come along.*
Ich **würde** nicht so viel **trinken**.	*I wouldn't drink so much.*

Note:

- Verbs that are generally not used with **würde** include **sein, haben, wissen,** and the modals.

Wenn die Studienkosten nur nicht so hoch **wären**.	*If only the cost of studying weren't so high.*
Wenn ich nur **wüsste**, wo meine Schlüssel sind.	*If I only knew where my keys were.*

Übung 8   Etwas höflicher, bitte!

Drücken Sie die folgenden Wünsche höflicher aus.

BEISPIEL: Leih mir bitte 50 Euro. →
           Würdest du mir bitte 50 Euro leihen? [*oder*]
           Könntest du mir bitte 50 Euro leihen?

1. Tu mir bitte einen Gefallen.

2. Tut mir bitte einen Gefallen.

3. Tun Sie mir den Gefallen und gehen Sie jetzt.

4. Leih mir bitte 100 Euro bis zum Monatsende.

5. Wechseln Sie mir bitte 200 Euro.

6. Geben Sie mir auch etwas Kleingeld.

7. Hilf mir bitte!

8. Helft mir bitte!

9. Unterschreiben Sie die Reiseschecks, bitte.

10. Zeigen Sie mir bitte Ihren Pass.

Übung 8. Note: Because subjunctive forms to express politeness are commonly used in German, use this exercise to elicit as many variations of individual sentences from students as possible.

Suggestion: One student requests something of another, using an imperative. The other in turn says *Etwas höflicher bitte: Würdest du bitte...* , etc.

Suggestion: Have students make up additional requests in the imperative. Ask individual students to rephrase the requests more politely.

Übung 9　Wie würden Sie darauf reagieren?

BEISPIEL:　Sie haben eine Sprachreise nach Österreich gewonnen. →
　　　　　　 Das wäre toll.

Sie sollen mit Freunden Bungeejumping
　gehen.
Sie haben eine Million Dollar gewonnen.
Sie haben ein Praktikum bei einer
　deutschen Firma bekommen.
Sie sind durch eine Prüfung gefallen (*failed
　a test*).
Sie haben Ihre Autoschlüssel verloren.
Ihre Freunde machen ohne Sie eine Reise
　in die Karibik.
Sie haben die Möglichkeit, eine Reise in
　einem Raumschiff zu machen.

Das wäre toll.
Das wäre nichts für mich.
Ich wäre sehr ärgerlich
　darüber.
Ich hätte Angst davor.
Ich wäre neidisch (*envious*).

Expressing Wishes and Hypothetical Situations

Wishes introduced with **wenn** require the subjunctive. The particles **doch,
nur,** and **doch nur** are frequently added to conversational **wenn-**clauses for
emphasis.

Wenn ich **doch** mehr Geld **hätte.**	*If only I had more money.*
Wenn ich **doch nur** mehr sparen **könnte.**	*If only I could save more money.*
Wenn Benzin nicht so teuer **wäre.**	*If only gasoline weren't so expensive.*
Wenn ich **nur wüsste,** wo meine Autoschlüssel sind.	*If I only knew where my car keys were.*
Wenn Stefan **doch** nicht so viel Geld für seinen Wagen **ausgeben würde.**	*If only Stefan didn't spend so much money on his car.*

Ich wünschte and **ich wollte** (*I wish*) are fixed expressions in the subjunctive. They are always followed by a verb in the subjunctive or **würde** +
infinitive.

Ich wollte, die Geschäfte in Deutschland **wären** länger geöffnet.	*I wish (that) the stores in Germany were open longer.*
Frau Schiff **wünschte,** sie **könnte** auch abends einkaufen.	*Ms. Schiff wishes she could go shopping in the evenings, too.*

The expression **an deiner Stelle** (*if I were you / in your place*) is always used with a verb in the subjunctive. The possessive adjective changes depending on the person in question.

An deiner Stelle würde ich alles bar bezahlen.

If I were you, I would pay cash for everything.

An seiner Stelle würde ich nicht mit Kreditkarte bezahlen.

If I were in his place, I would not pay with a credit card.

Übung 10   Was sind die Tatsachen hier?

Folgen Sie dem Beispiel.

BEISPIEL: Ich wünschte, ich könnte dir Geld leihen. →
Ich habe aber kein Geld. Ich kann dir nichts leihen.

1. Ich wünschte, ich hätte keine Kreditkarte. Dann hätte ich keine Schulden.
2. Ich wollte, die Kosten für das Studium wären nicht so hoch.
3. Ich wünschte, ich könnte genug Geld für eine Weltreise sparen.
4. Klaus wünschte, er würde nicht so viel Geld für Telefonieren ausgeben.
5. Wir wünschten, wir könnten eine preiswerte Wohnung in München finden.
6. Ich wollte, ich hätte mehr Zeit für Sport.
7. Mein Freund wollte, er könnte sich einen BMW kaufen.
8. Ich wünschte, das Semester wäre zu Ende.
9. Die Studenten wünschten, sie müssten nicht so schwer arbeiten.

Übung 11   Wenn doch nur...

Was wünscht Helga sich?

BEISPIEL: Helgas Katze ist weg. →
Wenn die Katze doch nur wieder da wäre!

1. Helga kann ihre Schlüssel nicht finden.
2. Sie hat keine Zeit, sie zu suchen.
3. Sie weiß nicht, wo sie sind.
4. Ihr Freund kommt erst spät nach Hause.
5. Sie ist ganz allein.
6. Sie kann nicht zu Hause bleiben.
7. Sie muss um drei zu einer Vorlesung gehen.

Übung 12   Wer wünscht sich was?

Drücken Sie aus, was sich diese Leute wünschen. Benutzen Sie dabei Konjunktivformen.

BEISPIEL: Gerhard hat nie Zeit. Was wünscht er sich? →
Er wünschte sich, er hätte mehr Zeit. [*oder*]
Wenn er doch mehr Zeit hätte!

1. Frau Schmidt fährt viel zu schnell auf der Autobahn. Was wünscht sich Herr Schmidt?
2. Herr Schmidt kann nicht gut Auto fahren. Was wünscht sich Frau Schmidt?

Suggestion: The expression *an seiner/ihrer Stelle* allows students to practice the subjunctive without having to formulate a complex conditional clause with *wenn*. Create short sentences with weak verbs, e.g., *sparen, kaufen, reisen, studieren, sagen, warten, mit Kreditkarte bezahlen, bar bezahlen*. Say *Hans spart nicht*. The student response is *An seiner Stelle würde ich sparen*. Have another student give the English meaning: "(If I were) in his place, I would save money." Other cues: *Er kauft ein Motorrad. Er reist allein. Er kauft auf Kredit. Er wartet stundenlang auf seine Freundin.*

Übung 10. Follow-up: Have students state their own wishes and then give the facts.

3. Es gibt nichts Interessantes im Fernsehen. Was wünsche ich mir?
4. Max ist total pleite. Was wünscht er sich?
5. Die Gäste bleiben viel zu lange, es ist schon nach Mitternacht. Was wünscht sich der Gastgeber?
6. Morgen fliegt mein Freund nach Tahiti. Ich muss leider zu Hause bleiben. Was wünsche ich mir?
7. Alex und Tanja besuchen Berlin, aber sie können leider kein Deutsch sprechen. Was wünschen sie sich?
8. Petra kann keine Wohnung finden. Was wünscht sie sich?
9. Die Kosten für Bücher sind zu hoch. Was wünschen die Studenten sich?

Übung 13. Suggestion: Have students focus on the situations in the drawings, asking them to describe the scenes. Then have them express what they would do if they found themselves in one of those situations. Encourage them to use the verbs given with the exercise, but also to go beyond them.

Übung 13   Heikle Situationen

Beschreiben Sie zuerst die Situation auf jedem Bild. Suchen Sie einen passenden Ausdruck aus der Liste. Überlegen Sie sich dann, was Sie an seiner oder ihrer Stelle tun würden.

BEISPIEL: An ihrer Stelle würde ich weggehen.

1.   2.   3.

1. weggehen; „Guten Tag" sagen; freundlich sein; nichts sagen; böse (*angry*) sein; nicht mit ihm reden; ??
2. eine Reparaturwerkstatt anrufen; sich ins Auto setzen und warten, bis der Regen aufhört; Hilfe anbieten (*offer*); um Hilfe bitten; zu Fuß weitergehen; den Reifen wechseln (*change the tire*); ??
3. nicht länger warten; allein ins Kino gehen; ungeduldig (*impatient*) sein; bei... anrufen; ??

Talking about Contrary-to-Fact Conditions

Compare the following sentences:

Wenn ich Geld **brauche, gehe** ich zur Bank.

When I need money, I go to the bank.

Wenn ich Geld **hätte, würde** ich mir einen neuen Wagen **kaufen.**

If I had money, I would buy a new car.

The first example states a condition of fact. The second example states a condition that is contrary to fact. The implication is that the speaker does not have enough money to buy a new car. In such cases, the subjunctive is used, in German as well as in English.

Die Schnecke in diesem Cartoon singt ein bekanntes deutsches Volkslied (*folk song*).

- Circle the verbs that express the snail's wishful thinking. Note that these verb forms differ from those you have learned: they have no **-e** ending. What could be the reason for this?

- State the three things the snail wishes to be, to have, or to do. (Note that the suffix **-lein,** when added to a noun, makes a diminutive of this noun.)

  > der Vogel (*bird*) → das Vöglein
  >
  > der Flügel (*wing*) → das Flüglein

  Sie möchte...

- Was sind die Tatsachen (*facts*) ihres Lebens?
  Eine Schnecke ist kein Vöglein; sie hat... und...

- Interessiert sich die zweite Schnecke für die Sängerin? Was würden Sie als Beweise (*evidence*) dafür anführen?

Analyse: Play or sing this well-known folk tune, which describes the longing of a young lover who is separated from his/her beloved. Point out that the text uses a form of the subjunctive of the strong verb *fliegen (flög[e])* that is less common in contemporary German but is still used and found in writing.

Unglückliche Verhältnisse[1]

[1]Unglückliche... *Unhappy conditions*
[2]*little bird*
[3]*little wings*
[4]Diese... *This lame snail gets on my nerves.*

Übung 14   Was würden Sie machen, wenn... ?

Sagen Sie, was Sie machen würden, wenn alles anders wäre.

BEISPIEL: Wenn ich Talent hätte, würde ich Opernsängerin werden.

Wenn ich Zeit hätte,	ein berühmter / eine berühmte __??__ (z.B. Sänger/Sängerin) werden.
Geld	interessante Leute kennen lernen.
Talent	öfter ins Kino gehen.
mehr Freizeit	eine Insel im Pazifik kaufen.
Präsident/Präsidentin wäre,	jeden Tag die Zeitung lesen.
??	??

Follow-up: Half the class writes *wenn*-clauses, the other half result-clauses only. Call on students to combine clauses; the attempt might produce some odd and amusing combinations!

Übung 15   Rat geben

Stellen Sie sich vor, ein Freund / eine Freundin hat ein Problem. Was raten Sie?

BEISPIEL: S1: Ich bin total pleite. Was soll ich nur machen?
           S2: Du solltest dir eine Arbeit suchen. [oder]
               Wenn ich total pleite wäre, würde ich mir eine Arbeit suchen.

PROBLEM	RAT
habe Zahnschmerzen	Arbeit suchen
kann nicht schlafen	Geld von jemand leihen
esse zu viel Schokolade	sofort zum Zahnarzt gehen
bin immer müde und schlapp	keine Schokolade mehr kaufen
habe kein Geld	Vitamintabletten einnehmen
??	nicht so spät schlafen gehen
	??

The Past Subjunctive°

Der Konjunktiv der Vergangenheit

The past subjunctive is used to express wishes and conjectures concerning events in the past.

> Wenn ich in der Lotterie **gewonnen hätte, wäre** ich überglücklich **gewesen.**

> *If I had won the lottery, I would have been ecstatic.*

The conjecture (*If I had...*) speculates about an event in the past: The speaker did not win the lottery. Both English and German require the past subjunctive in this case.

The past subjunctive forms are derived from the past perfect tense. Use the subjunctive form **hätte** or **wäre** plus the past participle of the main verb.

INFINITIVE	PAST PERFECT	PAST SUBJUNCTIVE
kaufen	ich hatte gekauft	ich hätte gekauft
sein	ich war gewesen	ich wäre gewesen

> Ich wünschte, ich **hätte** den neuen Porsche nicht **gekauft.**

> *I wish I had not bought the new Porsche.*

> Ein gebrauchter Wagen **wäre** billiger **gewesen.**

> *A used car would have been cheaper.*

Note:

- Use **hätte** or **wäre** according to the same rules that determine the use of **haben** or **sein** in the perfect tense (see **Kapitel 7**).

Ich **hatte** die Miete **bezahlt.**

Lars **hätte** die Miete nicht **bezahlt.**

Er **war** in die Stadt **gefahren.**

Ich **wäre** nicht in die Stadt **gefahren.**

- The **würde**-form is not used in the past subjunctive.

A clause stating a hypothetical situation usually begins with the conjunction **wenn.** As in English, the conjunction can be omitted, in which case the conjugated verb is placed at the beginning of the sentence.

Hätten wir nur gewusst, dass Ute hier ist, so wären wir sofort vorbeigekommen.

Had we only known that Ute was here, we would have come right over.

ANALYSE

Schauen Sie sich den Cartoon an.

- Find the verb forms in the past subjunctive and give their infinitives.
- What is the woman speculating about?
- What stereotype does the cartoon allude to? Formulate a conclusion to the hypothesis **"Wenn ich als Blondine geboren wär(e)..."**
- What is the reality of her life?

Analyse. Suggestion: Have students first describe the cartoon in German. Ask *Finden Sie diese Situation typisch? Komisch?*

Übung 16. Suggestion: Have students work in pairs. Ask each pair to come up with at least five things they would have done differently. Have several students briefly report what they would have done differently. Follow-up: Have students indicate what they would do differently.

Übung 16 Andreas ist total pleite

Wie ist das passiert? Sie sehen hier Andreas' Ausgaben für eine Woche. Schauen Sie sich die Liste an. Was hätten Sie anders gemacht?
Wofür hat er Ihrer Meinung nach (*in your opinion*) zu viel Geld ausgegeben? Machen Sie ein paar Vorschläge (*suggestions*), was Sie anders gemacht hätten.

	AUSGABEN
Geburtstagsgeschenk, Buch und Blumen für Freundin	€ 65,00
drei Sporthemden	120,00
Karte für „Phantom der Oper"	80,00
zweimal im Kino	22,00
Briefmarken	6,50
zweimal mit Freunden in der Kneipe	25,00
Bücher für Biologie und Computerwissenschaften (*computer science*)	125,00
Benzin fürs Auto	90,00
Zigaretten	48,00
dreimal zum Essen ausgegangen	59,00
Spende für Amnesty International	25,00
Telefon	<u>120,00</u>

REDEMITTEL

An seiner Stelle hätte ich nicht so viel für... ausgegeben.

Das wäre wirklich nicht nötig gewesen.

Braucht er wirklich... ? Ich hätte...

Zweimal... ? Einmal wäre genug (*enough*) gewesen.

Sprache im Kontext

Videoclips

A. Beatrice, Dennis und Jan sprechen über Geld und ihre monatlichen Ausgaben.

1. Alle drei beantworten diese Frage anders: „Was würdest du tun, wenn du eine Million Euro gewinnen würdest?". Was sagt Beatrice? Was sagt Dennis? Und Jan?

2. Wenn Sie eine Million in der Lotterie gewinnen würden, würden Sie dasselbe wie die drei machen oder etwas ganz anderes? Was?

B. Ergänzen Sie die Informationen in der Tabelle. Wenn es keine Information gibt, schreiben Sie „keine Information".

	BEATRICE	DENNIS	JAN
Wie viel Geld gibt er/sie aus für ...			
Miete?	_____	_____	_____
Telefon?	_____	_____	_____
Lebensmittel?	_____	_____	_____
Sonstiges?	_____	_____	_____
Woher bekommt er/sie sein/ihr Geld?	_____	_____	_____

C. Schauen Sie sich alle drei Interviews noch einmal an. Wen beschreiben diese Sätze? Schreiben Sie **B** für Beatrice, **D** für Dennis und **J** für Jan.

1. _____ kann nicht sehr gut mit Geld umgehen.
2. _____ will in der Zukunft Lehrer werden und kleine Kinder unterrichten.
3. _____ wohnt mit einer Freundin zusammen und teilt die Kosten.
4. _____ wohnt allein in einer Wohnung mit Kochnische.
5. _____ macht ein Magisterstudium in Kulturwissenschaften und studiert noch Politik dazu.
6. _____ lebt relativ sparsam.

Lesen

Zum Thema

Fragen zum Thema Geld. Beantworten Sie die folgenden Fragen erst selber, und interviewen Sie dann einige Personen im Kurs.

1. Haben Sie als Kind Taschengeld erhalten? Wie viel? Wie oft und wann?
2. Was war Ihr erster bezahlter Job? Was haben Sie mit dem Geld gemacht?
3. Können Sie gut sparen, oder geben Sie Ihr Geld impulsiv aus?

Auf den ersten Blick

A. Überlegen Sie sich, was Sie in den folgenden Situationen machen würden.

1. Sie sind im Restaurant und gerade mit dem Essen fertig. Da bemerken Sie, dass Sie weder Geld noch Kreditkarten bei sich haben. Was würden Sie machen?
2. Sie fahren durch Europa. Gewöhnlich übernachten Sie in Jugendherbergen, aber an einem Ort gibt es nur Hotels. Dafür haben Sie aber nicht genug Geld. Was würden Sie machen?

B. Lesen Sie die ersten zehn Zeilen der Geschichte „Fahrkarte bitte", und beantworten Sie die folgenden Fragen.

1. Wer sind die Hauptpersonen?
2. Wo findet die Geschichte statt? („Kiel" allein genügt nicht [*is not sufficient*] als Antwort.)
3. Zu welcher Tageszeit beginnt die Erzählung?
4. Was ist das Hauptproblem oder der Konflikt?

Auf den ersten Blick B: Have students write three questions about the rest of the story. As they read the story, they should try to find the answers to their questions.

von Helga M. Novak

Kiel sieht neu aus. Es ist dunkel. Ich gehe zum Hafen. Mein Schiff ist nicht da.
Es fährt morgen. Es kommt morgen vormittag an und fährt um dreizehn Uhr
wieder ab. Ich sehe ein Hotel. Im Eingang steht ein junger Mann. Er trägt einen
weinroten Rollkragenpullover.°   *turtleneck sweater*
5 Ich sage, haben Sie ein Einzelzimmer?
Er sagt, ja.
Ich sage, ich habe nur eine Handtasche bei mir, mein ganzes Gepäck ist auf
dem Bahnhof in Schließfächern.°   *lockers*
Er sagt, Zimmer einundvierzig. Wollen Sie gleich bezahlen? Ich sage, ach
10 nein, ich bezahle morgen.
Ich schlafe gut. Ich wache auf. Es regnet in Strömen.° Ich gehe hinunter. Der   *Es... It's pouring.*
junge Mann hat eine geschwollene Lippe.
Ich sage, darf ich mal telefonieren?
Er sagt, naja.
15 Ich rufe an.
Ich sage, du, ja, hier bin ich, heute noch, um eins, ja, ich komme gleich, doch
ich muß, ich habe kein Geld, mein Hotel, ach fein, ich gebe es dir zurück,
sofort, schön.
Der junge Mann steht neben mir. Er hat zugehört.
20 Ich sage, jetzt hole ich Geld. Dann bezahle ich.
Er sagt, zuerst bezahlen.
Ich sage, ich habe kein Geld, meine Freundin.
Er sagt, das kann ich mir nicht leisten.
Ich sage, aber ich muß nachher weiter.
25 Er sagt, da könnte ja jeder kommen.°   *da... anyone could say that*
Ich sage, meine Freundin kann nicht aus dem Geschäft weg.
Er lacht.
Ich sage, ich bin gleich wieder da.
Er sagt, so sehen Sie aus.°   *idiom: so... I bet you are (sarcastic)*
30 Ich sage, lassen Sie mich doch gehen. Was haben Sie denn von mir?
Er sagt, ich will Sie ja gar nicht.
Ich sage, manch einer wäre froh.°   *manch... many a man would be glad/*
Er sagt, den zeigen° Sie mir mal.   *show*
Ich sage, Sie kennen mich noch nicht.
35 Er sagt, abwarten und Tee trinken.°   *idiom: abwarten... let's wait and see*
Es kommen neue Gäste.
Er sagt, gehen Sie solange° in die Gaststube.   *for the time being*
Er kommt nach.
Ich sage, mein Schiff geht um eins.
40 Er sagt, zeigen Sie mir bitte Ihre Fahrkarte.
Er verschließt° sie in einer Kassette.°   *locks / box*
Ich sitze in der Gaststube und schreibe einen Brief.
Liebe Charlotte, seit einer Woche bin ich im „Weißen Ahornblatt" Serviererin.
Nähe Hafen. Wenn Du hier vorbeikommst, sieh doch zu mir herein. Sonst geht
45 es mir glänzend. Deine Maria.

Zum Text

1. Wer erzählt die Geschichte, ein Mann oder eine Frau? Welchen Beweis (*evidence*) können Sie dafür bringen?
2. Suchen Sie nach Wörtern und Äußerungen, die weitere Informationen über die Hauptpersonen geben. Was können Sie aus diesen Details schließen (*conclude*)? Es steht z.B. im Text, dass der junge Mann „eine geschwollene Lippe" hat.
3. Wann erfahren die Leser, dass eine der Hauptpersonen ein großes Problem hat? Wie würden Sie in dieser Situation handeln (*act*)? Welche Rolle spielt die Fahrkarte?
4. Sie hören nur eine Seite des Telefongesprächs. Was könnte die Person am anderen Ende sagen?
5. Sie sind Detektiv/Detektivin. Lesen Sie die Geschichte ein zweites Mal. Glauben Sie dieser Frau? Wenn nicht, was für Beweise haben Sie, dass sie lügt (*is lying*)?
6. Die Geschichte endet mit einem Brief. Was sagt uns der Brief über die Erzählerin? Ist Charlotte eventuell (*possibly*) dieselbe Person, mit der die Erzählerin am Telefon gesprochen hat? Welchen Beweis haben Sie dafür oder dagegen?

Sprechen und Schreiben

Aktivität 1   Ein kleines Theaterstück

Führen Sie die Geschichte „Fahrkarte bitte" als kleines Theaterstück auf. Teilen Sie die Geschichte in verschiedene Dialoge auf (z.B. Ankunft der Erzählerin, Gespräch am nächsten Morgen).

Aktivität 2   Wie könnte die Geschichte weitergehen?

Ein Monat ist vergangen. Was ist aus der Frau geworden? Schreiben Sie eine Fortsetzung (*continuation*) der Geschichte. Was macht die Frau jetzt? Ist sie noch in Kiel? Ist sie abgereist? Hat sie Geld? Ist sie glücklich?

Sprechen und Schreiben. Aktivität 2: Students can do this in groups and perform the continuation or read their stories aloud to the rest of the class.

Additional Activity: Assign students the task of playing Charlotte and answering Maria's letter.

Wortschatz

Geldangelegenheiten	Money Matters
die **Ausgabe, -n**	expense
das **Benzin**	gasoline
der **Bleistift, -e**	pencil
die **Computerdiskette, -n**	computer diskette
die **Einnahme, -n**	income
die **Ernährung**	food, nutrition
der **Haushalt, -e**	household
das **Heft, -e**	notebook

die **Heizung**	heat, heating system	**mieten**	to rent (*from someone*)
der **Kugelschreiber, -**	ballpoint pen	**sparen**	to save
der **Müll**	trash, garbage	**vergleichen, verglich,**	to compare
die **Nebenkosten**	utilities; extra costs	**verglichen**	
die **Reparatur, -en**	repair	**vermieten**	to rent out (*to someone*)
das **Sparkonto,** *pl.* **Sparkonten**	savings account		
der **Strom**	electricity		
die **Studiengebühren** (*pl.*)	tuition, fees		
die **Versicherung, -en**	insurance		

Das Haus	**The House**	**Adjektive und Adverbien**	**Adjectives and Adverbs**
das **Bauernhaus, ̈er**	farmhouse	**ab**	from, as of
das **Dach, ̈er**	roof	**ab 1. Juni (ab erstem Juni)**	as of June 1st
das **Dachgeschoss, -e**	top floor, attic		
die **Diele, -n**	front hall	**bald**	soon
der **Eingang, ̈e**	entrance	**deswegen**	because of that
die **Etage, -n**	floor, story	**durchschnittlich**	on average
der **Flur, -e**	hallway	**eigen**	own
die **Frühstücksnische, -n**	breakfast nook	**ganz**	very, completely, total(ly), entire(ly)
die **Garderobe, -n**	wardrobe; closet		
das **Gästezimmer, -**	guest room		
der **Kühlschrank, ̈e**	refrigerator	**monatlich**	monthly
der **Mikrowellenherd, -e**	microwave oven	**oben**	above; upstairs
der **Neubau, -ten**	modern building	**nach oben**	above; upstairs (*directional*)
die **Spülmaschine, -n**	dishwasher		
der **Teppichboden, ̈**	wall-to-wall carpeting	**pleite**	broke, out of money
		sparsam	thrifty
die **Treppe, -n**	staircase	**spätestens**	at the latest
die **Umgebung, -en**	area, neighborhood, vicinity	**übrig**	left over
		unten	below; downstairs
		nach unten	below; downstairs (*directional*)

Verben	**Verbs**	**Sonstiges**	**Other**
sich ärgern über (+ *acc.*)	to be annoyed about	**an deiner Stelle**	if I were you, (if I were) in your place
aus•geben (gibt aus), gab aus, ausgegeben	to spend (*money*)		
bauen	to build	die **Angst, ̈e**	fear
bitten um, bat, gebeten	to ask for, request	**Angst haben vor** (+ *dat.*)	to be afraid of
denken an (+ *acc.*), **dachte, gedacht**	to think about, of	der **Gruß, ̈e**	greeting
ein•richten	to furnish, equip	**viele Grüße**	best wishes
ein•ziehen in (+ *acc.*), **zog ein, ist eingezogen**	to move in	die **Katze, -n**	cat
sich freuen auf (+ *acc.*)	to look forward to	das **Tier, -e**	animal
sich freuen über (+ *acc.*)	to be glad about	die **Zeichnung, -en**	drawing

Use this checklist to verify that you can now . . .

- ☐ talk about money matters, your household budget, and the types of monthly expenses you have.

- ☐ describe features of typical homes, apartments, and rooms.

- ☐ understand German rental ads.

- ☐ talk and ask about things and ideas using **da-** and **wo-**compounds.

- ☐ make polite requests.

- ☐ express wishes using the subjunctive and **würde** forms.

- ☐ talk about hypothetical situations and conditions using **würde** + infinitive.

Viertes Zwischenspiel

Begegnung mit der Kunst der Gegenwart

Was ist Kunst? Das Wort „Kunst" kommt von „können". Ein Künstler oder eine Künstlerin ist ein „Könner"; jemand, der etwas „kann", z.B. malen, zeichnen, formen, komponieren, schreiben. Was erwarten Sie als Kunstbetrachter[1] von einem Kunstwerk? Soll es z.B. „schön" sein, provozieren, zum Nachdenken anregen[2] oder die Realität darstellen[3]?

Die Beispiele moderner und zeitgenössischer[4] deutscher Kunst auf diesen Seiten zeigen Kunst im Kontext von alltäglichen Dingen und ungewöhnlichen Medien. Viele Leute bewundern[5] diese Werke, andere nennen sie Werke von „Dilettanten und hochgemuten[6] Nichtskönnern". (S. 7, Faust / de Vries, „Hunger nach Bildern") Was meinen Sie?

Tisch mit Aggregat, 1958/87, Joseph Beuys

„Flaschenpost", 1990, Rolf Glasmeier

Aktivität 1   Kunstbewertung

A. Was halten Sie von diesen Kunstgebilden? Wie würden Sie sie charakterisieren?

BEISPIEL: Ich finde die „Flaschenpost" sehr witzig.

- ☐ aggressiv
- ☐ hässlich
- ☐ humorvoll
- ☐ komplex
- ☐ radikal
- ☐ schön
- ☐ verrückt
- ☐ kitschig
- ☐ witzig
- ☐ provozierend
- ☐ dilettantisch
- ☐ komisch
- ☐ originell
- ☐ faszinierend
- ☐ spektakulär
- ☐ kindisch
- ☐ phantasievoll
- ☐ kreativ
- ☐ tief[7]
- ☐ ??

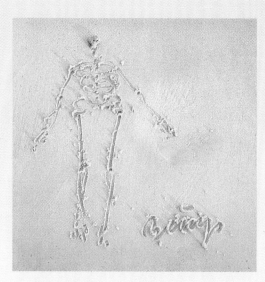

Sandzeichnung, 1975, Joseph Beuys

[1]*viewer of art* [2]*incite* [3]*represent* [4]*contemporary*
[5]*admire* [6]*arrogant* [7]*profound*

B. Besprechen Sie die folgenden Fragen im Plenum.

1. Welches dieser Kunstwerke gefällt Ihnen besonders gut? Wenn Ihnen keins davon gefällt, warum nicht?
2. Erinnert Sie das eine oder andere dieser Kunstwerke an etwas, was Sie schon einmal, vielleicht in einem Museum, gesehen haben? Sind Ihnen die Namen der Künstler bekannt? Wenn ja, welche Namen?
3. Wer ist Ihr Lieblingskünstler / Ihre Lieblingskünstlerin?
4. Was für Kunstwerke oder Reproduktionen von Kunstwerken haben Sie in Ihrem Zimmer oder in Ihrer Wohnung?
5. Wenn Sie eins dieser Kunstwerke erwerben[1] könnten, welches würden Sie wählen, und warum?

claus bremer

Konkrete Poesie

Hier sind zwei Beispiele konkreter Poesie. Charakteristisch für sie ist der visuelle Aspekt. Das Visuelle kann z.B. ein Piktogramm sein oder eine Figur, die mit Buchstaben und Wörtern gefüllt ist. Was halten Sie von Claus Bremers und Reinhard Döhls konkreter Poesie?

...elApfelApfelAp...
...pfelApfelApfelApfe...
...elApfelApfelApfelAp...
...ApfelApfelApfelApfelA...
...pfelApfelApfelApfelApfe...
...elApfelApfelApfelApfelAp...
...pfelApfelApfelApfelApfe...
...ApfelApfelApfelWurmApfelA...
...elApfelApfelApfelApfe...
...elApfelApfelApfelApfelAr...
...ApfelApfelApfelApfelA...
...ApfelApfelApfelA...
reinhard döhl ...ApfelApfelA...

Aktivität 2   Sie sind dran[2]

A. Schreiben Sie jetzt Ihr eigenes konkretes Gedicht.

B. Schreiben Sie ein Gedicht im Fünfzeilenformat:

Erste Zeile:	ein Substantiv
Zweite Zeile:	zwei Adjektive
Dritte Zeile:	drei Verben im Infinitiv
Vierte Zeile:	ein Satz, eine Frage oder ein Ausdruck
Fünfte Zeile:	Wiederholung der ersten Zeile, oder ein anderes Substantiv

„Der Leser", 1981, Georg Jiří Dokoupil

[1]*acquire*   [2]*Sie... Now it's your turn*

Medien und Technik

Was kaufen diese Leute?
a. einen Fernseher
b. eine Zeitung
c. eine Zeitschrift

Kapitel 13. Suggestion: Ask students to name any German newspapers or magazines they know, other than those pictured on the next page. Is there a German language newspaper in your area of the United States? If so, bring in a copy to show to your students. Bring in copies of any newspapers and magazines you have from Germany, Austria, or Switzerland.

Videoclips
In der Zeitung steht...

In diesem Kapitel

- **Themen:** Television, newspaper, and other media; technology
- **Grammatik:** Verbs **brauchen** and **scheinen,** infinitive clauses with **zu,** indirect discourse, infinitive clauses with **um... zu** and **ohne... zu**
- **Kultur:** Radio and television, inventions

Alles klar?

A. Hier sehen Sie Werbungen verschiedener deutscher Zeitungen für preiswerte Studenten-Abonnements (Abos). Welche Zeitung(en)

- liest man wahrscheinlich in München?
- trägt den Namen einer Stadt?
- kommt aus Düsseldorf?
- erscheint täglich?

B. Sie hören vier kurze Berichte aus dem Radio. Welche Schlagzeile passt zu welchem Bericht? Schreiben Sie die passende Zahl (1–4) vor die Schlagzeile.

_____3_____ Kluges (*smart*) Köpfchen vorm Mittagessen

_____4_____ Spender (*donor*) der Woche

_____2_____ Unbekanntes Dorf im Iran entdeckt

_____1_____ Autodieb (*car thief*) auf Surfbrett gefangen

Wörter im Kontext

Hier klicken!

Weiteres zum Thema
Medien finden Sie bei
Deutsch: Na klar! im
World-Wide-Web unter
www.mhhe.com/dnk.

THEMA 1: Medien

Was gibt's im Fernsehen?

THOMAS: Was gibt's denn heute Abend im Fernsehen?

BARBARA: Nach den **Nachrichten** um 19 Uhr kommt im zweiten **Programm** eine Familienserie, „Forsthaus Falkenau".

THOMAS: Eine Seifenoper, nein danke! Das ist nichts für mich! **Das ist mir zu blöd!** Was gibt's denn bei ARD?

BARBARA: Auch eine Seifenoper, „Gute Zeiten, schlechte Zeiten" und eine Komödie, „Die Nanny".

THOMAS: Auch **nichts Gescheites.**

BARBARA: Was möchtest du denn sehen?

Neue Wörter

Nachrichten news
Das ist mir zu blöd! I think that's really stupid!
nichts Gescheites nothing decent
das Programm program, channel
Bericht report
Spielfilm movie, feature film
ansehen watch
Such dir etwas aus! (sich etwas aussuchen) Choose something!
Wie wäre es mit... ? How about . . . ?
Na und? So what?
auf jeden Fall in any case
Sendung TV program
Wovon handelt er? (handeln von) What's it about?

THOMAS: Na, vielleicht einen Krimi oder Sport... oder einen **Dokumentarfilm.**

BARBARA: Um 20.15 gibt es einen Krimi, „Siska", und später, um 21.45, kommt „heute-journal" mit einem **Bericht** über die Fußballweltmeisterschaft. Aber keine Dokumentarfilme. Ich möchte mir mal einen guten **Spielfilm ansehen.**

THOMAS: Du hast ja das Programm für heute Abend. **Such dir was aus!**

BARBARA: **Wie wäre es mit** „Citizen Kane"?

THOMAS: So ein alter Schinken (*old hat*)!

BARBARA: **Na und?** Das ist **auf jeden Fall** ein guter, alter Klassiker.

THOMAS: Um 0.40 läuft die **Sendung** „Eine französische Frau".

BARBARA: Das ist mir viel zu spät.

THOMAS: Also dann „Citizen Kane". **Wovon handelt er** übrigens?

Was steht in der Zeitung?

Hier sind einige typische Rubriken aus der Zeitung, bzw. der **Zeitschrift.**

A. Welche Rubriken...

- lesen Sie immer? nie? manchmal?
- finden Sie am interessantesten?

B. Finden Sie nun eine passende **Schlagzeile** für die Rubriken.

Neue Wörter

Zeitschrift magazine
Schlagzeile headline
Inland at home, domestic, national
Aktuelles current events
Wirtschaft economy
Börse stock market
Forschen research

RUBRIKEN

Lokalnachrichten	**Aktuelles**	Sport
Inland	**Wirtschaft** und **Börse**	Reisen
Ausland	Arbeit und Karriere	**Horoskop**
Politik	Wissen und **Forschen**	Kultur

SCHLAGZEILEN

HIGHTECH-KRISE REISST DAX[1] IN DIE TIEFE

Asteroid auf Kollisionskur—möglicher Einschlag auf der Erde im Jahre 2010

Internet-Cafés: Berliner Polizei warnt vor illegalen Spielen

Was sagen die Sterne heute?

Panik an den Börsen

Scharfe Proteste gegen Luftangriff auf Zivilisten in Afghanistan

Traumjob: Diplomat werden Jobs aus dem Netz

Brandenburgs Justizminister tritt zurück

BERLIN: JEDER ACHTE LEBT IN ARMUT

Gentechnik: Embryonen-Patent umfasst keine menschlichen und tierischen Stammzellen mehr

Die 91. Bayreuther Festspiele eröffnen mit dem alten „Tannhäuser"

Schritt für Schritt nach Westen: Neuer Wanderweg führt quer durch die USA

Fußball-Weltmeisterschaft: vier Teams—zwei bleiben, zwei fahren heim

[1] *German stock market*

ARD+ZDF RADIO UND TV

Anmelden
leicht gemacht

Rundfunkgebühren
für Hörfunk und Fernsehen

GEZ 50656 Köln   **Anmeldung für den Privathaushalt**

Belegart 0100-4

Sind Sie bereits bei der
GEZ gemeldet?   Nein ☐ Ja ☐   Rundfunkteilnehmer-Nummer ☐☐☐☐☐☐☐☐

Bitte tragen Sie
hier Ihre **gültige
Anschrift** ein.

Name, Vorname (Umlaute ä, ö, ü, und ß bitte so schreiben: Häberle, Böhme, Hübner, Groß)

Geburtsdatum   Vorwahl   Rufnummer

Telefon-Nr. tagsüber
(Angabe freiwillig)

Straße, Hausnummer

PLZ   Ort

**Wo werden
die Geräte
bereitgehalten?**

Im Privathaushalt (Anschrift s. o.): In der Zweit- oder Ferienwohnung: Am Arbeitsplatz:

	Tag Monat Jahr		Tag Monat Jahr		Tag Monat Jahr
☐ Hörfunkgerät ab		☐ Hörfunkgerät ab		☐ Hörfunkgerät ab	
☐ Fernsehgerät ab		☐ Fernsehgerät ab		☐ Fernsehgerät ab	

**Ihre gewünschte
Zahlungsweise**
(bitte ankreuzen)

☐ durch Lastschrift von meinem/unserem Konto
Hiermit ermächtige(n) ich/wir Sie widerruflich, die
von mir/uns zu entrichtenden Rundfunkgebühren
bei Fälligkeit einzuziehen.

☐ durch Überweisung
oder mit Zahlschein

**Bitte tragen Sie hier Ihre
Kontonummer, Bankleitzahl**
und den Namen Ihrer Bank,
ggf. auch den Namen
des Kontoinhabers, für das
bequeme Abbuchen ein.

☐ jährlich
im voraus
(zum 1.1.)

☐ halbjährlich
im voraus
(zum 1.1., 1.7.)

☐ vierteljährlich
im voraus
(zum 1.1., 1.4., 1.7., 1.10.)

☐ in der Mitte eines
Dreimonatszeitraumes
(zum 15.)

Kontonummer   Bankleitzahl

◄ Bitte unbedingt angeben!

**Bitte
Datum/Unterschrift
nicht vergessen.**

Unterschrift des Rundfunkteilnehmers und ggf. des Kontoinhabers

Datum

GEZ 0100 03.96

KULTURTIPP

Lange Zeit gab es in Deutschland nur drei Programme. Die ARD (Arbeitsgemeinschaft der Rund-
funkanstalten Deutschlands)—auch „Erstes Programm" genannt—und das ZDF (Zweites Deutsches
Fernsehen) senden auch heute noch das erste und zweite Programm. Das „Dritte Programm" besteht
aus regionalen Sendern aus ganz Deutschland. In diesen drei Programmen werden die meisten
Sendungen nicht durch Werbung unterbrochen. Alle Werbespots werden blockweise zu einem
bestimmten Zeitpunkt gezeigt. Jeder Haushalt muss für Radio und Fernsehen eine Gebühr, die sogenannte Rundfunkgebühr, bezahlen.

Heutzutage gibt es in deutschsprachigen Ländern eine Vielfalt an Fernsehprogrammen. Kabelfernsehen und Satellitenprogramme, z.B. PRO 7, NBC Super-Channel und CNN, sind sehr beliebt
und zeigen viele Sendungen im amerikanischen Stil. Kabelfernsehen muss man abonnieren. Für
Sender wie Premiere (sogenannte Pay TV) muss man weitere Gebühren bezahlen.

Aktivität 1. Suggestion: Ask
your students if they recognize
any of the TV shows listed.

Suggestion: Show a German
TV program to your class.
Deutsche Welle now
broadcasts on cable stations
throughout the United States.

Aktivität ı   Das Fernsehprogramm

Suchen Sie im Fernsehprogramm auf Seite 387 eine Sendung, die zu jeder
der folgenden Kategorien passt.

BEISPIEL: Wetter →
Um 22.23 Uhr gibt es den Wetterbericht im Zweiten Programm.

1. Wetter   **3.** Spielfilm   **5.** Komödie
2. Nachrichten   **4.** Reportage   **6.** Unterhaltungssendung, z.B. Talk-Show

ARD 1

20.20

| INFO | **Monitor** |

Das Politmagazin sorgt immer wieder mit seinen kritischen Beiträgen für Furore. Seit Januar 2002 moderiert Sonia Mikich (Foto) die Sendung. Die ehemalige Russlandkorrespondentin hat sich auch als Autorin einen Namen gemacht.

20⁰⁰ **Tagesschau** ☑ 23·503
Mit Fußball-WM-Höhepunkten
20.20 Monitor ☑ 6-837-023
Politmagazin mit Sonia Mikich
21.00 Tatort (NDR) ⊙ 16:9 ☑ 13-752
Kriminalfilm, Deutschland 2001
Tod vor Scharhörn. Mit Manfred Krug, Charles Brauer, Kurt Hart, Anne Bennent, Ulrich Gebauer
Regie: Jürgen Bretzinger (Wh.)

Nachdem sie 1996 schon einmal einem „Tod auf Neuwerk" nachgegangen sind, führt ihr neuer und gleichzeitig letzter Fall Stoever (Manfred Krug, r.) und Brockmöller (Charles Brauer) wieder auf die Hamburger Inseln: Ihr Kollege Helmut Weckwört, zu dessen Pensionierung die Kommissare eben noch ein Ständchen geübt hatten, liegt erschossen im Straßengraben.
„Ein rechter Reif-für-die-Insel-Abschiedskrimi, noch einen Tick skurriler (,Leitkultur-Kohlsuppe mag er nicht, der Neger von Scharhörn') als gewohnt. Netter Rausschmeißer."
Werner Schmidtlein
22.30 Tagesthemen Nachrichten 85·874

23⁰³ **Das Wetter** 300-093-435
Mit Claudia Kleinert
23.05 Die Ehe der Maria Braun
Nachkriegsdrama, D 1978 2-853-232
Mit Hanna Schygulla, Klaus Löwitsch, Ivan Desny († 2002); Regie: Rainer W. Fassbinder († '82) Wh.
„Selten hat man so viele Schauspieler so gut in einem Fassbinder-Film gesehen" (Frankfurter Allgemeine)
1.00 Nachtmagazin 1-485-530
1.20 Warum läuft Herr R. Amok?
Gesellschaftsdrama, D 1969 8-128-820
Mit Kurt Raab († 1988), Hanna Schygulla, Amadeus Fengler
Regie: Rainer Werner Fassbinder († 1982), Michael Fengler (Wh.)
„Eine satanisch-satirische Studie des Alltagsgrauens" (AZ, München).
2.45 Tagesschau 13-838-191
2.50 Fliege Talk (Wh.) 1-092-172
3.50 Bahnstrecken Europas 4-516-066
4.00 ARD-Buffet ⊙ (Wh.) 7-188-998
4.50 Monitor ☑ (Wh.) 2-964-714

ZDF

20.15

| MUSIK | **Herzlichst Hansi …** |

Sommergrüße vom Wolfgangsee. Hansi Hinterseer (Foto) zieht es in den Ferien an den schönsten See seiner österreichischen Heimat. Viele Gäste sind ihm gefolgt, u. a. Peter Kraus, Johannes Heesters, Gaby Albrecht.

20¹⁵ **Herzlichst Hansi Hinterseer**
⊙ Sommergrüße 896-481
vom Wolfgangsee. Gäste: Geschwandtner, Hansi Hinterseer, Familie Leimer, Andrea Berg, Peter Kraus, Johannes Heesters, Seer, G. G. Anderson, Gaby Albrecht, Paldauer, Waltraut Haas, Lena Valaitis, Lothar Matthäus u. a.
■ Zwei weitere Hansi-Hinterseer-Specials folgen am 15. August (Ost-Tirol) und am 7. November (Besuch auf dem ZDF-„Traumschiff").
21.15 auslandsjournal ⊙ 767-145
Mit Dietmar Ossenberg
21.45 heute-journal/
⚽ **Fußball-WM 2002** ⊙ ☑ 7-259-706
Moderation: Wolf von Lojewski
22.23 Wetter 309-366-313
22.25 Berlin Mitte ⊙ 9-007-329
Talk-Show mit Maybrit Illner

Die kontroverse Gesprächsrunde mit Maybrit Illner (Foto) gehört mit 2,5 Millionen Zuschauern im Durchschnitt zu den beliebtesten Talk-Shows. Wie jeden Donnerstag hat die Moderatorin auch heute interessante Gäste nach Berlin ingeladen.

23¹⁰ **Die Johannes-B.-Kerner-Show** ⊙ 8-550-139
Gäste: Klaus Kinkel, Claudia Jung, Ivars Weide
0.10 heute nacht ⊙ 5-414-443
0.25 SOKO 5113 ⊙ (Wh.) 1-234-153
1.10 heute Nachrichten 80-009-608
1.15 Eine französische Frau ⊙ 16:9
(Une femme française) 1-105-795
Melodram, F/GB/D 1994. Mit Emmanuelle Béart, Daniel Auteuil, Gabriel Barylli, Jean-Claude Brialy, Heinz Bennent; Regie: R. Wargnier
Die Ehe des Offiziers Louis wird durch die Seitensprünge seiner jungen Frau Jeanne gestört. Als sie eine Affäre mit einem Deutschen beginnt, eskaliert der Konflikt. (Wh.)
„Feinfühlig inszeniert" (tz, München).
2.50 heute nacht 13-835-004
2.55 J.-B.-Kerner-Show 5-947-172
3.50 heute Nachrichten 61-656-882
3.55 Berlin Mitte ⊙ (Wh.) 2-348-608
4.40 citydreams 1-509-578
5.05 hallo Deutschland ⊙ 1-736-004

RTL 2

20.15

| SCI-FI | **Stargate** |

Die Goa'Uld unter Tanith (Peter Wingfield) bedrohen die friedliebenden Tollaner. Kanzler Travell (Marie Stillin) wird gezwungen, den Goa'Uld eine hochwirksame Waffe zu liefern, um sie gegen die Erde einzusetzen. Gibt es einen Ausweg?

20⁰⁰ **News** 682-763
Nachrichten und Wetter
20.15 Stargate 196-102
US-Science-Fiction-Serie
Der Kampf der Tollaner
Jack O'Neill....Richard D. Anderson
Daniel Jackson ......Michael Shanks
Major Carter........Amanda Tapping
Teal'C..............Christopher Judge
21.15 Andromeda 9-157-589
Science-Fiction-Serie. Planet Möbius
Captain Dylan Hunt .....Kevin Sorbo
Beka Valentine ....Lisa Ryder
Tyr Anasazi ....Keith Hamilton Cobb

Weil die Andromeda-Crew den demokratischen Planeten Möbius vor einer feindlichen Invasion retten will, muss Rommie (Lexa Doig) sich auf eine gefährliche Spionage-Mission begeben.
22.15 Lexx 9-275-270
Science-Fiction-Serie. TV-Planet Xev ....Xenia Seeberg
Stanley Tweedle........Brian Downey
Kai ....Michael McManus
Auf einem TV-Planeten erhalten die Lexx-Mitglieder die Chance, Fernsehstars zu werden. Vor allem Xev hat großen Erfolg.

23⁰⁵ **Poltergeist:**
Die unheimliche Macht 5-874-305
US-Horrorserie. John Doe -
Der unbekannte Kapitän
Rachel kümmert sich um einen Unbekannten, der seine wahre Identität nicht kennt und dem alles zu Eis gefriert, was er berührt.
0.00 exklusiv - die reportage 109-868
TV-Wahnsinn total - Fernseh-Helden aus der Provinz (Wh.)
0.50 News (Wh. von 20.00) 5-864-077
1.00 Das Zugunglück 9-061-313
(Day of the Roses) Katastrophenthriller, Austral. 1998. Mit Rebecca Gibney; Regie: Peter Fisk (Wh.)
3.00 Klippe des Todes 3-936-139
(Incident at Deception Ridge)
Krimi, USA 1994. Mit Michael O'Keefe, Ed Begley jr., Linda Purl
Regie: John McPherson (Wh.)
„Miserabel inszeniert" (film-dienst).
4.40 Adrenalin - Notärzte 5-668-416
im Einsatz Serie. Teuflische Kräfte

VOX

20.15

| SCI-FI | **J. Camerons Dark Angel** |

Tinga ist tot und Max (Jessica Alba, l., mit Michael Weatherly) sinnt auf Rache. Als sie sich auf Lydecker stürzt, wird sie überwältigt. Doch nicht Lydecker ist verantwortlich. Er entkommt und will Max dazu überreden, Manticore zu zerstören.

20¹⁵ **James Camerons** 259-594
Dark Angel (20) Letzte Folge der Sci-Fi-Serie. Das letzte Gefecht
Max Guevara..............Jessica Alba
Logan Cale ....Michael Weatherly
Original Cindy .....Valarie Rae Miller
Normal ..................J.C. MacKenzie
Sketchy ....Richard Gunn
Herbal Thought........Alimi Ballard
■ Ab nächsten Dienstag: Wh. dieser Staffel, ab November dann Staffel 2
21.10 stern TV-Reportage 9-176-614
Ein Herz für Nils - die dramatische Rettung eines Dreijährigen

Wann findet sich endlich ein Spenderherz für den todkranken Nils (Foto) ? Seit Monaten warten die Eltern auf den erlösenden Anruf, der für ihren Sohn die Rettung bedeuten würde.
22.10 Ally McBeal 1-107-481
US-Comedyserie. Duo im Abseits
Mit Calista Flockhart, Courtney Thorne-Smith, Greg Germann
Auf der Flucht vor ihren Verehrern, stolpert Ally im Restaurant über eine ehemalige Kommilitonin: Kimmy. Sie stellt Ally ihren Freundinnen als sehr prüde vor.

23⁰⁵ **Ally McBeal** 5-892-701
Comedy. Herz zu verschenken
0.00 Spätnachrichten 478-657
0.10 Halifax: Déjà-vu 5-845-675
(Halifax: Deja vu) Psychothriller, Austral. 1997. Mit Rebecca Gibney, Guy Pearce, Travis McMahon, Ross Williams, Philip Holder
Regie: Paul Moloney
Jane soll ihren ehemaligen Patienten Matthew begutachten. Ihm wird vorgeworfen, den Tod seiner Eltern verschuldet zu haben. Später nimmt er sich das Leben. Jane wendet sich an Matthews Bruder.
1.55 Tödlicher Verdacht 44-200-675
(Deep Family Secrets) Melodram, USA 1997. Mit Richard Crenna, Angie Dickinson, Molly Gross, Christie Lynn Smith (Wh.)
3.30 auto motor und sport tv 2-431-831
4.35 stern TV-Reportage 4-012-102
Ein Herz für Nils (Wh. von 21.10)
5.25 Rave Dance-Night 65-335-183

Aktivität 2 Hin und her: Wie informieren sie sich?

Wie informieren sich diese Personen? Was lesen sie zur Unterhaltung? Stellen Sie Fragen an Ihren Partner / Ihre Partnerin.

BEISPIEL: S1: Was sieht Martin gern im Fernsehen? Was liest er oft?
S2: Er _____.

PERSON	FERNSEHSHOWS	ZEITUNGEN UND ZEITSCHRIFTEN
Martin	Talk-Shows und Dokumentarfilme	*die Zeit* und *die TAZ*
Stephanie	klassische Spielfilme und Komödien	*der Spiegel*
Patrick	Quizsendungen wie „Der Preis ist heiß", die Nachrichten	*die Frankfurter Allgemeine* und *Stern*
Kristin	Sportsendungen, Krimi-Serien wie „Mord ist ihr Hobby"	*das Handelsblatt, die Welt* und *Brigitte*
Mein Partner / Meine Partnerin		

Aktivität 3 Das sehe ich gern!

Was mögen Sie im Fernsehen? Warum? Was finden Sie nicht besonders gut im Fernsehen? Geben Sie Beispiele.

BEISPIEL: Ich mag Serien, zum Beispiel „Friends". Die finde ich spannend. Aber Quizsendungen finde ich schrecklich langweilig.

Krimis	gewöhnlich	aktuell
Nachrichten	immer	interessant
Dokumentarfilme	meistens	komisch
Quizsendungen	schrecklich	langweilig
Talk-Shows	sehr	spannend
Seifenopern		schlecht
Sport		unterhalt-sam
Serien		
Musik		
Komödien		

Aktivität 4 Eine Sendung auswählen

Besprechen Sie mit einem Partner / einer Partnerin, was Sie heute Abend sehen möchten. Wählen Sie eine Sendung aus dem Fernsehprogramm in **Aktivität 1** aus.

S1	S2
1. Was gibt es heute Abend im Fernsehen?	**2.** Um _____ gibt es _____.
3. Was ist denn das?	**4a.** Das ist eine Sendung über _____. **b.** Keine Ahnung, klingt aber interessant.
5. Wer spielt mit?	**6.** Hier steht _____.
7. Wie lange dauert das?	**8a.** _____Stunden/Minuten **b.** Von _____ Uhr bis _____ Uhr.
9. Was gibt es sonst noch?	**10a.** Magst du _____? **b.** Wie wäre es mit _____?
11a. Ja, das finde ich _____. **b.** Nein, ich sehe lieber _____. **c.** Ich lese heute Abend lieber.	**12.** Na gut.

THEMA 2: Leben mit Technik

Blick in deutsche Wohnungen

Von je 100 Haushalten in Deutschland sind ausgestattet mit

Kühlschrank	99
Fernsehgerät	96
Telefon (stationär)	96
Waschmaschine	95
Fahrrad	78
Pkw	75
Gefriergerät	73
Videorecorder	69
Hi-Fi-Anlage	65
Mikrowellengerät	58
Mobiltelefon	56
Kabelanschluss	54
PC	53
Geschirrspülmaschine	51
Anrufbeantworter	43
Wäschetrockner	33
Satellitenempfangsanlage	32
Internetzugang	27
Modem	22
Videokamera, Camcorder	18
Faxgerät	16
ISDN-Anschluss	12

7881 © Globus   Stand 2001/aktualisiert Mitte 2002, Quelle: Stat. Bundesamt

Schauen Sie sich das Schaubild an und beantworten Sie die Fragen.

- Welche **Geräte,** die Sie für **nützlich** halten, besitzen Sie auch? Welche haben Sie nicht?

Neue Wörter

nützlich useful
Pkw = Personen-kraftwagen car
Geschirrspülma-schine dishwasher
Wäschetrockner clothes dryer
Geräte appliances, equipment
erfunden (erfinden) invented
Erfindungen inventions
unbedingt absolutely
auf... verzichten (verzichten auf) do without
Anrufbeantworter answering machine
Drucker printer
Staubsauger vacuum cleaner

- Welche Geräte hat man in den letzten fünfzig Jahren **erfunden**?
- Was sind **Erfindungen** der letzten zwanzig Jahre?

Elektrogeräte . . .

...im Arbeitszimmer		...im Schlafzimmer
Telefon	Lautsprecher-Boxen (2-4 Dosen)	Telefon
Anrufbeantworter	Kopierer	Fernsehgerät
Telefax-Gerät	Rechen-maschine	Videogerät
Fernsehgerät	Computer	Radio
Videogerät	Drucker	Radiowecker
Radio	Uhr	Alarmanlage
CD-Player	Aquarium (3-5 Dosen)	Staubsauger
DVD-Spieler	Staubsauger	Fernsehgerät
Cassettendeck		

- Welche von diesen Geräten haben Sie in Ihrem Arbeitszimmer oder Schlafzimmer?
- Welche sind für Sie **unbedingt** notwendig?
- **Auf** welche könnten Sie **verzichten**?

Aktivität 5 Wozu sind sie nützlich?

Was passt zusammen?

GERÄTE	DAMIT KANN MAN
1. _g_ Fernseher	a. schnell Essen zubereiten
2. _j_ Videogerät	b. die Wohnung sauber machen
3. _a_ Mikrowellenherd	c. Filme ansehen
4. _k_ Wäschetrockner	d. morgens rechtzeitig aufwachen
5. _h_ Heimcomputer	e. von unterwegs telefonieren
6. _i_ Anrufbeantworter	f. schriftliche Nachrichten per Telefon senden
7. _f_ Faxgerät	g. sich über Geschehnisse in der Welt informieren
8. _b_ Staubsauger	h. Texte verarbeiten
9. _d_ Radiowecker	i. telefonische Nachrichten hinterlassen
10. _e_ Handy	j. Filme und Sendungen aufnehmen
11. _c_ DVD-Spieler	k. Wäsche trocknen

Schauen Sie sich das Schaubild an und beantworten Sie dann die folgenden Fragen.

■ Wie viele Patentanmeldungen gibt es insgesamt für jedes Land?

■ Nennen Sie mindestens zwei Erfindungen (*inventions*) aus Ihrem Land.

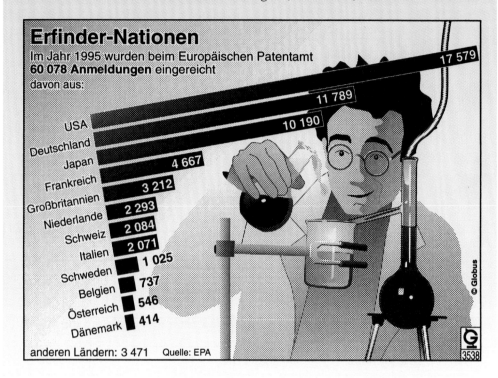

Erfinder-Nationen

Im Jahr 1995 wurden beim Europäischen Patentamt **60 078 Anmeldungen** eingereicht davon aus:

USA 17 579
Deutschland 11 789
Japan 10 190
Frankreich 4 667
Großbritannien 3 212
Niederlande 2 293
Schweiz 2 084
Italien 2 071
Schweden 1 025
Belgien 737
Österreich 546
Dänemark 414

anderen Ländern: 3 471   Quelle: EPA

© Globus

Aktivität 6   Haben Sie Erfindergeist?

Sind Sie erfinderisch (*inventive*)? Haben Sie Erfindergeist? Was wäre sehr nützlich?

BEISPIEL: BEREICH: Medizin
Ein Hustenbonbon, das wie Schokolade schmeckt.

BEREICHE

1. Medizin
2. Technik
3. Verkehr
4. Haushalt
5. Tiere
6. Stadtplanung
7. Umwelt
8. Häuser

Aktivität 7: The dearth of female inventors in this activity represents a gap in recorded history. If you know of more female inventors, you may wish to expand this activity.

Aktivität 7   Hin und her: Technische Erfindungen durch die Jahrhunderte

Sie möchten erfahren, wer was und wann erfunden hat. Arbeiten Sie zu zweit.

BEISPIELE: s1: Wer hat ＿＿＿ erfunden?
s2: ＿＿＿.
s1: Wann hat er / sie es erfunden?
s2: (Im Jahre) ＿＿＿.

[*oder:*] s1: Was hat ＿＿＿ erfunden?
s2: Er / Sie hat ＿＿＿ erfunden.
s1: In welchem Jahr?
s2: (Im Jahre) ＿＿＿.

ERFINDER	ERFINDUNG	JAHR
Johannes Gutenberg	Buchdruck mit beweglichen Lettern (*movable type*)	um 1450
Daniel Gabriel Fahrenheit	Alkoholthermometer	1709
Karl von Drais	Fahrrad (Draisine)	1817
Werner von Siemens	Dynamomaschine (*generator*)	1846
Gottlieb Daimler	Motorrad	1885
Rudolf Diesel	Dieselmotor	1893
Wilhelm Conrad Röntgen	Röntgenstrahlen (*X rays*)	1895
Hedy Lamarr (Hedwig Eva Maria Kiesler)	Wechselspektrum (*spread spectrum radio technology*)	1942

Heddy Lamar, the Austrian-born Hollywood star, along with George Antheil, invented a secret communication system that was patented in 1942, and although never used, is cited as the forerunner of subsequent communication systems.

Daimler is primarily known as the inventor of the internal combustion engine (**Verbrennungsmotor**), which he tried in four-wheel vehicles first, and then in 1885 he mounted his engine on a two-wheeler, a motorized bicycle, i.e., a motor-cycle.

Grammatik im Kontext

The Verbs brauchen and scheinen

The verbs **brauchen** (*to need*) and **scheinen** (*to seem*) are often used with a dependent infinitive preceded by **zu. Brauchen** is used instead of the modal **müssen** when the sentence has a negative meaning.

Heute muss ich arbeiten, aber morgen **brauche** ich **nicht zu arbeiten.**

Today I have to work, but tomorrow I don't have to work.

Ich **brauche keinen** neuen Computer **zu kaufen,** der alte ist noch gut genug.

I don't have to buy a new computer; the old one is still good enough.

Das Faxgerät **scheint** kaputt **zu sein.**

The fax machine seems to be broken.

Übung 1   Nichts scheint zu klappen°

Was scheint hier los zu sein? Folgen Sie dem Beispiel.

BEISPIEL: Das Telefon klingelt nicht. (Es ist kaputt.) →
Es scheint kaputt zu sein.

1. Der Computer funktioniert mal wieder nicht. (Er ist kaputt.)
2. Hast du meine Nachricht nicht bekommen? Ich habe nämlich eine Nachricht auf deinem Anrufbeantworter hinterlassen. (Er funktioniert nicht.)
3. Meine Uhr ist stehen geblieben. (Sie braucht eine neue Batterie.)
4. Bei Firma Bauer meldet sich niemand am Apparat. (Niemand ist im Büro.)
5. Drei von meinen Kollegen sind heute nicht zur Arbeit gekommen. (Sie sind alle krank.)

Übung 2   Nein, heute nicht

Fragen Sie einen Partner / eine Partnerin: Was musst du heute noch machen? Folgen Sie dem Beispiel.

BEISPIEL: s1: Musst du heute arbeiten?
s2: Nein, heute brauche ich nicht zu arbeiten.
s2: Musst du heute zur Uni gehen? usw.

1. im Labor arbeiten
2. eine Arbeit schreiben
3. in eine Vorlesung gehen
4. den Computer benutzen
5. ein Fax schicken
6. Rechnungen bezahlen
7. dein Zimmer / deine Wohnung sauber machen

Brauchen and **scheinen.**
Note: These verbs are similar to modal verbs, except of course that the dependent infinitive is preceded by *zu.* Students need to actively master only the present tense and be able to recognize other tenses in reading.

Point Out: Even though *brauchen ... zu* is used instead of *müssen* when a sentence contains *nicht* or *kein, müssen* can be used in a sentence with a negative whenever *müssen* is stressed (*Ich* **muss** *nicht arbeiten; aber ich will*). Make sure you point out the meaning "to not have to."

go right

Hoffentlich sieht Sie ein Professor bei der Lektüre!

Macht sich nicht schlecht, eine der renommiertesten Zeitungen der Welt zu lesen. Abos mit 40% Rabatt über Tel. 0130 81 58 98.

Neue Zürcher Zeitung

Dem Gesamtbild zuliebe.

Der Infinitivsatz

Infinitive Clauses with zu°

Infinitive phrases may function as complements of verbs, adjectives, or nouns. Without them, the sentence would be incomplete. When used this way, the infinitive is always preceded by **zu.**

Familie Baier hat sich entschlossen, einen neuen Computer **zu kaufen.**	*The Baiers have decided to buy a new computer.*
Es macht mir Spaß, E-Mail aus der ganzen Welt **zu bekommen.**	*I enjoy receiving e-mail from all over the world.*
Es ist leicht, einen Brief per E-Mail **zu schicken.**	*It is easy to send a letter via e-mail.*

Note:

- The infinitive with **zu** is always the last element of the sentence.
- With separable-prefix verbs, **zu** is placed between the prefix and the main verb.

Ich habe versucht, dich gestern **anzurufen.**	*I tried to call you yesterday.*
Du hast versprochen **vorbeizukommen.**	*You promised to come by.*

- A comma sets off an infinitive clause that includes more than just the infinitive with **zu.** No comma is used otherwise.

Übung 3   Meiner Meinung nach...

Sagen Sie, wie Sie das alles finden.

BEISPIEL: Seifenopern ansehen →
         Es macht mir (keinen) Spaß, Seifenopern anzusehen.

Ich habe keine Zeit	stundenlang am Computer sitzen
Es macht mir (keinen) Spaß	im Internet surfen
Ich finde es langweilig	Computerspiele/Videospiele spielen
wichtig	Kriegsfilme/Sportsendungen im Fernsehen ansehen
schwierig	Deutsch lernen
interessant	über Politik und Wirtschaft diskutieren
spannend	per E-Mail korrespondieren

Spaß machen. Note: Students previously learned *Lesen macht Spaß; Schwimmen macht Spaß.* When the infinitive is at the beginning of the sentence, it is the subject (the "*-ing*" form in English). As a verbal complement, the infinitive is used with *zu* and placed at the end of the sentence: *Es macht Spaß, im Garten zu arbeiten.* The infinitive clause generally contains more than just the infinitive with *zu.* Otherwise you would simply say *Essen macht Spaß.*

mein Horoskop in der Zeitung lesen

jeden Tag die Zeitung lesen

Nachrichten im Fernsehen ansehen

Radio hören

Übung 4   Aus dem Kalender

Schauen Sie sich Cornelias Kalender an. Was hat sie vor? Was darf sie nicht vergessen?

BEISPIEL: Sie hat vor, Sonntag mit Klaus ins Kino zu gehen.
            Sie darf nicht vergessen, Montag...

Sonntag	19.30 mit Klaus ins Kino gehen
Montag	Videogerät zur Reparatur bringen Reise nach Spanien buchen
Dienstag	Radio und Fernsehen anmelden 14.30 Prof. Hauser: Seminararbeit besprechen
Mittwoch	Job für den Sommer suchen
Donnerstag	nicht vergessen: Mutter anrufen, Geburtstag!
Freitag	Seminararbeit fertig schreiben 20.00 Vera treffen: Café Kadenz
Samstag	14.00 mit Klaus Tennis spielen 20.30 „Casablanca" im Fernsehen ansehen

Übung 5   Gute Vorsätze° für die Zukunft

intentions

A. Sie haben beschlossen (*decided*), in Zukunft alles besser zu machen. Was haben Sie sich versprochen? Was haben Sie vor? Überlegen Sie sich zwei gute Vorsätze (*resolutions*).

BEISPIELE: Ich habe vor, weniger Geld für CDs auszugeben.
            Ich habe mir versprochen, meine Eltern regelmäßig anzurufen.

B. Vergleichen Sie Ihre Vorsätze mit den Vorsätzen eines Partners / einer Partnerin. Haben Sie gemeinsame Vorsätze? Wenn ja, welche? Was sind die häufigsten guten Vorsätze im Kursus?

Indirect Discourse°

Die indirekte Rede

When you report what another person has said, you can quote that person verbatim, using direct discourse. In writing, this is indicated by the use of quotation marks. Note that in German, opening quotation marks are placed just below the line.

DIRECT DISCOURSE

Der Autofahrer behauptete: *The automobile driver claimed,*
    „Ich habe den Radfahrer   *"I did not see the bicyclist."*
    nicht gesehen."

Another way of reporting what someone said uses indirect discourse—a style commonly found in newspapers. In this case, German often uses subjunctive verb forms, especially the indirect discourse subjunctive.

Indirect Discourse. Note: The grammar introduces only a limited number of forms and verbs for active knowledge because the indirect discourse subjunctive is used less and less in spoken German. It is still quite common in writing, however, especially in newspapers.

Suggestion: Review the more common forms of the Subjunctive II. These are also used for indirect discourse whenever there is no special indirect discourse form available.

| Der Autofahrer behauptete, er **habe** den Radfahrer nicht **gesehen.** | *The driver claimed he did not see the bicyclist.* |

In using the indirect discourse subjunctive, a speaker or writer signals that the information reported does not necessarily reflect the speaker's own knowledge or views. The indirect discourse subjunctive establishes distance between the reporter and the topic. This is useful when people want to be objective or neutral.

With the exception of the verb **sein,** the indirect discourse subjunctive, or subjunctive I, is commonly used only in the third-person singular form. For other verb forms, German speakers increasingly tend to use the more common subjunctive II or **würde** plus infinitive (see **Kapitel 12**) instead of the indirect discourse subjunctive.

The Indirect Discourse Subjunctive: Present Tense

sein	
Singular	*Plural*
ich sei	wir seien
du sei(e)st	ihr sei(e)t
er sie es } sei	sie seien
Sie seien	

The present tense of the indirect discourse subjunctive (subjunctive I) is formed from the stem of the infinitive.

Note:

- All verbs, with the exception of **sein,** add **-e** to the stem to form the third-person singular of the indirect discourse subjunctive (subjunctive I).
- Use subjunctive II or **würde** plus infinitive for all other persons.

INFINITIVE	INDIRECT DISCOURSE SUBJUNCTIVE (I)		SUBJUNCTIVE II	
haben könnten wissen werden	er, sie, es {	habe könne wisse werde	er, sie, es {	hätte könnte wüsste würde

INFINITIVE	INDIRECT DISCOURSE SUBJUNCTIVE (I)		*WÜRDE* + INFINITIVE	
fahren tun sagen	er, sie, es {	fahre tue sage	ich {	würde fahren würde tun würde sagen

Der Politiker behauptete, er **sage** immer die Wahrheit.	*The politician claimed that he always tells the truth.*
Politiker behaupten, sie **würden** immer die Wahrheit **sagen.**	*Politicians claim they always tell the truth.*
Die Wähler meinten, man **könne** nichts glauben, was die Politiker sagen.	*The voters thought that one could not believe anything politicians say.*
Die Umfrage ergab, die Wähler **wüssten** nicht, wem sie noch vertrauen **könnten.**	*The survey showed that the voters did not know whom they could trust.*

ANALYSE

Lesen Sie die zwei Texte („Im Fernsehen…" und den Cartoon) und markieren Sie alle Verben in indirekter Rede. Was sind die Infinitive der Verben? Wie würden Sie diese Sätze auf English ausdrücken?

Im Fernsehen hat man berichtet, das Land sei in einer großen Krise. Niemand wisse, wie es weitergehen[1] soll. Niemand habe eine Lösung.[2]

[1]*to continue*   [2]*solution*   [3]*to close down*

Übung 6   Das stand in der Zeitung

Berichten Sie in indirekter Rede, was Sie in der Zeitung gelesen haben.

BEISPIEL: In der Zeitung stand, der Mensch denke am schnellsten vor dem Mittagessen.

1. Der Mensch denkt am schnellsten vor dem Mittagessen.
2. Man soll also schwierige Probleme zwischen 11 and 12 Uhr lösen.
3. Die Sinne (*senses*) funktionieren dagegen besser in der Dämmerung (*dusk*).
4. Das Abendessen schmeckt deshalb besser als das Frühstück.
5. Wir sind deshalb abends für Theater, Musik und auch für die Liebe am empfänglichsten (*most receptive*).
6. Für den Sport ist der Spätnachmittag ideal.
7. Nachmittags ist das Reaktionsvermögen (*capacity to react quickly*) auf dem Höhepunkt.
8. Man wird spätnachmittags nicht so schnell müde.

Übung 7   Immer diese Ausreden°

Sie hören drei Dialoge. Machen Sie sich zuerst Notizen. Erzählen Sie dann mit Hilfe Ihrer Notizen, was das Problem ist und was für Ausreden (*excuses*) die Personen in den Dialogen haben.

BEISPIEL: Peter hat gesagt, er könne nicht mit ins Kino...

SPRECHER/IN	PROBLEM	AUSREDE
1. Peter	kann nicht mit ins Kino	Wagen kaputt; hat Arbeit
2. Jens	Seminararbeit nicht fertig	Mutter krank
3. Ursula	30 Euro zurückzahlen	Scheck kommt morgen

¹*coffee grounds*

The Indirect Discourse Subjunctive: Past Tense

The past tense of the indirect discourse subjunctive I is formed with either **sei** or **habe** and the past participle of the main verb. Past subjunctive II forms are used for all but the third-person singular, and are increasingly used for all persons.

INFINITIVE	PAST SUBJUNCTIVE I	PAST SUBJUNCTIVE II
haben	habe gehabt	hätte gehabt
sein	sei gewesen	wäre gewesen
fahren	er/sie/es sei gefahren	ich wäre gefahren
sehen	habe gesehen	hätte gesehen
wissen	habe gewusst	hätte gewusst

Der Autofahrer behauptete, der Radfahrer **sei** bei Rot **gefahren.** Er **habe** ihn nicht rechtzeitig **gesehen.**

The driver claimed that the bicyclist had run a red light. He did not see him in time.

Übung 8   Ungewöhnliches° aus den Nachrichten

Unusual happenings

Schreiben Sie die folgenden Sätze in indirekter Rede der Vergangenheit um. Benutzen Sie dabei Konjunktiv I (*subjunctive I*) oder Konjunktiv II (*subjunctive II*).

Heute habe ich im Radio gehört:

1. Im Südwesten Irans hat man ein unbekanntes Dorf entdeckt.
2. Ein Mann im Gorillakostüm hat in den Straßen von Dallas 50-Dollar Scheine an Fußgänger verteilt (*distributed*).
3. Im Jahre 1875 haben die Leute noch 65 Stunden pro Woche gearbeitet. Heutzutage arbeiten die meisten nur noch 39 Stunden pro Woche im Durchschnitt.
4. Bei einer Verkehrskontrolle in Cocoa Beach ist ein Autodieb ins Meer gesprungen. Er ist immer weiter raus geschwommen. Ein Polizist in voller Uniform hat sich auf ein Surfbrett geschwungen und hat den Dieb nach zehn Minuten eingeholt.
5. Gestern ist auf einem Spielplatz in Russland ein UFO gelandet. Die Leute, die aus dem UFO gestiegen sind, sind sehr freundlich gewesen. Nach kurzer Zeit sind sie wieder abgeflogen.

Übung 9   Sensationelles aus der Presse

Lesen Sie zuerst den kurzen Bericht aus einer Zeitung und unterstreichen Sie die Verben in indirekter Rede. Wiederholen Sie dann die Sätze als Bericht in direkter Rede.

In der Zeitung stand, gestern Abend sei bei einer Geburtstagsfeier in einem Restaurant ein Geburtstagskuchen explodiert. Der Kellner habe zu viel Cognac über den Kuchen gegossen. Die Gäste und der Kellner seien, Gott sei Dank, unverletzt gewesen.

Infinitive Clauses with um ... zu and ohne ... zu

German uses many different ways to explain the reasons for an action. You have already learned a number of them. Compare the following sentences.

1. Stefan spart **für einen neuen CD-Spieler.**   ←   Prepositional phrase

2. Stefan will einen neuen CD-Spieler kaufen. **Deswegen** muss er jetzt sparen.   ←   Adverb: **deswegen** = *therefore*

3. Stefan spart. Er will **nämlich** einen CD-Spieler kaufen.   ←   Adverb: **nämlich** [*no English equivalent*]

4. Stefan spart, **denn** er will einen CD-Spieler kaufen.   ←   Coordinating conjunction: **denn**

5. Stefan spart, **weil** er einen CD-Spieler kaufen möchte.   ←   Subordinating conjunction: **weil**

Um ... zu. Point Out: The implied subject in an *um ... zu* clause is always the same as in the introductory clause.

Yet another way to explain one's reasons for an action is with an infinitive clause with **um ... zu.**

Stefan spart, **um** einen neuen CD-Spieler **zu kaufen.**	*Stefan is saving money in order to buy a new CD player.*
Manche Leute leben, **um zu arbeiten.**	*Some people live in order to work.*

Sie müssen kein Fisch sein, um Meerwasser[1] trinken zu können.

[1]*sea water*

Bessere Dinge für ein besseres Leben (DU PONT)

To express that you do one thing without doing another, use **ohne ... zu.**

Hubers wollen ein Haus bauen, **ohne** große Schulden **zu machen.**	*The Hubers want to build a house without going into heavy debt.*
Er ist an mir vorbeigegangen, **ohne** mich **zu erkennen.**	*He passed by me without recognizing me.*

Note the comma before an infinitive phrase beginning with **um** or **ohne.**

reasons

Übung 10   Was sind die Gründe° dafür?

Geben Sie die Gründe an. Benutzen Sie dabei **um ... zu, weil, nämlich, denn** oder **deswegen.**

BEISPIEL: Ich muss sparen. Ich möchte mir ein Videogerät kaufen. →
Ich spare, um mir ein Videogerät zu kaufen. [*oder:*]
Ich will mir ein Videogerät kaufen. Deswegen muss ich sparen.

1. Barbara macht den Fernseher an. Sie will die Nachrichten sehen.
2. Thomas setzt sich in den Sessel. Er will die Tageszeitung lesen.
3. Barbara schaut sich das Filmprogramm an. Sie sucht sich einen Spielfilm aus.
4. Thomas programmiert den Videorecorder. Er möchte die Fußballweltmeisterschaften im Fernsehen aufnehmen.

5. Stephanie füllt ein Formular aus. Sie muss ihr Radio und ihren Fernseher anmelden. (Sonst macht sie sich als Schwarzhörerin strafbar!)
6. Oliver überfliegt nur die Schlagzeilen in der Zeitung. Er will Zeit sparen.

Übung 11 Daran hat niemand gedacht!

Kombinieren Sie Sätze aus beiden Spalten mit Hilfe von **ohne ... zu.**

BEISPIEL: Oliver hat den gebrauchten Computer gekauft. ...hat ihn vorher nicht überprüft. →
Oliver hat den gebrauchten Computer gekauft, ohne ihn vorher zu überprüfen.

1. Erika hat das Videogerät gekauft.
2. Herr Wunderlich hat eine Wohnung gemietet.
3. Fritz ist nach den Nachrichten zu Bett gegangen.
4. Patrick hat wie hypnotisiert vor dem Fernseher gesessen.
5. Jemand hat eine Nachricht auf meinem Anrufbeantworter hinterlassen.

a. ...hat seinen Namen nicht hinterlassen.
b. ...hat nicht nach den Nebenkosten gefragt.
c. ...hat das Telefon nicht gehört.
d. ...hat den Fernseher nicht abgestellt.
e. ...hat nicht nach dem Preis gefragt.

Übung 11. Point Out:
Students need to remove negative *nicht* when changing to an infinitive phrase with *ohne ... zu.*

Sprache im Kontext

Videoclips

Jasmin, Peter und Maria sprechen über ihre Lese- und Fernsehgewohnheiten.

A. Schauen Sie sich die Interviews mit Jasmin und Maria an und füllen Sie die Tabelle aus. Wenn die Person keine Information zu dem Thema gibt, schreiben Sie „keine Information."

	MICHAEL	JASMIN	MARIA
Welche Zeitung liest du?			
Was liest du zuerst?			
Welchen Teil liest du ganz genau?			
Was überfliegst du?			
Was siehst du im Fernsehen?			
Welche Filme siehst du gern im Kino?			

B. Schauen Sie sich das Interview mit Peter an und beantworten Sie die Fragen.

1. Welche Tageszeitungen liest er?
2. Peter vergleicht drei verschiedene Zeitungen, den *Tagesspiegel,* die *Welt* und die *Süddeutsche Zeitung.* Wie beschreibt er jede Zeitung?
   a. der *Tagesspiegel:* _____.
   b. die *Welt:* _____.
   c. die *Süddeutsche Zeitung:* _____.
3. Welche Zeitung liest er nie? Warum?
4. Was liest Peter ganz genau? Was überfliegt er?

C. Ein Interview. Benutzen Sie die Tabelle in Teil A, um zwei andere Personen zu interviewen. Machen Sie Notizen zu jedem Interview und berichten Sie der Klasse darüber.

Lesen

Zum Thema

1. Wie oft sehen Sie fern?
   - überhaupt nicht
   - 1–5 Stunden pro Woche
   - 5–10 Stunden pro Woche
   - 10–20 Stunden pro Woche
   - über 20 Stunden pro Woche

2. Was für Sendungen gefallen Ihnen?
   - Seifenopern
   - Komödien
   - Spielfilme
   - Krimis
   - Dokumentarfilme
   - Zeichentrickfilme (*cartoons*)
   - Nachrichten
   - Sportsendungen
   - gar keine

3. Was würden Sie machen, wenn Ihr Fernseher kaputt wäre?
4. Falls Sie keinen Fernseher haben, wie verbringen Sie Ihre Freizeit?

Auf den ersten Blick. Note: The reading is by Loriot, which is the pen name of one of the best-known contemporary German humorists. Loriot, a Berliner born in 1923, is a master at demonstrating the comic absurdity in everyday life. **Note for #1:** Students need to look at the first eleven lines of the story to find the answers. Other words mentioned for *Fernseher* are *das Fernsehgerät, das Gerät, der Apparat,* and *der (blöde) Kasten* (colloquial).

Auf den ersten Blick

1. Suchen Sie Wörter aus dem Text, die...
   a. für Fernseher stehen.
   b. etwas mit sehen zu tun haben.
2. Schauen Sie sich den Titel an und lesen Sie die ersten zwei Sätze. Der Text ist...
   a. ein Interview.
   b. ein Dialog.
   c. ein Artikel.
3. Überfliegen Sie den Text in etwa dreißig Sekunden. Dieser Text handelt von...
   a. einem Ehepaar, dem ein Abend ohne Fernsehen bevorsteht.
   b. einem Ehepaar, das seinen kaputten Fernseher wegwerfen will.
   c. einem Ehepaar, das seinen Fernseher zur Reparatur bringt.

von Loriot

Fernsehabend. **Suggestion:** Depending on your students' acting talent, this humorous reading could be performed in class.

Ein Ehepaar sitzt vor dem Fernsehgerät. Obwohl die Bildröhre° ausgefallen° ist   tube / broken
und die Mattscheibe° dunkel bleibt, starrt das Ehepaar zur gewohnten° Stunde   screen / usual
in die gewohnte Richtung.

SIE: Wieso geht der Fernseher denn grade heute kaputt?

5 ER: Die bauen die Geräte absichtlich so, daß sie schnell kaputtgehen...
(*Pause*)

SIE: Ich muß nicht unbedingt fernsehen...

ER: Ich auch nicht... nicht nur, weil heute der Apparat kaputt ist... ich meine
sowieso°... ich sehe sowieso nicht gern Fernsehen...   in any case

10 SIE: Es ist ja auch wirklich nichts im Fernsehen, was man gern sehen
möchte... (*Pause*)

ER: Heute brauchen wir Gott sei Dank überhaupt nicht erst in den blöden
Kasten° zu gucken...   in... at the stupid box

SIE: Nee... (*Pause*)... Es sieht aber so aus, als ob° du hinguckst....   als... as if

15 ER: Ich?

SIE: Ja...

ER: Nein... ich sehe nur ganz allgemein in diese Richtung... aber du guckst
hin... Du guckst da immer hin!

SIE: Ich! Ich gucke da hin? Wie kommst du denn darauf?°   Wie... What makes you

20 ER: Es sieht so aus...°   think that? / Es... That's
   what it looks like.

SIE: Das *kann* gar nicht so aussehen... ich gucke nämlich vorbei... ich gucke
absichtlich vorbei... und wenn du ein kleines bißchen mehr auf mich
achten würdest, hättest du bemerken° können, daß ich absichtlich vor-   notice
beigucke, aber du interessierst dich ja überhaupt nicht für mich...

25 ER: (*fällt ihr ins Wort°*) Jaaa... jaaa... jaaa... jaaa...   fällt... interrupts

SIE: Wir können doch einfach mal ganz woandershin° gucken...   elsewhere

ER: Woanders?... Wohin denn?

SIE: Zur Seite... oder nach hinten...

ER: Nach hinten? Ich soll nach hinten sehen?... Nur weil der Fernseher
30 kaputt ist, soll ich nach hinten sehen? Ich laß mir doch von einem
Fernsehgerät nicht vorschreiben,° wo ich hinsehen soll!   Ich... I won't let a TV
(*Pause*)   dictate to me

SIE: Was wäre denn heute für ein Programm gewesen?

ER: Eine Unterhaltungssendung...

35 SIE: Ach...

ER: Es ist schon eine Un-ver-schämtheit,° was einem so Abend für Abend im   outrage
Fernsehen geboten wird!° Ich weiß gar nicht, warum man sich das über-   geboten... is offered
haupt noch ansieht!... Lesen könnte man statt dessen,° Kartenspielen   statt... instead
oder ins Kino gehen... oder ins Theater... statt dessen sitzt man da und
40 glotzt° auf dieses blöde Fernsehprogramm!   stares, watches (coll.)

SIE: Heute ist der Apparat ja nu kaputt...

ER: Gott sei Dank!

SIE: Ja...

ER: Da kann man sich wenigstens mal unterhalten°...   converse

45 SIE: Oder früh ins Bett gehen...

ER: Ich gehe nach den Spätnachrichten der Tagesschau ins Bett...

SIE: Aber der Fernseher ist doch kaputt!

ER: (*energisch*) Ich lasse mir von einem kaputten Fernseher nicht
vorschreiben, wann ich ins Bett zu gehen habe!

Zum Text

Richtig oder falsch? Wenn falsch, verbessern Sie die Aussagen.

1. _____ Der Fernseher ist kaputt. Aber es ist kein Problem, denn die zwei Leute haben einen zweiten Apparat im Schlafzimmer.
2. _____ Der Mann behauptet, dass er sowieso nicht gern fernsieht.
3. _____ Die zwei bleiben aber vor dem Fernseher sitzen und starren ihn einfach an.
4. _____ Die Frau schlägt eine Alternative zum Fernsehen vor.
5. _____ Der Mann meint, er darf hinschauen, wohin er will, auch wenn er den dunklen Fernseher anschaut.
6. _____ An diesem Abend gibt es Sport im Fernsehen.
7. _____ Der Mann behauptet, dass es normalerweise ausgezeichnete Sendungen im Fernsehen gibt.
8. _____ Die zwei unterhalten sich und gehen dann früh ins Bett.

Sprechen und Schreiben

Aktivität 1   Theater spielen

Wie stellen Sie sich die Kurzszene in „Fernsehabend" vor? Üben Sie die Szene mit einer Partnerin / einem Partner ein, um sie vor der Klasse vorzuführen.

Aktivität 2   Wie geht das Leben weiter?

Wie stellen Sie sich das Leben des Ehepaars vor? Schreiben Sie einen kurzen Dialog zwischen dem Ehepaar am nächsten Tag am Frühstückstisch.

Wortschatz

In der Zeitung — **In the Newspaper**

das **Abo(nnement), -s** — subscription
die **Börse, -n** — stock market
das **Horoskop, -e** — horoscope
das **Inland** — at home, domestic, national

   im Inland und Ausland — at home and abroad
die **Nachrichten** (*pl.*) — news
   die **Lokalnachrichten** — local news
die **Politik** — politics
die **Schlagzeile, -n** — headline
die **Wirtschaft** — economy

Im Fernsehen — **On Television**

der **Bericht, -e** — report
der **Dokumentarfilm, -e** — documentary (film)
das **Programm, -e** — station, TV channel; program

die **Sendung, -en** — TV or radio program
der **Spielfilm, -e** — feature film, movie
die **Unterhaltung** — entertainment
   zur Unterhaltung — for entertainment

Sonstige Substantive — **Other Nouns**

der **Anrufbeantworter, -** — answering machine
der **Drucker, -** — printer

die **Erfindung**, -en	invention	**sich melden**	to answer (phone)
das **Gerät**, -e	appliance; device;	Niemand meldet sich.	No one is answering.
	apparatus	**scheinen**	to seem, appear
die **Geschirrspül-**	dishwasher	**überfliegen, überflog,**	to skim (a text),
maschine, -n		**überflogen**	quickly read
der **Pkw (= Personen-**	automobile	**sich unterhalten**	to entertain (oneself);
kraftwagen, -)		**(unterhält),**	to converse
der **Staubsauger**, -	vacuum cleaner	**unterhielt,**	
der **Wäschetrockner**, -	clothes dryer	**unterhalten**	
die **Zeitschrift**, -en	magazine; periodical	**verzichten auf** (+*acc.*)	to do without

Verben / Verbs

abonnieren	to subscribe		
sich (*dat.*) **etwas**	to watch, look at		
an•schauen			
sich (*dat.*) **etwas**	to look at, watch		
an•sehen (sieht an),			
sah an, angesehen			
auf•nehmen (nimmt	to record (e.g., on		
auf), nahm auf,	video)		
aufgenommen			
sich (et)was	to select, find, choose		
aus•suchen	something		
behaupten	to claim, assert		
berichten	to report, narrate		
forschen	to do research		
erfinden, erfand,	to invent		
erfunden			
handeln (von)	to deal with, be about		
Wovon handelt es?	What's it about?		

Adjektive und Adverbien / Adjectives and Adverbs

aktuell	current, topical
Aktuelles	current events
blöd	stupid
gescheit	intelligent, bright;
	sensible, decent
nichts Gescheites	nothing decent
nützlich	useful
unbedingt	absolutely, by all means
unterhaltsam	entertaining

Ausdrücke / Expressions

auf jeden Fall	in any case
Das ist mir zu blöd!	I think that's really
	stupid!
Na und?	So what?
Wie wäre es mit... ?	How about . . . ?

LERNZIELE

Use this checklist to verify that you can now . . .

- ☐ talk about the mass media and various types of television and radio shows, films, newspapers, and magazines.

- ☐ express your own preferences with regard to television and radio shows as well as newspapers and magazines.

- ☐ use **brauchen** and **scheinen** and other verbal expressions with **zu** + infinitive.

- ☐ report what you have heard or read using indirect discourse subjunctive.

- ☐ expand sentences using **um ... zu** and **ohne ... zu** clauses.

KAPITEL 14

Die öffentliche Meinung

Hier gibt es Information über...
a. die Erhöhung von Studiengebühren
b. Umweltschutz

Kapitel 14. Suggestion: Introduce the chapter by brainstorming with the class about the problems of the world. What are the problems in your community? In your state? Are students involved in helping out with those problems?

Videoclips
Globale Probleme

In diesem Kapitel

- **Themen:** Global problems, environment, discussion strategies
- **Grammatik:** Passive voice, present participle
- **Kultur:** Global problems and issues, the environment, speed limits in Europe, recycling

Alles klar?

Ob es Politik, Wirtschaft oder Umwelt ist—Deutsche sind im Durchschnitt relativ gut informiert und äußern gern ihre Meinung zu verschiedenen Problemen.

A. Schauen Sie sich die Umfrage an. Welches Problem passt zu den folgenden Beschreibungen?

TV Hören Sehen UMFRAGE
Die drängendsten Probleme:

1. Arbeitslosigkeit

2. Fremdenhaß

3. Steuererhöhungen

4. Politiker

5. Geldmangel

6. Umwelt

7. Terrorismus

Alles klar. Have students do A and B either for homework or as an inclass activity.

A. Discuss with students the historical contexts for some of the problems, such as an influx of refugees to Germany after the dissolution of Eastern Europe, Germany's open-door policy toward political refugees and the continuing high costs of unification.

B. Discuss the results of the survey students carry out themselves and ask them to compare the problems in Germany to those they find in their own surroundings.

1. __1__ zu wenig Arbeitsplätze
2. __5__ nicht genug Geld
3. __2__ zu wenig Verständnis für Fremde im Land
4. __7__ Gewalt, Zerstörung
5. __3__ zu hohe Steuern
6. __4__ zu viele Skandale in der Politik
7. __6__ Naturzerstörung

B. Machen Sie eine Umfrage im Unterricht oder auf Ihrem Campus. Was sind die drängendsten Probleme in Ihrer Umgebung?

C. Sie hören jetzt eine Beschreibung von vier verschiedenen Seminaren über Probleme in der Welt. Welche Themen behandeln diese Seminare? Schreiben Sie die entsprechende Nummer vor jedes Thema.

___2___ Kriminalität/Gewalt

___3___ Umweltverschmutzung

___4___ Menschenrechte

___1___ Medizin/Umwelt

Wörter im Kontext

Neue Wörter

Welt world
Krankheiten diseases, illnesses
Arbeitslosigkeit unemployment
Armut poverty
Ausländerfeindlichkeit hatred of foreigners
Drogensucht drug addiction
Gewalttätigkeit violence
Regierung government
Krieg war
Obdachlosigkeit homelessness
Umweltverschmutzung environmental pollution
Verletzung der Menschenrechte abuse of human rights
mögliche Lösungen possible solutions
Fortschritte progress

THEMA 1: Globale Probleme

A. Was sind Ihrer Meinung nach die drei größten Probleme in der **Welt**, in Ihrem Staat und in Ihrer Heimatstadt?

	WELT	STAAT	STADT
AIDS und andere sexuell übertragbare **Krankheiten**	☐	☐	☐
Arbeitslosigkeit	☐	☐	☐
Armut	☐	☐	☐
Ausländerfeindlichkeit	☐	☐	☐
Drogensucht	☐	☐	☐
Gewalttätigkeit	☐	☐	☐
Hunger	☐	☐	☐
Korruption in der **Regierung**	☐	☐	☐
Krieg	☐	☐	☐
Obdachlosigkeit	☐	☐	☐
Rassismus	☐	☐	☐
Rechtsextremismus	☐	☐	☐
Terrorismus	☐	☐	☐
Umweltverschmutzung	☐	☐	☐
Verletzung der Menschenrechte	☐	☐	☐
??	☐	☐	☐

B. Mögliche Losungen. Was kann man gegen diese Probleme tun? Wie können **Fortschritte** gemacht werden? Suchen Sie aus der Liste auf der nächsten Seite passende Ausdrücke (*expressions*), um Ihre Meinung auszudrücken.

BEISPIEL: In meiner Heimatstadt ist Obdachlosigkeit ein großes Problem. Man sollte mehr Sozialbauwohnungen bauen.

- **an Demonstrationen teilnehmen**
- mehr **Fußgängerzonen** einrichten
- mehr Geld für **Forschung** ausgeben
- Alternativenergie entwickeln
- Giftstoffe (*toxics*) **vermindern** oder **verbieten**
- Hilfsorganisationen mit Geld **unterstützen**
- Informationen über die **Gefahren** von **Alkohol** und **Drogen verbreiten**
- Kinder besser **erziehen**
- mehr **Gefängnisse** bauen
- Recyclingprogramme **einführen**

- Safer Sex praktizieren
- Sozialbauwohnungen bauen
- Stressfaktoren (z.B. **Lärm**) reduzieren
- Umschulungsprogramme **fördern**
- Arbeitsplätze **schaffen**
- verantwortungsbewusste **Politiker/ Politikerinnen wählen**
- **sich** politisch **engagieren**
- **öffentliche Verkehrsmittel** fördern
- Umwelt **streng schützen**
- ??

Die Kunst der Diskussion

DISKUSSIONSREDEMITTEL

Achten Sie bitte auf die Redemittel in der folgenden Diskussion:

ich bin der Meinung	I am of the opinion
halte... für übertrieben	think . . . is exaggerated
außerdem	besides that
So ein Quatsch!	Nonsense!
meiner Meinung nach	in my opinion
ich bin total dagegen	I'm totally against that
ich bin dafür	I'm for that
So ein Unsinn!	Nonsense!
ich bedaure	I regret
ich schlage vor	I suggest

Suggestion: Focus on the expressions used to express an opinion. Use them in other contexts, e.g., Ich bin der Meinung, man sollte mehr Recycling-programme beginnen. Then go back to B above and have students do the exercise again incorporating these expressions.

*Neun **Bürger** und **Bürgerinnen** diskutieren über das Thema Obdachlosigkeit in ihrer Stadt.*

FRAU MAYER: **Ich bin der Meinung,** dass Obdachlosigkeit ein viel größeres Problem ist, als wir allgemein glauben.

HERR SACHS: Das **halte** ich **für übertrieben.** Das ist nur in Großstädten ein Problem, aber nicht hier bei uns in Kleinlichterhagen.

FRAU BECKER: Im Park an der Hauptstraße schlafen aber regelmäßig Leute auf den Bänken, und am Bahnhof sitzen auch welche, die nicht wissen wohin. Und...

HERR GRÜNKRAUT: Ja, und die sind so **schmutzig,** lassen überall ihren Dreck. **Außerdem** sind die meisten **Drogensüchtige.** Es ist ein Skandal, dass unsere Regierung nichts tut.

HERR SPITZ: **So ein Quatsch!**

FRAU RAST: **Meiner Meinung nach** hat die Regierung viel getan.

FRAU HOFFMANN: Ich finde, man sollte unbedingt Unterkunft für die **Obdachlosen** in unserer Stadt finden. Man sollte sie in Privatzimmern unterbringen.

FRAU NIKOLAI: Ich hoffe, Sie haben ein Zimmer frei! **Ich bin** nämlich

teilnehmen (an) participate (in)
Fußgängerzonen pedestrian zones
Forschung research
vermindern lessen
verbieten forbid
unterstützen support
Gefahren dangers
verbreiten spread
erziehen raise
Gefängnisse prisons
einführen introduce
Lärm noise
fördern promote
schaffen create
wählen elect
öffentliche Verkehrsmittel public transportation
streng strictly
schützen protect
Bürger/Bürgerinnen citizens
schmutzig dirty
Drogensüchtige drug addicts
Obdachlosen homeless (people)
entwickeln develop

total dagegen. Ich bin dafür, dass mehr Sozialbauwohnungen gebaut werden.

HERR SPITZ: **So ein Unsinn!**

FRAU LIESCHE: **Ich bedaure,** dass wir alle ohne Konzept um das Thema herum reden. **Ich schlage vor,** dass wir eine konkrete Strategie **entwickeln.** Nur so kann das Problem gelöst werden.

FRAU HOFFMANN: Was wohl die Obdachlosen über unsere Diskussion sagen würden!!!

HERR SPITZ: Das ist mir egal!

Aktivität 1 Hin und her: Probleme und Lösungen

Stellen Sie Ihrem Partner / Ihrer Partnerin Fragen zu den folgenden Problemen, um herauszufinden, welche möglichen Lösungen es gibt.

BEISPIEL: S1: Was kann man gegen Krieg tun?
S2: Man kann an Antikriegsdemonstrationen teilnehmen.

PROBLEME	MÖGLICHE LÖSUNGEN
Krieg	an Antikriegsdemonstrationen teilnehmen
Inflation	die Schulden der Regierung kontrollieren
Drogensucht	Informationen über die Gefahren von Drogen verbreiten
Umweltverschmutzung	alternative Energiequellen entwickeln
Verletzung der Menschenrechte	Organisationen wie Amnesty International unterstützen
Obdachlosigkeit	neue Wohnungen bauen
Arbeitslosigkeit	Arbeiter umschulen (*retrain*)

Aktivität 2 Probleme in der Stadt

Vier Leute sprechen über Probleme in ihrer Stadt und wie man sie lösen könnte. Setzen Sie die passende Nummer (1–4) vor das Problem, über das der Sprecher / die Sprecherin redet, und markieren Sie auch die Lösung, die er/sie vorschlägt.

SPRECHER	PROBLEM		LÖSUNG
_2_	Atomkraft (*nuclear power*)	**a.**	Solarenergie
		b.	Windenergie
_4_	Giftstoffe in Nahrungsmitteln	**a.**	strenge Staatskontrolle
		b.	keine Pestizide
_1_	Verkehr	**a.**	Tempolimit
		b.	Wagen am Stadtrand parken
_3_	Lärm	**a.**	weniger Flugzeuge
		b.	Autos verbieten

Aktivität 3 Um welche Probleme geht es hier?

A. Buttons—so heißen sie auch auf Deutsch—oder Aufkleber (*stickers*) sind eine beliebte Form, die Meinung zu äußern (*express*). Schauen Sie sich die Sprüche (*sayings*) auf den Buttons an, und stellen Sie fest, wofür oder wogegen sie sind. Schreiben Sie dann die passenden Zahlen in die Liste.

Aktivität 3.A. Follow-up: Which of these buttons would students wear?

¹AOK = Allgemeine Ortskrankenkasse *name of a health insurance company*   ²*pigeon*

Realia. The pictures of buttons were found on a calendar distributed by the Goethe Institut.

a. _____ fürs Faulenzen

b. _____ gegen Energieverschwendung

c. _____ für den Feminismus

d. _____ für die Sauberkeit (*cleanliness*) der Stadt

e. _____ gegen Autoabgase (*emissions*)

f. _____ für den Tierschutz

g. _____ gegen Rauchen

h. _____ für den Frieden, gegen den Krieg

i. _____ für höhere Gehälter

j. _____ gegen Giftstoffe in Nahrungsmitteln

k. _____ gegen Rassismus

l. _____ gegen Kernenergie

B. Wählen Sie ein Problem aus **Thema 1** und entwerfen Sie einen Spruch für einen Aufkleber. Lesen Sie der Klasse Ihre Sprüche vor.

Aktivität 4   Nehmen Sie Stellung!°

In Vierergruppen, äußern Sie sich zu einigen Problemen im **Thema 1.** Benutzen Sie dabei die Redemittel im **Thema 1.** Jemand nennt das Gesprächsthema; die anderen sagen ihre Meinung.

BEISPIEL: S1: Verkehrsbelästigung (*traffic disturbances*).

S2: Ich bin der Meinung, man sollte Autos in der Innenstadt verbieten.

S3: Meiner Meinung nach sollte man mehr Fußgängerzonen haben.

S4: Ich finde es schade, dass Leute immer ihren Wagen benutzen. Sie sollten öfter zu Fuß gehen.

THEMA 2: Umwelt

Was kann man für die Umwelt tun?

Realia. This article is from *Natur* magazine.

Die Zeitschrift „Natur" fragte ihre Leser „Bei welchen dieser Punkte auf der Liste glauben Sie, dass Sie mehr für die Umwelt tun könnten?" Hier sind die Antworten.

Neue Wörter

Wegwerfflaschen nonrecyclable bottles
Getränkedosen beverage cans
mit umweltfreundlicher Verpackung with environmentally friendly packaging
vorziehen prefer, use more than
Plastiktüten plastic bags
verbrauchen use; consume
Arzneimittel medication
sich (etwas) anschaffen buy, acquire (something)
isolieren to insulate; to isolate
Sammelstellen recycling centers
Abfälle waste

Keine Wegwerfflaschen oder Getränkedosen kaufen	35
Beim Einkauf auf Artikel mit umweltfreundlicher Verpackung achten	29
Öffentliche Verkehrsmittel dem Auto vorziehen	29
Aluminium getrennt vom Hausmüll sammeln	26
Beim Einkauf keine Plastiktüten verwenden	25
Weniger Strom verbrauchen	24
Alte Arzneimittel in der Apotheke abgeben	24
Energiesparende Haushaltsgeräte anschaffen	22
Heizwärme sparen, die Wohnung besser isolieren	21
Alte Batterien bei den Sammelstellen abgeben	20
Sonderabfälle[1] (z.B. Altöl) zur Deponie[2] bringen	18
Organische Abfälle kompostieren	16
Alte Kleider in die Sammlung geben	15
Auto mit Katalysator fahren	14
Altpapier in die Sammlung geben	13
Glas zum Container bringen	12
Nichts davon	18

[1] *special types of garbage*
[2] *garbage dump*

Was tun Sie persönlich für die Umwelt?

KULTURTIPP

Viele Menschen leben heutzutage viel umweltbewusster als früher. Sie sind daran interessiert, wie man die Umwelt schützen kann und wie man selbst mithelfen kann, umweltfreundlicher zu leben. Dieses Umweltbewusstsein zeigt sich auch in der modernen Sprache. So gebraucht man oft **alt** als Präfix, wenn man von Dingen spricht, die zur Deponie, zu Sammelstellen oder zur Wiederverwertung gebracht werden; z.B. **Altbatterien, Altöl, Altpapier, Altglas** und **Altkleidung.**

Recycling in Offenbach

Aktivität 5　Langsamer, bitte!

Sie hören zuerst ein Gespräch zwischen Andreas, einem deutschen Autofahrer, und Jennifer, seinem Gast aus den USA. Hören Sie zuerst den Dialog, und lesen Sie die Sätze unten. Bringen Sie dann die Sätze in die richtige Reihenfolge.

___3___ Bei uns ist die Höchstgeschwindigkeit (*speed limit*) 110 km pro Stunde.

___6___ Wahrscheinlich eine Baustelle (*construction zone*) in der Nähe.

___7___ Also doch ein Tempolimit. Gott sei Dank. Bei 100 km pro Stunde fühle ich mich direkt wie zu Hause.

___2___ Keine Angst. Der Wagen schafft das spielend.

___4___ Dann kann man gleich zu Fuß gehen.

___5___ Schau mal. Dort ist ein Schild. Höchstgeschwindigkeit 100 km pro Stunde.

___1___ Fliegen wir eigentlich oder fahren wir?

Kulturtipp. Note: The cameras use infrared light to take pictures after dark, so it is not safe to speed at any time.

KULTURTIPP

In allen Ländern Europas außer in der Bundesrepublik gibt es eine Höchstgeschwindigkeit auf der Autobahn. In Deutschland ist die Richtgeschwindigkeit (*suggested speed*) 130 km pro Stunde auf der Autobahn. Natürlich gibt es streckenweise (*for certain stretches*) Geschwindigkeitsbegrenzungen, zum Beispiel an Baustellen (*construction zones*). Über der Autobahn sind manchmal Kameras angebracht, die einen Wagen, der zu schnell fährt, filmen. Man bekommt dann einen Strafzettel (*ticket*) mit dem Bild des Wagens und dem Nummernschild ins Haus geschickt. Niemand kann dann sagen: Das war jemand anders.

Tempogrenzen in Europa
... auf Autobahnen

Norwegen, Rumänien, Türkei	**90**
Dänemark, Griechenland	**100**
Polen, Schweden*	**110**
Großbritannien	**112**
Belgien, Bulgarien, Finnland, Luxemburg, Niederlande, Portugal, Schweiz, Spanien, Ungarn	**120**
Frankreich, Italien,** Österreich	**130**
Deutschland (Richtgeschwindigkeit: 130 km/h)	

*90 km/h vom 20.6. bis 20.8.
**110 km/h an Wochenenden, Feiertagen, in der Ferienzeit

Aktivität 6 Ein Natur-Quiz

Wie gut kennen Sie Ihre Umwelt? Beantworten Sie die Fragen und vergleichen Sie dann Ihre Antworten mit denen eines Partners / einer Partnerin.

Suggestion: Have students compare statistics between the United States and Germany where appropriate.

1. Was ist am sparsamsten im Energieverbrauch?
   a. das Motorrad **b.** das Auto **c.** das Fahrrad **d.** die Bahn
2. In welchem Jahr und wo wurden erstmals Mülleimer (*garbage cans*) benutzt?
   a. 1213 in Rom **b.** 1473 in Amsterdam **c.** 1621 in Hamburg **d.** 1872 in Chicago
3. Wann und wo wurde die Konservendose erfunden?
   a. 1746 in Norwegen **b.** 1810 in England **c.** 1899 in Deutschland **d.** 1902 in der Schweiz
4. Wie viel Geld kostet die Umweltzerstörung in Deutschland jedes Jahr?
   a. 250 Millionen Mark   **b.** 13,7 Milliarden Euro
   c. 100 Milliarden Mark   **d.** 80 Milliarden Mark
5. Wie viel Papier wird in Deutschland pro Jahr verbraucht?
   a. 20 Millionen Tonnen   **b.** 40 Millionen Tonnen
   c. 250 Millionen Tonnen   **d.** 300 Millionen Tonnen
6. Wer ist der größte Müllproduzent?
   a. die Verpackungsindustrie **b.** die Autoindustrie
   c. die Bauindustrie   **d.** die Elektronikbranche

Hier klicken!

Weiteres zum Thema Umwelt finden Sie bei **Deutsch: Na klar!** im World-Wide-Web unter www.mhhe.com/dnk.

ANALYSE

Seit über zwanzig Jahren wächst das Umweltbewusstsein der Deutschen. Daher werden Berufe im Umweltbereich immer beliebter. Hier sind drei neue Berufe.

Holger Urban, 43, ist Raumplaner in einer süddeutschen Großstadt: „Mir macht die abwechslungsreiche Arbeit Freude. Vor allem, weil ich den ökologischen Stadtumbau als eine äußerst spannende Sache erlebe."

Dr. Ralph Hantschel, 34, zählt zu den ersten Studienabgängern der Geoökologie: „Die Ausbildung in Bayreuth war intensiv und gut." Heute sucht er Wege zu einer umweltverträglichen Landwirtschaft und ist beim Forschungszentrum für Umwelt und Gesundheit (GSF) tätig.

Siegfried Müller vom Amt für Abfallwirtschaft der Stadt München: „Es macht Spaß. Aber die Verwaltungswege erscheinen mir mitunter zu lang." Der 32jährige studierte Physik. Er arbeitet in der Entsorgungsplanung.

- Holger Urban. Raumplaner. Wo arbeitet er? Warum macht ihm die Arbeit Spaß?
- Dr. Ralph Hantschel. Geoökologe. Wo hat er studiert? Wo arbeitet er jetzt?
- Siegfried Müller. Entsorger (*waste management engineer*). Was hat er studiert? Wo arbeitet er jetzt?

Gibt es diese oder ähnliche (*similar*) Berufe in Ihrem Land? Wer befasst sich mit dem Folgenden? Schreiben Sie **R** (für Raumplaner/Raumplanerin), **G** (für Geoökologe/Geoökologin) oder **E** (für Entsorger/Entsorgerin).

1. _____ Altöl, Altbatterien und ihre Wirkung (*effect*) auf die Umwelt
2. _____ Kontrolle der Verpackungsflut (*glut of packaging*)
3. _____ Messung des sauren Regens
4. _____ organische Abfälle und Kompost
5. _____ Verkehrsbelastung
6. _____ Stromverbrauch
7. _____ Verschmutzung der Seen, Flüsse
8. _____ Grünanlagen für einen neuen Stadtteil

Grammatik im Kontext

The Passive Voice°

Das Passiv

So far you have learned to express sentences in German in the active voice. In the active voice, the subject of a sentence performs the action expressed by the verb. The person or thing performing the action is called the agent. In the passive voice, the subject is acted on by an agent that is not always named, because it is either understood, unimportant, or unknown. Compare the following sentences.

The Passive Voice. Note: It is important for students to learn to recognize a passive voice sentence in reading; however, active mastery—integrating passive voice sentences freely in conversation—should not be expected at this level. Students should merely be able to produce simple sentences in the passive voice.

ACTIVE VOICE

Viele Leute lesen täglich eine Zeitung. *Many people read a newspaper daily.*

Welche Zeitung lesen die Deutschen am häufigsten? *Which paper do Germans read most often?*

PASSIVE VOICE

In Deutschland werden viele Zeitungen verkauft. *Many newspapers are sold in Germany.*

Welche Zeitung wird am häufigsten gelesen? *Which newspaper is read most often?*

The active voice emphasizes the subject that carries out an activity; in the passive voice the emphasis shifts to the activity itself. For this reason, the passive voice tends to be more impersonal. It is commonly used in newspapers, scientific writing, and descriptions of procedures and activities.

Formation of the Passive Voice

The passive voice is formed with the auxiliary verb **werden** and the past participle of the main verb. (English uses *to be* and the past participle.) Although it can be used in all personal forms, the passive occurs most frequently in the third-person singular or plural.

Following are the commonly used tenses of the passive.

Formation of the Passive Voice. Suggestion: Review the conjugation of *werden*. To practice the passive with all personal forms, use *ich werde gefragt* or *ich werde eingeladen*.

PRESENT

Die Zeitung **wird verkauft.** *The newspaper is (being) sold.*

Die Zeitungen **werden verkauft.** *The newspapers are (being) sold.*

SIMPLE PAST

Die Zeitung **wurde verkauft.** *The newspaper was (being) sold.*

Die Zeitungen **wurden verkauft.** *The newspapers were (being) sold.*

PRESENT PERFECT

Die Zeitung **ist verkauft worden.** *The newspaper has been sold.*

Die Zeitungen **sind verkauft worden.** *The newspapers have been sold.*

Analyse. Suggestion:
Review the various functions of *werden* first; for example, *Hans wird Arzt. Was möchten Sie werden? Wir werden drei Wochen Ferien machen.* Then have students work in pairs to do the **Analyse.** When checking their answers, ask students to describe a possible context for each caption or headline.

Die Zeitung **war verkauft worden.**	*The newspaper had been sold.*
Die Zeitungen **waren verkauft worden.**	*The newspapers had been sold.*

Note:

- In the perfect tenses of the passive, the past participle **geworden** is shortened to **worden.**
- The presence of **worden** in any sentence is a clear signal that the sentence is in the passive voice.

ANALYSE

You now know three ways in which the verb **werden** can function.

1. **werden** as independent verb (*to become*)
2. **werden** + infinitive (future tense)
3. **werden** + past participle (passive voice)

Read the headlines and captions and determine . . .

- how the verb **werden** is used in each case (independent verb, future tense, passive)
- the position of the past participle in
  a. a main clause in the passive voice
  b. a dependent clause in the passive voice

KULTURSTADT

Weimar im Blickpunkt: Die deutsche Klassikermetropole wird 1999 Kulturstadt Europas

In jeder Minute werden 21 Hektar[1] Regenwald vernichtet[2]
Schon in wenigen Jahren wird es die „Grünen Lungen[3] der Erde" nicht mehr geben

Muß unser Dorf so häßlich werden?

GREENPEACE

Wie konnten Sie es zulassen[4], daß unsere Erde[5] in so kurzer Zeit vergiftet[6] wurde?

Realia. *Muß unser Dorf so hässlich werden?* is from a pamphlet published by the *Deutches Nationalkomitee für Denkmalschutz* in Bonn, which seeks to preserve the integrity and beauty of older buildings and monuments.

[1]*Hektar = 2.47 acres* [2]*destroyed* [3]*lungs* [4]*allow* [5]*earth* [6]*poisoned*

Expressing the Agent

As already noted, the agent causing the action in a passive voice sentence is often not stated. However, when it is stated, the agent is expressed with the preposition **von** (+ *dat.*).

> In einer Stunde werden 1,5 Millionen Briefe **von Deutschen** geschrieben.

> *In one hour 1.5 million letters are written **by Germans.***

When the action is caused by an impersonal force, the preposition **durch** (+ *acc.*) is used.

> Die Umwelt wird **durch Luftverschmutzung** zerstört.

> *The environment is being destroyed **by air pollution.***

Sentences in the passive voice that state the agent can also be expressed in the active voice. There is no difference in meaning, only in emphasis.

PASSIVE: In einer Stunde werden **1,5 Millionen Briefe** ⏞SUBJECT **von Deutschen** ⏞PREPOSITIONAL OBJECT (AGENT) geschrieben.

ACTIVE: **Die Deutschen** ⏞SUBJECT (AGENT) schreiben in einer Stunde **1,5 Millionen Briefe.** ⏞DIRECT OBJECT

Note that the subject in the passive voice sentence becomes the direct object in the active voice sentence, and the subject in the active voice sentence becomes the prepositional object (**von**) in the passive voice sentence.

Übung 1   Was passiert alles in 60 Minuten in Deutschland?

A. Bilden Sie Sätze im Passiv Präsens.

BEISPIEL: 1,5 Millionen Briefe werden geschrieben.

1. 1,5 Millionen Briefe	geboren
2. Mehr als eine Million Liter Bier	gegessen
3. 77 Kinder	gekauft
4. 458 Autos	geschrieben
5. 404 Fernsehgeräte	getrunken
6. Über eine Million Zeitungen	hergestellt
7. 38 Menschen / in Unfällen auf der Straße	produziert
8. 721 Tonnen Fleisch	verletzt

B. Drücken Sie die Sätze aus Teil A im Passiv Perfekt aus.

BEISPIEL: In einer Stunde sind 77 Kinder geboren worden.

Ihrer Haut zuliebe wurde auf jede Chemie verzichtet[1]

[1]*For the sake of your skin, all chemicals were avoided.*

Übung 2   Achtung, Uhren umstellen!

Lesen Sie folgende Nachricht über die Sommerzeit.

1. Identifizieren Sie alle Sätze im Passiv.
2. Was sind die Tatsachen?
   - **a.** Die Uhren...
   - **b.** Die Nacht...
   - **c.** Die Sommerzeit...
   - **d.** Das Ziel (*goal*)...

Achtung,[1] Uhren umstellen:[2] Die Sommerzeit beginnt

BM/dpa Hamburg, 26. März

Der Osterhase[3] bringt in diesem Jahr auch die Sommerzeit: In der Nacht zum Sonntag um 2 Uhr werden die Uhren auf 3 Uhr vorgestellt;[4] die Nacht wird um eine Stunde verkürzt.[5] Die Sommerzeit endet am 24. September – traditionsgemäß wieder eine Sonntag-Nacht.

   Die Sommerzeit war in der Bundesrepublik Deutschland – nach 30 Jahren Unterbrechung[6] – erstmals 1980 wieder eingeführt[7] worden. Das eigentliche[8] Ziel, Energie einzusparen, wurde jedoch nicht erreicht.[9] Dafür genießen[10] viele ihre Freizeit an den langen hellen Abenden.

In der Nacht zum Sonntag... ...Uhr 1 Stunde vorstellen

[1]*attention*   [2]*change*   [3]*Easter Bunny*   [4]*set ahead*   [5]*shortened*   [6]*interruption*
[7]*introduced*   [8]*real*   [9]*reached*   [10]*enjoy*

Expressing a General Activity

Sometimes a sentence in the passive voice expresses a general activity without stating a subject at all. In such cases, the "impersonal" **es** is generally understood to be the subject, and therefore the conjugated verb always appears in the third-person singular. This grammatical feature has no equivalent in English.

Hier wird gerudert.	*People are rowing here.*
Im Fernsehen wird viel über Terrorismus gesprochen.	*There's a lot of talk about terrorism on television.*
Hier wird Deutsch gesprochen.	*German (is) spoken here.*

Realia. Suggestion: Give students several minutes to figure out who sits where.

Eins – und eins – und eins . . .

Hier wird mächtig gerudert! **Jochen** sitzt zwischen **Peter** und **Stefan**, **Armin** sitzt zwischen **Martin** und **Thomas**. Vorn in einem Boot sitzt **Peter**, während **Martin** hinten sitzt. **Kalli** und **Stefan** rudern nicht in demselben Boot. Wer ist wer?

Lösung: 1. Stefan, 2. Jochen, 3. Peter, 4. Martin, 5. Armin, 6. Thomas, 7. Kalli

Übung 3   Was ist hier los?

Beschreiben Sie, was die Leute auf diesen Bildern machen. Gebrauchen Sie die Verben:

debattieren	feiern	reden
demonstrieren	lachen	tanzen
diskutieren	Musik machen	trinken
essen		

BEISPIEL: Bild 1: Da wird gefeiert und...

Übung 4   Eins nach dem andern!

Was kommt gewöhnlich zuerst?

BEISPIEL: Kuchen essen / Kuchen backen →
            Zuerst wird der Kuchen gebacken, dann wird er gegessen.

1. duschen / aufstehen
2. Haare trocknen / Haare waschen
3. Zeitung lesen / Kaffee machen
4. Zähne putzen / frühstücken
5. im Supermarkt einkaufen / Wohnung aufräumen
6. Dosen zum Recyclingcontainer bringen / Dosen sammeln
7. Freund/Freundin anrufen / stundenlang diskutieren

In zwei Städten, Neustadt und Altstadt, wird für eine bessere Umwelt gesorgt.

BEISPIEL: S1: Was ist zuerst in Neustadt gemacht worden?
　　　　　　 S2: Zuerst sind naturnahe Gärten angelegt worden.

	NEUSTADT	**ALTSTADT**
zuerst	naturnahe Gärten anlegen	Autos aus der Innenstadt verbannen
dann	Kinderspielplätze verbessern	neue Siedlungen am Stadtrand bauen
danach	Park im Zentrum säubern	Bürger über Umweltschutz informieren
schließlich	keine Wegwerfartikel in Geschäften verkaufen	neue, moderne Busse kaufen
zuletzt	nach Alternativenergie suchen	ein großes Umweltfest in der Innenstadt feiern

KULTURTIPP

In einigen Orten Deutschlands können alte Medikamente in die Apotheke zurückgebracht werden, damit sie nicht in den Abfall geworfen werden und als Giftstoffe die Umwelt gefährden. Andere potentiell gefährliche Substanzen wie alte Batterien und Farben werden von „Umweltbussen" abgeholt.

Beispiele für Gefahrensymbole

Gifte　　　Leicht entzündlich　　　Ätzend　　　Gesundheitsschädlich

The Passive with Modal Verbs

Modal verbs used with a passive infinitive convey something that should, must, or can be done. Only the present tense, the simple past tense, and the present subjunctive of modals are commonly used in the passive.

Die Umwelt **muss geschützt werden.**

The environment must be protected.

Die Natur **darf** nicht **zerstört werden.**

Nature must not be destroyed.

Recyclingprogramme **sollten gefördert werden.**

Recycling programs ought to be promoted.

The passive infinitive consists of the past participle of the main verb and **werden:**

geschützt werden (*to be protected*)

zerstört werden (*to be destroyed*)

gefördert werden (*to be promoted*)

Übung 6   Aus Liebe zur Umwelt

Was kann und muss gemacht werden? Folgen Sie dem Beispiel.

BEISPIEL: die Umwelt schonen / müssen →
Die Umwelt muss geschont werden.

1. alle Menschen über Umweltschutz informieren / müssen
2. mehr Energie sparen / sollen
3. Recyclingprogramme fördern / sollen
4. Altglas sammeln / können
5. Abfälle wie Plastiktüten und Einwegflaschen vermeiden / müssen
6. Altbatterien nicht in den Müll werfen / dürfen
7. Wegwerfprodukte (wie z.B. Einmal-Rasierer, Einmal-Fotoapparate) nicht kaufen / sollen
8. Verpackungen (wie die Mehrweg-Eierbox) wieder ins Geschäft bringen / können
9. Wälder und Flüsse schützen / müssen
10. Alternativenergie entwickeln / müssen
11. Luftverschmutzung vermindern / müssen

Schützt Flüsse und Auen

Diese Lebensräume vieler wildlebender Tier- und Pflanzenarten dürfen nicht weiter zerstört werden!

Spendenkonto: 1703-203, Postgiroamt Hamburg, oder werden Sie Mitglied im Bund der aktiven Naturschützer.

kompostierbar · recyclingfähig
aus 100% Altpapier

Aus Liebe zur Umwelt
Mehrweg-Eierbox
Bring'sie wieder mit

10x frische Eier, selbst ausgewählt
1x aktiv Umwelt geschont

GÜTE-KLASSE A

Verpackung aus 100% Altpapier recyclingfähig

Übung 7. Suggestion: Go over both columns to make sure students understand the vocabulary. This will probably bring up the questions of what one can bring back to a pharmacy and what an *Umweltbus* is.

Übung 7 Was ist das Problem?

Was soll, kann oder darf damit (nicht) gemacht werden?

BEISPIEL: Digitaluhren können nicht repariert werden.

1. Billiguhren (Digitaluhren)
2. Einmal-Fotoapparate
3. alte Batterien
4. Einwegflaschen
5. alte Medikamente
6. Giftstoffe

a. vom Umweltbus abholen
b. in fast alle Apotheken zurückbringen
c. nur für einen Film gebrauchen
d. nicht in den Müll werfen
e. nicht wieder füllen
f. nicht reparieren

Use of **man** as an Alternative to the Passive

Generally, the passive voice is used whenever the agent of an action is unknown. One alternative to the passive is to use the pronoun **man** in the active voice.

Note: Alternative publications often use *frau/man* in place of only *man*.

PASSIVE VOICE	ACTIVE-VOICE ALTERNATIVE
Die Gefahr ist nicht erkannt worden.	**Man hat** die Gefahr nicht **erkannt.**
The danger was not recognized.	*People (One) did not recognize the danger.*
Die Zerstörung der Altstadt ist verhindert worden.	**Man hat** die Zerstörung der Altstadt **verhindert.**
The destruction of the old city was prevented.	*People (One) prevented the destruction of the old city.*

Übung 8 Was kann man für die Umwelt tun?

Bilden Sie neue Sätze mit **man.**

BEISPIEL: Wegwerfprodukte sollen vermieden werden. →
           Man soll Wegwerfprodukte vermeiden.

1. Umweltschutz muss gelebt werden; er kann nicht befohlen werden.
2. Die Umwelt darf nicht weiter zerstört werden.
3. Altpapier und Glas sollten zum Recycling gebracht werden.
4. In Göttingen ist Geld für den Umweltschutz gesammelt worden.
5. Mehr Recycling-Container sind aufgestellt worden.
6. Chemikalien im Haushalt sollen vermieden werden.
7. Batterien sollen nicht in den Hausmüll geworfen werden.
8. Der Wald muss besonders geschützt werden.

Übung 9   Lebensqualität

Was kann man tun, um die Lebensqualität zu verbessern? Bilden Sie Sätze mit **man.**

BEISPIEL: alte Zeitungen →
           Man kann alte Zeitungen zum Recycling bringen.

alte Zeitungen	bauen
Plastiktüten	fördern
Windenergie	vermeiden
Kinderspielplätze	sammeln
Solarautos	entwickeln
Altpapier	schützen
öffentliche	benutzen
Verkehrsmittel	zum Recycling
Wälder	bringen

Übung 9. Suggestion: Use this exercise to review other possible passive voice substitutes (*Man soll...* , etc.). Also review modals with a passive infinitive (*Plastiktüten sollen vermieden werden,* etc.).

Das Partizip Präsens

The Present Participle°

The present participle (ending in *-ing* in English) is used in a more limited way in German than it is in English. In German it functions primarily as an adjective or an adverb. As an attributive adjective (preceding a noun), the participle takes appropriate adjective endings.

The present participle of a German verb is formed by adding **-d** to the infinitive.

INFINITIVE	PRESENT PARTICIPLE
kommen	kommend (*coming*)
steigen	steigend (*climbing, increasing*)

PRESENT PARTICIPLE AS ATTRIBUTIVE ADJECTIVE	
im **kommenden** Sommer	*in the coming (next) summer*
die **steigende** Arbeitslosigkeit	*increasing unemployment*

PRESENT PARTICIPLE AS ADVERB	
Jennifer spricht **fließend** Deutsch.	*Jennifer speaks German fluently.*

Übung 10   In der Zeitung

Worüber liest man fast täglich? Bilden Sie Sätze mit dem Partizip Präsens.

BEISPIEL: Man liest täglich über den wachsenden Verkehr.

1. die Menschen	steigen
2. die Preise	flüchten (*to flee*)
3. die Bürger	streiken
4. die Studenten	wachsen (*to grow*)
5. der Verkehr	protestieren
6. das Problem	sterben
7. der Wald	demonstrieren
8. die Arbeiter	

Sprache im Kontext

Videoclips

A. Claudia, Harald und Wiebke sprechen über die Probleme in der Welt.

    1. Was sind für sie die drei größten Probleme heute?

       Claudia: _____

                   _____

                   _____

       Harald: _____

                   _____

                   _____

       Wiebke: _____

                   _____

                   _____

    2. Und für Sie? Was sind für Sie die drei größten Probleme heute in der Welt?

B. Harald spricht über ein ganz spezifisches Problem in Berlin. Erklären Sie das Problem.

C. Wiebke spricht über AIDS und was dagegen gemacht wird. Was sagt sie? Ergänzen Sie ihre Worte.

   „Ich verfolge in der Zeitung ab und zu die Entwicklung von AIDS. Ich sehe, dass es in Afrika sehr stark _____ hat, dass auch die _____ Versorgung für AIDS noch nicht das _____, was es bringen könnte. Man arbeitet an Wirkstoffen und _____, aber die Versorgung zum Beispiel für _____ Leute in Afrika oder für Leute in den Ostblockländern ist nicht so gut. Und Medikamente sind auch nicht so verfügbar, wie man sich das _____.“

D. Was tun Claudia und Wiebke für die Umwelt? Schauen Sie sich die Interviews an und schreiben Sie vor jede Aussage entweder **C** für Claudia oder **W** für Wiebke.

   _____ sammelt Zeitungen

   _____ benutzt öffentliche Verkehrsmittel oder Fahrrad

   _____ bringt leere Flaschen zurück

   _____ benutzt Stoffbeutel statt Plastikbeutel

   _____ lässt das Wasser beim Zähneputzen nicht laufen

   _____ badet und duscht weniger und wäscht sich mehr, denn es ist gesünder für die Haut

   _____ gebraucht so wenig Strom wie möglich

E. Und Sie? Was machen Sie für die Umwelt?

Lesen

Zum Thema

Die Skandalpresse. In den meisten Ländern gibt es Zeitschriften, die von den jüngsten Sensationen und Skandalen berichten. Auch im Fernsehen wird oft von sensationellen und skandalösen Ereignissen (*events*) berichtet, die aber oft erfunden sind.

Machen Sie eine Umfrage im Kurs.

1. Wie heißen die Zeitungen und Zeitschriften, die sich auf Sensationen und Skandale spezialisieren?
2. Wer liest sie regelmäßig? Welche? Warum?

Auf den ersten Blick

Lesen Sie den Text, eine Ballade von Reinhard Mai, kurz durch.

1. Wovon handelt diese Ballade?
2. Wer sind die Hauptfiguren?
3. Wo spielt sich das Ereignis ab?

The Listening Comprehension Audio CD that accompanies the textbook contains a recording of the ballad of "Was in der Zeitung steht." You may wish to play this for your students in class, or recommend that they listen to it at home or in the lab.

Zum Thema. Suggestion: If possible, bring in a variety of German-language newspapers. Have students skim them and draw conclusions about the newspapers from a cursory examination.

WAS IN DER ZEITUNG STEHT

von Reinhard Mai

Wie jeden Morgen war er pünktlich dran, seine
Kollegen sahen ihn fragend an, „Sag' mal,
hast du noch nicht gesehen, was in der
Zeitung steht?"
5 Er schloß die Türe hinter sich,
hängte Hut und Mantel in den Schrank fein säuberlich,°   *neatly*
setzte sich, „da wollen wir erst mal sehen,
was in der Zeitung steht."

Und da stand es fett auf Seite zwei
10 „Finanzskandal", sein Bild dabei
und die Schlagzeile „Wie lang das wohl so weitergeht?"
Er las den Text,
und ihm war sofort klar,
eine Verwechslung,° nein, da war kein Wort' von wahr,   *mistake, mix-up*
15 aber wie kann so etwas verlogen° sein,   *fabricated*
was in der Zeitung steht?

Er starrte auf das Blatt,°   *paper*
das vor ihm lag,
es traf ihn wie ein heimtückischer° Schlag,°   *malicious / blow*
20 wie ist das möglich, daß so etwas in der Zeitung steht?
Das Zimmer ringsherum begann sich zu drehen,°   *sich... to turn*
die Zeilen konnte er nur noch verschwommen° sehen.   *as blurred*
Wie wehrt man sich° nur gegen das,   *wehrt... does one defend oneself*
was in der Zeitung steht?

25 Die Kollegen sagten, „stell dich einfach stur",°	*stell... be stolid*
er taumelte° zu seinem Chef über den Flur,	*staggered*
„aber selbstverständlich,	
daß jeder hier zu Ihnen steht,	
ich glaube, das Beste ist, Sie spannen erst mal aus,	
30 ein paar Tage Urlaub, bleiben Sie zu Haus,	
Sie wissen ja, die Leute glauben gleich alles,	
nur weil es in der Zeitung steht."	
Er holte Hut und Mantel, wankte° aus dem Raum,	*swayed*
nein, das war wirklich kalt, das war kein böser Traum,	
35 wer denkt sich sowas aus, wie das,	
was in der Zeitung steht?	
Er rief den Fahrstuhl,° stieg ein und gleich wieder aus,	*elevator*
nein, er ging doch wohl besser durch das Treppenhaus.°	*stairwell*
Da würde ihn keiner sehen, der wüßte,	
40 was in der Zeitung steht.	
Er würde durch die Tiefgarage gehen, er war zu Fuß.	
Der Pförtner° würde ihn nicht sehen,	*custodian*
der wußte immer ganz genau,	
was in der Zeitung steht.	
45 Er stolperte° die Wagenauffahrt° rauf,	*stumbled / driveway*
sah den Rücken des Pförtners,	
das Tor war auf,	
das klebt wie Pech° an dir,	*klebt wie... sticks like tar*
das wirst du nie mehr los,°	*wirst... you will never get rid of*
50 was in der Zeitung steht,	
was in der Zeitung steht,	
was in der Zeitung steht,	
was in der Zeitung steht.	
Er eilte° zur U-Bahnstation,	*hurried*
55 jetzt wüßten es die Nachbarn schon,	
jetzt war es im ganzen Ort herum,	
was in der Zeitung steht.	
Solange die Kinder in der Schule waren,	
solange würden sie es vielleicht nicht erfahren,°	*find out*
60 aber irgendwer hat ihnen längst erzählt,	
was in der Zeitung steht.	
Er wich den Leuten auf dem Bahnsteig aus,°	*wich... aus avoided*
ihm schien, die Blicke, alle richteten sich nur auf ihn,	
der Mann im Kiosk da, der wußte Wort für Wort,	
65 was in der Zeitung steht.	
Wie eine Welle° war es, die über ihm zusammenschlug,°	*wave / crashed down*
wie die Erlösung° kam der Vorortszug,°	*deliverance / local train*
du wirst nie mehr ganz frei, das hängt dir ewig an,	
was in der Zeitung steht.	
70 „Was wollen Sie eigentlich?" fragte der Redakteur,°	*editor*
„Verantwortung,° Mann, wenn ich das schon hör',	*responsibility*
die Leute müssen halt nicht gleich alles glauben,	

nur weil es in der Zeitung steht."

„Na, schön, so eine Verwechslung kann schon mal passieren,
75 da kannst du noch so sorgfältig° recherchieren.°   *carefully / research*
Mann, was glauben Sie, was Tag für Tag für ein Unfug°   *nonsense*
in der Zeitung steht?"

„Ja", sagte der Chef vom Dienst, „das ist wirklich zu dumm,
aber ehrlich,° man bringt sich doch nicht gleich um,°   *honestly / bringt... one*
80 nur weil mal aus Versehen°   *doesn't kill oneself / aus... by mistake*
was in der Zeitung steht."
Die Gegendarstellung° erschien am Abend schon,   *retraction, corrected version*
fünf Zeilen mit dem Bedauern° der Redaktion,   *regret*
aber Hand aufs Herz, wer liest, was so klein
85 in der Zeitung steht?

Zum Text

1. Lesen Sie die folgenden Sätze, und setzen Sie sie in die richtige
   Reihenfolge.

   _____ Er eilte zur U-Bahnstation, um nach Hause zu fahren.
   _____ Es war ganz klein gedruckt.
   _____ Der Chef fand, dass sein Selbstmord (*suicide*) übertrieben war.
   _____ Kein Wort war wahr. Es war eine Verwechslung.
   _____ Er verließ das Gebäude durch die Parkgarage, um die Leute zu
   vermeiden.
   __1__ Ein Mann ging ins Büro zur Arbeit und las zuerst die Zeitung.
   _____ Er sah sein Bild neben der Schlagzeile „Finanzskandal" in der
   Zeitung.
   _____ Er ging zu seinen Kollegen und zu seinem Chef.
   _____ Er warf sich vor den Zug.
   _____ In der Zeitung stand später, dass der Bericht ein Irrtum
   (*mistake*) war.
   _____ Sein Chef schickte ihn nach Hause.
   _____ Der Redakteur der Zeitung meinte, dass er keine
   Verantwortung trage.

2. Wie reagieren die Personen in der Ballade auf die falsche Information in
   der Zeitung?
3. Wie steht der Liedermacher zu der Presse?
4. „Was in der Zeitung steht" ist eine Ballade. Was ist charakteristisch für
   eine Ballade? Was macht dieser Text zu einer Ballade?

Sprechen und Schreiben

Aktivität 1   Informieren Sie sich!

Was finden Sie über die deutschsprachigen Länder in den Nachrichten und
Zeitungen? Suchen Sie sich mehrere Zeitungen oder Zeitschriften aus.
Schauen Sie nach, was in den letzten zwei Monaten über die
deutschsprachigen Länder berichtet wurde. Welche Themen über die

deutschsprachigen Länder kommen vor? Warum sind diese Themen wichtig? Wählen Sie ein Thema und geben Sie einen kurzen Bericht in der Klasse.

Aktivität 2 Reporter

Schreiben Sie einen kurzen Artikel über die Fakten in der Ballade von Reinhard Mai. Nehmen Sie dazu Stellung. Benutzen Sie dabei indirekte Rede.

Wortschatz

Weltweite Probleme	World Problems
die **Arbeitslosigkeit**	unemployment
die **Armut**	poverty
die **Ausländerfeindlichkeit**	xenophobia, hatred directed toward foreigners
die **Drogensucht** der/die **Drogensüchtige, -n**	drug addiction drug addict
die **Gewalttätigkeit, -en**	(act of) violence
der **Hunger**	hunger, famine
die **Korruption**	corruption
die **Krankheit, -en**	illness, disease, ailment
der **Krieg, -e**	war
das **Menschenrecht, -e**	human right (*usu. plural*)
der/die **Obdachlose, -n**	homeless person
die **Obdachlosigkeit**	homelessness
der **Rassismus**	racism
der **Rechtsextremismus**	right-wing extremism
der **Terrorismus**	terrorism
die **Umweltverschmutzung**	environmental pollution
die **Verletzung, -en**	injury, violation
die **Welt**	world, earth

Umwelt	Environment
der **Abfall, ⸚e**	waste, garbage, trash, litter
die **Dose, -n**	(tin or aluminum) can; jar
die **Getrankedose, -n**	beverage can
die **Flasche, -n**	bottle
die **Wegwerfflasche, -n**	nonrecyclable bottle
die **Fußgängerzone, -n**	pedestrian zone, mall
der **Lärm**	noise
die **Plastiktüte, -n**	plastic bag
die **Sammelstelle, -n**	recycling center
das **Verkehrsmittel, -**	vehicle, means of transportation
die **Verpackung, -en**	packaging, wrapping

Sonstige Substantive	Other Nouns
der **Alkohol**	alcohol
das **Arzneimittel, -**	medication
der **Ausländer, -** / die **Ausländerin, -nen**	foreigner
der **Bürger, -** / die **Bürgerin, -nen**	citizen
die **Demonstration, -en**	demonstration

die **Droge, -n**	drug; medicine	**unterstützen**	to support
die **Forschung, -en**	research	**verbieten, verbot, verboten**	to prohibit, forbid
der **Fortschritt, -e**	progress	**verbrauchen**	to consume
Fortschritte machen	to make progress	**verbreiten**	to spread, disseminate
die **Gefahr, -en**	danger		
das **Gefängnis, -se**	prison, jail	**vermeiden, vermied, vermieden**	to avoid
die **Lösung, -en**	solution		
die **Meinung, -en**	opinion	**vermindern**	to decrease, lessen
ich bin der Meinung...	I'm of the opinion . . .	**verwenden**	to use, apply
meiner Meinung nach...	in my opinion . . .	**vorschlagen (schlägt vor), schlug vor, vorgeschlagen**	to suggest
der **Politiker, -** / die **Politikerin, -nen**	politician	**vor•ziehen, zog vor, vorgezogen**	to prefer
die **Regierung, -en**	government	**wählen**	to vote, elect; to choose
die **Steuer, -n**	tax		

Verben — **Verbs**

sich etwas an•schaffen	to purchase or acquire something
bedauern	to regret
ein•führen	to introduce
sich engagieren	to get involved
entwickeln	to develop
erziehen, erzog, erzogen	to raise, bring up
fördern	to promote
halten (für) (hält), hielt, gehalten	to hold; to consider, think
isolieren	to isolate; to insulate
schaffen, schuf, geschaffen	to create
schützen	to protect
teil•nehmen an (+ *dat.*) **(nimmt teil), nahm teil, teilgenommen**	to participate (in)
(sich) trennen	to separate

Adjektive und Adverbien — **Adjectives and Adverbs**

möglich	possible, possibly
öffentlich	public
sauber	clean
schmutzig	dirty
streng	strict(ly)
übertrieben	exaggerated
umweltfreundlich	environmentally friendly

Andere Ausdrücke — **Other Expressions**

außerdem	besides, in addition to
Ich bin dafür.	I'm in favor of it.
Ich bin (total) dagegen.	I'm (totally) against it.
So ein Quatsch!	Nonsense!
So ein Unsinn!	Nonsense!

LERNZIELE

Use this checklist to verify that you can now . . .

- ☐ state your opinion about various problems in the world and possible solutions.
- ☐ state your opinion about the environment and what people can do to protect it.
- ☐ use a variety of discussion strategies to support your opinion.
- ☐ use the passive voice in simple sentences.
- ☐ create sentences using **man.**
- ☐ use the present participle as an attributive adjective or as an adverb.

Gestern und heute

Berlin ist die Hauptstadt
Europas und...
a. die größte Stadt
   Deutschlands
b. eins von 16 deutschen
   Bundesländern

Übergang. This chapter is
called *Übergang* because it is
considered a capstone for first-
year German and a transition to
second-year German. Begin the
chapter by discussing a
particular event from German
history. Ask students which
events from the recent past will
become important milestones in
history.

Videoclips

Berline: damals und
heute

In diesem Kapitel

- Short history of Germany (1939–present), remembrances of war and
  survival, Berlin—the capital

Kleine Chronik deutscher Geschichte von 1939–1999

1. September 1939	Der Zweite Weltkrieg beginnt mit der Invasion Polens durch deutsche Truppen.
9. Mai 1945	Um null Uhr eins endet der Zweite Weltkrieg in Europa offiziell mit der Kapitulation der Deutschen Wehrmacht.° Durch diesen Krieg verloren insgesamt 55 Millionen Menschen ihr Leben.

armed forces

Das zerbombte Reichstagsgebäude, Berlin 1945

Trümmerfrauen bei der Arbeit

Kleine Chronik. Suggestion: If it is available, show the film *Triumph des Willens* by filmmaker Leni Riefenstahl, which documents Hitler's effect on the German people, as shown in the annual ritual of the *Parteitag* in Nürnberg.

Suggestion: Assign the *Kleine Chronik* reading as homework. Discuss and elaborate on dates and events the following day, bringing in additional pictures and slides.

5. Juni 1945	Die vier Alliierten (die Vereinigten Staaten, die Sowjetunion, Großbritannien und Frankreich) übernehmen die oberste Regierungsgewalt in Deutschland. Deutschland wird in vier Besatzungszonen° aufgeteilt. Berlin, die ehemalige Hauptstadt, wird separat in vier Besatzungszonen aufgeteilt.

occupation zones

5. Juni 1947	Der Marshallplan wird für Deutschland die Grundlage° für das kommende Wirtschaftswunder.°

foundation
economic miracle

Menschenschlangen stehen 1946 nach Lebensmitteln an.

Die „Luftbrücke": Ein „Rosinenbomber" kurz vor der Landung in Berlin

20. Juni 1948	Es gibt neues Geld: die Deutsche Mark. Jeder Bürger der Westzonen und West-Berlins bekommt zu Anfang 40 Mark.
24. Juni 1948	Beginn der Berliner Blockade. Die Sowjetunion blockiert alle Wege nach West-Berlin außer den Luftwegen. Elf Monate lang werden die Berliner durch die „Luftbrücke" versorgt.
23. Mai 1949	Gründung der Bundesrepublik Deutschland (BRD).

7. Oktober 1949	Gründung der Deutschen Demokratischen Republik (DDR).	
17. Juni 1953	Volksaufstand° in Ost-Berlin und der DDR gegen das kommunistische Regime.	*popular uprising*
13. August 1961	Bau der Mauer° in Berlin.	*wall*
26. Juni 1963	Besuch Präsident John F. Kennedys in Berlin. Seine Erklärung der Solidarität mit Berlinern endet mit den oft zitierten Worten: „Ich bin ein Berliner."	
9. November 1989	Die Grenzen zwischen der DDR und der BRD werden geöffnet. Die Mauer zwischen Ost- und West-Berlin hat genau 10 315 Tage gehalten.	
18. März 1990	Erste freie, demokratische Wahl in der Deutschen Demokratischen Republik seit ihrer Gründung.	
3. Oktober 1990	Tag der offiziellen deutschen Einigung. Fünf neue Bundesländer (Brandenburg, Mecklenburg-Vorpommern, Sachsen, Sachsen-Anhalt und Thüringen) treten der Bundesrepublik bei.°	*treten... bei* *join*
20. Juni 1991	Der deutsche Bundestag wählt Berlin zum Regierungssitz° des vereinigten Deutschlands.	*seat of government*
1. Januar 1993	Der Vertrag über die Europäische Union tritt in Kraft.°	*tritt... Kraft* *comes into force*
8. September 1994	Offizieller Abschied der Besatzungstruppen von Berlin.	
19. April 1999	Der Bundestag tagt zum ersten Mal im neuen Reichstagsgebäude in Berlin.	

KULTURTIPP

Die Kaiser-Wilhelm-Gedächtniskirche liegt am Kudamm (Kurfürstendamm), dem großen Einkaufsboulevard Berlins. Die Kirche lag am Ende des Zweiten Weltkriegs in Trümmern (*ruins*). Man baute eine neue, moderne Kirche auf, ließ aber die schwarze Ruine des Turms als Mahnmal (*memorial*) an die dunklen Jahre des Krieges stehen.

Die Kaiser-Wilhelm-Gedächtniskirche in Berlin

Hier klicken!

Weiteres zum Thema
Geschichte finden Sie bei
Deutsch: Na klar! im
World-Wide-Web unter
www.mhhe.com/dnk.

Aktivität 1 Aus der deutschen Geschichte

Ordnen Sie zuerst die Daten und die Satzteile einander zu. Welches Bild
passt zu welchem Satz?

a. Am 9. Mai 1945

b. Am 13. August 1961

c. Am 9. November 1989

d. Am 19. April 1999

—— wurde die Grenze zwischen
Ost- und West-Berlin durch den Bau
der Mauer geschlossen. BILD ——.

—— feierte ganz Deutschland die
Öffnung der Grenze zwischen
Ost- und West-Berlin und zwischen
der DDR und der BRD. BILD ——.

—— tagte der Bundestag zum ersten Mal im
neuen Reichstagsgebäude. BILD ——.

—— als der Zweite Weltkrieg in Europa
endete, lag ganz Deutschland in
Trümmern. BILD ——.

1.

2.

3.

4.

Aktivität 2 Faktum oder nicht?

Stimmt das oder stimmt es nicht? Korrigieren Sie die falschen Aussagen.

	DAS STIMMT	DAS STIMMT NICHT
1. Der Zweite Weltkrieg begann mit der Invasion der Sowjetunion durch deutsche Truppen im September 1939.	☐	☒
2. Der Zweite Weltkrieg kostete 55 Millionen Menschen das Leben.	☒	☐
3. Deutschland wurde nach dem Zweiten Weltkrieg in vier Besatzungszonen geteilt.	☒	☐
4. Berlin gehörte ganz zur russischen Besatzungszone.	☐	☒
5. Die BRD und die DDR wurden 1945 gegründet.	☐	☒
6. Der Marshallplan spielte eine wichtige Rolle beim Wiederaufbau Europas.	☒	☐
7. Im Juni 1948 blockierte die Sowjetunion alle Transportwege nach Berlin.	☐	☒
8. Im Jahre 1953 rebellierten die Deutschen in Ost und West gegen die kommunistische Regierung.	☐	☒
9. Im Jahre 1991 wurden die DDR und die BRD vereinigt.	☐	☒
10. Im Jahre 1992 trat der Vertrag über die Europäische Union in Kraft.	☐	☒

Aktivität 3 Ein kleines Quiz

Bilden Sie mehrere Gruppen. Machen Sie mit Hilfe der kleinen Chronik deutscher Geschichte ein Quiz. Das Format bleibt jeder Gruppe überlassen. Es könnte z.B. in Form einer Quizshow sein: Wer bin ich?; es könnte eine Serie von Fragen sein, die Sie gemeinsam entwickeln; oder es könnte ein Wortratespiel sein. Die anderen im Kurs übernehmen die Rolle der Teilnehmer (*participants*).

Aktivität 3. Suggestion:
Assign the creation of the quiz to each group for homework. Brainstorm some ideas with students, and do the quiz in class the next day.

Große Freude nach der Öffnung der Grenzen: Eine Westberlinerin begrüßt eine DDR-Bürgerin.

Beiträge° zur deutschen Geschichte

Wie berührt (*touches*) Geschichte unser Leben? In diesem Teil des Kapitels erleben Sie Geschichte, indem Sie persönliche Dokumente, Auszüge aus einer Autobiographie und Briefe lesen. Diese persönlichen Dokumente bringen uns historische Ereignisse auf ungewöhnliche Weise näher.

Auf den ersten Blick 1.
Suggestion: Mention the different groups of people who were persecuted under Hitler: Jews, political opponents (particularly Communists), homosexuals, mentally retarded or mentally disturbed people, and other groups deemed racially inferior, such as Gypsies.

Auf den ersten Blick ı

Der folgende Text, ein kurzer Ausschnitt aus der Autobiographie der Zigeunerin (*Gypsy*) Ceja Stojka, *Wir leben im Verborgenen: Erinnerungen einer Rom-Zigeunerin,* ist im Jahre 1989 erschienen. Ceja Stojka wurde 1933 in einem Gasthaus in der Steiermark in Österreich geboren. Während des Dritten Reiches wurde sie als Zigeunerin—sie gehörte zu der Rom Gruppe— aus rassistischen Gründen verfolgt (*persecuted*). Sie kam zusammen mit ihrer Mutter und ihren Schwestern in die Konzentrationslager Auschwitz und Ravensbrück.

Überfliegen Sie den ersten Abschnitt des Textes. Welche der folgenden Namen und Wörter stehen im Text?

☐ Auschwitz
☐ Hitler
☐ experimentieren
☐ nach Hause gehen
☐ Berlin
☐ SS-Soldaten
☐ sterilisieren
☐ Ravensbrück
☐ SS-Frauen
☐ Konzentrationslager

KULTURTIPP

Die Aufseherinnen (*female guards*) in den Konzentrationslagern wurden automatisch zu Mitgliedern der SS. Daher die Bezeichnung SS-Frauen, die Ceja Stojka benutzt.

Für „arische" Frauen waren Verhütungsmittel (*birth control*), Abtreibungen (*abortions*) und Sterilisation gegen das Gesetz; aber für andere Frauen, die nicht der Norm entsprachen, gab es Zwangssterilisation (*forced sterilization*). In den Konzentrationslagern wurden Zwangssterilisationen an vielen Frauen vorgenommen, um mit neuen Methoden der Sterilisation zu experimentieren.

Kulturtipp. Note: The *SS (Schutzstaffel)* was created by Hitler in 1925 as a military organization within his party and was totally loyal to him. It became the most feared party organization during the Nazi years.

Realia. This is a *Wahlplakat* for Adolf Hitler: "Rettet die deutsche Familie. Wählt Adolf Hitler."

von Ceja Stojka

Ja, es war nicht einfach in diesem Frauenlager Ravensbrück. Die SS-Frauen waren schlechter als jeder Satan. Eines Tages kamen zwei von ihnen und sagten zu uns: „Hört alle gut zu, was wir euch sagen. Es ist ein Schreiben aus Berlin gekommen und das sagt, alle Frauen und Kinder, die sich sterilisieren
5 lassen, können bald nach Hause gehen." Und weiter sagten sie: „Na, ihr braucht ja keine Kinder mehr, also kommt morgen und unterschreibt,° daß ihr *sign* freiwillig dazu bereit seid. Der Oberarzt wird euch diesen Eingriff° machen. In *operation* ein paar Tagen könnt ihr dann das Lager verlassen." (Das war alles eine Lüge.° *lie* Ja, es war eine Lüge, denn wir standen alle schon auf der Liste.)
10 Die SS-Frauen wurden immer böser. So verging° ein Tag um den anderen. *passed* Täglich warf man Frauen in den Bunker, und sie kamen nicht mehr zurück. So ging es wochenlang.

Die Tage wurden nun schon länger und manchesmal war es nicht mehr so kalt. Ich, Mama, Kathi, Chiwe mit Burli und Rupa mußten in die Waschküche.
15 Wir machten dort unsere Arbeit und als wir zurückkamen, sahen wir, wie zwei Häftlinge° einen Bretterwagen° vor unsere Baracke zogen. Viele Frauen *inmates / wooden wagon* waren darauf, wie Schweine lagen sie übereinander. Ganz oben lag unsere kleine liebe Resi. Sie waren sterilisiert worden, alle hatten große Schmerzen, sie konnten nicht einmal ein einziges Wort sagen. Die kleine Resi starb° *died*
20 gleich, auch die anderen kamen nicht mehr durch. Alle waren tot. Die SS-Frauen sagten dann zu uns: „Ihr braucht keine Angst zu haben, der Oberarzt hat ein neues Gerät bekommen, das alte hatte einen Kurzschluß,° also ein Verse- *short circuit* hen.°" Wir wußten ganz genau, daß sie uns nur besänftigen° wollten, aber wir *accident / quiet* wußten auch, daß wir ihnen nicht entkommen.° Eines Tages kamen Binz und *escape*
25 Rabl und holten Mama, Kathi und mich ab. Sie sprachen nicht viel und sagten nur: „Marsch, Marsch". Wir gingen sehr schnell. In diesem Moment war uns alles egal. Wir kamen zu einem richtigen Haus. Es ging stockaufwärts. Die SS-Frauen machten im Vorraum dem Oberarzt ihre Meldung.° Nun warteten wir. *report* Mama zeigte uns mit ihren blauen Augen, daß wir mutig° sein sollten, *brave*
30 sprechen durften wir ja nicht. Die Zeit verging und es geschah nichts. Plötz- lich kam der Oberarzt und sagte: „Heute ist nichts mehr, wir haben leider keinen Strom." Er schaute uns mit großen Augen an und machte seine Tür zu. Zwei SS-Frauen brachten uns wieder in das Lager zurück. Unterwegs sahen wir eine Baracke. Drinnen waren viele Frauen mit Schreibmaschinen. Das war
35 die Schreibstube. Nun waren wir wieder in unserer Baracke. Alle fragten, was geschehen war, und alle Frauen weinten vor Freude.

Mama sagte: „*O swundo Dell gamel awer wariso de gerel amenza.*" (Der liebe Gott hat was anderes mit uns vor.)

Zum Text ı

1. Wie wurden Ceja und ihre Familie durch die Rassenpolitik der Nazis betroffen (*affected*)?

2. Welche Erfahrungen beschreibt die Autorin?

- Die SS-Frauen versprachen den Häftlingen, wenn sie sich freiwillig sterilisieren lassen,...
   a. bekommen sie besseres Essen.

b. brauchen sie eine Woche nicht zu arbeiten.

c. werden sie bald freigelassen.

■ Der Sterilisationsprozess im Lager war...
  a. freiwillig.
  b. ein medizinisches Experiment.
  c. eine Gesundheitsmaßnahme (*health precaution*).

■ Die Autorin erinnert sich daran, dass sie im Konzentrationslager...
  a. zur Schule ging.
  b. in der Waschküche arbeitete.
  c. auf der Schreibstube arbeitete.

■ Die ersten Frauen, die sterilisiert wurden,...
  a. starben an den Folgen der Sterilisation.
  b. kamen nie in die Baracken zurück.
  c. durften nach Hause gehen.

■ Die Autorin wurde nicht sterilisiert, weil...
  a. der Oberarzt Mitleid (*sympathy*) mit ihr hatte.
  b. man sie in der Waschküche brauchte.
  c. es keine Elektrizität gab.

Auf den ersten Blick 2

Auf den ersten Blick 2. Point Out: The letters reprinted on page 439 belong to a large collection of letters in the Hoover Institution Archives sent by German and Austrian children. The children's letters were the result of a nationwide effort to thank Hoover and the American people for their help. For many children, the *Schulspeisung* was the only regular meal of the day.

Im Frühjahr 1947 reiste der ehemalige Präsident Herbert Hoover nach Deutschland und Österreich, um die katastrophale Ernährungssituation zu untersuchen (*investigate*). Das Resultat war die Hoover-Speisung für Schulkinder in beiden Ländern. Kinder schickten Hoover Hunderte von Briefen, um ihm für seine Hilfe zu danken. Sie lesen hier zwei dieser Briefe, die jetzt in den Archiven des Hoover Instituts in Stanford, Kalifornien, gesammelt sind.

Überfliegen Sie die zwei Briefe kurz.

1. Wer hat die Briefe geschrieben? (Namen und Alter)
2. Aus welchem Jahr stammen die Briefe?
3. Wie reden (*address*) die Kinder Herbert Hoover an? Wie enden ihre Briefe?

Heike Leopold. Note: The style, spelling (*Aberika*), and handwriting show this to be the younger of the two writers. Heike is a refugee child who lost her home in Upper Silesia, now a part of Poland. Her keen interest in a doll with long hair, typical for young girls of that time, reflects a child's capacity to block out the harsh realities of survival. Those realities are only hinted at by her mention of her mother frequently standing in line for bread for a long time, leaving Heike and her sister by themselves.

THE HERBERT HOOVER ARCHIVES

Eckernförde, den 26.3.47.
Lieber Onkel Hoover!
Ich habe Dich neulich
im Kino gesehen und
da Du so lieb und gut
aussiehst, will ich Dir
heute schreiben. Wir
sind aus Oberschlesien
hierher gekommen und
haben dort unsre schönen
Sachen lassen müssen.

Giebt es in Amerika
schon Puppen mit lan=
gen Haaren zu kaufen?
Wir sind so oft allein,
weil unsre Mutti nach
Brot anstehen muß. Wer=
den bei euch alle Leute
satt? Nun willst Du
uns ja hier helfen in
Deutschland. Viele
Grüße, von Heike Leopold.

Margot Fränkel

Bayreuth, den 28.5.1947.
Sehr geehrter Herr Hoover!
Wir freuten uns sehr, als uns ver-
kündet[1] wurde, daß alle die Auslandsspeisen bekommen. Denn es wurde
durch Wiegen und Messen festgestellt,[2]
daß viele unterernährt[3] sind. Wir
sind schon immer auf die Minute
gespannt,[4] wenn es läutet[5] und wir
unser Essen bekommen. Heute gibt
es Teigwaren[6] mit Obsttunke.[7] Wenn
manchmal ein Rest übrig bleibt,
freuen wir uns am meisten, wenn
wir es bekommen. Es gibt jetzt schon
2½ Wochen Essen. Am meisten aber
freuen wir uns, wenn es am Ende
der Wochen Eiscremepaste gibt. Als es
das erstemal die Auslandsspeisen gab,

bekamen wir am Ende der Woche
eine Tafel Schokolade. Wir mußten
sie gleich anbeißen,[8] damit wir nicht
Schwarzhandel trieben.[9] Jeder geht jetzt
gerne in die Schule.
Ich danke Ihnen nochmals dafür,
für die guten Gaben.[10]
    Mit dankbarem Gruß
eine ergebene Schülerin
        Margot Fränkel

[1]announced   [2]es... it was found by weighing and
measuring   [3]malnourished   [4]eager   [5]the bell rings
[6]baked goods   [7]fruit syrup   [8]bite into it
[9]Schwarzhandel...   deal on the black market   [10]gifts

Das Nicolaiviertel

Zum Text 2

1. Was erfahren wir über die Folgen (*consequences*) des Krieges für die Kinder?
2. Welche Probleme erwähnen die Kinder? Wer schreibt davon, dass
   - die meisten Kinder unterernährt sind?
   - die Kinder wissen, wie man Schwarzhandel treibt?
   - die Familie aus ihrer Heimat geflüchtet (*fled*) ist?
   - sie oft allein ist, weil die Mutter nach Brot anstehen muss?

Zu guter Letzt

Berlin: Hauptstadt im Wandel

Im Juni 1991 wählte der deutsche Bundestag die Stadt Berlin zum offiziellen Regierungssitz. Mit etwa 3,4 Millionen Einwohnern ist Berlin die größte Stadt des vereinigten Deutschlands und dazu ein eigenständiger Staat der Bundesrepublik.

Von der Mauer, die von 1961 bis 1989 West-Berlin von Ost-Berlin trennte, ist kaum noch eine Spur zu sehen. Stattdessen sieht man überall moderne Bürohäuser, Einkaufszentren und Wohnhäuser, sowohl wie renovierte Regierungsgebäude. Das Stadtbild Berlin hat sich sehr verändert, vor allem am Potsdamer Platz und im früheren östlichen Teil. Berlin ist stolz auf seine Rolle als Metropole.

Das Kanzleramt

Das Wappen Berlins

Der Potsdamer Platz

Aktivität 1   Berlin erleben

Stellen Sie sich vor, dass Sie Berlin besuchen wollen. Machen Sie einen Plan, was Sie unbedingt sehen und tun möchten. Wählen Sie Veranstaltungen aus dem folgenden Programm aus. Suchen Sie sich zusätzliche Informationen über Berlin im Internet und planen Sie eine Stadtbesichtigung.

BEISPIEL: Ich möchte eine Bootstour auf der Spree machen und möglicherweise einen Spaziergang durch den Tiergarten. Ich möchte auch das Jüdisches Museum besuchen.

Hier klicken!

Weiteres zum Thema Berlin finden Sie bei **Deutsch: Na klar!** im World-Wide-Web unter www.mhhe.com/dnk.

PROGRAMM BERLIN

Die Symbole der Schaustelle

Objektbesichtigung

Objektbesichtigungen

Bustouren

Rundgänge

Radtouren

Bootstouren

Rundflüge

Events und Veranstaltungen

 9.30, 11.00, 13.00 und 14.30
Tour 42
Spreefahrt durch den zentralen Bereich
Karten € 10,-

 10.00, 12.00, 14.00 und 16.00
Bundesministerium der Justiz
Information auf Seite 6/7
Karten € 1,50,-

 10.00
Tour 11
Mauerpark Prenzlauer Berg
Karten € 8,- / 5,- (erm.)

 10.00, 12.00, 14.00 und 16.00
Museumsinsel
Information auf Seite 6/7
Karten € 1,50,-

 10.30
Tour 1
Innenstadttour
Karten € 15,- / 12,- (erm.)

 10.30
Tour 14
Spaziergang durch den Großen Tiergarten
Karten € 8,- / 5,- (erm.)

 11.00
Tour 40
Die Großbaustelle Berlin vom Wasser aus. Altbau – Neubau – Umbau
Karten € 10,- / 5,- (erm.)

 11.00 und 15.00
Tour 18
Die Hackeschen Höfe
Karten € 8,- / 5,- (erm.)

 11.00 und 13.30
KulturKaufhaus Friedrichstr.
Information auf Seite 10/11
Karten € 1,50,-

 11.00
Tour 37
Mit dem Fahrrad durch Mitte
Karten € 8,- / 5,- (erm.)

 11.00
Tour 19
Neue Architektur rund um den Checkpoint Charlie
Karten € 8,- / 5,- (erm.)

 15.00 und 17.00
Jüdisches Museum
Information auf Seite 56
Karten € 1,50,-

 15.00
Kultur und Ökologie auf dem Gelände der UFA-Fabrik
Information auf Seite 58
Karten € 1,50,-

 19.30
Tour 17
Die Zukunft hat begonnen.
Vom Reichstag zum Gendarmenmarkt
Karten € 8,- / 5,- (erm.)

Aktivität 2   Die Welt im Jahre 2050

Wie mag die Welt wohl in fünfzig oder hundert Jahren aussehen?
1. Arbeiten Sie zuerst in Gruppen, um Ideen zum Thema miteinander zu sammeln. Was sind Ihre Hoffnungen, Erwartungen, Fantasien, aber auch Ihre Ängste? Jemand in Ihrer Gruppe schreibt Hauptgedanken auf, und trägt sie im Plenum vor.
2. Schreiben Sie einen Bericht, wie Sie sich Ihr Leben im Jahr 2050 vorstellen: „Ein Tag in meinem Leben."

Appendix A

Einführung

Aktivität 12   Hin und her°: Wie ist die Postleitzahl?

This is the first of many activities in which you will exchange information with a partner. Take turns asking each other for the postal codes missing from your charts.

BEISPIEL: s1: Wie ist die Postleitzahl von Eisenach?
            s2: D-99817. Wie ist die Postleitzahl von Bitburg?
            s1: D-54634.

D-99817	Eisenach
D-54634	Bitburg
A-5020	Salzburg
CH-3800	Interlaken
D-94315	Straubing
D-06217	Merseburg
D-21614	Buxtehude
FL-9490	Vaduz

Kapitel 2
Aktivität 7   Hin und her: Machen sie das gern?

Find out what the following people like to do or don't like to do by asking your partner.

BEISPIEL: s1: Was macht Denise gern?
s2: Sie reist gern. Was macht Thomas nicht gern?
s1: Er fährt nicht gern Auto.

	GERN	NICHT GERN
Thomas	arbeiten	Auto fahren
Denise	reisen	kochen
Niko	Eis essen	Karten spielen
Anja	laufen	Bier trinken
Sie		
Ihr Partner / Ihre Partnerin		

Kapitel 3
relationships
Aktivität 8   Hin und her: Verwandtschaften°

Ask a partner questions about Bernd's family. How is each person related to Bernd?

BEISPIEL: s1: Wie ist Gisela mit Bernd verwandt?
s2: Gisela ist Bernds Tante.
s1: Wie alt ist sie denn?
s2: Sie ist 53.
s1: Wann hat sie Geburtstag?
s2: Im Februar.

PERSON	VERWANDTSCHAFT	ALTER	GEBURTSTAG
Gisela	Tante	53	Februar
Alexandra	Schwester	25	März
Werner	Schwager	36	Dezember
Andreas	Großvater	70	Juni
Sabine	Kusine	19	August

Kapitel 4

Aktivität 5 Hin und her: Zwei Stundenpläne

A. Sven und Frank sind 18 Jahre alt und gehen aufs Gymnasium (*secondary school*). Vergleichen Sie ihre Stundenpläne. Welche Kurse haben sie zusammen (*together*)?

BEISPIEL: S1: Welchen Kurs hat Sven dienstags um acht?
S2: Dienstags um acht hat Sven Informatik. Welchen Kurs hat Frank dienstags um acht?
S1: Dienstags um acht hat Frank Physik.

B. Sven und Frank möchten Tennis spielen. Wann ist die beste Zeit? Wann haben sie beide frei?

Zeit	Montag	Dienstag	Mittwoch	Donnerstag	Freitag	Samstag
8 – 8⁴⁵	Informatik	Physik	Kunst	Englisch	frei	Deutsch
8⁴⁵ – 9³⁰	Informatik	Physik	Kunst	Englisch	frei	Deutsch
9³⁵ – 10²⁰	Religion	Deutsch	Mathematik	Geschichte	Sozialkunde	
10⁴⁰ – 11²⁵	Religion	Mathematik	Deutsch	Mathematik	Deutsch	
11³⁰ – 12¹⁵	Erdkunde	frei	Sozialkunde	Erdkunde	Geschichte	
12¹⁵ – 13⁰⁰	Mathematik	Englisch	Physik	Informatik	frei	
13¹⁵ – 14⁰⁰			Sport			
14⁰⁰ – 14⁴⁵			Sport			

Franks Stundenplan

Kapitel 6

Übung 15   Hin und her: Warum nicht?

Fragen Sie Ihren Partner / Ihre Partnerin, warum die folgenden Leute nicht erschienen sind (*didn't show up*).

BEISPIEL: S1: Warum war Andreas gestern Vormittag nicht in der Vorlesung?
　　　　　S2: Er hatte keine Lust.

PERSON	WANN	WO	WARUM
Andreas	gestern Vormittag	in der Vorlesung	keine Lust haben
Anke	Montag	zu Hause	arbeiten müssen
Frank	gestern Abend	auf der Party	keine Zeit
Yeliz	heute Morgen	in der Vorlesung	schlafen wollen
Mario	Samstag	im Café	kein Geld haben
Ihr Partner / Ihre Partnerin			

Kapitel 7

Übung 9   Hin und her: Wochenende und Freizeit

Warum haben Sie das gemacht? Stellen Sie Ihrem Partner / Ihrer Partnerin Fragen, um die Gründe (*reasons*) zu erfahren.

BEISPIEL: S1: Warum ist Dagmar ins Alte Land gefahren?
　　　　　S2: Sie wollte auf einem Bauernhof Obst kaufen.

WER	WAS	WARUM
Dagmar	ins Alte Land fahren	auf einem Bauernhof Obst kaufen wollen
Thomas	in den Sportclub gehen	Bodybuilding machen wollen
Jürgen	zu Hause bleiben	seine Lieblingssendung im Fernsehen sehen wollen
Stefanie	Hans anrufen	auf die Party nicht kommen sollen
Susanne	sehr lange schlafen	die ganze Woche schwer arbeiten müssen

Kapitel 8

Aktivität 8   Hin und her: Meine Routine—deine Routine

Jeder hat eine andere Routine. Was machen diese Leute und in welcher Reihenfolge? Machen Sie es auch so?

BEISPIEL: S1: Was macht Alexander morgens?
            S2: Zuerst rasiert er sich und putzt sich die Zähne. Dann kämmt er sich. Danach setzt er sich an den Tisch und frühstückt.

WER	WAS ER/SIE MORGENS MACHT
Alexander	zuerst / sich rasieren / sich die Zähne putzen / dann / sich kämmen danach / sich an den Tisch setzen / frühstücken
Elke	zuerst / sich anziehen dann / sich die Zähne putzen danach / sich kämmen
Tilo	zuerst / sich duschen / sich rasieren / dann / sich an den Tisch setzen / frühstücken / danach / sich die Zähne putzen
Kamal	zuerst / sich das Gesicht waschen dann / frühstücken danach / sich rasieren / sich anziehen
Sie	zuerst / ? dann / ? danach / ?
Ihr Partner / *Ihre Partnerin*	zuerst / ? dann / ? danach / ?

Kapitel 9

Aktivität 6   Hin und her: In einer fremden° Stadt

Sie sind in einer fremden Stadt. Fragen Sie nach dem Weg. Benutzen Sie die Tabelle unten.

BEISPIEL: S1: Ist das Landesmuseum weit von hier?
S2: Es ist sechs Kilometer von hier, bei der Universität.
S1: Wie komme ich am besten dahin?
S2: Nehmen Sie die Buslinie 7, am Rathaus.

WOHIN?	WIE WEIT?	WO?	WIE?
Landesmuseum	6 km	bei der Universität	Buslinie 7, am Rathaus
Bahnhof	15 Minuten	im Zentrum	mit dem Taxi
Post	nicht weit	in der Nähe vom Bahnhof	zu Fuß
Schloss	15 km	außerhalb der Stadt	mit dem Auto
Opernhaus	ganz in der Nähe	rechts um die Ecke	zu Fuß, die Poststraße entlang

Übung 14   Hin und her: Was gibt es hier?

Fragen Sie einen Partner / eine Partnerin nach der fehlenden Information.

BEISPIEL: S1: Was gibt es beim Gasthof zum Bären?
S2: Warme Küche.
S1: Was gibt es sonst noch?
S2: Bayerische Spezialitäten.

WO?	WAS?	WAS SONST NOCH?
Gasthof zum Bären	Küche / warm	Spezialitäten / bayerisch
Gasthof Adlersberg	Biergarten / gemütlich	liegt in Lage / idyllisch
Gasthaus Schneiderwirt	Hausmusik / originell	Gästezimmer / rustikal
Hotel Luitpold	in Lage / idyllisch	Zimmer / rustikal

Kapitel 10

Aktivität 3 Hin und her: Was nehmen sie mit?

Wohin fahren diese Leute im Urlaub? Was nehmen sie mit? Ergänzen Sie die Informationen.

BEISPIEL: s1: Wohin fährt Angelika Meier in Urlaub?
            s2: Sie fährt in die Türkei.
            s1: Warum fährt sie in die Türkei?
            s2: Weil...
            s1: Was nimmt sie mit?
            s2: Sie nimmt...

PERSONEN	WOHIN?	WARUM?	WAS NIMMT ER/SIE MIT?
Angelika Meier	in die Türkei	sich am Strand erholen	Buch Sonnenbrille Badesachen
Peter Bayer	auf die Insel Rügen	windsurfen gehen	Sonnenschutzmittel Badehose
Roland Metz	nach Thüringen	wandern Weimar besichtigen	Stadtpläne Reiseführer Wanderschuhe
Sabine Graf	nach Griechenland	eine Studienreise machen	Reiseführer Wörterbuch Kamera

Übung 10 Hin und her: Wie war der Urlaub?

Herr Ignaz Huber aus München war drei Wochen im Urlaub in Norddeutschland. Er war zwei Tage in Hamburg, eine Woche in Cuxhaven und nicht ganz zwei Wochen auf der Insel Sylt. Stellen Sie Ihrem Partner / Ihrer Partnerin Fragen über seinen Urlaub. Benutzen Sie den Superlativ.

BEISPIEL: s1: Wo war es am wärmsten?
            s2: Am wärmsten war es in Cuxhaven.

	IN HAMBURG	IN CUXHAVEN	AUF DER INSEL SYLT
Wo war es (kalt/warm)?	20°C	25°C	15°C
Wo hat es (viel) geregnet?	zwei Tage	einen Tag	fünf Tage
Wo waren die Hotelpreise (günstig/teuer)?	150 Euro	60 Euro mit Vollpension	200 Euro
Wo war das Hotelpersonal (freundlich)?	freundlich	sehr freundlich	unfreundlich
Wo war der Strand (schön)?	kein Strand	sehr sauber, angenehm	zu windig

Kapitel 11

Aktivität 2 Hin und her: Wer macht was, und warum?

Ergänzen Sie die Informationen.

BEISPIEL: s1: Was macht Corinna Eichhorn?
s2: Sie ist Sozialarbeiterin.
s1: Warum macht sie das?
s2: Weil...

NAME	BERUF	WARUM?
Corinna Eichhorn	Sozialarbeiterin	Menschen helfen
Karsten Becker	Bibliothekar	sich für Bücher interessieren
Erika Lentz	Filmschauspielerin	mit Menschen zu tun haben
Alex Böhmer	Informatiker	mit Computern arbeiten

Aktivität 6 Hin und her: Berühmte° Personen

famous

Diese berühmten Menschen, die alle einen Beruf ausübten, hatten auch andere Interessen. Ergänzen Sie die Informationen.

BEISPIEL: s1: Was war Martin Luther von Beruf?
s2: Er war Priester.
s1: Was für andere Interessen hatte er?
s2: Er interessierte sich für Literatur, Musik und die deutsche Sprache.

NAME	BERUF	INTERESSEN
Martin Luther	Priester	Literatur, Musik, die deutsche Sprache
Rainer Werner Fassbinder	Filmregisseur	Literatur, Theater
Bertha von Suttner	Schriftstellerin	die europäische Friedensbewegung (*peace movement*)
Marlene Dietrich	Schauspielerin	Ski fahren
Käthe Kollwitz	Künstlerin	Politik
Willi Brandt	Politiker	Ski fahren, lesen

Kapitel 12

Aktivität 6 Hin und her: Meine Wohnung—deine Wohnung

Diese Leute haben entweder eine neue Wohnung oder ein neues Haus gekauft. Wer hat was gekauft? Wie viele Stockwerke gibt es? Wie groß ist das Wohnzimmer? Wie viele WCs oder Badezimmer gibt es?

BEISPIEL: S1: Was für eine Wohnung hat Bettina Neuendorf gekauft?
S2: Eine Eigentumswohnung.
S1: Wie viele Stockwerke hat die Wohnung?
S2: Eins.
S1: Und wie viele Schlafzimmer?...

PERSON	TYP	STOCKWERKE	SCHLAFZIMMER	WOHNZIMMER	WC/BAD
Bettina Neuendorf	Eigentums- wohnung	eins	eins, aber auch ein kleines Gästezimmer	mit Esszimmer kombiniert 30 Quadratmeter	eins
Uwe und Marion Baumgärtner	Haus	zwei	drei: Elternschlaf- zimmer, Kinder- schlafzimmer, Gästezimmer	sehr groß mit Balkon 37 Quadratmeter	zwei Badezim- mer: eins im Dachgeschoss und eins im Erdgeschoss
Sven Kersten	Eigentums- wohnung	zwei	zwei, eins als Gästezimmer benutzt	mit Esszimmer zusammen 35 Quadratmeter, Balkon von Wohnzimmer	zwei, ein WC und ein Bad
Carola Schubärth	Haus	eins	zwei: ein Schlaf- zimmer ist Arbeitszimmer	klein 25 Quadratmeter	ein Bad
ich					
mein Partner / meine Partnerin					

Kapitel 13

Aktivität 2 Hin und her: Wie informieren und unterhalten sie sich?

Wie informieren sich diese Personen? Was lesen sie zur Unterhaltung? Stellen Sie Fragen an Ihren Partner / Ihre Partnerin.

BEISPIEL: S1: Was sieht Martin gern im Fernsehen? Was liest er oft?
s2: Er _____.

PERSON	FERNSEHSHOWS	ZEITUNGEN UND ZEITSCHRIFTEN
Martin	Talkshows und Dokumentarfilme	*die Zeit* und *die TAZ*
Stephanie	klassische Spielfilme und Komödien	*der Spiegel*
Patrick	Quizsendungen wie „Der Preis ist heiß", die Nachrichten	die *Frankfurter Allgemeine* und *Stern*
Kristin	Sportsendungen, Krimi-Serien wie „Mord ist ihr Hobby"	das *Handelsblatt*, *Die Welt* und *Brigitte*
Mein Partner / Meine Partnerin		

Aktivität 7 Hin und her: Technische Erfindungen durch die Jahrhunderte

Sie möchten erfahren, wer was und wann erfunden hat. Arbeiten Sie zu zweit.

BEISPIELE: s1: Wer hat _____ erfunden?
  s2: _____.
  s1: Wann hat er es erfunden?
  s2: (Im Jahre) _____.
[oder:] s1: Was hat _____ erfunden?
  s2: Er hat _____ erfunden.
  s1: In welchem Jahr?
  s2: (Im Jahre) _____.

PERSON	ERFINDUNG	DATUM
Johannes von Gutenberg	Buchdruck mit beweglichen Lettern (*movable type*)	um 1450
Daniel Gabriel Fahrenheit	Alkoholthermometer	1716/18
Karl von Drais	Fahrrad (Draisine)	1817
Werner von Siemens	Dynamomaschine (*generator*)	1846
Gottlieb Daimler	Motorrad	1885
Rudolf Diesel	Dieselmotor	1893
Wilhelm Conrad Röntgen	Röntgenstrahlen (*X rays*)	1895
Hedy Lamarr (Hedwig Eva Maria Kiesler)	Wechselspektrum (*spread spectrum radio technology*)	1942

Kapitel 14

Stellen Sie Ihrem Partner / Ihrer Partnerin Fragen zu den folgenden Problemen, um herauszufinden, welche möglichen Lösungen es gibt.

BEISPIEL: S1: Was kann man gegen Krieg tun?
S2: Man kann an Antikriegsdemonstrationen teilnehmen.

PROBLEME	MÖGLICHE LÖSUNGEN
Krieg	an Antikriegsdemonstrationen teilnehmen
Inflation	die Schulden der Regierung kontrollieren
Drogensucht	Informationen über die Gefahren von Drogen verbreiten
Umweltverschmutzung	alternative Energiequellen (*energy sources*) entwickeln
Verletzung der Menschenrechte	Organisationen wie Amnesty International unterstützen
Obdachlosigkeit	neue Wohnungen bauen
Arbeitslosigkeit	Arbeiter umschulen

Übung 5   Hin und her: Zwei umweltbewusste Städte

In zwei Städten, Neustadt und Altstadt, wird für eine bessere Umwelt gesorgt.

BEISPIEL: S1: Was ist zuerst in Neustadt gemacht worden?
S2: Zuerst sind naturnahe Gärten angelegt worden.

	NEUSTADT	ALTSTADT
zuerst	naturnahe Gärten anlegen	Autos aus der Innenstadt verbannen
dann	Kinderspielplätze verbessern	neue Siedlungen am Stadtrand bauen
danach	Park im Zentrum säubern	Bürger über Umweltschutz informieren
schließlich	keine Wegwerfartikel in Geschäften verkaufen	neue, moderne Busse kaufen
zuletzt	nach Alternativenegie suchen	ein großes Umweltfest in der Innenstadt feiern

Appendix B

Studienfächer

Anthropologie	Anthropology
Architektur	Architecture
Astronomie	Astronomy
Bauingenieurwesen	Structural Engineering
Betriebswirtschaftslehre	Business Administration
Bibliothekswissenschaft	Library Science
Biochemie	Biochemistry
Biologie	Biology
Chemie	Chemistry
Elektrotechnik	Electrical Engineering
Ernährungswissenschaft	Nutritional Science
Forstwissenschaft	Forestry
Geographie/Erdkunde	Geography
Geologie	Geology
Geophysik	Geophysics
Germanistik	German Studies
Geschichte/Geschichtswissenschaft	History
Informatik	Computer Science
Journalistik/Publizistik	Journalism
Kerntechnik/Reaktortechnik	Nuclear Engineering
Kunstgeschichte	Art History
Maschinenbau	Mechanical Engineering
Mathematik	Mathematics
Medizin	Medicine
Musik	Music
Pädagogik	Education
Pharmakologie/Pharmazie	Pharmacy
Philosophie	Philosophy
Physik	Physics
Politikwissenschaft	Political Science
Psychologie	Psychology
Rechtswissenschaft/Jura	Law
Sport	Physical Education
Sprachwissenschaft/Linguistik	Linguistics
Städtebau/Stadtplanung	Urban Planning
Statistik	Statistics
Theaterwissenschaft	Dramatic Art
Theologie	Theology
Tiermedizin	Veterinary Science
Volkswirtschaftslehre	Economics
Zahnmedizin	Dentistry

Appendix C

GRAMMAR TABLES
1. Personal Pronouns

	SINGULAR					PLURAL		
Nominative	ich	du / Sie	er	sie	es	wir	ihr / Sie	sie
Accusative	mich	dich / Sie	ihn	sie	es	uns	euch / Sie	sie
Dative	mir	dir / Ihnen	ihm	ihr	ihm	uns	euch / Ihnen	ihnen

2. Definite Articles

	SINGULAR			PLURAL
	Masculine	*Neuter*	*Feminine*	*All genders*
Nominative	der	das	die	die
Accusative	den	das	die	die
Dative	dem	dem	der	den
Genitive	des	des	der	der

Words declined like the definite article: **jeder, dieser, welcher**

3. Indefinite Articles and the Negative Article kein

	SINGULAR			PLURAL
	Masculine	*Neuter*	*Feminine*	*All genders*
Nominative	(k)ein	(k)ein	(k)eine	keine
Accusative	(k)einen	(k)ein	(k)eine	keine
Dative	(k)einem	(k)einem	(k)einer	keinen
Genitive	(k)eines	(k)eines	(k)einer	keiner

Words declined like the indefinite article: all possessive adjectives (**mein, dein, sein, ihr, unser, euer, Ihr**)

4. Relative and Demonstrative Pronouns

| | SINGULAR | | | PLURAL |
	Masculine	Neuter	Feminine	Plural
Nominative	der	das	die	die
Accusative	den	das	die	die
Dative	dem	dem	der	denen
Genitive	dessen	dessen	deren	deren

5. Principal Parts of Strong and Irregular Weak Verbs

The following is a list of the most important strong and irregular weak verbs that are used in this book. Included in this list are the modal auxiliaries. Since the principal parts of compound verbs follow the forms of the base verb, compound verbs are generally not included, except for a few high-frequency compound verbs whose base verb is not commonly used. Thus you will find **anfangen** and **einladen** listed, but not **zurückkommen** or **ausgehen**.

INFINITIVE	(3RD PERS. SG. PRESENT)	SIMPLE PAST	PAST PARTICIPLE	MEANING
anbieten		bot an	angeboten	to offer
anfangen	(fängt an)	fing an	angefangen	to begin
backen		backte	gebacken	to bake
beginnen		begann	begonnen	to begin
begreifen		begriff	begriffen	to comprehend
beißen		biss	gebissen	to bite
bitten		bat	gebeten	to ask, beg
bleiben		blieb	(ist) geblieben	to stay
bringen		brachte	gebracht	to bring
denken		dachte	gedacht	to think
dürfen	(darf)	durfte	gedurft	to be allowed
einladen	(lädt ein)	lud ein	eingeladen	to invite
empfehlen	(empfiehlt)	empfahl	empfohlen	to recommend
entscheiden		entschied	entschieden	to decide
essen	(isst)	aß	gegessen	to eat
fahren	(fährt)	fuhr	(ist) gefahren	to drive
fallen	(fällt)	fiel	(ist) gefallen	to fall
finden		fand	gefunden	to find
fliegen		flog	(ist) geflogen	to fly
geben	(gibt)	gab	gegeben	to give
gefallen	(gefällt)	gefiel	gefallen	to like; to please
gehen		ging	(ist) gegangen	to go
genießen		genoss	genossen	to enjoy
geschehen	(geschieht)	geschah	(ist) geschehen	to happen
gewinnen		gewann	gewonnen	to win

INFINITIVE	(3RD PERS. SG. PRESENT)	SIMPLE PAST	PAST PARTICIPLE	MEANING
haben	(hat)	hatte	gehabt	to have
halten	(hält)	hielt	gehalten	to hold; to stop
hängen		hing	gehangen	to hang
heißen		hieß	geheißen	to be called
helfen	(hilft)	half	geholfen	to help
kennen		kannte	gekannt	to know
kommen		kam	(ist) gekommen	to come
können	(kann)	konnte	gekonnt	can; to be able
lassen	(lässt)	ließ	gelassen	to let; to allow
laufen	(läuft)	lief	(ist) gelaufen	to run
leihen		lieh	geliehen	to lend; to borrow
lesen	(liest)	las	gelesen	to read
liegen		lag	gelegen	to lie
mögen	(mag)	mochte	gemocht	to like
müssen	(muss)	musste	gemusst	must; to have to
nehmen	(nimmt)	nahm	genommen	to take
nennen		nannte	genannt	to name
raten	(rät)	riet	geraten	to advise
reiten		ritt	(ist) geritten	to ride
scheinen		schien	geschienen	to seem; to shine
schlafen	(schläft)	schlief	geschlafen	to sleep
schließen		schloss	geschlossen	to close
schreiben		schrieb	geschrieben	to write
schwimmen		schwamm	(ist) geschwommen	to swim
sehen	(sieht)	sah	gesehen	to see
sein	(ist)	war	(ist) gewesen	to be
singen		sang	gesungen	to sing
sitzen		saß	gesessen	to sit
sollen	(soll)	sollte	gesollt	should, ought; to be supposed
sprechen	(spricht)	sprach	gesprochen	to speak
stehen		stand	gestanden	to stand
steigen		stieg	ist gestiegen	to rise; to climb
sterben	(stirbt)	starb	(ist) gestorben	to die
tragen	(trägt)	trug	getragen	to carry; to wear
treffen	(trifft)	traf	getroffen	to meet
trinken		trank	getrunken	to drink
tun		tat	getan	to do
umsteigen		stieg um	(ist) umgestiegen	to change; to transfer
vergessen	(vergisst)	vergaß	vergessen	to forget
vergleichen		verglich	verglichen	to compare
verlieren		verlor	verloren	to lose
wachsen	(wächst)	wuchs	(ist) gewachsen	to grow
waschen	(wäscht)	wusch	gewaschen	to wash
werden	(wird)	wurde	(ist) geworden	to become
wissen	(weiß)	wusste	gewusst	to know
wollen	(will)	wollte	gewollt	to want
ziehen		zog	(ist/hat) gezogen	to move; to pull

6. Conjugation of Verbs

In the charts that follow, the pronoun **Sie** (*you*) is listed with the third-person plural **sie** (*they*).

Present Tense

Auxiliary Verbs

	sein	haben	werden
ich	bin	habe	werde
du	bist	hast	wirst
er/sie/es	ist	hat	wird
wir	sind	haben	werden
ihr	seid	habt	werdet
sie/Sie	sind	haben	werden

Regular Verbs, Verbs with Vowel Changes, Irregular Verbs

	REGULAR		VOWEL CHANGE		IRREGULAR
	fragen	finden	geben	fahren	wissen
ich	frage	finde	gebe	fahre	weiß
du	fragst	findest	gibst	fährst	weißt
er/sie/es	fragt	findet	gibt	fährt	weiß
wir	fragen	finden	geben	fahren	wissen
ihr	fragt	findet	gebt	fahrt	wisst
sie/Sie	fragen	finden	geben	fahren	wissen

Simple Past Tense

Auxiliary Verbs

	sein	haben	werden
ich	war	hatte	wurde
du	warst	hattest	wurdest
er/sie/es	war	hatte	wurde
wir	waren	hatten	wurden
ihr	wart	hattet	wurdet
sie/Sie	waren	hatten	wurden

	WEAK	STRONG		IRREGULAR WEAK
	fragen	**geben**	**fahren**	**wissen**
ich	fragte	gab	fuhr	wusste
du	fragtest	gabst	fuhrst	wusstest
er/sie/es	fragte	gab	fuhr	wusste
wir	fragten	gaben	fuhren	wussten
ihr	fragtet	gabt	fuhrt	wusstet
sie/Sie	fragten	gaben	fuhren	wussten

Present Perfect Tense

	sein	**haben**	**geben**	**fahren**
ich	bin	habe	habe	bin
du	bist	hast	hast	bist
er/sie/es	ist	hat	hat	ist
wir	sind } gewesen	haben } gehabt	haben } gegeben	sind } gefahren
ihr	seid	habt	habt	seid
sie/Sie	sind	haben	haben	sind

Past Perfect Tense

	sein	**haben**	**geben**	**fahren**
ich	war	hatte	hatte	war
du	warst	hattest	hattest	warst
er/sie/es	war	hatte	hatte	war
wir	waren } gewesen	hatten } gehabt	hatten } gegeben	waren } gefahren
ihr	wart	hattet	hattet	wart
sie/Sie	waren	hatten	hatten	waren

Future Tense

	geben
ich	werde
du	wirst
er/sie/es	wird } geben
wir	werden
ihr	werdet
sie/Sie	werden

Subjunctive

Present Tense: Subjunctive I (Indirect Discourse Subjunctive)

	sein	**haben**	**werden**	**fahren**	**wissen**
ich	sei	—	—	—	wisse
du	sei(e)st	habest	—	—	—
er/sie/es	sei	habe	werde	fahre	wisse
wir	seien	—	—	—	—
ihr	sei(e)t	habet	—	—	—
sie/Sie	seien	—	—	—	—

For those forms left blank in the chart above, the subjunctive II forms are preferred in indirect discourse.

Present Tense: Subjunctive II

	fragen	**sein**	**haben**	**werden**	**fahren**	**wissen**
ich	fragte	wäre	hätte	würde	führe	wüsste
du	fragtest	wär(e)st	hättest	würdest	führ(e)st	wüsstest
er/sie/es	fragte	wäre	hätte	würde	führe	wüsste
wir	fragten	wären	hätten	würden	führen	wüssten
ihr	fragtet	wär(e)t	hättet	würdet	führ(e)t	wüsstet
sie/Sie	fragten	wären	hätten	würden	führen	wüssten

Past Tense: Subjunctive I (Indirect Discourse)

	fahren		**wissen**	
ich	sei		—	
du	sei(e)st		habest	
er/sie/es	sei	gefahren	habe	gewusst
wir	seien		—	
ihr	sei(e)t		habet	
sie/Sie	sei(e)n		—	

Past Tense: Subjunctive II

	sein		**geben**		**fahren**	
ich	wäre		hätte		wäre	
du	wär(e)st		hättest		wär(e)st	
er/sie/es	wäre	gewesen	hätte	gegeben	wäre	gefahren
wir	wären		hätten		wären	
ihr	wär(e)t		hättet		wär(e)t	
sie/Sie	wären		hätten		wären	

Passive Voice

	einladen		
	Present	*Simple Past*	*Present Perfect*
ich	werde ⎫	wurde ⎫	bin ⎫
du	wirst ⎪	wurdest ⎪	bist ⎪
er/sie/es	wird ⎪ eingeladen	wurde ⎪ eingeladen	ist ⎪ eingeladen worden
wir	werden ⎪	wurden ⎪	sind ⎪
ihr	werdet ⎪	wurdet ⎪	seid ⎪
sie/Sie	werden ⎭	wurden ⎭	sind ⎭

Imperative

	sein	**geben**	**fahren**	**arbeiten**
Familiar Singular	sei	gib	fahr	arbeite
Familiar Plural	seid	gebt	fahrt	arbeitet
Formal	seien Sie	geben Sie	fahren Sie	arbeiten Sie

Appendix D

Alternate Spelling and Capitalization

As the result of the recent German spelling reform, some words now have an alternate, old spelling along with a new one. In some realia and literature selections, you may see alternate spellings. The vocabulary lists at the end of each chapter in this text present the new spelling. Listed here are words appearing in the end of chapter vocabulary lists that are affected by the spelling reform, along with their traditional alternate spellings. This list is not a complete list of words affected by the spelling reform.

NEW	ALTERNATE
Abschluss (¨e)	Abschluß (Abschlüsse)
Anschluss (¨e)	Anschluß (Anschlüsse)
auf Deutsch	auf deutsch
Dachgeschoss (-e)	Dachgeschoß (Dachgeschosse)
dass	daß
Erdgeschoss (-e)	Erdgeschoß (Erdgeschosse)
essen (isst), aß, gegessen	essen (ißt), aß, gegessen
Esszimmer (-)	Eßzimmer (-)
Fass (¨er)	Faß (Fässer)
Fitness	Fitneß
Fluss (¨e)	Fluß (Flüsse)
heute Abend / ...Mittag /...Morgen / ...Nachmittag / ...Vormittag	heute abend / ...mittag / ...morgen / ...nachmittag / ...vormittag
Imbiss (-e)	Imbiß (Imbisse)
lassen (lässt), ließ, gelassen Lass uns doch...	lassen (läßt), ließ, gelassen Laß uns doch...
morgen Abend / ...Mittag / ...Nachmittag / ...Vormittag	morgen abend / ...mittag / ...nachmittag / ...vormittag
müssen (muss), musste, gemusst	müssen (muß), mußte, gemußt
passen (passt), gepasst	passen (paßt), gepaßt
Rad fahren (fährt Rad), fuhr Rad, ist Rad gefahren	radfahren (fährt Rad), fuhr Rad, ist radgefahren
Reisepass (¨e)	Reisepaß (Reisepässe)
Samstagabend / -mittag / -morgen / -nachmittag / -vormittag	Samstag abend / ...mittag / ...morgen / ...nachmittag / ...vormittag
spazieren gehen (geht spazieren), ging spazieren, ist spazieren gegangen	spazierengehen (geht spazieren), ging spazieren, ist spazierengegangen
Stress	Streß
vergessen (vergisst), vergaß, vergessen	vergessen (vergißt), vergaß, vergessen
wie viel	wieviel

Vocabulary

GERMAN–ENGLISH

This vocabulary contains the German words as used in various contexts in this text, with the following exceptions: (1) compound words whose meaning can be easily guessed from their component parts; (2) most identical or very close cognates that are not part of the active vocabulary. (Frequently used cognates are, however, included so students can verify their gender.)

Active vocabulary in the end-of-chapter *Wortschatz* lists is indicated by the number of the chapter in which it first appears. The letter E refers to the introductory chapter, *Einführung.*

The following abbreviations are used:

acc.	accusative	*indef. pron.*	indefinite pronoun
adj.	adjective	*inform.*	informal
coll.	colloquial	**-(e)n** *masc.*	masculine noun ending in
coord. conj.	coordinating conjunction		**-n** or **-en** in all cases but the
dat.	dative		nominative singular
decl. adj.	declined adjective	*pl.*	plural
form.	formal	*sg.*	singular
gen.	genitive	*subord. conj.*	subordinating conjunction

A

das A und O (alpha and omega) essence

ab (+ *dat.*) from, as of; **ab 1. Juni** as of June 1st (12)

ab und zu now and then (8)

abbestellen (bestellt ab) to cancel

abbiegen (biegt ab), bog ab, ist abgebogen to make a turn (9); **nach rechts abbiegen** to make a right-hand turn

abbrechen (bricht ab), brach ab, abgebrochen to break off

der Abend (-e) evening (4); **am Abend** at night, in the evening; **guten Abend** good evening (E); **der Heilige Abend** Christmas Eve (3); **heute Abend** tonight; **jeden Abend** every night; **morgen Abend** tomorrow evening; tomorrow night; **Samstagabend** Saturday evening; Saturday night

das Abendessen (-) evening meal; dinner, supper (5); **zum Abendessen** for dinner, supper

das Abendkleid (-er) evening gown

abends in the evening, evenings (4); **eines Abends** one evening

das Abenteuer (-) adventure

der Abenteuerfilm (-e) adventure film

abenteuerlich adventurous

aber (*coord. conj.*) but, however (2); **Aber natürlich!** But of course! (1)

abfahren (fährt ab), fuhr ab, ist abgefahren to depart, leave (10)

die Abfahrt (-en) departure (10)

der Abfall (∹e) garbage (14)

der Abfallstoff (-e) waste product

die Abfallwirtschaft waste management

abfliegen (fliegt ab), flog ab, ist abgeflogen to depart, leave (by plane)

abfüttern (füttert ab) to feed

die Abgase (*pl.*) exhaust fumes

abgasfrei free of exhaust fumes

abgeben (gibt ab), gab ab, abgegeben to drop off, give to (8)

abgelegen in a remote area

der/die Abgeordnete (*decl. adj.*) (political) representative

abgesehen davon aside from that

abgucken (guckt ab) to copy

abhängig sein von (+ *dat.*) to be dependent on

abholen (holt ab) to pick up (4)

das Abi = Abitur

das Abitur *examination at the end of Gymnasium* (11)

der Abiturient (-en *masc.***) / die Abiturientin (-nen)** *graduate of the Gymnasium, person who has passed the Abitur*

der Ablauf duration

ablaufen (läuft ab), lief ab, ist abgelaufen to expire

ablenken (lenkt ab) to distract

abliefern (liefert ab) to hand in, deliver

ablösen (löst ab) to replace

(sich) abmelden (meldet ab) to check out (of a hotel)

abnehmen (nimmt ab), nahm ab, abgenommen to lose weight

das Abo(nnement) (-s) subscription (13)

abonnieren to subscribe (13)

die Abrechnung (-en) final account

abreisen (reist ab), ist abgereist to leave (on a trip) (9)

der Absatz (∹e) paragraph

abschaffen (schafft ab) to abolish

abschicken (schickt ab) to send off, mail

der Abschied (-e) farewell; **zum Abschied** when saying good-bye

abschließend in closing

der Abschluss (∹e) completion; degree (11)

der Abschnitt (-e) paragraph, section

absolut absolute(ly)

der Absolvent (-en) / die Absolventin (-nen) graduate (*higher education*) (11)

absolvieren: eine Lehre absolvieren to complete an apprenticeship

(sich) abspielen (spielt ab) to take place

abstammen von (+ *dat.*) **(stammt ab)** to be descended from

absteigen (steigt ab), stieg ab, ist abgestiegen to dismount, get off

abstellen (stellt ab) to turn off

das Abteil (-e) compartment

abtreiben (treibt ab), trieb ab, abgetrieben to have an abortion

die Abtreibung (-en) abortion

abwandern (wandert ab), ist abgewandert to migrate, move to another country

abwarten (wartet ab) to wait; **abwarten und Tee trinken** wait and see

abwechselnd taking turns

die Abwechslung (-en) diversion; change

abwechslungsreich varied, diverse (11)

abweisen (weist ab), wies ab, abgewiesen to reject

(sich) abzeichnen (zeichnet ab) to become evident

ach oh; **Ach so!** I see! **ach wo** not at all

Achsel zuckend shrugging (one's) shoulders

acht eight (E); **um acht Uhr** at eight o'clock

achtbar respectable

achte eighth (3)

achten auf (+ *acc.*) to pay attention (to), watch

Achtung! attention!

achtzehn eighteen (E)

achtzig eighty (E)

der Adel nobility

das Adjektiv (-e) adjective

die Adjektivendung (-en) adjective ending

die Adresse (-n) address (E)

das Adverb (-ien) adverb

das Aerobic aerobics; **Aerobic machen** to do aerobics

(das) Afrika Africa

AG = Aktiengesellschaft

der Agentenfilm (-e) spy movie

die Agrarreform (-en) agricultural reform

die Agressivität agression

ähnlich similar

Ähnliches (something) similar

die Ähnlichkeit (-en) similarity

Ahnung: Keine Ahnung! (I have) no idea!

das Ahornblatt (:er) maple leaf

Ah so! (*coll.*) (*also:* **Ach so!**) Oh, I get it!

der Akkusativ accusative case

der Akteur (-e) performer

die Aktie (-n) share (of stocks)

die Aktiengesellschaft (-en) corporation

der Aktienwert (-e) share value

die Aktion (-en) (political) action

aktiv active(ly) (10); **sportlich aktiv** engaged in sports (10)

die Aktivität (-en) activity

aktuell current, topical (13); **Aktuelles** current events (13)

der Alarm (air raid) warning; **Es ist Alarm.** There is an air raid.

die Alarmanlage (-n) alarm system

der Albaner (-) / die Albanerin (-nen) Albanian (person)

(das) Albanien Albania

albern silly

der Alkohol alcohol (14)

Alkoholeinfluss: unter Alkoholeinfluss under the influence of alcohol

alkoholfrei alcohol free (6)

der Alkoholiker (-) / die Alkoholikerin (-nen) alcoholic

der Alkoholismus alcoholism

all- all; **vor allem** above all

alle (*pl.*) all (5); **aller** of all; **alle fünf Jahre** every five years

allein alone

allein stehend single, unattached

aller- (+ *superlative*) absolutely the most (+ *adj.*)

allerdings however; to be sure

alles everything (10); **Alles Gute!** best wishes (3); **alles klar** everything (is) all right (E); **Das ist alles.** That is all. (5)

allgemein general; **im allgemeinen** in general

die Alliierten (*pl.*) the Allies, the Allied Forces

allmählich gradually

der Alltag everyday routine; workday

der Allwetterzoo (-s) all-weather zoo

allzu too (*emphatic*)

die Alpen (*pl.*) the Alps

das Alpenvorland foothills of the Alps

das Alphabet (-e) alphabet

alphabetisch alphabetical(ly)

als when; as; than (10); **als Kind** as a child

also thus; so; therefore; well

alt old (1); used

die Altbatterie (-n) used-up battery

der Altbau (Altbauten) old building (built before World War II)

die Altbauwohnung (-en) apartment in pre–World War II building

das Alter (-) age

alternativ alternative(ly)

der Alternativurlaub (-e) unusual vacation trip

das Altglas used glass

die Altkleider (*pl.*) used clothing

das Altöl used oil

das Altpapier used paper

die Altstadt old part of town

die Alufolie aluminum foil

das Aluminium aluminum

am = an dem; am 18. (achtzehnten) September on September 18 (3)

(das) Amerika America

der Amerikaner (-) / die Amerikanerin (-nen) American (*person*) (1)

amerikanisch American

die Ampel (-n) traffic light (9)

das Amt (:er) bureau, agency

amüsant entertaining

an (+ *acc./dat.*) at; near (6); up to; to

die Analyse (-n) analysis

anbeißen (beißt an), biss an, angebissen to take a bite (out of)

anbieten (bietet an), bot an, angeboten to offer

anbringen (bringt an), brachte an, angebracht to install

andere different, other; **der, die, das andere** the other one; **alles andere** everything else; **unter anderem** among other things; **ein Tag um den anderen** day after day; **(et)was anderes** something else; **am anderen Morgen** the next morning; **eins nach dem anderen** one thing at a time

der/die/das andere (*decl. adj.*) other, different

(sich) ändern to change

anders different(ly) in another way; **jemand/niemand anders** somebody/nobody else

anderswo somewhere/anywhere else

die Änderung (-en) change

anderweitig elsewhere

anerkannt recognized, acknowledged

der Anfang (:e) beginning, start; **am Anfang** in the beginning

anfangen (fängt an), fing an, angefangen to begin, start (4)

der Anfänger (-) / die Anfängerin (-nen) beginner

anfassen (fasst an) to touch

anfordern (fordert an) to request; to write away for

die Angabe (-n) statement, information; **persönliche Angaben** personal information

angeben (gibt an), gab an, angegeben to state

das Angebot (-e) (special) offer; selection (10)

angehaucht: französisch angehaucht (*coll.*) with a slight French tinge

angehören (gehört an) to be a member of

angeln to fish (7)

angenehm pleasant (7)

der/die Angestellte (*decl. adj.*) employee (9)

angrenzend adjacent

die Angst (:e) fear (12); **keine Angst** don't be afraid; **Angst haben** (**vor** + *dat.*) to be afraid of (12)

ängstlich afraid

Anhalter: per Anhalter hitchhiking

anhand (+ *gen.*) based on

(sich) anhören (hört an) to listen to

ankommen (kommt an), kam an, ist angekommen to arrive (9); **Es kommt darauf an.** It depends.

ankreuzen (kreuzt an) to mark; to check off

die Ankündigung (-en) announcement

die Ankunft (:e) arrival (10)

der Anlass (:e) occasion

anmachen (macht an) to turn on
(lights, etc.)

das Anmeldeformular (-e) registration
form (9)

(sich) anmelden (meldet an) to check in,
register (9)

die Anmeldung (-en) registration

annehmen (nimmt an), nahm an,
angenommen to accept

anno: pro anno per year, annual(ly)

anonym anonymous(ly)

anprobieren (probiert an) to try on (5)

der Anrufbeantworter (-) answering
machine (13)

anrufen (ruft an), rief an, angerufen to
call (on the phone) (4); Ruf mal an!
Call sometime.

der Anrufer (-) / die Anruferin
(-nen) caller

anrühren (rührt an) to touch

ans = an das

ansatzweise: nicht einmal ansatzweise
not even in the beginning stages, not
in the least

anschaffen: (sich) etwas anschaffen
(schafft an) to purchase or acquire
something (14)

sich (dat.) etwas anschauen (schaut an)
to watch, look at (13)

anschließend afterward

der Anschluss (::e) connection (10);
gleich Anschluss haben to make a
direct connection

(sich) anschnallen (schnallt an) to fasten
(one's) seatbelt

sich (dat.) etwas ansehen (sieht an),
sah an, angesehen to look at,
watch (13); Ich sehe mir das an.
I'm watching that.

das Ansehen (-) prestige (11)

ansprechen (spricht an), sprach an,
angesprochen to talk to somebody

(an)statt (+ gen.) instead of

anstehen (steht an), stand an,
angestanden to stand in line

anstellen (stellt an) to turn on
(radio, etc.)

der Anstieg (-e) increase

anstreichen (streicht an) to paint (a wall
or house) (4)

sich anstrengen (strengt an) to exert
oneself

anstrengend strenuous (8)

der Anteil (-e) share

die Antenne (-n) antenna

die Antwort (-en) answer

antworten to answer

der Anwalt (::e) / die Anwältin
(-nen) attorney

die Anzahl amount; number

das Anzeichen (-) sign

die Anzeige (-n) (newspaper)
advertisement

die Anzeigenannahme (-n) classified ad
department

das Anzeigenblatt (::er) classified
ad paper

(sich) anziehen (zieht an), zog an,
angezogen to get dressed (8)

der Anzug (::e) suit (5)

der Apfel (::) apple (5)

der Apfelsaft apple juice (5)

die Apfelsahne (whipped) cream mixed
with grated apples

der Apfelstrudel (-) apple pastry

die Apotheke (-n) pharmacy (5)

der Apparat (-e) appliance (such as TV,
telephone, camera) (9); sich am
Apparat melden to answer the
telephone

das Appartement (-s) one-room
apartment

die Appendizitis appendicitis

der Appetit appetite

die Aprikose (-n) apricot (5)

(der) April April (3)

das Aquarium aquarium

das Äquivalent (-e) equivalent

die Arbeit (-en) work; job (8)

arbeiten to work (1)

der Arbeiter (-) / die Arbeiterin
(-nen) worker

die Arbeiterpartei (-en) workers' party

der Arbeitgeber (-) / die Arbeitgeberin
(-nen) employer (11)

der Arbeitnehmer (-) / die
Arbeitnehmerin (-nen) employee

das Arbeitsamt (::er)
employment office (11)

das Arbeitsklima working atmosphere

arbeitslos unemployed

die Arbeitslosigkeit unemployment (14)

die Arbeitsmöglichkeit (-en) job
opportunity

der Arbeitsplatz (::e) workplace;
position (11)

die Arbeitsstelle (-n) work place

der Arbeitstag (-e) workday

die Arbeitsvermittlung (-en) employment
agency (11)

die Arbeitswelt world of work

die Arbeitszeit (-en) working hours

das Arbeitszimmer (-) workroom,
study (2)

der Arbeitszwang work obligation,
pressure to work

der Architekt (-en masc.) / die
Architektin (-nen) architect

die Architektur (-en) architecture

das Archiv (-e) archives

(das) Argentinien Argentina

argentinisch (adj.) Argentinian

der Ärger annoyance, trouble

sich ärgern (über + acc.) to be annoyed
about (12)

das Argument (-e) argument

der Arm (-e) arm (8)

arm poor

das Armband (::er) bracelet

die Armbanduhr (-en) wristwatch

die Armen (pl.) poor people

die Armut poverty (14)

arrangieren to arrange

die Art (-en) kind, type; manner

der Artikel (-) article

das Arzneimittel (-) medication (14)

der Arzt (::e) / die Ärztin (-nen)
physician, doctor (8)

(das) Aschenbrödel Cinderella

das Aspirin aspirin

die Assoziation (-en) association

assoziieren to associate

das Assoziogramm (-e) associogram

die Astronomie astronomy

astronomisch astronomical(ly)

das Asyl (-e) asylum

der Äther ether

die Atmosphäre atmosphere

die Atomenergie nuclear energy

die Atomkraft nuclear power

das Atomkraftwerk (-e) nuclear power
plant

die Atomwaffe (-n) nuclear weapon

die Atomwaffenfreiheit freedom from
nuclear weapons

attraktiv attractive(ly)

ätzend biting, horrible; caustic

auch also (1); ich auch me too (1)

auf (+ acc./dat.) on, upon; on top of (6);
Auf welche Namen? Under what
name? (9); auf Wiederhören good-bye
(on the phone); auf Wiedersehen
good-bye (E); auf jeden Fall in any
case (13)

aufbauen (baut auf) to build up,
rebuild

aufbewahren (bewahrt auf) to store

aufbleiben (bleibt auf), blieb auf, ist
aufgeblieben to stay up

aufblicken (blickt auf) to look up

der Aufenthalt (-e) stay; layover (9)

die Aufenthaltszeit (-en) length of
layover

auffordern (fordert auf): zum Tanzen
auffordern to ask (somebody) to dance

die Aufforderung (-en) request

aufführen (führt auf) to perform

die Aufführung (-en) performance

die Aufgabe (-n) task; exercise

aufgeben (gibt auf), gab auf, aufgegeben
to give up

aufgeschlossen outgoing

aufgeschnitten sliced

aufgrund (+ *gen.*) based on; because of

(sich) aufhalten (hält auf), hielt auf, aufgehalten to stay

die Aufheiterung (-en) clearing (of weather)

aufhören (mit + *dat.*) **(hört auf)** to quit, stop (doing something) (4)

der Aufkleber (-) sticker

aufmachen (macht auf) to open

die Aufnahme (-n) accommodation

aufnehmen (nimmt auf), nahm auf, aufgenommen to record (e.g., on video) (13)

aufräumen (räumt auf) to straighten up (a room) (4)

aufregend exciting

die Aufregung (-en) excitement

der Aufsatz (::e) essay

aufsaugen (saugt auf) to absorb

der Aufschnitt cold cuts (5)

aufschreiben (schreibt auf), schrieb auf, aufgeschrieben to write down

der Aufseher (-) / die Aufseherin (-nen) guard, overseer

der Aufstand (::e) rebellion, uprising

aufstehen (steht auf), stand auf, ist aufgestanden to get up (4)

aufsteigen (steigt auf), stieg auf, ist aufgestiegen to advance

aufstellen (stellt auf) to set up, put up

der Aufstieg (-e) advancement

die Aufstiegsmöglichkeit (-en) opportunity for advancement

aufstützen: ist aufgestützt is propped up

auftauchen (taucht auf), ist aufgetaucht to appear

aufteilen (teilt auf) to divide

auftreten (tritt auf), trat auf, ist aufgetreten to present oneself, appear

aufwachen (wacht auf), ist aufgewacht to wake up (4)

die Aufzeichnung (-en) drawing

der Aufzug (::e) elevator (9)

das Auge (-n) eye (8)

der Augenblick (-e) moment, instant; **im Augenblick** at the moment

der Augenzeuge (-n) / die Augenzeugin (-nen) eye witness

(der) August August (3)

aus (+ *dat.*) out of; from (5); **aus (Baumwolle)** made of (cotton); **aus dem Effeff** inside out; **aus Liebe** out of love; **Ich komme aus...** I'm from . . . (E)

ausbauen (baut aus) to add on (to a building)

ausbessern (bessert aus) to repair

die Ausbildung (-en) training (11)

der Ausbildungsplatz (::e) training position

die Ausbildungsstelle (-n) training position

ausbrechen (aus + *dat.*) **(bricht aus), brach aus, ist ausgebrochen** to break out (of, from)

die Ausdehnung (-en) dimension

sich etwas ausdenken (denkt aus), dachte aus, ausgedacht to think up something

der Ausdruck (::e) expression

ausdrücken (drückt aus) to express

auseinander fallen (fällt auseinander), fiel auseinander, ist auseinander gefallen to drift apart

die Auseinandersetzung (-en) altercation, argument

die Ausfahrt (-en) exit; off-ramp

ausfallen (fällt aus), fiel aus, ist ausgefallen to be canceled; to stop operating

der Ausflug (::e) excursion

ausfüllen (füllt aus) to fill out (9)

die Ausgabe (-n) expense (12)

der Ausgangspunkt (-e) starting point

ausgeben (gibt aus), gab aus, ausgegeben to spend (money) (12)

ausgehen (geht aus), ging aus, ist ausgegangen to go out (4); **Die Bananen gehen aus.** There are almost no more bananas.

ausgerechnet of all things

ausgeschildert marked by signs

ausgestattet furnished

ausgewählt select, chosen

ausgezeichnet excellent (E)

ausgleiten (gleitet aus), glitt aus, ist ausgeglitten to slip and fall

aushalten (hält aus), hielt aus, ausgehalten to endure

**auskommen (kommt aus), kam aus, ist ausgekommen; to make ends meet, to get by with (money)

die Auskunft (::e) information

das Ausland (*no pl.*) foreign countries (11); **im Ausland** abroad (11)

der Ausländer (-) / die Ausländerin (-nen) foreigner (14)

die Ausländerfeindlichkeit xenophobia; hatred directed toward foreigners (14)

ausländisch foreign

die Auslandsspeise (-n) foreign food

der Auslandsurlaub (-e) vacation abroad

auslassen (lässt aus), ließ aus, ausgelassen to leave out

die Ausnahme (-n) exception

auspacken (packt aus) to unpack

ausprobieren (probiert aus) to try out

die Ausrede (-n) excuse

ausrichten (richtet aus) to give a message

ausrotten (rottet aus) to eradicate

(sich) ausruhen (ruht aus) to rest (4); to recuperate

die Aussage (-n) statement

aussagefähig capable of testifying

aussagekräftig meaningful, pertinent

ausschauen (schaut aus) to look, appear

ausscheiden (scheidet aus), schied aus, ist ausgeschieden to be out of the game

ausschenken (schenkt aus) to pour, serve (beverage)

ausschließlich exclusively

der Ausschnitt (-e) excerpt, section

aussehen (sieht aus), sah aus, ausgesehen to look, appear; **gut aussehend** good-looking

außen outside; **nach außen hin** to the outside

der Außenminister (-) Secretary of State

außer (+ *dat.*) except for, besides

äußer- outer; **im äußeren Kreis** in the outer circle

außerdem besides, in addition (14)

außergewöhnlich extraordinary; extraordinarily

außerhalb (+ *gen.*) outside of (9); away from

die Äußerlichkeit (-en) formality

sich äußern to express oneself; **die Meinung äußern** to voice an opinion

äußerst extremely

die Äußerung (-en) statement

die Aussicht (-en) view; prospect

ausspannen (spannt aus) to rest, relax

aussteigen (steigt aus), stieg aus, ist ausgestiegen to get out of (a vehicle)

die Ausstellung (-en) exhibition

sich (et)was aussuchen (sucht aus) to select, find, choose something (13)

der Austausch (-e) exchange

austauschen (tauscht aus) to exchange

der Austauschschüler (-) / die Austauschschülerin (-nen) exchange student (*high school*)

der Austauschstudent (-en *masc.*) / **die Austauschstudentin (-nen)** exchange student (*college*)

(das) Australien Australia

austricksen (trickst aus) (*coll.*) to play a trick on

ausüben (übt aus) to practice

der Ausverkauf (::e) sale

die Auswahl (-en) choice; selection

auswählen (wählt aus) to choose, select

auswandern (wandert aus), ist ausgewandert to emigrate

auswechseln (wechselt aus) to change

ausweichen (weicht aus), wich aus, ist ausgewichen to avoid, evade

der Ausweis (-e) ID card

die Auszeichnung (-en) distinction

ausziehen (zieht aus), zog aus, ist ausgezogen to move out; **sich ausziehen** to get undressed (8)

der/die Auszubildende (*decl. adj.*) (*abbr.* Azubi [-s]) trainee, apprentice (13)

der Auszug (ːe) excerpt, extract

authentisch authentic

das Auto (-s) car, auto (2)

die Autoabgase (*pl.*) exhaust fumes

die Autobahn (-en) highway

die Autobahnbrücke (-n) freeway overpass

die Autobahnzubringerstraße (-n) road leading to the freeway

die Autobiografie (-n) autobiography

der (Auto)bus (-se) bus

der Autodieb (-e) car thief

der Autofahrer (-) / die Autofahrerin (-nen) (automobile) driver

die Autoindustrie (-n) automobile industry

der Automat (-en *masc.*) vending machine; **der Geldautomat** automatic teller

automatisch automatic

der Automechaniker (-) / die Automechanikerin (-nen) car mechanic

das Automobil (-e) automobile, car

das Automobilwerk (-e) automobile factory

der Autor (-en *masc.*) / die Autorin (-nen) author

das Autoradio (-s) car radio

autoritär authoritarian

die Autoschlange (-n) long line of cars

der Autoschlüssel (-) car key

Autostop: per Autostop reisen to hitchhike (10)

das Autotelefon (-e) car telephone

das Autozubehör car accessories

Azubi = der / die Auszubildende

B

das Baby (-s) baby

der Bach (ːe) creek, stream

backen (bäckt), backte, gebacken to bake

der Bäcker (-) / die Bäckerin (-nen) baker

die Bäckerei (-en) bakery (5)

der Backstein (-e) brick

die Backwaren (*pl.*) baked goods (5)

das Bad (ːer) bath; bathroom (2); spa

der Badeanzug (ːe) bathing suit (5)

die Badehose (-n) bathing trunks

der Bademantel (ː) bathrobe (5)

die Bademoden (*pl.*) beachwear

(das) Baden-Württemberg *one of the German states*

die Badesachen (*pl.*) beach wear; beach accessories

das Badezimmer (-) bathroom (2)

BAföG *abbreviation for German financial aid system for students*

die Baguette (-n) French bread

die Bahn (-en) train; railway (10); **mit der Bahn** by train; **die S-Bahn (-en)** light-rail line (9); **die U-Bahn (-en)** subway

der Bahnhof (ːe) train station (4)

der Bahnsteig (-e) (train) platform (10)

das Bahnticket (-s) train ticket

bald soon (12); **bis bald** see you later; **möglichst bald** as soon as possible (12)

der Baldrian valerian

der Balkon (-e) balcony (2)

der Ball (ːe) ball; **der Fußball** soccer

der Ballast ballast

das Ballett (-e) ballet (4)

die Banane (-n) banana (5)

das Band (ːer) tape; ribbon; **vom Band laufen** to be mass-produced

die Band (-s) (musical) band

die Bande (-n) gang

der Bandscheibenschaden slipped (vertebral) disc

die Bank (-en) bank (9)

die Bankkarte (-n) bank card

der Bankschalter (-) bank window

der Banktresor (-e) bank vault

bar in cash (9); **bar jeder Vernunft** devoid of any sense

die Bar (-s) bar

das Bargeld cash (10)

der Baron (-e) baron (*nobility title*)

der Bart (ːe) beard

(das) Baseball baseball

basteln to tinker; to build (as a hobby)

die Batterie (-n) battery

der Bau (Bauten) construction; building

der Bauch (ːe) belly, abdomen, stomach (8)

die Bauchschmerzen (*pl.*) belly ache

der Bauchtanz (ːe) belly dance

bauen to build

der Bauer (-n *masc.*) / die Bäuerin (-nen) farmer

das Bauernbrot (-e) farmer's bread

das Bauernfrühstück dish consisting of fried potatoes, bacon, and scrambled eggs

das Bauernhaus (ːer) farmhouse (12)

der Bauernhof (ːe) farm

der Bauernsalat (-e) farmer's salad

die Bauindustrie (-n) construction industry

der Baum (ːe) tree

die Baumwolle cotton; **aus Baumwolle** made of cotton

die Baustelle (-n) construction site

bayerisch (*adj.*) Bavarian

(das) Bayern Bavaria

beachten to notice; to observe, pay attention to; **Beachtung schenken** to pay attention to

der Beamte (*decl. adj.*) / **die Beamtin (-nen)** agent; government employee

beantragen to apply for

beantworten to answer

der Becher (-) beaker; container

der Bedarf demand, need; **bei Bedarf** as needed

das Bedauern regret

bedauern to regret (14)

bedeckt overcast

bedenken, bedachte, bedacht to consider, think about

bedeuten to mean, signify

bedeutend important, distinguished

die Bedeutung (-en) meaning, significance

bedienen to serve

die Bedienung service (6)

das Bedienungsgeld service charge

die Bedingung (-en) condition

bedingungslos unconditional

bedroht sein to be threatened

bedrücken to depress

das Bedürfnis (-se) need, desire

sich beeilen to hurry (up) (8)

beeindruckt impressed

beeinflussen to influence

beenden to complete, finish, end

befahren (*adj.*) traveled on

sich befassen mit (+ *dat.*) to occupy oneself with

befehlen (befiehlt), befahl, befohlen to order

das Befinden well-being

sich befinden, befand, befunden to be located; to be

die Begebenheit (-en) event

begehen, beging, begangen to commit

begeistert von enthusiastic about

beginnen, begann, begonnen to begin, start (10)

begleiten to accompany

begreifen, begriff, begriffen to understand, comprehend

begründen to substantiate

begrünt overgrown with greenery

begrüßen to greet, welcome

die Begrüßung (-en) greeting

behaglich comfortable

behandeln to treat

behaupten to claim, assert (13)

behausen to live in

sich behelfen (behilft), behalf, beholfen to make do
beherzigen to bear in mind
behindern to handicap, hinder
die Behörde (-n) regulatory authority, agency
bei (+ *dat.*) near; at; at the place of; with (5)
beibehalten (behält bei), behielt bei, beibehalten to maintain, keep up
beibringen (bringt bei), brachte bei, beigebracht to teach
beide (*pl.*) both
beifügen (fügt bei) to add; to enclose
beige beige (5)
die Beilage (-n) side dish (6)
beim = bei dem
das Bein (-e) leg (8)
das Beispiel (-e) example, model: **zum Beispiel** (*abbr.* **z.B.**) for example
beispielsweise for example
beißen, biss, gebissen to bite
der Beitrag (∴e) contribution
beitragen (trägt bei), trug bei, beigetragen to contribute
beitreten (+ *dat.*) **(tritt bei), trat bei, ist beigetreten** to join
bekannt acquainted; known; **bekannt werden** to become acquainted
der/die Bekannte (*decl. adj.*) acquaintance
bekannt geben (gibt bekannt), gab bekannt, bekannt gegeben to announce, report
sich beklagen to complain
die Bekleidung clothing, attire
bekommen, bekam, bekommen to receive, get (6); **Was bekommen Sie?** What will you have? (6)
belasten to burden
beleben to enliven
belegen: ein Seminar belegen to register for a seminar
die Beleuchtung (-en) lighting; illumination
(das) Belgien Belgium (E)
belgisch (*adj.*) Belgian
der Belichtungsmesser (-) exposure meter
beliebt popular
belohnen to reward
die Belohnung (-en) reward
bemerken to observe; to notice
die Bemerkung (-en) remark, comment
bemühen to bother
sich benehmen (benimmt), benahm, benommen to behave
benutzbar usable
benutzen to use
das Benzin gasoline (12)

der Benzinverbrauch gasoline consumption
beobachten to observe
bequem comfortable, comfortably (2)
beraten (berät), beriet, beraten to advise, counsel
die Beratung (-en) consultation
der Bereich (-e) area, field
bereit sein to be willing
bereiten to prepare
bereithalten (hält bereit), hielt bereit, bereitgehalten to hold in store
bereits already
bereuen to regret
der Berg (-e) mountain (7)
bergsteigen gehen (geht), ging, ist gegangen to go mountain climbing
der Bericht (-e) report (13)
berichten to report, narrate (13)
die Berichterstattung detailed reporting
Berliner (*adj.*) from/of Berlin
der Berliner (-) / die Berlinerin (-nen) person from Berlin
(das) Berlinerisch Berlin dialect
berücksichtigen to consider
der Beruf (-e) profession (1); occupation; **Was sind Sie von Beruf?** What do you do for a living? (1)
beruflich on business; professional
der Berufsberater (-) / die Berufsberaterin (-nen) employment counselor (11)
die Berufsberatung job counseling
berufsbildende Schule (-n) trade school
das Berufsleben professional life (11)
die Berufsschule (-n) vocational school
der/die Berufstätige (*decl. adj.*) working person
die Berufswahl (-en) career choice
der Berufswunsch (∴e) career goal
berühmt famous (11)
berühren to touch
besänftigen to appease, placate
die Besatzung (-en) (military) occupation
die Besatzungszone (-n) occupied zone
sich beschäftigen (mit) (+ *dat.*) to occupy oneself (with) (11); to spend time (with)
die Beschäftigung (-en) activity
Bescheid: Bescheid sagen (sagt Bescheid) to notify; to say definitely (10)
beschließen, beschloss, beschlossen to decide
beschreiben, beschrieb, beschrieben to describe
die Beschreibung (-en) description
die Beschwerde (-n) complaint
sich beschweren über (+ *acc.*) to lodge a complaint, complain about (9)
beseitigen to remove
der Besen (-) broom

der Besenstiel (-e) broomstick
besetzen to occupy
besetzt occupied, taken (6); **Hier ist besetzt.** This place is taken. (6)
besichtigen to view, see
die Besiedlung (-en) settlement
besitzen, besaß, besessen to own, possess (11)
die Besonderheit (-en) special feature
besonders especially, particularly (8); special; **etwas Besonderes** something special; **nicht besonders gut** not particularly well (E)
besorgen to purchase, procure, get
besprechen (bespricht), besprach, besprochen to discuss, talk about
die Besprechung (-en) conference
besser better (10)
die Besserung: Gute Besserung! Get well soon! (8)
besserwissend (*adj.*) in a know-all fashion
best-: am besten (the) best
der Bestandteil (-e) part
bestätigen to confirm, verify
bestechen (besticht), bestach, bestochen to bribe
das Besteck (-e) silverware
bestehen, bestand, bestanden to pass (an exam); **bestehen aus** (+ *dat.*) to consist of
bestellen to order; to reserve (6)
die Bestellung (-en) order; reservation
bestimmen to determine, decide
bestimmt definitely (1)
bestrafen to punish
bestreichen, bestrich, bestrichen to spread on
der Besuch (-e) visit; visitor; **zu Besuch haben** to have (somebody) as a visitor; **zu Besuch sein** to visit; **zu Besuch kommen** to come for a visit
besuchen to visit (1)
der Besucher (-) / die Besucherin (-nen) visitor, guest
betäubt stunned; anesthetized
beteiligt sein (an + *dat.*) to participate (in)
das Beton concrete
betonen to stress, emphasize
die Betonung (-en) emphasis
die Betonwüste (-n) concrete jungle
betragen (beträgt), betrug, betragen to amount to, come to; **die Miete beträgt** the rent comes to
betreffen (betrifft), betraf, betroffen to concern
betreffend regarding
betreten (betritt), betrat, betreten to walk into

der Betrieb (-e) enterprise, business
die Betriebsabteilung (-en) department of a business
die Betriebswirtschaft business management
das Bett (-en) bed (2)
die Bettkarte (-n) ticket, voucher for a bed (in a train)
der Bettler (-) / die Bettlerin (-nen) beggar
das Betttuch (:er) bed sheet
die Bettwaren (*pl.*) bedding
die Bettwäsche linens
beugen to bend
die Bevölkerung population
die Bevölkerungsexplosion population explosion
die Bevölkerungzahl population
der Bevölkerungszuwachs population increase
bevor (*subord. conj.*) before (10)
bevorzugt werden to be given priority
bewegen to move, move about
beweglich movable
die Bewegung (-en) exercise, movement
der Beweis (-e) proof, evidence
sich bewerben (um) (+ *acc.*) **(bewirbt), bewarb, beworben** to apply (for) (11)
der Bewerber (-) / die Bewerberin (-nen) applicant
die Bewerbung (-en) application (11)
das Bewerbungsformular (-e) application form (11)
bewerten to evaluate
bewohnen to reside in; to occupy
der Bewohner (-) / die Bewohnerin (-nen) resident, tenant
bewölkt cloudy, overcast (7)
die Bewölkungszunahme increasing cloudiness
bezahlbar payable; affordable
bezahlen to pay
die Bezeichnung (-en) label, term
bezeugen: Interesse bezeugen to show an interest
sich beziehen auf (+ *acc.*) to refer to
die Beziehung (-en) relationship; connection
beziehungsweise (bzw.) respectively, or
der Bezirk (-e) district, area (11)
bezweifeln to doubt
die Bibliothek (-en) library (4)
der Bibliothekar (-e) / die Bibliothekarin (-nen) librarian (11)
das Bier beer (5); **Bier vom Fass** draft beer (6)
der Biergarten (:) beer garden (*restaurant*) (6)
der Bierkeller (-) *type of restaurant where beer is served*
der Bierkrug (:e) beer stein

bieten, bot, geboten to offer, present
der Bikini (-s) two-piece bathing suit
die Bilanz (-en) financial balance, "bottom line"
das Bild (-er) picture
bilden to form
das Bildnis (-se) picture, image
das Bildsymbol (-e) pictogram
die Bildungswissenschaft (-en) science/field of education
das Billiard (-s) billiard
billig inexpensive(ly); cheap(ly) (2)
die Billiguhr (-en) cheap watch
binden, band, gebunden to tie
das Biobrot (-e) organic bread
biographisch biographical(ly)
der Bioladen (:) natural foods store (5)
die Biologie biology
der Biologielaborant (-en *masc.*) **/ die Biologielaborantin (-nen)** laboratory assistant
der Biologielehrer (-) / die Biologielehrerin (-nen) biology teacher
der Biologietechnologe (-n *masc.*) **/ die Biologietechnologin (-nen)** biotechnician
bis (+ *acc.*) until (6); up to; **bis zum/zur** as far as (9); **bis bald** see you later; **bis fünf Uhr** until five o'clock (6)
bisher so far, up to now
bisherig previous
ein bisschen a little (bit); somewhat
die Bistrobaguette (-n) special French bread
bitte please; you're welcome (E); **bitte schön** please; **bitte sehr** please; **Bitte sehr?** May I help you? (*in a store*); **Wie bitte?** Pardon? What did you say? (E)
bitten um (+ *acc.*), **bat, gebeten** to ask for, request (12)
bitter bitter(ly)
bizarr bizarre
blasen (bläst), blies, geblasen to blow
das Blatt (:er) sheet (of paper); leaf
blättern to leaf through
der Blattsalat (-e) green lettuce
blau blue (5); **in Blau** in blue
bleiben, blieb, ist geblieben to stay, remain (1); **stehen bleiben (bleibt stehen)** to stop walking; to stand still
der Bleistift (-e) pencil (12)
der Blick (-e) look; glance; **auf den ersten Blick** at first sight
der Blickpunkt (-e) focal point
der Blinddarm (:e) appendix
die Blinddarmreizung (-en) appendix irritation
blitzen to flash (7); **Es blitzt.** There is lightning. (7)

das Blitzgerät (-e) (photographic) flash unit
die Blockade (-n) blockade
blockieren to block; to blockade
blöd(e) (*coll.*) stupid (13)
blond blond
die Blondine (-n) blond woman
bloß merely; only; **bloß mal** only just; just once
blühen to blossom
die Blume (-n) flower
der Blumenkohl cauliflower (5)
die Bluse (-n) blouse (5)
die Blutorange (-n) blood orange
der BMW (-s) (Bayerische Motor Werke) BMW automobile
die Bockwurst (:e) *type of German hot dog*
der Boden (:) floor of a room, ground; attic
der Bodenbelag (:e) floor covering
der Bodenozon ground ozone
der Bodenozonwert (-e) level of ground ozone
der Bodenschatz (:e) ore
der Bodensee Lake Constance
das Bodybuilding body-building; **Bodybuilding machen** to do bodybuilding; weight training (7)
das Bogenschießen archery
die Bombe (-n) bomb
das Boot (-e) boat (1)
der Bootsverleih (-e) boat rental agency
Bord: an Bord on board
die Börse (-n) stock exchange (13)
böse angry (angrily), mad; mean; bad; **böse sein auf** (+ *acc.*) to be mad (at somebody)
(das) Bosnien Bosnia
botanisch botanical(ly)
die Boutique (-n) boutique store
die Bouzouki (-s) bouzouki (*Greek string instrument*)
das Bowlingcenter bowling center
die Boxen (*pl.*) stereo speakers
die Boxershorts (*pl.*) boxer shorts
boykottieren to boycott
die Branche (-n) type of business
(das) Brandenburg *one of the German states*
das Brandenburger Tor Brandenburg Gate (*in Berlin*)
(das) Brasilien Brazil
der Braten (-) roast
die Bratkartoffeln (*pl.*) fried potatoes (6)
die Bratwurst (:e) *special type of sausage*
brauchen to need (2)
brauen to brew
die Brauerei (-en) brewery
das Brauhaus (:er) brewery
braun brown (5)

BRD = Bundesrepublik Deutschland

brechen (bricht), brach, gebrochen to break

die Breite (-n) latitude

der Breitensport (-s) popular sport

die Bremse (-n) brake

bremsen to put on the brakes, brake

(das) Breslau *city in former German province of Silesia, now Wrocław, Poland*

das Brett (-er) board

das Brevier (-e) breviary

die Brezel (-n) pretzel (6)

der Brief (-e) letter

der Briefkasten (:) mailbox

die Briefmarke (-n) postage stamp

der Briefträger (-) / die Briefträgerin (-nen) mail carrier

die Brigade (-n) team of workers (in a factory)

die Brille (-n) eyeglasses (5)

bringen, brachte, gebracht to bring; to take (7); **es zu etwas bringen** to be successful (in life)

der Brockhaus *name of German encyclopedia*

der Brokkoli (-) broccoli (5)

die Broschüre (-n) brochure, pamphlet

das Brot (-e) bread (5); **das Butterbrot (-e)** sandwich

das Brötchen (-) bread roll (5)

der Bruch (:e) fraction

brüchig brittle

die Brücke (-n) bridge

der Bruder (:) brother (3)

brüllen to yell; to roar

die Brust (:e) breast, chest (8)

das Buch (:er) book (1)

der Buchdruck printing

buchen to book (a trip) (10)

das Bücherregal (-e) bookshelf (2)

der Bücherschrank (:e) bookcase

die Buchhandlung (-en) book store

das Büchlein (-) small book

der Buchmarkt (:e) book market

der Buchstabe (-n *masc.***)** letter of the alphabet

buchstabieren to spell; **Buchstabieren Sie!** Spell (it).

die Buchstabiertafel (-n) spelling chart

die Bucht (-en) bay

die Buchung (-en) reservation

die Bude (-n) (*coll.*) room (*slang term used by students*)

das Budget (-s) budget

die Bühne (-n) stage

das Bühnenbild (-er) stage decoration

der Bulle (-n *masc.***)** bull; (*derogatory*) policeman

bummeln to stroll

der Bund (-e) club; federation

das Bundesausbildungsförderungsgesetz (BAföG) *German law for the financial assistance of students*

der Bundesbürger (-) / die Bundesbürgerin (-nen) (German) citizen

der Bundeskanzler (-) (German or Austrian) chancellor

das Bundesland (:er) German state

der Bundespräsident (-en *masc.***)** German president

die Bundesrepublik Deutschland (BRD) German Federal Republic (E)

der Bundestag Federal German parliament

die Bundeswehr Federal German armed forces

der Bunker (-) bunker

bunt colorful

die Burg (-en) fortress, castle

der Bürger (-) / die Bürgerin (-nen) citizen (14)

die Bürgerinitiative (-n) grass-roots movement

der Bürgermeister (-) mayor

das Büro (-s) (11) office

die Büroarbeit (-en) office work

die Bürokauffrau (-en) (female) administrator

der Bürokaufmann (:er) (male) administrator

bürokratisch bureaucratical(ly)

der Bus (-se) bus (10)

die Busfahrt (-en) bus ride; bus trip

die Bushaltestelle (-n) bus stop

die Buslinie (-n) bus line

die Busreise (-n) bus trip

die Butter butter (5)

das Buttergemüse (-) buttered vegetable

der Butterkäse butter cheese

die Butterspätzle (*pl.*) buttered pasta dish

bzw. = beziehungsweise

C

ca. = circa, zirka about, approximately

das Café (-s) café (6)

campen to go camping

das Camping camping

der Campingplatz (:e) campground

die Campingtour (-en) camping tour

der Campus (-) (school) campus

der Cartoon (-s) cartoon

die CD (-s) CD

der CD-Spieler (-) CD player (2)

Celsius centigrade

der Champignon (-s) mushroom

die Chance (-n) chance

das Chaos chaos

der Charakter (-e) character, personality

die Checkliste (-n) checklist

der Chef (-s) / die Chefin (-nen) manager, boss, head (11)

die Chemie chemistry

der Chemielaborant (-en *masc.***) / die Chemielaborantin (-nen)** chemical technician

die Chemikalie (-n) chemical substance

der Chemiker (-) / die Chemikerin (-nen) chemist

die Chiffre (-n) code (number)

chinesisch (*adj.*) Chinese

der Chirurg (-en *masc.***) / die Chirurgin (-nen)** surgeon

der Chor (:e) choir, chorus; **im Chor** in a chorus

die Christianisierung christianization

christlich (*adj.*) Christian

die Chronik (-en) chronicle

der Chronobiologe (-n *masc.***) / die Chronobiologin (-nen)** chronobiologist

die Chronologie (-n) chronology

chronologisch chronological

circa = zirka about (12)

der Clown (-s) / die Clownin (-nen) clown

cm = Centimeter

die Cola (-s) cola (5)

der Computer (-) computer (2)

der Computeranschluss (:e) computer connection (2)

die Computerdiskette (-n) computer diskette (12)

das Computerspiel (-e) computer game (1)

der Computertisch (-e) computer table

die Computerwissenschaft (-en) computer science

der Container (-) recycling bin

der Containerstellplatz (:e) recycling center

die Cordhose (-n) corduroy pants

die Coronarsklerose (-n) coronary sclerosis, hardening of the arteries

die Couch (-en) couch

der Couchtisch (-e) coffee table (2)

der Cousin (-s) male cousin

die Cousine = Kusine female cousin

D

da there (2); since; **da drüben** over there (6)

dabei with that; in that context; **dabei sein** to be part of

das Dach (:er) roof (12)

das Dachgeschoss (-e) top floor, attic (12)

die Dachwohnung (-en) attic apartment

der Dackel (-) dachshund

dadurch for that reason; through that; because of

dafür for that; instead of that; **Ich bin dafür.** I am for it. (14)

dagegen against it (14); on the other hand; **Ich bin (total) dagegen.** I'm (totally) against it. (14)

daher from there; for that reason, therefore

dahin there (to that place) (9); **bis dahin** until then; **Wie komme ich am besten dahin?** What's the best way to get there?

dahinter behind that

daliegen (liegt da), lag da, dagelegen to lie there

damals formerly; (back) then, at that time

die Dame (-n) lady

der Damenhut (⸚e) ladies' hat

die Damenkonfektion (-en) ladies' wear

der Damenschuh (-e) ladies' shoe

die Damenwäsche lingerie

damit (*subord. conj.*) so that; with that

die Dämmerung dawn; dusk; twilight

der Dampf (⸚e) steam; **Dampf machen** (+ *dat.*) to make things uncomfortable (for somebody)

danach after that; afterward

der Däne (-n *masc.***) / die Dänin (-nen)** Dane, Danish person

daneben next to that

(das) Dänemark Denmark (E)

der Dank thanks; **vielen Dank** many thanks (6); **Gott sei Dank** thank God

dank (+ *gen.*) thanks to

dankbar grateful

danke thanks (E); **danke schön** thank you very much (E); **danke sehr** thanks a lot (1); **danke, es geht** O.K., thanks; **danke, gut** fine, thanks (E)

danken (+ *dat.*) to thank (5); **Nichts zu danken.** No thanks necessary., Don't mention it. (8)

dann then

(das) Danzig *German name for the town of Gdansk*

daran on that, at that, to that

darauf on that, for that; **bald darauf** soon after that

daraus from that

darin in that, in there

die Darmgegend (-en) intestinal area

die Darmgeschichten (*pl.*) intestinal troubles

darstellen (stellt dar) to portray, depict

darüber about that; above that; **darüber hinaus** moreover

darum therefore

darunter under, among (them)

das that, this; **Das ist...** This is . . . (E)

dass (*subord. conj.*) that (8)

dasselbe the same

der Dativ dative case

die Dativpräposition (-en) preposition governing the dative case

das Dativpronomen (-) pronoun in the dative case

das Dativverb (-en) verb requiring a dative object

das Datum (Daten) date (3); **Welches Datum ist heute/morgen?** What is today's/tomorrow's date? (3)

der Dauerbetrieb regular use

dauern to last; to take time (7)

dauernd constant(ly); all the time

die Dauerwelle (-n) permanent wave

der Daumen (-) thumb; **die Daumen drücken** to keep one's fingers crossed

davon of that, about that, on that; **abgesehen davon** apart from that

davor before that

dazu to that, for that

dazuverdienen (verdient dazu) to earn on the side

DB = Deutsche Bundesbahn

DDR = Deutsche Demokratische Republik

debattieren to debate

die Decke (-n) ceiling; blanket

decken to cover; **den Tisch decken** to set the table

die Deckenleuchte (-n) ceiling light

definieren to define

deftig hearty, solid

(sich) dehnen to stretch

dein your (*inform. sg.*) (3)

die Dekoration (-en) decoration

der Dekostoff (-e) decorator fabric

die Delikatesse (-n) delicacy

demnächst soon

die Demokratie (-n) democracy

demokratisch democratic(ally)

die Demonstration (-en) demonstration (14)

demonstrieren to demonstrate

denken, dachte, gedacht to think; **denken an** (+ *acc.*) to think about, of (12)

denkwürdig memorable

denn (*coord. conj.*) for, because (7); then; (*used in questions to express interest*) (1)

dennoch however; in spite of

die Deponie (-n) garbage dump

deportieren to deport

deprimiert depressed (8)

der, die, das the; that one

derjenige, diejenige, dasjenige the one (who)

derselbe the same

deshalb therefore, for that reason (8)

das Design (-s) design

der Designer (-) / die Designerin (-nen) designer

das Dessin (-s) pattern

desto: je... desto... the . . . the . . .

deswegen because of that (12)

das Detail (-s) detail

detailliert detailed

der Detektivroman (-e) detective story

deuten auf (+ *acc.*) to point to, refer to

deutlich clear, understandable

deutsch German; **(das) Deutsch** German (language) (1); **auf Deutsch** in German

der/die Deutsche (*decl. adj.*) German person

die Deutsche Demokratische Republik (DDR) German Democratic Republic (GDR)

die Deutsche Mark (DM) German mark

die Deutschklasse (-n) German class

der Deutschklub (-s) German club

der Deutschkurs (-e) German course

(das) Deutschland Germany (E)

der Deutschlehrer (-) / die Deutschlehrerin (-nen) German teacher

der/die Deutschlernende (*decl. adj.*) German learner

deutschsprachig German speaking

der Deutschunterricht German class

die Devisen (*pl.*) foreign currency

die Deviseneinfuhr (-en) importation of foreign currency

(der) Dezember December (3)

d.h. = (das heißt) that is, i.e. (8)

die Dialektik dialectics

der Dialog (-e) dialogue

die Diät (-en) diet

dich you (*acc. inform. sg.*)

der Dichter (-) / die Dichterin (-nen) poet

dichtmachen (macht dicht) to close

dick fat, plump; thick; **dick machen** to be fattening; **dick werden** to gain weight; **(ein) dickes Küsschen** (a) big kiss

der Dieb (-e) thief

der Diebstahl (⸚e) theft

die Diele (-n) front hall (12)

(der) Dienstag Tuesday (3)

dienstags Tuesdays, on Tuesday(s) (4)

dieselbe the same

der Dieselmotor (-en) diesel engine

dieser, diese, dies(es) this (5)

diesmal this time

digital digital

die Digitaluhr (-en) digital watch

das Dilemma (-s) dilemma

der Dill dill (*herb*)

der Dimmer (-) (*light switch*) dimmer

das Ding (-e) thing, object

Dipl. = Diplom (*academic degree*)

der Diplomat (-en *masc.***) / die Diplomatin (-nen)** diplomat

der Dirigent (-en *masc.***) / die Dirigentin (-nen)** musical conductor

das Dirndlkleid (-er) *traditional dress worn mostly in Southern Germany and Austria*

die Disko (-s) disco bar (4); **in die Disko gehen** to go to a disco (4)

die Diskriminierung (-en) discrimination

die Diskussion (-en) discussion

diskutieren to discuss (1); to debate

die Disziplin discipline

DM = die Deutsche Mark

doch yes (1); yes, of course; after all (4)

der Doktor (-en) physician; person holding doctorate; **Herr/Frau Doktor** *formal way of addressing individual with medical or doctoral degree*

das Dokument (-e) document

der Dokumentarfilm (-e) documentary (film) (13)

dokumentieren to document; to certify

der Dollarschein (-e) dollar bill

der Dolmetscher (-) / die Dolmetscherin (-nen) interpreter (11)

das Dolmetscherinstitut (-e) college for interpreters

der Dom (-e) cathedral; dome

die Donau Danube (*river*)

donnern to thunder; **Es donnert.** It is thundering. (7)

(der) Donnerstag Thursday (3)

donnerstags Thursdays, on Thursday(s) (4)

doof (*coll.*) dumb, stupid

doppelt double; twice

das Doppelzimmer (-) room with two beds; double room (9)

das Dorf (¨er) village (12)

der Dorfkrug (¨e) village inn

dort there

dorthin (to) there

die Dose (-n) (tin or aluminum) can; jar (14)

Dr. = Doktor

das Drachenfliegen hang gliding

der Draht (¨e) wire

das Drama (Dramen) drama

dramatisch dramatic(ally)

dran sein to have (one's) turn

sich drängen to crowd

das Drängendste (*decl. adj.*) the most urgent (matter)

drastisch drastically

(sich) drauflegen (legt drauf) to lie down on top of

draußen outside (7)

drehen to turn

drei three (E)

dreihundert three hundred (E)

das Dreikornbrot three-grain bread

dreimal three times (7)

dreißig thirty (E)

dreitausend three thousand (E)

dreizehn thirteen (E)

dreizehnte thirteenth (3)

drin (= darin) (*coll.*) inside

dringend urgent(ly) (2)

drinnen inside (7)

dritte third (3); **zu dritt** as a group of three

ein Drittel a third

die Droge (-n) drug; medicine (14)

drogenabhängig addicted to drugs

der/die Drogenabhängige (*decl. adj.*) drug addict

der Drogenhandel (-) drug trade

der Drogenkonsum drug consumption

die Drogensucht drug addiction (14)

der/die Drogensüchtige (*decl. adj.*) drug addict (14)

die Drogerie (-n) drugstore (*toiletries and sundries*) (5)

drüben, da drüben over there, on the other side (6)

drücken: die Daumen drücken to keep one's fingers crossed

der Drucker (-) printer (13)

du you (*inform. sg.*) (1)

düdeln to toot

dumm dumb, stupid

die Düne (-n) dune

dunkel dark (2)

dunkelblau dark blue

dunkellila dark purple

dunkelrot dark red

dünn thin; slender, skinny

durch (+ *acc.*) through; by (3)

das Durcheinander upheaval, commotion

durchaus by all means

durchfahren (fährt durch), fuhr durch, ist durchgefahren to travel without having to transfer

durchführen (führt durch) to carry out (an order)

durchkommen (kommt durch), kam durch, ist durchgekommen to get through

durchlesen (liest durch), las durch, durchgelesen to read through, peruse

durchs = durch das (3)

der Durchschnitt (-e) average; cross section; **im Durchschnitt** on the average

durchschnittlich on the average (12)

durchziehen (zieht durch), zog durch, durchgezogen to pull through

dürfen (darf), durfte, gedurft to be allowed to; may (4)

der Durst thirst; **Durst haben** to be thirsty (2)

die Dusche (-n) shower (9)

(sich) duschen to take a shower (8)

die Duschmilk shower lotion

das Dutzend (-e) dozen

der DVD-Spieler (-) DVD player (2)

dynamisch dynamic

die Dynamomaschine (-n) generator

E

eben just; simply

ebenfalls also

ebenso just like, the same as

ebensolch- similar

echt (*coll.*) really (1); **echt langweilig** really boring (1)

die Ecke (-n) corner

Effeff: aus dem Effeff inside out

die EG = Europäische Gemeinschaft

egal: Das ist mir egal. I don't care. (5)

der Egoist (-en *masc.***)** egotist

ehemalig former

das Ehepaar (-e) married couple

eher rather, sooner

ehest- soonest

die Ehre honor

der Ehrgeiz ambition

ehrlich honest

das Ei (-er) egg (5)

die Eierbox (-en) egg container

die Eieruhr (-en) egg timer

eigen own (12)

die Eigenschaft (-en) character trait; characteristic

eigentlich actually

die Eigentumswohnung (-en) condominium

die Eignung (-en) ability

eilen to hurry

der Eilzug (¨e) local train

der Eimer (-) bucket

ein, eine a(n); one

einander one another

die Einbahnstraße (-n) one-way street

einbiegen (biegt ein), bog ein, ist eingebogen to turn, make a turn (9)

der Einblick (-e) insight

der Einbrecher (-) / die Einbrecherin (-nen) burglar

der Einbruch (¨e) burglary

eindeutig obvious(ly)

der Eindruck (¨e) impression

einer one (of several)

einerseits on the one hand

einfach simple; simply; one-way (ticket) (10); **ganz einfach** quite simple

das Einfamilienhaus (¨er) single-family house

einfügen (fügt ein) to insert

der Einfluss (¨e) influence

einführen (führt ein) to introduce (14)

die Einführung (-en) introduction

der Eingang (:-e) entrance (12); entranceway
eingenäht sewn in
eingerichtet furnished; equipped
eingeschlossen included
eingesperrt caged in
der Eingriff (-e) (*medicine*) small operation
einhalten (hält ein), hielt ein, eingehalten to adhere to
einheimisch local
der/die Einheimische (*decl. adj.*) native person
die Einheit unity; union
einholen (holt ein) to catch up with
(ein) hundert (one) hundred (E)
einige (*pl.*) several, some
einiges several things
die Einigung (-en) unification
einjährig (*adj.*) one-year
der Einkauf (:-e) purchase
einkaufen (kauft ein); einkaufen gehen to shop, go shopping (4)
der Einkaufsboulevard (-s) shopping street
der Einkaufstag (-e) day for shopping
die Einkaufstasche (-n) shopping bag
das Einkaufszentrum (Einkaufszentren) shopping center
der Einkaufszettel (-) shopping list
der Einkauftipp (-s) shopping suggestion
das Einkommen (-) income (11)
einladen (lädt ein), lud ein, eingeladen to invite (4)
einladend inviting
die Einladung (-en) invitation
der Einlass (:-e) admission; **um Einlass bitten** to request admission
einlassen (lässt ein), ließ ein, eingelassen to let (somebody) in, admit
einlösen (löst ein) Reiseschecks einlösen to cash travelers' checks
einmal once (7)
einmalig unique
die Einnahme (-n) income (12)
einnehmen (nimmt ein), nahm ein, eingenommen to take (medicine); to seize (a city)
einrichten (richtet ein) to furnish, equip (12)
die Einrichtung (-en) furnishings
eins (*numeral*) one (E)
einsam lonely
einsammeln (sammelt ein) to gather, collect
der Einsatz (:-e) operation, use
einschicken (schickt ein) to send in; to forward
einschlafen (schläft ein), schlief ein, ist eingeschlafen to fall asleep (4)

die Einsendung: bei Einsendung upon mailing in
der Einspänner (-) one-horse carriage
einsparen (spart ein) to save
einsperren (sperrt ein) to lock in
einsteigen (steigt ein), stieg ein, ist eingestiegen to board, get into (*a vehicle*) (10)
der Einsteiger (-) / die Einsteigerin (-nen) beginner, newcomer
die Einstellung (-en) attitude
einstig- former
einstmals formerly
(ein) tausend (one) thousand (E)
eintreten (tritt ein), trat ein, ist eingetreten to enter
der Eintritt (-e) price of admission
der Eintrittspreis (-e) price of admission
einverstanden: einverstanden sein to be in agreement; to agree, approve (10); **Ich bin damit einverstanden.** I agree with that.
die Einwegflasche (-n) non-returnable bottle
der Einwohner (-) / die Einwohnerin (-nen) resident, inhabitant
einzahlen (zahlt ein) to pay in; to deposit
der Einzelhandel retail trade
der Einzelhandelskaufmann (:-er) / die Einzelhandelskauffrau (-en) retail merchant
der Einzelhandelsumsatz (:-e) retail trade
einzeln scattered; **jeder einzelne** every single one
der Einzelunterricht one-on-one instruction
der Einzelurlaub (-e) vacation alone
das Einzelzimmer (-) room with one bed; single room (9)
einziehen (zieht ein), zog ein, ist eingezogen to move in (12)
einzig only, sole; **nicht ein einziges Wort** not a single word
das Eis ice cream; ice (5)
der Eisbär (-en *masc.*) polar bear
der Eisbecher (-) dish of ice cream (6)
das Eiscafé (-s) ice cream parlor
die Eiscreme ice cream (5)
das Eishockey ice hockey
der Eiskaffee (-s) iced coffee mixed with ice cream and topped by whipped cream
der Eissalat (-e) iceberg lettuce
der Eisschrank (:-e) refrigerator
das Eisstadion (Eisstadien) ice-skating rink (7)
das Ekg = Elektrokardiogramm
die Elbe *German river flowing into the North Sea*
der Elefant (-en *masc.*) elephant
elegant elegant(ly)

elektrisch electrical
die Elektrizität electricity
die Elektroabteilung (-en) electrical department
der Elektroinstallateur (-e) / die Elektroinstallateurin (-nen) electrician
das Elektrokardiogramm (-e) electrocardiogram
das Elektronenmikroskop (-e) electron microscope
die Elektronikbranche (-n) (field of) electronics
der Elektroniker (-) / die Elektronikerin (-nen) electronic engineer
das Element (-e) item, element
elementar basic, easy
das Elend misery, need
elf eleven (E)
elfte eleventh (3)
der Ell(en)bogen (-) elbow (8)
(das) Elsass Alsace
die Eltern (*pl.*) parents (3)
das Elternschlafzimmer (-) master bedroom
der Elternteil (-e) parent
die Emanzipation (-en) emancipation
die Emission (-en) emission
der Emmentaler Käse (-) Emmental cheese
der Empfang (:-e) reception
der Empfänger (-) / die Empfängerin (-nen) recipient
empfehlen (empfiehlt), empfahl, empfohlen to recommend (5)
empfehlenswert recommendable
die Empfehlung (-en) recommendation
empfinden, empfand, empfunden to feel, consider
empfindlich sensitive
das Ende (-) end; **am Ende** in the end; **zu Ende sein** to be over
enden to end
endgültig final; finally; once and for all
endlich finally, at last
die Endung (-en) ending
die Energie energy
energieeffizient energy-efficient(ly)
Energie sparend energy-saving
die Energieverschwendung waste of energy
eng narrow, tight
sich engagieren to get involved (14)
engagiert involved, concerned
(das) England England
der Engländer (-) / die Engländerin (-nen) English person
englisch English; **auf Englisch** in English
das Englisch English language
der Englischlehrer (-) / die Englischlehrerin (-nen) English teacher

der Englischunterricht English instruction

der Enkel (-) / die Enkelin (-nen) grandson, granddaughter (3)

das Enkelkind (-er) grandchild

entdecken to discover

entfallen (entfällt), entfiel, ist entfallen auf (+ *acc.*) to be allotted to

entfernen to remove; **entfernt von** away from

entgegenlaufen (läuft entgegen), lief entgegen, ist entgegengelaufen (+ *dat.*) to run toward (somebody)

enthalten (enthält), enthielt, enthalten to contain, include; **im Preis enthalten** included in the price (9)

enthusiastisch enthusiastic(ally)

entkoffeiniert decaffeinated

entkommen, entkam, ist entkommen to get away

entlang (+ *acc.*) along; alongside; **die Straße entlang** along the street

entlanggehen (geht entlang), ging entlang, ist entlanggegangen to walk along (9)

entlaufen (entläuft), entlief, ist entlaufen to run away

entnehmen (entnimmt), entnahm, entnommen to gather (from)

entnervt unnerved

(sich) entscheiden, entschied, entschieden to decide

entscheidend decisive

die Entscheidung (-en) decision; **eine Entscheidung treffen** to make a decision

sich entschließen, entschloss, entschlossen to decide, make up one's mind

entschuldigen to excuse (6); **sich entschuldigen** to apologize; **Entschuldigen Sie bitte.** Excuse me, please. (6)

die Entschuldigung (-en) apology, excuse; **Entschuldigung.** Excuse me. (1)

sich entsinnen, entsann, entsonnen to remember

der Entsorger (-) / die Entsorgerin (-nen) (toxic) waste disposal worker

die Entsorgung (-en) (toxic) waste disposal

die Entsorgungsplanung waste disposal planning

sich entspannen to relax, take a rest (8)

die Entspannung relaxation

entsprechen (+ *dat.*) **(entspricht), entsprach, entsprochen** to correspond to; to comply with; to come up to

entsprechend appropriately

entstehen, entstand, ist entstanden to originate; to come about, happen

die Entstehung origin; creation

enttäuscht disappointed

entweder... oder either . . . or (8)

entwerfen (entwirft), entwarf, entworfen to design, develop

entwickeln to develop (14)

die Entwicklung (-en) development (11)

das Entwicklungsland (:er) developing country

entziehen, entzog, entzogen to take away

entzündlich flammable

die Enzyklopädie (-n) encyclopedia

epidemisch epidemic(ally)

er he; it (1)

Erachten: meines Erachtens in my view

erbauen to build

der Erbe (-n *masc.*) **/ die Erbin (-nen)** heir

erben to inherit

die Erdbeere (-n) strawberry (5)

die Erde Earth

das Erdgeschoss (-e) ground floor (9)

die Erdkunde geography

sich ereignen to happen

das Ereignis (-se) event

erfahren (erfährt), erfuhr, erfahren to find out; to experience; to learn

die Erfahrung (-en) experience (11)

erfinden, erfand, erfunden to invent (13)

der Erfinder (-) / die Erfinderin (-nen) inventor

der Erfindergeist inventiveness

erfinderisch inventive

die Erfindung (-en) invention (13)

der Erfolg (-e) success (11); **Erfolg haben** to be successful (11)

erfolgreich successful(ly) (11)

der Erfolgszwang pressure to succeed

erfordern to demand, require

erfragen to inquire

das Erfrischungstuch (:er) towelette

erfüllen to fulfill

ergänzen to complete, add

sich ergeben (ergibt), ergab, ergeben to be the result, to surrender

ergeben (*adj.*) devoted

erhalten (erhält), erhielt, erhalten to get, receive

die Erhebung (-en) elevation

erhöhen to increase; to heighten

sich erholen to recuperate; to rest (8)

die Erholung rest and recuperation

der Erholungspreis (-e) vacation price

sich erinnern an (+ *acc.*) to remember

die Erinnerung (-en) memory; remembrance

sich erkälten to catch a cold (8)

die Erkältung (-en) cold (8)

erkennen, erkannte, erkannt to recognize

erklären to explain

die Erklärung (-en) explanation

erklingen, erklang, ist erklungen to sound

sich erkundigen to seek information, inquire

erlauben to allow, permit (9); **erlaubt** permitted

erleben to experience (10)

das Erlebnis (-se) experience, event

die Erlösung (-en) rescue, salvation

ermöglichen to make possible, enable

ermüdend tiring

die Ernährung food, nutrition (12)

die Ernährungsaktion (-en) "operation nutrition"

das Ernährungsbewusstsein consciousness about nutrition

die Ernährungssituation (-en) food situation

erneuern to renew

ernst serious (1)

erntefrisch just harvested

erobern to conquer

die Eroberung (-en) conquest

eröffnen to open up

erraten (errät), erriet, erraten to guess

erreichbar mit able to be reached by, reachable via

erreichen to reach

erscheinen, erschien, ist erschienen to appear, come out

ersetzen to replace

ersparen to save

erst only, not until

erstaunt amazed

erste first (3); **erster Klasse** first-class (10); **zum ersten Mal** for the first time

erstklassig first class, excellent

erstmals (*adv.*) for the first time

ertönen to sound (off)

erträglich bearable

der/die Erwachsene (*decl. adj.*) adult, grownup

erwähnen to mention

erwarten to expect; to wait for

die Erwartung (-en) expectation

erweitern to expand

erwerben (erwirbt), erwarb, erworben to acquire, buy

erwünscht desired; desirable

erzählen to tell, narrate

der Erzähler (-) / die Erzählerin (-nen) narrator

die Erzählung (-en) story, narration

erzeugen to produce

erziehen, erzog, erzogen to raise, (14) bring up

die Erziehung upbringing, education

es it (1)

der Espresso (-s) espresso (coffee)

die **Espressomaschine (-n)** espresso machine
essbar edible
essen (isst), aß, gegessen to eat (1)
das **Essen (-)** food; meal; eating (1); **zum Essen** for dinner; **Essen und Trinken** food and drinks
die **Essgewohnheit (-en)** eating habits
der **Essig** vinegar
der **Esstisch (-e)** dining room table
das **Esszimmer (-)** dining room (2)
die **Etage (-n)** floor, story (12)
etwa approximately, about
etwas something; somewhat; a little (*adverb*) (2); **etwas anderes** something different
euch you (*acc. inform. pl.*) (3)
euer your (*inform. pl.*) (3)
euphorisch euphoric, enthusiastic
der **Euro (-s)** euro (*monetary unit*) (2)
die **Eurokarte (-n)** European bank card
(das) Europa Europe
europäisch (*adj.*) European
der **Euro-Schein (-e)** Euro bank note, bill
der **Euroscheck (-s)** *type of personal check used in Europe*
eventuell perhaps
evtl. = eventuell
ewig eternal(ly), constant(ly)
das **Examen (-)** examination
die **Ex-DDR** former East Germany
die **Existenz (-en)** livelihood
das **Experiment (-e)** experiment
experimentieren to experiment (11)
der **Experte (-n** *masc.*) / die **Expertin (-nen)** expert
explodieren to explode
exzentrisch eccentric (1)

F
fabelhaft fabulous, great
die **Fabrik (-en)** factory
das **Fabrikat (-e)** product
das **Fach (∵er)** subject (in school); **das Hauptfach** major subject; **das Lieblingsfach** favorite subject; **das Nebenfach** minor subject
die **Fachakademie (-n)** professional school (*university level*)
die **Fachbuchhandlung (-en)** textbook store
das **Fachgeschäft (-e)** specialty store
die **Fachhochschule (-n)** technical college
die **Fachoberschule (-n)** trade school
die **Fachrichtung (-en)** specific field of studies
die **Fachschule (-n)** technical school
die **Fahne (-n)** flag
fahren (fährt), fuhr, ist gefahren to drive, ride (1); to travel; to go; **Motorrad fahren** to ride (drive) a motorcycle (1)

der **Fahrer (-)** / die **Fahrerin (-nen)** driver
die **Fahrkarte (-n)** ticket (10)
der **Fahrkartenschalter (-)** ticket window (10)
der **Fahrplan (∵e)** schedule (10)
der **Fahrpreis (-e)** fare
das **Fahrrad (∵er)** bicycle (10)
die **Fahrradhose (-n)** bicycle pants
die **Fahrradtour (-en)** bicycle tour
der **Fahrschein (-e)** ticket
der **Fahrstuhl (∵e)** elevator
die **Fahrt (-en)** trip; ride (10)
die **Fahrtkosten** (*pl.*) traveling expenses
die **Fahrtstrecke (-n)** travel distance
die **Fakten** facts
der **Fall (∵e)** case; **auf jeden Fall** in any case (13)
fallen (fällt), fiel, ist gefallen to fall (7); to decline (value of money)
fallen lassen (lässt fallen), ließ fallen, fallen gelassen to drop (something)
falsch false, wrong, incorrect
fälschungssicher counterfeitproof
die **Familie (-n)** family (3)
die **Familienchronik (-en)** family chronicle
das **Familienfest (-e)** family celebration (3)
das **Familienleben** family life
das **Familienmitglied (-er)** family member
der **Familienname (-n** *masc.*) family name, last name
der **Familienpass (∵e)** pass for the entire family
der **Familienstammbaum (∵e)** family tree
der **Familienstand** marital status
die **Familienvorstellung (-en)** family performance
der **Fan (-s)** fan, admirer
fangen (fängt), fing, gefangen to catch
die **Fantasiewohnung (-en)** fantasy apartment
fantastisch fantastic (1)
die **Farbe (-n)** color (5)
der **Farbfernsehapparat (-e)** color TV set
das **Farbfernsehen** color TV
farbig colored
der **Fasching** Mardi Gras (*southern Germany*) (3)
das **Fass (∵er)** barrel, vat; **Bier vom Fass** beer on tap (6)
fassen to comprehend, grasp; **sich an den Kopf fassen** to take hold of one's head in disbelief; **Fuß fassen** to become acclimatized; **Ich kann es nicht fassen.** I can't comprehend it.
fast almost (8)
faszinieren to fascinate
faszinierend fascinating

fatal very serious(ly), fatal(ly)
faul lazy (1)
faulenzen to be lazy, not do anything (7)
das **Faxgerät (-e)** fax machine
FC = Fußballclub
(der) Februar February (3)
fehlen to be missing; to lack; to need; **Was fehlt Ihnen/dir?** What's the matter? (8)
fehlend missing
der **Feierabend (-e)** end of workday; **am Feierabend** after work
feiern to celebrate (3)
der **Feiertag (-e)** holiday
fein fine, delicate; all right; **fein säuberlich** nice(ly) and neat(ly)
das **Fenster (-)** window (2)
die **Fensterbank (∵e)** windowsill
die **Ferien** (*pl.*) vacation (10)
die **Ferienreise (-n)** vacation trip
der **Ferientraum (∵e)** dream vacation
die **Ferienwohnung (-en)** vacation apartment
das **Fernglas (∵er)** binoculars
der **Fernsehapparat (-e)** television set
fernsehen (sieht fern), sah fern, ferngesehen to watch television (4)
das **Fernsehen** television; watching television (4)
der **Fernseher (-)** TV set (2)
das **Fernsehgerät (-e)** television set
die **Fernsehnachrichten** (*pl.*) television news
das **Fernsehprogramm (-e)** TV program, schedule
der **Fernsehtechniker (-)** / die **Fernsehtechnikerin (-nen)** television technician
fertig finished, done; ready
das **Fest (-e)** festival; party, feast
fest stable, firm (11)
sich festlegen (legt fest) to commit oneself
feststellen (stellt fest) to establish, determine
die **Fete (-n)** (*coll.*) party
fett fat; greasy
das **Fett (-e)** fat
fettarm low-fat
fett gedruckt bold-face
das **Feuer (-)** fire
das **Feuerwerk (-e)** fireworks
das **Feuilleton (-s)** *cultural section of a newspaper*
das **Fieber** fever (8)
die **Figur (-en)** figure
die **Filialdirektion** head of a branch office
die **Filiale (-n)** branch office (11)
der **Film (-e)** film, movie (4); roll of film

der Filmabend (-e) evening of film showing

das Filmprogramm (-e) movie program

der Filmregisseur (-e) / die Filmregisseurin (-nen) movie director

der Filmschauspieler (-) / die Filmschauspielerin (-nen) movie actor/actress

der Filmstar (-e) movie star

der Filter (-) filter

der Finanzbeamte (decl. adj.) / die Finanzbeamtin (-nen) tax official

die Finanzen (pl.) finance(s)

finanziell financial (11)

finanzieren to finance

der Finanzskandal (-e) financial scandal

die Finanzzeitung (-en) financial newspaper

finden, fand, gefunden to find (1); to think, mean; **Wie findest du...?** How do you like . . .? What do you think of . . .? (1); **Ich finde...** I think . . . (14)

der Finderlohn (∶e) finder's reward

der Finger (-) finger (8)

das Fingerknipsen snapping of one's fingers

die Firma (Firmen) firm, company (11)

der Fisch (-e) fish

das Fischen fishing

das Fischerdorf (∶er) fishing village

die Fischerei (-en) fishery

der Fischfang fishing

die Fischverarbeitung fish processing

fit fit, in shape (8); **sich fit halten** to keep in shape (8)

die Fitness fitness (8)

der Fitnessberater (-) / die Fitnessberaterin (-nen) fitness consultant, personal trainer

das Fitnesscenter (-) fitness center; gym (4)

die Fitnessgewohnheiten (pl.) fitness habits

die Fitnessroutine (-n) fitness routine

das Fitnessstudio (-s) fitness studio

flach flat; even

die Fläche (-n) surface; area

das Fläschchen (-) little bottle

die Flasche (-n) bottle (14)

der Fleck (-e) spot

die Fledermaus (∶e) bat

das Fleisch meat (5)

die Fleischabteilung (-en) meat department

die Fleischwaren (pl.) meats

fleißig industrious, diligent (1)

die Flexibilität flexibility

fliegen, flog, ist geflogen to fly (7)

fließen, floss, ist geflossen to flow, run

fließend running; fluent(ly)

der Flohmarkt (∶e) flea market

(das) Florenz Florence (Italy)

die Flöte (-n) flute

flott quick, snappy

die Flotte (-n) fleet

flüchten (ist geflüchtet) to flee, escape

der Flüchtling (-e) refugee, fugitive

der Flug (∶e) flight

der Flugbegleiter (-) / die Flugbegleiterin (-nen) flight attendant

das Flugblatt (∶er) flyer

die Fluggesellschaft (-en) airline company

der Flughafen (∶) airport

der Flugingenieur (-e) / die Flugingenieurin (-nen) flight engineer

das Flüglein (-) small wing

die Flugreise (-n) airplane trip

der Flugschein (-e) airplane ticket

das Flugzeug (-e) airplane (10)

der Flugzeugbau airplane construction

der Flugzeuglärm airplane noise

der Flur (-e) hallway (12); **für den ganzen Flur** for the entire floor

der Fluss (∶e) river (7)

flüstern to whisper

die Folge (-n) consequence, result

folgen (+ dat.) to follow; **daraus folgt** the result of that is

folgend following

folglich consequently

der Fön, (-e) hair dryer (9)

fordern to demand

fördern to promote (14)

die Forelle (-n) trout

die Form (-en) form, shape

das Format (-e) format

formulieren to form, formulate

forschen to do research (13)

die Forschung (-en) research (14)

das Forschungszentrum (Forschungszentren) research center

fortschreitend advancing, progressive(ly)

der Fortschritt (-e) progress (14); **Fortschritte machen** to make progress (14)

die Fortsetzung (-en) continuation

der Fortsetzungsroman (-e) serialized novel (usually in a newspaper)

das Foto (-s) photograph (2)

das Fotoalbum (Fotoalben) photo album

die Fotoannahme (-n) photo processing place

der Fotoapparat (-e) camera

der Fotodesigner (-) / die Fotodesignerin (-nen) photographic designer

der Fotograf (-en masc.) / die Fotografin (-nen) photographer

das Fotografieren taking photographs

fotografieren to photograph

die Fotosammlung (-en) collection of photographs

die Frage (-n) question; **eine Frage stellen** to ask a question; **Das kommt nicht in Frage.** That is out of the question.; **Ich habe eine Frage.** I have a question. (E)

der Fragebogen (-) questionnaire

fragen to ask (1); **nach dem Weg fragen** to ask directions (9); **fragen nach** to ask about

fragend inquisitive(ly)

das Fragewort (∶er) interrogative pronoun (1)

(das) Frankreich France (E)

die Frankreichreise (-n) trip to/through France

der Franzose (-n masc.) / die Französin (-nen) French man/woman

französisch (adj.) French

die Frau (-en) Mrs., Ms.; woman (E); wife (3)

das Frauenlager (-) women's camp

das Fräulein (-) Miss; unmarried woman, young lady

frech naughty; risqué

frei free(ly) (2); vacant, available, unoccupied; **Ist hier noch frei?** Is this seat taken? (6); **im Freien** outdoors (11)

das Freibad (∶er) outdoor swimming pool (7)

Freien: im Freien outdoors (11)

freihaben (hat frei) to be off work

die Freiheit freedom, liberty

freilassen (lässt frei), ließ frei, freigelassen to release, set free

(der) Freitag Friday (3)

freitags Fridays, on Friday(s) (4)

freiwillig voluntary

die Freizeit free time (7)

die Freizeitaktivität (-en) leisure activity

die Freizeitpläne (pl.) plans for leisure time

der Freizeitservice leisure-time planning agency

der Freizeitspaß (∶e) leisure-time fun

Freizeitzwecke: nur für Freizeitzwecke not for business use

fremd strange; unknown; foreign

der/die Fremde (decl. adj.) stranger

der Fremdenführer (-) / die Fremdenführerin (-nen) tour guide

das Fremdenverkehrsamt (∶er) tourist information center

die Fremdsprache (-n) foreign language

das Fremdwort (∶er) foreign word

die Freude (-n) joy; **vor Freude** with joy; **Freude haben an (+ dat.)** to enjoy; **Freude machen (+ dat.)** to give pleasure, enjoy

freuen: Freut mich. Pleased to meet you. (E)

sich freuen auf (+ *acc.*) to look forward to (11); **sich freuen über** (+ *acc.*) to be happy about (12)

der Freund (-e) / die Freundin (-nen) friend (1)

freundlich friendly (1); pleasant

freundschaftlich friendly

der Friede (*also:* **der Frieden**) (**-n** *masc.*) peace

die Friedensbewegung (-en) peace movement

der Friedenssaal (Friedenssäle) peace-treaty hall

die Friedfertigkeit serenity

der Friedhof (:e) cemetery

friedlich peaceful

frieren, fror, gefroren to freeze; **Ich friere.** I am cold.

das Frisbee (-s) frisbee

frisch fresh(ly) (5)

der Friseursalon (-s) beauty parlor

der Frisiertisch (-e) dresser

froh glad, happy

fröhlich cheerful

der Fronteinsatz (:e) front-line duty

die Frottierware (-n) towels

die Frucht (:e) fruit

der Fruchtsaft (:e) fruit juice

früh early (4); **morgen früh** tomorrow morning

früher earlier; once; used to (*do, be, etc.*) (7)

das Frühjahr (-e) spring (7)

die Frühkartoffel (-n) new potato

der Frühling (-e) spring (7)

frühmorgens early in the morning

der Frühnebel (-) early morning fog

die Frührenaissance Early Renaissance

das Frühstück (-e) breakfast (5); **zum Frühstück** for breakfast

frühstücken to have breakfast (4)

das Frühstücksbuffet (-s) breakfast buffet

die Frühstücksnische (-n) breakfast nook (12)

der Frühstücksraum (:e) breakfast room (9)

das Frühstückstablett (-e) breakfast tray

der Frühstückstisch (-e) breakfast table

(sich) fühlen to feel (8)

führen to lead, guide, conduct; to carry (merchandise); **Gespräche führen** to hold conversations; **Tagebuch führen** to keep a diary

der Führer leader (*here:* Adolf Hitler)

der Führerschein (-e) driver's license

der Führungstag (-e) day with planned guided tour

der Fund (-e) find, finding

fünf five (E)

fünfmal five times

fünfte fifth (3)

ein Fünftel a fifth

fünfzehn fifteen (E)

fünfzig fifty (E)

funktionieren to function, work (9)

für (+ *acc.*) for (3); **was für** what kind of

fürchterlich horrible

fürs = für das

der Fürst (-en *masc.*) prince

der Fuß (:e) foot (8); **zu Fuß gehen** to go on foot, to walk (8)

der Fußball (:e) soccer, soccer ball (7); **Fußball spielen** to play soccer (7)

der Fußballclub (-s) soccer club

der Fußballfan (-s) soccer fan

der Fußballplatz (:e) soccer field

das Fußballspiel (-e) soccer game

der Fußgänger (-) / die Fußgängerin (-nen) pedestrian

die Fußgängerzone (-n) pedestrian zone, mall (14)

das Futonbett (-en) futon bed

füttern to feed

das Futur future tense

G

die Gabel (-n) fork (6)

der Gang (:e) course

die Gangschaltung (-en) gear shift

der Gangsterfilm (-e) gangster movie

ganz very (1); completely; total(ly), entire(ly) (12); fairly, rather; **ganz in der Nähe von** very close to; **den ganzen Tag** all day long; **ganz toll!** super! great! (1)

gar even; **gar kein** not any; **gar nicht** not at all; **gar nichts** nothing

die Garage (-n) garage (2)

garantieren to guarantee

die Garderobe (-n) check room; wardrobe; closet (12)

die Gardine (-n) curtain, drape

das Gardinenkomplet (-s) set of curtains

gären to ferment

der Garten (:) garden; yard (2)

das Gartenlokal (-e) garden restaurant

die Gartenmöbel (*pl.*) garden furniture

die Gasmaske (-n) gas mask

der Gast (:e) guest (1)

das Gästezimmer (-) guest room (12)

die Gastfamilie (-n) host family

gastfreundlich hospitable

der Gastgeber (-) / die Gastgeberin (-nen) host/hostess

das Gasthaus (:er) restaurant; inn

der Gasthof (:e) hotel; restaurant, inn

die Gastronomie gastronomy

die Gaststätte (-n) restaurant (6)

die Gaststube (-n) (hotel) dining room, lounge

die Gastversorgung guest service

geachtet respected

geb. = geboren(e)

das Gebäude (-) building

geben (gibt), gab, gegeben to give (3); **Bescheid geben** to inform, let someone know (5); **sich Mühe geben** to try hard; **Rat geben** to advise; **es gibt** there is, there are (3); **Es gibt Regen.** It is going to rain. (3)

das Gebiet (-e) area, region, district

gebietsweise in some areas

geblümt flowery

geboren born; **Ich bin geboren.** I was born. (1); **geboren werden** to be born; **geborene** née (*maiden name*)

der Gebrauch use

gebrauchen to use

gebraucht used

die Gebühr (-en) fee; **die Studiengebühren** (*pl.*) study fees, tuition (12)

das Geburtsdatum date of birth

der Geburtsort (-e) place of birth (1)

die Geburtsstätte (-n) place of birth

der Geburtstag (-e) birthday (3); date of birth (1); **Herzlichen Glückwunsch zum Geburtstag!** Happy Birthday! (3); **Wann hast du Geburtstag?** When is your birthday? (3)

die Geburtstagsfeier (-n) birthday celebration

die Geburtstagsfete (-n) (*coll.*) birthday party

der Geburtstagsgruß (:e) birthday wish

der Geburtstagskuchen (-) birthday cake

die Geburtstagstorte (-n) birthday cake

die Gedächtniskirche famous church in Berlin

gedämpft dimmed (*light*); steamed (*milk*)

das Gedicht (-e) poem

gedruckt printed; **klein gedruckt** printed in small letters

die Geduld patience

geehrt: sehr geehrter/geehrte (+ *proper name*) *formal letter address form*

geeignet suitable; appropriate

die Gefahr (-en) danger (14)

gefährden to endanger

das Gefahrensymbol (-e) danger symbol

gefährlich dangerous (10)

gefallen (+ *dat.*) **(gefällt), gefiel, gefallen** to like (5); **Wie gefällt Ihnen... ?** How do you like . . .? (5)

der Gefallen (-) favor, **einen Gefallen tun** to do a favor

das Gefängnis (-se) prison, jail (14)

gefasst sein auf (+ *acc.*) to be prepared for

gefroren frozen (5)

das Gefühl (-e) feeling; emotion

gefühllos insensitive

gefühlvoll sentimental; emotional
gefüttert lined
gegebenenfalls if necessary
gegen (+ *acc.*) against (3); around (+ *time*) (6); **(so) gegen fünf Uhr** around five o'clock (6)
die Gegend (-en) area, region
die Gegendarstellung (-en) opposing view
der Gegensatz (:e) contrast
die Gegenseite (-n) opposing side
gegenseitig mutual(ly)
das Gegenteil (-e) opposite; **im Gegenteil** on the contrary
gegenüber von (+ *dat.*) across from (9)
gegenüberliegend opposite
das Gehalt (:er) salary (11)
gehen, ging, ist gegangen to go (1); to walk; **zu Fuß gehen** to walk (8); **Na, wie geht's?** How are you? (*casual*) (E); **Wie geht's?** How are you? (*informal*) (E); **Wie geht es Ihnen?** (*formal*) How are you? (E); **Das geht auch.** That'll work too. (9)
die Gehirnoperation (-en) brain surgery
gehoben upper, elevated
das Gehör: (sich) Gehör verschaffen to make (oneself) be heard
gehorchen (+ *dat.*) to obey
gehören (+ *dat.*) to belong; to be part of (5)
die Geige (-n) violin
die Geisteswissenschaften (*pl.*) (academic field of) humanities
gelangweilt bored
gelaunt: schlecht gelaunt sein to be in a bad mood
gelb yellow (5)
das Geld (-er) money (2); **Geld verdienen** to earn money (11); **sich Geld leihen** to borrow money (12)
die Geldangelegenheit (-en) money matter
die Geldausgabe (-n) expenditure
der Geldautomat (-en *masc.*) automatic teller
der Geldschein (*also:* **der Schein**) **(-e)** bank note, paper money
gelegen situated, located; **zentral gelegen** centrally located (2)
die Gelegenheit (-en) opportunity (11); occasion
gelegentlich occasionally
der/die Geliebte (*decl. adj.*) beloved
gelingen, gelang, ist gelungen to succeed; **es gelingt mir** I am succeeding
gelten (+ *dat.*) **(gilt), galt, gegolten** to be valid; **gelten als** to be considered as
die Geltungsdauer period of validity; expiration date
das Gemälde (-) painting
die Gemeinde (-n) community

die Gemeindeverwaltung (-en) community administration
gemeinsam together; in common
der Gemeinschaftswaschraum (:e) communal washroom
gemeint für meant for
gemietet (*adj.*) rented
gemischt mixed
das Gemüse (-) vegetable (5)
die Gemüseabteilung (-en) produce department
der Gemüsegarten (:) vegetable garden
die Gemüsesorte (-n) type of vegetable
der Gemüsestand (:e) vegetable stand (5)
gemustert printed (*fabric*)
gemütlich cozy, comfortable, leisurely (4)
genau exact; precisely
genauso exactly like; just as
die Generation (-en) generation
genervt (*coll.*) annoyed, irritated
das Genie (-s) genius
genießen, genoss, genossen to enjoy, savor, relish
der Genießer (-) / die Genießerin (-nen) connoisseur
der Genitiv (-e) genitive case
genug enough, sufficient
genügen to suffice
das Genus (grammatical) gender
das Genussmittel (-) alcohol, tobacco, etc.; luxury articles
geöffnet open (6)
die Geographie geography
die Geographiestunde (-n) geography lesson
geographisch geographical(ly)
der Geoökologe (-n *masc.*) **/ die Geoökologin (-nen)** geo-ecologist
die Geoökologie (field of)
das Gepäck luggage (9)
die Gepäckaufbewahrung baggage check (10)
gepflegt well groomed
geplant planned
geprägt characterized (by)
gepunktet polka-dotted
gerade just, exactly (2); straight, erect; **Warum gerade Sie?** Why you of all people?
geradeaus straight ahead (9)
das Gerät (-e) appliance; device; apparatus (13); **das Fernsehgerät** TV set
geräuchert smoked
das Gerede talk
geregelt regulated; regular(ly)
das Gericht (-e) dish (*of prepared food*) (6)
gern (lieber, liebst-) gladly (2); **gern haben** to like (*a person or thing*) (2); **ich hätte gern** I would like to

have; **gern** (+ *verb*) to like to do something (2)
gesagt: kurz gesagt in a few words
gesamt total
gesamtdeutsch *referring to unified Germany*
die Gesamtleitung overall direction
die Gesamtschule (-n) German secondary school (*grades 6 to 12*)
der Gesang (:e) song; singing
das Geschäft (-e) store, shop; business (5)
der Geschäftsbrief (-e) business letter
die Geschäftsfrau (-en) business-woman (11)
die Geschäftsleute (*pl.*) business people (11)
der Geschäftsmann (Geschäftsleute) businessman (11)
geschehen (geschieht), geschah, ist geschehen to happen
gescheit intelligent, bright; sensible, decent (13); **nichts Gescheites** nothing decent (13)
das Geschenk (-e) present, gift (3)
der Geschenkartikel (-) gift item
die Geschenkboutique (-n) gift shop
die Geschichte (-n) story; history
die Geschirrspülmaschine (-n) dishwasher (13)
geschlossen closed (6)
die Geschmackssache matter of taste
geschmückt decorated
das Geschnetzelte (*decl. adj.*) special regional meat dish
geschützt protected
geschweige denn... let alone . . .
die Geschwindigkeit (-en) speed
die Geschwindigkeitsbegrenzung (-en) speed limit
die Geschwister (*pl.*) brothers and sisters, siblings (3)
geschwollen swollen
gesegnet blessed
die Gesellschaft (-en) company; party; society
gesellschaftlich social
das Gesetz (-e) law
das Gesicht (-er) face (8)
das Gespenst (-er) ghost
gesponsert sponsored
das Gespräch (-e) conversation
der Gesprächspartner (-) / die Gesprächspartnerin (-nen) conversation partner
der Gesprächsraum (:e) discussion room
die Gesprächssituation (-en) conversational setting
das Gesprächsthema (Gesprächsthemen) conversational topic
gestaltet created, designed
gestern yesterday (7)

die **Gestik** gesticulation
gestreift striped (5)
gestresst (*adj.*) under stress
gesucht/gefunden lost/found
gesund healthy (8)
die **Gesundheit** health (8)
gesundheitlich health related
die **Gesundheitsmaßnahme (-n)** health provisions
gesundheitsschädlich unhealthy
das **Gesundheitswesen** health-care system
geteilt divided
das **Getränk (-e)** beverage, drink (5)
die **Getränkedose (-n)** beverage can
der **Getränkeladen (ː)** beverage store (5)
getrennt separate (6); **zusammen oder getrennt?** together or separate (checks)?
gewählt selected, choice
die **Gewalt** violence
gewaltig enormous
die **Gewalttat (-en)** act of violence
die **Gewalttätigkeit (-en)** (act of) violence (14)
das **Gewehr (-e)** rifle
gewerblich commercial(ly)
die **Gewerkschaft (-en)** (labor) union
das **Gewicht (-e)** weight
gewinnen, gewann, gewonnen to win
die **Gewinnung (-en)** reclamation
gewiss certain(ly)
das **Gewitter (-)** thunderstorm (7)
gewöhnlich usual(ly) (4)
gewohnt an (+ *acc.*) accustomed to
das **Gewürz (-e)** spice
gewürzt spiced; spicy
gibt: es gibt there is, there are (3)
das **Gift (-e)** poison
die **Giftreaktion (-en)** toxic reaction
der **Giftstoff (-e)** toxic substance
gilt: Nichts gilt mehr. Nothing is valid anymore.
der **Gips** plaster; plaster cast
die **Gitarre (-n)** guitar
glänzend shiny; excellent
das **Glas (ːer)** glass
glatt smooth
glauben to believe (5)
gleich right away, immediately (8); same; **gleich da drüben** right over there
die **Gleichberechtigung** equality
das **Gleiche** (*decl. adj.*) the same
gleichfalls likewise (E)
gleichzeitig simultaneous(ly)
das **Gleis (-e)** track, platform (10)
das **Gleitschirmfliegen** hang gliding
der **Gletscher (-)** glacier
das **Glöckchen (-)** little bell
das **Glockenspiel (-e)** chimes, glockenspiel

das **Glück** fortune, luck; happiness; **Glück haben** to be lucky; **Glück wünschen** to congratulate; **Viel Glück!** Good luck! (1)
glücklich happy
das **Glücksrad (ːer)** wheel of fortune
der **Glückwunsch (ːe)** congratulations; **Herzlichen Glückwunsch zum Geburtstag!** Happy Birthday! (3)
GmbH = Gesellschaft mit beschränkter Haftung corporation
das **Gold** gold
der **Goldfisch (-e)** goldfish
die **Goldmedaille (-n)** gold medal
(das) Golf golf
der **Golfplatz (ːe)** golf course
das **Golfspielen** playing golf
der **Gönner (-) / die Gönnerin (-nen)** patron
das **Gorillakostüm (-e)** gorilla costume
gotisch gothic
der **Gott (ːer)** god; **Gott sei Dank** thank God; **grüß Gott** hello (*in southern Germany and Austria*)
der **Goudakäse (-)** Gouda cheese
Gr. = Größe
der **Grad (-e)** degree(s) (7); **35 Grad** 35 degrees (7)
die **Grafik (-en)** drawing
das **Gramm** gram
die **Grammatik (-en)** grammar; grammar book
der **Granit** granite
gratulieren (+ *dat.*) to congratulate (3)
grau gray (5)
graugetigert with gray stripes
greifen, griff, gegriffen to seize
das **Greifensymbol (-e)** griffin symbol
die **Grenze (-n)** border; limit
der **Grieche (-n** *masc.***) / die Griechin (-nen)** Greek (person)
(das) Griechenland Greece
griechisch (*adj.*) Greek
der **Grill (-s)** grill, barbecue (6)
grillen to barbecue, grill
grillfertig ready to be grilled
die **Grillparty (-s)** barbecue party, cookout
die **Grillscheibe (-n)** slice of barbecue meat
die **Grippe** flu (8)
groß big large (2); tall (1); **Ich bin 1,63 meter (groß).** I'm 1.63 meters tall. (1)
(das) Großbritannien Great Britain
die **Größe (-n)** size (5)
die **Großeltern** (*pl.*) grandparents (3)
größenwahnsinnig (*adj.*) megalomanic
die **Großmutter (ː)** grandmother (3)
der **Großonkel (-)** great-uncle
der **Großraumwagen (-)** rail car without compartments

die **Großstadt (ːe)** metropolis, large city
die **Großtante (-n)** great-aunt
der **Großvater (ː)** grandfather (3)
grün green (5); **ins Grüne fahren** to go on an outing (to where it is green)
die **Grünanlage (-n)** public gardens, park
der **Grund (ːe)** reason; ground
die **Grundausstattung (-en)** basic furnishings
gründen to found
der **Gründer (-) / die Gründerin (-nen)** founder
das **Grundgesetz (-e)** (German) constitution
die **Grundlage (-n)** basis, foundation
der **Grundlagenvertrag (ːe)** agreement about basic principles
grundlegend basic, fundamental
das **Grundrecht (-e)** fundamental right
der **Grundriss (-e)** outline; layout; blueprint
die **Grundschule (-n)** primary school (11)
das **Grundstudium (Grundstudien)** basic study program
die **Gründung (-en)** founding, establishment
die **Gruppe (-n)** group; team
der **Gruß (ːe)** greeting (12); **herzliche Grüße** kind regards; **viele Grüße** best wishes (12)
(sich) grüßen to say hello (to one another); **grüß dich** hello, hi (*among friends and family*) (E); **grüß Gott** hello, good day (*in Austria, southern Germany*)
die **Grütze: Rote Grütze** dessert made of red berries
gucken to look at, glance
die **Gulaschsuppe (-n)** spicy meat soup
gültig valid
der **Gummistiefel (-)** rubber boot
günstig (gut) advantageous(ly); good, well; favorable, favorably (10); reasonable (in price); **günstig liegen** to be conveniently located (9)
die **Gurke (-n)** cucumber; pickle (5)
der **Gürtel (-)** belt (5)
gut (besser, best) good; well (1); **Es geht mir gut.** I am fine; **Alles Gute!** Best wishes (3); **guten Abend** good evening (E); **Gute Besserung!** Get well soon! (8); **(guten) Morgen** good morning (E); **(guten) Tag** hello, good day (E); **gute Nacht** good night (E); **mach's gut** so long (E); **danke, gut** fine, thanks (E); **nicht besonders gut** not particularly well (E); **sehr gut** very well; fine; good (E)
das **Gutachten (-)** reference letter (11)

gut bezahlt well-paid
der Güterzug (-̈e) freight train
gutnachbarlich neighborly
das Gymnasium (Gymnasien) secondary school (11)

H

das Haar (-e) hair (8); **Mir stehen die Haare zu Berge.** My hair is standing on end.
das Haarshampoo (-s) shampoo
das Haarspitzenfluid (-s) hair conditioner
haben (hat), hatte, gehabt to have (2); **Durst haben** to be thirsty (2); **gern haben** to like (*a person or thing*) (2); **Hunger haben** to be hungry (2); **Lust haben** to feel like (*doing something*) (2); **Recht haben** to be correct (2); **Zeit haben** to have time (2)
der Hackbraten (-) meatloaf
der Hafen (-̈) harbor, port (9)
das Hafentor (-e) harbor gate
der Häftling (-e) prisoner
der Hagel hail (7)
das Hähnchen (-) chicken (5)
häkeln to crochet
der Haken (-) hook
halb half; **halb zwei** one thirty (4)
die Halbgeschwister (*pl.*) half-brothers and -sisters
halbieren to divide in half
die Halbpension accommodation with two meals per day included
die Hälfte (-n) half; fifty percent
der Halfter (-) (horse) harness
das Hallenbad (-̈er) indoor swimming pool (7)
hallo hello (*among friends and family*) (E)
die Halogenlampe (-n) halogen lamp
der Hals (-̈e) neck; throat (8)
das Halsband (-̈er) (animal) collar
die Halsschmerzen (*pl.*) sore throat (8)
halt (*particle*) just
Halt! Stop!
halten (hält), hielt, gehalten to hold, keep; to stop (14); **halten (für)** to hold; to consider, think (14); **halten von** to think of; **sich fit halten (hält sich fit)** to keep fit (8); **gerade halten** to keep straight
die Haltestelle (-n) (bus or streetcar) stop; **die Bushaltestelle** bus stop
die Haltung (-en) posture
die Hand (-̈e) hand (8)
die Handarbeit (-en) handicraft; needlework
der Handel trade, sales (11)
handeln to act; **handeln von** to deal with, be about (13); **es handelt sich**

um it is about; **Wovon handelt es?** What is it about? (13)
das Handgepäck carry-on luggage (10)
die Handlung (-en) plot
die Handschrift (-en) handwriting
handschriftlich handwritten
der Handschuh (-e) glove (10)
die Handtasche (-n) handbag
das Handtuch (-̈er) towel
das Handy (-s) cell phone (2)
hängen, hing, gehangen to hang (6); **es hängt davon ab...** it depends (on) . . .
die Hansestadt (-̈e) *town belonging to the old "Hanse" trade league*
harmlos harmless
die Harpune (-n) harpoon
hart hard
das Häschen (-) little rabbit (*term of endearment*)
hässlich ugly (2)
hauen to beat
häufig frequently, often; **am häufigsten** most often; most widely
der Hauptbahnhof (-̈e) main railroad station
der Haupteinkaufstag (-e) main shopping day
das Hauptfach (-̈er) major subject
die Hauptfigur (-en) main character; protagonist
das Hauptgebäude (-) main building
das Hauptgericht (-e) main dish; entrée (6)
die Hauptidee (-n) main idea
die Hauptindustrie (-n) chief industry
der Hauptkonflikt (-e) main conflict
die Hauptmahlzeit (-en) main meal of the day
das Hauptproblem (-e) main problem
hauptsächlich mainly, mostly
die Hauptsaison (-s) high season
der Hauptschulabschluss (-̈e) high school diploma
die Hauptschule (-n) junior high school (*grades 5–9/10*)
die Hauptstadt (-̈e) capital
die Hauptstraße (-n) main street
das Hauptthema (Hauptthemen) main topic
das Haus (-̈er) house (2); **nach Hause** home (indicating going home) (5); **zu Hause** at home (5)
die Hausarbeiten (*pl.*) homework, housework
die Hausaufgaben (*pl.*) homework
der Hausbewohner (-) / die Hausbewohnerin (-nen) tenant
die Hausfrau (-en) homemaker, housewife; **nach Hausfrauenart**

according to a special recipe, homestyle
hausgebeizt home-pickled
der Haushalt (-e) household; budget (12)
das Haushaltsgeld (-er) household money
das Haushaltsgerät (-e) household appliance
die Haushaltswaren (*pl.*) household utensils
häuslich domestic
der Hausmann (-̈er) house husband
der Hausmüll house trash
die Hausmusik music performed at home
die Hausnummer (-n) street address (number) (E)
der Hausschuh (-e) slipper (5)
das Haustelefon (-e) house telephone
das Haustier (-e) pet
die Haustür (-en) front door
die Haut skin
die Hautcreme (-s) skin cream
Hbf. = Hauptbahnhof
heben, hob, gehoben to lift; **Gewichte heben** to lift weights
das Heft (-e) notebook (12)
die Heide heath; **Lüneburger Heide** *area in North Germany*
das Heilbad (-̈er) spa
der Heilige Abend Christmas Eve (3)
das Heim (-e) home
die Heimat homeland, home town
die Heimatkunde local history
der Heimatort (-e) home town
die Heimatstadt (-̈e) home town
der Heimcomputer (-) home computer
heimlich secret
heimtückisch treacherous
der Heimwerker (-) / die Heimwerkerin (-nen) hobbyist
heiraten to marry, get married (3)
heiß hot (7)
heißen, hieß, geheißen to be called, be named (1); **Ich heiße...** My name is . . . (E); **Wie heißt...** What is the name of . . . (E); **Wie heißt du?** What's your name? (*informal*) (E); **Wie heißen Sie?** What's your name? (*formal*) (E)
der Heißluftballon (-s) hot air balloon
heiter pleasant, fair (7)
die Heizung (-en) heating
die Heizungsfirma (Heizungsfirmen) heating company
das Hektar (-e) hectare (= 2.471 acres)
hektisch hectic(ly)
helfen (+ *dat.*) **(hilft), half, geholfen** (5)
hell light, bright(ly) (2)
hellblau light blue

der Hellseher (-) / die Hellseherin (-nen) clairvoyant (person)
hellwach wide awake
das Hemd (-en) shirt (5)
her this way; here; **hin und her** back and forth; **um ... her** all around
heran to, onto; **sich heranwagen (wagt heran)** to dare to come close
herauf up; upstairs
herausbringen (bringt heraus), brachte heraus, herausgebracht to publish
herausfinden (findet heraus), fand heraus, herausgefunden to find out
herausfordern to challenge (11)
die Herausforderung (-en) challenge
herausgehen (geht heraus), ging heraus, ist herausgegangen to go outside
herb (*wine*) dry
der Herbst autumn, fall (7)
hereinkommen (kommt herein), kam herein, ist hereingekommen to come inside
hereinsehen (sieht herein), sah herein, hereingesehen to look in (on somebody)
herkommen (kommt her), kam her, ist hergekommen to come here
der Herr (-en, -n *masc.***)** Mr.; gentleman (E)
die Herrenabteilung (-en) men's department
die Herrenartikel (*pl.***)** men's accessories
das Herrenhemd (-en) men's shirt
die Herrenkonfektion men's ready-to-wear clothing
der Herrenschuh (-e) men's shoe
herrlich wonderful, magnificent
die Herrschaften (*pl.***)** ladies and gentlemen
herrschen to rule
herstellen (stellt her) to produce, manufacture (11)
herum: um ... herum around (*spatial*) (3)
herumgammeln (*coll.*) **(gammelt herum)** to fool around, be lazy
herumsuchen (sucht herum) to search all over
herunter (runter) down; downstairs
heruntergezogen (*adj.*) hanging
das Herz (-ens, -en) heart; **Hand auf's Herz** scout's honor; **von Herzen** from the bottom of my heart
herzhaft hearty; strong
herzlich cordial; heartfelt (E); **Herzlichen Glückwunsch zum Geburtstag!** Happy birthday! (3); **herzliche Grüße** kind regards; **herzlich willkommen** welcome (E)
(das) Hessen *German state*
hetzen to hurry; to chase; to agitate
heute today (1); **heute Abend** tonight (1); **heute Morgen** this morning (4); **heute**

Mittag this noon (4); **heute Vormittag** today before noon (4); **heute Nachmittag** this afternoon (4)
heutig today's
heutzutage nowadays
hier here (1)
hierher (to) here
hierher kommen (kommt hierher), kam hierher, ist hierher gekommen to come here
hiesig local
das Hifi-Regal (-e) entertainment center
die Hilfe help, assistance; **um Hilfe bitten** to ask for help
der Hilferuf (-e) call for help
die Himbeere (-n) raspberry
der Himmel (-) sky; heaven (7); **in den Himmel loben** to praise to high heavens
himmelblau sky blue
hin (to) there; **vor sich hin** to oneself; **nach außen hin** to the outside; **hin und her** back and forth; **hin und zurück** roundtrip (10)
hinaufgehen (geht hinauf), ging hinauf, ist hinaufgegangen to go upstairs
hinaus (to) outside; **darüber hinaus** beyond that
hinausgehen (geht hinaus), ging hinaus, ist hinausgegangen to go outside
hinauskommen (kommt hinaus), kam hinaus, ist hinausgekommen to come out; to get out
hinauslaufen (läuft hinaus), lief hinaus, ist hinausgelaufen to run outside
das Hindernis (-se) impediment
hineinschauen (schaut hinein) to look in; to drop by
hingehen (geht hin), ging hin, ist hingegangen to go there
hingehören (gehört hin) to belong (somewhere)
hinkommen (kommt hin), kam hin, ist hingekommen to get there
sich hinlegen (legt sich hin) to lie down (8)
sich hinsetzen (setzt sich hin) to sit down (8)
hinten in the back
hinter (+ *acc./dat.*) behind (6)
der Hintergrund (:e) background
die Hintergrundinformation (-en) background information
hinterher afterward
der Hinterhof (:e) courtyard behind apartment building
hinterlassen (hinterlässt), hinterließ, hinterlassen to leave behind
hinuntergehen (geht hinunter), ging hinunter, ist hinuntergegangen to go downstairs

der Hinweis (-e) tip, clue
hinzufügen (fügt hinzu) to add
hissen to hoist (a flag)
historisch historic(al)
das Hobby (-s) hobby (1)
der Hobbyarchäologe (-n *masc.***) / die Hobbyarchäologin (-nen)** amateur archeologist
hoch (hoh-) (höher, höchst) high(ly) (2); tall
hochaktuell extremely popular
das Hochhaus (:er) high-rise building
der Hochleistungssportler (-) / die Hochleistungssportlerin (-nen) high-powered athlete
hoch qualifiziert highly qualified
die Hochschule (-n) university, college
der Hochschullehrer (-) / die Hochschullehrerin (-nen) university instructor (1)
die Hochschulreife college qualification
höchstens at most
die Höchstgeschwindigkeit (-en) maximum speed, speed limit
die Höchstgrenze (-n) maximum limit
die Höchsttemperatur (-en) highest temperature, daily high
die Hochzeit (-en) wedding (3)
die Hochzeitsfeier (-n) wedding celebration
der Hochzeitstag (-e) wedding day; anniversary
hochziehen (zieht hoch), zog hoch, hochgezogen to pull up
der Hof (:e) farm
hoffen (auf) (+ *acc.*) to hope (for) (10)
hoffentlich I hope (6)
die Hoffnung (-en) hope
die Hoffnungslosigkeit hopelessness
höflich courteous, polite
der Höhepunkt (-e) climax; highlight
höher higher
holen to get, fetch
(das) Holland Holland, the Netherlands
holländisch Dutch
die Hölle hell
der Höllenlärm hellish noise
der Holzhammer (-) sledge-hammer, mallet
der Holzpantoffel (-n) wooden shoe, clog
der Honig honey
die Honigmelone (-n) honeydew melon
(das) Hoppelpoppel *dish made of fried potatoes and eggs*
hören to listen, hear (1)
der Hörer (-) / die Hörerin (-nen) listener
das Horoskop (-e) horoscope (13)
der Horrorfilm (-e) horror film
die Hose (-n) pants, trousers, slacks (5)
das Hosenbein (-e) pant leg

die Hosentasche (-n) pants pocket
das Hotel (-s) hotel (9); im Hotel
at the hotel
die Hotelfachfrau (-en) hotel
businesswoman
die Hotelpension (-en) hotel with meal
plan
das Hotelpersonal hotel employees
der Hotelpreis (-e) hotel charges
das Hotelzimmer (-) hotel room
hübsch pretty
die Hühnerbrust chicken breast (6)
die Hühnersuppe (-n) chicken soup
der Humor humor
humorvoll humorous; full of humor
der Hund (-e) dog (3)
das Hundehotel (-s) dog kennel
(ein)hundert one hundred (E); Hunderte
von... hundreds of . . .
hundertste hundredth
hundsmiserabel (coll.) sick as a dog (8)
der Hunger hunger (14); Hunger haben
to be hungry (2)
hungernd starving
die Hungersnot (:-e) famine
hungrig hungry
hurra hurrah
der Husten (-) cough (8)
husten to cough
der Hut (:-e) hat (5)
die Hüttenschuhe (pl.) slipper socks
die Hüttentür (-en) cottage door
hypnotisieren to hypnotize

I

ich I (1); ich auch me too (1)
ideal ideal(ly)
die Idee (-n) idea
identifizieren to identify
das Idyll (-e) idyllic setting
idyllisch idyllic, idyllical(ly)
ihm (to/for) him/it (5)
ihn him, it (3)
ihnen (to/for) them (5)
Ihnen (to/for) you (form.) (5)
Ihr (form.) your (3)
ihr (inform. pl.) you (1); her; its; their (3);
(to/for) her/it (5)
illegal illegal(ly)
die Illusion (-en) illusion
die Illustrierte (-n) illustrated magazine
im = in dem; im Januar in January (3)
der Imbiss (-e) fast-food stand (6)
immer always (1)
der Immobilienmakler (-) real
estate agent
der Imperativ (-e) imperative form
der Imperativsatz (:-e) imperative clause
das Imperfekt (-e) imperfect tense,
simple past
impliziert implied

in (+ acc./dat.) in, into; inside (6); in
zwei Tagen in two days (6)
incl. = inkl.
indem by (+ gerund)
der Indianer (-) / die Indianerin
(-nen) American Indian (person)
(das) Indien India
der Indikativ indicative voice
indirekt indirect(ly)
die Individualität individuality
(das) Indonesien Indonesia
die Industrialisierung industrialization
die Industrie (-n) industry
die Industriekauffrau (-en) industrial
businesswoman
der Industriekaufmann (:-er) industrial
businessman
industriell industrial
die Industriereform (-en) industrial
reform
die Industrieregion (-en) industrial area
der Infinitiv (-e) infinitive verb form
die Inflation (-en) inflation
die Informatik computer science
der Informatiker (-) / die Informatikerin
(-nen) computer scientist (11)
die Information (-en) information
sich informieren to inform oneself (8)
der Ingenieur (-e) / die Ingenieurin
(-nen) engineer
das Ingenieurbüro (-s) engineering office
der Inhaber (-) / die Inhaberin
(-nen) proprietor
der Inhalt content(s)
das Inland at home, domestic, national
(13); im Inland und Ausland at home
and abroad (13)
inkl. = inklusive
inklusive inclusive; included
innen inside
die Innenstadt (:-e) downtown (9)
inner-: im inneren Kreis in the
inside circle
die Innereien (pl.) inner organs
innerhalb within, inside of (9)
innovativ innovative
insbesondere in particular
das Insekt (-e) insect
die Insel (-n) island
insgesamt altogether, total (10)
inspirieren to inspire
der Installateur (-e) / die Installateurin
(-nen) installer, technician
das Institut (-e) institute
das Instrument (-e) instrument
intellektuell intellectual(ly)
intelligent intelligent(ly)
intensiv intense
die Interaktion (-en) interaction
Intercity referring to fast
intercity trains

interessant interesting (1); nichts
Interessantes nothing interesting
das Interesse (-n) interest (1)
sich interessieren für (+ acc.) to be
interested in (11)
international international
internieren to intern
die Interpretation (-en) interpretation
interpretieren to interpret
Interregio referring to fast trains
between regions
das Interrogativpronomen (-)
interrogative pronoun
das Interview (-s) interview
interviewen to interview
intravenös intravenous(ly)
die Invasion (-en) invasion
investieren to invest
involvieren to get involved
inzwischen in the meantime, meanwhile
(der) Iran Iran
irgend any at all; some; irgendetwas
anything at all; something;
irgendjemand anybody at all;
irgendwann anytime at all; irgendwer
somebody; irgendwo somewhere
(das) Irland Ireland
der Irrtum (:-er) error
das Isartal valley of the Isar River
isolieren to isolate; to insulate (14)
(das) Israel Israel
ital. = italienisch
(das) Italien Italy (E)
der Italiener (-) / die Italienerin
(-nen) Italian (person)
italienisch (adj.) Italian

J

ja yes (E)
die Jacke (-n) jacket (5)
das Jahr (-e) year (1); nächstes Jahr next
year (1); einmal im Jahr once a year
(7); mit 10 Jahren at age 10; die 90er
Jahre the nineties
die Jahresausgaben (pl.) annual
expenditures
die Jahreszeit (-en) season (7)
das Jahrhundert (-e) century
die Jahrhundertwende (-n) turn
of the century
der/die 12-Jährige (decl. adj.) twelve-
year old (person)
jährlich annual
die Jahrtausendwende (-n) turn of
the millenium
der Jammer suffering, sadness
der Jänner January (Austrian)
(der) Januar January (3)
(das) Japan Japan
der Japaner (-) / die Japanerin
(-nen) Japanese person

japanisch (*adj.*) Japanese
jawohl yes, of course
(der) Jazz jazz
der Jazzkeller (-) jazz bar
je ever, always; **je** (+ *comparative*)
   desto/umso (+ *comparative*)
   the (+ *comparative*) the
   (+ *comparative*); **je nachdem**
   depending on
die Jeans (*pl.*) jeans (5)
der Jeansrock (:e) denim skirt
jedenfalls in any case
jeder, jede, jedes each, every (5);
   everybody; **jeden Tag** every day (7);
   auf jeden Fall in any case
jedesmal every time
jedoch however, but
jemand somebody, someone (9)
jetzig current
jetzt now (1); immediately
jeweils in each case; individually;
   each time
Jh. = Jahrhundert
der Job (-s) (temporary) job
jobben to work at a temporary job
joggen to jog (7)
das Jogging jogging
der Jogginganzug (:e) jogging suit
der Joghurt (-e) yogurt (5)
der Journalist (-en *masc.*) **/ die**
   Journalistin (-nen) journalist (1)
Judo machen to do judo
die Jugend youth, young people
das Jugendgästehaus (:er) (type of)
   youth hostel
die Jugendgruppe (-n) youth group
die Jugendherberge (-n) youth
   hostel (9)
der/die Jugendliche (*decl. adj.*) young
   person; teenager
die Jugendreise (-n) trip for young people
der Jugendstil Art Nouveau (*artistic*
   style)
(das) Jugoslawien Yugoslavia
(der) Juli July (3)
jung young (10); **jungverheiratet**
   newly wed
der Junge (-n *masc.*) boy
jungverheiratet newly wed
(der) Juni June (3)
der Juniorpass (:e) student pass
die Jura law
der Juwelier (-e) jeweler's store

K

das Kabarett (-e) cabaret
das Kabel-TV cable TV
das Kabelfernsehen cable television
der Kabelkanal (:e) cable (TV) channel
das Kabrio (-s) convertible automobile
die Kachelplatte (-n) tile

der Käfer (-) bug, beetle
der Kaffee coffee
das Kaffeegetränk (-e) coffee drink
das Kaffeehaus (:er) café
die Kaffeehausküche coffeehouse
   cuisine
die Kaffeekanne (-n) coffee pot
die Kaffeemaschine (-n) electric
   coffeemaker
die Kaffeemenge (-n) amount of coffee
der Kaffeesatz coffee grounds
die Kaffeesorte (-n) type of coffee
Kaiser: die Kaiser-Wilhelm
   Gedächtniskirche *famous church*
   in Berlin
der Kaiserschmarren (-) *pancake-like*
   Austrian dessert
die Kalbsleberwurst (:e) veal liverwurst
der Kalender (-) calendar (3)
(das) Kalifornien California
kalkulieren to calculate
kalt cold (7)
kaltherzig coldhearted
die Kamera (-s) camera (10)
der Kamillentee camomile tea
der Kamin (-e) fireplace
sich kämmen to comb one's hair (8)
der Kampf (:e) battle, fight
kämpfen to fight, struggle
(das) Kanada Canada
der Kanarienvogel (:) canary
die Kanarischen Inseln (*pl.*) Canary
   Islands
das Kaninchen (-) rabbit
die Kaninchenbox (-en) rabbit hutch
Kännchen: ein Kännchen Kaffee
   a pot of coffee
das Kanufahren canoeing
das Kapitel (-) chapter
die Kapitulation (-en) capitulation
kapitulieren to capitulate
kaputt broken (9)
(das) Karate machen to do karate
die Karibik the Caribbean
kariert checkered, plaid (5)
karitativ charitable
die Karotte (-n) carrot (5)
der Karottensaft carrot juice
die Karriere (-n) career (11); **Karriere**
   machen to be successful in a career
die Karriereberatung (-en) career
   counseling
die Karrierechance (-n) career
   opportunity
die Karte (-n) card (7); ticket; **Karten**
   spielen to play cards
das Kartenspiel (-e) card game (7)
der Kartenvorverkauf (:e) advance
   ticket sale
die Kartoffel (-n) potato (5)
die Kartoffelchips (*pl.*) potato chips

der Kartoffelpuffer (-) potato pancake
das Kartoffelpüree mashed potatoes
der Kartoffelsalat potato salad
der Käse cheese (5)
die Käseabteilung (-en) cheese
   department
der Käsekuchen (-) cheese cake (6)
die Käsesauce (-n) cheese sauce
der Käseteller (-) cheese platter
die Kasse (-n) cash register; check-out
   (5); **vorne an der Kasse** up front at
   the cash register
der Kassenarzt (:e) / die Kassenärztin
   (-nen) physician accepting health
   insurance patients
die Kassette (-n) cash box; cassette
der Kassettenrecorder (-) tape recorder
der Kasten (:) box
der Kasus (grammatical) case
der Katalog (-e) catalogue
der Katalysator (-en) catalytic converter
katastrophal catastrophic
die Katastrophe (-n) catastrophe
der Kater (-) male cat
die Kathedrale (-n) cathedral
die Katze (-n) cat (12)
das Katzenhotel (-s) cat kennel
kaufen to buy (2)
die Kauffrau (-en) saleswoman (11)
das Kaufhaus (:er) department store (2)
die Kaufkraft (:e) purchasing power
der Kaufmann (Kaufleute) salesman (11)
kaufmännisch (*adj.*) business;
   businesslike
kaum hardly; barely (8); no sooner
der Kaviar caviar
kegeln to bowl
das Keglerheim (-e) clubhouse for
   bowlers
die Kehle (-n) throat
kein no, none, not any (2); **noch kein** no
   . . . yet; **kein ... mehr** no more . . .
keiner nobody
der Keks (-e) cookie (5)
der Keller (-) cellar, basement
der Kellner (-) / die Kellnerin (-nen)
   waiter, waitress; server (6)
kennen, kannte, gekannt to know, be
   acquainted with (3)
kennen lernen (lernt kennen) to meet; to
   get to know
die Keramik ceramics, pottery
die Kernenergie nuclear energy
die Kettengeschichte (-n) chain story
die Kettenreaktion (-en) chain reaction
der Kibbuz (-im) kibbutz
der Kick (-s) flair
das Kilo = Kilogramm kilogram
der Kilometer (-) kilometer
das Kind (-er) child (1); **als Kind**
   as a child

der **Kinderbrief (-e)** child's letter
die **Kinderermäßigung (-en)** reduced price for children
die **Kinderfreunde** children's friends
kinderfreundlich friendly to/comfortable for children
der **Kindergarten (ⁿ)** nursery school
die **Kinderhilfe** children's aid
die **Kinderkonfektion (-en)** children's wear
die **Kinderkrippe (-n)** childcare center
das **Kinderschlafzimmer (-)** children's bedroom
der **Kinderschutzbund (ⁿe)** association for the protection of children
der **Kinderspaß (ⁿe)** fun for children
die **Kinderspeisung** meals provided for children
die **Kinderspielecke (-n)** children's play corner
der **Kinderspielplatz (ⁿe)** children's playground
das **Kinderzimmer (-)** children's room
die **Kindheit** childhood
das **Kinn (-e)** chin (8)
das **Kino (-s)** movie house; movie theater (4); **ins Kino** to the movies; **ins Kino gehen** to go to the movies (4)
das **Kinoprogramm (-e)** movie program
der **Kiosk (-e)** kiosk
die **Kirche (-n)** church (9)
der **Kirchhof (ⁿe)** cemetery
kirchlich religious
der **Kirchturm (ⁿe)** church steeple
die **Kirschblüte (-n)** blossoming of the cherry trees
die **Kirsche (-n)** cherry
die **Kiwi (-s)** kiwi fruit
die **Klagemauer** Wailing Wall
die **Klammer (-n)** parenthesis
die **Klamotten** (*pl.*) (*slang*) clothes
klappen: nichts klappt nothing is working out
klappern to rattle
der **Klapptisch (-e)** folding table
klar clear; of course; **Na klar!** But of course!; You bet!; **Alles klar?** Everything clear?
der **Klarlack** clear lacquer
die **Klasse (-n)** class; classroom; **erster Klasse** first-class
der **Klassenkamerad (-en** *masc.*) / die **Klassenkameradin (-nen)** classmate
der **Klassenlehrer (-)** / die **Klassenlehrerin (-nen)** main teacher
das **Klassenzimmer (-)** classroom
der **Klassiker (-)** / die **Klassikerin (-nen)** classical writer
klassisch classical (4)
die **Klausur (-en)** written exam

das **Klavier (-e)** piano; **Klavier spielen** to play the piano
die **Klaviermusik** piano music
das **Klavierspielen** piano playing
der **Klavierunterricht** piano instruction
kleben to glue; to stick
das **Kleid (-er)** dress (5)
das **Kleidchen (-)** child's dress
die **Kleiderfrage (-n)** clothes problem
der **Kleiderschrank (ⁿe)** clothes closet (2)
der **Kleiderständer (-)** clothes rack
die **Kleidung** clothing
das **Kleidungsstück (-e)** garment, piece of clothing (5)
klein small (2); little
die **Kleinanzeige (-n)** classified ad
das **Kleingerät (-e)** small appliance
das **Kleinhirn (-e)** cerebellum
Kleinigkeit: eine Kleinigkeit essen to have a bite to eat
das **Kleinkind (-er)** small child, toddler
die **Kleinkinderbetreuung** child care
die **Kleinstadt (ⁿe)** small city; town
der **Klempner (-)** / die **Klempnerin (-nen)** plumber
klettern to climb
der **Klient (-en** *masc.*) / die **Klientin (-nen)** client
das **Klima** climate (10)
die **Klimaanlage (-n)** air conditioning
klingeln to ring
klingen, klang, geklungen to sound (8); **Das klingt nicht gut.** That doesn't sound good. **Du klingst so deprimiert.** You sound so depressed. (8)
die **Klinik (-en)** hospital
klopfen to knock
der **Klub (-s)** club
klug smart, intelligent
km = Kilometer
knabbern to nibble
das **Knäckebrot** crisp bread
knacken to crack
knackig crisp
die **Knackwurst (ⁿe)** *special German sausage*
knallen to slam
knallig flashy, gaudy
knapp just about
die **Kneipe (-n)** pub, bar (6); die **Kneipentour (-en)** bar-hopping
das **Knie (-)** knee (8)
der **Knoblauch** garlic
die **Knoblauchbutter** garlic butter
die **Kobra (-s)** cobra (snake)
der **Koch (ⁿe)** / die **Köchin (-nen)** cook, chef
das **Kochbuch (ⁿer)** cookbook
kochen to cook (1); boil
das **Kochgeschirr (-e)** mess kit

der **Kochlöffel (-)** cooking spoon
die **Kochnische (-n)** kitchen nook
der **Koffer (-)** suitcase (5)
das **Kofferpacken** packing the suitcase
das **Kofferradio (-s)** portable radio
der **Kofferschlüssel (-)** suitcase key
die **Kohle** (*slang*) money
das **Kokain** cocaine
der **Kollege (-n** *masc.*) / die **Kollegin (-nen)** colleague, coworker
(das) **Köln** Cologne
der **Kolonialwarenladen (ⁿ)** grocery store
kombinieren to combine
der **Komfort (-s)** comfort
komfortabel comfortable
komisch strange, funny
kommen, kam, ist gekommen to come (1); **Woher kommst du?** Where do you come from? (E); **der kommende Sommer** next summer
die **Kommode (-n)** dresser (2)
die **Kommunikation (-en)** communication
das **Kommunikationssystem** communication system
das **Kommunikationswesen** communications
kommunistisch communist
die **Komödie (-n)** comedy (4)
die **Kompanie (-n)** (military) company
die **Komparativform (-en)** comparative form (of adjective)
kompetent competent
komplett complete(ly)
kompliziert complicated (1)
der **Komponist (-en** *masc.*) / die **Komponistin (-nen)** composer
der **Kompost (-e)** compost
kompostierbar compostable
kompostieren to compost
das **Kompott (-e)** compote, stewed fruit
die **Konditorei (-en)** pastry shop (5); café
die **Konfektion** ready-made clothing
der **Konferenzraum (ⁿe)** conference room
der **Konflikt (-e)** conflict
der **Kongress (-e)** congress, convention
die **Konjunktion (-en)** conjunction
die **Konjunktivform (-en)** subjunctive form
konkret concrete(ly)
der **Konkurrent (-en** *masc.*) / die **Konkurrentin (-nen)** competitor
können (kann), konnte, gekonnt to be able to, can; to know how (4)
konsequent consequent(ly)
konservativ conservative (1)
die **Konservendose (-n)** can
(das) **Konstanz** Constance (*town in southern Germany*)
konstruieren to build, construct

der Konstrukteur (-e) / die Konstrukteurin (-nen) technical designer

das Konsulat (-e) consulate

der Konsum consumption

der Konsument (-en *masc.***) / die Konsumentin (-nen)** consumer

der Konsumentenkredit (-e) consumer credit

die Konsumexplosion (-en) consumption explosion

der Konsumzwang pressure to buy

der Kontakt (-e) contact (11)

der Kontext (-e) context

kontinuierlich continual(ly)

das Konto (Konten) bank account

der Kontrast (-e) contrast

kontrollieren to inspect, keep under control

konventionell conventional(ly)

die Konversation (-en) conversation

die Konzentration concentration

das Konzentrationslager (-) concentration camp

sich konzentrieren (auf + *acc.***)** to concentrate (on)

das Konzept (-e) concept

das Konzert (-e) concert (4); **ins Konzert gehen** to go to a concert (4)

die Konzertveranstaltung (-en) concert performance

koordinierend coordinating

der Kopf (-̈e) head (8); **pro Kopf** per head; per capita

die Kopfbedeckung (-en) headgear

Köpfchen: kluges Köpfchen clever little person

das Kopfkissen (-) pillow

der Kopfsalat (-e) lettuce

die Kopfschmerzen (*pl.*) headache (8)

der Kopierer (-) copying machine

die Koproduktion (-en) coproduction

das Korn (-̈er) grain

der Körper (-) body

das Körpergewicht (-e) (body) weight

die Körpergröße (-n) (body) height

die Körperpflege personal grooming

der Körperteil (-e) body part

korrespondieren to correspond

korrigieren to correct

die Korruption (-en) corruption (14)

die Kosmetik cosmetics

kosmopolitisch cosmopolitan

kosten to cost (2)

die Kosten (*pl.*) expense

kostengünstig reasonably priced

kostenlos free of charge

köstlich delicious

das Kostüm (-e) women's suit

der Krabbencocktail (-s) shrimp cocktail

der Krach loud noise; quarrel; **mit Ach und Krach** with great difficulty

der Kraftfahrzeugmechaniker (-) / die Kraftfahrzeugmechanikerin (-nen) automobile mechanic

kräftig strong

(das) Krakau Cracow (*city in Poland*)

krank sick, ill (8)

das Krankenhaus (-̈er) hospital

die Krankenkasse health insurance company (8)

der Krankenpfleger (-) / die Krankenschwester (-n) nurse (8)

die Krankenversicherung (-en) health insurance

die Krankheit (-en) illness, disease, ailment (14)

das Kraut (*short for* **Sauerkraut**) sauerkraut

der Kräutertee (-s) herbal tea (8)

die Kräutervinaigrette (-n) herbal salad dressing

der Krautsalat (-e) coleslaw

die Krawatte (-n) tie (5)

kreativ creative(ly)

die Kreativität creativity

der Krebs cancer

die Kreditkarte (-n) credit card (9)

der Kreis (-e) circle

kreisen to circle

der Kreislauf (-̈e) cycle

die Kreislaufbeschwerden (*pl.*) circulatory problems

die Kreuzung (-en) intersection (9)

das Kreuzworträtsel (-) crossword (1)

der Krieg (-e) war (14)

kriegen to receive, get

der Kriegsfilm (-e) war movie

die Kriegsgewalt (-en) violence of war

der Krimi (-s) detective story/show (4)

die Krimikomödie (-n) detective comedy

die Kriminalität criminality

die Krise (-n) crisis

die Kriterien (*pl.*) criteria

die Kritik (-en) critique, review; criticism

der Kritiker (-) / die Kritikerin (-nen) critic

kritisch critical (1)

die Krücke (-n) crutch

der Krug (-̈e) jug, pitcher

sich krümmen to bend over, double up (with pain)

die Küche (-n) kitchen (2); cuisine, food (6)

der Kuchen (-) cake (5)

der Küchenchef (-s) chief cook

das Küchenrezept (-e) recipe

der Küchentisch (-e) kitchen table

die Kuckucksuhr (-en) cuckoo clock

der Kudamm = Kurfürstendamm

der Kugelschreiber (-) ballpoint pen (12)

die Kuh (-̈e) cow

kühl cool (7)

der Kühlschrank (-̈e) refrigerator (12)

kulinarisch culinary

die Kultur (-en) culture

der Kulturamtsleiter (-) / die Kulturamtsleiterin (-nen) head of the Department of Culture

der Kulturbummel (-) stroll through the cultural sights

kulturell cultured; cultural

die Kulturnotiz (-en) cultural comment

die Kulturstadt (-̈e) city of culture

die Kulturstätte (-n) place of culture

das Kulturzentrum (Kulturzentren) cultural center

sich kümmern um (+ *acc.*) to take care of, look after

der Kunde (-n *masc.***) / die Kundin (-nen)** customer (2)

der Kundenberater (-) / die Kundenberaterin (-nen) customer service representative

der Kundendienst customer service

die Kundenkarte (-n) store credit card

künftig future; in the future

die Kunst art

die Kunstgeschichte art history

die Kunsthalle (-n) museum, exhibition hall

der Künstler (-) / die Künstlerin (-nen) artist (11)

künstlerisch artistic (11)

das Kunstmuseum (Kunstmuseen) art museum

die Kunstseide rayon

die Kur (-en) health cure, treatment (at a spa)

das Kuramt (-̈er) resort administration

der Kurfürstendamm *name of famous shopping street in Berlin*

der Kurgast (-̈e) spa guest

das Kurhaus (-̈er) hotel and center for all spa activities

der Kurort (-e) health spa, resort

der Kurs (-e) (*also:* **Kursus**) course; exchange rate

die Kursivschrift italic type

das Kursprogramm (-e) course program

kurz for a short time; short, brief (10); **vor kurzem** recently

der Kurzdialog (-e) short dialogue

kürzlich recently (11)

der Kurzschluss (-̈e) electrical short circuit

die Kurzwaren (*pl.*) notions

die Kusine (-n) female cousin (3)

Küsschen: ein dickes Küsschen a big kiss

die Küste (-n) coast
die Küstenlänge (-n) coastal span

L

das Labor (-s) laboratory
der Laborant (-en *masc.*) / die Laborantin (-nen) laboratory technician
die Laborarbeit (-en) lab work
lächeln to smile
lächelnd smiling
lachen to laugh
lächerlich ridiculous
der Lachs (-e) salmon
der Lackregenmantel (:) shiny plastic raincoat
der Laden (:) store, shop (5)
die Lage (-n) location (9); situation
das Lager (-) camp
die Lagerzeit (-en) storage time
lagig: 2-lagig double-layered, 2-ply
die Lampe (-n) lamp (2)
das Lampenstudio (-s) lamp store
das Land (:er) country; nation, land (1); auf dem Land in the country
landen, hat/ist gelandet to land
die Landeshauptstadt (:e) state capital
das Landesmuseum (Landesmuseen) regional museum
die Landflucht (-en) massive migration from the country
die Landkarte (-n) map
der Landkreis (-e) (rural) district
das Landleben country life
die Landschaft (-en) scenery; landscape; nature
die Landstraße (-n) country road; highway
die Landwirtschaft agriculture
lang long (10); jahrelang for years and years
lange (*temporal*) long; wie lange (for) how long (1); noch lange still a long time
lang gestreckt stretched-out
langsam slow(ly) (10); Langsamer, bitte. Slower, please. (E)
längst- the longest; längst nicht mehr not for the longest time
(sich) langweilen to bore; to be bored
langweilig boring (1); echt langweilig really boring (1)
die Lappalie (-n) mere trifle
der Lärm noise (14)
die Lasagna (Lasagne) lasagna
lassen (lässt), ließ, gelassen to leave; to let (6); to have something done; Lass uns (doch)... Let's . . . (6) Was lässt sich machen? What can be done?
(das) Latein Latin language
(das) Lateinamerika Latin America

lateinisch (*adj.*) Latin
der Lattenrost (-e) slatted mattress platform
Lauf: im Laufe der Zeit in the course of time
laufen (läuft), lief, ist gelaufen to run, jog (2); to walk; Der Film läuft im... The film is playing at . . .; Schlittschuh laufen to ice skate (7); ski laufen to ski
laut loud(ly); according to
läuten: es läutet the bell is ringing
der Lautsprecher (-) loudspeaker, public address system
die Lautsprecherbox (-en) (stereo) loudspeaker
lauwarm lukewarm
das Lazarett (-e) military hospital
das Leben life (11)
leben to live
der/die Lebende (*decl. adj.*) living (person)
der Lebensabschnitt (-e) period of (one's) life
lebensbedrohend life-threatening
die Lebensdaten (*pl.*) biographical dates
die Lebensfreude zest for life
lebensgefährlich life-threatening
die Lebensgewohnheiten (*pl.*) personal lifestyle
der Lebensinhalt purpose in life
das Lebensjahr: seit seinem zweiten Lebensjahr since he was two years old
der Lebenslauf (:e) résumé (11); handschriftlicher Lebenslauf handwritten résumé; tabellarischer Lebenslauf résumé in outline form
die Lebensmittel (*pl.*) food, groceries (5)
das Lebensmittelgeschäft (-e) grocery store
die Lebensmittelhilfe humanitarian aid
die Lebensqualität quality of life
der Lebensraum (:e) habitat (of animals)
der Lebensstandard (-e) standard of living
der Lebensunterhalt livelihood
der Lebensweg (-e) (course of) life
die Leber (-n) liver
der Leberkäs(e) Bavarian-style dish made of liver (6)
der Leberknöd(e)l (-) liver dumpling
die Leberwurst liverwurst
der Lebkuchen (-) gingerbread
lecker tasty, delicious
das Leder leather
die Lederbekleidung leatherwear
die Lederhose (-n) leather pants (*mostly worn in southern Germany*)
die Lederjacke (-n) leather jacket
die Ledernadel (-n) leathercraft needle
die Ledersandalen (*pl.*) leather sandals

die Lederwaren (*pl.*) leather goods
ledig unmarried, single
legen to lay, place (6)
sich (hin)legen (legt sich hin) to lie down (8)
legendär legendary
das Lehrbuch (:er) textbook
die Lehre (-n) apprenticeship
der Lehrer (-) / die Lehrerin (-nen) teacher (E)
der Lehrling (-e) apprentice, trainee
die Leibesübungen (*pl.*) physical education; gymnastics
leicht easy; light
das Leid sorrow, grief; Das tut mir Leid. I am sorry. (9)
leiden, litt, gelitten to suffer
leidenschaftlich passionate(ly)
leider unfortunately (3)
leihen, lieh, geliehen to lend; to borrow (5); Ich leihe mir Geld. I borrow money.; Ich leihe ihm Geld. I lend him money.
das Leinen linen
das Leintuch (:er) (bed) sheet
die Leinwand (:e) movie screen; canvas
leise quiet(ly); softly
sich (+ *dat.*) etwas leisten to afford; Das kann ich mir nicht leisten. I can't afford that.
die Leistung (-en) accomplishment; soziale Leistungen social benefits
der Leitartikel (-) lead editorial
die Leitung direction
die Lektüre (-n) reading (material)
lernen to learn, study (1); Ich lerne Deutsch. I'm learning German.
die Lernmittel (*pl.*) school supplies
das Lernziel (-e) educational goal
das Leseexemplar (-e) book copy
die Lesegewohnheiten (*pl.*) reading habits
die Leseleuchte (-n) reading lamp
lesen (liest), las, gelesen to read (1)
der Leser (-) / die Leserin (-nen) reader
der Leserbrief (-e) letter to the editor
die Leserschaft readers
der Leserservice readers' service
letzt- last; zum letzten Mal for the last time
der Leuchtturm (:e) lighthouse
die Leute (*pl.*) people
das Lexikon (Lexika) dictionary, encyclopedia
das Licht (-er) light; lamp
der Lichtschalter (-) light switch
lieb dear
die Liebe love; alles Liebe all my love (*at end of letter*)

lieben to love

lieber (+ *verb*) rather; preferably (4); **ich möchte lieber** I would prefer, I would rather (4)

der Liebesfilm (-e) romantic movie

lieblich (*wine*) aromatic

das Lieblingsauto (-s) favorite car

die Lieblingsbeschäftigung (-en) favorite activity

das Lieblingsbuch (:er) favorite book

das Lieblingscafé (-s) favorite café

das Lieblingsfach (:er) favorite subject (in school)

die Lieblingsfarbe (-n) favorite color

das Lieblingsgetränk (-e) favorite drink

der Lieblingskomponist (-en *masc.*) / die Lieblingskomponistin (-nen) favorite composer

das Lieblingslokal (-e) favorite eating place

das Lieblingsrestaurant (-s) favorite restaurant

die Lieblingssendung (-en) favorite (TV) program

der Lieblingssport favorite sport

das Lieblingsthema (Lieblingsthemen) favorite topic

der/die/das Liebste (*decl. adj.*) dearest; best

am liebsten (+ *verb*) the best; the most (4); **möchte am liebsten** would like to (do) most (4)

(das) Liechtenstein Liechtenstein (E)

das Lied (-er) song

der Liedermacher (-) / die Liedermacherin (-nen) (folk) songwriter

liefern to supply; to deliver

die Liegekarte (-n) ticket for sleeping compartment

liegen, lag, gelegen to lie; to be located (6)

liegen bleiben (bleibt liegen), blieb liegen, ist liegen geblieben to stay down

die Liegewiese (-n) lawn for sunning oneself

der Lift (-e) elevator

lila purple, violet (5)

die Limonade (-n) lemonade; any fruit-flavored soda, soft drink

das Linguistikseminar (-e) linguistics seminar

die Linie (-n) line; **in erster Linie** first and foremost

der Linienflug (:e) regularly scheduled flight

links left (9); **nach links** to the left (9)

die Lippe (-n) lip

die Liste (-n) list

der Liter (-) liter

literarisch literary

das Literatenkaffeehaus (:er) café frequented by intellectuals

die Literatur literature

loben to praise (11)

locker loose(ly); relaxed

der Löffel (-) spoon (6)

logisch logical

der Lohn (:e) wage

sich lohnen to be worthwhile

das Lokal (-e) restaurant, pub, bar (6)

die Lokalnachrichten (*pl.*) local news (13)

der Lokalpatriotismus regional patriotism

los loose; off; **dann los!** let's go!; **Was ist denn los?** What's the matter? (2)

lösen to solve (a problem)

losgehen (geht los), ging los, ist losgegangen to start; to be off

loslegen (legt los) (*coll.*) to start

die Lösung (-en) solution (14)

loswerden (wird los), wurde los, ist losgeworden (*coll.*) to get rid of

losziehen (zieht los), zog los, ist losgezogen (*coll.*) to take off, leave

die Lotterie (-n) lottery

das Lotto (-s) number-drawing, lottery

die Lücke (-n) gap, hole

der Lückentext (-e) text with blanks to be filled in

die Luft air (8)

die Luftbrücke (-n) "air bridge"; 1949 Berlin airlift

die Luftpumpe (-n) bicycle pump

der Lüftungsbau ventilation system construction

die Luftverschmutzung air pollution

der Luftweg (-e) via air

die Lüge (-n) lie

die Lüneburger Heide Luneburg Heath (*sandy area in northern Germany*)

Lust haben to feel like (*doing something*) (2)

lustig cheerful; fun (1)

(das) Luxemburg Luxembourg (E)

der Luxusartikel (-) luxury article

die Luxusjacht (-en) luxury yacht

(das) Luzern Lucerne (Switzerland)

M

machen to do; to make (1); **Kreuzworträtsel machen** to do crossword puzzles (1); **sich Sorgen machen** to worry; **Mach's gut.** Take care., So long. (E); **Was macht... ?** How is . . . ?; **Das macht zusammen...** That comes to . . . (5); **eine Reise machen** to take a trip; **Urlaub machen** to go on vacation; **Das macht dick.** That is fattening.; **Das macht nichts.** That doesn't

matter. (8); **Das macht mir Spaß.** That's fun. (1)

mächtig powerful; tremendous, strenuous

das Mädchen (-) girl

der Magen (:) stomach

die Magenbeschwerden (*pl.*) stomach troubles

die Magenvergiftung (-en) food poisoning

der Magerquark low-fat farmer's cheese

das Mahl (-e) meal

die Mahlzeit (-en) meal

das Mahnmal (:er) memorial

(der) Mai May (3)

das Make-up makeup (5)

mal = einmal once; just; **erstmal** first of all; **Ruf mal an!** Call sometime! (*softening particle*) (4); **Moment mal** just a moment

das Mal (-e) time(s); **ein zweites Mal** a second time

malen to paint (7)

die Mama (-s) mom, mommy

man (*indef. pron.*) one; you; they; people (4)

der Managementberater (-) / die Managementberaterin (-nen) management consultant

mancher, manche, manches some; **manch ein** many a

manches Mal many a time

manchmal sometimes (8)

der Mangel (:) lack, deficiency

der Mann (:er) man (1); husband (3)

das Männlein (-) little man

männlich masculine

die Mannschaft (-en) team; league

die Mansarde (-n) room under the roof of a building; garret

der Mantel (:) (over)coat (5)

die Mantelgröße (-n) coat size

das Märchen (-) fairy tale

marineblau navy blue

marinieren to marinate

die Mark mark (*German money*); **die DM (Deutsche Mark)** German mark

die Marke (-n) brand (name)

markieren to mark

der Markt (:e) (open air) market, market place (5)

der Marktplatz (:e) market square

die Marmelade (-n) jam

der Mars Mars

marschieren to march; **marsch!** march!

der Marshallplan Marshall Plan (*American recovery program for Europe after World War II*)

(der) März March (3)

das Marzipan *sweet almond paste for candy and cakes*

die Maschine (-n) machine
der Maschinenbau mechanical engineering
der Maskenball (∵e) masked ball
das Maskulinum (Maskulina) masculine noun
die Maß Bier a mug of beer (*about one liter*)
die Massage (-n) massage
mäßig moderate
massiv (*coll.*) total(ly)
maßlos endless(ly), immeasurably
das Material (-ien) material, fabric
materialistisch materialistic
(die) Mathe = (*coll.*) Mathematik
die Mathematik mathematics
der Matjeshering (-e) young, slightly salted herring
die Matratze (-n) mattress
die Matura = das Abitur (*in Austria and Switzerland*)
die Mauer (-n) wall
die Maueröffnung (-en) opening of the (Berlin) wall
die Maus (∵e) mouse (*term of endearment*)
maximal (*adj.*) maximum
der Mechaniker (-) / die Mechanikerin (-nen) mechanic (11)
(das) Mecklenburg-Vorpommern *one of the German states*
die Medien (*pl.*) media
das Medikament (-e) medicine (pills, etc.), medication
der Meditationsurlaub (-e) meditating vacation; retreat
meditieren to meditate
die Medizin (field of) medicine; Medizin studieren to go to medical school
medizinisch medical
das Meer (-e) sea; ocean (7); am Meer at the seaside
das Meerwasser sea water
mehr more (10); kein... mehr no . . . more . . . ; nicht mehr not anymore; nie mehr never again
das Mehrbettzimmer (-) room with several beds
mehrere (*pl.*) several
die Mehrheit majority
mehrmals often, several times, on several occasions
mehrtägig lasting for several days
die Mehrwegbox (-en) recyclable box
die Mehrwertsteuer (-n) value-added tax; national sales tax
die Mehrzahl majority (14); plural
die Meile (-n) mile
mein my (3)
meinen to mean; to observe

die Meinung (-en) opinion (14); meiner Meinung nach in my opinion (14); ich bin der Meinung I'm of the opinion (14)
die Meinungsforschung (-en) public opinion research
meist mostly
der, die, das Meiste the most (10); am meisten (the) most
meistens mostly (8)
die Meisterhand: von Meisterhand zugeschnitten custom-cut by the hand of a master
die Melange (-n) coffee with milk
sich melden to answer (phone) (13); Niemand meldet sich. No one is answering. (13)
die Meldung (-en) message
die Mensa (-s) student cafeteria (1)
der Mensch (-en *masc.*) human being, person (2)
die Menschenrecht (-e) human rights (*usually pl.*) (14)
menschlich human
die Mentalität (-en) mentality
das Menü (-s) set meal, menu
merken to notice, observe
merkwürdig strange; remarkable
das Mesolithikum Mesolithic Age
messbar measurable
das Messer (-) knife (6)
das Metall (-e) metal
der Meteorologe (-en *masc.*) / die Meteorologin (-nen) meteorologist
der/das Meter (-) meter
die Methode (-n) method
der Metzger (-) butcher
die Metzgerei (-en) butcher shop (5)
der Metzgermeister (-) / die Metzgermeisterin (-nen) master butcher
(das) Mexiko Mexico
mich me (*acc.*) (3)
die Miederwaren (*pl.*) intimate apparel
das Mietangebot (-e) for-rent ad
die Miete (-n) rent (2); die Miete beträgt the rent comes to
mieten to rent (from someone) (12)
der Mieter (-) / die Mieterin (-nen) tenant, renter
das Mietgesuch (-e) rental want ad
die Mietkosten (*pl.*) rental expenses
das Mietshaus (∵er) apartment building
der Mietwagen (-) rental car
der Mikrowellenherd (-e) microwave oven (12)
die Milch milk (5)
der Milchkaffee coffee with milk
das Milchprodukt (-e) dairy product
mild mild
das Militär army
militärisch military

die Milliarde (-n) billion
der Milliliter (-) one thousandth of a liter
die Million (-en) million
der Millionär (-e) / die Millionärin (-nen) millionaire
die Milz spleen
die Mimik mimicry
mindestens at least (8)
die Mindestmietdauer minimum rental time
die Mineralölbranche (-n) mineral oil business
das Mineralwasser mineral water (5)
die Minibar (-s) minibar
das Minigolf miniature golf (game)
der Minister (-) / die Ministerin (-nen) (political) minister
das Ministerium (Ministerien) ministry; government department
die Minute (-n) minute (4)
Mio = Million
mir (to/for) me (5)
mischen to mix, blend
die Mischform (-en) mixed form
das Mischgewebe (-) blended fabric
miserabel miserable
mit (+ *dat.*) with (5)
der Mitarbeiter (-) / die Mitarbeiterin (-nen) co-worker, colleague (11)
der Mitbegründer (-) / die Mitbegründerin (-nen) co-founder
der Mitbewohner (-) / die Mitbewoh-nerin (-nen) roommate (2)
mitbringen (bringt mit), brachte mit, mitgebracht to bring/take along
miteinander together
miterziehen (erzieht mit), erzog mit, miterzogen to co-educate
mitfahren (fährt mit), fuhr mit, ist mitgefahren to ride/drive/come along, share the ride
die Mitfahrgelegenheit (-en) ride-sharing opportunity
die Mitfahrzentrale (-n) ride-sharing center
mitgehen (geht mit), ging mit, ist mitgegangen to come along; to join
das Mitglied (-er) member
mitkommen (kommt mit), kam mit, ist mitgekommen to come along (4, 7R)
mitkriegen: sie hat gar nichts mitgekriegt (*coll.*) she didn't understand a thing
das Mitleid compassion, pity
mitmachen (macht mit) to participate
der Mitmensch (-en *masc.*) fellow human being
mitnehmen (nimmt mit), nahm mit, mitgenommen to take along (4); zum Mitnehmen to go; take-out (6)
mitsamt together with, including

**der Mitschüler (-) / die Mitschülerin
(-nen)** classmate
der Mitstudent (-en *masc.***) / die
Mitstudentin (-nen)** fellow student
der Mittag (-e) noon (4); **heute Mittag**
today at noon; **morgen Mittag**
tomorrow noon; **Samstagmittag**
Saturday noon
das Mittagessen midday meal;
lunch (5)
mittags at noon (4)
die Mittagszeit (-en) noontime
die Mitte (-n) middle, center (9);
in der Mitte (der Stadt) in the center
(of the city) (9)
mitteilen (teilt mit) to convey, tell
das Mittelalter Middle Ages
mittelalterlich medieval
die Mittelklasse (-n) middle class
das Mittelmeer Mediterranean Sea
der Mittelpunkt (-e) center
der Mittelwesten (USA) Midwest
mitten in the midst
die Mitternacht midnight; **um
Mitternacht** at midnight (3)
mittler-: die mittlere Reife high school
diploma (*not sufficient for
university studies*)
(der) Mittwoch Wednesday (3)
mittwochs Wednesdays, on
Wednesday(s) (4)
mitunter sometimes
mitverantwortlich also responsible
der/die Mitwirkende (*decl. adj.*)
performer
ml = Milliliter
die Möbel (*pl.*) furniture
die Möbelbeleuchtung (-en) furniture
illumination
möbl. = möbliert
möbliert furnished (2)
möchte: ich möchte I would like (4)
das Modalpartikel (-n) flavoring particle
das Modalverb (-en) modal verb
die Mode (-n) fashion
das Modell (-e) example, model
das Modellbeispiel (-e) model example
der Modeunsinn fashion craze
die Modewaren (*pl.*) fashion articles
modisch fashionable (5)
mögen (mag), mochte, gemocht to like
(4); **Ich möchte** I would like (4)
möglich possible (14)
die Möglichkeit (-en) opportunity;
possibility (10)
möglichst as . . . as possible; **möglichst
bald** as soon as possible
der Mohnkuchen (-) poppy-seed cake
die Möhre (-n) carrot
der Moment (-e) moment; **Moment (mal)**
just a moment

der Monat (-e) month (3); **einmal
im Monat** once a month (7)
monatlich monthly (12)
das Monatsende (-n) end of the month
der Mönch monk
(der) Montag Monday (3)
montags Mondays, on Monday(s) (4)
das Moped (-s) motor scooter
der Mord (-e) murder
der Morgen (-) morning (4); **(guten)
Morgen** good morning (E); **am
Morgen** in the morning
morgen tomorrow (3); **morgen früh**
tomorrow morning (4); **morgen
Vormittag** tomorrow morning; **heute
Morgen** this morning; **morgen Mittag**
tomorrow noon; **morgen Nachmittag**
tomorrow afternoon; **morgen Abend**
tomorrow evening; tomorrow night;
Samstagmorgen Saturday morning
die Morgengymnastik morning exercise
der Morgenmuffel (-) morning grouch
die Morgenroutine (-n) morning routine
morgens in the morning, mornings (4)
die Mosel Moselle River
das Motel (-s) motel
das Motorrad (¨er) motorcycle (2);
Motorrad fahren to ride (drive) a
motorcycle (1)
das Mountainbike (-s) mountain bike
(das) Mountainbiking mountain biking
müde tired (8)
die Mühe: sich Mühe geben to do one's
best; **Mühe haben** to have trouble
der Müll trash, garbage (12)
der Mülleimer (-) garbage can
die Müllhalde (-n) garbage dump
der Müllproduzent (-en *masc.***)** waste
producer
(das) München Munich
Münchner Weißwurst (¨e) Bavarian
veal sausage
der Mund (¨er) mouth (7)
mündlich oral, verbal
die Münze (-n) coin (7)
der Münzfernsprecher (-) coin-
operated public telephone
das Museum (Museen) museum (9)
das Musical (-s) musical
die Musik music (1)
musikalisch (*adj.*) musical
der Musikant (-en *masc.***) / die
Musikantin (-nen)** music maker;
musician
**der Musiker (-) / die Musikerin
(-nen)** (professional) musician
das Musikfest (-e) music festival
die Musikindustrie (-n) music industry
die Musikschule (-n) music school
der Musikstudent (-en *masc.***) / die
Musikstudentin (-nen)** music student

musizieren to play an instrument
der Muskel (-n) muscle (8)
das Müsli *type of granola cereal* (5)
müssen (muss), musste, gemusst to have
to, must (4)
das Muster (-) model; sample; example;
pattern; **nach... Muster** patterned after
. . .; **nach dem folgenden Muster**
according to the following model
mutig brave
die Mutter (¨) mother (3)
mütterlicherseits on the mother's side
der Muttertag (-e) Mother's Day (3)
die Mutti (-s) mommy, mom
die Mütze (-n) cap (5)
Mwst. = Mehrwertsteuer

N

na well; so; **na, dann mach's gut** well,
see you later; **na gut** all right then; **Na
klar!** But of course!; You bet! (14); **Na
und?** So what? (13); **Na, wie geht's?**
How are you? (*casual*) (E)
nach (+ *dat.*) to (*place name*) (5); after
(6); **meiner Meinung nach** in my
opinion; **nach links/rechts** to the
left/right (8); **nach Hause** home
(*indicating going home*) (5); **fünf nach
zwei** five after two (4); **nach oben**
above, upstairs (12); **nach unten**
below, downstairs (12)
der Nachbar (-n *masc.***) / die Nachbarin
(-nen)** neighbor
die Nachbarwohnung (-en) apartment
next door
nachdem (*subord. conj.*) after (10)
nachdenken (über) (+ *acc.*) **(denkt
nach), dachte nach, nachgedacht** to
think (about) (11)
die Nacherzählung (-en) retelling
die Nachfrage (-n) demand
**nachgießen (gießt nach), goss nach,
nachgegossen** to add liquid
nachher afterward
**nachkommen (kommt nach), kam
nach, ist nachgekommen** to follow,
come later
Nacht: gute Nacht good night (E)
der Nachmittag (-e) afternoon (4);
heute Nachmittag this afternoon;
morgen Nachmittag tomorrow
afternoon; **Samstagnachmittag**
Saturday afternoon
nachmittags in the afternoon,
afternoons (4)
der Nachname (-ns, -n) family name,
surname (1)
die Nachricht (-en) message; **die
Nachrichten** (*pl.*) news (13); **die
Lokalnachrichten** (*pl.*) local
news (13)

das **Nachrichtenprogramm (-e)** news broadcast

der **Nachrichtensprecher (-) / die Nachrichtensprecherin (-nen)** anchor person

das **Nachschlagewerk (-e)** reference book

die **Nachspeise (-n)** dessert (6)

nächst- next, following; closest, nearest (10); **nächstes Jahr** next year (1)

die **Nacht (ː̈e)** night (4); **gute Nacht** good night (E)

der **Nachteil (-e)** disadvantage

der **Nachtisch (-e)** dessert (6)

das **Nachtlager (-)** place to sleep; night's lodging; bed

nachts at night, nights (4)

der **Nachttisch (-e)** nightstand (2)

die **Nachttischleuchte (-n)** bedside lamp

nah (näher, nächst-) close by, near

die **Nähe** vicinity; **in der Nähe** nearby, in the vicinity (9); **ganz in der Nähe von** very close to; **nähere Umgebung** close vicinity

die **Naherholung (-en)** vacation close by

der **Nähkasten (ː̈)** sewing box

die **Nahrung** nutrition; food

das **Nahrungsmittel (-)** food

das **Nähzeug** sewing utensils

naiv naive

der **Name (-ns, -n)** name (1); **im Namen (+ gen.)** on behalf of; **Wie ist Ihr(dein) Name?** What's your name? (E)

namens called by; the name of

nämlich namely, that is to say (3)

nanu? now what?

die **Narbe (-n)** scar

narkotisieren to anesthetize

die **Nase (-n)** nose (8)

die **Nasenlänge (-n)** nose length

der **Nasenring (-e)** nose ring

national national(ly)

die **Nationalität (-en)** nationality

die **Nationalsozialisten (Nazis) (pl.)** members of the German National Socialist Party (1933–1945)

die **Natur** nature (10)

das **Naturbett (-en)** health bed

die **Naturfaser (-n)** natural fiber

das **Naturheilmittel (-)** non-medical remedy

der **Naturkostladen (ː̈)** health food store

die **Naturkraft (ː̈e)** organic energy

natürlich natural(ly); of course (3); **Aber natürlich!** But of course! (1)

naturnah (adj.) close to nature

die **Naturoase (-n)** place with undisturbed nature

der **Naturkostladen (ː̈)** health food store (8)

der **Naturpark (-s)** nature park

der **Naturschützer (-) / die Naturschützerin (-nen)** nature preservationist

der **Naturschutzverband (ː̈e)** nature preservation organization

die **Naturwissenschaft (-en)** natural science

naturwissenschaftlich scientific(ly)

der **Nazi (-s) (abbreviation for)** member of the German National Socialist Party (1933–1945)

das **Neandertal** valley near Düsseldorf

der **Nebel (-)** fog (7)

neben (+ acc./dat.) next to, beside (6)

nebenan next door

nebenbei on the side

das **Nebenfach (ː̈er)** minor subject (at school)

das **Nebeninteresse (-n)** hobby

der **Nebenjob (-s)** second job

die **Nebenkosten (pl.)** utilities; extra costs (12)

die **Nebensache (-n)** something of secondary importance

die **Nebensaison (-s)** off-season

der **Nebentisch (-e)** next table

neblig foggy (7)

nee (coll.) = nein

der **Neffe (-n masc.)** nephew (3)

negativ negative(ly)

nehmen (nimmt), nahm, genommen to take (2); **Platz nehmen** to take a seat

neidisch envious

die **Neigung (-en)** tendency

nein no (E)

nennen, nannte, genannt to name

nennenswert worth mentioning

die **Nerven (pl.)** nerves

nerven (coll.) to get on one's nerves, irritate; **Das nervt mich.** That gets on my nerves.; That Irritates me.

nervös nervous (1)

die **Nervosität** nervousness

nett nice (1); pleasant

das **Netz (-e)** net

neu new (3); **nichts Neues** nothing new

der **Neubau (Neubauten)** modern building (12)

die **Neubauwohnung (-en)** apartment in a new building

neugierig curious, nosy

(das) Neuguinea New Guinea

das **Neujahr** New Year's Day (3)

neulich the other day

neun nine (E)

neunte ninth (3)

neunzehn nineteen (E)

neunzig ninety (E)

(das) Neuseeland New Zealand

neutral (adj.) neutral

der **Neuwagen (-)** new car

die **Neuzeit** modern time (from ca. 1500 C.E. to the present)

die **Nibelungen:** *Der Ring der Nibelungen* opera by Richard Wagner

nicht not (1); **nicht mehr** no longer (11); **noch nicht** not yet; **nicht wahr?** isn't that so?

die **Nichte (-n)** niece (3)

der **Nichtraucher (-)** no-smoking car (10)

nichts nothing (2); **Das macht nichts.** That doesn't matter. (8); **gar nichts** nothing at all; **nichts mehr** nothing (any)more; **Nichts zu danken.** No thanks necessary.; Don't mention it. (8)

nie never (8)

der **Niedergang** decline and fall

die **Niederlande (pl.)** the Netherlands (E)

die **Niederlassung (-en)** branch office

der **Niederschlag (ː̈e)** precipitation

niedlich cute

niedrig low (2)

niemand nobody; **Niemand meldet sich.** No one is answering. (13)

die **Niere (-n)** kidney

noch still; yet (2); else; another; **noch nicht** not yet; **noch etwas** something else; **noch einmal** once more; **sonst noch** otherwise

nochmals once again

die **Nockerln (pl.)** Austrian dumplings

das **Nomen (-)** noun

der **Nominativ (-e)** nominative case

(das) Norddeutschland northern Germany

der **Norden** north; **im Norden** (in the) north

nördlich (von) north (of)

der **Nordpol** north pole

(das) Nordrhein-Westfalen one of the German states

die **Nordsee** North Sea

die **Norm (-en)** norm

normal normal(ly)

normalerweise normally

(das) Norwegen Norway

nostalgisch nostalgic

die **Note (-n)** grade (on a report card)

notieren to write down

nötig necessary

die **Notiz (-en)** note; **sich Notizen machen** to take notes

das **Notlicht (-er)** emergency light

notwendig necessary

(der) November November (3)

Nr. = Nummer

das **Nudelgericht (-e)** pasta dish

die **Nudeln (pl.)** noodles

nuklear nuclear

die **Nuklearmacht (ː̈e)** nuclear power

null zero (E)
nummerieren to number
die Nummer (-n) number (E)
nun now
nur only (2)
(das) Nürnberg (city of) Nuremberg
die Nuss (∵e) nut
nützen to make use of
nützlich useful (13)

O

ob (*subord. conj.*) if, whether (or not) (8)
obdachlos homeless
der/die Obdachlose (*decl. adj.*) homeless person (14)
die Obdachlosigkeit homelessness (14)
oben at the top; above; upstairs (12); **da oben** up there; **nach oben** above, upstairs (12)
der Ober (-) waiter (6); **Herr Ober!** Waiter!
ober upper (12); outer
der Oberarzt (∵e) / die Oberärztin (-nen) chief physician
(das) Oberbayern Upper Bavaria
die Oberbekleidung (-en) outer wear
oberflächlich superficial
(das) Oberschlesien Upper Silesia
das Obst fruit (5)
der Obst- und Gemüsestand (∵e) fruit and vegetable stand (5)
die Obstsorte (-n) type of fruit
die Obsttorte (-n) fruit torte
die Obsttunke (-n) fruit sauce
obwohl (*subord. conj.*) although, even though
oder (*coord. conj.*) or (7)
die Ofenkartoffel (-n) baked potato
offen open
öffentlich public(ly) (14)
offiziell official(ly)
öffnen to open (1)
die Öffnung (-en) opening
die Öffnungszeiten (*pl.*) business hours
oft often (1)
öfter frequently
oh je! oh, dear!
ohne (+ *acc.*) without (3)
das Ohr (-en) ear (8)
der Ohrring (-e) earring
der Ökoarchitekt (-en *masc.***) / die Ökoarchitektin (-nen)** environmental architect
die Ökolebensmittel (*pl.*) organic foods (8)
ökologisch ecological(ly)
der Ökonom (-en *masc.***) / die Ökonomin (-nen)** economist
das Oktett (-e) octet
(der) Oktober October (3)
der Ölberg Mount of Olives

die Olive (-n) olive (6)
der Ölprinz (-en *masc.***) / die Ölprinzessin (-nen)** oil prince/oil princess
die Olympischen Spiele (*pl.*) Olympic Games
die Oma (-s) grandma (3)
die Omi (-s) grandma
der Onkel (-) uncle (3)
der Opa (-s) grandpa (3)
der Opel (-) (*automobile*) Opel
die Oper (-n) opera (4); **in die Oper gehen** to go to the opera (4)
die Operation (-en) operation, surgery
die Operette (-n) operetta
das Opernhaus (∵er) opera house
der Opernsänger (-) / die Opernsängerin (-nen) opera singer
die Optik (-en) optical shop
die Orange (-n) orange (5)
orange (*adj.*) (color of) orange (5)
der Orangensaft orange juice (5)
das Orchester (-) orchestra
ordentlich neat
die Ordinalzahl (-en) ordinal number
ordnen to put in order
die Ordnung order; **geht in Ordnung** that's all right, sure; **in Ordnung bringen** to clean up; **in Ordnung sein** to function properly
die Organisation (-en) organization
organisch organic
organisieren to organize
die Orientierung (-en) orientation
die Orientierungsstufe (-n) *level in German school system*
der Orientteppich (-e) oriental rug
original original(ly)
originell inventive, unique
der Ort (-e) place; locality
örtlich local(ly)
die Ortschaft (-en) town
der Ortsteil (-e) section of town
(das) Ostberlin East Berlin
der Ostberliner (-) / die Ostberlinerin (-nen) person from East Berlin
der/die Ostdeutsche (*decl. adj.*) East German (person)
(das) Ostdeutschland East Germany
der Osten east
der Osterhase (-n *masc.***)** Easter bunny
(das) Ostern Easter (3)
(das) Österreich Austria (E)
österreichisch Austrian
östlich (von) east (of)
die Ostsee Baltic Sea
die Ostseite (-n) east side
der Ozean (-e) ocean
der Ozon (-e) ozone
das Ozonloch (∵er) ozone hole

das Ozonproblem (-e) ozone problem
die Ozonschicht (-en) ozone layer

P

das Paar (-e) pair
ein paar a few, a couple of; **ein paarmal** a few times
packen to pack
die Packung (-en) package; box
das Paket (-e) package
die Pantomime (-n) pantomime, gesturing
der Papa (-s) daddy
der Papagei (-en) parrot
das Papier (-e) paper (2); **ein Blatt Papier** a sheet of paper
das Papiergeld (-er) paper money
der Papierkorb (∵e) wastebasket (2)
die Papierlaterne (-n) paper lantern
die Paprika (-s) / Paprikaschote (-n) bell pepper (6)
die Parfümerie (-n) cosmetics store
der Park (-s) park
der Parka (-s) parka
die Parkanlage (-n) public park grounds
parken to park
das Parkett main floor of a theater, orchestra seat section
die Parkgarage (-n) parking garage
das Parkhaus (∵er) high-rise parking garage
der Parkplatz (∵e) parking lot; parking space (9)
das Parkproblem (-e) parking problem
das Parkverbot: hier ist Parkverbot no parking here
das Parlament (-e) parliament
das Partizip (-ien) participle
der Partner (-) / die Partnerin (-nen) partner
die Party (-s) party (3)
das Partymenü (-s) party menu
der Pass (∵e) pass; passport
der Passagier (-e) / die Passagierin (-nen) passenger
der Passagierkai (-s) boardwalk
der Passant (-en *masc.***) / die Passantin (-nen)** passer-by (9)
passen (+ *dat.*) to match, fit (5); **Das passt mir.** That fits (me).
passend matching, suitable
passieren, ist passiert to happen (7)
das Passiv passive voice
der Patient (-en *masc.***) / die Patientin (-nen)** patient
die Pauke (-n) kettle drum
das Pauschalangebot (-e) package tour offer
die Pauschalreise (-n) package tour
die Pause (-n) pause, break
pausenlos continuous, without a break

der **Pazifik** Pacific Ocean
das **Pech** pitch; bad luck; **So ein Pech!**
What a shame! (What bad luck!) (8)
der **Pelz** (-e) fur
pendeln to commute; to go back
and forth
die **Pension** (-en) small, family-run hotel;
bed-and-breakfast inn (9)
sich **pensionieren lassen** to retire
per via; by way of; **per Autostop reisen**
to hitchhike (10)
das **Perfekt** present perfect tense
perfekt (*adj.*) perfect
die **Periode** (-n) period, time
perplex amazed, confused
die **Person** (-en) person; **pro Person**
per person (10)
der **Personalausweis** (-e) (personal) ID
card (10)
der **Personalchef** (-s) / die **Personal-
chefin** (-nen) head of personnel
das **Personalpronomen** (-) personal
pronoun
der **Personenkraftwagen** (Pkw) (-)
automobile, car (13)
persönlich personal
die **Persönlichkeit** (-en) personality
die **Perspektive** (-n) perspective
das **Pestizid** (-e) pesticide
der **Pfad** (-e) path; **der Trimm-Pfad**
(-e) parcourse, jogging path
die **Pfanne** (-n) frying pan (6)
der **Pfarrer** (-) / die **Pfarrerin**
(-nen) minister
der **Pfeffer** pepper (5)
der **Pfeifton** (⸚e) (electronic) beep
die **Pfeilspitze** (-n) arrowhead
der **Pfennig** (-e) penny (*German
monetary unit*)
das **Pferd** (-e) horse; **zu Pferde** on
horseback
das **Pferderennen** (-) horse race
Pfiff: mit Pfiff with style, class
der **Pfirsich** (-e) peach
die **Pflanze** (-n) plant
pflanzen to plant
die **Pflanzenart** (-en) type of plant
das **Pflanzenschutzmittel** (-) pesticide
die **Pflanzensorte** (-n) plant species
der **Pförtner** (-) / die **Pförtnerin**
(-nen) doorkeeper
das **Pfund** (-e) pound
das **Phantom** (-e) phantom
die **Pharmaziebranche** (-n)
pharmaceutical business
die **Philologie** philology
die **Philosophie** philosophy
philosophisch philosophical
die **Physik** physics
der **Physiker** (-) / die **Physikerin**
(-nen) physicist

das **Picknick** (-s) picnic
picknicken to have a picnic
der **Picknickkorb** (⸚e) picnic basket
der **Picknickplatz** (⸚e) picnic area
der **Pilot** (-en *masc.*) / die **Pilotin**
(-nen) pilot
die **Pilsbar** (-s) beer bar
das **Pilsener** (-) pilsner beer (6)
die **Pistole** (-n) pistol, revolver
die **Pizza** (-s) pizza
der **Pkw = Personenkraftwagen**
automobile, car (13)
die **Plakette** (-n) button, sticker
der **Plan** (⸚e) plan
planen to plan (3)
das **Plastik** plastic
das **Plastikgeld** plastic money
das **Plastikrechteck** (-e) plastic square
die **Plastiktüte** (-n) plastic bag (14)
die **Platte** (-n) record; platter
der **Plattenspieler** (-) record player
der **Platz** (⸚e) place; seat (6); **Platz
nehmen** to take a seat; **Da ist kein
Platz.** There is no room.
die **Platzkarte** (-n) seat reservation
card (10)
die **Platzreservierung** (-en) seat
reservation
plaudern to chat
pleite (*coll.*) broke, out of money (12)
das **Plenum: im Plenum** all together
plötzlich suddenly; unexpected
der **Plural** (-e) plural form
der **Pluspunkt** (-e) plus point
das **Plusquamperfekt** past perfect tense
die **Poesie** poetry
(**das**) **Polen** Poland (E)
die **Politik** politics (13)
der **Politiker** (-) / die **Politikerin** (-nen)
politician (14)
politisch political
die **Politologie** political science
die **Polizei** police, police station (9)
der **Polizist** (-en *masc.*) /die **Polizistin**
(-nen) police officer
die **Pommes frites** (*pl.*) French
fries (6)
die **Popeline** (-) poplin
populär popular
der **Porsche** (-) Porsche (*automobile*)
das **Portemonnaie** (-s) wallet; coin purse
die **Portion** (-en) portion; order of
(**das**) **Portugal** Portugal
das **Porzellan** China
die **Posaune** (-n) trombone
positiv positive(ly)
das **Possessivpronomen** (-) possessive
adjective
die **Post** postal system; post office (9);
mail; **bei der Post Karriere machen** to
have a career in the postal service

das **Postamt** (⸚er) post office
das **Poster** (-) poster (2)
das **Postfach** (⸚er) post office box
das **Postgiroamt** (⸚er) post office bank
die **Postkarte** (-n) postcard
die **Postleitzahl** (-en) postal code (E)
postwendend by return mail
potenziell potential(ly)
das **Präfix** (-e) prefix
prägen to shape
das **Praktikum** (Praktika) internship (1);
ein Praktikum machen to do an
internship (1)
praktisch practical (1)
die **Präposition** (-en) preposition
das **Präsens** present tense
präsentieren to present
der **Präsident** (-en *masc.*) / die
Präsidentin (-nen) president
die **Praxis** (Praxen) practice;
professional practice
der **Preis** (-e) price; cost; **im
Preis enthalten** included in
the price (9)
preisgeben (gibt preis), gab preis,
preisgegeben to reveal
preiswert inexpensive, a bargain (2);
recht preiswert quite
inexpensive (2)
die **Premiere** (-n) premiere
die **Presse** press (*newspapers, etc.*)
das **Prestige** prestige
der **Preuße** (-n *masc.*) / die **Preußin**
(-nen) Prussian (person)
der **Priester** (-) / die **Priesterin**
(-nen) priest
prima great, super (E)
privat private; **privat wohnen** to have
a room in somebody's house
or apartment
das **Privatleben** personal life
das **Privatzimmer** (-) private room
pro per; **pro Kopf** per head; **pro Person**
per person (10); **pro Woche**
per week (4)
das **Problem** (-e) problem (2); **ein
Problem lösen** to solve a problem
problemlos without any problem
das **Produkt** (-e) product
die **Produktion** (-en) production
produzieren to produce
der **Professor** (-en) / die **Professorin**
(-nen) professor (1)
der/die **Profi** (-s) professional (person)
das **Programm** (-e) station, TV channel;
program (13); **im ersten Programm**
on channel 1
progressiv progressive
das **Projekt** (-e) project
die **Promenade** (-n) place for strolling
promenieren to stroll

die Prominenz prominent people, socialites
das Pronomen (-) pronoun
das Pronominaladverb (-ien) pronominal adverb
propagiert publicly advocated
prophezeien to predict
der Prospekt (-e) brochure
protestieren to protest
provisorisch temporary, temporarily
provozierend provoking
die Prozedur (-en) procedure
das Prozent (-e) percent
prüfen to test
die Prüfung (-en) test, exam
der Prüfungsraum (ːe) examination room
der Psychologe (-n *masc.***) / die Psychologin (-nen)** psychologist (11)
die Psychologie psychology
der Psychothriller (-) psycho-thriller (movie)
das Publikum public; audience
der Pudding (-e) pudding
der Pudel (-) poodle
pudelnackt stark naked
der Pullover (-) sweater, pullover (5)
der Puls (-e) pulse
Pump: auf Pump (*coll.*) on credit
der Punkt (-e) point; period
pünktlich punctual, on time
die Puppe (-n) doll
die Puppenstube (-n) dollhouse
pusten to blow
putzen to polish, clean (8); **sich die Zähne putzen** to clean, brush one's teeth (8)

Q

qm = Quadratmeter
das Quadrat (-e) square
der/das Quadratmeter (-) square meter
die Qualifikation (-en) qualification
qualifizieren to qualify
die Qualität (-en) quality
der Quark curd cheese
das Quartal (-e) (*academic*) quarter
der Quatsch (*coll.*) nonsense; **So ein Quatsch!** Nonsense! (14)
quatschen (*coll.*) to talk, chat
das Quecksilber mercury, quicksilver
die Quelle (-n) source; spring
quer durch across
das Quiz (-) quiz
der Quizmaster (-) quizmaster
die Quizsendung (-en) quiz program
die Quizshow (-s) quiz show

R

das Racket (-s) (tennis) racket
das Rad (ːer) wheel; bicycle
das Radabzeichen (-) bike emblem

die Radbekleidung (-en) biking clothes
Rad fahren (fährt Rad), fuhr Rad, ist Rad gefahren to ride a bicycle (7)
der Radfahrer (-) / die Radfahrerin (-nen) cyclist
das Radio (-s) radio (2); **im Radio** on the radio
die Radiosendung (-en) radio broadcast
der Radiotechniker (-) / die Radio-technikerin (-nen) radio technician
der Radiowecker (-) clock radio
der Radius (Radien) radius
die Radreise (-n) bike trip
die Radtour (-en) bicycle tour
die Radtourfahrt (-en) bicycle trip
der Radweg (-e) bike path
raffiniert smart; sophisticated
der Rahm cream
die Rakete (-n) rocket
der Rand (ːer) edge; **am Rande** at the edge, outskirts
der Rang balcony, circle (*in the theater*); **der erste Rang** mezzanine; **der dritte Rang** upper balcony
rar rare
das Rascheln rustling
die Raserei rushing around, driving too fast
die Rasiercreme (-s) shaving cream (5)
sich rasieren to shave (8)
das Rasierzeug shaving kit
die Rassenpolitik politics of racism
der Rassismus racism (14)
rassistisch racist
der Rastplatz (ːe) rest area
der Rat advice (8)
raten (rät), riet, geraten to guess; to advise
der Ratgeber (-) advisor; advice column
das Rathaus (ːer) city hall
der Ratschlag (ːe) advice
das Rätsel (-) puzzle, riddle
der Ratskeller (-) (cellar) restaurant near town hall
die Räuberhöhle (-n) thieves' den
der Rauch smoke (8)
das Rauchen smoking
rauchen to smoke (8)
der Rauchtisch (-e) coffee table
rauf = herauf
der Raum (ːe) room; space; **der Abstellraum** storage room
der Raumplaner (-) / die Raumplanerin (-nen) interior decorator
raus = heraus, hinaus; er muss raus he has got to go; **rein und raus** in and out
rausgehen (geht raus), ging raus, ist rausgegangen to go outside

rauskommen (kommt raus), kam raus, ist rausgekommen to come outside; to get out
rausschwimmen (schwimmt raus), schwamm raus, ist rausgeschwommen to swim out into the sea/lake
reagieren auf (+ *acc.*) to react to
die Reaktion (-en) reaction
real real, genuine
der Realschulabschluss (ːe) diploma attained at the end of the Realschule
die Realschule (-n) *secondary school with a commercially oriented curriculum*
der Rebell (-en *masc.***)** rebel
rebellieren to rebel
das Rebland (ːer) wine country
die Rechenmaschine (-n) calculator
recherchieren to investigate, research
rechnen (mit + *dat.***)** to count (on), expect
die Rechnung (-en) bill (6)
recht quite, rather (2); **auf der rechten Seite** on the right-hand side; **nicht so recht** not quite; **Das ist mir recht.** That's fine with me.
das Recht (-e) right; law; **Recht haben** to be correct (2)
rechtfertigen to justify
rechtlich legal(ly)
rechts on the right (9); **nach rechts** to the right (9)
der Rechtsanwalt (ːe) / die Rechtsan-wältin (-nen) attorney, lawyer (11)
rechtsextrem (*adj.*) on the extreme political right
der Rechtsextremismus right-wing extremism (14)
der/die Rechtsradikale (*decl. adj.*) radical (person) on the political right
rechtzeitig in (on) time
das Recycling recycling
recyclingfähig recyclable
der Recyclingingenieur (-e) / die Recyclingingenieurin (-nen) recycling engineer
das Recyclingprogramm (-e) recycling program
der Redakteur (-e) / die Redakteurin (-nen) chief editor
die Rede (-n) speech
das Redemittel (-) speech
reden to talk about (4); **reden über** (+ *acc.*) to talk about; **um das Thema herumreden** to beat around the bush
reduzieren to reduce
das Reflexivpronomen (-) reflexive pronoun
das Reflexivverb (-en) reflexive verb
die Reformkost health food

das Regal (-e) shelf (2)
die Regel (-n) rule
regelmäßig regularly (8)
der Regen rain (7); Es gibt Regen. It is going to rain.
die Regenbekleidung (-en) rainwear
der Regenmantel (¨) raincoat
der Regenschauer (-) rain shower (7)
der Regenschirm (-e) umbrella (7)
der Regenwald (¨er) rain forest
die Regie (-n) (film) direction
die Regierung (-en) government (14)
die Regierungsgewalt (-en) government power
das Regime (-) regime
die Region (-en) region, area
regional regional(ly)
der Regisseur (-e) / die Regisseurin (-nen) (film) director
regnen to rain; Es regnet. It's raining. (7)
regnerisch rainy (7)
das Reich (-e) empire; realm
reich rich
reichen to reach; to suffice; to hand; Das reicht. That's enough.
reichhaltig abundant, plentiful
die Reichskanzlei (-en) (former) German Chancellery
die Reife: mittlere Reife diploma attained at the end of the Realschule
der Reifen (-) tire
die Reihe (-n) row
die Reihenfolge sequence; order
das Reihenhaus (¨er) town house (12)
sich reimen to rhyme
rein = herein; rein und raus in and out
die Reinigung (-en) dry cleaning
reinkommen (kommt rein), kam rein, ist reingekommen to come in, enter
der Reis rice (6)
die Reise (-n) trip (10)
die Reiseapotheke (-n) portable first-aid kit
die Reiseberatung (-en) travel consultation
der Reisebericht (-e) travel report
das Reisebüro (-s) travel agency (10)
der/die Reisebüroangestellte (decl. adj.) travel agency employee
die Reisebürokauffrau (-en) / der Reisebürokaufmann (¨er) licensed travel agent
der Reisebüroleiter (-) / die Reisebüroleiterin (-nen) travel agency manager
die Reisecheckliste (-n) travel checklist
der Reisefilm (-e) travel film
der Reiseführer (-) travel guide (book) (10)
das Reisegepäck luggage

der Reiseleiter (-) / die Reiseleiterin (-nen) tour guide
die Reiselektüre vacation reading material
der Reisemantel (¨) travel coat
die Reisemöglichkeit (-en) travel opportunity
reisen, ist gereist to travel (1); das Reisen traveling
der/die Reisende (decl. adj.) traveler
der Reisepass (¨-e) passport (9)
das Reisepersonal travel staff
der Reiseprospekt (-e) travel brochure (10)
der Reiseproviant food for a trip
der Reisescheck (-s) traveler's check (10)
die Reiseverbindung (-en) travel connection
die Reisevorbereitungen (pl.) travel preparations
die Reisewettervorhersage (-n) traveler's weather forecast
reiten, ritt, ist geritten to ride on horseback (7)
die Reitschule (-n) riding school
die Reklame (-n) advertising
der Rekord (-e) record
relativ relative(ly)
das Relativpronomen (-) relative pronoun
der Relativsatz (¨-e) relative clause
die Religion (-en) religion
die Remouladensauce (-n) dressing made of mayonnaise and herbs
die Renaissance Renaissance (period)
der Rennfahrer (-) / die Rennfahrerin (-nen) race driver
renovieren to renovate
die Renovierungskosten (pl.) remodeling costs
rentabel profitable
die Rente (-n) pension
das Rentiergeweih (-e) reindeer antlers
der Rentner (-) / die Rentnerin (-nen) retired person
die Reparatur (-en) repair (12)
die Reparaturwerkstatt (¨-e) repair shop
reparieren to repair (9)
der Reporter (-) / die Reporterin (-nen) reporter
der Repräsentant (-en masc.) / die Repräsentantin (-nen) representative
repräsentieren to represent
die Republik (-en) republic
reservieren to book, reserve (7)
die Reservierung (-en) reservation
die Residenzstadt (¨-e) government capital
der Rest (-e) remainder
das Restaurant (-s) restaurant (6)
restaurieren to restore

das Resultat (-e) result
retten to save, rescue
das Rezept (-e) recipe
die Rezeption (-en) reception desk (9)
die Rezession (-en) recession
der Rhein Rhine (River)
das Rheinland area along the river Rhine
(die) Rheinland-Pfalz one of the German states
sich richten an (+ acc.) to address; sich richten auf (+ acc.) to be directed at
richtig correct, right (1)
die Richtung (-en) direction; in Richtung in the direction of
der Riese (-n masc.) giant
das Rieseneisbein (-e) gigantic pork hock
riesig enormous, gigantic
der Rinderbraten (-) beef roast (5)
die Rinderroulade (-n) beef roulade
das Rindfleisch beef (5)
der Ring (-e) ring
ringen, rang, gerungen to wrestle
ringsum all around
der Ritter (-) knight
das Roastbeef roast beef
der Rock (¨-e) skirt (5)
die Rockband (-s) rock band
die Rockgruppe (-n) rock group
das Rockkonzert (-e) rock concert
die Rockmusik rock music
roh raw
die Rohmilch raw milk
die Rolle (-n) role
rollen to roll
das Rollenspiel (-e) role play
der Rollkragen (-) turtleneck
der Rollkragenpullover (-) turtleneck sweater
der Rollschuh: Rollschuh laufen roller-skating
der Roman (-e) novel
die Romanfortsetzung (-en) continuation of novel
romantisch romantic (1)
die Röntgenstrahlen (pl.) X rays
das Rostbratwürstl (-) grilled sausage
rot red (5)
(das) Rotkäppchen Little Red Riding Hood
der Rotwein (-e) red wine
die Routine (-n) routine
das Rübenkraut sugar-beet syrup
rüber = herüber
die Rubrik (-en) category; column
der Rücken (-) back (8)
rücken (+ dir. obj.) to move (something)
die Rückenschmerzen (pl.) backache
die Rückfahrt (-en) return trip
der Rucksack (¨-e) backpack (5)
der Rückstrahler (-) rear reflector
rückwärts backward

rudern, ist gerudert to row
der Ruf (-e) call, shout
rufen, rief, gerufen to call (out)
die Ruhe rest, calm (8); **in Ruhe** in peace and quiet, at one's leisure; **in Ruhe lassen** to leave alone
der Ruhetag (-e) *day that a business is closed* (6)
ruhig quiet (1); calm
das Rührei (-er) scrambled egg
(sich) rühren to stir
die Ruine (-n) ruin
(das) Rumänien Rumania
das Rumpsteak (-s) steak
rund round; around
der Rundfunk radio; broadcasting
die Rundfunkanstalt (-en) broadcasting corporation
rundum all around
der Russe (-n *masc.***) / die Russin (-nen)** Russian (person)
russisch (*adj.*) Russian
(das) Russland Russia
rustikal rustic
die Rüstung (-en) armament
das Rüstzeug equipment

S

die Sache (-n) thing, object; event; **in Sache** concerning; **mit 200 Sachen** (*coll.*) driving at 200 km an hour
(das) Sachsen *one of the German states*
(das) Sachsen-Anhalt *one of the German states*
die Sackgasse (-n) dead end
die Safari (-s) safari
der Saft (-̈e) juice (5)
saftig juicy
sagen to say, tell (1); **sag mal** tell me (1); **Wie sagt man... auf Deutsch?** How does one say . . . in German? (E)
die Sahne cream (6)
das Sahneeis ice cream
die Sahnehaube (-n) (whipped) cream topping
die Saison (-s) season
der/das Sakko (-s) man's jacket, coat (5)
der Salat (-e) salad; lettuce (6); **der Kartoffelsalat** potato salad
die Salatbar (-s) salad bar
der Salatkranz (-̈e) bed of lettuce
die Salatplatte (-n) mixed salad dish
das Salz salt (5)
sammeln to collect (7)
die Sammelstelle (-n) recycling center (14)
der Sammler (-) / die Sammlerin (-nen) collector
die Sammlung (-en) collection
(der) Samstag Saturday (3); **Samstagmorgen** Saturday morning (4);

Samstagvormittag Saturday before noon (4); **Samstagmittag** Saturday noon (4); **Samstagabend** Saturday evening; Saturday night (4)
samstags Saturdays, on Saturday(s) (4)
sämtlich total, all
die Sandale (-n) sandal
der Sänger (-) / die Sängerin (-nen) singer
die Sanierung (-en) renovation
der Satan (-e) devil
das Satansweib (-er) devilish woman
das Satellitenprogramm (-e) satellite program
die Satire (-n) satire
satt full, having had enough to eat; **satt werden** to get enough to eat
der Sattel (-̈) saddle
der Satz (-̈e) sentence
die Satzklammer (-n) sentence bracket
der Satzteil (-e) part of a sentence, clause
sauber clean (14)
(sich) sauber halten (hält sauber), hielt sauber, sauber gehalten to keep (oneself) clean
die Sauberkeit cleanliness
säuberlich neatly
sauber machen (macht sauber) to clean house
das Sauerfleisch marinated meat
das Sauerkraut sauerkraut, pickled cabbage (6)
säuerlich sour-tasting
der Sauerregen (-) acid rain
die Sauna (-s) sauna
die S-Bahn (-en) light-rail inner city train
(das) Schach chess; **Schach spielen** to play chess (7)
die Schachtel (-n) box
schade too bad
schaden to harm
der Schaden (-̈) damage; **ohne Schaden** without being hurt
schädlich harmful
das Schäfchen (-) lamb
schaffen, schuf, geschaffen to create (14)
schaffen, schaffte, geschafft to accomplish, succeed; **Wir schaffen es nicht.** We're not going to make it.
der Schaffner (-) / die Schaffnerin (-nen) conductor
der Schal (-s) shawl, scarf (5)
die Schale (-n) bowl
die Schande disgrace
scharf sharp
die Schärfe (-n) sharpness
der Schatz: mein Schatz my darling
das Schaubild (-er) diagram

die Schaubühne (-n) theater
schauen to look; **Schau mal!** Look! (2)
der Schauer (-) (rain) shower (8)
das Schaufenster (-) store window
der Schauspieler (-) / die Schauspielerin (-nen) actor, actress (11)
der Scheck (-s) check
die Scheckkarte (-n) bank card
die Scheibe (-n) slice
scheiden, schied, ist geschieden to divorce
der Schein (-e) (paper) money; **der Euro-schein** Euro note, bill
scheinbar apparently
scheinen, schien, geschienen to shine; to seem, appear (13); **Die Sonne scheint.** The sun is shining.
schenken to give (a gift) (5)
scheußlich horrible
schick stylish
schicken to send (5)
das Schicksal (-e) fate
schieben, schob, geschoben to push
schießen, schoss, geschossen to shoot
das Schiff (-e) ship (10)
die Schiffsfahrt (-en) boat trip
die Schiffsreise (-n) voyage
das Schild (-er) sign, road sign
der Schilling (-e) *Austrian monetary unit*
schimpfen to scold
der Schinken (-) ham (5)
der Schirm (-e) umbrella
die Schlacht (-en) battle
der Schlaf sleep
der Schlafanzug (-̈e) pajama
schlafen (schläft), schlief, geschlafen to sleep (2); **schlafen gehen** to go to bed
das Schlafmittel (-) sleeping pills
der Schlafraum (-̈e) sleeping room
der Schlafsack (-̈e) sleeping bag
die Schlaftablette (-n) sleeping pill
das Schlafzimmer (-) bedroom (2)
der Schlag (-̈e) blow
schlagartig sudden(ly)
der Schlägel (-) drumstick; mallet
schlagen (schlägt), schlug, geschlagen to beat
der Schlager (-) hit song; hit
das Schlagobers whipped cream topping
die Schlagzeile (-n) headline (13)
das Schlagzeug (-e) (set of) drums; percussion instruments
die Schlämmkreide fine chalk
schlank slender
schlapp without energy, rundown, listless; worn out (8)
schlecht bad (E); **schlecht erreichbar** hard to reach; **Mir ist schlecht.** I feel sick to my stomach. (8)
schleifen, schliff, geschliffen to sharpen

schleppen to drag, lug

(das) Schleswig-Holstein *one of the German states*

schließen, schloss, geschlossen to close; **schließen aus** (+ *dat.*) to conclude (from)

das Schließfach (∵er) locker

schließlich finally, in the end

schlimm bad

das Schlimme (*decl. adj.*) the bad thing

der Schlips (-e) tie (5)

der Schlittschuh (-e) ice skate

Schlittschuh laufen (läuft), lief, ist gelaufen to ice skate (7)

das Schloss (∵er) castle; palace

der Schlossgarten (∵) palace garden

der Schluckauf hiccup

schlucken to swallow (8)

der Schlüssel (-) key (9)

schmecken to taste; **Das schmeckt (mir) gut.** That tastes good (to me). (5)

schmelzen (schmilzt), schmolz, ist geschmolzen to melt; to thaw

die Schmerzen (*pl.*) pains (8); **vor Schmerz schreien** to cry out with pain; **die Halsschmerzen** (*pl.*) sore throat (8); **die Kopfschmerzen** (*pl.*) headache (8)

(sich) schminken to put on makeup (8)

der Schminktisch (-e) makeup table

der Schmuck jewelry

der Schmutz dirt

die Schmutzarbeit (-en) menial work

schmutzig dirty (14)

die Schnecke (-n) snail

der Schnee snow (7)

die Schneekette (-n) snow chain

der Schneemann (∵er) snowman

schneiden, schnitt, geschnitten to cut

schneien to snow (7); **Es schneit.** It is snowing. (7)

schnell quick; fast (10)

der Schnittkäse sliced cheese

das Schnitzel (-) cutlet (5)

der Schnupfen cold; sniffle (8)

schnurlos cordless

der Schnurrbart (∵e) mustache

die Schokolade chocolate

die Schokoladentorte (-n) chocolate torte

der Schokoriegel (-) chocolate bar

schon already (2); yet; ever

schön nice(ly), beautiful(ly) (2); **bitte schön** please (E); **danke schön** (many) thanks (E); **schön warm** nice and warm

schonen to protect

die Schönheit (-en) beauty

der Schonkaffee low-acid decaffeinated coffee

schöpfen to scoop; to draw (from a well)

der Schornsteinfeger (-) chimney sweep

der Schrank (∵e) cupboard; closet; wardrobe

schrecklich horrible

der Schrei (-e) scream; **der letzte Schrei** the latest fashion

schreiben, schrieb, geschrieben to write (2); **Wie schreibt man ___?** How do you write ___? (E)

die Schreibmaschine (-n) typewriter

die Schreibstube (-n) office; writing room

der Schreibtisch (-e) desk (2)

die Schreibwaren (*pl.*) stationery goods

schreien, schrie, geschrien to scream

schriftlich in writing

der Schriftsteller (-) / die Schriftstellerin (-nen) writer, author

der Schritt (-e) step (11)

die Schublade (-n) drawer

der Schuh (-e) shoe (5)

das Schuhgeschäft (-e) shoe store

die Schuhgröße (-n) shoe size

der Schuhkauf (∵e) shoe purchase

das Schuhwerk footwear

der Schulabgänger (-) / die Schulabgängerin (-nen) school graduate

die Schularbeiten (*pl.*) homework

die Schuld guilt; blame

die Schulden (*pl.*) debts; **Schulden machen** to go into debt

schuldig guilty

die Schule (-n) school; **Schule machen** to set an example

der Schüler (-) / die Schülerin (-nen) pupil, student in primary or secondary school

das Schulessen (-) school lunch

die Schulferien (*pl.*) school vacation, holidays

der Schulfreund (-e) / die Schulfreundin (-nen) school friend

das Schuljahr (-e) school year; **im zehnten Schuljahr** in tenth grade

das Schulkind (-er) pupil

der Schulort (-e) town in which one attends school

die Schulsachen (*pl.*) school supplies

die Schulspeisung meal provided at school

die Schulter (-n) shoulder (8)

das Schultergelenk (-e) shoulder joint

die Schulterpartie (-n) shoulder area

der Schultyp (-en *masc.*) type of school

die Schüssel (-n) bowl

der Schutz (-e) protection

schützen to protect (14)

schwach weak

die Schwäche (-n) weakness

schwachsinnig (*coll.*) crazy

der Schwager (∵) brother-in-law (3)

die Schwägerin (-nen) sister-in-law (3)

schwanger pregnant

schwarz black (5)

das Schwarzbrot black bread

schwarzhaarig dark-haired

der Schwarzhandel black market

der Schwarzwald Black Forest

die Schwarzwälder Kirschtorte (-n) Black Forest cake

der Schwarzweißfilm (-e) black-and-white film

(das) Schweden Sweden

das Schwefeldioxyd (-e) sulfur dioxide

das Schwein (-e) pig; **kein Schwein** (*coll.*) nobody

der Schweinebraten (-) pork roast (6)

das Schweinefleisch pork (5)

das Schweinegulasch pork goulash

das Schweineschnitzel (-) pork cutlet

die Schweineschulter (-n) pork shoulder

die Schweinshaxe (-n) pork knuckle

das Schweinskotelett (-s) pork cutlet

der Schweiß perspiration

die Schweiz Switzerland (E)

der Schweizer Käse Swiss cheese

schwer heavy; difficult; **schwer arbeiten** to work hard

der Schwerpunkt (-e) focus, emphasis

die Schwester (-n) sister (3)

die Schwiegermutter (∵) mother-in-law (3)

der Schwiegervater (∵) father-in-law (3)

schwierig difficult

die Schwierigkeit (-en) difficulty

das Schwimmbad (∵er) swimming pool (7)

schwimmen, schwamm, ist geschwommen to swim (2)

die Schwimmflosse (-n) flipper

die Schwimmhalle (-n) indoor pool

die Schwimmstufe (-n) swimming level

schwitzen to sweat

schwül muggy (7)

der Schwung: voll Schwung full of zest

sechs six (E)

sechste sixth (3)

sechzehn sixteen (E)

sechzig sixty (E)

die sechziger Jahre the sixties

der See (-n) lake (7); **auf dem See** on the lake; **die See** ocean

der Seekanal (∵e) sea channel

das Segelflugzeug (-e) glider

der Segelkurs (-e) sailing course

segeln to sail (7)

sehen (sieht), sah, gesehen to see (2)

sehenswert worth seeing

sehenswürdig remarkable

die Sehenswürdigkeit (-en) (tourist) attraction

sehr very (1); **sehr gut** very well (E)

die Seide silk

die Seidenblume (-n) silk flower

die Seidenbluse (-n) silk blouse
das Seil (-e) rope
sein (ist), war, ist gewesen to be (1)
sein his, its (3)
seit (+ *dat.*) since; for (5); **seit wann** since when (6); **seit zwei Jahren** for two years (6)
seitdem since then
die Seite (-n) side; page
der Sekretär (-e) / die Sekretärin (-nen) secretary
der Sekt champagne
die Sekunde (-n) second (4)
selb- (*adj.*) same; **derselbe, dieselbe, dasselbe** the same
selber self; **selber machen** to do (*something*) oneself
selbst self
selbständig independent(ly) (11)
die Selbstbedienung self-service
das Selbstbewusstsein self-confidence
selten rare(ly) (2); seldom
das Semester (-) semester (1)
das Seminar (-e) seminar (2)
die Seminararbeit (-en) paper written for a seminar
die Semmel (-n) bread roll (*southern Germany and Austria*)
senden, sandte, gesandt to send
die Sendung (-en) TV or radio program (13)
der Senf mustard (6)
(der) September September (3)
die Serie (-n) series
servieren to serve
die Serviette (-n) napkin
der Sessel (-) armchair (2)
setzen to set; to put (6); **sich (hin)setzen** to sit down (8)
das Shampoo (-s) shampoo
sicher safe(ly) (10)
die Sicherheit security
die Sicherheitskraft (∵e) security force
sicherlich certainly
sichern to secure
sichtbar visible
Sie (*form.*) you (1)
sie she; it; they (1); her, it; them (*acc.*) (3)
sieben seven (E)
sieb(en)te seventh (3)
siebzehn seventeen (E)
siebzig seventy (E)
die Siedlung (-en) housing development
das Signal (-e) signal
signalisieren to signal, indicate
das Silber silver
das Silbergeld silver pieces of money
die Silbermünze (-n) silver coin
silbern silver(y)
(das) Silvester (-) New Year's Eve (3)
singen, sang, gesungen to sing

sinken, sank, ist gesunken to sink; to drop
der Sinn (-e) sense; meaning; feeling; **Sinn für Humor** sense of humor
sinnlos senseless
die Situation (-en) situation
der Sitz (-e) seat
sitzen, saß, gesessen to sit (6)
sitzen bleiben (bleibt sitzen), blieb sitzen, ist sitzen geblieben to be left behind; to fail a class
die Sitzgruppe (-n) living room set
der Sitzplatz (∵e) seat
die Sitzung (-en) session
(das) Sizilien Sicily
das Skalpell (-e) scalpel
das Skeetschießen skeet shooting
skeptisch skeptical
der Sketch (-e) sketch
Ski fahren (fährt), fuhr, ist gefahren to ski
die Skihose (-n) ski pants
Ski laufen (läuft), lief, gelaufen to ski
der Skiläufer (-) / die Skiläuferin (-nen) skier
der Skipass (∵e) lift pass
die Skulptur (-en) sculpture
der Slawenfürst (-en *masc.*) Slavic prince
slawisch Slavic
(die) Slowakei Slovakia (E)
(das) Slowenien Slovenia (E)
so so (2); like that; **So ein Pech!** What a shame! (8); **So ein Quatsch!** Nonsense! (14); **So ein Unsinn!** Nonsense! (14); **so gegen fünf uhr** around five o'clock (6); **so lala** OK, so-so (E); **so... wie** as . . . as (10)
sobald (*subord. conj.*) as soon as
die Socke (-n) sock (5)
das Sofa (-s) sofa (2)
sofort immediately (9)
sogar even (8)
sogenannt so-called
der Sohn (∵e) son (3)
solange (*subord. conj.*) as long as
das Solarauto (-s) solar automobile
die Solarenergie (-n) solar energy
das Solarium (Solarien) solarium
das Solarmobil (-e) solar car
solch ein- such a
der Soldat (-en *masc.*) / die Soldatin (-nen) soldier
die Solidarität solidarity
solide solid, sound
sollen (soll), sollte, gesollt shall; to be supposed to; ought; should (4); said to be
der Sommer (-) summer (7)
der Sommergarten (∵) summer garden

das Sommerstipendium (Sommerstipendien) summer scholarship
der Sommertag (-e) summer day
die Sommerzeit (-en) daylight savings time
der Sonderabfall (∵e) radioactive waste
die Sonderaktion (-en) special (sales) offer
das Sonderangebot (-e) special offer (at a store)
sonderbar strange
sondern but rather (7)
der Sonderpreis (-e) special price
(der) Sonnabend Saturday (3)
sonnabends Saturdays (4)
die Sonne (-n) sun (7); **Die Sonne scheint.** The sun is shining. (7)
die Sonnenblume (-n) sunflower
die Sonnenbrille (-n) sun glasses
die Sonnenenergie (-n) solar energy
der Sonnenschein sunshine (7)
das Sonnenschutzmittel (-) suntan lotion, sunscreen (10)
sonnig sunny (7)
(der) Sonntag Sunday (3)
sonntags Sundays, on Sunday(s) (4)
sonst (noch) otherwise; else; other than that; **Sonst noch etwas?** Anything else? (10)
sonstig other, additional (10)
Sonstiges other items, miscellaneous
die Sorge (-n) worry; **sich Sorgen machen** to worry
sorgenfrei carefree
sorgfältig careful
die Sorte (-n) kind; variety
das Souvenir (-s) souvenir
der Souvenirverkauf (∵e) souvenir sale
so viel so much
so viele (*pl.*) so many
so was something like that
so weit: Endlich ist es so weit. It's finally happening.
sowie as; as well as; like
sowieso anyway
die Sowjets (*pl.*) Soviets
die Sowjetunion Soviet Union
sowohl... als auch... . . . as well as . . .
sozial social
der Sozialarbeiter (-) / die Sozialarbeiterin (-nen) social worker
der Sozialismus socialism
die Sozialkunde social science
die Sozialwissenschaften (*pl.*) social sciences
die Soziologie sociology
die Spalte (-n) (printed) column
das Spanferkel (-) roasted suckling pig
(das) Spanien Spain
spanisch (*adj.*) Spanish

spannend exciting, suspenseful (4)

das Sparen saving

sparen to save (12)

der Spargel (-) asparagus

die Sparkasse (-n) savings bank

das Sparkonto (Sparkonten) savings account (12)

der Sparpreis (-e) discount price

sparsam thrifty (12)

das Sparschweinchen (-) piggy bank

der Spartopf (⸚e) cookie jar for savings

der Spaß fun; **Spaß machen** to joke; **Das macht mir Spaß.** That's fun. (1); **Viel Spaß!** Have fun! (1)

spät late (4); **Wie spät ist es?** What time is it? (4)

spätestens at the latest (12)

spazieren to go for a walk, stroll

spazieren führen (führt spazieren) to take for a walk

spazieren gehen (geht spazieren), ging spazieren, ist spazieren gegangen to go for a walk (4)

der Spaziergang (⸚e) walk, stroll

der Speck bacon

der Speditionskaufmann (Speditions-kaufleute) / die Speditionskauffrau (-en) forwarding agent

speichern to store

die Speise (-n) meal

die Speiseauswahl (-en) food selection

die Speisekarte (-n) menu (6)

speisen to eat; to dine

der Speisewagen (-) dining car

die Speisung (-en) food distribution

spektakulär spectacular

die Spekulation (-en) speculation

spekulieren to speculate; to gamble

die Spende (-n) donation, contribution

spenden to donate

das Spendenkonto (Spendenkonten) account for donations

der Spender (-) / die Spenderin (-nen) donor

die Spezialausrüstung (-en) special clothing

das Spezialgericht (-e) (*food*) specialty

sich spezialisieren auf (+ acc.) to specialize in

die Spezialität (-en) specialty

spezifisch specific

der Spiegel (-) mirror

das Spiegelei (-er) fried egg (6)

das Spiel (-e) play; game

die Spielecke (-n) play corner

spielen to play (1); **Computerspiele spielen** to play computer games (1); **Karten spielen** to play cards (1)

spielend (*adv.*) without effort, easily

der Spieler (-) / die Spielerin (-nen) player

der Spielfilm (-e) feature film, movie (13)

die Spielkarte (-n) playing card (7)

der Spielplatz (⸚e) playground

das Spielzeug (-e) toy, toys

der Spinat spinach

die Spinne (-n) spider

der Spiritus (-se) spirit, alcohol

die Spitze (-n) tip; (pointed) top

das Spitzenprodukt (-e) top product

spontan spontaneous

der Sport sports (7)

Sport treiben, trieb, getrieben to engage in sports (7)

die Sportanlage (-n) sports grounds

die Sportart (-en) type of sport

der Sportartikel (-) sports equipment

die Sportbekleidung (-en) sporting clothes

das Sportcamp (-s) sports camp

die Sporthalle (-n) gymnasium (7)

das Sporthemd (-en) casual shirt (5)

der Sportlehrer (-) / die Sportlehrerin (-nen) gym teacher

sportlich athletic (1); casual; **sportlich aktiv** active in sports (10)

die Sportnachrichten (*pl.*) sports news

der Sportplatz (⸚e) athletic field, stadium (7)

die Sportschau (-s) sports show

der Sportschuh (-e) athletic shoe

die Sportsendung (-en) sports program

das Sporttreiben playing sports

der Sportwagen (-) sports car

das Sportzentrum (Sportzentren) athletic center

die Sprache (-n) language; **die Fremdsprache** foreign language

der Sprachkurs (-e) language course

das Sprachlabor (-s) language lab

sprechen (spricht), sprach, gesprochen to speak (2)

der Sprecher (-) / die Sprecherin (-nen) speaker

die Sprechstunde (-n) office hour (8)

der Springbrunnen (-) fountain

springen, sprang, ist gesprungen to jump

spritzen to spray

der Spruch (⸚e) saying; message

der Sprudel (-) mineral water (6)

die Spülmaschine (-n) dishwasher (12)

das Squash squash (game)

der Staat (-en) state, nation

staatlich by the government

der Staatsbesuch (-e) state visit

das Staatsexamen (-) state examination

die Staatsgewalt (-en) government power

die Staatskontrolle (-n) government control

die Staatsprüfung (-en) examination administered by a national board

stabil stable; solid

der Stacheldraht barbed wire

das Stadion (Stadien) stadium (7)

die Stadt (⸚e) town; city (E)

das Stadtarchiv (-e) city archives

das Stadtbad (⸚er) municipal bath

der Stadtbewohner (-) / die Stadtbewohnerin (-nen) city dweller

das Stadtbild (-er) urban picture

das Städtchen (-) little town

stadteinwärts toward the center of town

der Stadtführer (-) city guide

die Stadtführung (-en) city tour

der Stadtgraben (-) town moat

das Stadtkino (-s) city movie theater

das Stadtklima urban climate

das Stadtleben (-) city life

die Stadtmitte (-n) town center

der Stadtpark (-s) city park

der Stadtplan (⸚e) city street map

die Stadtplanung urban planning

der Stadtrand (⸚er) edge of town

der Stadtrundgang (⸚e) city tour

der Stadtteil (-e) city district

das Stadttheater (-) municipal theater

das Stadttor (-e) city gate

der Stadtumbau (-ten) town reconstruction

die Stadtverwaltung (-en) city administration

der Stadtwall (⸚e) town wall

das Stadtzentrum (Stadtzentren) town center

stagnieren to stagnate

der Stamm (⸚e) stem

der Stammbaum (⸚e) family tree

stammen aus (+ *dat.*) to come from; to originate

der Stammgast (⸚e) regular guest

der Stammtisch (-e) permanently reserved table

das Standesamt (⸚er) hall of records

ständig always; permanent

der Standort (-e) position

die Standuhr (-en) grandfather clock

der Star (-s) (film, etc.) star

stark strong

starr rigid

starren to stare

der Start (-s) start

starten to start

die Starthilfe (-n) starting assistance

der Startpunkt (-e) starting point

die Statistik (-en) statistics

statistisch statistical(ly)

(an)statt (+ *gen.*) instead of

stattdessen instead of (that)

stattfinden (findet statt), fand statt, stattgefunden to take place

der Stau (-s) traffic jam

der Staubsauger (-) vacuum cleaner (13)

staunen to be amazed

der Stausee (-n) artificially created lake behind a dam

das Steak (-s) steak (5)

stecken to place, put (*inside*); to be (*inside*) (6); **seine Hände in die Hosentasche stecken** to put one's hands in one's pocket

stecken bleiben (bleibt stecken), blieb stecken, ist stecken geblieben to be stuck

stehen, stand, gestanden to stand; to be located (6); to look good (*on a person*) (5); **Die Farbe steht mir.** The color looks good on me. (5); **(im Text) stehen** to say (in the text)

stehen bleiben (bleibt stehen), blieb stehen, ist stehen geblieben to stop (running)

die Stehlampe (-n) floor lamp

stehlen (stiehlt), stahl, gestohlen to steal

der Stehplatz (¨e) standing room

die Steiermark one of the Austrian states

steigen, stieg, ist gestiegen to climb, go up, rise

steigend increasing

steigern to increase

der Stein (-e) stone

die Steinzeit Stone Age

die Stelle (-n) place, position (11); **an deiner Stelle** if I were you, (I if were) in your place (12); **auf der Stelle** right away, immediately; on the spot; **an erster Stelle** in first place; **eine feste Stelle** permanent position

stellen to stand up; to place, put (*upright*) (6); **eine Frage stellen** to ask a question

das Stellenangebot (-e) job offer; help-wanted ad (11)

die Stellenanzeige (-n) want ad

der Stellenmarkt (¨e) job market

die Stellensuche job search

die Stellung (-en) position; **Stellung nehmen zu** (+ *dat.*) to state one's opinion on

die Steppdecke (-n) comforter

sterben (stirbt), starb, ist gestorben to die

die Stereoanlage (-n) stereo (2)

die Sterilisation (-en) sterilization

sterilisieren to sterilize

der Stern (-e) star

stetig regularly

das Steuer (-) steering wheel

die Steuer (-n) tax (14)

die Steuerberatung (-en) tax consultant

die Steuereinnahme (-n) tax revenue

die Steueroase (-n) tax-free country

das Stichwort (¨er) key word, cue

sticken to embroider

der Stiefel (-) boot (5)

der Stil (-e) style

die Stimme (-n) voice; vote

stimmen to be correct; **(Das) stimmt.** That's correct.

stinken, stank, gestunken to smell bad

das Stipendium (Stipendien) scholarship

der Stock (*pl.* **die Stockwerke**) floor, story (9); **im ersten Stock** on the second floor

stockaufwärts up to the next floor

das Stockwerk (-e) = Stock floor, story (9)

der Stoff (-e) fabric

der Stoffbezug (¨e) fabric cover

stöhnen to moan, sigh

der Stollen (-) (type of) fruit cake

stolpern, ist gestolpert to stumble

stolz proud; **stolz sein auf** (+ *acc.*) to be proud of

stören to bother, disturb

stoßen (stößt), stieß, gestoßen to push

der Strand (¨e) beach (9)

die Straße (-n) street (E); **die Straße entlang** along the street; **auf der Straße** in the street

die Straßenbahn (-en) streetcar

der Straßenverkehr street traffic

die Strategie (-n) strategy

die Strecke (-n) stretch of the road; route

(sich) strecken to stretch (8)

streckenlang for stretches on end

der Streifen (-) strip

das Streifendesign (-s) stripe pattern

streiken to go on strike

streng strictly (14)

der Stress stress (8)

der Stressfaktor (-en) stress factor

stressfrei stress-free

stressig stressful (1)

stricken to knit

die Strickwaren (*pl.*) knitwear

der Strohhut (¨e) straw hat

der Strom electricity (12); **Es regnet in Strömen.** It is pouring rain.

der Stromverbrauch electricity consumption

der Strumpf (¨e) stocking, sock (5)

die Strumpfboutique (-n) hosiery store

das Stübchen (-) / das Stuberl (-n) small room (*used in restaurant names*)

die Stube (-n) room

das Stück (-e) piece; (theater) play (4); **pro Stück** each, per piece

der Student (-en *masc.***) / die Studentin (-nen)** student (1)

das Studentenabonnement (-s) student subscription

der Studentenalltag (-e) student's daily routine

das Studentenbudget (-s) student budget

das Studentenheim (-e) dormitory (2)

die Studentenkneipe (-n) student pub

das Studentenleben (-) student life

das Studentenwohnheim (-e) dormitory (2)

die Studentenzeitung (-en) student newspaper

das Studentenzimmer (-) student's room

der Studienabgänger (-) graduate

die Studienbedingung (-en) university requirement

die Studiendauer length of study program

das Studienfach (¨er) academic subject

die Studiengebühren (*pl.*) fees, tuition (12)

das Studienjahr (-e) academic year

der Studienplatz (¨e) place at a university

die Studienreise (-n) study trip

studieren to study (1)

das Studio (-s) studio

das Studium (Studien) course of studies

der Stuhl (¨e) chair (2)

die Stunde (-n) hour (4)

stundenlang for hours

der Stundenplan (¨e) hourly class schedule

stur stubborn, obstinate

das Substantiv (-e) noun

die Substanz (-en) substance

die Suche search; **auf der Suche nach** searching for

suchen to look for (2)

(das) Südamerika South America

süddeutsch southern German

(das) Süddeutschland southern Germany

der Süden south; **im Süden** (in the) south

südlich von (+ *dat.*) to the south of

die Südseite (-n) south side

südwestlich (*adj.*) southwest

der Südwesten southwest

die Summe (-n) sum, amount

die Superlativform (-en) superlative form

der Supermarkt (¨e) supermarket (5)

die Supermarktanzeige (-n) supermarket ad

die Suppe (-n) soup (6)

das Surfbrett (-er) surfboard

surfen to surf

süß sweet; **etwas Süßes** something sweet

die Süßigkeiten (*pl.*) sweets

die Süßwaren (*pl.*) sweets

das Sweatshirt (-s) sweatshirt

(das) Sylt German island in the North Sea

das Symbol (-e) symbol

sympathisch likable, pleasant, nice (1)

das Symptom (-e) symptom

synkron synchronous(ly)

die Synthetik (-en) synthetic material

die Szene (-n) scene

T

der **Tabak** tobacco
die **Tabakpflanze** (-n) tobacco plant
der **Tabaksamen** (-) tobacco seed
tabellarisch in tabular form
die **Tabelle** (-n) table; index
das **Tablett** (-s) tray
die **Tablette** (-n) pill
die **Tafel** (-n) chalkboard; **die Tafel Schokolade** chocolate bar
der **Tag** (-e) day (2); **(guten) Tag** hello, good day (E); **eines Tages** one of these days; **jeden Tag** every day (7)
das **Tagebuch** (-̈er) diary; **Tagebuch führen** to keep a diary
die **Tagebucheintragung** (-en) diary entry
der **Tagesablauf** daily routine
die **Tageshälfte** (-n) half of the day
die **Tageshöchsttemperatur** (-en) maximum temperature during the day
das **Tagesprogramm** (-e) daily program
die **Tagesschau** *German television news program*
die **Tagestemperatur** (-en) temperature during the day
die **Tageszeit** (-en) time of day
die **Tageszeitung** (-en) daily newspaper
täglich daily (6)
tagsüber during the day
das **Tagungshotel** (-s) convention hotel
das **Talent** (-e) talent
der **Taler** (-) old German coin
die **Talkshow** (-s) talk show
tanken to get gasoline
die **Tankstelle** (-n) gas station (9)
die **Tante** (-n) aunt (3)
der **Tanz** (-̈e) dance (1)
das **Tanzen** dancing; **jemanden zum Tanzen auffordern** to ask someone to dance
tanzen to dance (1); **Er tanzt gut.** He dances well. (1)
die **Tasche** (-n) bag, handbag (5); pocket
das **Taschenbuch** (-̈er) paperback book
das **Taschengeld** allowance
die **Taschenuhr** (-en) pocket watch
die **Tasse** (-n) cup (4); **eine Tasse Kaffee** a cup of coffee (4)
tätig sein to be active; to work
die **Tätigkeit** (-en) position, activity (11)
der **Tätigkeitsbereich** (-e) field of activity
die **Tatsache** (-n) fact
tatsächlich in fact; actual
die **Taube** (-n) pigeon
tauchen to dive (7)
die **Taucherausrüstung** (-en) diving equipment
taumeln, ist getaumelt to sway, stagger
tauschen to exchange; to swap
tausend thousand (E)

tausendste thousandth
das **Taxi** (-s) taxicab (10)
der **Taxifahrer** (-) / die **Taxifahrerin** (-nen) taxi driver
das **Team** (-s) team
die **Technik** technology; technique (11); technical engineering
der **Technikberater** (-) / die **Technikberaterin** (-nen) technical advisor
technisch technical; mechanical
das/der **Techno** techno
der **Teddy** = **Teddybär**
der **Teddybär** (-en *masc.*) teddy bear
der **Tee** tea (5)
der **Teener** (-) teenager
die **Teigwaren** (*pl.*) pasta
(sich) teilen to share; to divide
teilhaben (hat teil), hatte teil, teilgehabt to have a share in
teilnehmen (an + *dat.*) (nimmt teil), nahm teil, teilgenommen to participate (14)
der **Teilnehmer** (-) / die **Teilnehmerin** (-nen) participant
die **Teilung** (-en) division
teilweise partly
das **Telefaxgerät** (-e) fax machine
das **Telefon** (-e) telephone (2)
der **Telefonanruf** (-e) telephone call
das **Telefonbuch** (-̈er) telephone directory
das **Telefongespräch** (-e) telephone call, conversation
telefonieren to telephone
telefonisch over the telephone
die **Telefonkarte** (-n) telephone card (*for use in public telephones instead of coins*)
die **Telefonnummer** (-n) telephone number; **Wie ist deine/Ihre Telefonnummer?** What is your telephone number? (E)
die **Telefonrechnung** (-en) telephone bill
das **Telegramm** (-e) telegram
der **Teller** (-) plate (6)
das **Temperament** (-e) temperament
die **Temperatur** (-en) temperature (7)
das **Tempo** (-s) speed
das **Tempolimit** (-s) speed limit
(das) Tennis tennis; **Tennis spielen** to play tennis (7)
die **Tennisanlage** (-n) tennis court
der **Tennisplatz** (-̈e) tennis court (7)
der **Tennisschuh** (-e) tennis shoe (5)
die **Tennissocke** (-n) tennis sock
das **Tennistraining** tennis practice
der **Teppich** (-e) rug, carpet (2)
der **Teppichboden** (-̈) wall-to-wall carpeting (12)
der **Termin** (-e) appointment (8)
die **Terrakotta** (**Terrakotten**) terracotta

die **Terrasse** (-n) terrace (2)
der **Terror** terror
der **Terrorismus** terrorism (14)
der **Terrorist** (-en *masc.*) / die **Terroristin** (-nen) terrorist
das **Testergebnis** (-se) test result
teuer expensive(ly) (2)
teuflisch devilish
der **Text** (-e) text
der **Textausschnitt** (-e) (text) excerpt
das **Theater** (-) theater (4); **ins Theater gehen** to go to the theater (4)
die **Theaterkarte** (-n) theater ticket
das **Theaterstück** (-e) play (4)
das **Thema** (**Themen**) theme; topic
die **Theorie** (-n) theory
das **Thermalbad** (-̈er) thermal bath
der **Thermalbrunnen** (-) thermal spring
die **Thermalkur** (-en) thermal cure
das **Thermometer** (-) thermometer
der **Thunfisch** (-e) tuna fish
(das) Thüringen *one of the German states*
der **Tick** (-s) tic, twitching
das **Ticket** (-s) ticket
tief low; deep; **tief schlafen** to be in a deep sleep
die **Tiefgarage** (-n) underground garage
tiefgekühlt frozen
das **Tier** (-e) animal (12)
der **Tierarzt** (-̈e) / die **Tierärztin** (-nen) veterinarian
der **Tiger** (-) tiger
der **Tipp** (-s) hint, piece of advice
tippen to type
der **Tiroler Hut** Tyrolean hat
der **Tisch** (-e) table (2); **den Tisch decken** to set the table
das **Tischchen** (-) little table
die **Tischreservierung** (-en) table reservation
(das) Tischtennis table tennis
die **Tischwäsche** table linen
der **Titel** (-) title
der **Toast** (-e) toast
die **Tochter** (-̈) daughter (3)
der **Tod** death
tödlich deathly; to death
die **Toilette** (-n) toilet
der **Toilettenartikel** (*pl.*) toiletries
das **Toilettenpapier** toilet paper (5)
die **Toilettensachen** (*pl.*) toiletries
toll! (*coll.*) super! (1); **ganz toll!** super! (1), great!
die **Tomate** (-n) tomato (5)
der **Ton** (-̈e) sound
die **Tonne** (-n) ton
das **Tor** (-e) gate; (*soccer*) goal
der **Tornister** (-) field pack
die **Torte** (-n) torte, pie, cake
tot dead

total total(ly); **Ich bin total dagegen.** I'm totally against it. (14)

die Tour (-en) tour

das Tourenprogramm (-e) tour program

der Tourismus tourism

der Tourist (-en *masc.***) / die Touristin (-nen)** tourist

die Touristeninformation (-en) tourist information

das Tourrad (⸚er) touring bike

die Tracht (-en) traditional costume

die Tradition (-en) tradition

traditionell traditional

traditionsgemäß traditionally

tragen (trägt), trug, getragen to wear; to carry (5); **die Verantwortung tragen** to be responsible

die Tragik tragedy

die Tragödie (-n) tragedy (4)

trainieren to train; to practice

das Training training, practice

der Trainingsanzug (⸚e) jogging suit

trampen, ist getrampt to hitchhike

die Transportbranche (-n) transportation business

das Transportmittel (-) means of transportation

der Transportweg (-e) transport road

trauen to trust

der Traum (⸚e) dream

träumen (von + *dat.***)** to dream (of)

traumhaft: traumhaft schön unbelievably beautiful

traurig sad (1)

die Traurigkeit sadness

(sich) treffen (mit + *dat.***) (trifft), traf, getroffen** to meet (8)

der Treffpunkt (-e) meeting place

treiben, trieb, getrieben: Sport treiben to engage in sports (7); **Schwarzhandel treiben** to trade on the black market

trennbar separable

(sich) trennen to separate (14)

die Trennung (-en) separation

die Treppe (-n) staircase (12)

das Treppenhaus (⸚er) stairwell

treten (tritt), trat, ist getreten to step (on)

die Tretmühle (-n) daily grind

treu loyal (1); faithful

der Trimm-Pfad (-e) jogging path

sich trimmen to exercise in order to lose weight

trinken, trank, getrunken to drink (2)

die Trinkkur (-en) mineral-water drinking cure

trocken dry

die Trompete (-n) trumpet

trompeten to play the trumpet

der Tropfen (-) drop

trotz (+ *gen.***)** in spite of (9)

trotzdem nevertheless

die Trümmer (*pl.***)** rubble, ruins

die Truppen (*pl.***)** troops

der Truthahn (⸚e) turkey (5)

das Truthahnschnitzel (-) turkey cutlet

(das) Tschechien Czech Republic (E)

(das) Tschernobyl Chernobyl

tschüss (*coll.***)** so long, bye (E)

das T-Shirt (-s) T-shirt (5)

das Tuch (⸚er) scarf; piece of cloth

die Tüchtigkeit efficiency

der/die Tumorkranke (*decl. adj.***)** person suffering from a tumor

tun, tat, getan to do (8); **Was tun?** What can be done?; **viel zu tun haben** to be busy; **weh tun (***dat.***) (tut weh)** to hurt (8); **Das tut mir Leid.** I'm sorry. (9)

der Tuner (-) (radio) tuner

der Tunnel (-) tunnel

die Tür (-en) door (2); **die Türen knallen** to slam the doors

der Türke (-n *masc.***) / die Türkin (-nen)** Turk, Turkish person

die Türkei Turkey

türkisch Turkish

der Turm (⸚e) tower

turnen to do gymnastics (7)

die Turnhalle (-n) gymnasium (7)

die Turnschuhe (*pl.***)** gym shoes; sneakers

der Typ (-en) type

typisch typical

U

die U-Bahn (-en) subway

die U-Bahnstation (-en) subway station

übel nauseated; **Mir ist übel.** I feel nauseated.

üben to practice

über (+ *acc./dat.***)** over, above (6); about

überall everywhere

überarbeitet overhauled; overworked

überblicken to overlook, have a good view of

die Überdachung (-en) roof cover

überdurchschnittlich above average

übereinander one on top of the other

überfliegen, überflog, überflogen to skim (a text), read quickly (13)

überfordert asked too much; overtaxed

überfüllt overcrowded

überglücklich overjoyed

überhaupt at all; **überhaupt nicht** not at all

überheblich arrogant

überholen to pass (a vehicle)

überlassen (überlässt), überließ, überlassen to leave to

sich (*dat.***) etwas überlegen** to think about something; **Ich will es mir überlegen.** I want to think about it.

die Überlegung (-en) consideration

der Übermut exuberance

übernachten to stay overnight (9)

die Übernachtung (-en) overnight stay (9)

die Übernachtungskosten (*pl.***)** lodging expenses

übernehmen (übernimmt), übernahm, übernommen to take over (11)

überprüfen to double-check

überqueren to cross (a street)

überraschen to surprise

überreden to talk into, persuade

die Überredungskunst (⸚e) persuasiveness, ability to persuade

überregional national (for a newspaper)

überschwemmt flooded

der Übersetzer (-) / die Übersetzerin (-nen) translator, interpreter

übertragen (überträgt), übertrug, übertragen to transfer

die Übertragung (-en) (live) show; broadcast

übertreiben, übertrieb, übertrieben to exaggerate

übertrieben exaggerated (14)

übertrumpfen to outdo

überwiegend predominant(ly)

überzeugen to convince

das Übliche (*decl. adj.***)** the usual (thing)

übrig left over (12)

übrigens by the way, furthermore (9)

die Übung (-en) exercise

das Ufer (-) bank (of a body of water)

das Ufo (-s) UFO (flying saucer)

die Uhr (-en) clock (2); **Wie viel Uhr ist es?** What time is it? (4); **Die Uhr geht nicht.** The clock isn't working.

der Uhrmacher (-) / die Uhrmacherin (-nen) watchmaker

die Uhrzeit (-en) time of day (4)

die Ukraine Ukraine

ultramodern extremely modern

um (+ *acc.***)** at (3); **um fünf Uhr** until five o'clock (6); **Um wie viel Uhr?** At what time? (4); **um ... herum** around (*spatial*) (3); **um zwei** at two (4); **um ... zu** in order to

umarmen to embrace, hug

der Umfang size

umfassen to include, consist of

die Umfrage (-n) poll, survey

umgebaut remodeled

die Umgebung (-en) area, neighborhood, vicinity (12); **nähere Umgebung** close vicinity

umgehen mit (geht um), ging um, ist umgegangen to deal with, treat

umgekehrt the other way around

umgestalten (gestaltet um) to remodel

das Umland (⸚er) surrounding countryside
der Umlaut (-e) mark indicating change of vowel sound
die Umleitung (-en) detour
ums = um das
umsatteln (sattelt um) to change, switch
der Umsatz (⸚e) sales, turnover
die Umsatzstatistik (-en) sales statistic(s)
die Umschulung (-en) vocational retraining
der Umstand (⸚e) condition
umsteigen (steigt um), stieg um, ist umgestiegen to transfer, change (trains) (10)
umstellen (stellt um) to reset
die Umwälzung (-en) upheaval
die Umwelt environment
die Umweltbelastung (-en) environmental pollution
umweltbewusst conscious of the environment
die Umweltbranche (-n) environmental business
der Umweltbus (-se) ecological bus
umweltfreundlich environmentally friendly (14)
umweltschädlich environmentally harmful, polluting
der Umweltschutz environmental protection
die Umweltverschmutzung environmental pollution (14)
umweltverträglich environmentally safe
umziehen (zieht um), zog um, ist umgezogen to move (residence)
der Umzug (⸚e) move
unabhängig independent
unbedingt absolutely, by all means (13)
unbegrenzt unlimited
unbehandelt untreated
unbekannt unknown
unbemerkt unnoticed
unbeschadet unharmed
unbestimmt uncertain
unbewohnt vacant
und and (E)
und so weiter and so on (etc.)
unentschieden: Das Spiel ist unent- schieden. The game ends in a tie.
unerlaubt forbidden, not permitted
unerträglich unbearable
unerwartet unexpected
der Unfall (⸚e) accident
unfreundlich unfriendly (1)
der Unfug nonsense
(das) Ungarn Hungary (E)
ungeduldig impatient
ungefähr approximately, about (9)
ungeheuer immense(ly)
ungehindert unobstructed

ungemütlich uncomfortable
ungenügend insufficient
ungern (+ verb) to dislike . . . (2)
ungestört undisturbed(ly)
ungesund unhealthy
ungewöhnlich unusual
das Ungeziefer vermin, bugs
ungezwungen casual, relaxed
unglaublich unbelievable
das Unglück (-e) accident
unheimlich terrific
unhöflich impolite
die Uni = Universität
die Unibibliothek (-en) university library
die Uniform (-en) uniform
die Universität (-en) university; college (1)
der Universitätsprofessor (-en) / die Universitätsprofessorin (-nen) university professor
die Universitätsstadt (⸚e) university town
unkompliziert uncomplicated
unkonventionell unconventional
die Unkosten (pl.) expenses
unkritisch uncritical (1)
unlogisch illogical
unmittelbar direct(ly)
unmöbiliert unfurnished (2)
unmöglich impossible
unnötig unnecessary
die Unordnung disorder, mess
unpersönlich impersonal
unpraktisch impractical (1)
unregelmäßig irregular
die Unruhe unrest
uns us (acc.) (3); (dat.) (5)
unser our (3)
unsicher insecure
der Unsinn nonsense (14); **So ein Unsinn! Nonsense!** (14)
unsympathisch unlikable (1)
unteilbar indivisible
unten downstairs; below
unten erwähnt mentioned below
unter (+ acc./dat.) under, below; among, beneath (6); **unter anderem** among other things; **unter uns** between (the two of) us
unterbrechen (unterbricht), unterbrach, unterbrochen to interrupt
die Unterbrechung (-en) interruption
unterernährt malnourished
untergehen (geht unter), ging unter, ist untergegangen to go down; (sun) to set
die Untergrundbahn (-en) subway
der Unterhalt upkeep, support
sich unterhalten (unterhält), unterhielt, unterhalten to entertain (oneself); to converse (13)

unterhaltsam entertaining (13)
die Unterhaltung entertainment (13); **zur Unterhaltung** for entertainment (13)
die Unterkunft (⸚e) accommodation (9)
die Unterkunftsmöglichkeit (-en) accommodations
die Unterlagen (pl.) documentation, papers (11)
die Untermiete sublet (11); **zur Untermiete wohnen** to rent a room
das Unternehmen (-) business, enterprise
unternehmen (unternimmt), unternahm, unternommen to undertake (10); **eine Reise unternehmen** to take a trip
die Unternehmensberatung business consultant
das Unterrichtsfach (⸚er) subject of instruction
der Unterrichtstag (-e) day of school
unterschätzen to underestimate
der Unterschied (-e) difference
unterschreiben, unterschrieb, unterschrieben to sign
die Unterschrift (-en) signature
unterstreichen, unterstrich, unterstrichen to underline
unterstützen to support (14)
untersuchen to examine
untertags during the day
der Untertitel (-) subtitle
die Unterwäsche (pl.) underwear
unterwegs on the road
die Unterwürfigkeit servility
unterzeichnen to sign
untrennbar inseparable
unübersehbar incalculable
unverletzt unharmed
unverschämt impertinent
unwichtig unimportant
unwohnlich not livable; uncomfortable
unzumutbar unacceptable
der Urenkel (-) / die Urenkelin (-nen) great-grandson; great-granddaughter
die Urgroßeltern (pl.) great-grandparents
die Urgroßmutter (⸚) great-grandmother
der Urgroßvater (⸚) great-grandfather
der Urlaub (-e) vacation; **Urlaub machen** to go on vacation (8)
das Urlaubshotel (-s) resort hotel
die Urlaubspläne (pl.) vacation plans
die Urlaubstipps (pl.) vacation advice
die Ursache (-n) cause
ursprünglich original(ly)
die USA (pl.) the United States; **aus den USA** from the United States
usw. = und so weiter and so on

V

der Valentinstag (-e) Valentine's Day (3)
der Vampir (-e) vampire
das Vanilleeis vanilla ice cream

die Vanillesauce (-n) vanilla sauce
der Vater (∴) father (3)
väterlicherseits on the father's side
Vati Daddy
der Vegetarier (-) / die Vegetarierin (-nen) vegetarian (*person*)
vegetarisch vegetarian (6)
(das) Venedig Venice (Italy)
die Verabredung (-en) date; appointment
verabschieden: ein Gesetz verabschieden to pass a law
verändern to change
die Veränderung (-en) change
veranstalten to put on (an event)
die Veranstaltung (-en) event
verantwortlich responsible (11)
die Verantwortung (-en) responsibility (11)
verarbeiten to process
das Verb (-en) verb
verbessern to correct; to improve
die Verbesserung (-en) improvement; correction
verbieten, verbot, verboten to prohibit (14); **Rauchen verboten** no smoking
verbinden, verband, verbunden to connect
die Verbindung (-en) connection
verborgen: im Verborgenen leben to live in isolation
der Verbrauch consumption
verbrauchen to consume (14)
der Verbraucher (-) / die Verbraucherin (-nen) consumer
verbreiten to spread, disseminate (14)
verbringen, verbrachte, verbracht to spend (7); **Zeit verbringen** to spend time
verbunden connected
verdanken (+ *dat.*) to be indebted to
verdienen to earn; to deserve (11); **Geld verdienen** to earn money (11); **es sich** (*dat.*) **verdient haben** to deserve it
der Verdruss dissatisfaction
der Verein (-e) club
die Vereinbarung: nach Vereinbarung by appointment
vereinfachen to simplify
vereinigt united; **die Vereinigten Staaten** (*pl.*) United States
die Vereinigung (-en) unification
vereint: vereintes Europa united Europe
die Verfassung (-en) constitution
verfolgen to follow; to persecute
verfügen über (+ *acc.*) to control
Verfügung: zur Verfügung stehen to be available, be at one's disposal
die Vergangenheit past
vergehen, verging, ist vergangen to pass; **Ein Monat ist vergangen.** A month

has passed.; **Die Zeit vergeht wie im Flug.** Time flies by.
vergessen (vergisst), vergaß, vergessen to forget (10)
vergiften to poison
die Vergiftung (-en) poisoning
der Vergleich (-e) comparison
vergleichen, verglich, verglichen to compare (12)
das Vergnügen (-) pleasure
vergnüglich amusing
die Vergnügung (-en) amusement, entertainment
sich verhalten (verhält), verhielt, verhalten to act, behave
das Verhältnis (-se) condition; relationship, affair
sich verhaspeln to get muddled (speaking)
verheiratet married
verhindern to prevent
verhüten to prevent
das Verhütungsmittel (-) contraceptive
verkaufen to sell
der Verkäufer (-) / die Verkäuferin (-nen) salesperson (2)
das Verkaufsgebiet (-e) sales region
das Verkaufstalent (-e) salesmanship
das Verkaufstraining sales training
der Verkehr traffic
das Verkehrsamt (∴er) tourist office
die Verkehrsbelästigung (-en) traffic disturbance
der Verkehrsknotenpunkt (-e) traffic junction
die Verkehrskontrolle (-n) vehicle checkpoint
der Verkehrsminister (-) / die Verkehrsministerin (-nen) transportation minister
das Verkehrsmittel (-) vehicle, means of transportation (14)
die Verkehrsplanung traffic planning
verkehrsreich heavily traveled (*street*)
das Verkehrsschild (-er) traffic sign
das Verkehrssystem (-e) traffic system
das Verkehrswesen (-) transportation system
verkehrt the other way around; **Kaffee verkehrt** more milk than coffee
verkleidet dressed up (in costume)
das Verknoten wringing (of hands)
verkraften to handle, cope with
verkrüppelt crippled
die Verkündigung (-en) announcement
verkürzen to shorten
der Verlag (-e) publishing house
verlangen to demand
verlängern to lengthen
verlassen (verlässt), verließ, verlassen to leave

verlässlich reliable
verlegen to relocate
der Verleger (-) / die Verlegerin (-nen) publisher
die Verlegung (-en) relocation
verleihen: Farbe verleihen to give color
sich verletzen to injure oneself (8)
die Verletzung (-en) injury; violation (14)
sich verlieben in (+ *acc.*) to fall in love with
verlieren, verlor, verloren to lose
sich verloben (mit + *dat.*) to get engaged (to)
verlogen sein to be full of lies
der Verlust (-e) loss
sich vermehren to multiply
vermeiden, vermied, vermieden to avoid (14)
vermieten to rent out (to someone) (12); **zu vermieten** for rent
der Vermieter (-) / die Vermieterin (-nen) landlord, landlady
vermindern to decrease, lessen (14)
vermitteln to arrange; to mediate
das Vermögen (-) capital
vermuten to assume
vernichten to destroy
die Vernunft: bar jeder Vernunft totally senseless
verordnen to prescribe
die Verpackung (-en) packaging, wrapping (14)
die Verpackungsflut (-en) excess use of packaging
die Verpackungsindustrie (-n) packaging industry
sich verpflichten to commit oneself; **Adel verpflichtet** nobility has a responsibility, noblesse oblige
verraten (verrät), verriet, verraten to betray
verräterisch treacherous
verreisen, ist verreist to go on a trip (10); **verreist sein** to be on a trip
verringern to reduce
verrückt crazy, mad (8)
der Versandkatalog (-e) mail-order catalogue
versäumen to miss
verschaffen: (sich) Gehör verschaffen to make (oneself) heard
verschieden different
verschliessen, verschloss, verschlossen to lock up
verschmutzen to pollute
die Verschmutzung (-en) pollution
verschoben (*adj.*) postponed
verschreiben, verschrieb, verschrieben to prescribe (8)
verschrotten to scrap
verschuldet in debt

verschwenden to waste

das Versehen (-) mishap; **aus Versehen** by accident

die Versicherung (-en) insurance (12)

der Versicherungsfachmann (:er) / die Versicherungsfachfrau (-en) insurance expert

der Versicherungskaufmann (Versicherungskaufleute) / die Versicherungskauffrau (-en) insurance sales agent

die Version (-en) version

versorgen to supply (with)

verspätet delayed

die Verspätung (-en) delay

versprechen (verspricht), versprach, versprochen to promise

versprühen to spray around

der Verstand reason

verständlich understandable; understandably

das Verständnis (-se) understanding

verstehen, verstand, verstanden to understand; **sich verstehen mit** to get along with; **Ich verstehe das nicht.** I don't understand. (E)

versteigern to auction off

verstopfen to clog up

verstoßen: gegen das Gesetz verstoßen to do something illegal

versuchen to try (8)

verteidigen to defend

verteilen to distribute

vertonen to set to music

der Vertrag (:e) contract; lease; **einen Vertrag schließen** to sign a contract

vertrauensvoll trusting

der Vertreter (-) / die Vertreterin (-nen) sales representative

der/die Vertriebene (*decl. adj.*) refugee

der Vertriebsrepräsentant (-en *masc.*) / **die Vertriebsrepräsentantin (-nen)** marketing representative

verunsichert insecure

verursachen to cause

vervollkommnen to make perfect

vervollständigen to complete

die Verwaltung (-en) administration

der Verwaltungsweg (-e) administrative route

das Verwaltungszentrum (Verwaltungszentren) administrative center

die Verwandlung (-en) transformation

verwandt mit related to (3)

die Verwandschaft (-en) relationship

der/die Verwandte (*decl. adj.*) relative

die Verwechslung (-en) mistake, confusion

verwenden to use, apply (14)

verwirklichen to make real

verwirrt confused

der/die Verwundete (*decl. adj.*) injured person

verzehren to consume

verzeichnet sein to be marked/listed

das Verzeichnis (-se) list, index

verzichten auf (+ *acc.*) to do without (13)

verziert decorated

der Vetter (-n) male cousin (3)

das Video (-s) video(tape) (2)

das Videogerät (-e) VCR

die Videokamera (-s) video camera

der Videorecorder (-) video recorder (VCR) (2)

das Videospiel (-e) video game

das Vieh cattle; animals

viel (mehr, meist-) a lot, much (1); **Viel Glück!** Good luck! (1); **Vielen Dank!** Many thanks! (6); **Viel Spaß!** Have fun! (1)

viele (*pl.*) many (2); **wie viele** how many

die Vielfalt diversity

vielleicht maybe, perhaps (2)

vielmehr rather

vier four (E); **zu viert** with four people

das Viermächteabkommen (-) four-power pact

viermal four times

viertägig (*adj.*) four-day

vierte fourth (3)

das Viertel (-) quarter; **Es ist Viertel nach/vor zwei.** It is a quarter after/to two. (4)

vierzehn fourteen (E)

vierzig forty (E)

die Villa (Villen) villa

vis-à-vis across from

das Visum (Visen) visa

das Vitamin (-e) vitamin

die Vitamintablette (-n) vitamin pill

der Vogel (:) bird

der Vogelkäfig (-e) bird cage

der Vogelschutz bird preservation

das Vöglein (-) little bird

die Vokabeln (*pl.*) vocabulary

die Vokabelsuche vocabulary search

die Vokabelübung (-en) vocabulary exercise

die Vokaländerung (-en) vowel change

das Volk (:er) nation; people

der Volksaufstand (:e) people's revolt

das Volksfest (-e) public festival; fair

die Volksfeststimmung (-en) party mood

das Volkslied (-er) folk song

die Volksschule elementary school

der Volkssport national sport

die Volkswirtschaft economics

voll full; crowded (6); **in voller Uniform** dressed in full uniform

vollenden to achieve, complete

völlig total(ly)

das Vollkornbrot (-e) whole-grain bread

die Vollkornnudeln (*pl.*) whole-grain pasta

die Vollmilch whole milk

die Vollpension accommodation and three meals per day included

vollständig complete

voll tanken (tankt voll) to get gasoline, fill up

vollwert full nutritional value

vom = von dem

von (+ *dat.*) from; by (5); of; out of; **von... bis** from . . . to (6)

vor (+ *acc./dat.*) before (4); in front of; ago (6); **vor allem** above all; **vor kurzem** recently; **vor sich hin** to oneself; **vor Florida** off the coast of Florida; **fünf vor zwei** five to/of two (4); **vor zwei Tagen** two days ago (6)

vorankommen (kommt voran), kam voran, ist vorangekommen to get ahead

die Voraufführung (-en) preview performance

voraus; im voraus in advance; **voraus sein** to be ahead

die Voraussetzung (-en) prerequisite

vorbei past, gone, over (9); **vorbei sein** to be gone

vorbeifahren (fährt vorbei), fuhr vorbei, ist vorbeigefahren to drive past

vorbeigehen (geht vorbei), ging vorbei, ist vorbeigegangen to pass by

vorbeikommen (kommt vorbei), kam vorbei, ist vorbeigekommen to drop in, come by (4)

vorbeimarschieren (marschiert vorbei) to march past

sich vorbereiten (auf) (bereitet vor) to prepare (for) (11)

die Vorderseite (-n) front side

der Vorfall (:e) incident

vorgebeugt bent forward

vorgestern day before yesterday

vorhaben (hat vor) to plan, have plans (4)

vorhanden sein to exist

vorher before that; before

die Vorhersage (-n) forecast

vorig previous, last

vorkommen (kommt vor), kam vor, ist vorgekommen to occur

die Vorlesung (-en) (university) lecture

vorletzt-: die vorletzte Woche week before last

vorliegend at hand

der Vormittag (-e) before noon; **morgen Vormittag** tomorrow morning; **heute Vormittag** today before noon; **Samstagvormittag** Saturday before noon

vormittags before noon (4)

vorn in the front; **nach vorne** toward the front

der Vorname (-ns, -n) first, given name (1)

vorne in front (6); **ganz vorne** way in front

vornehmen (nimmt vor), nahm vor, vorgenommen to plan, carry out

der Vorort (-e) suburb

der Vorortszug (:e) commuter train

der Vorraum (:e) front hall

der Vorsatz (:e) resolution

die Vorschau (-en) preview

der Vorschlag (:e) suggestion

vorschlagen (schlägt vor), schlug vor, vorgeschlagen to suggest (10)

vorsetzen (setzt vor) to place in front

vorsichtig careful, cautious

der/die Vorsitzende (*decl. adj.*) chairperson

die Vorspeise (-n) appetizer (6)

die Vorstadt (:e) suburb

sich (*dat.*) **vorstellen (stellt vor)** to imagine (11); **sich** (*acc.*) **vorstellen** to introduce oneself (11); **die Uhr vorstellen** to set the clock forward; **Stell dir vor!** Just imagine!

die Vorstellung (-en) performance; introduction; concept

das Vorstellungsgespräch (-e) job interview (11)

der Vorteil (-e) advantage

der Vortrag (:e) lecture (4)

der Vorverkauf (:e) advance sale

die Vorverkaufsstelle (-n) advance sales agency

vorwärts forward

vorwärts kommen (kommt vorwärts), kam vorwärts, ist vorwärts gekommen to get ahead

vorweisen (weist vor), wies vor, vorgewiesen to show, present

das Vorwort (-e) preface

vorziehen (zieht vor), zog vor, vorgezogen to prefer (14)

vorzüglich excellent

der VW (-s) (*automobile*) Volkswagen

W

wach werden (wird wach) to wake up

wachsen (wächst), wuchs, ist gewachsen to grow

wachsend increasing, growing

die Waffe (-n) weapon

der Waffenexport (-e) arms export

der Wagen (-) car (10)

die Wagenauffahrt (-en) driveway

der Waggon (-s) (train) car

die Wahl (-en) election

wählen to vote, elect; to choose (14)

wahlweise optional

der Wahnsinn madness

wahr true; **nicht wahr?** isn't it true?

während (+ *gen.*) during; while (9)

die Wahrheit truth

wahrscheinlich probably (11)

die Währung (-en) currency

die Währungsreform (-en) *1948 introduction of new German currency*

die Währungsunion (-en) *equalization of East- and West-German monetary systems*

der Wald (:er) forest (7)

der Waldweg (-e) forest trail

die Walküre *opera by Richard Wagner*

der Walzer (-) waltz

die Wand (:e) wall (2); **die vier Wände** (*fig.*) one's home

die Wanderfahrt (-en) field trip

die Wanderkarte (-n) trail map

das Wandermagazin (-e) magazine for hikers

wandern, ist gewandert to hike (1)

die Wanderreise (-n) walking tour

die Wanderschuhe (*pl.*) hiking shoes

der Wanderstock (:e) hiking stick

die Wandertour (-en) hiking tour

die Wanderung (-en) hike; walking tour

der Wanderweg (-e) hiking trail

wanken, ist gewankt to stagger, sway

wann when (1); **seit wann** since when

das Wappen (-) coat of arms

das Wappentier (-e) heraldic animal

wäre: Wie wäre es mit... ? How about . . . ? (13)

die Ware (-n) goods, product

warm warm (7); heated; **schön warm** nice and warm (7); **warme Küche** hot food

die Wärme warmth

warmherzig warm-hearted

(das) Warschau Warsaw (Poland)

warten auf (+ *acc.*) to wait for (6)

warum why (2)

was what (1); **was für ein** what kind of (a) (11); **Was ist denn los?** What's the matter? (2)

das Waschbecken (-) sink

die Wäsche underwear; linens; **Wäsche waschen** to do one's laundry

die Wäschegarnitur (-en) lingerie ensemble

(sich) waschen (wäscht), wusch, gewaschen to wash (oneself) (8); **Ich wasche mir die Hände.** I am washing my hands.

der Wäschetrockner (-) clothes dryer (13)

das Wäschewaschen doing laundry

die Waschküche (-n) laundry room

die Waschmaschine (-n) washing machine

das Waschmittel (-) laundry detergent

der Waschraum (:e) washroom

der Waschvollautomat (-en *masc.***)** washing machine

das Wasser water (5)

die Wassermusik water music

das Wasserskifahren waterskiing

die Watte absorbent cotton

das WC toilet; bathroom (9)

der Wechsel (-) change

der Wechselkurs (-e) exchange rate

wechseln to change, exchange; **Geld wechseln** to exchange money

der Wecker (-) alarm clock (2)

das Weckglas (:er) preserving jar

weg away, off; **weit weg von...** far away from the . . . (2)

der Weg (-e) path, way; road (9); **jemand nach dem Weg fragen** to ask someone for directions (9)

wegbleiben (bleibt weg), blieb weg, ist weggeblieben to stay away

wegen (+ *gen.*) because of, on account of (9)

weggehen (geht weg), ging weg, ist weggegangen to leave

wegnehmen (nimmt weg), nahm weg, weggenommen to take away

wegwerfen (wirft weg), warf weg, weggeworfen to throw away

die Wegwerfflasche (-n) non-recyclable bottle (14)

das Wegwerfprodukt (-e) disposable product

der Wehrdienst military service

sich wehren to defend oneself

(sich *dat.***) weh tun (tut weh), tat weh, weh getan** to hurt (oneself) (8); **Das tut mir weh.** That hurts. (8)

weiblich feminine

weich soft

der Weichkäse (-) soft (young) cheese

(das) Weihnachten Christmas (3)

der Weihnachtsbaum (:e) Christmas tree (3)

das Weihnachtsgeschenk (-e) Christmas present

weil (*subord. conj.*) because (8)

die Weile while, span of time (11); **eine Weile lang** for a while

weilen: unter den Lebenden weilen to be alive

der Wein (-e) wine (6); **eine Flasche Wein** a bottle of wine

weinen to cry

die Weinflasche (-n) wine bottle

die Weintraube (-n) grape (5)

die Weise (-n) manner, way

weisen, wies, gewiesen to point

weiß white (5)

das Weißbier (-e) wheat beer
das Weißbierglas (:er) *special glass used for* **Weißbier**
der Weißwein (-e) white wine
die Weißwurst (:e) white sausage (6)
weit far (9); **weit von hier** far from here; **ganz schön weit** pretty far; **weit weg von** far away from (2)
weitaus by far
weiter further, farther; (+ *verb*) to continue to . . .
weiter bestehen (besteht weiter), bestand weiter, weiter bestanden to continue to exist
weiterentwickeln (entwickelt weiter) to develop further
weitergehen (geht weiter), ging weiter, ist weitergegangen to continue walking
weitermachen (macht weiter) to continue
welcher, welche, welches which (5)
der Wellensittich (-e) parakeet
die Welt world, earth (14)
weltbekannt world famous
der Welthunger world hunger
die Welthungerorganisation (-en) world hunger organization
die Weltkonferenz (-en) world conference
der Weltkrieg (-e) world war
die Weltreise (-n) trip around the world
weltweit throughout the world, global
wem (to/for) whom (5)
wen whom (*acc.*)
wenig little (8); **zu wenig** too little
wenige (*pl.*) few, a few
weniger less
wenigstens at least
wenn (*subord. conj.*) when; if; whenever (8)
wer who (1)
die Werbeagentur (-en) advertising agency
das Werbeplakat (-e) advertising poster
der Werbetext (-e) advertising copy
der Werbespruch (:e) advertising slogan
die Werbung (-en) commercial (13)
werden (wird), wurde, ist geworden to become (3); **leiser werdend** becoming more and more quiet
werfen (wirft), warf, geworfen to throw
das Werk (-e) work, opus
die Werkstatt (:en) workshop
das Werkzeug (-e) tool
der Wert (-e) value
das Wertpapier (-e) bond, stock
die Wertvorstellung (-en) concept of values
wesentlich essential(ly)
wessen whose
(das) Westberlin West Berlin

westberliner (*adj.*) (from) West Berlin
westdeutsch (*adj.*) West German
der Westen west (9); **im Westen** (in the) west; **nach Westen** to the west
die Western Musik Western music
(das) Westfalen Westphalia
westfälisch Westphalian
die Westküste (-n) west coast
westlich western, from the west
westlich von (+ *dat.*) to the west of
die Westmächte (*pl.*) Western powers (France, Great Britain, USA)
(das) Westpommern West Pomerania (*former German province*)
die Westzone (-n) western zone (*parts of Germany that later became the Federal Republic*)
der Wettbewerb (-e) contest
wetten to bet
das Wetter weather (7)
der Wetterbericht (-e) weather report (7)
der Wetterdienst weather service
der Wetterexperte (-n *masc.*) / **die Wetterexpertin (-nen)** weather expert
der Wetterhahn (:e) weathercock
die Wetterlage (-n) weather condition
die Wettervorhersage (-n) weather forecast
die WG = Wohngemeinschaft
Whg. = Wohnung
wichtig important (3)
wie how (1); **Wie bitte?** Pardon? What did you say? (E); **wie lange** how long; **wie viel** how much, **wie viele** how many; **Wie viel Uhr ist es?, Wie spät ist es?** What time is it? (4); **Wie wäre es mit...?** How about . . .? (13)
wieder again (2); back; **schon wieder** yet again (*emphatic*) (2)
der Wiederaufbau reconstruction
wieder aufbauen (baut wieder auf) to rebuild
wieder finden (findet wieder), fand wieder, wieder gefunden to find again, rediscover
wieder hochkommen (kommt wieder hoch), kam wieder hoch, ist wieder hochgekommen to come back up
wiederholen to repeat; to review (E)
die Wiederholung (-en) review; **zur Wiederholung** as a review
Wiederhören: auf Wiederhören good-bye (*only on the phone*) (9)
wiederkommen (kommt wieder), kam wieder, ist wiedergekommen to come back
Wiedersehen: (auf) Wiedersehen good-bye (E)
wiederum again
wieder verwenden (verwendet wieder) to reuse

wieder verwerten (verwertet wieder) to recycle
(das) Wien Vienna
das Wiener Schnitzel (-) breaded veal cutlet (6)
die Wiese (-n) meadow
wieso why
wildfremd: wildfremde Leute total strangers
das Wildgehege (-) game preserve
wild lebend wild, free
der Wildwestfilm (-e) Western (*movie*)
willkommen (*adj.*) welcome (E); **herzlich willkommen** welcome (E)
der Wind (-e) wind (7)
die Windenergie wind energy
windig windy (7)
das Windsurfen windsurfing
(das) Windsurfing machen to do windsurfing (7)
der Winter (-) winter (7)
der Wintermantel (:) winter coat
wir we (1)
wirken to have an effect
wirklich really (1)
die Wirklichkeit reality; **in Wirklichkeit** in fact, actually
die Wirkung (-en) effect
die Wirtschaft economy (13)
wirtschaftlich economic
das Wirtshaus (:er) pub (6)
die Wirtschaftswissenschaft (-en) economics
das Wirtschaftswunder (-) economic miracle
die Wirtschaftszeitung (-en) business magazine
das Wirtshaus (:er) pub
das Wissen knowledge
wissen (weiß), wusste, gewusst to know (a fact) (3); **Das weiß ich nicht.** I don't know. (E)
die Wissenschaft (-en) science
der Wissenschaftler (-) / die Wissenschaftlerin (-nen) scientist
wissenschaftlich scientific(ally), scholarly
die Witterung (-en) weather
der Witterungshinweis (-e) weather advisory
die Witwe (-n) widow
der Witz (-e) joke
wo where (1)
woanders elsewhere
wobei whereby
die Woche (-n) week (4); **einmal die Woche** once a week (7); **pro Woche** per week (4)
das Wochenende (-n) weekend (4); **am Wochenende** on the weekend
wochenlang for weeks

der Wochenplan (:e) weekly plan

der Wochentag (-e) day of the week (3)

die Wochenzeitung (-en) weekly newspaper

wodurch through what; by what

wofür for what; why

wogegen against what

woher from where (1); **Woher kommst du/kommen Sie?** Where are you from? (E)

wohin where (to) (5); **Wohin gehst du?** Where are you going?

wohinter behind what

wohl probably (11); **sich wohl fühlen (fühlt wohl)** to feel well; **wohl geachtet** respected

der Wohlstand affluence

wohnbar livable

der Wohnbereich (-e) living space

wohnen to reside, live (1)

die Wohngemeinschaft (-en) (WG) shared housing (2)

das Wohnheim (-e) (student) dormitory

der Wohnort (-e) place of residence (1)

das Wohnumfeld (-er) living environment

die Wohnung (-en) apartment (2)

das Wohnungsangebot (-e) for-rent ad

der Wohnungsschlüssel (-) house key

die Wohnungssuche apartment search

der Wohnungstyp (-en) type of apartment

der Wohnwagen (-) camper, trailer

das Wohnzimmer (-) living room (2)

die Wolke (-n) cloud (7)

das Wolkenband (:er) cloud bank

wolkenlos without clouds (7)

wolkig cloudy

die Wolle wool

wollen (will), wollte, gewollt to want (to) (4)

die Wollqualität (-en) wool quality

womit with what

wonach after what; according to what

woneben next to what

woran on what; about what

worauf on what; for what

woraus from what; of what

worin in what

das Wort (:er) word

das Wortelement (-e) word element

das Wörterbuch (:er) dictionary

das Wortratespiel (-e) word-guessing game

der Wortschatz vocabulary

die Wortschatzübung (-en) vocabulary exercise

der Wortteil (-e) part of word

worüber about what

worum about what; around what

worunter under what

wovon of what

wovor before what; in front of what; of what

wozu for what; why

wozwischen between what

wuchern to grow abundantly

wund (*adj.*) sore

das Wunder (-) miracle; **kein Wunder** no wonder

wunderbar wonderful

das Wunderkind (-er) child prodigy

der Wunsch (:e) wish

wünschen to wish (3)

würden: Würden Sie bitte... ? Would you please . . . ? (9)

der Wurmfortsatz (:e) (*anatomy*) appendix

die Wurst (:e) sausage (5)

das Würstchen (-) small sausage; hot dog

der Wurstsalat (-e) salad made of strips of cold cuts

würzen to season

Z

zaghaft timid(ly)

die Zahl (-en) number; amount; **die Postleitzahl** zip code (E)

zahlen to pay (5); **Zahlen, bitte!** Check, please! (6); **bar zahlen** to pay in cash

zählen to count

das Zahlenlotto (-s) number lottery

zahm tame

der Zahn (:e) tooth

der Zahnarzt (:e)/die Zahnärztin (-nen) dentist (11)

die Zahnpasta (Zahnpasten) toothpaste (5)

die Zahnschmerzen (*pl.*) toothache

zappeln to jerk

zart tender (5)

zärtlich affectionate

der Zauberer (-) / die Zauberin (-nen) magician

zaubern to do magic

z.B. (= zum Beispiel) for example

(das) ZDF *German television station*

die Zehe (-n) toe (8)

zehn ten (E)

der Zehner (-) ten-mark bill

der Zehnmarkschein (-e) ten-mark bill

zehnte tenth (3)

zehntreichst- tenth richest

das Zeichen (-) sign

zeichnen to draw, sketch (7)

der Zeichner (-) / die Zeichnerin (-nen) graphic artist (11)

die Zeichnung (-en) drawing (12)

zeigen to show (5)

die Zeile (-n) line

die Zeit (-en) time (2); **die ganze Zeit** all the time; **eine Zeit lang** for a while; **mit der Zeit** as time goes by; **um diese Zeit** at this time; **zur Zeit** now; **Die Zeit vergeht wie im Flug.** Time flies by. (10); **Zeit haben** to have time (2)

die Zeitansage (-n) time recording

das Zeitbudget (-s) time budget

die Zeitform (-en) time expression

der Zeitpunkt (-e) moment; time

die Zeitschrift (-en) magazine; periodical (13)

die Zeitung (-en) newspaper (1)

das Zeitunglesen reading newspapers

der Zeitungsleser (-) / die Zeitungsleserin (-nen) newspaper reader

zeitweise temporary; temporarily

das Zelt (-e) tent (10)

die Zensur (-en) grade (on a report card)

der Zentimeter (-) centimeter

zentral central(ly); **zentral gelegen** centrally located (2)

die Zentralheizung (-en) central heating

das Zentralnervensystem (-e) central nervous system

das Zentrum (Zentren) center; **im Zentrum** in the center of town

zerbrochen broken

zerschlagen shattered

zerstören to destroy

die Zerstörung (-en) destruction

der Zettel (-) piece of paper

das Zettelchen (-) small piece of paper

der Zeuge (-n *masc.*) / **die Zeugin (-nen)** witness

das Zeugnis (-se) report card; transcript; evaluation (from a former employer) (11)

ziehen, zog, ist/hat gezogen to pull; to move (somewhere)

das Ziel (-e) aim, goal, target; destination

die Zielstrebigkeit determination

ziemlich rather (6)

die Zigarette (-n) cigarette

der Zigeuner (-) / die Zigeunerin (-nen) gypsy

das Zimmer (-) room (2); **Dreizimmerwohnung** three-room apartment

die Zimmerbestellung (-en) room reservation

der Zimmergenosse (-n *masc.*) / **die Zimmergenossin (-nen)** roommate

der Zimmerkollege (-n *masc.*) / **die Zimmerkollegin (-nen)** roommate

die Zimmerpflanze (-n) houseplant (2)

die Zimmervermittlung (-en) room rental agency

zirka about, approximately

zitieren to quote

die Zitrone (-n) lemon

der Zivildienst community service (*as an alternative to military conscription*)

die Zivilisation (-en) civilization

der Zivilist (-en *masc.*) / die Zivilistin (-nen) civilian
zögern to hesitate
zögernd hesitant(ly)
der Zoll customs
die Zone (-n) zone; die Fußgängerzone (-n) pedestrian zone
der Zoo (-s) zoo
das Zoogelände (-) zoo grounds
zu (+ *dat.*) to (5); too; zu Hause at home (5)
das Zubehör accessories
zubereiten (bereitet zu) to prepare
zubetonieren (betoniert zu) to fill in with concrete
die Zucchini (*pl.*) zucchini
zucken: mit den Achseln zucken to shrug one's shoulders
der Zucker sugar (5)
zuckerkrank diabetic
zueinander to one another
zuerst (erst) first, at first (9)
zufrieden content, satisfied
der Zug (:e) train (10); mit dem Zug by train
der Zugang (:e) access
zugeben (gibt zu), gab zu, zugegeben to admit
zugeschneit covered with snow, snowed in
zügig fast
zugreifen (greift zu), griff zu, zugegriffen to grab
die Zugreise (-n) train trip
das Zugrestaurant (-s) train restaurant
die Zugspitze *name of Germany's highest mountain*
zu Hause home
das Zuhause home
zuhören (hört zu) to listen
die Zukunft future
zulassen (lässt zu), ließ zu, zugelassen to allow
zuletzt last, last time, finally
zum (= zu dem); zum Geburtstag for (your) birthday (3)
die Zunge (-n) tongue
zumachen (macht zu) to close
zumindest at least
zunächst first; for the time being
zunehmen (nimmt zu), nahm zu, zugenommen to increase, gain
zur = zu der

zurechtmachen (macht zurecht) to prepare
(jemandem) zureden (redet zu) to encourage
zurück back; hin und zurück roundtrip
zurückbringen (bringt zurück), brachte zurück, zurückgebracht to return (something)
zurückgeben (gibt zurück), gab zurück, zurückgegeben to give back
zurückhaltend reserved
zurückkommen (kommt zurück), kam zurück, ist zurückgekommen to come back, return (4)
zurückrufen (ruft zurück), rief zurück, zurückgerufen to call back
zurücktreten (tritt zurück), trat zurück, ist zurückgetreten to resign
zurückzahlen (zahlt zurück) to pay back
zurückziehen (zieht zurück), zog zurück, ist zurückgezogen to move back
zusagen: Es sagt mir nicht zu. I don't like it.
zusammen together (5); Das macht zusammen... That comes to . . . (5); zusammen oder getrennt together or separate (checks)
die Zusammenarbeit team work
zusammenfassen (fasst zusammen) to summarize
die Zusammenfassung (-en) summary
zusammengehören (gehört zusammen) to belong together
zusammengesetzt compounded
der Zusammenhang (:e) connection
zusammenhängen (hängt zusammen), hing zusammen, zusammengehangen to be connected
zusammenkrampfen: Mein Herz krampft sich zusammen. It breaks my heart.
zusammenleben (lebt zusammen) to live together
zusammenpassen (passt zusammen) to match
zusammenschlagen (schlägt zusammen), schlug zusammen, ist zusammengeschlagen *here:* to engulf (of a wave)
sich zusammenschließen zu (+ *dat.*) (schließt zusammen), schloss zusammen, zusammengeschlossen to form a group

zusammenschrauben (schraubt zusammen) to assemble with screws
die Zusammensetzung (-en) combination
zusammenstellen (stellt zusammen) to put together
der Zusammenstoß (:e) clash
zusammenwachsen (wächst zusammen), wuchs zusammen, ist zusammengewachsen to grow together
zusammenwohnen (wohnt zusammen) to live together
zusätzlich additional
der Zuschlag (:e) surcharge
zuschneiden (schneidet zu), schnitt zu, zugeschnitten to custom-cut
Zuschr. = Zuschriften
die Zuschrift (-en) letter; reply
(jemandem) zusprechen (spricht zu), sprach zu, zugesprochen to comfort; to give friendly advice
der Zustand (:e) condition
zutreffen (trifft zu), traf zu, zugetroffen to be correct
das Zutreffende (*decl. adj.*) the correct (answer)
zuverlässig reliable
die Zuversicht confidence
zu viel too much
zu wenig too little, not enough
der Zwang pressure, stress
die Zwangssterilisation (-en) forced sterilization
zwanzig twenty (E)
der Zwanziger (-) twenty-mark bill
zwar however; admittedly; und zwar that is to say
zwei two (E); zu zweit two of (us, them)
der Zweifel (-) doubt
zweifelnd doubtful
zweihundert two hundred (E)
zweimal twice (7)
zweitausend two thousand (E)
zweite second (3); zweiter Klasse second class (10)
die Zwiebel (-n) onion (6)
die Zwiebelringe (*pl.*) onion rings
die Zwillinge (*pl.*) twins
zwischen (+ *acc./dat.*) between (6); zwischen zwei und drei Uhr between two and three o'clock (6)
zwischendurch in between
zwölf twelve (E)
zwölfte twelfth (3)
zypriotisch (*adj.*) Cyprian (*from Cyprus*)

ENGLISH–GERMAN

This list contains all the words from the end-of-chapter vocabulary sections.

A

able: to be able to, can können (kann), konnte, gekonnt (4)

about über (+ *acc.*); (+ *time*) gegen; ungefähr (9); **to be about** handeln von (+ *dat.*) (13); **it is about** es handelt sich um (13); **What is it about?** Wovon handelt es? (13)

above über (+ *acc./dat.*) (6); (nach) oben (12)

abroad im Ausland (11); **at home and abroad** im Inland und Ausland (13)

absolutely unbedingt (13)

academic quarter das Quartal (-e)

accommodation die Unterkunft (⸚e) (9)

account (12); **savings account** das Sparkonto; **on account of** wegen (+ *gen.*) (9)

accusative case der Akkusativ (4)

acquainted: to be acquainted with (to know) kennen, kannte, gekannt; **to get acquainted (with)** bekannt werden mit

across from gegenüber (+ *dat.*) (9)

act of violence die Gewalttätigkeit (-en)

active(ly) aktiv (10); **active in sports** sportlich aktiv (10)

activity die Tätigkeit (-en) (11)

actor/actress der Schauspieler (-)/die Schauspielerin (-nen) (11)

ad: classified ad die Kleinanzeige (-n) (13); **help-wanted ad** das Stellenangebot (-e) (11)

addict: drug addict der/die Drogensüchtige (*decl. adj.*) (14)

address die Addresse (-n) (E); **street address** die Hausnummer (-n); **What's the address?** Wie ist die Adresse? (E)

adjective das Adjektiv (-e) (2)

advantageous(ly) günstig gut (10)

adverb das Adverb (-ien) (2)

advertisement (*commercial*) die Werbung (-en)

advice der Rat (8)

afraid: to be afraid (of) Angst haben (vor + *dat.*); (hat Angst) (12)

after nach (+ *dat.*) (6); **a quarter after two** ein Viertel nach zwei (4); nachdem (*subord. conj.*) (10)

afternoon der Nachmittag (-e) (4); **this afternoon** heute Nachmittag; **Sunday afternoon** Sonntagnachmittag; **tomorrow afternoon** morgen Nachmittag (4)

afternoons: in the afternoon nachmittags (4)

again wieder (2)

against gegen (+ *acc.*) (3); **I'm totally against it.** Ich bin total dagegen. (14)

ago: two days ago vor zwei Tagen (6)

to agree (be in agreement) einverstanden sein (10); **I agree with that.** Ich bin damit einverstanden. (10)

ahead: straight ahead (immer) geradeaus (9)

ailment die Krankheit (-en) (14)

air die Luft (8)

airplane das Flugzeug (-e) (10)

alarm clock der Wecker (-) (2)

alcohol der Alkohol (14)

all alle (*pl.*) (5); **All the best!** Alles Gute! (3); **all right** in Ordnung

allowed: to be allowed to dürfen (darf), durfte, gedurft (4)

almost fast (8)

along: to come along mitkommen (kommt mit), kam mit, ist mitgekommen (4); **to take along** mitnehmen (nimmt mit), nahm mit, mitgenommen (4)

already schon (2)

also auch (1)

altogether insgesamt (10)

aluminum can die Dose (-n) (14)

always immer (1)

American (*person*) der Amerikaner (-) / die Amerikanerin (-nen) (1)

among unter (+ *acc./dat*) (6)

to amount to betragen (beträgt), betrug, betragen (12)

and und (*coord. conj.*) (E)

animal das Tier (-e) (12)

annoyed: to be annoyed about sich ärgern über (+ *acc.*) (12)

to answer antworten (3); (*phone*) sich melden (13); **No one is answering.** Niemand meldet sich. (13)

answering machine der Anrufbeantworter (-) (13)

any kein (2); **in any case** auf jeden Fall (13)

anything: Anything else? sonst noch etwas? (10)

apartment die Wohnung (-en) (2)

apparatus das Gerät (-e) (13)

to appear scheinen, schien, geschienen (13)

appetizer die Vorspeise (-n) (6)

apple der Apfel (⸚) (5)

apple juice Apfelsaft (5)

appliance der Apparat (-e) (9); das Gerät (-e) (13)

application die Bewerbung (-en) (11)

application form das Bewerbungsformular (-e) (11)

to apply verwenden (14); **to apply (for)** sich bewerben (um + *acc.*) (bewirbt), bewarb, beworben (11)

appointment der Termin (-e) (8)

to approve einverstanden sein (10)

approximately ungefähr (9)

April (der) April (3)

are: there are/there is es gibt (4)

area der Bezirk (-e) (11); die Umgebung (-en) (12)

arm der Arm (-e) (8)

armchair der Sessel (-) (2)

around (*spatial*) um ... herum (3); (+ *time*) gegen (3); **around five o'clock** (so) gegen fünf Uhr (6); **to lie around** faulenzen (7)

arrival die Ankunft (⸚e) (10)

to arrive ankommen (kommt an), kam an, ist angekommen (9)

article der Artikel (-); **leading (newspaper) article** der Leitartikel (13); **article of clothing** das Kleidungsstück (-e)

artist der Künstler (-)/die Künstlerin (-nen) (11)

as als (10); **as far as** bis zum/zur (+ *acc.*) (9); **as of (June 1st)** ab (1. Juni) (12); **as soon as possible** möglichst bald

to ask fragen (1); **to ask for** bitten um (+ *acc.*) (bittet), bat, gebeten (12); **to ask about** fragen nach (+ *dat.*) (12); **to ask someone for directions** jemand nach dem Weg fragen (9)

to assert behaupten (13)

assignment die Arbeit (-en) (8)

at an, auf (+ *acc./dat.*) (6); bei (+ *dat.*) (5); um (+ *time*) (3); **at least** wenigstens; **at most** höchstens (8); **at night** abends (4); **at noon** mittags (4); **At what time?**

Um wie viel Uhr? (3); **at two** um zwei (4)

athletic sportlich (1)

athletic field der Sportplatz (∹e) (7)

to attempt versuchen (8)

attic das Dachgeschoss (12)

attorney der Rechtsanwalt (∹e) / die Rechtsanwältin (-nen) (11)

August (der) August (3)

aunt die Tante (-n) (3)

Austria (das) Österreich (E)

auto(mobile) das Auto (-s) (2); der Wagen (-) (10); der Personenkraftwagen (Pkw) (-) (13)

autumn der Herbst (7)

available frei; **Is this seat available?** Ist dieser Platz frei? (6)

average: on average durchschnittlich (12)

to avoid vermeiden, vermied, vermieden (14)

away: far away from weit weg von (2)

B

back zurück; **to come back** zurückkommen (kommt zurück), kam zurück, ist zurückgekommen (4); **in back of** hinter (+ *acc./dat.*) (6)

back der Rücken (-) (8)

backpack der Rucksack (∹e) (5)

bad(ly) schlecht (E); **What bad luck!** So ein Pech! (8)

bag die Tüte (-n); **plastic bag** die Plastiktüte (14)

baggage das Gepäck (9)

baggage check die Gepäckaufbewahrung (10)

baked goods die Backwaren (*pl.*) (5)

bakery die Bäckerei (-en) (5)

balcony der Balkon (-s) (2)

ballet das Ballett (-e) (4)

ballpoint pen der Kugelschreiber (-) (12)

banana die Banane (-n) (5)

bank die Bank (-en) (9)

bar die Kneipe (-n), das Lokal (-e) (6)

barbecue der Grill (-s) (6)

(a) bargain preiswert (2)

bathing suit der Badeanzug (∹e) (5)

bathroom das Bad (∹er), das Badezimmer (-) (2); das WC (-s) (9)

to be sein (ist), war, ist gewesen (1)

to be able to können (kann), konnte, gekonnt (4)

to be about handeln von (+ *dat.*) (13)

to be acquainted with kennen, kannte, gekannt (E)

to be afraid Angst haben (hat Angst) (12)

to be allowed dürfen (darf), durfte, gedurft (4)

to be annoyed (about) sich ärgern (über + *acc.*) (12)

to be called heißen, hieß, geheißen (E)

to be correct Recht haben (2)

to be glad (about) sich freuen (über + *acc.*) (12)

to be hungry Hunger haben (hat Hunger) (2)

to be interested in sich interessieren für (+ *acc.*) (11)

to be lazy faulenzen (7)

to be located liegen, lag, gelegen (6)

to be missing fehlen (10)

to be permitted to dürfen (darf), durfte, gedurft (4)

to be right Recht haben (hat Recht) (2)

to be supposed to sollen (soll), sollte, gesollt (4)

to be thirsty Durst haben (hat Durst) (2)

beach der Strand (∹e) (9)

beautiful(ly) schön (2)

because denn (*coord. conj.*) (7); weil (*subord. conj.*) (8)

because of wegen (+ *gen.*) (9); **because of that** deswegen (12)

to become werden (wird), wurde, ist geworden (3)

bed das Bett (-en) (2); **bed-and-breakfast hotel** die Pension (-en) (9); **room with one bed** das Einzelzimmer (-) (9); **room with two beds** das Doppelzimmer (9)

bedroom das Schlafzimmer (-) (2)

beef das Rindfleisch (5)

beer das Bier (-e) (5); **draft beer** Bier vom Fass (6); **pilsner beer** das Pilsner (6)

beer garden der Biergarten (∹) (6)

before vor (+ *acc./dat.*) (6); **before noon** am Vormittag (4)

to begin anfangen (fängt an), fing an, angefangen (4); beginnen, begann, begonnen

behind hinter (+ *acc./dat.*) (6)

beige beige (5)

Belgium (das) Belgien (F)

to believe glauben (+ *dat.*); glauben an (*acc.*) (5)

bell pepper die Paprikaschote (-n) (6)

belly der Bauch (∹e) (8)

to belong gehören (+ *dat.*) (5)

below (nach) unten (12); unter (+ *acc./dat.*) (6)

belt der Gürtel (-) (5)

beneath unter (6)

beside neben (+ *acc./dat.*) (6)

besides außerdem (14)

best best-; **All the best!** Alles Gute! (7); **best wishes** viele Grüße (12)

better besser (7)

between zwischen (+ *acc./dat.*) (6)

beverage das Getränk (-e) (5)

beverage (liquor) store der Getränkeladen (∹) (5)

bicycle das Fahrrad (∹er) (10)

to bicycle Rad fahren (fährt Rad), fuhr Rad, ist Rad gefahren (7)

big groß (2)

bill die Rechnung (-en) (9)

birth: date of birth der Geburtstag (-e) (1)

birthday der Geburtstag (-e) (3); **When is your birthday?** Wann hast du Geburtstag? (3); **Happy birthday!** Herzlichen Glückwunsch zum Geburtstag! (3)

birthplace der Geburtsort (-e) (1)

black schwarz (5)

blouse die Bluse (-n) (5)

blue blau (5)

to board (*train, etc.*) einsteigen (steigt ein), stieg ein, ist eingestiegen (10)

body der Körper (-); **parts of the body** die Körperteile (*pl.*) (8)

body-building: to do body-building Bodybuilding machen (7)

book das Buch (∹er) (1); **notebook** das Heft (-e) (12)

to book buchen (10); **to book (a trip)** reservieren (10)

bookcase das Bücherregal (-e) (2); der Bücherschrank (∹e)

bookshelf das Bücherregal (-e) (2)

boot der Stiefel (-) (5)

boring langweilig (1); **really boring** echt langweilig (1)

born: I am born ich bin geboren (1)

to borrow (from) leihen (von + *dat.*) (5); **to borrow money** sich Geld leihen (12)

boss der Chef (-s) / die Chefin (-nen) (11)

bottle die Flasche (-n); **nonrecyclable bottle** die Wegwerfflasche (14)

branch office die Filiale (-n) (11)

bread das Brot (-e) (5)

breakfast das Frühstück (-e); **to eat breakfast** frühstücken (5)

breakfast nook die Frühstücksnische (-n) (12)

breakfast room Frühstücksraum (∹e) (9)

breast die Brust (∹e) (8)

bright(ly) hell (2); (*weather*) heiter; (*intelligent*) gescheit (13)

to bring bringen, brachte, gebracht (7)

to bring up (children) erziehen, erzog, erzogen (14)

broadcast die Sendung (-en) (13)

broccoli der Brokkoli (-) (5)

brochure der Prospekt (-e); **travel brochure** der Reiseprospekt (10)

broke (*coll.*) pleite (12)

broken kaputt (9)

brother der Bruder (ː) (3)

brother-in-law der Schwager (ː) (3)

brown braun (5)

to brush (one's teeth) sich (die Zähne) putzen (8)

budget das Budget (-s); der Haushalt (-e) (12)

building: modern building der Neubau (Neubaute) (12)

bus der Bus (-se) (10)

businessman / businesswoman Geschäftsmann (Geschäftsleute)/ Geschäftsfrau (-en) (11)

but aber (2); **But of course!** Aber natürlich! (1); **but rather** sondern (*coord. conj.*) (7)

butcher shop die Metzgerei (-en) (5)

butter die Butter (5)

to buy kaufen (2)

by von (+ *dat.*); **to come by** vorbeikommen (kommt vorbei), kam vorbei, ist vorbeigekommen (4); **by all means** unbedingt (13); **by the way** übrigens (9)

bye tschüss (E)

C

café das Café (-s) (6)

cafeteria: student cafeteria die Mensa (Mensen) (1)

cake der Kuchen (-) (5); **cheese cake** der Käsekuchen (6)

calendar der Kalender (-) (3)

call: telephone call der Telefonanruf (-e) (12)

to call up anrufen (ruft an), rief an, angerufen (4)

called: to be called heißen, hieß, geheißen (1)

camera die Kamera (-s) (10)

can (*tin or aluminum*) die Dose (-n) (14)

can, to be able to können (kann), konnte, gekonnt (4)

cap die Mütze (-n) (5)

car der Wagen (-) (10); das Auto (-s) (2); der Pkw (Personenkraftwagen) (-) (13); **no-smoking car** der Nichtraucher (-) (10); **to drive a car** Auto fahren (fährt Auto), fuhr, ist gefahren (2)

card die Karte (-n) (7); **playing card** die Spielkarte (-n) (7); **personal ID card** der Personalausweis (-e) (10); **report card** das Zeugnis (-se) (11); **seat reservation card** die Platzkarte (-n) (10); **to play cards** Karten spielen (1)

care: take care mach's gut (E); **I don't care.** Das ist mir egal. (5)

to care for, like mögen (mag), mochte, gemocht (4)

carpet der Teppich (-e) (2)

carpeting (wall-to-wall) der Teppichboden (ː) (12)

carrot die Karotte (-n) (5)

to carry tragen (trägt), trug, getragen (5)

carry-on luggage das Handgepäck (10)

case: in any case auf jeden Fall (13)

cash das Bargeld; **in cash** bar (9)

cash register die Kasse (-n) (5)

casual shirt das Sporthemd (-en) (5)

cat die Katze (-n) (12)

to catch a cold sich erkälten (8)

cauliflower der Blumenkohl (5)

CD player der CD-Spieler (-) (2)

to celebrate feiern (3)

cell phone das Handy (-s) (2)

center: center (of the city) Mitte (der Stadt) (9); **recycling center** die Sammelstelle (-n) (14)

centrally located zentral gelegen (2)

cereal das Müsli (5)

chair der Stuhl (ː-e) (2); **armchair** der Sessel (-) (2)

to challenge herausfordern (11)

to change (trains) umsteigen (steigt um), steig um, umgestiegen (11)

channel (*TV*) das Programm (-e) (13); **on Channel 1** im ersten Programm

characteristics die Eigenschaften (*pl.*) (1)

cheap(ly) billig (2)

check der Scheck (-s); **Check, please.** Zahlen, bitte! (6); **traveler's check** der Reisescheck (-s) (10); **baggage check** die Gepäckaufbewahrung (10)

to check in (*hotel*) sich anmelden (meldet an) (9)

check-out die Kasse (-n) (5)

to check out (*of hotel*) sich abmelden (meldet ab) (9)

cheerful lustig (1)

cheese der Käse (5); **cheese cake** der Käsekuchen (-) (6)

chess: to play chess Schach spielen (7)

chest die Brust (8)

chicken das Hähnchen (-) (5)

chicken breast die Hühnerbrust (ː-e) (6)

child das Kind (-er) (1)

chin das Kinn (-e) (8)

to choose wählen (14); **to choose something** sich (et)was aussuchen (sucht aus) (13)

Christmas Weihnachten; **Christmas Eve** der Heilige Abend (3); **Christmas tree** der Weihnachtsbaum (ː-e) (3)

church die Kirche (-n) (9)

cinema das Kino (-s) (4)

citizen der Bürger (-)/die Bürgerin (-nen) (14)

city die Stadt (ː-e) (E); **in the city** in der Stadt; **inner city** die Innenstadt (9)

to claim behaupten (13)

class die Klasse (-n); **first-class** erster Klasse (6)

classified ad die Kleinanzeige (-n) (13)

clean sauber (14)

to clean (one's teeth) sich (die Zähne) putzen (8); **to clean up** aufräumen (räumt auf) (4)

cleaner: vacuum cleaner der Staubsauger (-) (13)

clock die Uhr (-en) (2); **alarm clock** der Wecker (-) (2); **five o'clock** fünf Uhr

closed geschlossen; **day a business is closed** der Ruhetag (-e) (6)

clothes closet der Kleiderschrank (ː-e) (2)

clothing die Kleidung; **article of clothing** das Kleidungsstück (-e) (5)

cloud die Wolke (-n) (7)

cloudless wolkenlos (7)

coat der Mantel (ː); **sports coat** das Sakko (-s) (5)

coffee table der Couchtisch (-e) (2)

cola die Cola (-s) (5)

cold (*adj.*) kalt (10)

cold die Erkältung (-en); **to catch a cold** sich erkälten; **head cold** der Schnupfen (8)

cold cuts der Aufschnitt (5)

colleague der Mitarbeiter (-) / die Mitarbeiterin (-nen) (11)

to collect sammeln (7)

color die Farbe (-n) (5)

columnist: advice columnist der Ratgeber (-) (13)

to comb (one's hair) sich (das Haar) kämmen (8)

to come kommen, kam, ist gekommen (1); **That comes to . . .** Das macht zusammen... (5)

to come along mitkommen (kommt mit), kam mit, ist mitgekommen (4)

to come back zurückkommen (kommt zurück), kam zurück, ist zurückgekommen (4)

to come by vorbeikommen (kommt vorbei), kam vorbei, ist vorbeigekommen (4)

comedy die Komödie (-n) (4)

comfortable (comfortably) bequem (2)

commercial die Werbung (-en) (13)

company die Firma (Firmen) (11)

comparative die Komparativform (-en) (7)

to compare vergleichen, verglich, verglichen (12)

to complain sich beschweren (9)

completely ganz (12)

completion (*of training or school*) der Abschluss (¨e) (11)

complicated kompliziert (1)

computer der Computer (-) (2); **computer connection** der Computeranschluss (¨e) (2); **computer diskette** die Computerdiskette (-n) (12); **to play computer games** Computerspiele spielen (1)

computer scientist der Informatiker (-) /die Informatikerin (-nen) (11)

concert das Konzert (-e) (4)

congestion: nasal congestion der Schnupfen (8)

to congratulate gratulieren (+ *dat.*) (3)

conjunction die Konjunktion (-en) (8)

connection der Anschluss (¨e) (10); (computer) der Computeranschluss (¨e) (2)

conservative konservativ (1)

to consider sich überlegen; halten für (+ *acc.*) (hält), hielt, gehalten (14)

to consume verbrauchen (14)

contact der Kontakt (-e) (11)

conveniently located günstig liegen (9)

to converse sich unterhalten (unterhält), unterhielt, unterhalten (13)

to cook kochen (1)

cookie der Keks (-e) (5)

cool kühl (7)

correct: to be correct Recht haben (2)

corruption die Korruption (14)

to cost kosten (2)

costs die Kosten (*pl.*) (12); **extra costs** die Nebenkosten (*pl.*) (12)

cough, coughing der Husten (8)

counselor der Berater (-) / die Beraterin (-nen); **employment counselor** der Berufsberater (-) / die Berufsberaterin (-nen) (11)

country das Land (¨er); **foreign country** das Ausland (14)

course (*food*) der Gang (¨e) (6)

course: of course natürlich, allerdings (3); **But of course!** Aber natürlich! (1)

cousin (*female*) die Kusine (-n); (*male*) der Vetter (-n)

coworker der Mitarbeiter (-) / die Mitarbeiterin (-nen) (11)

cozy, cozily gemütlich (4)

crazy verrückt (8)

cream die Sahne (6); **ice cream** das Eis (5)

to create schaffen, schuf, geschaffen (14)

credit card die Kreditkarte (-n) (9)

crossword puzzle: to do crossword puzzles Kreuzworträtsel machen (1)

crowded voll (6)

cucumber die Gurke (-n) (5)

cuisine die Küche (6)

cup die Tasse (-n); **a cup of coffee** eine Tasse Kaffee (4)

current aktuell (13); **current events** Aktuelles (13)

customer der Kunde (-n *masc.*) / die Kundin (-nen) (2)

cutlet das Schnitzel (-) (5); **breaded veal cutlet** das Wiener Schnitzel (6)

Czech Republic (das) Tschechien (E)

D

daily täglich (6)

dairy product das Milchprodukt (-e) (5)

to dance tanzen (1); **He dances well.** Er tanzt gut. (1)

dangerous gefährlich (10)

dark dunkel (2)

date of birth der Geburtstag (-e) (1)

dative case der Dativ (5)

daughter die Tochter (¨) (3)

day der Tag (-e) (2); **every day** jeden Tag (7); **good day** guten Tag (E); **day that a business is closed** der Ruhetag (6)

day of the week der Wochentag (-e) (3)

to deal with handeln von (+ *dat.*) (13)

December (der) Dezember (3)

decent gescheit (13); **nothing decent** nichts Gescheites (13)

definitely bestimmt (1); **to say definitely** Bescheid sagen (10)

degree (*school*) der Abschluss (¨e) (11); (*temperature*) Grad (-e) (7); **35 degrees** 35 Grad (7)

demonstration die Demonstration (-en) (14)

Denmark (das) Dänemark (E)

dentist der Zahnarzt (¨e)/die Zahnärztin (-nen) (11)

to depart abreisen (reist ab), ist abgereist (10); abfahren (fährt ab), fuhr ab, ist abgefahren (9)

department store das Kaufhaus (¨er) (2)

departure die Abfahrt (-en) (10)

depressed deprimiert (8); **You sound so depressed.** Du klingst so deprimiert. (8)

to deserve verdienen (11)

desire die Lust; **to feel like (doing something)** Lust haben (2)

desk der Schreibtisch (-e) (2)

dessert die Nachspeise (-n); der Nachtisch (-e) (6)

detective (*film or book*) der Krimi (-s) (3)

to develop entwickeln (14)

development die Entwicklung (-en) (11)

device das Gerät (-e) (13)

diligent fleißig (1)

dining room das Essimmer (-) (2)

directions: to ask someone for directions jemand nach dem Weg fragen (9)

dirty schmutzig (14)

disco die Disko (-s); **to go to a disco** in die Disko gehen (4)

to discuss diskutieren (1)

disease die Krankheit (-en)(14)

dish (*of prepared food*) das Gericht (-e) (6); **main dish** das Hauptgericht (6); **side dish** die Beilage (-n) (6); **dish of ice cream** der Eisbecher (-) (6)

dishwasher die Geschirrspülmaschine (-n) (12)

diskette (*computer*) die Computerdiskette (-n) (12)

disloyal untreu (1)

to disseminate verbreiten (14)

district der Bezirk (-e) (11)

to dive tauchen, ist getaucht (7)

diverse abwechslungsreich (11)

to do machen (1); tun, tat, getan (8); **What do you do for a living?** Was sind Sie von Beruf? (1); **to do gymnastics** turnen; **to do sports** Sport treiben, trieb, getrieben (7); **to do without** verzichten auf (+ *acc.*) (13); **to do crossword puzzles** Kreuzworträtsel machen (1); **What do you do for a living?** Was sind Sie von Beruf? (1)

dock der Hafen (¨) (9)

doctor der Arzt (¨e) / die Ärztin (-nen) (8)

documentary (film) der Dokumentarfilm (-e) (13)

documentation die Unterlagen (*pl.*) (11)

dog der Hund (-e) (3); **sick as a dog** hundsmiserabel (8)

door die Tür (-en) (2)

domestic das Inland (13)

dormitory das Studenten(wohn)heim (-e) (2)

downstairs nach unten (12)

downtown die Innenstadt (¨e) (9)

draft beer das Bier vom Fass (6)

drama das Theaterstück (-e) (3)

to draw zeichnen (7)

drawing die Zeichnung (12)

dress das Kleid (-er) (5)

dressed: to get dressed sich anziehen (zieht an), zog an, angezogen (8)

dresser die Kommode (-n) (2)

drink das Getränk (-e) (5)

to drink trinken, trank, getrunken (2)

to drive fahren (fährt), fuhr, ist gefahren (1); **to drive a motorcycle** Motorrad fahren (1)

to drop off abgeben (gibt ab), abgegeben (8)

drug addict der/die Drogensüchtige (*decl. adj.*) (14)

drug addiction die Drogensucht (14)

drugstore (*toiletries and sundries*) die Drogerie (-n) (5)

dryer der Wäschetrockner (-) (13)

during während (+ *gen.*) (9)

DVD player der DVD-Spieler (-) (2)

E

each jeder, jede, jedes (5)

ear das Ohr (-en) (8)

early früh (4); **earlier** früher (7)

to earn verdienen (11)

earth die Welt (14)

Easter (das) Ostern (3)

to eat essen (isst), aß, gegessen (1); **to eat breakfast** frühstücken (4)

eating das Essen (1)

economy die Wirtschaft (13)

eccentric exzentrisch (1)

egg das Ei (-er) (5); **fried egg** das Spiegelei (6)

eight acht (E)

eighteen achtzehn (E)

eighty achtzig (E)

elbow der Ell(en)bogen (-) (8)

to elect wählen (14)

electricity der Strom (12)

elevator der Lift (-e) (9)

eleven elf (E)

else: Anything else? Sonst noch etwas? (6)

employer der Arbeitgeber (-) / die Arbeitgeberin (-nen) (11)

employment counselor der Berufsberater (-) / die Berufsberaterin (-nen) (11)

employment office das Arbeitsamt (¨er) (11)

to entertain (oneself) sich unterhalten (unterhält), unterhielt, unterhalten (13)

entertaining unterhaltsam (13)

entertainment die Unterhaltung (-en) (13); **for entertainment** zur Unterhaltung (13)

entire(ly) ganz (12)

environment die Umwelt (14)

environmental pollution die Umweltverschmutzung (14)

environmentally friendly umweltfreundlich (14)

to equip einrichten (richtet ein) (12)

especially besonders (8)

euro der Euro (-s) (2)

evaluation (*from a former employer*) das Zeugnis (-se) (11)

even sogar (8)

evening der Abend (-e) (4); **good evening** guten Abend (E); **this evening** heute Abend (4); **in the evening, evenings** abends (4); **evening meal** das Abendessen (5)

every jeder, jede, jedes; **every day** jeden Tag (5)

everything alles (10)

exactly gerade (2)

exaggerated übertrieben (14)

examination (*at the end of Gymnasium*) das Abitur (-e) (11)

excellent ausgezeichnet (E)

except for außer (+ *dat.*) (5)

to excuse entschuldigen (6); **Excuse me.** Entschuldigung. (1)

to exert oneself sich anstrengen (strengt an) (8)

expense die Ausgabe (-n) (12)

expensive(ly) teuer (2)

experience die Erfahrung (-en) (11)

to experience erleben (10)

eye das Auge (-n) (8)

F

face das Gesicht (-er) (8)

fair (*weather*) heiter (7)

fall (*autumn*) der Herbst (7)

to fall fallen (fällt), fiel, ist gefallen (7)

to fall asleep einschlafen (schläft ein), schlief ein, ist eingeschlafen (4)

familiar: to be familiar with, to know kennen, kannte, gekannt (3)

family die Familie (-n) (3)

family gathering das Familienfest (-e) (3)

family name der Nachname (-n *masc.*) (1)

family tree der Stammbaum (¨e) (3)

famine der Welthunger (14)

fantastic fantastisch (1)

far weit (9); **as far as** bis (+ *acc.*) (9); **far away from** weit weg von (2)

farmhouse das Bauernhaus (¨er) (12)

fashionable modisch (5)

fast schnell (10)

fast-food stand der Imbiss (-e) (6)

father der Vater (¨) (3)

favor: I'm in favor of it. Ich bin dafür. (14)

favorable günstig (gut) (10)

fear die Angst (¨e); **to be afraid** Angst haben (12)

feature film der Spielfilm (-e) (13)

February der Februar (3)

to feel (sich) fühlen (8); **to feel like** (*doing something*) Lust haben (2)

fees die Studiengebühren (*pl.*) (12)

female cousin die Kusine (-n) (3)

fever das Fieber (8)

few wenige (*pl.*) (8)

fifteen fünfzehn (E)

fifty fünfzig (E)

to fill out ausfüllen (füllt aus) (9)

film der Film (-e) (4); **feature film** der Spielfilm (-e) (13)

financial finanziell (11)

to find finden, fand, gefunden (1); sich (et)was aussuchen (sucht aus) (13)

fine: sehr gut (E); **fine, thanks** danke, gut (E)

finger der Finger (-) (8)

firm (*n.*) die Firma (Firmen) (11)

firm (*adj.*) fest (11)

first erst (3); **at first** zuerst (9)

first name der Vorname (-n *masc.*) (1)

to fish angeln (7)

fit fit; **to keep fit** sich fit halten (hält fit), hielt fit, fit gehalten (8)

to fit passen (+ *dat.*) (5)

fitness die Fitness (8)

fitness center das Fitnesscenter (-) (4)

five fünf (E)

to flash blitzen (7)

floor der Stock (Stockwerk -e) (9), die Etage (-n) (12); **ground floor** das Erdgeschoss (-e) (9); **top floor** das Dachgeschoss (-e) (12)

flu die Grippe (8)

to fly fliegen, flog, ist geflogen (7)

fog der Nebel (7)

food(s) die Lebensmittel (*pl.*) (5); die Speise (-n) (6); das Essen (1); die Küche (6); (*nutrition*) die Ernährung (12); **organic foods** die Ökolebensmittel (*pl.*) (8); **organic foods store** der Bioladen (¨) (5)

foot der Fuß (¨e) (10); **on foot** zu Fuß

for denn (*coord. conj.*); (*time*) seit (+ *dat.*) (5); für (3)

foreign countries das Ausland (*no pl.*) (11)

forest der Wald (⸚er) (7)

to forget vergessen (vergisst), vergaß, vergessen (10)

fork die Gabel (-n) (6)

form das Formular (-e); **registration form** das Anmeldeformular; **application form** das Bewerbungsformular (-e) (11)

forty vierzig (E)

forward: to look forward to sich freuen auf (+ *acc.*) (11)

four vier (E)

fourteen vierzehn (E)

France (das) Frankreich (E)

free(ly) frei (2)

free time die Freizeit (7)

French fries die Pommes frites (*pl.*) (6)

fresh frisch (5)

Friday (der) Freitag (3); **Fridays, on Friday(s)** freitags (4)

fried egg das Spiegelei (-er) (6)

fried potatoes die Bratkartoffeln (*pl.*) (6)

friend der Freund (-e)/die Freundin (-nen) (1)

friendly freundlich (1)

from aus (+ *dat.*), von (+ *dat.*) (5); ab (+ *dat.*); **from (June 1)** ab (1. Juni) (12); **I'm from . . .** Ich komme aus... (E); **from where** woher (1); **across from** gegenüber (+ *dat.*); **from . . . to** von... bis; **from two to three** von zwei bis drei (6); **Where are you from?** Woher kommst du/kommen Sie? (E)

in front of vor (+ *acc./dat.*) (6)

front hall die Diele (-n) (12)

frozen gefroren (5)

fruit das Obst (5)

fruit and vegetable stand der Obst- und Gemüsestand (⸚e) (5)

full voll (6)

fun: That's fun. Das macht mir Spaß. (1); **Have fun!** Viel Spaß! (1)

fun lustig (1)

to function funktionieren (11)

to furnish einrichten (richtet ein) (12)

furnished möbliert (2)

G

game das Spiel (-e); **computer game** das Computerspiel (1)

garage die Garage (-n) (2)

garbage der Müll, der Abfall (⸚e) (12)

garden der Garten (⸚) (2); **beer garden** der Biergarten (⸚) (6)

gasoline das Benzin (12)

gas station die Tankstelle (-n) (9)

genitive case der Genitiv (9)

gentleman der Herr (-en, -n *masc.*) (E)

German deutsch; (*language*) (das) Deutsch (1); **How does one say . . . in German?** Wie sagt man ... auf Deutsch? (E)

German mark die Deutsche Mark (DM) (2)

Germany Deutschland (E)

to get (receive) bekommen, bekam, bekommen (6); **(turn)** werden (wird), wurde, ist geworden

to get acquainted (with) bekannt werden (mit + *dat.*) (wird bekannt) wurde, ist geworden (E)

to get dressed sich anziehen (zieht an), zog an, angezogen (8)

to get into (*a vehicle*) einsteigen (steigt ein), stieg ein, ist eingestiegen (10)

to get undressed sich ausziehen (zieht aus), zog aus, ausgezogen (8)

to get up aufstehen (steht auf), stand auf, ist aufgestanden (4)

to get well sich erholen; **Get well soon!** Gute Besserung! (8)

to give geben (gibt), gab, gegeben (2); **to give** (*as a gift*) schenken (5); **to give to** abgeben (gibt an), angegeben (8)

given name der Vorname (-n *masc.*) (1)

glad: to be glad about sich freuen über (+ *acc.*) (12)

gladly gern (2)

glasses (eyeglasses) die Brille (-n) (5)

glove der Handschuh (-e) (10)

to go gehen, ging, ist gegangen (1); fahren (fährt), fuhr, ist gefahren (1); **to go to the movies** ins Kino gehen; **to go for a walk** spazieren gehen (geht spazieren); **to go on a trip** verreisen, ist verreist (10); **to go out** ausgehen (geht aus) (4); **to go on vacation** Urlaub machen (8); **food "to go"** zum Mitnehmen (6)

good sehr gut (E); gut (1); günstig (gut) (10); **good day** (guten) Tag (E); **good evening** guten Abend (E); **good night** gute Nacht (E); **Good luck!** Viel Glück! (1); **good morning** (guten) Morgen (E); **good-bye** (auf) Wiedersehen (E); **good-bye** (*telephone*) auf Wiederhören! (9)

goods: baked goods die Backwaren (*pl.*) (5)

graduate (*higher education*) der Absolvent (-en) / die Absolventin (-nen) (11); (*graduate of the*

Gymnasium; person who has completed the Abitur) der Abiturient (-en) / die Abiturientin (-nen)

graphic artist der Zeichner (-) / die Zeichnerin (-nen) (11)

granddaughter die Enkelin (-nen) (3)

grandfather der Großvater (⸚) (3)

grandma die Oma (-s) (3)

grandmother die Großmutter (⸚) (3)

grandpa der Opa (-s) (3)

grandparents die Großeltern (*pl.*) (3)

grandson der Enkel (-) (3)

granola (cereal) das Müsli (5)

grape die Weintraube (-n) (5)

gray grau (5)

Great! Prima! (E); (Ganz) toll! (1)

green grün (5)

greeting die Begrüßung (-en), der Gruß (⸚e) (12)

grill der Grill (-s) (6)

guest der Gast (⸚e) (12)

guest room das Gästezimmer (-) (12)

guide: travel guide (book) der Reiseführer (-) (10)

gym das Fitnesscenter (-) (4)

gymnasium die Turnhalle (-n) (7)

gymnastics: to do gymnastics turnen (7)

H

hail der Hagel (7)

hair das Haar (-e) (8)

hair dryer der Fön (-e) (9)

half: half past one halb zwei (4)

hall: front hall die Diele (-n) (12)

hallway der Flur (-e) (12)

ham der Schinken (-) (5)

hand die Hand (⸚e) (8)

handbag die Tasche (-n) (5)

handsome hübsch, gut aussehend (7)

to hang (something) hängen; **to be hanging** hängen, hing, gehangen (6)

to happen passieren, ist passiert (7)

happiness das Glück; **Much happiness!** Viel Glück! (3)

happy glücklich; **Happy birthday!** Herzlichen Glückwunsch zum Geburtstag! (3)

harbor der Hafen (⸚) (9)

hat der Hut (⸚e) (5)

hatred directed toward foreigners die Ausländerfeindlichkeit (14)

to have haben (hat), hatte, gehabt (2); **to have time** Zeit haben (2); **I have a question.** Ich habe eine Frage.; **Have fun!** Viel Spaß! (1)

to have time Zeit haben (2)

to have to (must) müssen (muss), musste, gemusst (4)

he er (1)

head der Kopf (∹e) (8); (*boss*) der Chef (-s) / die Chefin (-nen) (11)

headache die Kopfschmerzen (*pl.*) (8)

head cold der Schnupfen (8)

headline die Schlagzeile (-n) (13)

health die Gesundheit (8); **health food store** der Naturkostladen (∹) (8)

healthy gesund (8)

to hear hören (1)

heavy (*weather*) stark (7)

hello grüß dich (*inform.*) (E); (guten) Tag (E); hallo (*among friends and family*) (E)

to help helfen (+ *dat.*) (hilft), half, geholfen

help-wanted ad das Stellenangebot (-e) (11)

her ihr; sie (3)

herbal tea der Kräutertee (s) (8)

here hier (1)

hi grüß dich (*inform.*) (E)

high(ly) hoch (hoh-) (2)

to hike wandern, ist gewandert (1)

him ihn (3); ihm (5)

his sein (3)

to hitchhike per Autostop reisen (10)

hobby das Hobby (-s) (1)

to hold halten (hält), hielt, gehalten (14)

holiday der Feiertag (-e) (13)

home: (to) home nach Hause; **(at) home** zu Hause (5); das Inland (13); **at home and abroad** im Inland und Ausland (13)

homelessness die Obdachlosigkeit (14)

homeless person der/die Obdachlose (*decl. adj.*) (14)

to hope (for) hoffen (auf + *acc.*) (10); **I hope** hoffentlich (6)

horoscope das Horoskop (-e) (13)

horseback: to ride horseback reiten, ritt, ist geritten (7)

hostel: youth hostel die Jugendherberge (-n) (9)

hot heiß (7)

hotel das Hotel (-s); die Pension (-en) (bed and breakfast) (9); **at the hotel** im Hotel (9)

hour die Stunde (-n) (4); **office hour** die Sprechstunde (-n) (8)

house das Haus (∹er) (2)

household der Haushalt (-e) (12)

household appliance das Haushaltsgerät (-e) (12)

houseplant die Zimmerpflanze (-n) (2)

housing: shared housing die Wohngemeinschaft (-en) (WG) (2)

how wie (1); **How about . . . ?** Wie wäre es mit...? (13); **how long** wie lange; **how much** wie viel; **how many** wie viele (1); **How are you?** (*inform.*) (Na,) wie geht's? Wie geht es dir?; (*form.*) Wie geht es Ihnen? (E); **How do you say . . . in German?** Wie sagt man ... auf Deutsch? (E)

however aber (2)

human being der Mensch (-en *masc.*) (2)

human rights das Menschenrecht (-e) (*usually pl.*) (14)

humid schwül (7)

hundred (ein) hundert (E)

Hungary (das) Ungarn (E)

hunger der Hunger (14); **world hunger** der Welthunger (14)

hungry: to be hungry Hunger haben (2)

to hurry up sich beeilen (8)

to hurt weh tun (tut weh), tat weh, weh getan (8); **That hurts.** Das tut mir weh. (8)

husband der Mann (∹er) (3)

I

I ich; **I am** ich bin (E); **I'm from . . .** ich komme aus . . . (E); **I'm sorry.** Das tut mir leid. (9) **I don't know.** Das weiß ich nicht. (E) **I don't care.** Das ist mir egal. (5)

ice das Eis (5)

ice cream das Eis (5); **dish of ice cream** der Eisbecher (-) (6)

to ice skate Schlittschuh laufen (läuft), lief, ist gelaufen (7)

ice-skating rink das Eisstadion (Eisstadien) (7)

identification card (ID) Personalausweis (-e) (10)

i.e. das heißt (8)

if wenn (*subord. conj.*) (8); **if I were you** an deiner Stelle (12)

ill krank (8)

illness die Krankheit (-en) (14)

to imagine sich (*dat.*) vorstellen (11)

immediately sofort (8)

important wichtig (3)

impractical unpraktisch (1)

in in (+ *acc./dat.*) (6); **in the morning(s)** morgens (4); **in shape** fit (8); **in spite of** trotz (+ *gen.*) (9); **in German** auf Deutsch (E); **in your place** an deiner Stelle (12)

included in the price im Preis enthalten (9)

income das Einkommen (-) (11)

independent(ly) selbständig (11)

indoor swimming pool die Schwimmhalle (-n) (9)

industrious fleißig (1)

inexpensive(ly) billig (2); preiswert (2); **quite inexpensive** recht preiswert (2)

to inform (oneself) sich informieren (8)

information die Information (-en) (10)

to injure oneself sich verletzen (8)

injury die Verletzung (-en) (14)

inner city die Innenstadt (∹e) (9)

inside drinnen (7)

instructor: university instructor der Hochschullehrer (-) / die Hochschullehrerin (-nen) (1)

to insulate isolieren (14)

insurance die Versicherung (-en) (12)

intelligent gescheit (13)

interest das Interesse (-n) (1)

interested: to be interested in sich interessieren für (+ *acc.*) (11)

interesting interessant (1)

internship das Praktikum (Praktika) (1); **to do an internship** ein Praktikum machen (1)

interpreter der Dolmetscher (-) / die Dolmetscherin (-nen) (11)

interrogative das Fragewort (∹er) (1)

intersection die Kreuzung (-en) (9)

into: to get into (*a vehicle*) einsteigen (steigt ein), stieg an, ist eingestiegen (10)

to introduce sich (*acc.*) vorstellen (stellt vor) (11)

to invent erfinden, erfand, erfunden (13)

invention die Erfindung (-en) (13)

to invite einladen (lädt ein), lud ein, eingeladen (14)

involved; to get involved sich engagieren (14)

irregular unregelmäßig (7)

is: there is/there are es gibt (3)

to isolate isolieren (14)

it es, er, sie (1); ihn, sie, es (3); ihm, ihr (5)

Italy (das) Italien (E)

its sein; ihr (3)

J

jacket die Jacke (-n); **sports jacket** das Sakko (-s) (5)

jail das Gefängnis (14)

January der Januar; **in January** im Januar (3)

jeans die Jeans (*pl.*) (5)

job die Stelle (-n); der Arbeitsplatz (∹e) (11)

job interview das Vorstellungsgespräch (-e) (11)

job offer das Stellenangebot (-e) (11)

to jog laufen (2)

journalist der Journalist (-en *masc.*) / die Journalistin (-nen) (1)
juice der Saft (⸚e) (5)
juicy saftig (5)
July der Juli (3)
June der Juni (3)
just gerade (2); **in just ten minutes** in knapp zehn Minuten

K

keep halten (hält), hielt, gehalten (14)
keep on going straight immer geradeaus gehen (9)
key der Schlüssel (-) (9)
kitchen die Küche (-n) (2)
knee das Knie (-) (8)
knife das Messer (-) (6)
to know (be acquainted with) kennen, kannte, gekannt (3); **to know something as a fact** wissen (weiß), wusste, gewusst (3); **I don't know.** Das weiß ich nicht. (E)

L

lake der See (-n) (7)
lamp die Lampe (-n) (2)
large groß (2)
to last dauern (7)
late spät; **at the latest** spätestens (12)
lawyer der Rechtsanwalt (⸚e) / die Rechtsanwältin (-nen) (11)
to lay (something) down legen (6)
lazy faul (1); **to be lazy** faulenzen (7)
leading editorial der Leitartikel (-) (13)
to learn lernen (1)
least: at least wenigstens; mindestens (8)
to leave abfahren (fährt ab), fuhr ab, ist abgefahren (10)
lecture der Vortrag (⸚e) (4)
left links; **to the left** nach links (9)
left over übrig (12)
leg das Bein (-e) (8)
to lend leihen (5)
to let lassen (lässt), ließ, gelassen; **Let's . . .** Lass uns (doch)... (6)
letter der Brief (-e) (13)
lettuce der Salat (-e) (6)
level (in a building) die Etage (-n); der Stock; das Stockwerk (-e) (9)
librarian der Bibliothekar (-e) / die Bibliothekarin (-nen) (11)
library die Bibliothek (-en) (4)
to lie liegen, lag, gelegen (6); **to lie around** faulenzen (7)
Liechtenstein (principality of) (das) Liechtenstein (E)
to lie down sich hinlegen (legt sich hin) (8)
life das Leben (11); **professional life** das Berufsleben (11)

light (*adj.*) hell (2)
light: traffic light die Ampel (-n) (9)
lightning: There's lightning. Es blitzt. (7)
likable sympathisch (1)
to like (*a person or thing*) gern haben (hat gern) (2); mögen (mag), mochte, gemocht (4); (*be pleasing to*) gefallen (*dat.*) (5); (*to do something*) gern (+ *verb*) (2); **would like to** möchte(n) (4); **How do you like . . .?** Wie findest du ...? (1); Wie gefällt Ihnen ...? (5); **What do you like to do?** Was macht dir Spaß? (4); **to feel like** (*doing something*) Lust haben (2)
likewise gleichfalls (E)
line die Linie (-n); **bus line** die Buslinie (10)
to listen hören (1)
litter der Abfall (⸚e) (14)
little wenig; **a little** etwas (*adverb*) (2)
to live wohnen (1)
living: What do you do for a living? Was sind Sie von Beruf? (1)
living room das Wohnzimmer (-) (2)
loaf of bread das Brot (-e) (5)
local news die Lokalnachrichten (*pl.*) (13)
located: to be located liegen, lag, gelegen (6); stehen, stand, gestanden (6); **centrally located** zentral gelegen (2); **conveniently located** günstig liegen (9)
location die Lage (-n) (9)
long lang(e) (10); **how long** wie lange (1); **so long** mach's gut, tschüss (E)
to look at sich etwas ansehen (sieht an) (13); **The color looks good on me.** Die Farbe steht mir. (5)
to look for suchen (2)
to look forward to sich freuen auf (+ *acc.*) (11)
to lose verlieren, verlor, verloren (7)
lot: a lot viel (1)
lotion: suntan lotion das Sonnenschutzmittel (-) (10)
low niedrig (2)
loyal treu (1)
luck: Good luck! Viel Glück! (1); **What bad luck!** So ein Pech! (8)
luggage das Gepäck (9); **carry-on luggage** das Handgepäck (10)
lunch das Mittagessen (-) (5)
Luxembourg (das) Luxemburg (E)

M

machine: answering machine der Anrufbeantworter (-) (12)
magazine die Zeitschrift (-en) (13)

main dish das Hauptgericht (-e) (6)
to make machen (1)
makeup das Make-up (5)
male cousin der Vetter (-n) (3)
mall die Fußgängerzone (-n) (14)
man der Mann (⸚er) (1)
manager der Chef (-s) / die Chefin (-nen) (11)
to manufacture herstellen (stellt her) (11)
many viele (*pl.*) (2); **how many** wie viele (1)
March (der) März (3)
Mardi Gras der Karneval (*Rhineland*), der Fasching (*southern Germany*) (3)
to marry heiraten (3)
matter: What's the matter? Was ist (denn) los? (2) Was fehlt Ihnen (dir)? (8); **That doesn't matter.** Das macht nichts. Das ist mir egal. (8)
May (der) Mai (3)
may, to be permitted to dürfen (darf), durfte, gedurft (4)
maybe vielleicht (2)
me too ich auch (1)
meadow die Wiese (-n) (7)
meal: evening meal das Abendessen; **midday meal** das Mittagessen (5)
to mean: What does . . . mean? Was bedeutet...? (E)
means: by means of mit (+ *dat.*) (5)
meat das Fleisch (5)
meatloaf (*Bavarian style*) der Leberkäs (6)
meats die Fleischwaren (*pl.*) (5)
mechanic der Mechaniker (-) / die Mechanikerin (-nen) (11)
medication das Arzneimittel (14)
medicine das Medikament (-e) (5)
to meet (sich) treffen (trifft), traf, getroffen (8); **Pleased to meet you.** Freut mich. (E)
mention: Don't mention it. Nichts zu danken. (8)
menu die Speisekarte (-n) (6)
microwave oven der Mikrowellenherd (-e) (12)
midnight: at midnight am Mitternacht (3)
milk die Milch (5)
mineral water das Mineralwasser (5); der Sprudel (6)
minute die Minute (-n) (4)
modal verb das Modalverb (-en) (4)
modern building der Neubau (Neubauten) (12)
Monday (der) Montag (3); **on Monday** am Montag; **(on) Mondays** montags (4)

money das Geld (2); **to borrow money** sich Geld leihen (12); **to earn money** Geld verdienen (11)

month der Monat (-e) (3); **once a month** einmal im Monat (7)

monthly monatlich (12)

more mehr (10); **once more** noch einmal (7)

morning der Morgen (4); **good morning** (guten) Morgen (E); **tomorrow morning** morgen früh; **in the morning, mornings** morgens (4)

most meist-

mother die Mutter (⋮) (3)

Mother's Day der Muttertag (-e) (3)

motorcycle das Motorrad (⋮er) (2); **to ride a motorcycle** Motorrad fahren (fährt Motorrad), fuhr, ist Motorrad gefahren (1)

mountain der Berg (-e) (7)

mouth der Mund (⋮er) (7)

to move in einziehen (zieht ein), zog ein, ist eingezogen (12)

movie der Film (-e) (4); der Spielfilm (-e) (13); **watching movies** Filme sehen (9)

movie theater das Kino (-s) (4); **to go to the movies** ins Kino gehen (4)

Mr. . . . Herr... (E)

Mrs. . . . Frau... (E)

Ms. . . . Frau... (E)

much viel (1); **how much** wie viel (1)

muggy schwül (7)

muscle der Muskel (-n) (8)

museum das Museum (Museen) (9)

mushroom der Champignon (-s)

music die Musik (1); **listening to music** Musik hören

must, to have to müssen (muss), musste, gemusst (4)

mustard Senf (6)

my mein (3)

mystery (*film or book*) der Krimi (-s) (9)

N

name der Name (-ns, -n) (1); **What's your name?** (*form.*) Wie ist Ihr (dein) Name? Wie heißen Sie?; (*inform.*) Wie heißt du? (E); **My name is . . .** Mein Name ist... (E); **family name (surname)** der Nachname (1); **first name (given name)** der Vorname (1); **Under what name?** Auf welchen Namen? (9); **What is the name of . . .?** Wie heißt...? (E)

named: to be named heißen, hieß, geheißen (1)

namely nämlich (3)

napkin die Serviette (-n) (6)

to narrate berichten (13)

nasal congestion der Schnupfen (8)

natural foods store der Bioladen (⋮) (5)

natural(ly) natürlich (3)

nature die Natur (10)

near bei (+ *dat.*) (5); in der Nähe (von + *dat.*) (9)

necessary nötig (3)

neck der Hals (⋮e) (8)

necktie die Krawatte (-n) (5)

to need brauchen (2); **What size do you need?** Welche Größe brauchen Sie? (5)

neighborhood die Umgebung (-en) (12)

nephew der Neffe (-n *masc.*) (3)

Netherlands (die) Niederlande (*pl.*) (E)

never nie (8)

new neu (5)

New Year's Day das Neujahr (3)

New Year's Eve (der) Silvester (3)

news die Nachrichten (*pl.*) (13)

newspaper die Zeitung (-en) (1); **reading the newspaper** Zeitung lesen (liest Zeitung), las, gelesen

newspaper cultural section das Feuilleton (-s) (13)

next nächst- (10); **next to** neben (6); **next year** nächstes Jahr (1)

nice(ly) nett (1); schön (2)

niece die Nichte (-n) (3)

night die Nacht (⋮e) (4); **at night (nights)** nachts (4); **good night** gute Nacht (E)

nightstand der Nachttisch (-e) (2)

nine neun (E)

nineteen neunzehn (E)

ninety neunzig (E)

no nein (E); **no (not any)** kein (2); **no longer** nicht mehr; **no more** nicht mehr; **no . . . yet** noch kein (2)

nonalcoholic alkoholfrei (6)

none kein (2)

nonrecyclable bottle die Wegwerfflasche (-n) (14)

Nonsense! So ein Quatsch! (14); So ein Unsinn! (14)

noon der Mittag (4); **at noon** mittags (4); **afternoon** der Nachmittag

no one: No one is answering. Niemand meldet sich. (13)

nose die Nase (-n) (8)

no-smoking car der Nichtraucher (-) (10)

not nicht (1); **not any** kein (2); **not yet** noch nicht (2)

nothing nichts (2)

to notify Bescheid sagen (sagt Bescheid) (10)

noun das Substantiv (-e) (1)

novel der Roman (-e)

November der November (3)

now jetzt (1); **now and then** ab und zu (8)

number die Nummer (-n), die Zahl (-en) (E); **telephone number** die Telefonnummer (E)

nurse der Krankenpfleger (-) / die Krankenschwester (-n) (8)

O

occasionally ab und zu (8)

occupied besetzt (6)

to occupy oneself (with) sich beschäftigen (mit + *dat.*) (11)

ocean das Meer (7)

o'clock: It's one o'clock. Es ist eins. Es ist ein Uhr. (4); **until five o'clock** um fünf Uhr (6)

October (der) Oktober (3)

of (+ *time*) vor; **five of two** fünf vor zwei (4); **made of** aus (+ *dat.*); **out of** aus (+ *dat.*); von (+ *dat.*) (5); **of course** allerdings; natürlich (13); **But of course!** Aber natürlich! (1)

offer das Angebot (-e) (10); **job offer** das Stellenangebot (11)

office das Büro (-s) (11); **branch office** die Filiale (-n) (11); **employment office** das Arbeitsamt (⋮er) (11); **office hour** die Sprechstunde (-n) (8)

often oft (1)

OK so lala (E)

old alt (1)

olive die Olive (-n) (6)

on an (+ *acc./dat.*); **on (top of)** auf (+ *acc./dat.*) (6); **on Monday** am Montag (4); **on television** im Fernsehen (13)

once einmal; früher (7); **once a year** einmal im Jahr (7)

one eins (E); (*indef. pron.*) man (4)

oneself sich (8)

one-way ticket einfach (10)

onion die Zwiebel (-n) (6)

only nur (2)

open geöffnet (6)

opera die Oper (-n) (4)

opinion die Meinung (-en); **in my opinion** meiner Meinung nach (14)

opportunity die Gelegenheit (-en) (11)

or oder (*coord. conj.*) (8)

orange (*color*) orange (5)

order die Ordnung; **in order** in Ordnung (14)

organic foods die Ökolebensmittel (*pl.*) (8)

to order bestellen (6)

other ander-, sonstig (10)

ought to sollen (soll), sollte, gesollt (4)

our unser (3)

outdoors im Freien (11)

out of aus (+ *dat.*) (5)

outside draußen (7); **outside of** außerhalb (+ *gen.*) (9)

oven: microwave oven der Mikrowellenherd (-e) (12)

over über (+ *acc./dat.*); **over there** da drüben (6); **left over** übrig (12)

overcast bewölkt (7)

overnight stay die Übernachtung (-en) (9)

own eigen (12)

to own besitzen, besaß, besessen (11)

P

packaging die Verpackung (-en) (14)

pain der Schmerz (-en) (8)

to paint (*a wall or house*) anstreichen (streicht an) (4); malen (7)

pair of eyeglasses die Brille (-n) (5)

pan die Pfanne (-n) (6)

pants die Hose (-n) (5)

paper das Papier (-e) (2); **toilet paper** das Toilettenpapier (5)

papers die Unterlagen (*pl.*) (11)

Pardon? Wie bitte? (E)

parents die Eltern (*pl.*) (3)

parking space, parking lot der Parkplatz (⸚e) (9)

part der Teil (-e); **parts of the body** die Körperteile (*pl.*) (8)

to participate teilnehmen an (+ *dat.*) (nimmt teil), nahm teil, teilgenommen (14)

particular(ly) besonders (8); **not particularly well** nicht besonders gut (E)

party die Party (-s) (3)

passer-by der Passant (-en *masc.*) (9)

passport der Reisepass (⸚e) (9)

past: half past one halb zwei (4)

pastry shop die Konditorei (-en) (5)

path der Weg (-e) (9)

patio die Terrasse (-n) (2)

to pay zahlen (5); bezahlen (9); **Check, please!** Zahlen, bitte! (6)

to pay attention (to) achten (auf + *acc.*) (8)

pedestrian zone die Fußgängerzone (-n) (14)

pen: ballpoint pen der Kugelschreiber (-) (12)

pencil der Bleistift (-e) (12)

people (*indef. pron.*) man (4)

pepper der Pfeffer (5); **bell pepper** die Paprikaschote (-n) (6)

percent das Prozent (-e)

per: per person pro Person (10); **per week** pro Woche (4)

perhaps vielleicht (2)

to permit erlauben (9)

to be permitted to dürfen (darf), durfte, gedurft (4)

person die Person (-en); der Mensch (-en *masc.*) (2); **per person** pro Person (10)

pharmacy die Apotheke (-n) (5)

phone: cell phone das Handy (-s) (2)

photograph das Foto (-s) (2)

physician der Arzt (⸚e) / die Ärztin (-nen) (8)

to pick up (*from a place*) abholen (holt ab) (4)

pilsner beer das Pilsner (-) (6)

place der Platz (⸚e); **This place is taken.** Hier ist besetzt. (6); **place of birth** der Geburtsort (-e) (1); **place of residence** der Wohnort (-e) (1); **if I were in your place** an deiner Stelle (12)

to place (*in a standing position*) stellen (6); (*inside*) stecken (6)

plaid kariert (5)

to plan planen; vorhaben (hat vor), hatte vor, vorgehabt (3); **plan to do (something)** (etwas) vorhaben (4)

plane ticket der Flugschein (-e) (10)

plant: house plant die Zimmerpflanze (-n) (2)

plastic bag die Plastiktüte (-n) (14)

plate der Teller (-) (6)

platform (*train*) der Bahnsteig (-e) (10)

play (*theater*) das Theaterstück (-e) (4)

to play spielen (1); **to play computer games** Computerspiele spielen (1); **to play cards** Karten spielen (1); **to play tennis** Tennis spielen (7)

player: CD player der CD-Spieler (-) (2); **DVD player** der DVD-Spieler (-) (2)

playing card die Spielkarte (-n) (7)

pleasant angenehm (7)

please bitte (E)

Pleased to meet you. Freut mich. (E)

to be pleasing to gefallen (+ *dat.*) (gefällt), gefiel, gefallen (5)

Poland (das) Polen (E)

police, police station die Polizei (9)

politician der Politiker (-) / die Politikerin (-nen) (14)

politics die Politik (13)

pollution: environmental pollution die Umweltverschmutzung (14)

pool: swimming pool das Schwimmbad (⸚er) (7)

poor(ly) schlecht (E)

pork das Schweinefleisch (5); **pork roast** der Schweinebraten (-) (6)

position (*job*) der Arbeitsplatz (⸚e), die Tätigkeit (-en), die Stelle (-n) (11)

possibility die Möglichkeit (-en) (10)

possible möglich (14)

postal code die Postleitzahl (-en) (E)

poster das Poster (-) (2)

post office die Post (Postämter) (9)

potato die Kartoffel (-n) (5); **fried potatoes** die Bratkartoffeln (6)

poverty die Armut (14)

practical praktisch (1)

to prefer (to do something) lieber (+ *verb*) (4); vorziehen (zieht vor), zog vor, vorgezogen (14)

to prepare (for) sich vorbereiten (auf + *acc.*) (bereitet vor) (11)

preposition die Präposition (-en) (5)

to prescribe verschreiben, verschrieb, verschrieben (8)

present das Geschenk (-e) (3)

prestige das Ansehen (11)

pretty hübsch (1)

pretzel die Brezel (-n) (6)

price der Preis (-e) (9); **reasonable in price** günstig; **included in the price** im Preis enthalten (9)

primary school die Grundschule (-) (11)

printer der Drucker (-) (13)

prison das Gefängnis (-se) (14)

probably wahrscheinlich (11); wohl (11)

problem das Problem (-e) (2)

to produce herstellen (stellt her) (11)

product das Produkt (-e); **dairy products** die Milchprodukte (*pl.*) (5)

profession der Beruf (-e) (1)

professional life das Berufsleben (11)

professor der Professor (-en) / die Professorin (-nen) (1)

program das Programm (-e) (13)

progress der Fortschritt (-e); **to make progress** Fortschritte machen (14)

to promote fördern (14)

pronoun das Pronomen (-) (1)

to propose vorschlagen (schlägt vor), schlug vor, vorgeschlagen (10)

to protect schützen (14)

psychologist der Psychologe (-n *masc.*) / die Psychologin (-nen) (11)

pub die Kneipe (-n), das Lokal (-e), das Wirtshaus (⸚er) (6)

pullover sweater der Pullover (-) (5)

punctual(ly) pünktlich (10)

to purchase (something) sich (etwas) anschaffen (schafft an) (14)

purple lila (5)

to put (*in a lying position*) legen; (*in a standing position*) stellen (6)

puzzles: to do crossword puzzles Kreuzworträtsel machen (1)

Q

quarter: a quarter to two Viertel vor zwei (12)

question die Frage (-n); **I have a question.** Ich habe eine Frage. (E)

question word das Fragewort (¨er) (6)

quick(ly) schnell (10)

quiet ruhig (1)

quite recht (2)

R

racism der Rassismus (14)

radio das Radio (-s) (2)

railway die Bahn (-en) (10)

rain der Regen (7)

to rain regnen; **It's raining.** Es regnet. (7)

rain shower der Regenschauer (-) (7)

rainy regnerisch (7)

to raise (*a child*) erziehen, erzog, erzogen (14)

rare(ly) selten (2)

rather recht (2); **would rather** möchte lieber (4)

to read lesen (liest), las, gelesen (1); **to read quickly** überfliegen, überflog, überflogen (13); **to read books/the newspaper** Bücher/Zeitung lesen

really wirklich (1); (*coll.*) echt (1)

reasonable (*in price*) recht preiswert (2); günstig (10)

to receive bekommen, bekam, bekommen (6)

reception der Empfang (¨e); **reception desk** die Rezeption (9)

to recommend empfehlen (empfiehlt), empfahl, empfohlen (5)

to record (on video) aufnehmen (nimmt auf), nahm auf, aufgenommen (13)

recorder: video recorder der Videorecorder (-) (2)

to recover sich erholen (8)

recycling das Recycling; **recycling center** die Sammelstelle (-n) (14)

red rot (5)

to reduce vermindern (14)

refrigerator der Kühlschrank (¨e) (12)

register: cash register die Kasse (-n) (5)

registration form das Anmeldeformular (-e) (9)

to regret bedauern (14)

regular(ly) regelmäßig (8)

related to verwandt mit (3)

to relax sich entspannen (8)

to remain bleiben, blieb, ist geblieben (1)

rent die Miete (-n) (2)

to rent (*from someone*) mieten (12); **to rent out** (*to someone*) vermieten (12)

repair die Reparatur (-en) (12)

to repair reparieren (9)

to repeat wiederholen; **Please repeat.** Wiederholen Sie, bitte. (E)

report der Bericht (-e) (13)

to report berichten (13)

report card das Zeugnis (-se) (11)

to request bitten um (+ *acc.*), bat, gebeten (12)

research die Forschung (-en) (14); **to do research** forschen (13)

reservation: seat reservation card die Platzkarte (-n) (10)

to reserve reservieren (7)

to reside wohnen (1)

residence: place of residence der Wohnort (-e) (1)

responsible verantwortlich (11)

to rest (sich) ausruhen (ruht aus) (4)

restaurant das Restaurant (-s), das Lokal (-e), die Gaststätte (-n) (6); Biergarten (¨) (*beer garden*) (6)

restroom die Toilette (-n) (9)

résumé Lebenslauf (¨e) (11)

rice der Reis (6)

to ride fahren (fährt), fuhr, ist gefahren (1); **to ride a motorcycle** Motorrad fahren (1); **ride (on horseback)** reiten, ritt, ist geritten (7)

right rechts; **to the right** nach rechts (9)

right das Recht; **human rights** das Menschenrecht (-e) (*usually pl.*) (14); **to be right** Recht haben (2)

right-wing extremism der Rechtsextremismus (14)

river der Fluss (¨e) (7)

road der Weg (-e) (9)

roast: pork roast der Schweinebraten (-) (6)

roll das Brötchen (-) (5)

romantic romantisch (1)

roof das Dach (¨er) (12)

room das Zimmer (-); **bathroom** das Badezimmer (2); **bedroom** das Schlafzimmer; **breakfast room** der Frühstücksraum (¨e); **room with two beds** das Doppelzimmer (9); **room with one bed** das Einzelzimmer, das Einbettzimmer (9)

roommate der Mitbewohner (-) / die Mitbewohnerin (-nen) (2)

round-trip (*adj.*) hin und zurück (10)

rug der Teppich (-e) (2)

to run laufen (läuft), lief, ist gelaufen (2)

S

sad traurig (7)

safe sicher (10)

to sail segeln (7)

salad der Salat (-e) (6)

salary das Gehalt (¨er) (11)

sales der Handel (11)

salesperson der Verkäufer (-) / die Verkäuferin (-nen) (2); der Kaufmann (*pl.* Kaufleute) / die Kauffrau (-en) (10)

salt das Salz (5)

Saturday (der) Samstag, Sonnabend (3); **Saturdays, on Saturday** samstags (4)

sauerkraut das Sauerkraut (6)

sausage die Wurst (¨e) (5); **white sausage** die Weißwurst (6)

to save sparen (12)

saving: savings account das Sparkonto (Sparkonten) (12)

to say sagen (1); **to say definitely** Bescheid sagen (10); **How do you say . . . in German?** Wie sagt man... auf Deutsch? (E); **What did you say?** Wie bitte? (E)

saying good-bye beim Abschied (E)

scarcely kaum (8)

scarf der Schal (-s) (5)

schedule (train) der Fahrplan (¨e) (10)

school: secondary school das Gymnasium (Gymnasien) (11)

scientific wissenschaftlich (13)

season die Jahreszeit (-en) (7)

seat der Platz (¨e) (6); **seat reservation card** die Platzkarte (-n) (10)

second die Sekunde (-n) (4)

to see sehen (sieht), sah, gesehen (2)

to seem scheinen, schien, geschienen (13)

to select something (for oneself) sich (et)was aussuchen (sucht aus) (13)

semester das Semester (-) (1)

to send schicken (3)

sensible gescheit (13)

separate getrennt (6)

to separate (sich) trennen (14)

September (der) September (3)

serious ernst (1)

service die Bedienung (-en) (6)

to set (*put in a sitting position*) setzen (6)

seven sieben (E)

seventeen siebzehn (E)

seventy siebzig (E)

shame: What a shame! So ein Pech! (8)

shampoo das Shampoo (-s) (5)

shape: in shape fit; **to keep in shape** sich fit halten (hält), hielt, gehalten (8)

shared housing die Wohngemeinschaft (WG) (-en) (2)

to shave sich rasieren (8)

shaving cream die Rasiercreme (-s) (5)

she sie (1)

shelf das Regal (-e) (2)

shirt das Hemd (-en) (5); **casual shirt** das Sporthemd (-en) (5)

shoe der Schuh (-e); **tennis shoe** der Tennisschuh (5)

to shop einkaufen (kauft ein); **to go shopping** einkaufen gehen (geht), ging, ist gegangen (4)

short kurz; (*person*) klein (10)

shoulder die Schulter (-n) (8)

show die Show; (*TV*) die Sendung (-en) (13)

to show zeigen (5)

shower die Dusche (-n) (9)

to shower (sich) duschen (8)

siblings die Geschwister (*pl.*) (3)

sick krank; **sick as a dog** hundsmiserabel (8)

side dish die Beilage (-n) (6)

simple einfach (10)

since seit (+ *dat.*) (5); da (*subord. conj.*)

sister die Schwester (-n) (3)

sister-in-law die Schwägerin (-nen) (3)

to sit sitzen, saß, gesessen (6)

to sit down sich (hin)setzen (setzt sich hin) (8)

six sechs (E)

sixteen sechzehn (E)

sixty sechzig (E)

size die Größe (-n) (5)

skate: ice skate der Schlittschuh (-e); **to skate: to ice skate** Schlittschuh laufen (läuft) lief, ist gelaufen (7)

skating rink (*ice*) das Eisstadion (Eisstadien) (7)

to sketch zeichnen (7)

to skim (*a text*) überfliegen, überflog, überflogen (13)

skirt der Rock (¨e) (5)

sky der Himmel (7)

to sleep schlafen (schläft), schlief, geschlafen (2)

slipper der Hausschuh (-e) (5)

Slovakia (die) Slowakei (E)

Slovenia (das) Slowenien (E)

slow(ly) langsam (10); **Slower, please.** Langsamer, bitte. (E)

small klein (2)

to smoke rauchen (8); **no-smoking car** der Nichtraucher (-) (10)

snow der Schnee (7)

to snow schneien (8); **It's snowing.** Es schneit. (7)

so so (2); **so long** mach's gut, tschüss (E); **so-so** so, lala (E); **So what?** Na und? (13)

soccer der Fußball; **to play soccer** Fußball spielen (7)

sock die Socke (-n); der Strumpf (¨e) (5)

sofa das Sofa (-s) (2)

solution die Lösung (-en) (14)

something etwas (2)

sometimes manchmal (8)

somewhat etwas (2); ziemlich (6)

son der Sohn (¨e) (3)

soon bald (12)

sooner eher (13)

sore throat die Halsschmerzen (*pl.*) (8)

sorry: I'm sorry. Das tut mir Leid. (9)

so-so so lala (E)

to sound klingen, klang, geklungen (8); **You sound so depressed.** Du klingst so deprimiert. (8)

soup die Suppe (-n) (6)

to speak sprechen (2)

special offer das Angebot (-e) (10)

to spend (*money*) ausgeben (gibt aus), gab aus, ausgegeben (12); (*time*) verbringen (8)

spite: in spite of trotz (+ *gen.*) (9)

spoon der Löffel (-) (6)

sport der Sport (Sportarten); **to do sports** Sport treiben, trieb, getrieben (7); **engaged in sports** sportlich aktiv (10)

sports arena die Sporthalle (-n) (7)

sports coat das Sakko (-s) (5)

to spread verbreiten (14)

spring das Frühjahr, der Frühling (7)

stable (*adj.*) fest (11)

stadium das Stadion (Stadien) (7)

stairway die Treppe (-n) (12)

to stand stehen, stand, gestanden (6)

to stand up aufstehen (steht auf), stand auf, ist aufgestanden (4); (*to put in a standing position*) stellen (6)

station: train station der Bahnhof (¨e) (10); **television station (channel)** das Programm (-e) (13)

to start beginnen, begann, begonnen (10)

stay der Aufenthalt (-e); **overnight stay** die Übernachtung (-en) (9)

to stay bleiben, blieb, ist geblieben (1); **to stay overnight** übernachten (10)

to stay up aufbleiben (bleibt auf), blieb auf, ist aufgeblieben

steak das Steak (-s) (5)

stereo die Stereoanlage (-n) (2)

still noch (2); **still none/no** noch kein

stock exchange die Börse (-n) (13)

stocking der Strumpf (¨e) (5)

stomach der Bauch (¨e) (8)

stop (*e.g., bus*) die Haltestelle (-n) (10)

to stop: (*doing something*) aufhören (hört auf) (4); halten (hält), hielt, gehalten (14)

store das Geschäft (-e); der Laden (¨) (5); **department store** das Kaufhaus (¨er) (2); **drugstore** (*toiletries and sundries*) die Drogerie (-n) (5); **health food store** der Naturkostladen (¨) (8)

story (*level*) der Stock (Stockwerke) (9); die Etage (-n) (12)

straight ahead (immer) geradeaus (9)

to straighten up aufräumen (räumt auf) (4)

strawberry die Erdbeere (-n) (5)

street die Straße (-n) (E)

street address die Hausnummer (-n) (E)

strenuous anstrengend (8)

stress der Stress (8)

stressful stressig (1)

to stretch sich strecken (8)

strictly streng (14)

striped gestreift (5)

student der Student (-en *masc.*) / die Studentin (-nen) (1)

student cafeteria die Mensa (Mensen) (1)

study das Arbeitszimmer (-) (2)

to study studieren; lernen (1)

to subscribe to abonnieren (13)

subscription das Abonnement (-s) (13)

success der Erfolg (-e) (11)

successful(ly) erfolgreich (11); **to be successful** Erfolg haben (11)

successfully erfolgreich (11)

sugar der Zucker (5)

to suggest vorschlagen (schlägt vor), schlug vor, vorgeschlagen (10)

suit der Anzug (¨e); **bathing suit** der Badeanzug (¨e) (5)

suitcase der Koffer (-) (5)

summer der Sommer (7)

sun die Sonne (7); **The sun is shining.** Die Sonne scheint. (7)

Sunday (der) Sonntag (3); **(on) Sundays** sonntags (4)

sunny sonnig (7)

sunscreen das Sonnenschutzmittel (-) (10)

sunshine der Sonnenschein (7)

suntan lotion das Sonnenschutzmittel (-) (10)

super prima (E); (Ganz) toll (1)

superlative die Superlativform (-en) (7)

supermarket der Supermarkt (¨e) (5)

to support unterstützen (14)

to be supposed to sollen (soll), sollte, gesollt (4)

surname der Nachname (-n *masc.*) (1)

to be suspended hängen, hing, gehangen (6)

suspenseful spannend (4)

to swallow schlucken (5)

sweater der Pullover (-) (5)

to swim schwimmen, schwamm, ist geschwommen (2)

swimming pool das Schwimmbad (:er) (7)

Switzerland die Schweiz (E)

T

table der Tisch (-e) (2); **coffee table** der Couchtisch (2)

to take nehmen (nimmt), nahm, genommen (2); dauern (7); **take-out** (*food*) zum Mitnehmen (6); **to take along** mitnehmen (nimmt mit), nahm mit, mitgenommen (4); **to take over** übernehmen (übernimmt), übernahm, übernommen (11); **Take care.** Mach's gut. (E)

tall groß (1); **How tall are you?** Wie groß sind Sie/bist du? (1); **I'm 1.63 meters (tall).** Ich bin 1,63 (meter groß). (1)

tape (*video*) das Video (-s) (2)

to taste (good) schmecken (+ *dat.*); **That tastes good (to me).** Das schmeckt (mir). (5)

tax die Steuer (-n) (14)

taxi das Taxi (-s) (10)

taxi driver der Taxifahrer (-) / die Taxifahrerin (-nen) (10)

tea der Tee (-s) (5); **herbal tea** der Kräutertee (-s) (8)

teacher der Lehrer (-) / die Lehrerin (-nen) (E)

technique die Technik (-en) (11)

technology die Technik (-en) (11)

telephone das Telefon (-e) (2)

telephone number die Telefonnummer (-n) (E)

television (media) das Fernsehen; **on television** im Fernsehen; **watching television** das Fernsehen (4); **to watch television** fernsehen (sieht fern), sah fern, ferngesehen (13)

television set der Fernseher (-) (2)

television station (channel) das Programm (-e) (13)

to tell sagen; **tell me** sag mal (1)

temperature die Temperatur (-en) (7)

ten zehn (E)

tender zart (5)

tennis: to play tennis Tennis spielen (7)

tennis court der Tennisplatz (:e) (7)

tennis shoe der Tennisschuh (-e) (5)

tent das Zelt (-e) (10)

terrace die Terrasse (-n) (2)

terrible scheußlich (7)

terrorism der Terrorismus (14)

thank you danke (E)

thanks danke; **thank you very much** danke schön (E); **thanks a lot** danke sehr (1); **fine, thanks** danke, gut (E)

thanks: Many thanks! Vielen Dank! (6); **No thanks necessary.** Nichts zu danken. (8)

that (*subord. conj.*) dass (8)

that is das heißt (8)

the der, die, das (E)

theater das Theater (-) (4); **movie theater** das Kino (-s) (4); **to go to the Theater** ins Theater gehen (4)

their ihr (3)

then dann (1); **now and then** ab und zu (8)

there da (2); **over there** da drüben (6); **there is/there are** es gibt (3)

therefore deshalb (8)

they sie; man (*indef. pron.*) (1)

to think (about/of) denken (an + *acc.*), dachte, gedacht (12); nachdenken (über + *acc.*) (denkt nach), dachte nach, nachgedacht (11)

to think (of) finden, fand, gefunden; halten für (+ *acc.*) (hält), hielt, gehalten (14); **What do you think of . . . ?** Wie findest du...? (1); **I think . . .** Ich finde... (14); **I think it is a pity.** Ich finde es schade. (12)

to be thirsty Durst haben (2)

thirteen dreizehn (E)

thirty dreißig (E)

this dieser, diese, dies(es); das (5); **This is . . .** Das ist... (E); **this evening** heute Abend (1)

thousand (ein) tausend (E)

thrifty sparsam (12)

three drei (E)

three times dreimal (7)

throat der Hals (:e); **sore throat** die Halsschmerzen (*pl.*) (8)

through durch (+ *acc.*) (3)

to thunder donnern; **It's thundering.** Es donnert. (7)

thunderstorm das Gewitter (-) (7)

Thursday (der) Donnerstag (3); **(on) Thursdays** donnerstags (4)

ticket die Fahrkarte (-n); **airplane ticket** der Flugschein (-e); **one-way** (*ticket*) einfach (10)

ticket window der Fahrkartenschalter (-) (10)

time die Zeit (2); die Uhrzeit (-en); **free time** die Freizeit (7); **to have time** Zeit haben (2); **What time is it?** Wie spät ist es? (4); **At what time?** Um wie viel Uhr? (4)

time of day die Tageszeit (-en) (2)

tin can die Dose (-n) (14)

tired müde (8)

to an (+ *acc./dat.*) (6); zu (+ *dat.*); nach (+ *dat.*); bis zum/zur; **(to) home** nach Hause; **to the theater** ins Theater (5)

today heute (1)

toe die Zehe (-n) (8)

together gemeinsam, zusammen (6)

toilet das WC (-s) (9)

toilet paper das Toilettenpapier (5)

toiletries die Toilettenartikel (*pl.*) (5)

toiletries and sundries store die Drogerie (-n) (5)

tomato die Tomate (-n) (5)

tomorrow morgen (3); **tomorrow morning** morgen früh (4)

tonight heute Abend (4)

toothpaste die Zahnpasta (5)

topical aktuell (13)

total ingesamt (10); **The total is . . .** Das macht zusammen... (6)

total(ly) ganz (12); **I'm totally against it.** Ich bin total dagegen. (14)

town die Stadt (:e) (E)

trade der Handel (11)

track (*train*) das Gleis (-e) (10)

tradition die Tradition (-en) (3)

traffic light die Ampel (-n) (9)

tragedy die Tragödie (-n) (4)

trail: hiking trail der Wanderweg (-e) (10)

train die Bahn (-en), der Zug (:e) (10)

train platform der Bahnsteig (-e) (10)

train station der Bahnhof (:e) (4)

training die Ausbildung (11)

transcript (*school*) das Zeugnis (-se) (11)

to transfer (*trains*) umsteigen (steigt um), stieg um, ist umgestiegen (10)

transcript das Zeugnis (-se) (11)

trash der Abfall (:e) (14)

to travel reisen, ist gereist (1)

travel agency das Reisebüro (-s) (10)

travel brochure der Reiseprospekt (-e) (10)

traveler's check der Reisescheck (-s) (10)

travel guide (*person*) der Reiseleiter (-) / die Reiseleiterin (-nen); (*book*) der Reiseführer (-) (10)

tree der Baum (:e); **family tree** der Stammbaum (3)

trip die Fahrt (-en) (10); **to go on a trip** verreisen, ist verreist (10)

trousers die Hose (-n) (5)

to try probieren, versuchen (8); **to try on** anprobieren (probiert an) (5)

T-shirt das T-Shirt (-s) (5)

Tuesday (der) Dienstag (3); **(on) Tuesdays** dienstags (4)

tuition die Studiengebühren (*pl.*) (12)

turkey der Truthahn (¨e) (5)

to turn into einbiegen in (+ *acc.*) (9)

turnover der Umsatz (¨e) (11)

TV set der Fernseher (-) (2)

twelve zwölf (E)

twenty zwanzig (E)

twice zweimal (7)

two zwei (E)

type die Art (-en), die Sorte (-n); **types of fruit** die Obstsorten (*pl.*) (5)

U

ugly hässlich (2)

umbrella der Regenschirm (-e) (7)

uncle der Onkel (-) (3)

under unter (+ *acc./dat.*) (6); **Under what name?** Auf welchen Namen? (9)

to understand: I don't understand. Ich verstehe das nicht. (E)

to undertake unternehmen (unternimmt), unternahm, unternommen (10)

undressed: to get undressed sich ausziehen (zieht sich aus), zog sich aus, hat sich ausgezogen (8)

unfortunately leider (3)

unfriendly unfreundlich (1)

unfurnished unmöbliert (2)

university die Universität (-en) (1)

university instructor der Hochschullehrer (-) / die Hochschullehrerin (-nen)(1)

unlikable unsympathisch (1)

until five o'clock bis (um) fünf Uhr (6)

upstairs oben; nach oben (12)

urgent(ly) dringend (2)

to use verwenden (14)

useful nützlich (13)

usually gewöhnlich (4)

utilities die Nebenkosten (*pl.*) (12)

V

vacation: to go on vacation Urlaub machen (8)

vacuum cleaner der Staubsauger (-) (13)

Valentine's Day der Valentinstag (-e) (3)

varied abwechslungsreich (11)

veal cutlet (*breaded*) das Wiener Schnitzel (-) (6)

veal sausage (*white*) die Weißwurst (¨e) (6)

vegetable das Gemüse; **type of vegetable** die Gemüsesorte (-n); **fruit and vegetable stand** der Obst- und Gemüsestand (¨e) (5)

vegetarian vegetarisch (6)

verb das Verb (-en) (1); **modal verb** das Modalverb (5)

very sehr (1); ganz (1); **very well** sehr gut (E)

vicinity die Nähe (9); die Umgebung (-en) (12)

video(tape) das Video (-s) (2)

video recorder (VCR) der Videorecorder (-) (2)

view: in my view meines Erachtens (14)

violation die Verletzung (-en) (14)

violence: (act of) violence die Gewalttätigkeit (-en) (14)

to visit besuchen (1)

W

to wait (for) warten (auf + *acc.*) (6)

waiter der Kellner (-); der Ober (-) (6)

waitress die Kellnerin (-nen) (6)

to wake up aufwachen (wacht auf), ist aufgewacht (4)

walk: to go for a walk spazieren gehen (geht), ging spazieren, ist spazieren gegangen (4); **to walk along** entlanggehen (geht entlang), ging entlang, ist entlanggegangen (9)

wall die Wand (¨e) (2); **wall-to-wall carpeting** der Teppichboden (¨) (12)

to want wollen (will), wollte, gewollt (4)

war der Krieg (-e) (14)

warm warm (7)

to wash oneself sich waschen (wäscht), wusch, gewaschen (8)

waste der Abfall (¨e) (14); **wastebasket** der Papierkorb (¨e) (2)

to watch sich (*dat.*) etwas ansehen (sieht an), sah an, angesehen (13); anschauen (schaut an) (13); **to watch television** fernsehen (sieht fern), sah fern, ferngesehen (4)

watching television das Fernsehen (4)

water das Wasser; **mineral water** das Mineralwasser (5)

way der Weg (-e) (9); **along the way** unterwegs; **by the way** übrigens (9)

we wir (1)

weak schlapp (8)

wear tragen (trägt), trug, getragen (5)

weather das Wetter (7)

weather report der Wetterbericht (-e) (7)

wedding die Hochzeit (-en) (3)

Wednesday (der) Mittwoch (3); **(on) Wednesdays** mittwochs (4)

week die Woche (-n) (4); **once a week** einmal die Woche (7)

weekend das Wochenende (-n) (4)

weight training: to do weight training Bodybuilding machen (7)

welcome: (a hearty) welcome herzlich willkommen; **you're welcome** bitte (E)

well gut (1); günstig (gut) (10); **not so well** nicht besonders gut (E); **very well** sehr gut (E); **to get well** sich erholen (8); **Get well soon!** Gute Besserung! (8)

were: if I were you an deiner Stelle (12)

what was (1); **What a shame!** So ein Pech! (8); **What is . . . ?** Wie ist...? (E); **What's your name?** (*form.*) Wie ist Ihr Name? / Wie heißen Sie? (*inform.*) Wie heißt du? (E); **what kind of (a)** was für (ein) (11); **What does . . . mean?** Was bedeutet...? (E); **What time is it?** Wie spät ist es? (4); **So what?** Na und? (13)

when als (*subord. conj.*) (10); wann (1); wenn (*subord. conj.*) (8); **When is your birthday?** Wann hast du Geburtstag? (3)

where wo; **from where** woher (1); **(to) where** wohin (5); **Where are you from?** (*form.*) Woher kommst du/kommen Sie? (E)

whether ob (*subord. conj.*) (8)

which welcher, welche, welches (5)

whipped cream die Sahne (6)

white weiß (5)

who wer (1)

whom wen (*acc.*) (2); wem (*dat.*) (5)

why warum (2)

wife die Frau (-en) (3)

wind der Wind (7)

window das Fenster (-) (2); **ticket window** der Fahrkartenschalter (-) (10)

windy windig (7)

wine der Wein (-e) (6)

winter (der) Winter (7)

to wish wünschen (3)

wishes: best wishes viele Grüße (12)

with mit (+ *dat.*); bei (+ *dat.*) (5)

without ohne (3); **to do without** verzichten auf (+ *acc.*) (13)

woman die Frau (-en) (1)

wonderful fabelhaft (E)

word das Wort (¨er); **question word** das Fragewort (¨er) (1)

work die Arbeit (8)

to work arbeiten (1); funktionieren (9); **That'll work too.** Das geht auch. (9)

workplace der Arbeitsplatz (¨e) (11)

workroom das Arbeitszimmer (-) (2)
world die Welt (14)
world hunger der Welthunger (14)
would: would like (to) möchte; **would rather** möchte lieber; **would like best** möchte am liebsten (4); **Would you please . . . ?** Würden Sie bitte...? (9)
to write schreiben, schrieb, geschrieben (2); **How do you write____?** Wie schreibt man____? (E)

X

xenophobia die Ausländerfeindlich-keit (14)

Y

yard der Garten (·:) (2)
year das Jahr (-e) (1); **next year** nächstes Jahr (1); **once a year** einmal im Jahr (7)
yellow gelb (5)
yes ja (E); doch (1)
yesterday gestern (7)
yet noch (2); **no . . . yet** noch kein; **not any . . . yet** noch kein; **not yet** noch nicht
yogurt der Joghurt (5)
you du (*inform. sg.*); ihr (*inform. pl.*); Sie (*form sg./pl.*) (1); dich (*acc. inform. sg.*); euch (*acc./dat.*

inform. pl.); Sie (*acc. form.*) (3); dir (*dat. inform. sg.*); Ihnen (*dat. form.*) (5)
young jung (10)
your dein (*inform. sg.*); euer (*inform. pl.*); Ihr (*form sg./pl.*) (3)
youth hostel die Jugendherberge (-n) (9)

Z

zero null (E)
zip code die Postleitzahl (-en) (E)

Index

The index is followed by a list of major topics ("Culture") appearing in the **Kulturtipp** boxes along with other pertinent cultural topics and a list of vocabulary items grouped by category ("Vocabulary"). References to reading strategies are incorporated in the index under *reading strategies*. *Note: KT* = **Kulturtipp;** *ST* = **Sprachtipp;** *N* = footnote.

A

aber vs. **sondern,** 217
accusative case
  of definite articles, 64 (*charts*)
  of demonstrative pronouns, 73
  of **der-**words, 64
  direct object in, 64, 155
  es gibt with, 146 *ST*
  of indefinite articles, 66
  of interrogative pronouns, 66
  of negative article **kein,** 69–70 (*chart*)
  of nouns, 58 *ST,* 64
  of personal pronouns, 95 (*chart*)
  of possessive adjectives, 92
  prepositions requiring, 97. 186–87, 194
  of reflexive pronouns, 245–46 (*chart*)
  of relative pronouns, 335
  of weak masculine nouns, 65, 158
  word order of, 64, 159
active voice, 415, 417
address
  mailing, 11, 12–13
  street, 11
address, forms of
  du vs. **Sie,** 3 *KT,* 29 *ST,* 35
  Herr, Frau, Fräulein, 3 *KT*
adjectival nouns, 306–7 (*chart*). *See also* adjective endings
adjective endings, 55 *ST,* 271–72 (*charts*), 299–300, 304. *See also* attributive adjectives; weak adjective endings
adjectives. *See also* adjective endings; attributive adjectives; comparative form; predicate adjectives; superlative form
  comparative form, 294 *ST,* 299–300, 300 *ST*
  demonstrative, 165
  possessive, 91–92 (*charts*)
  possessive, with dative case, 157
  without preceding article, 275
  present participles used as, 423
  referring to city names, 278
  superlative form, 302–3, 304
  used as nouns, 306–7 (*chart*)
  viel/mehr, 300 *ST*
  wenig/weniger, 300 *ST*

adverbs
  comparative form, 294 *ST,* 299–300, 300 *ST*
  dahin, 361
  deswegen, 397
  gern, 60 *ST,* 299, 303
  immer, with comparative, 300
  nämlich, 399
  nicht, 69
  present participles used as, 423
  superlative form, 302–3
  of time, 117 *ST,* 118 *ST,* 388
agent
  in passive sentences, 413, 415
  passive without (using **es**), 416
alle, 165
alphabet, German, 4–5
als
  with comparative form, 299
  as subordinating conjunction, 311
alternatives to passive
  with impersonal **es,** 416
  with **man,** 420
antecedent
  personal pronouns agreeing with, 35
  relative pronouns referring to, 335
arbeiten vs. **lernen/studieren,** 29 *ST*
articles. *See* definite articles; indefinite articles; **kein**
attributive adjectives
  city names used as, 278
  comparative form, 294 *ST,* 299–300, 300 *ST*
  endings of, 55 *ST,* 271–72 (*chart*), 272 *ST,* 274 (*chart*) 275 (*charts*), 277 *ST*
  present participles used as, 423
  superlative form, 304
aus, 162
auxiliary verbs. *See also* **haben;** modal auxiliary verbs; **sein; werden**
  with past participles, 218, 224, 313

B

be-, 223
bei, 146 *ST,* 162
Beuys, Joseph, 378
bevor, with past perfect tense, 313

bitte, 133
bleiben, 222
brauchen, with dependent infinitive plus **zu,** 391
Brecht, Bertolt, 229
Bremer, Claus, 379

C

capitalization. *See also* Appendix E
  of adjectival nouns, 306
  of adjectives referring to cities and regions, 278
  of nouns, 33
  of pronouns, 35, 92
  of **Sie,** 35
cardinal numbers, 10, 89 *ST*
cases. *See* accusative case; dative case; genitive case; nominative case
city names, attributive adjectives referring to, 278
clauses. *See also* sentences; word order
  dependent clauses, 241
  infinitive clauses, 391, 392
  main clauses, 241
  relative clauses, 335–36
clock, 112, 113 *ST,* 114 *ST,* 117
cognates, 15
commands. *See* imperative
comparative form, 298. *See also* superlative form
  of adjectives, 299–300, 300 *ST*
  of adverbs, 299–300
compound nouns, 34
compounds
  da-, 360–61
  noun, 34, 201
  wo-, 363
conjunctions
  coordinating, 217
  subordinating, 241, 311
connectors: **zuerst, deshalb, dann, zuletzt,** 152 *ST*
contractions of prepositions and articles, 163, 187
contrary-to-fact conditions, 368. *See also* subjunctive mood
coordinating conjunctions, 217

Photos *Page 1* © Ulrike Welsch; *2* (top) © Ulrike Welsch; *2* (bottom) © Beryl Goldberg; *3* © Ulrike Welsch; *22* © argus/ Schwarzbach; *24* (top left) © Kevin Galvin; *24* (middle) © Ulrike Welsch; *24* (bottom) © Owen Franken/Stock Boston; *32* © Beryl Goldberg; *50* © plus 49/Dirk Vogel; *61* (left) © Tony Stone/Getty; *61* (right) © Joseph Guido Gianetti/Stock Boston; *65* © Benja Weller/Das Fotoarchiv; *80* © Ulrike Welsch; *81* © Wolfgang Kaehler; *85* © Koelbl Stern; *88* (top) © Schmied-Helga Lade Fotoagentur/Peter Arnold, Inc.; *88* (bottom) © BAV-Helga Lade Fotoagentur/Peter Arnold, Inc.; *89* © McGraw-Hill, Inc.; *100* © Bob Krist/Corbis; *101* © Archive Fur Kunst und Geschichte, Berlin; *108* (all) © Archive Fur Kunst und Geschichte, Berlin; *109* (top and bottom) © Archive Fur Kunst und Geschichte, Berlin; *110* © Adam Jones/Danita Delimont, Agent; *122* © Zefa/Damm; *138* Courtesy Miguel Guglielminpietro © Express Newspaper Ltd./Dist. Bulls; *142* © Wolfgang Kaehler; *174* © argum; *177* Courtesy Miguel Guglielmienpietro; *179* © Kevin Galvin/Stock Boston; *182* © Daniel Aubry; *200* © CARO/Hechtenberg; *204* (left) © Helga Lade/Peter Arnold, Inc.; *204* (right) © Rudy Muller/Envision; *205* © Hugh Rogers; *206* © Kevin Galvin; *213* (top left) © Julie Marcotte/Stock Boston; *213* (top right) © Reichmann; *213* (bottom left) © Fridmar Dann/eStock; *213* (bottom right) © David Ulmer/Stock Boston; *219* © Ulrike Welsch/PhotoEdit; *229* © Topham/The Image Works; *232* © Werner H. Mulle/Peter Arnold, Inc.; *234* (top) © Michael P. Gadomski/Photo Researchers; *234* (bottom) © Helga Lade/Peter Arnold, Inc.; *235* © Photodisc; *243* © Ulrike Welsch; *258* © Lange/Helga Lade Fotoagentur/Peter Arnold, Inc.; *272* © Courtesy of Monica D. Clyde; *277* © Shaun Egan/Getty; *279* © Jochen Kallhardt/BlueBox; *286* (top and bottom left) © Helga Lade/Peter Arnold, Inc.; *286* (bottom right) © Zefa/Waldkirch; *288* © Kevin Galvin; *293* © Ulrike Welsch; *309* © Ulrike Welsch/PhotoEdit; *310* © Visum/The Image Works; *320* © vario-press; *331* © Helga Lade/Peter Arnold, Inc.; *348* © Ulrike Welsch; *378* (top) © 1995 Artists Rights Society, NY/Bild Kunst, Bonn © AKG London; *378* (middle) © 1995 Artists Rights Society, NY/Bild Kunst, Bonn; *378* (bottom) © 1995 Artists Rights Society, NY/Bild Kunst, Bonn © AKG London; *379* "Der Leser" by Jiri Georg Dokoupil. Reproduced with permission; *380* © CARO Fotoagentur/A. Bastian; *404* © Kevin Galvin; *411* © Ulrike Welsch; *428* © Paul Thompson/ImageState; *429* (left) © Topham/The Image Works: *429* (right) © UPI Bettman/Corbis; *430* (top) © Keystone Pressedi/The Image Works; *430* (bottom) © Bettman/Corbis; *431* © Dallas and John Heaton/Stock Boston; *432* (top left) Reuters/Bettman/Corbis; *432* (top right) © UPI Bettman/Corbis; *432* (bottom left) © Bojan Brecelli/Corbis; *432* (bottom right) © Topham/The Image Works; *433* © Michael Schwarz/The Image Works; *438* (top) © Jose Fuste Raga/Corbis; *438* (middle) © Paul Langrock/Laif/AURORA; *438* (bottom) © Tim Matsui/IPN/AURORA.

Realia *Page 4* Beate and Klaus Stetten; *6* © Eva Heller. From *Vielleicht sind wir eben zu verschieden;* *7* Michel & Co.; *9 Funk Uhr;* *10* © *Berliner Morgenpost;* *11* Helma Koch; *12* Volkswagen AG; *16* (bottom) Kino International; *38* Volksbanken Raiffeisenbanken; *39* Saxacon Verlag; *40* From *Huhnstage von Peter Gaymann* © Fakelträger Verlag 1984; *41* From *Huhnstage von Peter Gaymann* © Fakelträger Verlag 1984; *43* Reprinted with permission of Galerie in der Töpferstube; *52* Pro Fertighaus, Fachschriften-Verlag; *66* Reprinted with permission of Werner Buchi/*Brückenbauer;* *70* Reprinted with permission of Wolfgang Horsch; *85* Courtesy of DSM-Heerlen; *98* Reprinted with permission of Deutsche Welthungerhilfe; *100 Känguru: Stadtmagazin für Familien in Köln;* *104 Die Ganze Woche;* *113* P.M./Hurzlmeier; *118* Reprinted with permission of Langenscheidt-Verlag, Berlin and Munich; *121* (top left) ICC Berlin; *121* (middle and middle right) Reprinted with permission of Thilo Beu; *128* (top left) © Droemer Knauer Verlag, Munich; *128* (bottom) Reprinted with permission of Christine Sielung, Düsseldorf; *129* Beate Heinen, Kunstverlag, D 56653 Maria Laach, Nr. 2705; *175* Reprinted with permission of Offenbach-Stuben; *178* Deutsche Telekom; *195* Detlef Kersten/Cartoon-Caricature-Contor, Munich; *207* © Globus Infografik GmbH; *209* Jugendamt und Sport- und Bäderamt, Göttingen; *215* BZ/Image Presseservice Gensler GmbH; *220* Reprinted with permission of Kalkberg GmbH, Bad Segeberg; *225* Reprinted with permission of Fremdenverkehrsverein Altes Land e.V., D 21635 Jork; *228 Focus* 24/97; *242* Reprinted with permission of René Fehr, Brückenbauer; *245 Rheinische Post,* Düsseldorf; *247* © Tribune Media Services. All Rights Reserved. Reprinted with permission; *248* Reprinted with permission of Uli Stein; *253–54* Illustrations reprinted with permission of Reinhard Wendlinger; text: *Focus* 24/97; *264* Warmemünde-Prospekt 1992/Kuramt; *299* Villa Media; *304* ADAC Hessen-Thüringen, Schumannstrasse 4-6, Thüringen D 60325; *315 Sports—Die Sportzeitschrift,* Jahr-Verlag GmbH; *321* Globus Infografik GmbH; *323* WestLB; *324–25* From *Berufswahl—Trips, Trends, Tests,* Commerzbank, Frankfurt am Main; *327* Plus Warenhandelsgesellschaft mbH; *331 Tatsachen über Deutschland* © Societäts-Verlag, Frankfurt; *333* Erich Rauschenbach, Cartoon-Caricature-Cartoon, Munich; *336* Handelsblatt GmbH, Düsseldorf; *351* © Globus Infografik GmbH; *354 Pro Fertighaus;* *369* © Eva Heller. From *Vielleicht sind wir eben zu verschieden;* *370* Reprinted with permission of Wolfgang Horsch; *371* © Eva Heller. From *Vielleicht sind wir eben zu verschieden;* *379* "Der Leser" by Georg Jiři Dokoupil; *379* Illustration by Claus Bremer from *Konkrete Poesie* (Ditzingen: Philipp Reclam Jun. Verlag, 1976); *379* Illustration by Reinhard Döhl from *Konkrete Poesie* (Ditzingen: Philipp Reclam Jun. Verlag, 1976); *381 Rheinische Post* 2002, Düsseldorf; *382 Bild und Funk,* Gong Verlag GmbH; *383* www.BerlinOnline.de; *384* Gebühreneinzugszentrale; *385 Bild und Funk,* Gong Verlag GmbH; *387* Globus Infografik GmbH; *389* Globus Infografik GmbH; *392 Neue Zürcher Zeitung;* *395* Detlev Kersten © Lappan Verlag; *396 Volkszeitung;* *398* © Du Pont de Nemours GmbH; *405 TV Hören & Sehen;* *410 Natur,* Ringier Verlag; *411 Natur,* Ringier Verlag; *412 Natur,* Ringier Verlag; *414* Reprinted with permission of Greenpeace Germany; *416* Index Funk/*Berliner Morgenpost;* *416* © ALI Press Agency; *434, 436, 437* Herbert Hoover Collection, Memorabilia, Hoover Institution Archives; *439* Partner für Berlin—Gesellschaft für Haupstadt-Marketing mbH.

Readings *Page 46* "Dialog" by Nasrin Siege from *Text dagegen,* Silvia Bartholl (Hrsg.), 1993 Beltz Verlag, Weinheim und Basel Programm Beltz & Gelberg, Weinheim; *138* "Immer das gleiche" © Christine Wuttke; *168* Karl Valentin, "Im Hutladen" from *Gesammelte Werke in einem Band* © Piper Verlag GmbH, Munich, 1985; *200* From *live Wien für junge Leute,* Vienna Tourist Board; *229* "Vergnügungen" from *Gesammelte Werke* by Bertolt Brecht © Surhkamp Verlag, Frankfurt am Main, 1967; *281* "Die Gitarre des Herrn Hatunoglu" by Heinrich Hannover from *Als der Clown die Grippe hatte.* Copyright © 1992 by Rowohlt Taschenbuch Verlag GmbH, Reinbek bei Hamburg; *316* From *Outdoor,* 4/97, Rotpunkt Verlag; *345 Für Sie;* *374* "Fahrkarte bitte" by Helga M. Novak from *Palisaden* © 1980 Luchterhand Literaturverlag; *401* Loriot, *Loriots Dramatische Werke.* Copyright © 1981 by Diogenes Verlag AG Zürich; *423* "Was in der Zeitung steht" by Reinhard Mai, *Alle meine Lieder,* Maikäfer Musik Verlagsgesellschaft, Berlin; *435* From *Wir leben im Verborgenen* by Ceja Stojka, reprinted with permission of Picus Verlag.

About the Authors

Robert Di Donato   is Professor of German and Chair of the German, Russian, and East Asian Languages Department at Miami University in Oxford, Ohio. He received his Ph.D. from the Ohio State University. He is the chief academic and series developer of *Fokus Deutsch,* a telecourse with accompanying texts and materials for teaching and learning German. He has also written articles about language methodology and has given numerous keynote speeches, workshops, and presentations—both in the United States and abroad—on teaching methods and teacher education. He has won a number of awards for his work in language education including the Florence Steiner Award for Leadership in foreign language education.

Monica D. Clyde   is a native of Düsseldorf. She received her Ph.D. in German Literature from the University of California at Berkeley. She has taught German language and literature at Mills College, Cañada College, the Defense Language Institute, and the College of San Mateo. She is currently Director of Faculty Development and Scholarship at Saint Mary's College of California. She has co-authored *Texte und Kontexte* and was a contributor to *Mosaik: Deutsche Kultur und Literatur,* Third Edition, both intermediate college-level German textbooks.

Jacqueline Vansant   received her Ph.D. from the University of Texas at Austin. She has taught at Hamilton College and Miami University in Oxford, Ohio, and currently teaches at the University of Michigan-Dearborn, where she also heads the German section of the Department of Humanities. She is the main author of *Blickwechsel,* an intermediate German reader. Her particular interest in language pedagogy lies in reading and reading strategies. In addition, she has written widely on contemporary Austrian literature and culture and is currently co-editor of *Modern Austrian Literature.*

Listening Comprehension Scripts

EINFÜHRUNG
Hallo! Guten Tag! Herzlich willkommen!

(*See textbook pages 2–3.*)

Aktivität 8   Wie geht's?

Dialog 1
URSEL: 'n Abend, Thomas.
THOMAS: 'n Abend, Ursel.
URSEL: Na, wie geht's?
THOMAS: Ach, nicht besonders gut. Und dir?
URSEL: Danke, gut.

Dialog 2
FRAU ENGELHARDT: Grüß Gott, Herr Kümmerli.
HERR KÜMMERLI: Grüß Gott, Frau Engelhardt.
FRAU ENGELHARDT: Wie geht es Ihnen?
HERR KÜMMERLI: Danke, gut. Und wie geht es Ihnen?
FRAU ENGELHARDT: Danke, auch gut.
HERR KÜMMERLI: Na, dann, auf Wiedersehen.
FRAU ENGELHARDT: Auf Wiedersehen, Herr Kümmerli.

Dialog 3
NINA: Grüß dich, Dieter.
DIETER: Nina. Wie geht's?
NINA: Ach, es geht nicht besonders gut und nicht besonders schlecht. Und dir?
DIETER: Ausgezeichnet.
NINA: Na, dann mach's gut!
DIETER: Tschüss.

Aktivität 10   Wichtige Telefonnummern

Polizei	1 10
Kinoprogramme	1 15 11
Küchenrezepte	11 67
Sportnachrichten	11 63
Konzerte	1 15 17
Feuerwehr/Rettungsleitstelle	1 12
Wetter	38 53
Zahlenlotto	11 62
Zeit	19 94

Aktivität 11   Die Adresse und Telefonnummer, bitte!

1. A: Wie ist die Adresse von Professor Hauser, bitte?
   B: Moment mal. Gartenstraße 19.
   A: Und die Postleitzahl?
   B: 82067 Ebenhausen/Isartal.
   A: Und wie ist die Telefonnummer?
   B: 41 34 76.
   A: Vielen Dank.
   B: Bitte schön.

2. A: Bitte schön, die Adresse von Margas Fitnessstudio?
   B: Bautzner Straße 15.
   A: Wissen Sie übrigens die Postleitzahl?
   B: Jawohl. 01093 Dresden.
   A: Und die Telefonnummer?
   B: Die Telefonnummer ist 20 86 73.
   A: Danke sehr. Wiederhören!
   B: Wiederhören!

3. A: Könnten Sie mir bitte die Adresse von Autohaus Becker sagen?
   B: Freilich. Das wäre Landstuhler Straße 54.
   A: Haben Sie die Postleitzahl?
   B: Ja. Die ist 66482 Zweibrücken-Ixheim.
   A: Und die Telefonnummer?
   B: 1 88 42.
   A: Vielen Dank. Wiederhören!
   B: Wiederhören!

Aktivität 15   Sie verstehen schon etwas Deutsch!

1. Der neue Opel Astra: Komfort, Sicherheit und Technik. Das neue Auto für die 90er Jahre.
2. Im Neuen Theater Hamburg spielt heute Abend um 20.00 Uhr „Das Phantom der Oper" von Andrew Lloyd Webber.
3. Lillehammer, Norwegen, Olympische Spiele. Die Deutschen gewinnen 9 Goldmedaillen.
4. Café-Restaurant Schönberger sucht einen Koch oder eine Köchin mit klassischer Ausbildung.
5. Bei Kinderfreude haben wir Freude an Kindern. Unsere Kinderkrippe ist kinderfreundlich, sauber, modern und sicher.

KAPITEL 1
Alles klar?

B. 1. Grüß Gott. Mein Name ist Nikolaus Euba. Ich bin Student und komme aus München.
   2. Guten Tag. Mein Name ist Marco Berger. Ich bin Journalist und komme aus Köln.
   3. Guten Tag. Ich heiße Andrea Rubik. Ich bin Sportlehrerin. Ich komme aus Wien.
   4. Mein Name ist Marion Hintze. Ich bin Architektin und komme aus Leipzig.
   5. Guten Tag. Ich heiße Zafir Brückner. Ich bin Physiker und komme aus Zürich.

Wörter im Kontext
Aktivität 1   Interessante Personen

1. Haralds Nachname ist Lohmann.
   Er ist Journalist.
   Er kommt aus Deutschland.
   Er wohnt in Regensburg.

Seine Adresse ist
Bahnhofstraße 20.
Er ist 1,82 groß.
2. Die Frau heißt Daniela Lercher.
Sie wohnt in Salzburg.
Sie kommt aus Österreich.
Sie ist Studentin.
Sie ist 1,75 groß.
3. Herr Rütli ist Architekt von Beruf.
Er heißt Anton mit Vornamen.
Er kommt aus Luzern in der Schweiz.
Seine Adresse ist Kirchplatz 76.
Er ist 1,74 groß.

Aktivität 2   Eine neue Studentin

BEAMTER: Ihr Name, bitte?
JULIE: Julie Harrison.
BEAMTER: Buchstabieren Sie das bitte.
JULIE: Vorname: J-u-l-i-e
Nachname: H-a-r-r-i-s-o-n
BEAMTER: Beruf?
JULIE: Studentin.
BEAMTER: Und woher kommen Sie?
JULIE: Aus den USA, Cincinnati.
BEAMTER: Ihr Pass, bitte.
JULIE: Hier, bitte.
BEAMTER: Ihre Adresse hier in Berlin?
JULIE: Brandenburgerstraße 37.
BEAMTER: Geburtstag?
JULIE: Vierter April 1980.
BEAMTER: Danke, jetzt brauche ich nur noch Ihre
Unterschrift.

Thema 2:   Glücksrad Fortuna

(*See textbook page 27.*)

Ein Gespräch an der Uni

(*See textbook page 28.*)

Aktivität 9   Kurzdialoge

1. A: Wie heißt du?
B: Ich heiße Dieter.
2. A: Woher kommen Sie?
B: Ich studiere hier.
3. A: Was machen Sie hier?
B: Wir besuchen Freunde.
4. A: Wie heißen Sie?
B: Mein Name ist Lentz.
5. A: Hallo. Grüß dich, Helmut!
B: Auf Wiedersehen.
6. A: Woher kommst du?
B: Aus Berlin.
7. A: Wie finden Sie Berlin?
B: Ich komme aus den USA.

8. A: Wo ist denn das?
B: Das ist in den USA.
9. A: Auf Wiedersehen, Frau Keller.
B: Guten Tag!
10. A: Was studieren Sie?
B: Englisch.

Grammatik im Kontext

Übung 1   Was hören Sie?

1. Wie bitte, wie ist der Name?
2. Die Frau kommt aus Amerika.
3. Wie heißt das Land?
4. Wie ist die Adresse von McDonald's?
5. Woher kommt der Student?
6. Die Studentin lernt Deutsch in Erfurt.
7. Was macht das Mädchen in Berlin?
8. Wo wohnt der Professor?

Übung 20   Das Studentenleben

A. Karin Renner kommt ursprünglich aus Dresden. Familie Renner wohnt immer noch da. Jetzt wohnt Karin aber in Göttingen. Sie studiert da nämlich Informatik. Sie ist sehr gut in Mathematik. Karin wohnt in einem Studentenwohnheim am Rosenbachweg. Das Wohnheim ist sehr groß und modern, aber auch unpersönlich. Karin arbeitet viel für ihre Kurse.

Sie ist auch sportlich sehr aktiv. Sie geht regelmäßig schwimmen. Sie geht auch oft ins Café. Sie findet das Café Kadenz besonders nett. Sie trifft da oft ein paar Freunde, und dann diskutieren sie über ihre Kurse, die Arbeit, die Politik und natürlich die Professoren.

KAPITEL 2
Alles klar?

B. 1. INGRID: Was suchst du in der Zeitung?
KIRSTEN: Eine Wohnung. Ich brauche eine Dreizimmerwohnung.
INGRID: Warum so groß?
KIRSTEN: Für mich und Angelika.
2. GERD: Suchst du eine neue Wohnung?
JOCHEN: Ja. Die alte ist zu klein. Ich suche eine Zweizimmerwohnung mit Küche und Bad.
3. GABI: Suchst du im Moment ein Zimmer?
ANJA: Ja. Bei einer Familie.
GABI: Ein Appartement ist besser. Es ist privater.

Wörter im Kontext

Thema 1:   Auf Wohnungssuche

(*See textbook pages 52–53.*)

Aktivität 1   Wir brauchen eine Wohnung oder ein Zimmer.

1. Fotodesignerin, 22, sucht preiswertes Zimmer in junger Wohngemeinschaft, zum ersten Juli.
2. Freundlicher Schauspieler aus Hamburg sucht Zimmer in Wohngemeinschaft vom ersten Mai bis ersten August in München.
3. Architekturstudentin, 25, sucht zum ersten oder fünfzehnten Mai ruhiges Zimmer bis 200 Euro inklusive, in Wohngemeinschaft.
4. Freundlicher, junger 37-jähriger Englischlehrer sucht ein Zimmer in Wohngemeinschaft, um mit euch Deutsch zu sprechen und es besser zu lernen.
5. Musiker, 24, sucht Zimmer oder Raum in Wohngemeinschaft zum ersten Juni oder etwas früher. Zahle bis 250 Euro inklusive.

Aktivität 4   Ulla hat jetzt endlich ein Zimmer.

KARIN: Tag, Ulla. Wie geht's dir denn?

ULLA: Tag, Karin. Es geht mir prima. Ich habe jetzt endlich ein Zimmer.

KARIN: Wo denn?

ULLA: Schillerstraße 13.

KARIN: Toll, zentral gelegen. Ist das Zimmer möbliert?

ULLA: Ja. Es hat ein Bett, einen Schreibtisch, einen Stuhl, einen Tisch und einen Sessel. Ich brauche nur noch eine Lampe für den Schreibtisch und ein Bücherregal.

KARIN: Wie hoch ist die Miete?

ULLA: Nur 125 Euro.

KARIN: Hast du Telefon?

ULLA: Nein, noch nicht.

Aktivität 6   Ein Gespräch im Kaufhaus

VERKÄUFER: Bitte sehr?

ULLA: Ich suche eine Lampe für meinen Schreibtisch.

VERKÄUFER: Hier haben wir Lampen.

ULLA: Was kostet die Lampe hier?

VERKÄUFER: 200 Euro. Die ist aus Italien.

ULLA: Die ist sehr schön, aber zu teuer.

VERKÄUFER: Hier ist eine Lampe für 25 Euro, sehr preiswert und modern. Ein Sonderangebot.

ULLA: Gut, die nehme ich. Und wo finde ich hier Bücherregale?

VERKÄUFER: Tut mir Leid. Wir führen keine Bücherregale.

Grammatik im Kontext

Übung 3   Neu in Göttingen

STEFAN: Hallo, Birgit. Komm bitte rein.

BIRGIT: Tag Stefan. Also das ist deine neue Wohnung. Du hast wirklich Glück. Ich suche nämlich immer noch eine Wohnung.

STEFAN: Komm, ich zeige dir die Wohnung erst mal. Hier ist das Wohnzimmer mit Kochnische. Und hier ist das Bad.

BIRGIT: Na, das Zimmer ist ja ein bisschen klein. Wo schläfst du denn?

STEFAN: Ich brauche noch ein paar Möbel, ein Bett zum Beispiel. Im Moment schlafe ich auf dem Boden im Schlafsack.

BIRGIT: Kauf doch so ein japanisches Futon-Bett. Das ist ganz praktisch. Tagsüber ist es eine Couch, und dann kannst du es ausziehen, und es ist ein Bett.

STEFAN: Gute Idee. Bitte, setz dich doch. Leider habe ich nur einen Stuhl im Moment.

BIRGIT: Nein, danke, ich sitze gern auf dem Boden.

STEFAN: Morgen kaufe ich einen Schreibtisch und ein Bücherregal. Möchtest du einen Kaffee?

BIRGIT: Gern. Komm, ich helfe.

STEFAN: Ach, da fällt mir gerade ein: Ich habe Kaffee, aber ich brauche noch eine Kaffeemaschine. Gehen wir doch ins Café. Kennst du das Café Kadenz? Das ist mein Lieblingscafé.

BIRGIT: Na, gut.

Übung 8   Immer diese Ausreden!

1. KALLE: Grüß dich, Reinhard! Heute Abend spielt ein toller Film im Kino. Kommst du mit?
   REINHARD: Tut mir Leid, es geht wirklich nicht. Ich habe nur noch einen Euro.
2. ALEXANDRA: Morgen gehen wir in die Disko. Kommst du mit, Erika?
   ERIKA: In die Disko? Wer geht denn sonst noch mit?
   ALEXANDRA: Nur Peter und ich. Helmut kommt doch sicher mit, nicht?
   ERIKA: Helmut ist nicht da. Und allein habe ich keine Lust.
3. FRAU WEISS: Frau Becker, haben Sie jetzt Zeit für eine Tasse Kaffee?
   FRAU BECKER: Tut mir wirklich Leid, aber ich trinke keinen Kaffee. Kaffee trinken macht mich zu nervös.
4. FRANK: Hallo, Jens! Servus, Ulla! Kommt ihr heute Abend zur Party? Wir haben Pizza und Bier.
   JENS: Hmmm, wir möchten gerne, aber wir müssen leider morgen unsere Examen schreiben. Ich habe noch viel Arbeit und brauche die Zeit heute Abend zum Lernen.
5. LYDIA: Peter, hast du Lust, mit ins Museum zu gehen?
   PETER: Ins Museum? Heute? Ach, ich bin kein Museumsfan. Ins Museum gehen macht mir überhaupt keinen Spaß. Ich bin eher Fußballfan.

KAPITEL 3

Alles klar?

B. Hallo, ich bin Alexandra Thalhofer aus Köln. Auf dem Foto seht ihr meine Familie vor dem Standesamt in Köln. Mein Bruder Bernd hat geheiratet. Bernd und seine Frau, Bettina, sind beide Lehrer an einem Gymnasium. Bernd unterrichtet Mathematik und Physik und Bettina ist Deutschlehrerin. Die beiden reisen gern und machen ihre Hochzeitsreise nach Kanada.

Ich habe noch einen Bruder Werner. Er steht ganz rechts auf dem Bild. Er ist vierzig Jahre alt, ist verheiratet und hat zwei Kinder, einen Jungen und ein Mädchen. Seine Frau, Antje, ist auch auf dem Bild. Sie ist die Frau mit Hut in der Mitte. Meine Eltern sind auch auf dem Foto. Mein Vater steht neben mir. Meine Mutter steht vorne neben Bernd.

Wörter im Kontext

Aktivität 7   Eine Einladung zum Geburtstag

TOM: Tom McKay.
HEIKE: Hallo, Tom? Hier ist Heike.
TOM: Tag, Heike.
HEIKE: Du, Tom, ich mache eine kleine Party zu Hause. Ich habe nämlich Geburtstag. Ich möchte dich einladen.
TOM: Vielen Dank für die Einladung. Ich komme gern. Wann ist die Party denn?
HEIKE: Am Samstag.
TOM: Schön. Wer kommt sonst noch?
HEIKE: Du kennst doch die Gabi? Die kommt auch. Und vielleicht Jürgen. Sonst sind nur meine Eltern und Geschwister da.
TOM: Also gut, bis Samstag dann.
HEIKE: Mach's gut. Tschüss.

Grammatik im Kontext

Übung 1   Herzlichen Glückwunsch!

Guten Morgen, liebe Hörerinnen und Hörer. Willkommen zu unserem Programm: Von Haus zu Haus. Unsere Hörer senden Glückwünsche zum Geburtstag. Außerdem ist heute ein ganz besonderer Tag: Valentinstag.

1. Unsere liebe Mutter, Frau Sibille Heinemann aus Krefeld, ist heute achtzig. Herzlichen Glückwunsch senden dir deine Kinder.
2. Unser Opa, der beste Opa der Welt, wird heute sechzig. Es gratulieren deine Enkel Kai, Inge, Uwe, Sandra und Claudia aus Würzburg.
3. Hallo, Uwe! Endlich ist es so weit. Du bist achtzehn. Alles Gute wünscht dir deine Freundin Elke.
4. Hurra, unser Vater wird heute vierzig Jahre. Er ist der beste. Wir wünschen dir noch viele schöne Jahre. Alles Liebe zum Geburtstag, deine Söhne Helmut, Friedrich und Klaus-Daniel.
5. Unsere Tochter Hannelore wird heute einundzwanzig. Wir wünschen dir alles Liebe und Gute, deine Eltern.
6. Liebe Eltern, zum Valentinstag liebe Grüße aus Dresden, eure Kinder Wolfgang und Martina.
7. Für meine Kinder Steffi und Sebastian in Weimar alles Liebe, viel Spaß und alles Gute zum Valentinstag, eure Mutter.
8. Liebe Gabi, zum Valentinstag alles Liebe und Gute, dein Tiger.

Übung 12   Die neue Mitbewohnerin

1. Wann beginnt das Semester?
2. Kennst du das Buch von Professor Seufert?
3. Wo ist die Unibibliothek?
4. Ist das Theater hier gut?
5. Wie sind die anderen Mitbewohner hier im Wohnheim?
6. Ist das Wetter hier immer so schlecht?
7. Kennst du den Professor Kreuzer?
8. Weißt du, wo das Sportzentrum ist?

KAPITEL 4
Alles klar?

B. DIRK: Hier Dirk Krekel. Ich bin im Moment nicht zu Hause. Hinterlassen Sie bitte eine kurze Nachricht. Warten Sie bitte auf den Pfeifton.
ERIKA: Hallo, Dirk! Hier ist Erika. Hast du Samstagnachmittag schon etwas vor? Thomas und ich machen nämlich eine kleine Fete bei uns zu Hause. Um vier gibt's Kaffee und Kuchen. Hast du Zeit? Ruf uns bitte zurück!

Wörter im Kontext

Aktivität 1   Zeitansagen

1. Die Zeit ist 17 Uhr 35.
2. Die Zeit ist 3 Uhr 6.
3. Die Zeit ist 14 Uhr 15.
4. Die Zeit ist 11 Uhr 25.
5. Die Zeit ist 19 Uhr 45.
6. Die Zeit ist 13 Uhr 40.
7. Die Zeit ist 0 Uhr 15.
8. Die Zeit ist 21 Uhr 50.

Thema 3:   Kino, Musik und Theater

(*See textbook page 119.*)

Aktivität 8   Zwei Einladungen

Dialog 1
PETER: Möchtest du heute Abend ins Kino?
KARLA: Leider kann ich nicht. Ich habe nämlich am Montag eine Klausur.
PETER: Eine Klausur?
KARLA: Ja, in Physik. Ich muss noch dafür arbeiten.
PETER: Na, dann wünsche ich dir viel Glück.
KARLA: Danke, ich kann es brauchen.

Dialog 2
GABI: Hallo, Hans. Hast du heute Abend Zeit? Im Olympia läuft ein toller Film, „Ich und Er".
HANS: Ich möchte schon mitgehen. Wann fängt er denn an?
GABI: Um 17 Uhr.
HANS: Das ist mir zu früh. Ich habe nämlich noch eine Vorlesung bis fünf.
GABI: So spät am Freitag noch?
HANS: Ja, leider.

Grammatik im Kontext

Übung 1 Daniels Tagesablauf

Ich wache morgens schon früh auf und stehe um fünf Uhr auf. Ich wohne zusammen mit meinem Bruder Mark in einer alten Villa in Berlin. Wir haben ein Zimmer unter dem Dach. Das kostet uns nichts. Wir beide sind nämlich so etwas wie Hausmänner für die Familie Schröder: Wir gehen für sie einkaufen, reparieren Sachen und arbeiten im Garten.

Ich habe zwei Tagesabläufe: einen für das Geld und einen für die Kunst. An drei Tagen arbeite ich im Hotel als Junge für alles. Um sieben fängt die Arbeit an. Im Hotel arbeiten Leute aus Jugoslawien, Afghanistan, Italien und Amerika. Ich arbeite gern da. So gegen drei Uhr nachmittags komme ich nach Hause zurück. Dann schlafe ich erst mal ein bis zwei Stunden. Da habe ich die Illusion, mein Tag fängt noch einmal neu an. Dann fängt nämlich mein Leben für die Kunst an. Meistens habe ich ein Projekt vor. Ich mache Skulpturen aus Metall und Plastik. Abends rufe ich manchmal ein paar Freunde an. Die kommen dann vorbei, und dann reden wir und trinken Bier bis Mitternacht. Vor ein Uhr nachts schlafe ich nie ein. Ich brauche auch nicht viel Schlaf.

Übung 9 Im Deutschen Haus

CHRIS: Ich will schlafen.
　　Du willst schlafen.
　　Er will schlafen.
　　Wir wollen schla...
JEFF: Chris, was machst du da?
CHRIS: Ich lerne deutsche Grammatik.
JEFF: Das kann ich hören.
CHRIS: Morgen haben wir einen Test über Modalverben. Ich muss unbedingt ein A bekommen.
JEFF: Musst du das denn so laut machen? Kannst du das nicht leise machen?
CHRIS: Ich kann leider nur laut Deutsch lernen.
JEFF: Ich muss aber auch arbeiten, und ich höre nur immer „Ich will schlafen". Du hypnotisierst mich. Jetzt will ich auch schon schlafen.
CHRIS: Also gut, ich gehe ins Badezimmer. Da kannst du mich nicht hören. Ich will dich nicht stören.

Übung 14 In der Sprechstunde

1. PROFESSOR: Guten Tag, Frau Lerner, bitte, kommen Sie herein!
2. PROFESSOR: Bitte, nehmen Sie Platz!
3. MARY: Herr Professor, erklären Sie mir bitte, was dieser Satz heißt!
4. PROFESSOR: Verstehen Sie das nicht?
5. MARY: Sprechen Sie etwas langsamer, bitte!
6. PROFESSOR: Gehen Sie regelmäßig jede Woche ins Sprachlabor?
7. PROFESSOR: Warten Sie einen Moment, bitte.
8. STUDENT: Hallo, Herr Professor Schwermut, kommen Sie heute Abend zu unserm Filmabend im Deutschklub?
9. PROFESSOR: Rufen Sie mich bitte später wieder an! Ich habe im Moment keine Zeit.
10. PROFESSOR: Haben Sie ein Wörterbuch zu Hause, Frau Lerner?
11. PROFESSOR: Lesen Sie jeden Tag eine Stunde Deutsch?
12. PROFESSOR: Kommen Sie nächste Woche wieder vorbei!
13. MARY: Haben Sie nächsten Mittwoch Zeit?
14. PROFESSOR: Vergessen Sie Ihre Bücher nicht! Also dann, auf Wiedersehen.
　　MARY: Auf Wiedersehen.

KAPITEL 5
Alles klar?

B. 1. Heute im vierten Stock. Preiswerte Kameras. Nur 150 Euro.
2. Modische italienische Herrenschuhe im zweiten Stock. Aus Leder von hoher Qualität. Nur 85 Euro.
3. In unserer Elektroabteilung im vierten Stock bieten wir Krups Kaffeemaschinen. Heute Sonderpreis 29 Euro 50.
4. Zu Hause haben Sie bestimmt Platz für einen zweiten Videorecorder. Heute im Sonderangebot für 249 Euro. Im vierten Stock.

Wörter im Kontext
Aktivität 1 Eine Reise nach Südspanien

BETTINA: Ich weiß nicht, was ich mitnehmen soll.
MARKUS: Ich nehme nur einen Rucksack mit. Da passt sowieso nicht viel rein.
BETTINA: Ich nehme auch nur einen Rucksack mit. Sind Jeans und T-Shirts genug?
MARKUS: Ich nehme nur Shorts und ein paar T-Shirts mit. Jeans sind mir zu warm. Es ist nämlich unglaublich heiß da im Sommer. Ach ja, und Sandalen natürlich.
BETTINA: Ich nehme Tennisschuhe mit, zwei Paar ... Ich brauche unbedingt einen neuen Badeanzug. Mein Badeanzug ist bestimmt schon fünf Jahre alt.
MARKUS: Also in Südspanien am Strand... das kann ich dir sagen, da brauchst du gar keinen Badeanzug!
BETTINA: (laughs) Also nein,... das ist nichts für mich... Und was machst du mit deinem Geld?
MARKUS: Ich habe einen besonderen Gürtel für mein Geld. Da ist es ganz sicher.
BETTINA: Ich stecke mein Geld immer in die Schuhe.
MARKUS: In die Schuhe?
BETTINA: Ja, in die Schuhe im Rucksack. Mein zweites Paar Tennisschuhe.
MARKUS: Ach so, ich kann mir auch nicht vorstellen, dass du mit Geld im Schuh durch Südspanien läufst.
BETTINA: Also, mach's gut. Tschüss!
MARKUS: Servus, Bettina.

Thema 2: Beim Einkaufen im Kaufhaus

(See textbook page 147.)

Aktivität 6   Gespräche im Geschäft

Dialog 1

VERKÄUFER: Bitte schön, kann ich Ihnen helfen?
KUNDE: Ich brauche ein Paar Schuhe.
VERKÄUFER: Welche Größe bitte?
KUNDE: Größe 44.
VERKÄUFER: Und welche Farbe?
KUNDE: Schwarz bitte.

Dialog 2

VERKÄUFERIN: Guten Tag. Kann ich Ihnen helfen?
KUNDIN: Ich brauche eine Hose.
VERKÄUFERIN: Welche Größe, bitte?
KUNDIN: Ich glaube Größe 38. Aber ich bin nicht sicher.
VERKÄUFERIN: Und welche Farbe soll es sein?
KUNDIN: Haben Sie etwas in Blauweiß gestreift?

Dialog 3

VERKÄUFERIN: Guten Tag, kann ich Ihnen helfen?
KUNDE: Ja, ich suche ein Geschenk für meine Freundin. Eine Bluse vielleicht.
VERKÄUFERIN: Und welche Größe hat Ihre Freundin?
KUNDE: Hmm, ich weiß nicht, sie ist ziemlich klein. Ich glaube ungefähr Größe 44.
VERKÄUFERIN: Das ist aber ziemlich groß. Sie sagen, sie ist ziemlich klein?
KUNDE: Ja.
VERKÄUFERIN: Ich empfehle Ihnen Größe 38.
KUNDE: Vielen Dank. Also, Größe 38.
VERKÄUFERIN: Und welche Farbe?
KUNDE: Rot.

Dialog 4

VERKÄUFER: Bitte schön. Kann ich Ihnen helfen?
KUNDE: Ich suche einen Wintermantel.
VERKÄUFER: Und welche Größe brauchen Sie?
KUNDE: Größe 44.
VERKÄUFER: Und welche Farbe?
KUNDE: Haben Sie was in Dunkelblau?
VERKÄUFER: Ja, da bin ich ganz sicher.

Aktivität 10   Wo? Was? Wie viel?

Dialog 1

VERKÄUFERIN: Bitte schön. Was darf's sein?
KUNDE: Ich möchte gern ein Dutzend Würstchen.
VERKÄUFERIN: Sonst noch etwas?
KUNDE: Ja, ein Pfund Aufschnitt.
VERKÄUFERIN: Und sonst noch etwas?
KUNDE: Nein, danke. Das ist alles.
VERKÄUFERIN: Das macht zusammen 8 Euro 50.

Dialog 2

VERKÄUFERIN: Guten Morgen, Frau Linder.
KUNDIN: Guten Morgen. Haben Sie frische Brötchen?
VERKÄUFERIN: Ja, natürlich. Ganz frisch von heute Morgen. Wie viele möchten Sie?
KUNDIN: Sechs Brötchen, bitte, und noch ein Schwarzbrot.
VERKÄUFERIN: Sonst noch etwas?
KUNDIN: Nein, danke.
VERKÄUFERIN: Das macht zusammen 3 Euro 20.

Dialog 3

VERKÄUFERIN: Bitte schön?
KUNDIN: Haben Sie frische Tomaten?
VERKÄUFERIN: Ja, Tomaten haben wir, ganz frisch aus Holland.
KUNDIN: Wie viel kosten die denn?
VERKÄUFERIN: 5 Euro das Kilo.
KUNDIN: Das ist aber teuer. Was haben Sie denn an Obst?
VERKÄUFERIN: Erdbeeren sind sehr preiswert. Nur 1 Euro 70 für 500 Gramm.
KUNDIN: Na, dann nehme ich ein Pfund Erdbeeren und ungefähr ein Pfund Tomaten.
VERKÄUFERIN: Das macht zusammen 4 Euro 20.

Grammatik im Kontext

Übung 2   Situationen im Alltag

Dialog 1

HANS: Du, Werner, ich brauche unbedingt etwas Geld. Kannst du mir ein paar Euro leihen bis morgen? Meine Mutter hat nämlich Geburtstag, und ich möchte ihr unbedingt ein paar Blumen schicken.
WERNER: Es tut mir Leid, Hans, aber ich habe selber kein Geld. Schreib ihr doch einen Brief.

Dialog 2

STUDENTIN: Können Sie uns bitte sagen, wo das Café Kadenz ist?
PASSANT: Natürlich. Kommen Sie. Ich zeige es Ihnen. Es liegt in der Berliner Straße.

Dialog 3

MARIANNE: Helmut hat morgen Geburtstag. Was soll ich ihm bloß schenken? Er hat ja alles.
UTE: Schenk ihm doch eine CD.
MARIANNE: Ich glaube, ich schreibe ihm nur eine Karte.

Dialog 4

STUDENTIN: Ich stehe jeden Morgen um fünf Uhr auf und mache Yoga.
STUDENT: Und das soll ich dir glauben? Wieso kommst du denn dann immer zu spät in die Vorlesung?
STUDENTIN: Doch, ich mache das schon lange. Ich kann es dir nur empfehlen.

Dialog 5

STUDENT: Achim sagt, er lebt nur von Wasser und Brot.
STUDENTIN: Du musst ihm nicht alles glauben, was er sagt. Er geht doch fast jeden Abend aus.

Übung 7   Ein typischer Tag

Maxi wohnt seit einem Monat in Göttingen. Sie studiert da Geschichte. Sie wohnt mit drei anderen Studentinnen zusammen in einer Wohnung. Sie wohnen nicht zu weit von der Universität. Sie können zu Fuß gehen.

Maxi kommt gerade mit ihrer Freundin Inge aus dem Café Kadenz. Jetzt muss sie noch schnell einkaufen. Inge geht gleich mit. Sie braucht auch einiges. Zuerst gehen sie zum

Supermarkt. Da kaufen sie aber nur ein paar Bananen. Dann kaufen sie frische Brötchen beim Bäcker direkt um die Ecke. Ach, da ist der neue Laden mit den tollen CDs! Die beiden möchten ja gerne mal schnell hineinschauen, aber es wird spät, und Maxi muss noch zur Bank. Sie gehen schnell durch die Fußgängerzone zur Bank. Maxi muss etwas Geld von der Bank holen. Es ist inzwischen fünf Uhr, und die Bank ist zu. Gott sei Dank kann sie mit der Bankkarte am Geldautomaten Geld bekommen.

KAPITEL 6

Alles klar?

B. DORIS: So. Jetzt wo ich das Problem mit dem BAföG gelöst habe, hätte ich gern eine weitere Information.

REFERENTIN: Gern. Wie kann ich dir weiter helfen?

DORIS: Meine Eltern kommen am Wochenende zu Besuch, und ich möchte mit ihnen im Restaurant essen. Ich bin ja neu hier in Berlin und kenne mich nicht so gut aus.

REFERENTIN: Du hast Glück. Wir haben gerade einen Kneipenführer zusammengestellt. Aber Berlin ist eine riesige Stadt. Wo seid ihr dann am Wochenende?

DORIS: Wohl in Mitte oder Prenzlauerberg.

REFERENTIN: Wenn einer von euch vegetarisch isst, dann kann ich den Kartoffelkeller im Nikolaiviertel empfehlen. Außer Kartoffeln gibt es verschiedene Salate, und man sitzt dort sehr gemütlich.

DORIS: Ich habe von einem Restaurant im Brecht Haus gehört. Warst du schon mal dort? Meine Eltern interessieren sich für Brecht.

REFERENTIN: Nein, aber Freunde von mir waren dort. Es heißt einfach „Kellerrestaurant" und serviert österreichische Küche. Einige Gerichte sollen nach Rezepten von Helene Weigel, Brechts Frau, sein.

DORIS: Kennst du ein gutes italienisches Restaurant?

REFERENTIN: Ja. Da geht ihr am besten in die Oranienburger Straße. So weit ich weiß, heißt das Restaurant einfach „Ristorante Italiano". Dort kann man eine sehr gute Pizza bekommen, und es ist nicht so teuer. Mir fällt auch ein neues Restaurant in der Gormann Straße ein. Es heißt „Brazil" und bietet brasilianische Spezialitäten, vor allem Fleischgerichte—sehr beliebt unter Studenten und jungen Leuten. Es ist immer rappelvoll und für deine Eltern vielleicht ein wenig laut, aber es macht viel Spaß, dort zu essen.

DORIS: Vielen Dank. Berlin hat wirklich viele tolle Lokale. Tschüss.

REFERENTIN: Tschüss.

Wörter im Kontext

Aktivität 5   Was bestellen Norbert und Dagmar?

NORBERT: Was möchtest du essen?

DAGMAR: Ich nehme Nürnberger Rostbratwürst'l mit Kraut und Kartoffelpüree.

NORBERT: Nimmst du eine Vorspeise?

DAGMAR: Ich nehme Gulaschsuppe. Und du?

NORBERT: Auch Gulaschsuppe und Spanferkel mit Bratkartoffeln. Und was willst du trinken?

DAGMAR: Ich sehe hier alkoholfreies Bier auf der Speisekarte. Das muss ich unbedingt mal probieren.

NORBERT: Ich nehme auch Bier, aber kein alkoholfreies. Herr Ober, wir möchten bestellen.

Aktivität 8   Im Brauhaus Matz

STEFANIE: Hier ist es aber ziemlich voll. Hoffentlich finden wir noch Platz.

JENS: Da drüben ist noch etwas frei. Da sitzen nur zwei Leute am Tisch. Ich gehe mal dahin und frage.

JENS: Entschuldigen Sie bitte! Ist hier noch frei?

HERR AM TISCH: Nein, hier ist besetzt.

JENS: Entschuldigen Sie. Ist hier noch frei?

DAME AM TISCH: Ja, hier ist noch frei. Bitte sehr.

JENS: Danke schön.

Aktivität 10   Wir möchten zahlen, bitte.

Dialog 1

HERR X: Bedienung, ich möchte zahlen.

KELLNERIN: Jawohl. Drei Bier, zwei Knackwürste und Sauerkraut. Und hatten Sie auch Brot?

HERR X: Nein.

KELLNERIN: Das macht zusammen 18 Euro 50.

Dialog 2

FRAU X: Herr Ober, wir möchten zahlen.

OBER: Zwei Tassen Kaffee, ein Stück Käsekuchen und ein Stück Obsttorte. Das macht zusammen 9 Euro 55.

Dialog 3

HERR Y: Bedienung, wir möchten zahlen.

KELLNERIN: Zusammen oder getrennt?

HERR Y: Zusammen, bitte.

KELLNERIN: Dreimal Leberknödelsuppe, zweimal Schweinskotelett mit Salat und einmal zwei Münchner Weißwürste.

HERR Y: Und fünf Brezeln.

KELLNERIN: Ja, und fünf Bier und eine Portion Emmentaler Käse. Das macht zusammen 39 Euro 40.

KAPITEL 7

Alles klar?

B. 1. X: Was machst du so in deiner Freizeit?

ULRIKE: Ich lese sehr sehr viel und ich tanze.

X: Wo tanzt du denn? In der Disko?

ULRIKE: Nein, nein, ich gehe einmal die Woche zum Ballettunterricht.

X: Ach so.

2. X: Und wie verbringst du deine Freizeit?

WOLFGANG: Na, mit Fernsehen.

X: Und sonst nichts?

WOLFGANG: Ab und zu spiele ich Fußball mit ein paar Freunden. Fußball spielen macht mir Spaß.

3. X: Sag mal, Antje, was machst du so in deiner Freizeit?

ANTJE: Freizeit, kenn' ich nicht. Ich studiere und habe eine Nebenbeschäftigung. Da bleibt mir keine Freizeit.

X: Na, hör mal, das gibt's doch wohl nicht.

ANTJE: Na ja, gelegentlich gehe ich mal ins Kino. Ach ja, und ich habe übrigens einen neuen Computer. Da surfe ich schon mal im Internet. Das macht mir Spaß.

Wörter im Kontext

Aktivität 3   In der Freizeit

1. NINA: Ich bin Kunststudentin und verbringe meine Zeit hauptsächlich mit Malen, auch meine Freizeit! Malen ist für mich Leben. In letzter Zeit habe ich aber ein neues Hobby für die Freizeit: Fotografieren. Ich habe nämlich eine Digitalkamera zum Geburtstag bekommen. Das macht mir auch Spaß. Malen und fotografieren das mache ich also in meiner Freizeit. Dann höre ich aber auch gern mal Musik, brasilianische Musik, die finde ich besonders toll, die hat wirklich Rhythmus. Ja, und dann gehe ich natürlich auch mal mit Freunden aus, tanzen oder einfach gemütlich ins Café oder in eine Kneipe. Hier ist ja immer was los mit den vielen Studenten in der Stadt.

2. THOMAS: Ich arbeite den ganzen Tag von morgens bis abends fürs Studium. Ich mache jetzt Staatsexamen und habe keine Freizeit. Aber ich träume von der Freizeit! Also, ich träume, ich schwinge mich auf meine neue Harley-Davidson und brause wie ein Easy Rider die Autobahn runter und überhole alle die dicken Mercedes und BMWs. Motorrad fahren, das ist was ich in der Freizeit mache! Im Winter fahre ich dann zum Ski fahren, nach Österreich. Ja, das ist mein Traum von der Freizeit. So, und jetzt muss ich zur Uni.

3. ANNETTE: In meiner Freizeit gehe ich gewöhnlich zum Flohmarkt in unserer Stadt. Ich sammle nämlich alte Spielkarten und so was kann man gut auf dem Flohmarkt finden. Und dann gehe ich auch ins Internet in meiner Freizeit. Da habe ich eine Gruppe gefunden. Die machen Auktionen für Spielkarten im Internet. Also, das ist super. Ich habe Spielkarten aus Indien, aus Deutschland, Amerika und Russland, und England. Natürlich spiele ich auch gern Karten in meiner Freizeit, Bridge und Rommé, mit Freunden. Das macht auch Spaß. Ja, das ist alles. Wer hat schon viel Freizeit?

Aktivität 6   Pläne für einen Ausflug

VERENA: Sag mal, wie wäre es mit einem Ausflug am Wochenende?

ANTJE: Prima Idee! Ich brauche unbedingt Abwechslung. Die Arbeit geht mir im Moment auf die Nerven. Was schlägst du denn vor?

VERENA: Warst du schon mal im Neandertal?

ANTJE: Nein, noch nie. Wie weit ist das von hier?

VERENA: Nicht zu weit. Wir können mit dem Rad dahin. Man kann bequem in zwei Stunden da sein. Der Weg führt fast nur durch den Wald.

ANTJE: Soll ich Stefan auch einladen?

VERENA: Schön. Wenn er Lust hat.

ANTJE: Ich weiß, dass er gern mitkommt. Hoffentlich bleibt das Wetter schön.

Aktivität 9   Wetterberichte im Radio

Der Wetterbericht aus Zürich: Sonnig und warm. Temperaturen zwischen 20 und 25 Grad.

Und aus Wien: Bewölkt. Vor allem in der zweiten Tageshälfte Neigung zu Gewittern. Höchsttemperaturen um 18 Grad.

Und nun unser Wetterbericht für Berlin: Morgens noch Schauer, dann nachmittags bewölkt bis heiter. Tagestemperaturen bis zu 20 Grad.

Der Wetterbericht aus Paris: Schön mit leichtem Wind aus Südwest. Tagestemperatur: 29 Grad.

Und aus London: Morgens Nebel, später stark bewölkt und Regen. Tagestemperaturen nicht über 10 Grad.

Grammatik im Kontext

Übung 3   In meiner Kindheit

1. HERR HARTER: Was hat mir als Kind Spaß gemacht? Also, ich habe immer viel gesammelt, zum Beispiel Briefmarken, tote Insekten, Bilder mit Fußballspielern. Und dann habe ich Trompete gespielt. Ich habe dann in der Schule in unserer Band gespielt. Das hat mir immer viel Spaß gemacht.

2. FRAU BEITZ: Ich mochte Tiere immer gern, und als Kind hatte ich einen Hund. Das war der Charly. Ich habe mit meinem Hund gespielt. Ich war auch gern im Zoo und habe die Tiere gefüttert. Ja, das hat mir Spaß gemacht. Und ich habe auch immer gemalt und gezeichnet.

3. HERR HUPPERT: Als Junge habe ich leidenschaftlich gern Cowboy gespielt. Meine Eltern haben mir immer Bücher von Karl May zum Geburtstag geschenkt. Ich bin immer noch ein großer Karl-May-Fan, und ich fahre manchmal nach Bad Segeberg zu den Karl-May-Spielen. Ich habe alle Bücher von Karl May gesammelt. Ich war auch in einem Fußballverein und habe Fußball gespielt. Das hat wirklich Spaß gemacht.

KAPITEL 8

Alles klar?

B. HERR LOHMANN: Jeden Tag gehen wir ins Thermalbad. Danach bekommen wir auch eine Massage. In die Sauna gehen wir nie. Mittags essen wir gern vegetarisch. Nachmittags spielen wir manchmal Karten mit einigen anderen Kurgästen. Und natürlich gehen wir viel spazieren.

HERR KRANZLER: Ich bin allein hier. Meine Familie wohnt in Mainz. Ich spiele viel Golf, gehe auch gern wandern und schwimmen. Danach gehe ich immer in die Sauna und ins Thermalbad. Und dann mache ich eine Trinkkur. Da trinke ich jede Stunde ein Glas Wasser.

FRAU DIETMOLD: Ja, ich mache auch eine Trinkkur, und dann gehe ich ins Thermalbad und bekomme Massagen. Tischtennis macht mir viel Spaß. Ich gehe hier abends oft ins Theater. Ich spiele auch Mini-Golf, und dann tanze ich gern.

Wörter im Kontext

Thema 1:   Fit und gesund

(*See textbook pages 234–35.*)

Thema 2:   Der menschliche Körper

(*See textbook pages 236–37.*)

Aktivität 3   Im Aerobic-Kurs

AEROBIC-LEHRERIN: Strecken Sie die Arme nach oben. Langsam den Rücken nach vorne beugen. Die Knie gerade halten. Mit den Fingern bis an die Füße reichen. Langsam wieder hoch kommen.

Drehen Sie den Kopf erst nach rechts, dann nach links, dann langsam rollen. Das ist gut für den Hals. Jetzt die Schultern bis an die Ohren hoch ziehen und langsam wieder fallen lassen. So und jetzt geht's etwas flotter. Fünf Minuten auf der Stelle laufen. Eins, zwei, eins, zwei, eins, zwei!

MANN: Morgen tun mir bestimmt alle Muskeln weh.

Aktivität 5   Beschwerden

Dialog 1

LENI: Ich fühle mich hundsmiserabel.

DORIS: Was fehlt dir denn?

LENI: Ich hab' 'ne Erkältung. Ich muss immer husten, habe Kopfschmerzen, und ich kann mich auf nichts konzentrieren.

DORIS: Du siehst auch wirklich müde aus. Geh doch nach Hause, und leg dich ins Bett. Gute Besserung!

LENI: Danke.

Dialog 2

DORIS: Na, geht's dir wieder besser?

LENI: Ja, ich habe mich ein paar Tage zu Hause ausgeruht. Jetzt bin ich wieder fit.

DORIS: Ich fühle mich heute überhaupt nicht gut. Ich glaube, ich werde auch krank.

LENI: Na, hoffentlich nicht. Was ist denn los?

DORIS: Also, es ist mein Bauch. Ich habe irgendetwas gegessen.

LENI: Geh lieber gleich zum Arzt. Übrigens, trink viel Kamillentee. Der ist gut gegen Bauchschmerzen.

Dialog 3

ARZT: Was fehlt Ihnen denn?

PATIENT: Ach, Herr Doktor. Ich habe überhaupt keine Energie, fühle mich immer schlapp. Und nachts kann ich nicht schlafen. Ich bin immer nervös. Ich kann mich nicht konzentrieren.

ARZT: Hmm. Wie lange haben Sie diese Symptome schon?

PATIENT: Schon seit Monaten.

ARZT: Sie brauchen Urlaub. Sie haben zu viel Stress in Ihrem Leben. Ich empfehle Ihnen eine Kur im Schwarzwald. Ich schreibe Ihnen auch ein Rezept für Schlaftabletten.

Grammatik im Kontext

Übung 7   Beim Arzt

HERR SCHNEIDER: Guten Tag, Herr Doktor.

ARZT: Guten Tag, Herr Schneider. Bitte, setzen Sie sich. Was fehlt Ihnen denn?

HERR SCHNEIDER: Ich fühle mich so schlapp, ich kann mich überhaupt nicht konzentrieren.

ARZT: Seit wann fühlen Sie sich schon so schlapp?

HERR SCHNEIDER: Schon seit Wochen.

ARZT: Müssen Sie sich bei der Arbeit zu sehr anstrengen?

HERR SCHNEIDER: Ja, leider ist meine Arbeit mit sehr viel Stress verbunden. Ich bin Vertreter für eine Firma und bin ständig unterwegs, Termine mit Kunden, Staus auf der Autobahn. Ich habe einfach keine Zeit, mich mal zu entspannen.

ARZT: Sie müssen sich aber einfach entspannen. Der ständige Stress ist sehr schlecht für Ihre Gesundheit. Ich empfehle Ihnen eine Kur im Schwarzwald. Da können Sie sich vom Stress erholen.

HERR SCHNEIDER: Ja, das sagt meine Frau auch. Ich habe leider keine Zeit, in Urlaub zu fahren.

ARZT: Interessieren Sie sich für Sport? Etwas Aerobic kann Ihnen nicht schaden.

HERR SCHNEIDER: Leider interessiere ich mich nicht für Sport. Aerobic ist mir zu anstrengend.

ARZT: Nun, dann verschreibe ich Ihnen ein paar Vitamintabletten. Nehmen Sie abends und morgens 125 Stück. Und kommen Sie in vier Wochen wieder.—Übrigens, seit wann haben Sie diesen Schluckauf schon?

HERR SCHNEIDER: Schluckauf? Welchen Schluckauf?

ARZT: Herr Schneider, ich muss Ihnen dringend raten, sofort auf Kur zu gehen. Sie brauchen dringend Entspannung. Sie sind mit Ihren Nerven am Ende!

KAPITEL 9
Alles klar?

B. Jedes Jahr kommen rund vier Millionen Touristen in die sächsische Hauptstadt Dresden. Heute leben in der Stadt etwa 470 000 Einwohner. Dresden ist bekannt für viele Sachen. Zum Beispiel, die erste deutsche Lokomotive kommt aus Dresden. Und hier hat man Bierdeckel, Kaffeefilter und Zahnpasta entwickelt! Dresden ist aber auch eine Stadt der Musik. Heinrich Schütz hat hier die erste deutsche Oper geschrieben. Und später hat der Komponist Richard Wagner viele Jahre in Dresden verbracht. Zwei seiner Opern, „Tannhäuser" und „Der fliegende Holländer", wurden hier uraufgeführt. Den Dresdener Besucher erwartet ein großes kulturelles

Angebot: Musik, Museen und Theater. Dresden gilt auch als die europäische Hauptstadt des Dixieland. Der alte Zoologische Garten in Dresden ist einer der ältesten deutschen Tiergärten—gebaut im Jahr 1861.

Wörter im Kontext

Aktivität 1   Zwei telefonische Zimmerbestellungen

Erstes Telefongespräch

REZEPTION: Hotel Mecklenheide, guten Tag.

HERR DEGENER: Guten Tag. Haben Sie noch ein Zimmer frei?

REZEPTION: Brauchen Sie ein Einzelzimmer oder ein Doppelzimmer?

HERR DEGENER: Ich hätte gern ein Doppelzimmer mit Bad für drei Nächte.

REZEPTION: Wir haben noch ein Doppelzimmer frei, aber leider ohne Bad.

HERR DEGENER: Hmmm. Na gut. Und was kostet das Zimmer?

REZEPTION: 50 Euro, mit Frühstück.

HERR DEGENER: Also gut. Ich nehme es. Übrigens, ich habe einen Hund, einen Pudel. Ich hoffe, Sie haben nichts dagegen.

REZEPTION: Oh, es tut mir schrecklich Leid, aber Hunde sind leider nicht erlaubt.

HERR DEGENER: Na, dann muss ich es eben woanders versuchen. Auf Wiederhören.

REZEPTION: Auf Wiederhören.

Zweites Telefongespräch

FRAU BETZ: Jugendgästehaus am Stadtgraben.

GABRIELE: Ich möchte ein Zimmer für August bestellen. Haben Sie noch ein Einzelzimmer?

FRAU BETZ: Wir haben überhaupt keine Einzelzimmer. Unsere Schlafräume haben jeweils zehn Betten.

GABRIELE: Hmm, zehn Betten?

FRAU BETZ: Ja, aber die Räume sind sehr gemütlich. Unser Haus ist fast 800 Jahre alt. Es liegt ganz in der Nähe der Innenstadt.

GABRIELE: Gibt es auch Bad und Dusche und WC im Haus?

FRAU BETZ: Aber natürlich. Jedes Zimmer hat einen Waschraum mit Dusche und Toilette.

GABRIELE: Eine Dusche für zehn Leute? Hm. Und was kostet die Übernachtung?

FRAU BETZ: 15 Euro pro Übernachtung, mit Frühstück.

GABRIELE: Na, das ist ja sehr günstig. Bitte reservieren Sie mir ein Bett für vier Nächte vom ersten August an.

FRAU BETZ: Gut, geht in Ordnung. Und wie ist Ihr Name?

GABRIELE: Holzschuh, Gabriele.

Thema 2:   Im Hotel

(*See textbook pages 262–63.*)

Thema 3:   Nach dem Weg fragen

(*See textbook page 265.*)

Aktivität 5   Drei Touristen

Dialog 1

JULIA: Entschuldigung, wie kommt man hier zum Markt?

KATRIN: Gehen Sie immer geradeaus bis zur Ampel, dann links.

Dialog 2

ULRICH: Bitte, können Sie mir sagen, wo das Hotel Continental ist?

GISELA: Gehen Sie zwei Straßen geradeaus, dann rechts.

Dialog 3

PETER: Entschuldigung, wo ist hier eine Post?

SEPP: Tut mir leid. Ich bin Tourist und kenne die Stadt auch nicht.

Grammatik im Kontext

Übung 12   Kurze Gespräche

Dialog 1

GERD: Sag mal, seit wann hast du denn blaue Haare?

GABI: Seit letzter Woche. Gefallen sie dir?

GERD: Na ja, ich war an deine braunen Haare gewöhnt.

GABI: Ich habe ja auch blaue Augen. Die blauen Haare passen gut zu meinen blauen Augen.

GERD: Ein merkwürdiger Grund. Na ja, meine Oma hat lila Haare.

Dialog 2

PASSANT: Entschuldigung, wo ist das Rathaus?

PASSANTIN: Meinen Sie das alte oder das neue?

PASSANT: Oh, es gibt zwei? Ein altes und ein neues? Ich suche das Rathaus mit dem berühmten Glockenspiel.

PASSANTIN: Also, das ist das alte Rathaus. Gehen Sie geradeaus, dann die zweite Straße links. Das Rathaus liegt auf der rechten Seite.

KAPITEL 10

Alles klar?

B. Dialog 1

TONI: Wo wart ihr denn im Urlaub?

ELKE: An der Ostsee. In Warnemünde. Es war einfach herrlich! Strand, Wind und Meer!

TONI: Habt ihr dort viel unternommen?

ELKE: Wir wollten unbedingt segeln lernen—und das haben wir auch getan. Karl ist ein begeisterter Segler. Nächstes Jahr will er wieder dahin.

Dialog 2

UTE: Wo hast du denn dieses Jahr Urlaub gemacht?

BERND: In Südamerika, in Bolivien.

UTE: In Bolivien? Wie war es denn?

BERND: Fantastisch. Ich wollte ja immer schon mein Spanisch verbessern. Da habe ich mich zu einem Sprachurlaub in Bolivien entschlossen.

UTE: Hast du im Hotel gewohnt?

BERND: Nein. Ich hatte Glück. Ich habe eine Privatunterkunft bei einer Familie gefunden. Die waren alle unheimlich nett. Wir haben natürlich nur Spanisch gesprochen. Wir haben auch gemeinsam was unternommen. So habe ich viel gesehen und erlebt. Ich kann das nur empfehlen. So, ich muss jetzt gehen. Also, hasta mañana.

UTE: Tschüss.

Dialog 3

HANS: Einen Aktivurlaub habt ihr gemacht? Wieso?

JENS: Ganz einfach. Wir wollten mal was anderes machen. Da haben wir uns für einen Aktivurlaub entschieden— Wandern und Bergsteigen in den Dolomiten. Am aufregendsten war das Bergsteigen. Das war ein Erlebnis. Es hat mir unheimlich viel Spaß gemacht.

Wörter im Kontext

Thema 2:   Im Reisebüro

(*See textbook pages 294–95.*)

Aktivität 6   Pläne für einen interessanten Urlaub

Dialog 1

NICOLA: Ja, guten Tag. Ich möchte bitte Information über italienische Sprachkurse für Reisende.

ANGESTELLTE: Was halten Sie von Sizilien?

NICOLA: Das wäre nicht schlecht. Sizilien soll traumhaft schön sein.

ANGESTELLTE: Sehen Sie, hier im Reiseprospekt: „Italienisch für Anfänger"—vier Wochen lang in der Nähe von Palermo. Sie fliegen von hier aus direkt nach Palermo.

NICOLA: Das klingt fantastisch. Aber ich möchte natürlich nicht nur arbeiten, sondern auch etwas von der Gegend sehen.

ANGESTELLTE: Der Unterricht findet am Morgen statt, die Nachmittage und Wochenenden stehen Ihnen zur freien Verfügung.

Dialog 2

ANGESTELLTER: Guten Tag. Kann ich Ihnen helfen?

MARIANNE: Wir suchen Urlaubstipps für einen Alternativurlaub. Wir interessieren uns nämlich für Meditation. Können Sie etwas vorschlagen?

ANGESTELLTER: Es gibt ein paar interessante Möglichkeiten. Hier ist zum Beispiel ein Angebot auf der griechischen Insel Korfu—eine Woche Meditationsurlaub mit Workshops.

ASTRID: Hm, Korfu und Meditation? Na, was meinst du, Marianne?

MARIANNE: Ich weiß noch nicht. Ich will es mir überlegen.

Dialog 3

ANGESTELLTE: Grüß Gott, kann ich Ihnen helfen?

SABINE: Wir haben vor, Urlaub in Alaska zu machen. Haben Sie Reiseprospekte über Alaska?

ANGESTELLTE: Natürlich. Alaska ist ein sehr beliebtes Ziel. Natur, spektakuläre Berge, Gletscher, Eisbären, um nur ein paar Sehenswürdigkeiten zu nennen. Wie lange wollen Sie insgesamt bleiben?

HERBERT: Zwei bis drei Wochen.

ANGESTELLTE: Hier ist ein Angebot für eine vierzehntägige Reise. Sie fliegen zuerst nach Anchorage. Von dort aus kommen Sie mit Bus und Schiff weiter.

SABINE: Haben Sie gesagt Eisbären? Davor habe ich aber Angst.

ANGESTELLTE: Keine Sorge! Das war nur im Spaß gemeint. Sie sehen sie höchstens aus der Ferne, wenn überhaupt.

Dialog 4

SEBASTIAN: Guten Tag. Ich möchte bitte Information über eine Studienreise nach Israel. Haben Sie einen Reiseprospekt?

ANGESTELLTER: Ich kann Ihnen den Studiosus-Prospekt geben.

SEBASTIAN: Ich interessiere mich sehr für die Kulturstätten in Israel.

ANGESTELLTER: Wie wäre es mit diesem Angebot: Felsendom, Ölberg, Klagemauer, Schwimmen im Toten Meer und Aufenthalt im Kibbuz.

SEBASTIAN: Das klingt ja alles sehr interessant.

ANGESTELLTER: Wie viel Zeit haben Sie?

SEBASTIAN: Drei Wochen. Können Sie die Reise noch heute buchen?

ANGESTELLTER: Selbstverständlich.

SEBASTIAN: Danke schön.

ANGESTELLTER: Bitte sehr.

Thema 3:   Eine Fahrkarte, bitte!

(*See textbook page 297.*)

Aktivität 9   Am Fahrkartenschalter

Dialog 1

HERR BÖLL: Zwei Fahrkarten nach Hamburg, hin und zurück, erster Klasse.

HERR STEIN: Zweimal, hin und zurück. Das macht 200 Euro.

HERR BÖLL: Hat der Zug einen Speisewagen?

HERR STEIN: Ja.

HERR BÖLL: Ich möchte auch Platzkarten.

HERR STEIN: Raucher oder Nichtraucher?

HERR BÖLL: Nichtraucher.

Dialog 2

HERR FRANK: Ich möchte gern fünf Fahrkarten, hin und zurück, nach Salzburg.

FRAU BETZ: Alles Erwachsene?

HERR FRANK: Nein, zwei Erwachsene und drei Kinder.

FRAU BETZ: Kinder fahren zum halben Preis.

HERR FRANK: Gibt es ein Restaurant im Zug?

FRAU BETZ: Ja.

Dialog 3

FRAU SACHS: Einmal einfache Fahrt nach Bonn.

FRAU BETZ: Das macht 40 Euro.

FRAU SACHS: Und wann fährt der nächste Zug?

FRAU BETZ: In fünf Minuten fährt ein Zug nach Bonn.

FRAU SACHS: Danke, da muss ich mich aber beeilen.

Grammatik im Kontext

Übung 4   Werners Reisevorbereitungen

SEBASTIAN: Sag mal, Werner. Hast du eigentlich schon gepackt?

WERNER: Ach wo. Ich hatte einfach noch keine Zeit. Ich musste bis um sieben Uhr arbeiten.

SEBASTIAN: Wann fährt denn dein Zug?

WERNER: Morgen um vierzehn Uhr fünfzig. Übrigens kannst du mir einen Koffer leihen? Mein alter ist zu klein.

SEBASTIAN: Hast du schon alles für die Reise?

WERNER: Fast alles. Ich brauche noch Film für meine Kamera.

SEBASTIAN: Welche nimmst du mit?

WERNER: Die kleine. Sie nimmt nicht so viel Platz wie die Videokamera. Ich kann sie praktisch in meine Hosentasche stecken.

SEBASTIAN: Wie lange bleibst du weg?

WERNER: Insgesamt sechs Wochen.

SEBASTIAN: So eine lange Reise?

WERNER: Ja, so lange habe ich noch nie Urlaub gemacht.

Übung 17   Münchhausens Reise

Münchhausens Reise nach Russland begann im Winter. Er reiste mit Pferd und Wagen, weil das am bequemsten war. Leider trug er nur leichte Kleidung, und er fror sehr. Da sah Münchhausen eine alte Frau im Schnee. Er gab ihr etwas zu essen und ritt weiter. Er konnte leider kein Gasthaus finden. Er war müde und stieg vom Pferd ab. Dann band er das Pferd an einen Baumast im Schnee und legte sich hin. Er schlief tief und lange. Als Münchhausen am Morgen aufwachte, fand er sich mitten auf dem Marktplatz eines Dorfes. Wo war sein Pferd? Er konnte es über sich hören. Er schaute in die Höhe und sah sein Pferd vom Dach des Rathauses hängen. Was war passiert? Das Dorf war in der Nacht zugeschneit gewesen. In der Sonne war der Schnee geschmolzen. Der Baumast, an den Münchhausen sein Pferd gebunden hatte, war in Wirklichkeit die Spitze des Rathauses gewesen. Nun nahm er seine Pistole und schoss nach dem Halfter des Pferdes. Das Pferd landete ohne Schaden direkt neben Münchhausen. Dann reiste er weiter.

KAPITEL 11
Alles klar?

B. INTERVIEWER: Frau Sommer, wie sind Sie darauf gekommen, Tierärztin zu werden?

GABRIELE: Schon als Kind habe ich mich sehr für Tiere interessiert. Ich bin zu Hause mit Hunden, Katzen, drei Kanarienvögeln und sogar einem Pferd aufgewachsen. Meine Familie wohnte damals nämlich am Rande der Lüneburger Heide und da hatten wir Kinder immer ein Reitpferd. In der Schule war ich in naturwissenschaftlichen Fächern immer am besten. Ich hatte Glück, denn ich habe nach dem Abitur sofort einen Studienplatz in Erlangen bekommen. In Tiermedizin bekommt man schon eher einen Studienplatz. Ich bin jetzt im letzten Studienjahr. Mein Traum ist eine eigene Praxis in einer Kleinstadt, aber das wird noch lange dauern.

Wörter im Kontext

Aktivität 1   Drei junge Leute

INTERVIEWERIN: Tina, was möchtest du beruflich tun?

TINA: Eigentlich möchte ich gerne im Freien arbeiten, als so etwas wie Landschaftsarchitektin oder als Gärtnerin. Ich habe keine Lust, Büroarbeit zu machen. Großes Ansehen zu haben oder viel Geld zu verdienen—das ist mir nicht wichtig.

INTERVIEWERIN: Und du, Markus? Was würde dich am meisten beruflich interessieren?

MARKUS: Am liebsten würde ich in meinem Beruf viel reisen und vielleicht sogar im Ausland arbeiten. Meine Tätigkeit soll abwechslungsreich sein. Mit Menschen zu tun haben— das gefällt mir.

INTERVIEWERIN: Und du, Andrea? Wofür interessierst du dich beruflich?

ANDREA: Ich arbeite gerne mit meinen Händen und interessiere mich für technische Sachen—wie zum Beispiel Maschinen. Computer interessieren mich auch—ich würde gern mit Computern arbeiten.

Aktivität 9   Ein Gespräch unter Freunden

GÜNTHER: Wie steht's denn mit deiner Suche nach einem Ausbildungsplatz? Hast du schon was gefunden?

PETRA: Ich habe noch nichts Definitives. Gestern war ich mal wieder beim Arbeitsamt.

GÜNTHER: Na, da kannst du lange warten, bevor die was für dich finden.

PETRA: Man kann nie wissen. Vor ein paar Tagen stand eine Anzeige in der Zeitung für Ausbildungsstellen für Laboranten.

GÜNTHER: Bei welcher Firma?

PETRA: Alpha Pharma. Die suchen Bewerber.

GÜNTHER: Muss man Abitur haben?

PETRA: Für die Ausbildung als Biologielaborantin braucht man Abitur. Aber für die Ausbildung zur Chemielaborantin braucht man nur Realschulabschluss.

GÜNTHER: Ist ja super. Hast du dich schon beworben?

PETRA: Ja, ich habe gleich meine Unterlagen eingeschickt, das Übliche: Lebenslauf, Foto und Zeugnisse.

GÜNTHER: Hast du schon mal angerufen?

PETRA: Nein, noch nicht. Wenn die Firma einen will, muss man noch einen Test machen.

GÜNTHER: Weißt du irgendetwas über die Firma?

PETRA: Nur, was in der Anzeige stand. Ich muss erst mal abwarten und sehen, ob sie mich zum Test einladen.

Grammatik im Kontext

Übung 7   Ein unkonventioneller Klub

SVEN: Was liest du denn da?

ANJA: Ein Buch.

SVEN: Na, das kann ich auch sehen! Was für ein Buch ist das denn?

ANJA: Es heißt *Das literarische Oktett.*

SVEN: Was für ein merkwürdiger Titel ist das denn?

ANJA: Das ist ein Buch, das acht Studenten geschrieben haben. Sie haben einen Klub der Dichter gegründet. Der Klub nennt sich auch „das literarische Oktett".

SVEN: Was für Gedichte schreiben sie denn? Komplizierte Gedichte, die kein Mensch verstehen kann?

ANJA: Nein, sie schreiben hauptsächlich kleine, freche Geschichten. Aber es gibt auch ein paar Gedichte im Buch.

SVEN: Über was für Themen schreiben die denn?

ANJA: Na, für was für Themen interessieren sich Studenten schon? Sex, Liebe, Studentenalltag, Essen, Trinken, und so weiter. Es ist alles recht provozierend, aber auch originell und unkonventionell.

SVEN: Ich möchte es auch mal lesen.

ANJA: Gut, wenn ich fertig bin, gebe ich es dir.

KAPITEL 12
Alles klar?

B. INTERVIEWER: Jens, was bedeutet dir Geld?

JENS: Geld bedeutet für mich zwei Dinge: etwas für andere damit tun, aber auch etwas für mich selbst tun. Ich habe nicht viel, denn ich bin Student, aber wenn ich genug Geld hätte, würde ich einen Teil davon für medizinische Forschung spenden. Ich bin aber auch ein bisschen Egoist und würde mir vielleicht einen neuen Wagen oder eine neue Wohnung kaufen.

INTERVIEWER: Welche Bedeutung hat Geld für dich, Lucia?

LUCIA: Ja, ich meine auch, mit Geld muss man anderen Menschen helfen, besonders den Armen. Wenn ich Geld nur für mich ausgeben würde, würde ich wahrscheinlich weiter studieren—vielleicht im Ausland. Ich musste mein Studium unterbrechen, weil ich im Moment kein Geld habe. Später aber möchte ich vielleicht mein eigenes Geschäft aufmachen.

INTERVIEWER: Und für dich, Elke?

ELKE: Wenn ich viel Geld hätte, würde ich es bestimmt investieren. Ich würde einen langen Urlaub machen, aber dann würde ich wieder arbeiten. Wichtig für mich sind die Welthungerorganisationen—denen würde ich soviel Geld wie möglich geben.

Wörter im Kontext

Aktivität 2   Andreas Dilemma

ANDREA: Sag mal, könntest du mir einen Gefallen tun?

STEFAN: Was denn?

ANDREA: Würdest du mir bis Ende der Woche 50 Euro leihen? Ich bin total pleite.

STEFAN: Fünfzig Euro? Das ist viel Geld.

ANDREA: Ich musste 100 Euro für Bücher ausgeben. Und jetzt habe ich keinen Cent mehr übrig. Ich warte auf Geld von meinen Eltern.

STEFAN: Hm, ich würde es dir gern leihen. Aber 50 Euro habe ich selber nicht mehr. Ich kann dir höchstens 20 Euro leihen.

ANDREA: Ich zahle es dir bis Ende des Monats bestimmt zurück.

STEFAN: Eben hast du gesagt, bis Ende der Woche.

ANDREA: Ja, ja. Das Geld von meinen Eltern kann jeden Tag kommen.

STEFAN: Na gut. Hier ist ein Zwanziger.

ANDREA: Vielen Dank.

Aktivität 4   Einnahmen und Ausgaben

Dialog 1

INTERVIEWER: Woher bekommst du monatlich Geld, Stefanie?

STEFANIE: Hauptsächlich von meinen Eltern, aber während der Semesterferien arbeite ich und verdiene mir etwas Geld zum Studium.

INTERVIEWER: Als was arbeitest du denn?

STEFANIE: Gewöhnlich als Kellnerin. Während des Semesters habe ich aber keine Zeit zum Jobben.

INTERVIEWER: Und wo wohnst du?

STEFANIE: Ich habe Glück. Ich habe nämlich ein Zimmer im Studentenwohnheim. Da kostet die Miete nur 100 Euro im Monat.

Dialog 2

INTERVIEWER: Woher bekommst du monatlich Geld, Gert?

GERT: Ich bekomme BAföG. Und in den Semesterferien arbeite ich dann. Letztes Jahr habe ich bei der Post als Briefträger gearbeitet.

INTERVIEWER: Und wo wohnst du?

GERT: Ich wohne privat bei Bekannten von meinen Eltern. Ich habe da ein Zimmer.

INTERVIEWER: Und was musst du dafür bezahlen?

GERT: Es ist sehr günstig. Nur 150 Euro pro Monat. Das Haus liegt allerdings etwas außerhalb. Ich muss jeden Tag mit der U-Bahn zur Uni fahren.

Dialog 3

INTERVIEWER: Und wie finanzierst du dein Studium, Susanne?

SUSANNE: Meine Eltern unterstützen mich. Aber ich arbeite auch während des Semesters nebenbei.

INTERVIEWER: Was machst du denn?

SUSANNE: Ich gebe Englischunterricht. Ich habe drei Schüler.

INTERVIEWER: Und wo wohnst du?

SUSANNE: Ich wohne mit drei anderen Studentinnen in einer Wohngemeinschaft. Wir teilen uns die Miete für eine Vierzimmerwohnung. Jeder bezahlt 150 Euro im Monat.

Dialog 4

INTERVIEWER: Und nun zu Martin. Woher bekommst du Geld fürs Studium?

MARTIN: Ich bekomme Geld von meinen Eltern, aber es ist nicht genug. Ich muss also nebenbei arbeiten, auch während des Semesters und in den Semesterferien.

INTERVIEWER: Und wo wohnst du?

MARTIN: Seit letztem Jahr wohne ich in der Studentenstadt. Da habe ich eine kleine Wohnung. Die kostet nur 200 Euro.

Aktivität 5   Die ideale Wohnung

Dialog 1

INTERVIEWER: Frau Heine, Sie suchen eine Wohnung. Wie stellen Sie sich Ihre ideale Wohnung vor?

FRAU HEINE: Die Wohnung muss in der Innenstadt liegen. Ich arbeite nämlich dort. Ich möchte gern einen Neubau mit Zentralheizung. Ich bin gern an der frischen Luft. Deswegen muss meine Wohnung einen Balkon haben. Ich habe keinen Wagen. Eine Garage brauche ich deshalb nicht.

Dialog 2

INTERVIEWER: Ich spreche jetzt mit Herrn und Frau Zumwald aus Hannover. Herr und Frau Zumwald, was für eine Wohnung wäre für Sie und Ihre Kinder ideal?

HERR ZUMWALD: Wir suchen ein komfortables Haus außerhalb der Stadt. Wir brauchen einen großen Garten für unsere zwei Kinder und unseren Hund. Wir möchten gern ein älteres Haus, weil Altbauten oft gemütlicher sind. Allerdings muss das Haus Zentralheizung haben. Unwichtig ist uns, ob das Haus Teppichboden hat.

Dialog 3

INTERVIEWER: Meine Herren, Sie studieren hier an der Uni?

THOMAS: Ja. Meine zwei Freunde hier und ich suchen eine komfortable Altbauwohnung in der Innenstadt. Die Mietkosten dürfen natürlich nicht zu hoch sein. Wir haben alle Fahrräder. Deswegen ist eine Garage nicht so wichtig. Eine Waschmaschine im Haus ist wichtig, aber ein Teppichboden in der Wohnung interessiert uns überhaupt nicht. Aber ohne Zentralheizung möchten wir nicht sein. Die ist sehr wichtig.

Aktivität 9   Ist die Wohnung noch frei?

FRAU KRENZ: Hier Krenz.

HERR BRUNNER: Brunner. Guten Tag. Ich rufe wegen der Anzeige in der Zeitung an. Ist die Wohnung noch frei?

FRAU KRENZ: Ja, die ist noch frei.

HERR BRUNNER: Ich hätte einige Fragen. Ist Heizung in den Nebenkosten eingeschlossen?

FRAU KRENZ: Nein, Heizung ist extra.

HERR BRUNNER: In welchem Stock liegt die Wohnung?

FRAU KRENZ: Im vierten Stock.

HERR BRUNNER: Gibt es denn einen Aufzug im Haus?

FRAU KRENZ: Aber natürlich. Sind Sie allein stehend, oder haben Sie Familie?

HERR BRUNNER: Ich bin allein stehend. Kann ich mir die Wohnung mal ansehen?

FRAU KRENZ: Ja, gerne. Wann können Sie vorbeikommen?

HERR BRUNNER: Möglichst bald. Am besten direkt nach der Arbeit.

FRAU KRENZ: Schön, wie wäre es mit morgen so um 18.00 Uhr?

HERR BRUNNER: Das ist mir recht. Übrigens, bevor ich es vergesse, wie ist die Adresse?

FRAU KRENZ: Augustinerstraße 27. Es ist ganz leicht zu finden. Das Haus steht nämlich direkt gegenüber vom Museum.

HERR BRUNNER: Vielen Dank. Bis morgen dann. Auf Wiederhören.

FRAU KRENZ: Auf Wiederhören.

KAPITEL 13
Alles klar?

B. Bericht 1

Bei einer Verkehrskontrolle in Cocoa Beach sprang ein 21jähriger Autodieb ins Meer und schwamm immer weiter raus. In voller Uniform schwang sich ein Polizist auf ein Surfbrett und hatte den Mann nach 10 Minuten eingeholt und als Ballast auf das Surfbrett gehoben.

Bericht 2

Im Südwesten des Irans hat man ein unbekanntes Dorf entdeckt, das bisher auf keiner Karte verzeichnet ist. Die Bewohner leben ohne jeden Kontakt mit der modernen Zivilisation.

Bericht 3

Am schnellsten denkt der Mensch vor dem Mittagessen, fanden amerikanische Chronobiologen heraus. Wer also ein schwieriges Problem lösen muss, soll sich zwischen 11 und 12 Uhr damit befassen.

Bericht 4

Ein Mann im Gorillakostüm verteilte in den Straßen von Dallas, Texas, 6 000 Dollar in 50-Dollar-Scheinen an Fußgänger. In einem Interview sagte er: „Ich mache das, um die erstaunten Gesichter der Menschen zu sehen, denen ich das Geld gebe. Das macht unheimlichen Spaß." Beim Interview trug er sein Gorillakostüm, seinen Namen gab er nicht preis.

Wörter im Kontext

Thema 1: Medien

(*See textbook pages 384–85.*)

Grammatik im Kontext

Übung 7   Immer diese Ausreden

Dialog 1

PETER: Du, Jan, hier ist Peter.

JAN: Grüß dich, Peter.

PETER: Also, ich kann heute Abend leider nicht mit ins Kino. Ich muss noch für morgen eine Arbeit fertig schreiben und 150 Seiten Psychologie lesen. Außerdem ist mein Wagen kaputt.

JAN: Schade, aber mach dir weiter keine Sorgen. Bis demnächst dann. Tschüss.

PETER: Tschüss, bis bald.

Dialog 2

JENS: Hier Jens Hertling. Ist Herr Professor Hauser in seinem Büro?

SEKRETÄR: Nein, er hat heute keine Sprechstunde.

JENS: Würden Sie ihm bitte sagen, dass ich meine Seminararbeit heute nicht einreichen kann. Meine Mutter ist

nämlich krank und ich muss sie ins Krankenhaus
bringen.

SEKRETÄR: Ich werde es ihm ausrichten. Auf Wiederhören.

Dialog 3

KARIN: Sag mal, Ursula, kannst du mir vielleicht die 30 Euro
zurückzahlen, die ich dir vor drei Wochen geliehen habe?

URSULA: Oh, das tut mir Leid. Ich kann dir das Geld aber
heute leider noch nicht zurückzahlen. Ich erwarte morgen
einen Scheck von meinen Eltern. Ich bringe dir das Geld
morgen Abend.

KARIN: Schön. Bis morgen Abend dann.

URSULA: Wiedersehen.

KAPITEL 14

Alles klar?

C. Seminar 1

In diesem Seminar werden verschiedene Ursachen
der Vergiftung untersucht. Der Schwerpunkt liegt auf
Ursachen der Magenvergiftung. Heutzutage vermehren
sich allergische Reaktionen auf Nahrungsmittel sowie auf
die Umwelt dramatisch. Insbesondere wird in diesem
Seminar das Thema Giftreaktionen im Magen behandelt.

Seminar 2

In den letzten zehn Jahren hat die Zahl der Gewalttaten
drastisch zugenommen. Im Fernsehen und in den
Zeitungen wird das Thema heiß debattiert. Dieses
Seminar befasst sich mit der steigenden Gewaltbereit-
schaft von Jugendlichen und Kindern und dem Zulauf
zu rechtsextremen Gruppen.

Seminar 3

Die Umweltbelastung durch Luftverschmutzung und
Lärm ist das Hauptthema dieses Seminars. Weiter wird
untersucht, wie man durch Verkehrsplanung und die
Entwicklung umweltfreundlicher Verkehrsmittel die
Autoabgase und insgesamt die Verkehrsbelästigung in
den Innenstädten reduzieren kann.

Seminar 4

Dieses Seminar behandelt als Hauptthema menschliche
Grundrechte und Freiheiten und wie sie in verschiede-
nen Ländern interpretiert werden. Die Lektüre für das
Seminar besteht hauptsächlich aus Dokumenten und
Berichten von Amnesty International und von der Welt-
konferenz über Menschenrechte, die in Wien stattfand.

Wörter im Kontext

Thema 1: Die Kunst der Diskussion

(*See textbook pages 409–10.*)

Aktivität 2 Probleme in der Stadt

INTERVIEWER: Was halten Sie für das größte Problem?

SPRECHER 1: Das größte Problem ist der Verkehr. Wir wohnen
etwas außerhalb der Stadt. Der Verkehr in der Stadt wird
jährlich immer stärker. Früher haben wir fast eine Stunde
mit Fahren und im Stau auf der Landstraße verbracht. Da
kam man schon genervt zur Arbeit. Seit etwa einem halben
Jahr parken wir unseren Wagen am Rande der Stadt und
nehmen von dort einen Bus in die Innenstadt.

SPRECHERIN 2: Der Staat investiert zu viel Geld in die Forschung von Atomenergie. Jetzt soll hier in der Nähe ein
neues Atomkraftwerk gebaut werden. Aber niemand kann
garantieren, dass wir nicht eines Tages ein Tschernobyl-
Unglück bei uns haben. Ich finde, der Staat soll mehr Geld
in die Forschung für alternative Energie stecken, zum
Beispiel Windenergie. Wind haben wir doch genug hier.

SPRECHER 3: Wir wohnen in der Nähe des Flughafens. Der
ständige Lärm durch die Flugzeuge, die hier landen, ist
unerträglich geworden. Den ganzen Tag hören wir über
unseren Dächern die Flugzeuge. Man könnte die Zahl der
Flugzeuge reduzieren. Aber die Fluggesellschaften haben
eine starke Lobby.

SPRECHERIN 4: Ich mache mir Sorgen um die Qualität
unserer Nahrungsmittel, besonders Obst und Gemüse. Da
hört man, wie immer stärkere Pestizide für Gemüse und
Obst verwendet werden. Und das Fleisch ist auch voller
Giftstoffe. Man sollte diese Sachen streng vom Staat
kontrollieren lassen und viele Pestizide verbieten.

Aktivität 5 Langsamer, bitte!

JENNIFER: Sag mal, fliegen wir eigentlich oder fahren wir?

ANDREAS: Wieso?

JENNIFER: Wie kannst du mit 200 Sachen durch die Landschaft
fahren? Mir stehen die Haare zu Berge.

ANDREAS: Keine Angst. Mein BMW schafft das spielend. Der
liegt doch wie ein Brett auf der Straße.

JENNIFER: Ich bin an so ein Tempo nicht gewöhnt. Bei uns ist
die Höchstgeschwindigkeit nur etwa 105 km pro Stunde.

ANDREAS: Dann kann man ja gleich zu Fuß gehen.

JENNIFER: Zu Fuß gehen würde weniger Abgase verursachen.
Und bei dieser Raserei verbraucht man auch viel mehr
Benzin.

ANDREAS: Das ist alles übertrieben. Und außerdem ist mein
Wagen für hohe Geschwindigkeiten gebaut.

JENNIFER: Du, schau mal, da ist ein Schild über der Autobahn:
Höchstgeschwindigkeit 100 km.

ANDREAS: Wahrscheinlich eine Baustelle in der Nähe.

JENNIFER: Also doch ein Tempolimit. Gott sei Dank. Bei
100 km fühle ich mich direkt wie zu Hause.